# AFRICAN DEVELOPMENT REPORT
## 2004

**AFRICA IN THE WORLD ECONOMY**

**AFRICA IN THE GLOBAL TRADING SYSTEM**

**ECONOMIC AND SOCIAL STATISTICS ON AFRICA**

PUBLISHED FOR THE AFRICAN DEVELOPMENT BANK
BY
OXFORD UNIVERSITY PRESS

# OXFORD

UNIVERSITY PRESS

*Great Clarendon Street, Oxford OX2 6DP*

Oxford University Press is a department of the University of Oxford.
*It furthers the University's objective of excellence in research, scholarship,
and education by publishing worldwide in*

Oxford  New York

*Auckland  Bangkok  Buenos Aires  Cape Town  Chennai
Dar es Salaam  Delhi  Hong Kong  Istanbul  Karachi  Kolkata
Kuala Lumpur  Madrid  Melbourne  Mexico City  Mumbai  Nairobi
São Paulo  Shanghai  Singapore  Taipei  Tokyo  Toronto
with an associated company in Berlin*

*Oxford is a registered trade mark of Oxford University Press
in the UK and in certain other countries*

*Published in the United States
by Oxford University Press Inc., New York*

© 2004 by African Development Bank

*The moral rights of the author have been asserted
Database right Oxford University Press (maker)*

*First published 2004*

*The African Development Report 2004 is produced by the staff of the African Development Bank,
and the views expressed therein do not necessarily reflect those of the Boards of Directors
or the countries they represent. Designations employed in this Report do not imply the expression
of any opinion, on the part of the African Development Bank, concerning the legal status of any
country or territory, or the delineation of its frontiers.*

*British Library Cataloguing in Publication Data
Data available
Library of Congress Cataloging-in-Publication Data
Data available
ISBN  0-19-927179-8*

*Typeset by Hope Services, Abingdon, Oxon
Printed in Great Britain
on acid-free paper by
Ashford Colour Press Limited, Gosport, Hampshire*

# FOREWORD

The *African Development Report*, a staff report prepared by the Development Research Department of the Bank, has over the years become an important source of analysis and information on developments in the African economy. Each year it provides an update on key macroeconomic and sectoral developments and provides an in-depth analysis of an important development topic critical for Africa's development prospects. In keeping with this tradition, the first part of this year's report is devoted to an analysis of the African economy in 2003, viewed from continental, regional and national perspectives. The second part examines in detail Africa's position in the global trading system.

As discussed more fully in the report, Africa's economic performance registered some marked improvements in 2003. Despite the fragile recovery of the world economy, initial estimates point to an increase of the growth rate of real GDP in Africa from 2.9 percent in 2002 to 3.7 percent in 2003, with some 18 countries achieving growth rates in excess of 5 percent (compared to only 10 in 2002), and 16 others registering rates between 3 and 5 percent. Inflation has largely stabilized, with some 40 countries achieving single-digit levels. The fiscal deficit also declined from 3.4 percent in 2002 to 3.0 percent in 2003, while the external current account improved, with a positive trade balance for the fourth year in a row.

Several factors account for the continent's improved performance: the strengthening of the domestic macroeconomic environment; the recovery of non-fuel commodity prices; favorable weather conditions; and debt relief under the enhanced HIPC Initiative. It is gratifying to note that most countries have continued to follow prudent fiscal and monetary policies, resulting in improved macroeconomic stability. In addition, important structural reforms continued to be implemented, including further price liberalizations, privatization of state-owned enterprises, and the strengthening of regulatory frameworks. A large number of countries also enhanced their Poverty Reduction Strategy Papers (PRSPs) to serve as a comprehensive framework to reduce poverty, promote economic growth, and coordinate donor support.

A favorable external environment supported the domestic reform efforts. The price of oil continued to rise and the price of non-oil commodities increased significantly. In addition, the trend decline in the debt burden of African economies has continued, with the ratio of debt to GDP declining to 47.6 percent, and the ratio of debt service to exports also falling to 15.2 percent.

While developments in the African economy were on the whole positive in 2003, the difficulties that some countries continued to face should not be overlooked. Although a number of long-standing conflicts, such as those in the Great Lakes Region, came to an end and the prospects for ending others are promising, many of the affected countries have yet to launch effective reconstruction and rehabilitation programs. Others continue to face political instability and civil strife, resulting in a contraction of their economies. Clearly, the international community will need to bolster its efforts to find peaceful solutions for countries in conflict and to provide the much-needed assistance to post-conflict countries.

While the improvement in the performance of the African economy in 2003 is most welcome, it needs to be stressed that on current trends, growth is still inadequate in most countries, particularly with respect to achieving the Millennium Development Goals (MDGs). The only exceptions are South Africa and the countries of North Africa. Other countries therefore need to redouble their efforts and put in place the required policies and structures to accelerate and sustain growth rates in the order of 6-8 percent. A few countries, such as Mozambique, have demonstrated the possibility of doing so. And for its part, the international donor community needs to continue to provide the requisite assistance in terms of increasing ODA flows, reducing external debt to sustainable levels, and improving market access for Africa's exports.

Indeed, Africa's future economic performance will in large part be determined by its trade relations with the rest of the world. As the findings in this report make clear, Africa has fared quite poorly in its international trade performance over the last two decades. Its share in world exports has declined to 2 percent in 2002, compared to 3 percent in 1990, and to 6 percent in 1980.

To reverse this trend, African countries need to pursue a development strategy that is export-oriented while at the same time seeking to transform their production and exports base. Such a strategy must necessarily start with strengthening Africa's comparative advantage in traditional exports, where the continent has lost market share in primary commodities such as coffee, cocoa and cotton. In addition, enhanced diversification programs should start by strengthening the linkages between agriculture and the industrial sector, as the comparative advantage of many African countries may initially lie in the processing of agricultural goods. Further, African countries should exploit the potential that exists in the export of services, including the substantial comparative advantage that they enjoy in tourism. These sectors should be given high priority while African countries seek to build up their comparative advantage in manufacturing.

Successful promotion of exports and diversification will require that domestic policies do not discriminate against exporters and that the physical and marketing infrastructure required to help African producers become more competitive in the global market be developed. In most countries, there is an urgent need for investments to reduce key constraints such as inefficient transportation and marketing systems.

Export diversification also requires the scaling-up of local capacity with the support of foreign firms. Partnerships with foreign capital create access to the needed technologies as well as access to managerial and marketing know-how. In addition, African countries will continue to require technical assistance from their development partners in such critical areas as capacity development in exports promotion, industrial research, information management, and quality control.

Africa's quest to increase and diversify its exports will also necessitate the support of its development partners to put in place a development-oriented international trade regime. In this regard, important steps such as the *Everything but Arms* (EBA) initiative of the European Union and the Africa Growth and Opportunity Act (AGOA) of the United States are yielding positive results. These initiatives will, however, need to be broadened to cover other important trade-related issues such as agricultural subsidies, quotas, and non-tariff barriers.

The Doha Development Agenda of the WTO sought to address these issues within a negotiated multilateral framework. The failure of the Ministerial talks at Cancún in 2003 therefore represents a major setback for African and other developing countries. It is evident that the international community needs to re-commit itself to pursuing a rules-based global trading system that takes full account of the needs of poor countries. It is for this reason that we urge the resumption of the Doha Round and its timely conclusion.

This year's *African Development Report* provides a rich and extensive discussion of these and other trade-related matters that are likely to have a major impact on Africa's development prospects. I am confident that policy-makers, researchers, as well as representatives of civil society and the private sector, both in Africa and elsewhere, will find the analysis useful.

**Omar Kabbaj**
**President**
**African Development Bank**

The *African Development Report 2004* has been prepared by a staff team in the Development Research Department of the African Development Bank under the direction of Henock Kifle.

The research team was led by Mohamed Nureldin Hussain and comprised Obadiah Mailafia, John C. Anyanwu, Charlotte Vaillant (consultant) and Barfour Osei (consultant) from the Research Division.

The Economic and Social Statistics on Africa were prepared by the Statistics Division led by Charles L. Lufumpa and comprised André Portella, Beejaye Kokil, Maurice Mubila and Koua Louis Kouakou.

Rhoda R. Bangurah provided production services, Richard Synge editorial services and Bakri Abdul-Karim publication coordination.

Preparation of the *Report* was aided by the background papers listed in the bibliographical note. Comments from outside the Bank are noted with appreciation. Chukwuma Soludo of the African Institute for Applied Economics; Milton Iyoha of the African Economic Research Consortium; Christopher Stevens of the Institute of Development Studies; Oliver Morrissey of the University of Nottingham; V.N. Balasubramanyan of the University of Lancaster; Farid Ben Youcef, University of Alger all made comments and suggestions to improve the *Report*. Dominic Byatt and Claire Croft at Oxford University Press oversaw the editorial and publication process.

# ABBREVIATIONS

| | |
|---|---|
| AAEU | Association Agreement with the European Community |
| ACP | African, Caribbean and Pacific |
| ACP-EU | African, Caribbean and Pacific-European Union |
| ADF | African Development Fund |
| ADMARC | Agricultural Development and Marketing Corporation (Malawi) |
| ADR | The African Development Report |
| AEO | African Economic Outlook |
| AGOA | Africa Growth and Opportunity Act |
| AIDS | Acquired Immune Deficiency Syndrom |
| AMU | Arab Maghreb Union |
| APEC | Asia Pacific Economic Cooperation |
| APIX | Investment Promotion & Major Projects (Senegal) |
| APRM | African Peer Review Mechanism |
| ASEM | Asia-Europe Meeting |
| ATLEs | Africa's Ten Largest Economies |
| BCC | Banque Centrale du Congo |
| BCCE | Banque Congolaise du Commerce Extérieur |
| BCEAO | Banque Centrale des Etats de l'Afrique de l'ouest |
| BCI | Banco de Comércio e Indústria |
| BEAC | Banque des Etats d'Afrique Centrale |
| BMCE | Banque Marocaine du Commerce Exterieur (privatized in 1995) |
| BPC | Banco de Poupança e Credito |
| bpd | Barrels per day |
| BPRS | Botswana National Poverty Reduction Strategy |
| BRVM | Bourse régionale des valeurs mobilières |
| BTD | Bank Togoloise du Development |
| BVMAC | Bourse de valeurs mobilières de l'Afrique centrale |
| BWIs | Bretton Woods Institutions |
| CAA | Caisse Autonome d'Amortissement |
| CAIC | Crédit pour l'agriculture, l'industrie et le commerce |
| CAP | Common Agricultural Policy |
| CAR | Central African Republic |
| Caricom | Caribbean Community |
| CAT | Central Transport Authority |
| CBE | Central Bank of Egypt |
| CBE | Commercial Bank of Ethiopia |
| CBN | Central Bank of Nigeria |

| | |
|---|---|
| CDCRO | Commonwealth Developing Countries Remission Order |
| CEAO | Communauté des États de l'Afrique d'Ouest (West African Economic Community) |
| CEB | Central Electricity Board (Mauritius) |
| CEMAC | Communauté économique et monétaire de l'Afrique centrale |
| CEN-SAD | Community of Sahel-Saharan States |
| CEPGL | Economic Community of the Great Lakes Countries |
| CET | Common External Tariff |
| CFA | Communauté Financière Africaine |
| CFCO | Congo Ocean Railways Corporation |
| CGE | Computable General Equilibrium |
| CIF | Cost, Insurance and Freight |
| CIPR | International Commission on Intellectual Property Rights |
| CM | Common Market |
| CMA | Common Monetary Area |
| CMDT | Compagnie Malienne pour le Développement des Textiles |
| COMESA | Common Market for Eastern and Southern Africa |
| COPIREP | Committee on the Reform of Public Sector |
| CPA | Crédit Populaire Algérien |
| CRTA | Committee on Regional Trade Agreements |
| CTD | Committee on Trade and Development |
| CU | Customs Unions |
| DCP | Debt Conversion Program |
| DRC | Democratic Republic of Congo |
| DUP | Directly Unproductive Profit-Seeking Activities. |
| EAC | East African Community |
| EAGB | The Electricity and Water Company of Guinea Bissau |
| EALF | East Asia-Latin America Forum |
| EBA | Everything But Arms |
| ECCAS | Economic Community of Central African States |
| ECOWAS | Economic Community of West African States |
| EERm | Effective Exchange Rate for Imports |
| EERx | Effective Exchange rate for Exports |
| EMAE | Water and Electricity Power Utility (Sao Tomé) |
| EMU | Economic and Monetary Union |
| EP | Export Promotion |
| EPA | Economic Partnership Agreement |
| EPZ | Export Processing Zone |
| ERP | Economic Recovery Program |
| EU | European Union |
| FAO | UN Food and Agriculture Organization |

| | |
|---|---|
| FDI | Foreign Direct Investment |
| FERTIMA | Société Marocaine des Fertilisants |
| FOB | Free on Board |
| FTA | Free Trade Area |
| GATS | General Agreement on Trade in Services |
| GATT | General Agreement on Tariffs and Trade |
| GCB | Gabbia Commercial Bank |
| GCC | Gambia Groundnut Corporation |
| GDP | Gross Domestic Output |
| GECAMINES | Generale des Carrieres et des Mines (DRC) |
| GPT | General Preferential Tariff |
| GSM | Global System of Mobiles |
| GSP | Generalised Scheme of Preferences |
| HIPC | Heavily-Indebted Poor Countries |
| HIV | Human Immunodeficiency Virus |
| HS | Harmonized System |
| ICT | Information & Communications Technologies |
| IDA | International Development Association |
| IMF | International Monetary Fund |
| IOC | Indian Ocean Commission |
| IS | Import Substitution |
| JSE | Johannesburg Stock Exchange |
| KCM | Konkola Copper Mines (Zambia) |
| LDC | Least Developed Country |
| LRA | Lesotho Revenue Authority |
| LTC | Lesotho Telecommunication Corporation |
| m/bd | Million barrels per day |
| MDB | Multilateral Development Bank |
| MDGs | Millennium Development Goals |
| MEDIFA | Laboratoire des médicaments du Faso (Burkina Faso) |
| MERCOSUR. | Southern Common Market Agreement |
| MFN | Most Favoured Nation |
| MNC | Multinational corporation |
| MRU | Mano River Union |
| MTAs | Multilateral Trade Agreements on Goods |
| MVA | Manufacturing Value-Added |
| NBR | National Bank of Rwanda |
| NCP | National Commission for Privatization |
| NEPAD | New Partnership for Africa's Development |
| NERP | National Economic Revival Program (Zimbabwe) |

| | |
|---|---|
| NIGELEC | Société Nigérienne d'Electricité |
| NNPC | Nigerian National Petroleum Corporation |
| NPL | Non-Performing Loan |
| NPV | Net Present Value |
| NT | National Treatment |
| NTB | Non-Tariff Barrier |
| OCTRA | l'Office du chemin de fer du Transgabonais |
| ODA | official development assistance |
| OECD | Organisation for Economic Co-operation and Development |
| OFIDA | Office des Douanes et Accises (DRC) |
| ONATEL | Office National des Telecommunications du Burkina Faso |
| ONEA | Office national de l'eau et de l'assainissement (Burkina Faso) |
| ONPE | National Postal and Savings Office (Niger) |
| OPEC | Organization of Petroleum Exporting Countries |
| OPRAG | Office des Portes et Rodes du Gabon |
| PARPA | Action Plan for the Reduction of Absolute Poverty Mozambique |
| PAT | Eastern and Southern African Preferential Trade Area |
| PDRE | Development Research Department (ADB) |
| PEEPA | Public Enterprise Evaluation & Privatization Agency (Botswana) |
| PRGF | Poverty Reduction and Growth Facility |
| PRGF | Poverty reduction and growth facility |
| PRSP | Poverty Reduction Strategy Paper |
| PTA | Preferential Trade Agreement |
| R&D | Research and Development |
| REC | Regional Economic Community |
| RMC | regional member country |
| RBM | Reserve Bank of Malawi |
| RTA | Regional Trade Agreement |
| SACU | South African Customs Union |
| SADC | Southern African Development Community |
| SARB | South African Reserve Bank |
| SARS | Severe Acute Respiratory Syndrome |
| SBEE | Benin Electricity and Water Company |
| SDR | Special Drawings Right |
| SDT | Special and Differential Treatment |
| SENELEC | Société Sénégalaise d'Electricité |
| SIR | Societe Ivoirienne de Raffinage |
| SNE | Société nationale d'électricité (Cameroon) |
| SNEC | Société Nationale des Eaux du Cameroun |
| SNPC | Société Nationale de Pétrole du Congo |

| | |
|---|---|
| SOE | State-Owned Enterprise |
| SOFITEX | Société des Fibres Textiles du Burkina Faso |
| SONABEL | Société Nationale d' Electricité du Burkina |
| SONACOS | Senegal's Oil/Groundnut Refinery |
| SONAPRA | Société nationale pour la promotion agricole (Benin) |
| SONIDEP | Société nigérienne des produits pétroliers |
| SSA | Sub-Saharan Africa |
| STB | State Trading Corporation (Mauritius) |
| TACV | Transportes Aéreos de Cabo Verde |
| T-bill | treasury bill |
| TDCA | Trade, Development and Co-operation Agreement |
| TDE | Société Togolaise des Eaux |
| TdM | Telecommunications de Mozambique |
| TELMA | Telecommunications Madagascar |
| TFP | Total factor productivity |
| TOR | Tema Oil Recovery (Ghana) |
| TQ | Tariff Quota |
| TRC | Tanzanian Railway Company |
| TRIMs | Trade-Related Investment Measures |
| TRIPs | Trade-Related Aspects of Intellectual Property Rights |
| TTCL | Tanzania Telecommunications Company Ltd |
| UDEAC | Central African Customs and Economic Union |
| UEMOA | Union Economique et Monétaire Ouest Africaine |
| UN | United Nations |
| UNCTAD | United Nations Conference on Trade and Development |
| UNECA | UN Economic Commission for Africa |
| UNIDO | UN    Industrial Development Organization |
| UNITA | União Nacional para a Independência Total de Angola |
| UTB | Union Toglaise de Banque. |
| VAT | Value-Added Tax |
| VER | Voluntary Export Restraint |
| WAEMU | West African Economic and Monetary Union |
| WTO | World Trade Organisation |
| ZAMTEL | Zambia Telecommunications Limited |
| ZESA | Zimbabwe Electricity Supply Authority |
| ZESCO | Zambia Electricity Supply Corporation |
| ZNCB | Zambia National Commercial Bank |

# CONTENTS

## PART ONE: AFRICA IN THE WORLD ECONOMY

## PART TWO:  AFRICA IN THE GLOBAL TRADING SYSTEM

## PART THREE:  ECONOMIC AND SOCIAL STATISTICS ON AFRICA

# BOXES

## Text Figures

## Text Tables

# PART ONE

# AFRICA IN THE WORLD ECONOMY

# CHAPTER 1

# The African Economy in 2003

This chapter reviews the performance of the African economy in 2003. In the first half, the overall growth of the African economy and other macroeconomic indicators of performance are discussed. The analysis is then disaggregated into a discussion of the performance of Africa's ten largest economies that account for some three-quarters of Africa's GDP. A brief overview of regional performances is then presented, although this is discussed in much greater detail in Chapter 2. This is followed by a discussion of the performance of the major sectors of the African economy — agriculture, industry, and services.

In the second half of the chapter, the factors that underpinned Africa's economic performance in 2003 are discussed. The improved external environment, particularly with respect to trade — as evidenced by higher commodity prices, growth in volume of exports, and higher receipts from tourism — is first presented. The improving domestic policy and regional environment, which also underlined the improved economic performance, is then discussed. The chapter closes with a brief discussion of Africa's medium- and long-term prospects.

## The Performance of African Economies[1]

### Growth Rebound against a Background of a Fragile Global Recovery

Africa's growth rate, in 2003, at 3.7 percent, was the highest for the last four years, and significantly higher than the 2.9 percent rate achieved in 2002. The improved growth rate was, however, broadly in line with the trend growth observed since 1995 (see Figure 1.1). The higher output growth was achieved despite a fragile world output growth and continued constraints to improved economic performance in some parts of the continent. Remarkably, Africa's growth rate in 2003 was higher than the global growth rate and also higher than that recorded by the advanced countries and Latin America and the Caribbean. It, however, lagged behind Asia and the countries in transition of Europe and Central Asia (see Table 1.11 and Figure 1.2).

World output increased by 3.2 percent in 2003 as compared to 3.0 percent in 2002, with the marginal improvement driven mainly by increases in growth of output of developing economies. Output growth in the advanced economies remained at its 2002 level — 1.8 percent. By contrast, output growth in

---

[1] The cut-off date for the 2003 data used in this chapter is 28 February 2004. The estimates provided may, therefore, change slightly as they are firmed up in the course of the year.

### Table 1.1: Africa: Macroeconomic Indicators, 1999–2003

| Indicators | 1999 | 2000 | 2001 | 2002 | 2003[a] |
|---|---|---|---|---|---|
| 1. Real GDP Growth Rate | 3.0 | 3.2 | 3.6 | 2.9 | 3.7 |
| 2. Real Per Capita GDP Growth Rate | 0.6 | 0.8 | 1.3 | 0.7 | 1.5 |
| 3. Inflation (%) | 11.9 | 13.6 | 11.9 | 9.4 | 11.2 |
| 4. Investment Ratio (% of GDP) | 20.2 | 18.5 | 19.2 | 19.7 | 20.5 |
| 5. Fiscal Balance (% of GDP) | –3.3 | –1.9 | –2.8 | –3.4 | –3.0 |
| 6. Growth of Money Supply (%) | 16.9 | 17.3 | 20.2 | 19.2 | 15.8 |
| 7. Export Growth, volume (%) | 3.9 | 8.4 | 0.2 | 2.0 | 4.8 |
| 8. Import Growth, volume (%) | 5.5 | 2.2 | 2.9 | 2.8 | 4.6 |
| 9. Terms of Trade (%) | 6.6 | 13.3 | –4.6 | 0.2 | 2.7 |
| 10. Trade Balance ($ billion) | –5.7 | 24.8 | 10.2 | 6.7 | 15.6 |
| 11. Current Account ($ billion) | –17.6 | 3.7 | –2.2 | –5.4 | –2.7 |
| 12. Current Account (% of GDP) | –3.4 | 0.7 | –0.4 | –1.0 | –0.4 |
| 13. Debt Service (% of Exports) | 19.8 | 16.2 | 17.4 | 21.2 | 15.2 |
| 14. National Savings (% of GDP) | 16.4 | 18.7 | 17.9 | 18.3 | 19.1 |
| 15. Net Capital Inflows ($ billion) | 20.5 | 14.7 | 20.3 | 23.1 | ... |
| 16. FDI ($ billion) | 12.2 | 8.5 | 18.8 | 11.0 | ... |
| 17. FDI (% of FDI to developing countries) | 5.3 | 3.5 | 9.0 | 6.8 | ... |

Notes: a/ Preliminary estimates
... Not available
Source: ADB Statistics Division and IMF.

developing countries rose from 4.6 percent in 2002 to 5 percent in 2003. South and East Asia maintained their high growth performance of 6.4 percent in 2003. Latin America and the Caribbean reversed their 2002 negative growth and posted a modest positive growth of 1.1 percent. Worldwide, the 2002 slump was partly due to geopolitical uncertainties, continued concerns about terrorism, persistence of the slowdown in global trade and investment, and the lingering effects of the financial crisis in Latin America and East Asia. Many regions still face a number of impediments to investment and trade and the current forecasts do not as yet foresee speedy recovery towards the attainment of long-term growth potentials.

### Economic Fundamentals Continue to Strengthen

The improved output growth on the continent was accompanied by a strengthening of economic fundamentals. Although the continent's average inflation rate increased from 9.4 percent in 2002 to 11.2 percent in 2003, this was largely due to hyperinflation in a few countries such as Zimbabwe, which recorded an inflation rate of 420 percent and higher agricultural prices in others as a result of food shortages (see Figure 1.3). Africa's

## Table 1.2: Africa: Frequency Distribution of Countries According to Real GDP and Real Per Capita GDP Growth Rates, 1999-2003

|  | 1999 | 2000 | 2001 | 2002 | 2003[a] |
|---|---|---|---|---|---|
| **Real GDP Growth Rate (%)** | | | | | |
| Negative | 10 | 11 | 5 | 7 | 6 |
| 0–3 | 14 | 13 | 14 | 18 | 11 |
| Above 3 to 5 | 14 | 11 | 11 | 16 | 16 |
| Above 5 | 13 | 16 | 21 | 10 | 18 |
| Not available | 2 | 2 | 2 | 2 | 2 |
| Total | 53 | 53 | 53 | 53 | 53 |
| **Real Per Capita GDP Growth Rate (%)** | | | | | |
| Negative | 20 | 19 | 13 | 16 | 12 |
| 0–1.5 | 9 | 10 | 9 | 14 | 7 |
| Above 1.5 to 5 | 19 | 17 | 22 | 16 | 28 |
| Above 5 | 3 | 5 | 7 | 5 | 4 |
| Not available | 2 | 2 | 2 | 2 | 2 |
| Total | 53 | 53 | 53 | 53 | 53 |

*Note*: a/ Preliminary estimates
*Source*: ADB Statistics Division.

## Figure 1.1:  Africa: Real GDP Growth Rate (%) — 1990–2004

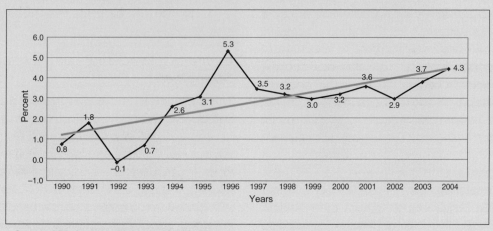

*Source*: ADB Statistics Division and IMF, 2004

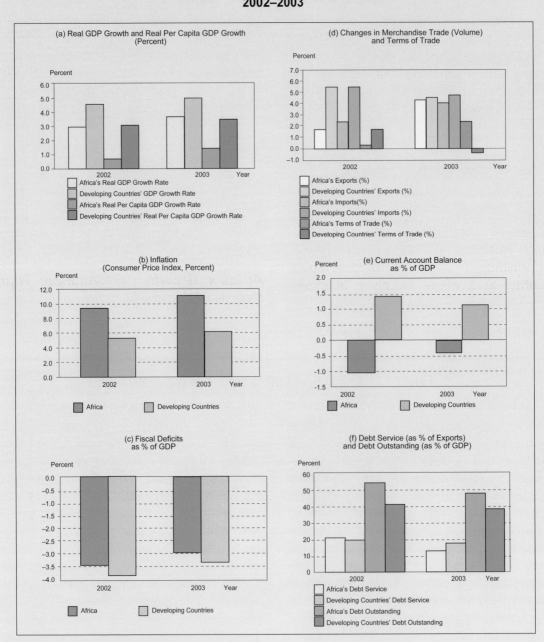

Figure 1.2: Developing Countries vis-à-vis Africa's Major Performance Indicators, 2002–2003

Source: ADB Statistics Division, 2004

median inflation rate was only 5.6 with some 40 countries recording single-digit inflation rates. The fiscal deficit for the continent declined to 3.0 percent from 3.4 percent in 2002, reflecting both tighter monetary policies as well as higher receipts from exports.

The trade performance of the continent registered a major improvement in 2003, with the trade balance increasing to US$15.6 billion from US$6.7 billion in 2002. This was reflected in the current account deficit declining from 1.0 percent of GDP in 2002 to 0.4 percent in 2003. Significantly, the debt service of African countries continued its trend decline, reaching 15.2 percent of exports in 2003 from the 21.2 percent level of 2002. Indicators of Africa's economic performance in relation to developing countries as a whole are given in Figure 1.2.

## Investment: Considerable Variability among Countries

Africa's investment ratio (to GDP) improved slightly from 19.7 percent in 2002 to 20.5 percent in 2003. This average masks considerable variations in investment ratios among African countries, with the levels closely related to their policy stance. Those African countries that have improved their macroeconomic policy and investment climate have made significant progress in increasing their overall domestic investment, and in particular private investment, in recent years. For example, during the period 1998–2002, the following countries experienced fairly high investment ratios: Botswana (28.4 %), Ghana (23.0 %), Mauritius (24.7 %), Mozambique (36.7 %), and Tunisia (26.7 %). These higher levels of investment were

associated with reasonably high economic growth rates.

On the other extreme, the countries that have experienced political and economic instability recorded poor investment performance and diminishing economic growth. For instance, during the period 1998–2002 Sierra Leone had an average investment ratio of 5.9 percent and an associated economic growth rate of 1.3 percent while Burundi had an average investment ratio of 8.7 percent and an average economic growth rate of 1.9 percent. Also, during the same period, Zimbabwe had an investment rate of 10.9 percent and the economic growth rate declined to a negative 6.3 percent.

## Africa's Growth Performance: High Degree of Variability

As in previous years, there was considerable variation in the growth performance of African countries, although, on the whole, there was marked improvement. Significantly, countries with growth rates in excess of 5 percent increased from 10 to 18 in 2003 (see Table 1.2). These included Equatorial Guinea (14.7%), Madagascar (9.6%), Chad (9.1%), Gambia (7.3%), Mozambique (7.0%), Algeria (6.7%), Sierra Leone (6.5%), Senegal (6.5%), Malawi (5.9 %), Sudan (5.8%), Libya (5.6%), Tunisia (5.5%), Tanzania (5.5%), Benin (5.5%), Uganda (5.4%), Mauritania (5.3%), Eritrea (5.03%) and Nigeria (5.01%). Major factors that contributed to these high growth rates include: economic reforms, increased oil revenues, and improved supply response in agriculture. For instance, in the oil-producing economies of Algeria, Equatorial Guinea, Libya and Nigeria, a sharp increase in oil

## Figure 1.3: Africa: Major Economic Indicators, 1999–2003

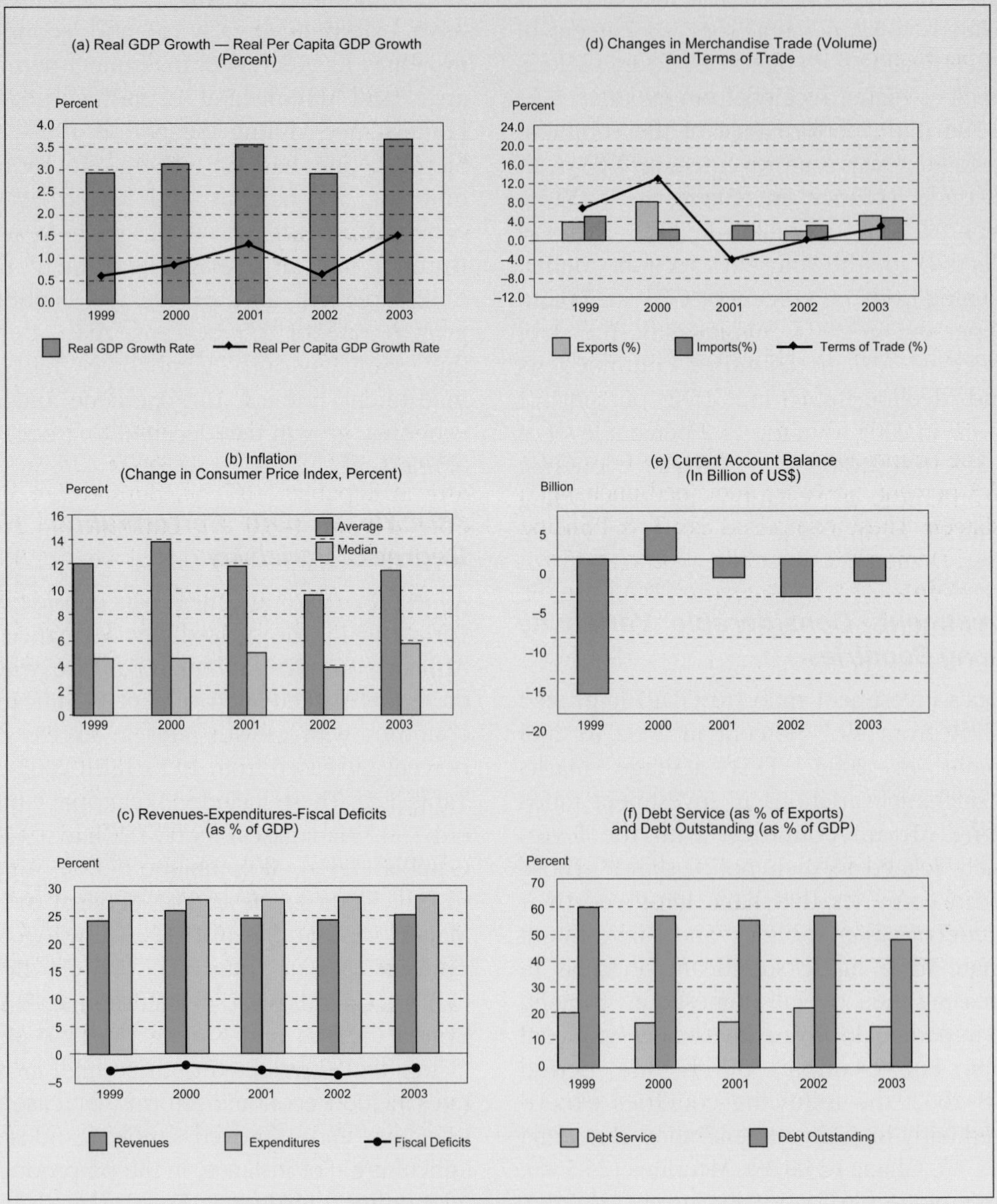
(a) Real GDP Growth — Real Per Capita GDP Growth (Percent)
Percent
4.0
3.5
3.0
2.5
2.0
1.5
1.0
0.5
0.0
1999
2000
2001
2002
2003
Real GDP Growth Rate
Real Per Capita GDP Growth Rate
(d) Changes in Merchandise Trade (Volume) and Terms of Trade
Percent
24.0
20.0
16.0
12.0
8.0
4.0
0.0
−4.0
−8.0
−12.0
1999
2000
2001
2002
2003
Exports (%)
Imports(%)
Terms of Trade (%)
(b) Inflation (Change in Consumer Price Index, Percent)
Percent
16
14
12
10
8
6
4
2
0
Average
Median
1999
2000
2001
2002
2003
(e) Current Account Balance (In Billion of US$)
Billion
5
0
−5
−10
−15
−20
1999
2000
2001
2002
2003
(c) Revenues-Expenditures-Fiscal Deficits (as % of GDP)
Percent
30
25
20
15
10
5
0
−5
1999
2000
2001
2002
2003
Revenues
Expenditures
Fiscal Deficits
(f) Debt Service (as % of Exports) and Debt Outstanding (as % of GDP)
Percent
70
60
50
40
30
20
10
0
1999
2000
2001
2002
2003
Debt Service
Debt Outstanding

*Source*: ADB Statistics Division, 2004

export revenue helped boost income growth. On the other hand, in the Sudan, increases in productivity both within and outside the oil industry spurred growth. Senegal and the Gambia regained their high growth trajectory after the large exogenous shock associated with the drought in 2002. Similarly in Malawi, Tanzania, and Uganda an improvement in agricultural production contributed to strong growth. In Sierra Leone, progress on the peace front allowed the restoration of macro-economic stability and growth. Economic activity in Tunisia gained from some of the improvement in the international economic environment as well as the improved performance of the agricultural sector.

The countries with growth rates between 3 and 5 percent, however, remained unchanged at sixteen. These comprised Sao T. & Principe (5 %), Democratic Republic of Congo (5.%), Cape Verde (5.%), Ghana (4.7%), Angola (4.4%), Mauritius (4.4%), Zambia (4.3 %) Morocco (4.2 %), Lesotho (4.2 %), Cameroon (4.0 %), Niger (4.0 %), Namibia (3.7 %), Botswana (3.7 %), Guinea (3.6 %), Rwanda (3.2 %), and Mali (3.2 %). These growth rates are generally above population growth, indicating some gain in per capita income. In the Democratic Republic of Congo, the economy responded to the stimulus of macroeconomic stabilization, structural reforms, and growth in output across a range of sectors, including services, transportation and communication. Improvement in the agricultural sector in Ghana, especially a strong recovery of the cocoa sector, helped boost growth. Also, in Mali, Zambia, and Rwanda. growth was

spurred by the marked improvement in the agricultural sector. Botswana saw an increase in diamond output and in Mauritius, the healthy performance of the service sector continued to lead economic growth.

The number of countries with growth rates between 0 and 3 percent fell from 18 in 2002 to 11 in 2003. These comprise Togo (3.0 %), Djibouti (3.0 %), Egypt (2.8 %), Burkina Faso (2.6 %), Comoros (2.4 %), Guinea Bissau (2.4 %), Swaziland (2.3 %), South Africa (2.2 %) Kenya (1.4 %), Congo (1.2 %), and Gabon (0.8 %). Also, the number of countries with negative growth rate fell from seven in 2002 to six in 2003. This group consists mainly of countries in conflict or countries affected by drought and natural disasters — Central African Republic (–0.7 %), Burundi (–1.3 %), Côte d'Ivoire (–3.0 %), Ethiopia (–4.2 %), Seychelles (–4.9 %), and Zimbabwe (–11.0 %).[2]

Many African countries have faced difficulties in sustaining high growth rates, resulting in great variability in economic growth rates from year to year. This is most evident in the performance of the sub-regions. Growth in East Africa declined rather sharply from 5.3 percent in 2001 to 2.1 percent in 2002 and only registered a modest rebound of 2.6 percent in 2003. Similarly, growth in North Africa decelerated from 3.8 percent in 2001 to 2.8 percent in 2002, but rose significantly to 4.7 percent in 2003. West Africa also showed a great variation its output growth, falling to 1.9 percent in 2002 but rising to 4 percent in 2003. In Southern Africa, the region's performance is dominated by the performance of the South African economy. Output growth of the South African economy had increased to 3.6 percent in 2002 from 2.6

---

[2] The growth performance for Somalia and Liberia are not included because of lack of data.

percent in 2001, but declined to 2.2 percent in 2003. The growth performance of central African countries, at around 4 percent, has been more consistent in recent years owing to the post-conflict rebound and sharp increases in oil revenue, although there exists considerable variation in growth rates among the countries as well.

The annual variability in Africa's growth performance is accounted for by a number of factors. These include major variations in climatic conditions affecting agricultural output, which still contributes a substantial share to the GDP of most counties. In addition, variations in the export prices of primary commodities result in a high variability in export revenues and growth, given the dependence of most countries on the export of a few commodities for their export revenues. The variability of Africa's economic performance is also driven by the incidence of civil conflicts — their frequency, geographical location within the continent, the number of countries negatively affected, and the extent of such effects. The unpredictability of donors' support also contributes to Africa's performance variability. Despite the growing use of medium-term expenditure frameworks in many countries, most donor funding is still committed annually, with the amount and timing rarely communicated in advance.

### Improvements in Output per Capita

Accompanying the higher overall growth rate, Africa's output per capita grew by 1.5 percent in 2003. This represents a marked improvement over the 2002 GDP per capita growth of 0.7 percent. The per capita income of most countries also improved over their 2002 levels. The number of countries with negative per capita growth in 2003 fell from 16 to 12 . Similarly, the number of countries with per capita growth rates between 0 and 1.5 percent fell by half from 14 to seven, while the number of countries with per capita growth rates between 1.5 percent and 5 per-cent rose from 16 to 28. On the other hand, countries with per capita output growth above 5 percent fell marginally from five to four.

The achievement of higher output per capita, a necessary condition for lowering poverty levels and for making progress towards the Millennium Development Goals (MDGs), depends on a number of factors. In the first instance, African countries would need to accelerate their GDP growth rates and sustain them over time. As importantly, they will need to pursue appropriate population-related development policies — such as family planning services, maternal and child care, and improving the access of girls to education — to improve the standards of living of their populations. Such policies are essential to curb the increasing pressure on both the socioeconomic infrastructure and natural resources that has been caused by continuous and rapid increases in population levels over the past four decades. In this connection, it is, however, important to keep in mind the serious adverse demographic impact — such as high mortality rates and a lowering of average life expectancy — that the HIV/AIDS is having on a number of African countries, particularly in Southern Africa.

## The Performance of Africa's Ten Largest Economies

Continental averages of economic outcomes are heavily influenced by the performance of

'Africa's Ten Largest Economies' (ATLEs). The ATLEs account for about 55 percent of the region's population and contribute 75 percent of its GDP (see Table 1.3). In 2003, the ATLEs grew by 3.9 percent, slightly above the continental average of 3.7 percent, although there was considerable variation in output growth among the countries that belong to this group.

The higher growth of the ATLEs was attributable to the strong performance of four of the six North African countries that belong to this group — Algeria, Libya, Sudan and Tunisia. These countries registered growth rates above 5 percent (see Tables 1.3 and 1.4). Of the remaining two North African countries, the Moroccan economy grew at 4.2 percent, while Egypt, probably more disproportionately affected by negative developments in the Middle East, grew by only 2.8 percent.

The growth of the South African economy — the largest on the continent — slowed down in 2003, partly as a result of the weak European recovery (Europe being its major trading partner) and a decline in the growth of tourism as a result of the considerable appreciation of the rand. These developments, combined with lower agricultural production, resulted in a growth rate of 2.2 percent in 2003 compared to the 3.0 percent registered in 2002. Similarly, Nigeria is estimated to have a high growth rate of 5 percent in 2003 compared to 3.3 percent in 2002, as a result of larger oil revenues in 2003. Angola registered a growth rate of 4.4 percent, sustaining its higher growth rate achieved following the end of the civil war in 2002. On the other hand, Kenya's growth rate did not rise above 1.4 percent, owing in part to investor uncertainties and infrastructural

### Table 1.3: Africa's Ten Largest Economies (ATLE), 2003

| Country | GDP at current US$ (Billions) | Population (Millions) | GDP Growth Rate | Country Weight in Total African GDP (%) |
|---|---|---|---|---|
| SOUTH AFRICA | 160.8 | 45.03 | 2.2 | 24.9 |
| EGYPT | 78.7 | 71.93 | 2.8 | 12.2 |
| ALGERIA | 65.7 | 31.80 | 5.9 | 10.2 |
| NIGERIA | 48.0 | 124.01 | 5.0 | 7.4 |
| MOROCCO | 44.7 | 30.57 | 4.2 | 6.9 |
| TUNISIA | 24.9 | 9.83 | 5.5 | 3.9 |
| LIBYA | 21.4 | 5.55 | 5.6 | 3.3 |
| SUDAN | 14.6 | 33.61 | 5.8 | 2.3 |
| ANGOLA | 14.3 | 13.63 | 4.4 | 2.2 |
| KENYA | 14.2 | 31.99 | 1.4 | 2.2 |
| **TOTAL ATLE** | **487** | **398** | **4.0** | **75.4** |

*Source*: ADB Statistics Division, UN and IMF.

constraints, as well as limited inflows of international financial assistance.

In addition to the improvement in real GDP growth in 2003, which contributed to the rise in income per capita, most other macroeconomic fundamentals also improved in 2003 in the ALTEs. The fiscal deficit remained relatively stable at 2.7 percent of GDP compared with the annual average of 2.6 percent over the period 1999–2002. Significant improvement in the fiscal balance was recorded in 2003 in Algeria, Egypt, Tunisia and Morocco, while the deficit worsened in South Africa and Kenya. As a result of the sharp increase in oil export revenues of Algeria, Nigeria, and Libya, the trade balance of the ALTE increased significantly from the annual average of about US$6.0 billion more than 1999–2002 to over US$20.7 billion in 2003. The sharp increase in the trade balance contributed to an improvement also in the current account balance, from the average surplus of US$1.0 billion in 1999–2002 to nearly US$4 billion in 2003. Improved export receipts in 2003 contributed to the fall in the debt service ratio from the annual average 16.2 percent in 1999–2002 to 15.4 percent. Similarly, national savings in the ALTE improved in 2003, buoyed by the rise in export revenues. On the other hand, the rate

### Table 1.4: Macroeconomic Indicators for ALTE*, 1999–2003

| Indicators | 1999 | 2000 | 2001 | 2002 | 2003 |
|---|---|---|---|---|---|
| 1. Real GDP Growth Rate | 3.0 | 3.6 | 3.3 | 3.0 | 4.0 |
| 2. Real Per Capita GDP Growth Rate | 0.9 | 1.5 | 1.2 | 1.0 | 2.0 |
| 3. Inflation (%) | 5.0 | 3.9 | 3.6 | 4.9 | 5.8 |
| 4. Investment Ratio (% of GDP) | 20.6 | 18.6 | 19.2 | 20.2 | 21.1 |
| 5. Fiscal Balance (% of GDP) | −3.1 | −1.0 | −2.7 | −3.5 | −2.7 |
| 6. Growth of Money Supply (%) | 13.4 | 13.6 | 16.7 | 13.8 | 12.4 |
| 7. Export Growth, volume (%) | 3.1 | 11.2 | 0.6 | 1.9 | −2.5 |
| 8. Import Growth, volume (%) | 5.5 | 5.0 | 1.6 | 2.5 | −10.8 |
| 9. Terms of Trade (%) | 5.6 | 18.5 | −4.0 | −1.5 | 5.0 |
| 10. Trade Balance ($ billion) | −6.6 | 16.1 | 8.5 | 6.8 | 20.7 |
| 11. Current Account ($ billion) | −9.8 | 9.1 | 4.7 | 0.3 | 3.6 |
| 12. Current Account (% of GDP) | −2.5 | 2.2 | 1.2 | 0.1 | 0.9 |
| 13. Debt Service (% of Exports) | 19.6 | 14.9 | 15.9 | 14.3 | 15.4 |
| 14. National Savings (% of GDP) | 18.5 | 21.4 | 20.3 | 20.5 | 21.6 |
| 15. Net Capital Inflows ($ billion) | 6.6 | 2.0 | 7.4 | 9.1 | ... |
| 16. FDI ($ billion) | 8.6 | 5.9 | 15.6 | 6.9 | ... |
| 17. FDI (% to developing countries) | 1.0 | 0.5 | 2.6 | 1.5 | ... |

* ALTE: South Africa, Egypt, Algeria, Nigeria, Morocco, Tunisia, Libya, Sudan, Angola and Kenya.
   ... Not available
Source: ADB Statistics Division and IMF, 2004

of inflation rose in the ALTE in 2003 mainly as a result of higher inflation rates recorded in South Africa and Kenya.

## Regional Performance

As in previous years, and as noted above, there was considerable variation in 2003 in the growth performance of the continent's sub-regions. The growth of output in the countries of North Africa showed a substantial increase from 2.8 percent in 2002 to 4.7 percent in 2003. A similar increase was registered in West Africa with the growth in output doubling to 4.0 percent from the 1.9 percent of 2002. Central Africa's growth rate fell marginally from 4.6 percent to 4.4 percent. The strong performance in these three regions accounted for the increase in

### Table 1.5: Real GDP Growth Rates by Sub-Region, 1999–2003

| | 1999 | 2000 | 2001 | 2002 | 2003[a/] |
|---|---|---|---|---|---|
| **ADB Geographical sub-regions** | | | | | |
| Central Africa | 0.0 | 0.2 | 3.6 | 4.6 | 4.4 |
| Eastern Africa | 4.4 | 4.2 | 5.3 | 2.1 | 2.6 |
| Northern Africa | 3.9 | 3.7 | 3.8 | 2.8 | 4.7 |
| Southern Africa | 2.1 | 2.8 | 2.6 | 3.6 | 2.2 |
| Western Africa | 2.5 | 2.8 | 3.7 | 1.9 | 4.0 |
| **ADB Operational groupings** | | | | | |
| ADF-eligible countries (incl. Blend countries) | 2.8 | 2.5 | 3.8 | 2.9 | 3.6 |
| ADF-only Countries | 3.6 | 2.7 | 4.6 | 4.1 | 3.8 |
| Blend countries | 0.1 | 1.9 | 1.0 | −1.6 | 2.8 |
| Non-ADF countries | 3.0 | 3.6 | 3.4 | 2.9 | 3.8 |
| **Regional & economic groups** | | | | | |
| AMU | 2.3 | 2.3 | 3.5 | 2.7 | 5.6 |
| CAEMC | 2.2 | 3.5 | 6.5 | 4.9 | 4.6 |
| COMESA | 4.2 | 3.5 | 3.2 | 2.7 | 2.8 |
| ECCAS | 0.6 | 0.7 | 3.5 | 6.6 | 4.4 |
| ECOWAS | 2.5 | 2.9 | 3.7 | 1.9 | 4.0 |
| FRANC ZONE | 2.9 | 1.8 | 5.2 | 3.2 | 3.3 |
| SADC | 1.6 | 2.4 | 2.5 | 3.6 | 2.6 |
| WAEMU | 3.3 | 0.8 | 4.3 | 2.1 | 2.4 |
| HIPC Countries | 4.8 | 3.8 | 6.2 | 3.9 | 4.2 |
| Net Oil Exporters | 3.7 | 3.9 | 3.2 | 2.7 | 4.7 |
| Net Oil Importers | 2.5 | 2.6 | 3.8 | 3.1 | 3.0 |
| **ALL RMCs** | **3.0** | **3.2** | **3.6** | **2.9** | **3.7** |

Note: a/ Preliminary estimates.
Source: ADB Statistics Division, 2004

the continent's overall output from 2.9 to 3.7 percent. By contrast, there was only a marginal improvement in the growth performance of countries in East Africa — from 2.1 in 2002 to 2.6 percent in 2003, while the Southern Africa region experienced a deceleration in growth from 3.6 percent in 2002 to 2.2 percent in 2003. The latter was in large part due to the slower growth of the South African economy and the sharp contraction in the Zimbabwean economy, which registered a negative growth rate of 11 percent. The highlights of the growth performance in 2003 of each sub-region are detailed in Boxes 1.1 to 1.5.

---

**Box 1.1: Highlights of Regional Performances — Central Africa**

Central Africa's growth in 2003 at 4.4 percent, remained virtually the same as in 2002 at 4.6 percent, despite great variation in the performance of individual countries. Two countries, Burundi and the Central African Republic, recorded negative growth of 1.3 percent and 0.7 percent respectively. A number of other countries registered modest growth rates. For example, the Congo Republic saw its growth rate decline from 3.5 percent in 2002 to 1.2 percent in 2002 and Gabon reversed its negative growth in 2002 and recorded a modest increase of 0.8 percent. The performance of post-war countries in the region was mixed. Rwanda's growth rate dropped sharply to 3.2 percent in 2003 after registering a high of 9.4 percent in 2002. By contrast the Democratic Republic of Congo accelerated its pace of growth to 5 percent in 2003 from 3.0 percent in 2002. And driven mainly by high oil production, the Republic of Chad and Equatorial Guinea maintained their exceptionally high growth during the year with the former reaching 9.1 percent while the latter grew by 14.7 percent.

---

**Box 1.2: Highlights of Regional Performances — East Africa**

Growth in output of 2.6 percent in 2003 for East Africa was an improvement from the 2.1 percent growth of 2002. As in other regions, there was considerable variation in the performance of individual countries. Ethiopia recorded a negative growth rate of 4.2 percent due to the major reduction in agricultural output in 2003 because of severe drought conditions in the 2002/2003 cropping season. Kenya's economy — the largest in the region — continued with its trend growth which has averaged around 1 percent for the last five years, with output growth at 1.4 percent despite relatively large earnings from tourism. By contrast, the economies of Tanzania and Uganda grew by over 5 percent each. A major improvement was also recorded by Madagascar, which reversed its negative growth of 12.7 percent in 2002, occasioned by the political crisis, to positive growth of 9.6 percent in 2003. Mauritius also improved on its 2002 growth of 2.1 percent to reach 4.4 percent in 2003.

## Box 1.3: Highlights of Regional Performances — Southern Africa

Output growth in Southern Africa declined to 2.2 percent in 2003 from 3.6 percent in 2002. This was in large part due to the slower growth rate of the South African economy, the largest economy in the region, whose growth rate declined to 2.2 percent from 3.6 percent registered in 2002. But more broadly, the lower performance of Southern African economies is also accounted for by the incidence of drought, political instability in some countries, and the severe economic and social impact of the HIV/AIDS pandemic. Although food production has started to recover from the severe drought that reduced harvests by as much as 50 percent in 2001/02, several countries in the region still faced severe shortages in 2003. Political instability in Zimbabwe continued in 2003 and contributed to the country posting a negative output growth for the fifth consecutive year, with the economy contracting by 11.0 percent in 2003. Economic output in Botswana continues to be highly affected by the HIV/AIDS pandemic as its growth of 3.7 percent in 2003 is the second lowest in the last seven years. Angola's impressive growth of 15.3 percent of 2002, precipitated by post-war reconstruction, could not be sustained for a second year. However, the growth of 4.4 percent in 2003 is still well above the sub-regional average of 2.2 percent. A few countries in the region also performed better both relative to the sub-regional average and also relative to their 2002 performance levels. Malawi grew by 5.9 percent as against its average of less than 1.5 percent growth since 2000. Mozambique maintained the exceptionally high growth it has recorded over a seven-year period with output increasing by 7 percent in 2003.

## Box 1.4: Highlights of Regional Performances — North Africa

North Africa accounts for nearly 40 percent of the African economy, and the sub-region recorded impressive performance in 2003. With the exception of Egypt and Morocco, all the countries in the region grew by over 5 percent in 2003. The repercussions of the Iraqi crisis, which raised oil prices to a monthly average peak of US$32 per barrel, contributed to the higher growth rates. The Algerian economy, with its heavy dependence on oil and gas exports, grew by 5.9 percent. Similarly, the Libyan economy grew by more than 5 percent, after negative growth of 0.2 percent in 2002. Sudan, which had maintained a very high growth of over 5 percent per annum for most of the last decade, maintained its strong performance growing by 5.8 percent in 2003. In Morocco and Tunisia, the higher growth rates achieved in 2003 largely reflected the rebound in agricultural production after the devastating drought of 2002. The Moroccan economy grew by 4.2 percent and the Tunisian by 5.5 percent. By contrast, the growth of the Egyptian economy was affected by the build-up to the war in Iraq. Uncertainty over security issues led to sharply lower receipts in the tourism sector, which accounts for approximately 10 percent of GDP. In addition, lower volumes of non-oil trade led to a loss of revenue from trade along the Suez Canal. This combined with extended domestic macroeconomic weakness, especially subdued private investment, to curb the Egyptian economy's growth at below potential.

**Box 1.5: Highlights of Regional Performances — West Africa**

West Africa's regional average growth of 4 percent was double the 1.9 percent rate achieved in 2002. Nigeria's growth rate, which is estimated to have risen to 5 percent in 2003 — up from 3.3 percent in 2002 — was a major factor in the growth outcome for the region, as Nigeria accounts for about 60 percent of the region's GDP. The increased regional growth rate was also supported by the performance of the traditionally high-growing economies — Benin, Cape Verde, Senegal, and The Gambia — as these maintained good growth rates. Mali, which had posted an exceptional growth rate of 11.8 percent in 2002, saw its rate decline to 3.2 percent, although in 2003 there were record cereal and cotton harvests. Part of the slowdown was explained by a reduction on activity in other sectors, due to the adverse impact of the crisis in Côte d'Ivoire. Post-war Sierra Leone also recorded high growth on account of reconstruction and restoration of political stability in the country. The majority of the remaining countries, however, posted modest growth rates. Côte d'Ivoire, with the second largest economy in the region and experiencing significant civil disturbance since 2002, registered negative growth for the second consecutive year.

## Major Sectoral Developments

In the sectoral division of Africa's GDP, agriculture contributes 20 percent, industry (including mining, quarrying, and the energy sector) 32 percent, and the services sector the remaining 48 percent. In 2003, all three sectors continued to grow, albeit at relatively low rates. The industrial sector had the highest growth rate at 4.1 percent, although the growth of the manufacturing sector fell to 2.3 percent from the 3.5 percent registered in 2002. Developments within each sector are discussed in more detail below.

### Agriculture and Food Security

The agriculture sector continues to be a critical sector for Africa as it provides employment for some 50 percent of Africa's labor force and a means of livelihood for over 70 percent of the poor. It also accounts for about 35 percent of the region's GDP. Its performance is therefore decisive for overall economic welfare of the region. In 2003, agricultural growth increased

marginally, with a growth rate of 3.1 percent relative to 2.8 percent in 2002 (see Tables 1.6 and 1.7). This performance was characterized by mixed performance of crop production on the continent, with bumper harvests in a number of countries but poor harvests in others. In the latter countries, factors responsible included drought in some East and Southern African countries and continued political instability in countries such as Zimbabwe and Côte d'Ivoire.

In 2003, cereal production on the continent was mixed. Though some regions in SSA enjoyed bumper crops, food shortages existed in some 23 African countries. According to estimates of the FAO, Africa's cereal production in 2003 increased slightly by about 8.9 million tonnes, up to 126.1 million tonnes compared with 117.2 million tonnes in 2002 (see Table.1.7). Africa's total cereal imports in 2003 stood at 38.2 million tonnes, comprising 23.2 million tonnes of wheat and 15 million tonnes of coarse grains. Imports by

| Table 1.6: Sectoral Growth Rates, 1999–2003 | | | | | |
|---|---|---|---|---|---|
| (Percentage changes from preceding year) | | | | | |
| | 1999 | 2000 | 2001 | 2002 | 2003[a] |
| Agriculture | 2.1 | 1.4 | 4.7 | 2.8 | 3.1 |
| Industry | 2.4 | 4.3 | 3.6 | 2.6 | 4.1 |
| Manufacturing | 3.3 | 4.3 | 4.1 | 3.5 | 2.3 |
| Services | 3.7 | 3.4 | 2.9 | 3.4 | 3.6 |
| GDP at constant market prices | 3.0 | 3.2 | 3.6 | 2.9 | 3.7 |

Note: a/ Preliminary estimates.
Source: ADB Statistics Division.

| Table 1.7: Africa's Cereal Production, 2000–2003 | | | | |
|---|---|---|---|---|
| (million tonnes) | | | | |
| | 2000 | 2001 | 2002 | 2003 |
| North Africa | 28.0 | 33.7 | 31.1 | 37.7 |
| Eastern Africa | 20.1 | 22.8 | 21.9 | 21.4 |
| Southern Africa | 23.2 | 17.7 | 19.3 | 19.0 |
| Western Africa | 36.4 | 36.9 | 39.8 | 43.2 |
| Central Africa | 4.5 | 5.1 | 5.1 | 5.3 |
| Africa | 112.2 | 116.2 | 117.2 | 126.5 |

Source: Adapted from FAOSTAT (2004) February

North African countries remained high, totaling 23.4 million tones or about 61 percent of total African cereal imports. Also, cereal import requirements in SSA in 2003 remained high, reflecting mainly the effects of 2002 droughts in Southern, East and West Africa. The total food aid requirement was estimated at 4.6 million tonnes, against 2.0 million tonnes estimated in 2001/02. Cereal food aid pledges for 2002/03, including those carried over from 2001/02, amounted to 4.0 million tonnes.

In spite of the modest improvements in agricultural production in the region, the food security situation in Africa remains the worst for all regions of the world. Current estimates indicate that Africa's food insecurity may increase in the coming decade, making it unlikely for the region to achieve the Millennium Development Goal 1 Target 2 of halving the number of people living in hunger by 2015. In addition to the limited progress being achieved in increasing per capita agricultural output, other causes for the food

insecurity in Africa include the impact of the HIV/AIDS pandemic on rural households, great variability of weather conditions often leading to drought in a number of sub-regions, and continued civil strife and instability in a number of countries. As a consequence, the number of people facing chronic as opposed to transitory food insecurity has increased, necessitating continuous supply of food aid from developing countries. The specific food security situations in the five sub-regions of the continent is given below.

### Food Security by Region

In **Southern Africa**, although weather conditions improved in 2003, food aid needs remained substantial because of erratic wea- ther patterns, the deteriorating Zimbabwean economy, and the devastating impact of the HIV/AIDS pandemic across the region. Production of the 2003 cereals was estimated at 19 million tonnes, virtually the same as in 2002. While in most countries of the region the output recovered from the reduced levels of the previous two years, it decreased in Botswana and remained below average in Zimbabwe. In Zimbabwe, aggregate cereal production in 2003 was estimated close to 1 million tonnes, 39 percent above the poor crop of the previous year but 48 percent below the 2000/01 harvests, which was itself significantly below average. The reduced harvest in 2003 reflected drought conditions during the growing season and the impact of land reform activities. During 2003, some 5.5 million people were estimated to be in need of food.

In Lesotho and Swaziland, as well as in parts of Namibia, Madagascar, and Mozambique, substantial amounts of emergency food aid were still required. In Angola, following the return of the displaced population to their areas of origin, and as a result of generally favorable weather conditions as well as substantial increase in areas sown, the aggregate cereal production rose by almost 25 percent to 670,000 tonnes in 2003. Output from other crops — including cassava, pulses, and sweet potatoes — was also estimated to have increased, reflecting larger areas sown and good yields. However, food assistance was required for about 1.1 million returnees. In Zambia and Malawi, the food security situation, while still requiring attention in 2003, improved over the last year. In both countries good rains and timely and targeted distribution of agricultural inputs to farmers made the difference between the poor harvest of 2002 and the better outcome in 2003. In Zambia, the production of maize, the country's main staple crop, was estimated at about 1.16 million tonnes, which was almost double the output of the 2002 season (602,000 tonnes) and about 28

percent above the average of the previous five years. In Malawi, maize production in 2003 increased by 22 percent over the 2002 harvest. As with Zambia, however, several parts of the country experienced crop failures. It was estimated that about 132,000 Malawians required food aid in 2003.

In **East Africa,** abundant rains during 2003 generally improved the cereal crop output. However, there were trouble spots with regard to food security as severe floods and erratic rains in some areas affected yields. Several countries in the sub-region still face serious food shortages. In Eritrea, a crop assessment put the 2003 cereal harvest at about 190,000 tonnes, a strong recovery from the decimated crop of 2002, but about 12 percent below the average for the five previous years and the food situation remained precarious. Some 2.3 million people were estimated to face severe food shortages as a result of last year's drought, poverty and the lingering effects of the war with Ethiopia. In Ethiopia, the number of people who needed food assistance in 2003 was about 13.2 million. In Tanzania, estimates of the 2002/03 food crop production indicated a 10 percent decline compared to the preceding year, caused mainly by extended dry weather in eastern, central, western and southern areas of the country. Also in Tanzania, an estimated 1.9 million people were in need of food assistance during 2003. Similarly the food situation in northern and eastern areas of Uganda deteriorated with the escalation of armed conflict. In 2003 more than 820,000 people were displaced by the conflict, bringing the total number of those in need of emergency food assistance to more than 1.6 million.

In **Central Africa**, agricultural production continued to suffer from the aftermath of conflict in the two largest countries of the sub-region. Food production in the Central African Republic did not increase in 2003 due to insecurity at planting time and a lack of seeds. Also, in the Democratic Republic of the Congo and Burundi, food production continued to be hampered by insecurity. In Burundi, in 2003, the production of all food crops declined and remained below the pre-civil conflict average (1988–93), an outcome which, coupled with the increase in population, lowered per capita food production. As the most marked reduction was in pulses, which are the protein source of the majority of the population, food-ration quality consequently deteriorated as well. In Rwanda, output of the 2003 food crops was estimated to be lower than last year's average level.

**West Africa** saw some improvement in agricultural production in 2003. There was a bumper crop in the Sahel, following generally favorable weather throughout the growing season. However, Cape Verde, Guinea-Bissau, and Mauritania still faced food shortages. In Côte d'Ivoire the food situation was critical, particularly in the west and north. In Liberia, the humanitarian situation improved following a peace agreement in mid-August and the deployment of a West African peacekeeping force. But the overall security situation remains precarious, affecting agricultural production. In neighboring Sierra Leone, despite below-normal rainfall, the overall food security situation improved with returning refugees and displaced farmers resuming farming activities. Record harvests were recorded in Burkina Faso in 2003. Also, Niger was favored with good weather conditions, leading to improved food production and good access to cereals. In Nigeria and Ghana, agricultural production in 2003 gained from the improved weather conditions marked by a steady and evenly distributed rainfall nationwide.

In **North Africa,** the aggregate wheat output for the sub-region was estimated by the FAO at 15.1 million tonnes, which compared favorably with the 11.6 million tonnes in 2002, when crops were severely affected by drought. In Algeria, wheat production in 2003 was double the output in 2002, and barley production was nearly three times higher. In Egypt, wheat output declined by some 33,000 tonnes in 2003, while maize production was estimated to be about 6.4 million tonnes. In Morocco, wheat production was estimated at 5.1 million tonnes, compared to 3.4 million tonnes harvested in 2002 and the previous five-year average of 3.1 million tonnes. Production of barley also increased from 1.7 million tonnes in 2002 to 2.6 million tonnes in 2003. In Tunisia, wheat output more than tripled in 2003 compared with the 2002 production level, while barley output reached 345,000 tonnes in 2003, compared to the poor 90,200 tonnes in 2002 and the five-year average of 265,840 tonnes.

## Industry

Industrialization is essential for Africa's economic growth as it contributes to raising employment and productivity and enhances the income-generating assets of the poor. It is also critical to helping countries diversify their export base and lessen the risks from the variability of the prices of primary commodities. Although in recent years the privatization programs implemented by many

African countries have given industrialization a boost, the industrial base, with the exception of South Africa and some of the North African countries, generally remains weak. Sub-Saharan Africa (excluding South Africa) continues to lag behind all other regions with respect to manufacturing activity and the intensity of industrialization, measured by manufacturing value-added per capita. In 2003, the industrial sector showed an increase in output, due to an increase in mining activities, reflected in an increase of its growth rate from 2.6 percent in 2002 to 4.1 percent in 2003.

However, the manufacturing sub-sector saw its growth rate decline from 3.5 percent in 2002 to 2.3 percent in 2003. Individual country performances were diverse, but the underlying factors behind the poor manufacturing activity remained similar across most SSA countries. Weak domestic demand continued to constrain expansion of manufacturing output. In addition, high interest rates have slowed the level of local demand for manufactured goods, especially durables. In the North African countries and in South Africa the slowdown was due to weakening global economic conditions, worsened by the Iraq war in 2003, which hindered the growth of export demand. Also, in South Africa, the sustained appreciation of the rand dampened export demand; consequently manufacturing output contracted for most of 2003.

The poor performance of manufacturing in most African countries in 2003 is in line with the limited gains made by African countries over the last decade. UNIDO data indicate that manufacturing value-added (MVA) increased only marginally from 3.0 percent between 1992–1997 to 4.2 percent

between 1997–2002 (see Table 1.8). Over the two sub-periods, North Africa's MVA rose from 3.3 percent to 5.1 percent while that of Central Africa rose significantly from minus 2.4 percent to 4.6 percent. The growth rate in MVA for East and Southern Africa fell during the two sub-periods from 4.6 percent to 2.7 percent while it declined in West Africa from 2.6 percent to 2.1 percent. The growth rate of per capita MVA followed the same trend as the growth rate in MVA, increasing from 0.5 percent in 1992–1997 to 1.7 during the 1997–2001 period. North Africa witnessed an increase from 1.3 percent to 3.2 percent while that of Central Africa rose from minus 5.0 percent to 1.6 percent during the period. On the other hand, West Africa continued to remain in the negative zone recording a decrease from minus 0.2 percent to minus 0.5 percent, with East and Southern Africa also recording a decrease from 2.0 percent to 0.3 percent in their per capita MVA growth.

### Services

The services sector grew by 3.6 percent in 2003, marginally up from growth of 3.4 percent in 2002. A major contributor was the tourism sub-sector. International tourist arrivals in Africa increased marginally to 30.5 million from its 2002 level of 29.1 million (Table 1.9). In North Africa, international tourist arrivals rose slightly from 10.3 million in 2002 to 10.8 million in 2003, while SSA experienced a higher increase from 18.8 million to 19.8 million during the period. Africa's market share of international tourism has risen from 3.6 percent in 1995 and 4.0 percent in 2002 to 4.4 percent in 2003. Although North Africa's share increased only marginally from 1.3 percent in 1995 and 1.4

Table 1.8: Annual Growth of MVA, 1992–2002 and Per Capita MVA, 2002a/

| Country Group or Country/Area | Total MVA | | | | | | Per Capita MVA | | | | | | |
| --- | --- | --- | --- | --- | --- | --- | --- | --- | --- | --- | --- | --- | --- |
| | Growth Rate Percentage | | Index (1995 = 100) | | | | Growth Rate Percentage | | Index (1995 = 100) | | | | Value (dollars) |
| | 1992–1997 | 1997–2002 | 1999 | 2000 | 2001/b | 2002/c | 1992–1997 | 1997–2002 | 1999 | 2000 | 2001/b | 2002/c | 2002/c |
| Africa /d | 3.0 | 4.2 | 120 | 125 | 130 | 135 | 0.5 | 1.7 | 109 | 110 | 112 | 114 | 68 |
| North Africa | 3.3 | 5.1 | 122 | 129 | 134 | 137 | 1.3 | 3.2 | 113 | 117 | 120 | 121 | 190 |
| UMA | 1.2 | 3.3 | 109 | 113 | 118 | 118 | -0.8 | 1.5 | 102 | 104 | 106 | 104 | 220 |
| Central Africa | -2.4 | 4.6 | 114 | 117 | 125 | 137 | -5.0 | 1.6 | 102 | 101 | 105 | 112 | 28 |
| Western Africa (ECOWAS) | 2.6 | 2.1 | 116 | 117 | 120 | 126 | -0.2 | -0.5 | 104 | 103 | 103 | 105 | 31 |
| Eastern and Southern Africa /d | 4.6 | 2.7 | 120 | 120 | 123 | 132 | 2.0 | 0.3 | 108 | 106 | 106 | 111 | 34 |
| Latin America | 3.0 | 0.7 | 108 | 113 | 111 | 113 | 1.3 | -0.8 | 101 | 104 | 101 | 102 | 678 |
| South and East Asia | 9.8 | 6.6 | 127 | 140 | 145 | 155 | 8.2 | 5.2 | 120 | 131 | 133 | 141 | 338 |
| West Asia and Europe | 4.3 | 1.8 | 114 | 120 | 118 | 126 | 2.0 | -0.4 | 104 | 107 | 103 | 108 | 554 |
| World | 3.3 | 2.9 | 112 | 118 | 119 | 122 | 1.8 | 1.5 | 106 | 111 | 110 | 111 | 1 162 |

a/ At constant 1995 prices.
b/ Provisional.
c/ Estimate.
d/ Excluding South Africa
Source: Adapted from UNIDO Database (2004), January

## Table 1.9: International Tourism Arrivals by Sub-region

| | International Tourism Arrivals (million) | | | | | Market Share (%) | | Growth Rate | | | | Average Annual growth (%) |
|---|---|---|---|---|---|---|---|---|---|---|---|---|
| | 1995 | 2001 | 2002 | 2003* | | 1995 | 2003* | 01/00 | 02/01 | 03*/02 | | 90–00 |
| Africa | 20.0 | 28.3 | 29.1 | 30.5 | | 3.6 | 4.4 | 3.2 | 2.8 | 4.9 | | 6.3 |
| North Africa | 7.3 | 10.6 | 10.3 | 10.8 | | 1.3 | 1.6 | 4.8 | -2.4 | 4.8 | | 1.8 |
| Sub-Saharan Africa | 12.7 | 17.8 | 18.8 | 19.8 | | 2.3 | 2.8 | 2.3 | 6.0 | 4.9 | | 10.2 |
| Americas | 108.8 | 120.2 | 114.9 | 112.4 | | 19.8 | 16.2 | -6.1 | -4.4 | -2.1 | | 3.2 |
| North America | 80.5 | 84.4 | 81.6 | 76.1 | | 14.6 | 11.0 | -7.5 | -3.3 | -6.7 | | 2.4 |
| Caribbean | 14.0 | 16.9 | 16.1 | 17.3 | | 2.5 | 2.5 | -1.6 | -5.0 | 7.6 | | 4.2 |
| Central America | 2.6 | 4.4 | 4.7 | 4.9 | | 0.5 | 0.7 | 1.7 | 6.4 | 3.4 | | 8.4 |
| South America | 11.7 | 14.4 | 12.5 | 14.2 | | 2.1 | 2.0 | -5.0 | -13.6 | 13.5 | | 6.8 |
| Asia and the Pacific | 85.6 | 121.1 | 131.3 | 119.1 | | 15.6 | 17.2 | 5.1 | 8.4 | -9.3 | | 7.2 |
| North-East Asia | 44.1 | 65.6 | 73.6 | 67.2 | | 8.0 | 9.7 | 5.0 | 12.2 | -8.8 | | 8.4 |
| South-East Asia | 29.2 | 40.2 | 42.2 | 35.7 | | 5.3 | 5.1 | 8.7 | 4.9 | -15.4 | | 5.6 |
| Oceania | 8.1 | 9.5 | 9.6 | 9.4 | | 1.5 | 1.4 | -1.6 | 0.8 | -1.9 | | 6.5 |
| South Asia | 4.2 | 5.8 | 5.9 | 6.8 | | 0.8 | 1.0 | -4.5 | 0.9 | 16.5 | | 6.8 |
| Europe | 322.3 | 390.8 | 399.8 | 401.5 | | 58.6 | 57.8 | -0.5 | 2.3 | 0.4 | | 3.4 |
| Northern Europe | 41.4 | 44.6 | 46.4 | 47.1 | | 7.5 | 6.8 | -4.7 | 4.1 | 1.5 | | 3.8 |
| Western Europe | 116.7 | 139.2 | 141.1 | 139.1 | | 21.2 | 20.0 | -2.6 | 1.4 | -1.4 | | 2.3 |
| Central and Eastern Europe | 61.4 | 63.4 | 65.2 | 68.3 | | 11.2 | 9.8 | 1.8 | 2.9 | 4.7 | | 4.8 |
| Southern Europe | 102.7 | 143.7 | 147.0 | 147.0 | | 18.7 | 21.2 | 2.1 | 2.3 | 0.0 | | 4.0 |
| Middle East | 13.6 | 23.6 | 27.6 | 30.4 | | 2.5 | 4.4 | -1.3 | 16.7 | 10.3 | | 9.5 |
| World | 550.4 | 684.1 | 702.6 | 694.0 | | 100.0 | 100.0 | -0.5 | 2.7 | -1.2 | | 4.2 |

*Source:* World Tourism Organization (2004), January

* Estimates

percent in 2002 to 1.6 percent in 2003, SSA's share increased from 2.3 percent in 1995 and 2.6 percent in 2002 to 2.8 percent in 2003. Significantly, growth in international arrivals in Africa maintained a higher momentum in 2003, declining from 3.2 percent in 2001 to 2.8 percent in 2002 and then rising 4.9 percent in 2003. Africa's performance was above average.

The start of the Iraq war in March 2003 caused an immediate drop in demand, particularly in air traffic, interregional travel, and travel to destinations perceived as close to the conflict zone. Very few destinations and sectors were immune from the impact. Destinations in North Africa, in particular, were adversely affected. For example, Morocco, Tunisia, and Egypt, all started 2003 with a substantial increase in tourism, but registered sizeable drops from March. Similarly, in the major tourism countries of East Africa, there were increased arrivals in January and February, but decreases in March. However, South Africa maintained the good rate registered in 2002, when tourism increased by 11 percent. Even during the month of March, when most destinations around the world were suffering from the geopolitical tension, South Africa saw only a slight decrease of 0.3 percent. Significantly, from the start of the Iraq war, national tourism administrations, tourism boards, and tourism businesses in Africa were much better prepared and attempted to adapt quickly to the changing conditions.

In 2003, a number of countries in Africa undertook projects to boost tourism. These ranged from the virtually untapped tourist destination of Malawi in the south to the better established destination of Senegal in the west. In Malawi, a strategic tourism development plan and a priority action program were initiated to focus in particular on promoting eco-tourism. The country's principal attraction is Lake Malawi, one of the biggest lakes in Africa. By contrast, Senegal has been developing its tourism since the early 1970s and is now receiving some half a million tourists a year. The country began in 2003 to assess tourism's impact on the country's economy, with a view to developing the sector further.

## Energy

In 2003, the output of African oil-producing countries totaled 8.2 mb/d of crude oil (or 11.8 percent of global production) while the entire OPEC countries produced 27.8 mb/d of crude oil or 40.3 percent of the global production. Total world crude oil production was estimated to have risen from 66.8 mb/d in 2002 to 69.0 mb/d in 2003 (Table 1.10). Five countries — Algeria, Angola, Egypt, Libya, and Nigeria — continued to dominate Africa's oil production, accounting for 83 percent of its 2003 total. Next in importance to the African oil sector are many small-to-medium sized oil producers, including Equatorial Guinea, Sudan, Gabon, Congo, Cameroon, and Tunisia. Combined crude oil production in Nigeria, Libya, and Algeria — the three OPEC members in Africa — rose to 5.2 mb/d in 2003 from their 2002 level of 4.7 mb/d. In terms of prices, the average basket price of crude oil in 2003 stood at US$28.9 per barrel (as against US$25 in 2002).

To date, there are proven oil reserves of 75.4 billion barrels (7 percent of the world's total) in the continent, and production of oil in Africa is projected to rise from current

## Table 1.10 Africa Crude Oil Production[a/], 1995–2003

| (Thousand Barrels per Day) Country | 1995 | 1996 | 1997 | 1998 | 1999 | 2000 | 2001 | 2002 | 2003* |
|---|---|---|---|---|---|---|---|---|---|
| Algeria | 1,202 | 1,242 | 1,277 | 1,246 | 1,202 | 1,254 | 1,270 | 1,306 | 1,604 |
| Angola | 646 | 709 | 714 | 735 | 745 | 746 | 742 | 896 | 909 |
| Cameroon | 111 | 108 | 124 | 121 | 100 | 85 | 77 | 69 | 67 |
| Congo | 188 | 201 | 253 | 265 | 270 | 280 | 275 | 242 | 217 |
| Egypt | 920 | 922 | 856 | 834 | 852 | 748 | 698 | 631 | 620 |
| Equatorial Guinea | 5 | 17 | 52 | 83 | 102 | 168 | 181 | 231 | 248 |
| Gabon | 365 | 368 | 370 | 352 | 331 | 315 | 301 | 294 | 240 |
| Libya | 1,390 | 1,401 | 1,446 | 1,390 | 1,319 | 1,410 | 1,367 | 1,319 | 1,418 |
| Nigeria | 1,993 | 2,001 | 2,132 | 2,153 | 2,130 | 2,165 | 2,256 | 2,118 | 2,202 |
| Sudan | n.a. | 2 | 5 | 10 | 69 | 186 | 209 | 245 | 280 |
| Tunisia | 89 | 87 | 84 | 80 | 83 | 79 | 70 | 72 | 66 |
| Other Countries | 45 | 54 | 54 | 71 | 69 | 72 | 69 | 270 | 286 |
| | | | | | | | | | |
| Africa | 6,954 | 7,112 | 7,368 | 7,340 | 7,272 | 7,507 | 7,516 | 7,693 | 8,157 |
| OPEC | 26,004 | 26,461 | 27,710 | 28,774 | 27,579 | 29,262 | 28,317 | 26,370 | 27,809 |
| World Total | 62,335 | 63,711 | 65,690 | 66,921 | 65,848 | 68,342 | 68,057 | 66,842 | 69,032 |

na: Not available
* Estimates
a/ Crude Oil (Including Lease Condensate)
*Sources*: Energy Intelligency Administration, Economist Intelligence Unit, Etudes et Statistiques BEAC and ADB Statistics Division estimates

levels of 8 mb/d to 11–13 mb/d over the next ten years. Apart from the main existing oil producers, other countries also aim to increase their output or become first-time producers, including Chad, Sudan, Namibia, South Africa, and Madagascar, while Mozambique and Tanzania are potential gas producers.

New investments and other developments to boost production took place in the oil sector in 2003. In Côte d'Ivoire, preparations intensified for production to start from the first Ivorian deepwater block, which is part of the larger Baobab oil reservoir. In Angola, two fresh oilfields began producing oil, and have the potential to increase national production to more than 1 mb/d. The Chad–Cameroon oil development and pipeline project began production in 2003. By contrast, Nigeria's crude oil production and plans to expand the national reserve to 40 billion barrels by 2010 suffered a setback, following the reclassification of about one billion barrels of crude oil reserves from 'proven' to 'probable'.

## Factors Impacting Economic Development in Africa: the External Environment

### Global Growth and Africa's Performance

Africa is arguably more vulnerable to changes in the international markets than any other region in the world. This is due to a number of factors: the composition and direction of its trade — particularly its excessive dependence on primary commodities and on the EU as its main export market — and the size of its aggregate output; its dependence on external flows, with the potential for attendant macroeconomic shocks; and its low technological manufacturing base, which necessitates imports from other regions. Individual country and regional responses to these external environment variables differ widely, depending, *inter alia*, on the nature of domestic macroeconomic policies and the reliance on inflows.

As noted earlier, global recovery continued to proceed at sluggish rates during 2003, rising marginally to 3.2 percent from 3.0 percent in 2002 (see Table 1.11). Growth in the advanced economies remained stagnant at 1.8 percent while the economies of developing countries increased their growth rates from 4.6 to 5.0 percent. In the advanced countries, fiscal stimulation failed to produce the expected growth result. The factors for the limited impact included: geopolitical uncertainties, continuing concerns about terrorism; persistence of the slowdown in trade and investment; and the fall in business and consumer confidence. Consequently, a number of countries were forced to look inwards (particularly towards domestic macroeconomic

reforms) to engender further growth. An additional weakness in the global economy was the large international imbalances, evidenced in the substantive external deficit of the US and a matching aggregate of surpluses in other economies. Nonetheless, 2003 saw an increased demand for Africa's exports, while recoveries in global commodity prices helping to boost Africa's economic performance.

### Improved Trade Performance

Noticeable changes in the external trade sector underpinned much of Africa's improved growth performance in 2003. Terms of trade improved significantly from 0.2 percent in 2002 to 2.7 percent in 2003. Trade balance, which had been on the downturn since 2000, increased by US$8.9 billion in the year alone. In 2003 (for the first time since 2001) export growth volume marginally outpaced import growth. While export volume increased by 4.8 percent, import volume increased by 4.6 percent. However, owing to debt-related transfers and capital flows out of the region, the current account declined by US$2.7 billion.

Africa's commodity prices firmed up during the year. This was attributable partly to increased demand not from Europe but from China and other Asian countries, as well as to supply bottlenecks and shortages for some commodities. In the year, Africa's export volume grew, but so too did the prices of major export commodity items (Table 1.11). Oil prices rose (averaging US$28.9 in 2003 against US$25 in 2002) (Table 1.12) due to the war in Iraq and supply constraints in Venezuela and Nigeria. Production quotas of the Organization of Petroleum Exporting Countries (OPEC) also increased.

## Table 1.11: Selected International Economic Indicators, 1999–2003

(Percentage changes from preceding year, unless otherwise specified)

|  | 1999 | 2000 | 2001 | 2002 | 2003[a] |
|---|---|---|---|---|---|
| **Changes in output** | | | | | |
| World | 3.6 | 4.8 | 2.4 | 3.0 | 3.2 |
| Advanced economies b/ | 3.4 | 3.9 | 1.0 | 1.8 | 1.8 |
| Developing countries | 3.9 | 5.7 | 4.1 | 4.6 | 5.0 |
| -Asia | 6.2 | 6.8 | 5.8 | 6.4 | 6.4 |
| -Latin American and Caribbean countries | 0.2 | 4.0 | 0.7 | –0.1 | 1.1 |
| -Africa c/ | 3.0 | 3.2 | 3.6 | 2.9 | 3.7 |
| Countries in transition | 4.1 | 7.1 | 5.1 | 4.2 | 4.9 |
| **Changes in Consumer Price Index** | | | | | |
| Advanced economies | 1.4 | 2.2 | 2.2 | 1.5 | 1.8 |
| Developing countries | 6.5 | 5.8 | 5.8 | 5.3 | 5.9 |
| -Asia | 2.5 | 1.8 | 2.7 | 2.0 | 2.5 |
| -Latin American and Caribbean countries | 7.4 | 6.8 | 6.4 | 8.7 | 10.9 |
| -Africa c/ | 11.9 | 13.6 | 11.9 | 9.4 | 11.2 |
| **Changes in Merchandise Trade (volume)** | | | | | |
| World Trade | 5.8 | 13.3 | –0.6 | 3.3 | 2.9 |
| Advanced economies | | | | | |
| -Exports | 5.3 | 12.6 | –1.6 | 2.0 | 1.1 |
| -Imports | 8.7 | 12.6 | –1.7 | 2.4 | 2.9 |
| Developing countries | | | | | |
| -Exports | 4.6 | 15.4 | 2.2 | 6.3 | 5.0 |
| -Imports | 1.7 | 17.1 | 1.2 | 6.2 | 5.3 |
| Africa c/ | | | | | |
| -Exports | 3.9 | 8.4 | 0.2 | 2.0 | 4.8 |
| -Imports | 5.5 | 2.2 | 2.9 | 2.8 | 4.6 |
| **Changes in Terms of Trade** | | | | | |
| Advanced economies | 0.0 | –2.9 | 0.4 | 0.8 | 1.1 |
| Developing countries | 5.8 | 7.2 | –3.9 | 1.8 | –0.4 |
| -Asia | –0.9 | –3.6 | –0.8 | 1.2 | –2.2 |
| -Africa c/ | 6.6 | 13.3 | –4.6 | 0.2 | 2.7 |
| Countries in transition | 2.4 | 5.9 | 0.2 | –0.5 | –0.0 |
| **Changes in FDI** | | | | | |
| World | 57.3 | 29.1 | –40.9 | –21.0 | ... |
| Advanced economies | 74.6 | 35.9 | –47.4 | –21.9 | ... |
| Developing countries | 19.9 | 7.3 | –14.9 | –22.6 | ... |
| -Asia | 8.5 | 30.9 | –24.9 | –11.0 | ... |
| -Latin American and Caribbean countries | 32.0 | –11.9 | –12.2 | –33.1 | ... |
| -Africa c/ | 37.0 | –30.6 | 121.1 | –41.4 | ... |

**Table 1.11: (Continued)**

| (Percentage changes from preceding year, unless otherwise specified) | 1999 | 2000 | 2001 | 2002 | 2003[a] |
|---|---|---|---|---|---|
| FDI (as percent of global FDI flows) | | | | | |
| Advanced economies | 76.4 | 80.4 | 71.5 | 70.7 | ... |
| Developing countries | 21.2 | 17.7 | 25.4 | 24.9 | ... |
| -Asia | 10.1 | 10.2 | 13.0 | 14.6 | ... |
| -Latin American and Caribbean countries | 10.0 | 6.8 | 10.2 | 8.6 | ... |
| -Africa c/ | 1.1 | 0.6 | 2.3 | 1.7 | ... |

*Notes*: a/ Preliminary estimates
b/ Comprises the industrial market economies, Israel and four newly industrialized Asian economies.
c/ ADB Regional Member Countries.
*Sources*: IMF, World Economic Outlook, September 2003 and ADB Statistics Division.

Of the non-oil export commodities, cotton performed very well, rising by 37.3 percent, while gold prices increased by 17.3 percent, and copper 14 percent. On the aggregate, agricultural export prices for the continent increased by over 20.5. For Sub-Saharan Africa, the export-weighted price of non-energy commodities rose by 13.5 percent while non-oil exports terms of trade gained 4.2 percent. Equally important to the positive terms of trade performance within the year was the relative fall in the price of manufactured goods, which constitute the bulk of Africa's imports.

Diverse preferential trade arrangements for the region also yielded positive returns for the continent. The share of non-oil exports under the US Africa Growth and Opportunity Act (AGOA) improved in 2003. A number of African countries have benefited from the AGOA program, including non-oil exporters such as South Africa, Kenya, and Lesotho, which together with Nigeria and a few other countries, account for about 93 percent of total exports to the US under the AGOA concessions. Significantly, the share of non-traditional export items such as textiles and processed agricultural products rose, with the former doubling and the latter rising by about 38 percent.

As noted above, exports revenues in 2003 were also boosted by an increase in receipts from tourism. Some 30.5 million tourists visited the continent in 2003. Compared to North Africa, Sub-Saharan Africa recorded a larger increase in the number of tourist arrivals, from 18.8 million in 2002 to 19.8 million in 2003. This partly reflects the growing popularity of South Africa as a global tourist destination; indeed, the country is estimated to have the world's fastest-growing tourist industry in recent times.

## Official Development Assistance (ODA), Foreign Private Capital Inflows, and External Debt

Africa's economic performance is also dependent on capital flows generated through both official development assistance (ODA) and private capital flows, as these provide essential resources to augment domestic investment. The resources that can be made available to support investment also depend in part on the volume of outstanding external debt and the resources that would need to be diverted to service it. Important developments occurred in ODA and private capital flows in 2002 (the latest year for which data are available). Africa's debt burden and debt servicing also continued their downward trend.

After declining through most of the 1990s, net ODA to Africa has begun to recover, rising from a total US$ 15.7 billion in 2001 to US$ 21.2 billion in 2002. By contrast, foreign direct investment (FDI) inflows to Africa have remained low compared with other developing regions. The most recent data of the UN Conference on Trade and Development (UNCTAD) indicate that in 2002 FDI inflows to Africa declined by an average of 41 percent, affecting 23 countries on the continent. The downturn, from US$19 billion in 2001 to US$10.9 billion in 2002, occurred at a time of worldwide slumps in FDI flows, although domestic factors were also a contributory factor. In particular, the reduction in FDI is in part attributable to a slower pace of privatization in some of the larger countries of the continent. Furthermore, perceived risks of policy reversals, particularly with respect to pricing of infrastructural services, also dampened FDI.

A major concern regarding FDI inflows into Africa is its heavy concentration in natural resources exploitation. Of the major recipient countries, most of the FDI flows are directed to Angola, Algeria, Sudan, Nigeria, and Gabon for oil and gas projects. Similarly, over 50 percent of the flows into South Africa and Tanzania went into gold mining. Indeed, the primary sector was the largest recipient of accumulated FDI to Africa, with a 55 percent share for the period 1996–2000. Service industries have, however, become more important in recent years, registering a 25 percent share of FDI.

## Factors Impacting Economic Development in Africa: the Domestic Policy Environment

Africa's improved economic performance since 1996 is also in part explained by improvements in the policy environment in many countries. Increasingly, the institutionalization of macroeconomic policy and the deepening of policy reforms are gaining ground across the continent. Equally important, a sea-change is taking place in the approach to and structure of, ownership of the instruments and methods of these reforms. At the national level, country-owned Poverty Reduction Strategy Papers (PRSPs) are increasingly becoming the principal instruments for directing national development as well as providing a framework for donor coordination. At the regional level, under the aegis of the New Economic Partnership for Africa's Development (NEPAD), there have been strong commitments to promote good governance and sound economic management on the part of various African governments. In this regard, some 16 countries have signed up

## Table 1.12: Selected Commodity Prices Data

| Commodity | Unit | 2002 | 2003 |
|---|---|---|---|
| Crude Oil, Brent | $/bbl | 25.0 | 28.9 |
| | | | |
| Agricultural Commodities | | | |
| Wheat, U. S., HRW | $/mt | 148.1 | 146.1 |
| Rice, Thai, 5 percent | $/mt | 191.9 | 197.6 |
| Soybeans | $/mt | 212.7 | 264 |
| Sugar, world | Cents/kg | 15.18 | 15.63 |
| Coffee, other milds | Cents/kg | 135.7 | 141.5 |
| Coffee, robusta | Cents/kg | 66.2 | 81.5 |
| Cocoa | Cents/kg | 177.8 | 175.1 |
| Tea, auctions (3) average | Cents/kg | 150.6 | 151.7 |
| Cotton | Cents/kg | 101.9 | 139.9 |
| | | | |
| Metals and Minerals | | | |
| Aluminum | $/mt | 1,350 | 1431 |
| Copper | $/mt | 1,559 | 1779 |
| Gold | $/toz | 310 | 363.5 |
| Iron ore, Carajas | cents/dmtu | 29.31 | 31.95 |
| Lead | cents/dmtu | 45.3 | 51.5 |
| Nickel | $/mt | 6,772 | 9629 |
| Silver | cents/toz | 462.5 | 491.1 |
| Tin | cents/kg | 406.1 | 489.5 |
| Zinc | cents/kg | 77.9 | 82.8 |

*Source*: Adapted from World Bank, Commodity Price Data (Pink Sheets), January 2004.

to the African Peer Review Mechanism (APRM) under NEPAD (see below).

In addition, African leaders have made impressive progress in resolving major conflicts in the region, for example, in the DRC, Congo Republic, and Sierra Leone. The political turmoil and armed conflicts experienced during 2002–2003 in such countries as Côte d'Ivoire and Liberia are also being addressed, mainly through African-led initiatives, although the massive challenges of rebuilding war-torn nations remain.

## Fiscal Policy Stance

An important aspect of the improved policy framework is the greater discipline shown by governments in managing their public finances. As is well known, prudent fiscal and monetary policies are essential for maintaining macroeconomic stability and for reining in inflationary pressures. Noticeable improvements have taken place in recent years in these areas in many African countries.

In 2003, the improvement in fiscal management in the region resulted in a decline in the fiscal deficit as a ratio of GDP from 3.4 percent in 2002 to 3 percent. On the whole, the evidence points in favor of a greater fiscal prudence in the region than was the case in the early 1990s. However, while the 3 percent deficit GDP is an improvement over the 2002 figure, it is above the average for the 5-year period 1999–2003 and therefore indicates room for further improvement. Moreover, this performance masks the diversities in country-level performance. While a number of the oil-importing countries face serious fiscal pressures, for many of the oil and mineral resource-exporting countries, by contrast, fiscal prudence remained a big challenge, given the significant increase in export receipts.

## Monetary Policy

As well as prudent fiscal policies, many African countries pursued tight monetary policies as witnessed in 2002. Growth in broad money in the region fell further from 19.2 percent in 2002 to 15.8 percent in 2003.

Some examples of tight monetary policies that prevailed on the continent were those followed by South Africa and Nigeria. In South Africa, such a policy led to the appreciation of the rand in 2003. In the case of Nigeria, the Central Bank of Nigeria (CBN) continued to tighten monetary policy in response to the threat of fiscal political-economy pressures.

A tighter monetary policy stance has resulted in a major curb on inflation, especially given the improved terms of trade of the region. In 2003, only 11 countries recorded inflation rates in excess of 10 percent, with few countries experiencing high inflation rates as a result of political instability or armed conflicts. Countries like Angola and Zimbabwe had very high inflation rates, at 95 percent and 420 percent respectively. For the vast majority of the countries, monetary and inflation performance were at reasonable levels. Even countries like Côte d'Ivoire, with significant macro-economic and political problems, maintained satisfactory inflation rates. All the oil-exporting countries, with the exception of Nigeria and Angola, also registered single-digit inflation rates.

Among the countries belonging to the Banque Centrale des Etats de l'Afrique de l'Ouest (BCEAO), inflation also was kept low. The coverage of base money by foreign reserves was also adequate in the WAEMU countries, despite a weaker economic performance by member countries and intensified political crises in the region. The regional group management also made a significant advance in budget financing policy by shifting such financing from direct advances by the Central Bank to issuing securities on the regional capital market. The WAEMU Council of Ministers also adopted an anti-money-laundering directive and a regulation mandating the freezing of funds linked to terrorist activities.

## Regional Policy Development: NEPAD

The New Partnership for Africa's Development (NEPAD) initiative — a major regional initiative launched by African leaders in October 2001, gained further momentum in 2003. In February 2003, the UN Development Program (UNDP) agreed to provide US$ 1.9 million to support the Initiative. The UNDP contribution is part of a broader US$ 3.5 million plan expected to draw funding from additional international partners. The UNDP will provide institutional support to the NEPAD Secretariat and help in 6 key areas, including promotion of political governance and democracy; the development of a communications and popularization strategy; and the promotion of the Millennium Development Goals within the framework of the NEPAD objectives.

Concrete steps have also been taken on NEPAD's economic and social priorities. A number of regional infrastructure projects have been elaborated to develop Africa's roads, railways, energy, and communications projects, with the support of the African Development Bank. Under NEPAD, the Bank plays a leadership role in the areas of regional banking standards and codes and infrastructure development. In 2003, the Bank prioritized a number of projects that fell under NEPAD regional economic integration initiatives. Large-scale programs and projects included a road program linking landlocked Burkina Faso and Mali to Ghanaian ports, the natural gas pipeline project in South Africa and Mozambique undertaken by SASOL, and Assistance to the Preventive Control of the Desert Locust in Mauritania, Mali, Niger, and Chad. Other sectoral developments included the Comprehensive Africa Agriculture Development Program (CAADP) drawn up and approved in July 2003, with the support of the UN Food and Agriculture Organization. The New Partnership has also worked towards the elaboration of its health and education programs.

The creation of the African Peer Review Mechanism (APRM) has been one of NEPAD's most significant achievements to date. The overall objective of the APRM is to ensure that the policies and practices of Participating States conform to agreed political, economic, and corporate governance values, codes, and standards. The APRM is defined as "a system of voluntary self-assessment and constructive peer dialogue and persuasion." The APRM was formally launched at the Seventh Meeting of NEPAD Heads of State and Government Implementation Committee (HSGIC) in May 2003, when a 6-member panel was appointed to operate the peer review mechanism. The members of the panel are all Africans of proven eminence and integrity. By mid-2003, 16 countries had signed the APRM's memorandum of understanding. Reviews of 4 participating countries were scheduled to begin before the end of the year (see African Development Bank, *Annual Report 2003*).

## Medium- and Long-Term Economic Prospects

Despite Africa's considerable progress over the last ten years, as evidenced by the restoration of macroeconomic stability and the resump-tion of economic growth, the continent faces daunting challenges as it seeks to accelerate growth, reduce poverty, and attain the Millennium Development Goals. A major challenge facing most countries is raising growth rates from the current average of 3 to 4 percent and, as important, sustaining them over the medium to long term. As noted above, one of the prominent features of recent African economic performance is its variability from year to year, making it difficult to sustain the growth and recovery process in the long-term. Improving economic performance in the medium to long term will require a number of measures: improving the domestic macro-economic environment, particularly the investment climate, to stimulate private investment, both domestic and foreign, improving systems of governance — particularly the legal and judicial framework — and mobilizing adequate resources for key investments to develop the human capital of the continent.

### Medium-Term Prospects

In the medium term, the anticipated recovery of the global economy and moderate gains in commodity prices are expected to help African economies achieve higher growth rates. Estimates of the IMF and ADB for the region as a whole indicate a pick-up of the growth rate to 4.3 percent in 2004. For SSA, growth is forecast to reach 5.1 percent in 2004, while over the long term, per capita growth is expected to average 1.5 percent. This would imply a significant improvement over recent historical trends, though still well below what is needed to achieve the MDGs.

Clearly, Africa's future growth performance is highly dependent on economic recovery in its major trading partners, particularly the EU. Recent trends in growth rates in the EU point to a longer and slower rebound than in most other regions. According to the OECD, the estimate of growth in the euro zone shows that growth will reach about 2.2 percent on average in 2004, with a projected growth of 2.5 percent in 2005. This has important implications for Africa's growth prospects as Europe is still the principal end-user of African products and its slower growth may result in lower than anticipated demand for African export commodities. The slackening demand from Europe may, however, be compensated by increased demand from the rapidly growing economies of Asia, particularly China. Africa's export performance will also depend on improved market access for African products in the EU and other industrialized nations. Further efforts are therefore required to remove tariff and non-tariff barriers and in particular tariff escalation, which inhibits the growth of African processed exports as opposed to primary commodities.[3]

## Longer-term Prospects

Ultimately, Africa's longer-term prospects will depend on improved economic management and adequate support from the international community. More specifically, African countries will need to: (a) deepen macro-economic reforms and enhance domestic competitiveness and efficiency as foundations for a favorable investment climate and growth, (b) strengthen democratic institutions and systems of public budget and financial management to ensure that governments are accountable to their people, especially in the use of public resources, (c) invest adequate resources in human development, and (d) strengthen regional cooperation and inte-gration efforts in the context of NEPAD.

In turn, developed countries should support Africa's development efforts by (a) sustaining the reverse in the decline in ODA to meet the resource needs of low-income countries, (b) making future assistance more predictable, (c) harmonizing their policies and procedures, (d) reducing agricultural subsidies and removing remaining trade barriers, and (d) helping to reduce the external debt of poor countries to sustainable levels.[4]

---

[3] These issues are discussed in greater detail in Part II of the Report.

[4] See African Development Bank *et al.*, *Achieving the Millennium Development Goals in Africa: Progress, Prospects, and Policy Implications,* Abidjan, 2002 .

# CHAPTER 2
# Regional Economic Profiles

## Introduction

In addition to providing an overview of the performance of each sub-region of Africa, this chapter discusses individual country performances in some detail, highlighting the major changes that occurred during the year. The analysis focuses on the recent economic trends, policy developments and performance outlook for the years immediately ahead. The five sub-regions' real GDP growth rates, as well as their shares in Africa's GDP, trade and population are summarized in Table 2.1. This shows that growth in Central, Western and North Africa led continental growth in 2003. By contrast, East and Southern Africa recorded the lowest growth rates on the continent in 2003, at 2.6 percent and 2.2 percent respectively. North Africa remained the largest sub-regional wealth contributor in Africa, accounting for 38.8 percent of its GDP in 2003. This highlights the many disparities that exist across Africa's sub-regional groupings.

### Table 2.1: A Sub-Regional Overview of African Economies

| | | 2003[a/] | | | |
|---|---|---|---|---|---|
| | Average Real GDP Growth 1999–2002 | Real GDP Growth | Share in Africa's GDP | Share in Africa's Exports[b/] | Share in Total Population |
| Central Africa | 2.1 | 4.4 | 5.8 | 6.7 | 12.0 |
| Eastern Africa | 4.0 | 2.6 | 8.0 | 6.1 | 23.5 |
| Northern Africa | 3.6 | 4.7 | 38.8 | 36.4 | 21.9 |
| Southern Africa | 2.8 | 2.2 | 32.1 | 32.0 | 14.1 |
| Western Africa | 2.7 | 4.0 | 15.3 | 18.9 | 28.4 |
| Franc Zone | 3.3 | 3.3 | 10.3 | 11.9 | 13.3 |
| Net Oil Exporters | 3.4 | 4.7 | 43.0 | 52.3 | 32.8 |
| Net Oil Importers | 3.0 | 3.0 | 57.0 | 47.7 | 67.2 |
| **ALL RMCs** | **3.2** | **3.7** | – | – | – |

*Notes*: a/ Preliminary estimates
b/ Exports of Goods & Nonfactor Services at Current Market Prices
Source: ADB Statistics Division, 2004

# Central Africa

Central Africa encompasses ten countries: Burundi, Cameroon, Central African Republic (CAR), Chad, the Democratic Republic of Congo (DRC), Congo, Equatorial Guinea, Gabon, Rwanda and Sao Tome & Principe. Cameroon, Congo, Gabon, Equatorial Guinea, and now Chad, are all major oil exporters in the region. But political instability, most notably in the Great Lakes region, has long prevented Central Africa from exploiting its abundant natural resources and rich agricultural land to the full. As a result, its contribution to continental GDP is the lowest amongst all regions and accounted for 5.8 percent of the continental gross output in 2003. Cameroon is by far the largest economy in the region and contributed about 32.2 percent of its GDP in 2003.

The total population in Central Africa was 107.6 million in 2003, equivalent to 12 percent of the continental total. Economic growth in the region failed to match that of the population through most of the 1990s, but resumed growth in post-conflict countries has led to an encouraging increase in per capita GDP since 2002. The region's GDP per capita averaged US$355 in 2003, against a continental average of US$761. This hides wide disparities, however, with GDP per capita in Gabon and Equatorial Guinea reaching US$4,336 and US$5,849 respectively in 2003.

## Recent Trends in the Domestic Economy

### Economic Growth and Inflation

Growth in Central Africa outpaced continental growth by 0.7 percentage point in 2003, largely indicating good performance in Chad, DRC and Equatorial Guinea (Table 2.2). Other countries in the sub-region experienced an economic slowdown in 2003, owing to political instability and/or adverse weather conditions. Inflation in Central Africa averaged 8 percent in 2003, against a continental average of 11.2 percent. This reflected tight monetary and fiscal policies in the CFA zone — which comprises Cameroon, CAR, Chad, Congo, Equatorial Guinea, and Gabon — and successful macroeconomic stabilization in DRC (Figure 2.1**).**

Renewed fighting between the regular army and Hutu rebels in **Burundi** has threatened the peace process. Adverse weather conditions resulted in a contraction in agricultural output in 2003 and the scarcity of foreign exchange, coupled with poor security conditions, continued to restrict activity in manufacturing and services. Real GDP growth was negative as a result, at –1.3 percent. This compares poorly with 2002, when bumper crops led to growth accelerating to 4.5 percent. Inflation, which had fallen since 2001, as a result of a recovery in food production and tighter fiscal and monetary policy, accelerated to 7.1 percent in 2003, owing to food shortage and higher oil prices.

Economic performance in **Cameroon** was mixed in 2003. Agricultural output increased following abundant and widespread rains, and activity in some services, notably in telecommunications, was robust. By contrast, oil production declined and the manufacturing sector performed poorly, owing to the energy crisis and the lack of new investment. The construction of the Chad-Cameroon pipeline was meanwhile

# Figure 2.1: Central Africa, Selected Economic Indicators, 1999–2003

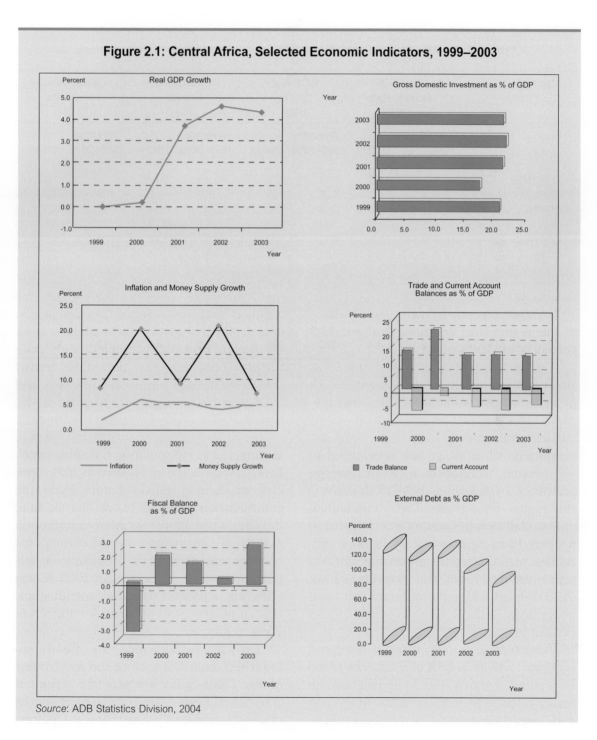

**Table 2.2: Central Africa: Gross Domestic Product and Export Performances**

| Country | Real GDP Growth Rate (%) | | GDP Per Capita (US$) | | Real Exports[c] Growth (%) | | Exports[b] Per Capita (US$) | |
|---|---|---|---|---|---|---|---|---|
| | Average 1999–2002 | 2003[a] | Average 1999–2002 | 2003[a] | Average 1999–2002 | 2003[a] | Average 1999–2002 | 2003[a] |
| BURUNDI | 1.2 | –1.3 | 111 | 87 | –0.5 | 50.7 | 8 | 8 |
| CAMEROON | 4.5 | 4.0 | 595 | 753 | 0.0 | 1.0 | 169 | 173 |
| CENTRAL AFRICAN REP. | 1.1 | –0.7 | 269 | 336 | 1.0 | 19.5 | 47 | 48 |
| CHAD | 5.0 | 9.1 | 204 | 319 | –4.0 | 36.8 | 29 | 49 |
| CONGO | 3.1 | 1.2 | 813 | 1,137 | 0.8 | 3.8 | 729 | 747 |
| CONGO, DEM. REP. OF | –2.4 | 5.0 | 102 | 115 | –3.2 | 6.8 | 20 | 23 |
| EQUATORIAL GUINEA | 25.9 | 14.7 | 3,176 | 5,849 | 12.8 | 12.4 | 3,387 | 5,861 |
| GABON | –2.3 | 0.8 | 3,794 | 4,336 | –6.2 | –0.8 | 2,359 | 2,460 |
| RWANDA | 7.2 | 3.2 | 224 | 209 | 8.2 | 3.3 | 18 | 17 |
| SAO TOME & PRINCIPE | 3.4 | 5.0 | 322 | 374 | 6.5 | 97.5 | 124 | 154 |
| **CENTRAL AFRICA** | **2.1** | **4.4** | **287** | **355** | **–2.0** | **4.6** | **112** | **128** |

*Notes*: a/ Preliminary estimates    b/: Exports of Goods and Nonfactor Services at Market Prices
c/: Real Exports of Goods Growth
*Source*: ADB Statistics Division, 2004

completed. All in all, growth decelerated to 4.0 percent, compared with an average growth of 4.5 percent in 1999–2002; this was still higher than regional and continental growth. Inflation in Cameroon accelerated to 6.3 percent in 2002, as a result of poor agricultural performance the previous year. Food supply returned to satisfactory levels in 2003. This, coupled with tight monetary and fiscal policy, led to a deceleration in inflation to 2.5 percent in 2003.

Persistent insecurity strongly disrupted economic activity in **CAR** in 2003. Prior to the *coup d'état* of March 2003, there had been an earlier attempt in October 2002, leading to widespread destruction of physical assets,

looting, and population displacement. Economic growth was negative in 2003. Food crop production remained unchanged, but cotton production fell by about one-third despite satisfactory weather conditions. Activity in construction, manufacturing, and services was meanwhile brought to a halt. Inflation rose to 3.2 percent in 2003, mostly reflecting depressed consumer spending and tight liquidity conditions under the Franc Zone.

Growth performance in **Chad** has improved dramatically since the construction of the Chad-Cameroon pipeline started in 2001. As oil fields in Doba came on stream by mid-2003, real GDP growth was 9.1 percent over the year. Agriculture and livestock, which provide a livelihood for most Chadians, performed well, but activity in construction and services slowed down following the completion of the pipeline, while power cuts and high energy costs continued to hinder manufacturing. Inflation decelerated to 4.3 percent in 2003, reflecting satisfactory harvests and a stabilization in the domestic demand.

National reconciliation in **DRC** made good overall progress in 2003, despite resumed fighting among rebel groups in the northeast. Troops from neighboring countries, including Rwanda, have withdrawn and a new Constitution was signed in April 2003, with a transition government installed in Kinshasa two months later. Resumed external assistance, improved security conditions, fiscal consolidation and other reforms have all helped to end a decade of continuous economic decline, with growth resuming in 2002, before accelerating to 5 percent in 2003. Inflation fell to a single-digit figure for the first time in 2003, when it averaged 9.1 percent. This reflected significant progress in tightening fiscal and monetary policy.

In **Congo**, the normalization of the political situation, coupled with favorable oil market conditions, have helped to compensate for a decline in oil production (owing to depleted reserves). Fighting in the southwest Pool region became less frequent in 2003, after the government and rebel leaders signed a ceasefire in March. But resources for post war reconstruction and public investment are still lacking because of fiscal mismanagement and delays in normalizing relations with the IMF and other external creditors. As a result, real GDP grew

by a subdued 1.2 percent in 2003. Inflation decelerated to 2 percent in 2003, as supply routes to Brazzaville were re-opened.

The most impressive economic performance in the region was recorded by **Equatorial Guinea**, which has experienced significant growth since large oil reserves started to be exploited in the mid-1990s. Real GDP grew by a yearly average 25.9 percent in 1999–2002 and by 14.7 percent in 2003. Activity in the oil sector has boosted GDP in construction and services, but the economy has stagnated elsewhere, most notably in agriculture and manufacturing. Inflation averaged 10 percent in 2003, reflecting a strong demand for housing and services.

**Gabon**, which is the second most important economy in the region, relies heavily on oil. Domestic oil production has fallen since 1997, because of depleting reserves. Growth averaged a negative 2.3 percent a year between 1999 and 2002, as a result, and real GDP grew by an estimated 0.8 percent in 2003. Momentum to diversify the economy away from the oil sector has been slow, the country still having one of the highest GDP per capita rates in Africa. Inflation rose to 2 percent in 2003, reflecting low demand pressure and tight liquidity conditions.

Economic prospects in **Rwanda** have steadily improved since the end of the military and civil conflict in 1995. A new Constitution was passed by referendum in May, followed by presidential and legislative elections. Large inflows of external assistance (primarily from the EU, IDA and the UK) have continued to finance activities in construction, manufacturing and services, but agricultural output in 2003 did not match the exceptional harvests of 2002, because of delayed rains. As a result, economic growth slowed to 3.2 percent in 2003, whereas inflation accelerated to 4.7 percent, owing to tighter food supplies and rising fuel prices.

Growth in **São Tomé & Príncipe** accelerated to 5 percent in 2003 and was not greatly affected by the failed coup attempt in July. This mostly reflected activity in agriculture, the backbone of the economy, and construction. Oil licensing kicked-started in October, one year after a joint settlement was signed with Nigeria over oil exploration. Inflation averaged 9.0 percent in 2003, reflecting relatively expansive monetary and fiscal policy.

### Fiscal Developments

Central Africa was the only region in Africa to record a fiscal surplus in 2003. The region's fiscal position largely reflects fluctuations in earnings from the oil sector. Overall, the region achieved a fiscal surplus equivalent to 2.7 percent of GDP in 2003, as a result of firm oil prices, increased donor support in post-conflict recovering countries, and the introduction of cost-cutting measures in Cameroon, Congo, Gabon and Sao Tome (Table 2.3).

The government in **Burundi** pursued an expansionary fiscal policy in 2003, with notably a significant rise in capital expenditures associated with the World Bank's Economic Recovery Credit and the IMF's Post-Conflict Emergency Assistance. This, coupled with lower earnings due to the planned reduction in external tariffs and the economic slowdown, caused the fiscal deficit to surge to 6.2 percent of GDP in 2003, against an average fiscal deficit of 3.7 percent

of GDP in 1999–2002. The government aimed at regularizing all external payment arrears by end-2003.

**Cameroon**'s overall government balance has been in surplus since 2000, in the context of robust world oil prices and fiscal consolidation. The fiscal surplus remained largely unchanged in 2003, at 1.8 percent of GDP, despite lower oil receipts. Tax reforms and the strengthening of administrative capacity have helped to boost non-oil revenues in recent years. Public expenditures, especially social spending, fell below target in 2003, although measures to increase the share of expenditures towards social sectors and improve public expenditure management were taken recently.

Revenue-generating sectors, such as timber and mining, have been the main targets of an anti-corruption campaign in **CAR** under the new administration. The Ministry of Economy and Finances has taken drastic measures to trim public expenditures, with a civil servants census in July revealing the presence of 'ghost workers'. The new administration has struggled to pay salaries on time, and there are up to 36 months of salary arrears. Some donors have resumed their assistance to the country, with China and France notably supporting the public sector wage bill.

Oil revenues in **Chad** are expected to flow in at the beginning of 2004, turning the overall budget balance as a percentage of GDP from a deficit of 7.0 percent in 2003 into a surplus of 3.4 percent in 2004. Concerns over the possible misuse of oil revenues have led to the adoption of a new law on the management of oil revenues, effective since 1999. Under the law, all oil revenues are to be

**Table 2.3: Central Africa: Macroeconomic Management Indicators**

| Country | Inflation (%) | | Fiscal Balance as % of GDP | | Gross Domestic Investment | | Gross National Savings | |
|---|---|---|---|---|---|---|---|---|
| | | | | as % of GDP | | | | |
| | Average 1999–2002 | 2003[a/] | Average 1999–2002 | 2003[a/] | Average 1999–2002 | 2003[a/] | Average 1999–2002 | 2003[a/] |
| BURUNDI | 8.9 | 7.1 | –3.7 | –6.2 | 8.5 | 11.5 | 0.7 | 4.6 |
| CAMEROON | 3.2 | 2.5 | 0.6 | 1.8 | 18.1 | 17.4 | 14.4 | 11.9 |
| CENTRAL AFRICAN REP. | 2.0 | 3.2 | –1.1 | –1.6 | 9.6 | 7.1 | 7.0 | 4.0 |
| CHAD | 3.2 | 4.3 | –6.0 | –7.0 | 33.4 | 41.6 | 2.8 | 7.0 |
| CONGO | 1.9 | 2.0 | –3.4 | 3.1 | 24.6 | 22.4 | 22.1 | 21.0 |
| CONGO, DEM. REP. OF | 302.3 | 9.1 | –3.8 | –4.9 | 8.7 | 15.0 | 4.9 | 11.4 |
| EQUATORIAL GUINEA | 7.6 | 10.0 | 9.0 | 23.2 | 47.6 | 26.9 | 18.0 | 25.1 |
| GABON | 0.5 | 2.0 | 5.0 | 8.9 | 24.0 | 25.5 | 24.3 | 25.2 |
| RWANDA | 1.7 | 4.7 | –1.8 | 0.9 | 18.0 | 19.9 | 11.5 | 8.6 |
| SAO TOME & PRINCIPE | 11.5 | 9.0 | –19.7 | –10.2 | 35.0 | 30.2 | 12.4 | 18.2 |
| **CENTRAL AFRICA** | **5.5** | **8.0** | **0.0** | **2.7** | **19.9** | **21.0** | **14.1** | **15.0** |

*Note*: a/ Preliminary estimates
*Source*: ADB Statistics Division, 2004

included into the general budget and direct receipts (royalties and dividends) will be earmarked to priority expenditures. A medium term expenditure framework has also been drawn up.

The government in **DRC** has made good progress in fighting extra-budgetary spending and enhancing revenue collection. The fiscal deficit rose to 4.9 percent of GDP in 2003, against an average 3.8 percent of GDP in 1999–2002. There was some slippage in early 2003, when military and security spending was higher than anticipated and the central bank's net credit to the government exceeded its target. The shift in the composition of

expenditure toward poverty reduction spending meanwhile failed to materialize. Measures aimed at fiscal consolidation were taken in March 2003, and the tax structure was streamlined. The government adopted a supplementary 2003 budget in June, which uses a new expenditure classification system and centralizes all receipts and expenditures in line with the country's reunification.

The government in **Congo** adopted an austerity budget in 2003, after public finances deteriorated sharply in 2002 because of overspending. As a result, the fiscal balance turned into a surplus of 3.1 percent of GDP in 2003, reflecting a combination of belt-tightening and fiscal consolidation measures and buoyant oil revenue. Measures were notably taken to address administrative weaknesses in budget execution and tax and custom collection, while capital spending was kept to the minimum.

The overall government surplus in **Equatorial Guinea** rose to 23.2 percent of GDP in 2003, owing to strong oil revenue inflows. Transparency and discipline are still lacking, however, as evidenced by the plethora of extra-budgetary procedures, especially in the oil sector.

The government in **Gabon**, which adopted an austerity budget in 2003, has stepped up its efforts to increase non-oil tax revenue, while cutting down on recurrent expenditures to bring them into line with shrinking oil revenue. The government is also committed to wage and civil service reforms. The overall surplus rose to 8.9 percent of GDP in 2003.

Strong donor support and privatization proceeds helped the **Rwanda** government to finance the cost of holding elections and proceed with the demobilization and reintegration of the armed forces in 2003. The overall government deficit turned into a small surplus of 0.9 percent of GDP in 2003. Progress was made in strengthening the domestic tax base, following the increase in the VAT rate from 15 to 18 percent since 2001 and the introduction of new excise taxes in the 2003 budget. There was meanwhile a substantial increase in priority spending.

The coup attempt in **São Tomé & Príncipe** dented revenue inflows in 2003. But the government has taken steps to improve public expenditure management and reduce the number of civil servants, bringing the overall government deficit down to 10.2 percent of GDP in 2003.

## Monetary and Exchange Rate Developments

Monetary policy in the Central African CFA zone is dictated by the regional central bank, Banque des Etats d'Afrique centrale (BEAC). The BEAC's inter-bank and money market has lacked effectiveness, because of the region's excess liquidity and poor regional financial integration. Statutory reserve requirements for commercial bank were introduced in September 2001 and tightened in March 2003. Government bonds were to be introduced by January 2004, as BEAC's financing of government deficits is phased out. Interest rate adjustments remain rare and limited, although the BEAC cut its rediscount rate from 6.35 percent to 6.30 percent in December 2002, in the context of falling regional inflation and lower world interest rates. Central Africa witnessed a deceleration in money supply growth in 2003 to 7.2 percent against 21.3 percent in 2002.

All CFA countries share the same currency, the CFA franc, which is pegged to the euro at a rate of CFA656:Euro1 since January 1999. Foreign reserves are pooled together in an operation account held at the French Public Treasury, which in turn guarantees the stability and convertibility of the regional currency. In line with the euro, the CFA franc appreciated from an average of CFA697:US$1 in 2002 to CFA584:US$1 in 2003, which dented the region's external competitiveness.

The central bank of **Burundi** has taken steps to develop indirect monetary control instruments, with the adoption of weekly liquidity auctions. A tight monetary stance was maintained in 2003. Mandatory reserve requirements were raised from 7.5 percent to 8.5 percent in January and stricter penalties for banks that exceed their refinance ceilings were introduced in March. Exchange restrictions were meanwhile relaxed, as part of the reforms initiated in August 2002 to improve the functioning of the foreign exchange auctions market. Foreign currencies remained scarce, however, as indicated by the continued gap between the official and parallel exchange rates.

In the **DRC**, the Banque centrale du Congo (BCC) aims to achieve price stability within the framework of a floating exchange rate system that was introduced in May 2001. A new board of governors was appointed in May 2003, which is in line with the bank's newly acquired independent statutes (the BCC had to print money through most of the 1990s to cover growing central government and public enterprises deficits). The bank launched a new financial instrument (*billet de trésorerie*) in mid-December 2002 to help regulate the country's liquidity, and the refinancing rate was raised from 12 percent to 27 percent in January 2003, down to 25 percent in May. Another main challenge for the BCC is to normalize and unify the DRC's payment system without jeopardizing macroeconomic stability. The bank issued new banknotes of small denominations in October, as a first step towards facilitating monetary transactions in Congolese francs. Tight liquidity conditions also helped to maintain a relatively stable exchange rate against the US dollar in 2003, after a 23 percent depreciation in 2002.

Inflationary pressures prompted the central bank of **Rwanda** to tighten liquidity conditions through open market operations in 2003. As a result, the yields on treasury bills rose from 10.5 percent in January to 11.5 percent in August, while the bank pension rate rose from 13 percent to 14.5 percent over the same period. The Rwanda franc/dollar exchange rate, which depreciated by 12.0 percent in 2002, continued to weaken in 2003, notwithstanding interventions by the central bank in its weekly auctions.

There has been a marked improvement in money aggregates in **São Tomé & Príncipe** since 1998, as a result of a tightening in reserve requirements, greater fiscal discipline, and a substantial fall in net bank credit to the government. The discount rate was gradually reduced from 43 percent in end-1997 to 15 percent in end-2002, as a result of lower inflation. The depreciation of the dobra has slowed in recent years.

## Poverty Alleviation Strategies

All countries, except medium-income **Equatorial Guinea**, have sought to formulate their poverty reduction programs within the framework of the enhanced HIPC debt relief initiative. Three countries — **Rwanda** in 2002 and **Cameroon** and **Chad** in 2003 — have completed their Poverty Reduction Strategy Papers (PRSPs), whereas **CAR**, **DRC**, and **São Tomé & Príncipe**, have released interim versions.

The government in **Burundi** has prepared a national poverty reduction program, launched in April 2002, which it plans to use as the basis for an interim PRSP. The government in **Congo** has also made good progress in the preparation of an interim PRSP, which it hoped to finalize at the end of 2003 after engaging in participatory consultations.

While not qualifying for HIPC debt relief, the **Gabon** government submitted an interim PRSP to donors in mid-2003 as part of its negotiation for a financial deal with the IMF. The government in **Equatorial Guinea** has no poverty alleviation program. Income inequality is particularly high in this country, most citizens living well beyond the reach of the average per capita income of US$5,849.

## Structural Reforms

The pace of structural reforms in 2003 remained slow for most oil-producing countries in Central Africa, although governments have pledged to increase transparency in the oil sector. Major developments took place elsewhere, with notably the sale of Rwanda's electricity parastatal and the creation of a privatization unit in DRC.

**Burundi**'s government hopes to initiate a privatization program once security conditions have improved. There are more than 50 public enterprises in the country. Other structural adjustment reforms focused on improving the transparency and control of public finances, by notably undertaking a civil service census and planning the liberalization of the coffee sector.

**Cameroon**'s privatization program has made little progress since the Sonel electricity firm was sold in 2001. Negotiations with Ondeo Services over its participation in SNEC (the national water company) fell through in 2003, and plans to privatize Sodecoton, Cameroon Development Corporation (banana, rubber and palm oil), Camtel (telecommunications) and Camair (air) also stalled. Four strategic investors have been short-listed to take over the commercial side of the port of Douala. The government is soon to hire an international consultant to revive the liberalization of the cotton sector and Tunisian and Cameroonian interests have been mandated to rehabilitate the Camrail railway company.

The *coup d'état* in **CAR** has rendered the sale of some state-owned enterprises (SOEs) uncertain. Castel of France still plans to take over Sogesca (sugar), but shares in BARC (freight) could remain unsold. Funds are needed to undertake financial audits in Enerca (electricity), Socatel (telecommunications), and SNE (water) ahead of privatization.

In **Chad**, Sudan-based Azoum and Arcory International have been selected to take over DHS, the oil and soap unit of Cotontchad but the government has yet to choose one of the privatization options that were drawn up for Cotonchad in early 2003. Other enterprises mooted for sale include Air Chad and Sotel Chad (telecommunications).

A Steering Committee on the Reform of Public Enterprises was established in the **DRC** in October 2002 and became operational at end-2003. The Committee is to prepare a draft law on public enterprise reforms for 2004. Restructuring plans will include Cohydro (oil). Also in 2003, the government decided to liquidate the BCCE bank as part of its ongoing reforms to strengthen the banking sector. New regulations were introduced in the mining sector and progress was made in preparing the restructuring of Gecamines (copper).

The government in **Congo** pushed through its program of structural reforms in 2003, albeit with some delays. Preparations for the sale of SNE (electricity) and CFCO (railway) went ahead, while the post and telecommunication utility was split into two separate units. Meanwhile, BMCE of Morocco bought a 25 percent share in the state-owned CAIC bank, and three state-owned hotels were handed over to private interests. The financial audit of the national oil company (SNPC) was launched in March 2003, eight months later than planned, as a first move to enhancing transparency in the oil sector.

The government in **Equatorial Guinea** has made a nominal commitment to privatization but has yet to draw up a program.

Privatization in **Gabon** made little progress in 2003, although the government stepped up its commitment to reforms by issuing new tenders for the sale of OPRAG (ports) and Gabon Telecom. Meanwhile, lease contracts for OCTRA (railway) and Agrogabon (palm oil) were repealed, after private operators failed to meet their commitments. Other enterprises mooted for privatization include Air Gabon and Hevegab (rubber). Other structural reforms focused on enhancing the private investment climate, by notably adopting anti-corruption legislation, reforming the procurement code, and creating a one-stop investment shop.

The pace of privatization accelerated in **Rwanda** in 2003, when a five-year management contract for the electricity and gas parastatal, Electrogaz, was signed and the government sold 23.5 percent of its shares in the tea processor, Sorwathe. A lease contract was also signed for Akagera hotel. Preparations for the sale of the public telecommunications company, Rwandatel, are well advanced, and the government has issued tenders for two state-owned tea estates, Mulindi and Pfunda. Other reforms are pending, including the sale of the Banque Commerciale du Rwanda, which will help to strengthen the banking sector.

**São Tomé e Príncipe** has focused on preparations for the sale of EMAE (water and electricity), implying a rise in water and electricity rates in line with production and marketing costs.

## Recent Trends in the External Sector

### Trade Liberalization

Central Africa as a whole is relatively open by continental standards. Countries in Central Africa that have the highest trade-to-GDP ratios are economies that are heavily dependent on oil exports, notably Congo, Equatorial Guinea, and Gabon, as well as São Tomé & Príncipe, the latter bearing the characteristics of a small island economy. By contrast, the trade-to-GDP ratios in the region's landlocked countries, notably Rwanda and Burundi, remain low by regional and continental standards, at less than 40 percent. The importance of trade has grown with oil development in Chad.

All countries, except Equatorial Guinea and São Tomé e Príncipe, are members of the WTO, which means that they are committed to multilateral trade liberalization and must grant most-favored nation treatment to all their trading partners. Cameroon, CAR, Chad, Congo, Gabon and Equatorial Guinea are working towards the adoption of a common external tariff and the lifting of intra-regional import barriers within the economic grouping, Communauté économique et monétaire de l'Afrique centrale (CEMAC). Trade regimes in **Cameroon** and **Congo** are relatively open. There have been some delays elsewhere, however. **Chad** in particular has yet to implement an action plan for the reform of customs administration, after serious irregularities were exposed in an audit in 2002.

The regional grouping, Common Market for Eastern and Southern Africa (COMESA), to which DRC, Rwanda, and Burundi belong, is scheduled to form a free trade area by January 2004. Governments in DRC, Rwanda and Burundi have all committed to the adoption of a common external tariff. The **Burundi** government adopted the new tariff structure ahead of schedule in 2003. Indirect taxation was reformed to compensate for the revenue losses expected from the reform. Also in 2003, the government in **DRC** adopted a simplified three-band tariff structure and eliminated the surtax applicable to a list of specific products. The domestic tax base was widened to help make up for the loss of earnings. Efforts were also made to simplify custom procedures. The reform of the Custom and Excise Office (OFIDA) was approved in 2003, with the one-stop window due to open by mid-year. The DRC is also a member of the Southern African Development Community (SADC). The government in **Rwanda** has also made progress in opening its trade regime, although the 2003 budget introduced new excise taxes. The adoption of a common external tariff is scheduled no later than end 2004.

### Current Account Developments

The region's external position improved in 2003, with the current account deficit standing at 3.4 percent of GDP, compared with 5.1 percent of GDP in 1999–2002 (Table 2.4). Important changes are taking place in the region's export composition: oil will soon replace cotton and livestock as Chad's main source of foreign exchange earnings, while peace in DRC should gradually bring formerly smuggled commodities into the fold of the formal economy. São Tomé e Príncipe should also start producing oil in the years to come. Only Cameroon currently has a relatively wide export base, although this mostly entails crude oil and low value-added agricultural products. The terms of trade for oil-exporting countries in Central Africa were satisfactory in 2003, with world oil prices rising, although not enough to compensate for the strengthening of the CFA franc against the US dollar. This contributed to sluggish export performance in some of the CFA zone countries in 2003.

The external current account deficit in **Burundi** widened to 6.8 percent of GDP in 2003, despite fresh disbursements of foreign assistance and a slight recovery in world arabica coffee prices. While imports increased with world oil prices, food assistance requirements, and donor-funded reconstruction projects, export earnings slumped, in large part because of lower coffee production.

**Cameroon**'s trade surplus improved in 2003, as a result of higher earnings from non-oil exports (notably coffee, cocoa, and timber) and falling imports following the completion of the Chad-Cameroon oil pipeline. Oil revenues continued to fall, despite higher world prices. The current account deficit declined to 5.6 percent of GDP in 2003, reflecting movements in the trade balance and lower debt servicing obligations.

Net trade in goods and services has traditionally been negative in **CAR**, because of heavy freight costs. Export earnings, mostly from diamond, timber, and to a lesser extent, cotton, are nonetheless high enough for the country to occasionally post a small

## Table 2.4: Central Africa: The External Sector

| Country | Trade balance as % of GDP | | Current Account as % of GDP | | Terms of Trade (%) | | Total External Debt as % of GDP | | Debt Service as % of Exports | |
|---|---|---|---|---|---|---|---|---|---|---|
| | Average | | Average | | Average | | Average | | Average | |
| | 1999–2002 | 3002[/a] | 1999–2002 | 2003[a/] | 1999–2002 | 2003[a/] | 1999–2002 | 2003[a/] | 1999–2002 | 2003[a/] |
| BURUNDI | −7.6 | −11.9 | −8.2 | −6.8 | −1.1 | −8.6 | 130.1 | 172.9 | 47.7 | 40.0 |
| CAMEROON | 5.0 | −0.4 | −3.4 | −5.6 | 0.7 | −6.1 | 88.5 | 48.4 | 18.4 | 13.9 |
| CENTRAL AFRICAN REP. | −18.1 | −21.7 | −4.7 | −6.2 | −3.9 | 0.0 | 82.1 | 100.0 | 13.5 | 94.7 |
| CHAD | 0.3 | 1.1 | −2.4 | −1.5 | −0.9 | 12.4 | 60.4 | 55.9 | 3.9 | 9.5 |
| CONGO, DEM. REP. OF | 6.8 | −2.3 | −4.1 | −3.3 | 4.1 | −8.5 | 221.1 | 143.3 | 149.2 | 14.1 |
| CONGO, REPUBLIC OF | 39.0 | 37.7 | −16.7 | −1.6 | 4.5 | −5.1 | 212.2 | 174.7 | 12.6 | 13.5 |
| EQUATORIAL GUINEA | 16.7 | −19.2 | −46.3 | −1.4 | 0.1 | −0.6 | 84.9 | 9.8 | 19.5 | 2.1 |
| GABON | 34.4 | −1.5 | 0.2 | −0.3 | 7.8 | −1.9 | 69.6 | 42.8 | 19.8 | 50.3 |
| RWANDA | −12.8 | −4.1 | −7.6 | −4.7 | 2.2 | −8.3 | 72.5 | 86.0 | 21.7 | 28.6 |
| SAO TOME & PRINCIPE | −36.6 | −33.3 | −48.8 | −33.3 | 0.1 | −2.4 | 567.5 | 450.0 | 26.9 | 100.0 |
| **CENTRAL AFRICA** | **11.9** | **0.6** | **−5.1** | **−3.4** | **2.4** | **−5.1** | **119.4** | **79.8** | **32.0** | **21.4** |

*Note*: a/ Preliminary estimates
*Source*: ADB Statistics Division, 2004

trade surplus in FOB terms. In addition, the demand for the import of machinery and consumption goods is often depressed. Political instability, a fall in official transfers, and sluggish activity in mining contributed to keep the current account deficit at an equivalent to 6.2 percent of GDP in 2003.

Cotton and livestock remained **Chad**'s main sources of export earnings in 2003, although oil revenue began accruing to the country in the third quarter of the year. Rising world cotton prices, coupled with higher cotton seed production and a decline in the imports of capital and intermediary goods

following the completion of the pipeline brought the current account deficit down from 2.4 to 1.5 percent of GDP in 2003.

**DRC** is rich with natural resources, with a well–diversified export base, comprising diamonds, crude oil, copper, cobalt and coffee. The current account balance improved substantially and turned into a surplus of 2.1 percent of GDP in 2002, reflecting an upturn in diamond exports and a rise in external grants. In 2003, the external current account balance turned into a deficit of −3.3 percent of GDP, in line with the resumption of foreign-financed investment and with it, aid-related imports of goods and services.

**Congo**'s external position deteriorated in 2003, owing to falling oil production and the weakening of the US dollar. Up to 90 percent of the country's export earnings come from oil. The growth in imports was meanwhile lower than expected, reflecting delays in post-war reconstruction efforts. This, coupled with higher-than-projected world oil prices and lower transport costs, helped to contain the deficit in the current account to 1.6 percent of GDP.

**Equatorial Guinea**'s fast growing oil production has led to an exponential growth in exports earnings. Imports of consumer and capital goods, freight and insurance costs, and profit remittances have also surged, leading to a widening in the current account deficit over the years, the bulk of which is being financed by private capital flows. The current account deficit has nonetheless shrunk since 2001, owing to the falling demand for foreign capital equipment and the strong increase in oil output and prices. In 2003, the current account deficit fell to an equivalent 1.4 percent of GDP.

**Gabon** enjoys a relatively modest import bill because of its small population, while oil export earnings contribute up to 80 percent of the country's export receipts. The trade surplus, which averaged 39.2 percent of GDP in 1999–2002, has slowly eroded, however, because of falling oil production. The current account balance turned into a small deficit of 0.3 percent of GDP in 2003.

**Rwanda**'s terms of trade have deteriorated sharply over the years, as a result of falling tea and coffee prices and a sharp reduction in mining receipts (mostly cobalt). Exports increased moderately in 2003, because of slightly higher coffee and tea export volumes and prices. Growth in imports was meanwhile robust, reflecting higher oil prices and growing aid-related expenditures. The deficit on the external current account, including grants, fell to 4.7 percent of GDP in 2003, as a result. Concessional loans and debt rescheduling mostly financed this deficit.

**São Tomé & Príncipe**'s export base is very narrow (mostly cocoa beans), while imports comprise essential goods, such as food, oil and capital equipment. Transport and insurance freights are also high in this island economy, which has yet to fully develop its tourism industry, also a main source of foreign exchange earnings. Exports were above average in 2003, reflecting robust world cocoa prices. The current account deficit fell to 33.3 percent of GDP in 2003.

### External Debt

Central Africa's external debt burden is the highest in Africa and amounted to 79.8 percent of the region's GDP in 2003, down an average 119.4 percent of GDP in 1999–2002. The debt service ratio stood at 21.4 percent in 2003. Five out of eight low income countries in the region have qualified for debt relief under the HIPC initiative. This in large part indicates difficulties in regularizing relations with external creditors and/or concluding an IMF-sponsored Poverty Reduction and Growth Facility (PRGF).

Foreign direct investment, another source of external financing, has increased significantly in Central Africa in recent years, but it remains largely confined to the oil sector, political instability being the main hindrance to FDI elsewhere. According to UNCTAD's *World Investment Report 2003*, FDI inflows to the region totaled US$1.7 billion in 2002,

US$901 million of which went to Chad. In terms of FDI inward stocks, Gabon and Equatorial Guinea were the main recipients in 2003, with stocks totaling more than US$2 billion each. Central Africa CFA zone countries created a regional stock exchange market, Bourse de valeurs mobilières de l'Afrique centrale (BVMAC), in Libreville, Gabon, in July 2003, but the bourse is unlikely to be operational before mid-2004. Cameroon opened its own national stock exchange in Douala in 2002.

Total debt in **Burundi** amounted to a high 172.9 percent of GDP in 2003, while the debt service ratio fell to 40.0 percent of exports. While current with the World Bank, its main lender, the country is in arrears with other multilateral institutions, including the African Development Bank, and a number of bilateral creditors. The government has given priority to the settlement of arrears owed to multilateral creditors. A multidonor trust fund was set up by the World Bank in December 2000 to help the government clear its stock of payment arrears, and eventually qualify to HIPC assistance, but available resources in 2003 remained insufficient to step up debt service payments to external creditors.

Improved fiscal position and prudent borrowing policy, combined with successive debt relief deals with the Paris Club of official, bilateral creditors, have led to a continuous decline in **Cameroon**'s external debt burden. The government hoped to reach completion point under the enhanced HIPC initiative by end-2003. The external debt-GDP ratio stood at 48.4 percent in 2003, while the debt service ratio rose to a still manageable 13.9 percent.

**CAR**'s external debt is mostly made of highly concessional, multilateral, long-term loans. The country has yet to qualify for debt relief under the enhanced HIPC initiative, reflecting multilateral debt payment arrears and delays in securing an IMF financial deal. The debt-to-GDP ratio rose to 100 percent in 2003, reflecting negative growth, while the debt service ratio totaled 94.7 percent

External debt in **Chad** declined to 55.9 percent of GDP in 2003, reflecting high economic growth and access to non-debt capital inflows. The HIPC initiative, for which Chad qualified in May 2001, will lead to an estimated US$260 million in debt relief. The government hopes to reach completion point by end-2004. The debt service ratio decline to 9.5 percent in 2003, due to HIPC interim assistance and a Paris Club debt relief deal in June 2001, it is expected to fall significantly in 2004, as export earnings increase with oil production.

**DRC** reached decision point under the enhanced HIPC Initiative in July 2003. Debt relief from all of the country's creditors will amount to approximately US$10 billion in nominal terms over time. This indicates the country's remarkable progress in pushing through economic reforms and regularizing its situation with external creditors since reconciliation began in 2001. The stock of debt to GDP ratio was estimated at 143.4 percent of GDP in 2003, following the approval of a debt rescheduling deal with the Paris Club in September 2002.

**Congo** faces a very heavy debt burden, because of excess borrowing against future oil earnings in the past. Taking advantage of the high oil prices, the government resumed current external debt service and made partial payments on debt arrears to some multilateral donors, including the African Development

Bank, in 2003 — this led to the resumption by the AfDB of its institutional support project. In addition, there has been no recourse to oil-collateralized borrowing since October 2002. External debt declined to 174.7 percent of GDP in 2003, as a result, while the debt service ratio rose to 13.5 percent, as the government remained current on its debt payment obligations that year.

**Equatorial Guinea** is not eligible for concessional assistance, being a middle-income economy. Most of the country's external public debt has been contracted on a bilateral basis, as a result. The debt burden is low: owing to remarkable growth rates and rising oil export earnings, total debt amounted to less than 10 percent of GDP in 2003 and the debt service ratio stood at 2.1 percent. The government has nonetheless been reluctant to clear principal and interest payments arrears contracted by previous administrations.

The government in **Gabon** has restricted external borrowing since the mid-1990s, with the debt-to-GDP ratio falling to 42.8 percent in 2003, despite poor economic performance. But the debt service ratio has failed to decline, instead rising to 50.3 percent in 2003, as a result of falling export earnings. All non-reschedulable debt payment arrears were cleared by June 2003, when the government entered a new round of negotiations with the IMF. Gabon does not qualify for HIPC debt relief, being classified as a middle-income economy.

**Rwanda**'s external debt amounted to US$1.5 billion (86.0 percent of GDP) at end-2003. The government continued to depend on interim debt relief from its creditors to meet its debt payment obligations. A new debt rescheduling and relief deal was signed with the Paris Club in March 2002 under the Cologne terms. A debt rescheduling agreement with the Kuwait Fund was signed in February 2003. The country qualified for debt relief under HIPC in May 2001, which will lead to a nominal US$810 million in debt relief at completion point, which the government hopes to reach in 2004.

At 450 percent, **São Tomé & Príncipe**'s external debt-to-GDP ratio is the highest in Africa. Sao Tome qualified for the HIPC initiative in December 2000, which will lead to a nominal debt relief of US$200 million at completion point. About 65 percent of the country's debt is owed to multilateral lenders. The debt service ratio declined to 100 percent in 2003, reflecting HIPC interim debt relief, the impact of a Paris Club debt rescheduling deal in May 2000, and strong export earnings that year.

## Outlook

Central African GDP is forecast to grow faster than the 4.4 percent of 2003, assuming peace consolidation in the region. Growth in **Burundi** is expected to resume in 2004, assuming peace consolidation and a return to satisfactory weather conditions. Rising donor assistance (the IMF approved a second post-conflict emergency assistance for the country in May 2003) will support the country's reconstruction efforts. In **Cameroon**, reduced activity in construction and services will tend to undermine growth targets. Annual rates around 4–5 percent could be achieved, with acceleration in structural reforms and the implementation of poverty alleviation measures. Economic recovery in **CAR** will hinge on success in fostering peace and stability, through notably organizing fair and transparent elections in 2004 and negotiating a staff monitored program with the IMF. Oil production will become the main source of growth in **Chad** in 2004, although construction activity will continue outside the Doba oil project. Economic growth is set to accelerate to 40 percent in 2004, as oil production reaches a peak of 225,000 to 250,000 barrels per day (bpd). The government will need to show strong commitment to poverty alleviation measures. But fiscal slippage is likely, which could delay completion point under the enhanced HIPC initiative.

Growth in **DRC** will remain robust, driven by an increase in externally financed investment, macroeconomic stabilization, and the implementation of structural and sectoral reforms. Real GDP in **Congo** is expected to rise by 4–5 percent, on the back of rising investment and activity in the non-oil sector. Recent progress in fiscal consolidation and structural reforms could pave the way for an IMF deal in 2004. This will prompt other donors to return. Meanwhile, oil production will continue to decline. Growth performance will remain exceptionally strong in **Equatorial Guinea**, as oil production continues to expand at Zafiro, Ceiba and Oukoume, the country's main fields. The IMF is expected to approve a three-year facility for **Gabon** in 2004, on the back of improved performance in economic policy and reforms. Rising external assistance will help to boost activity in the non-oil sector, partly compensating for falling oil production and prices. In **Rwanda**, the ongoing program of privatization, notably in the commercial agricultural sector, will help to achieve annual rates of growth of around 6 percent. The government will

continue heavily to rely on external assistance to finance its budget. Continued investment in petroleum exploration and infrastructure development will drive economic performance in **São Tomé & Príncipe**.

# East Africa

The East Africa region is made up of 11 countries: Comoros, Djibouti, Eritrea, Ethiopia, Kenya, Madagascar, Mauritius, Seychelles, Somalia, Tanzania and Uganda. East Africa's GDP accounted for 8.0 percent of continental output in 2003. Most countries in East Africa thrive on tourism and the exports of primary commodities, notably tea and coffee. Other countries, like Mauritius, have been more successful in diversifying their export base away from traditional products. The region is a net importer of oil. Kenya is the largest economy of the zone, followed by Tanzania, Ethiopia, and Uganda. Taken together, these four countries generated 69.7 percent of the regional GDP in 2003.

The population in East Africa was estimated at 209.5 million in 2003, representing about 23.6 percent of the continent's population. Seychelles and Mauritius are middle-income countries, their GDP per capita being estimated at US$8,660 and US$4,593 respectively in 2003. By contrast, Eritrea and Ethiopia, which suffered from a severe drought in 2002, the worst in many years, are among the poorest countries in Africa, their per capita income being below US$200. The region's GDP per capita remains the lowest in Africa, averaging US$263 in 2003 (Table 2.5).

Political stability in the region has remained fragile. The UN-sponsored discussions between Ethiopia and Eritrea over the demarcation border have dragged on, further delaying the demobilization process. The national reconciliation process launched in 2001 in Comoros has meanwhile proved slow and legislative elections due in April 2003 have been postponed indefinitely. In Uganda, the government has stepped up its campaign against rebels in the north, while withdrawing its last troops from neighboring DRC. On a more positive side, a ceasefire was signed between the transitional government in Somalia and 21 warring factions in October 2002 and first presidential elections were held in Somaliland in April 2003. Madagascar has meanwhile recovered from the severe political crisis that hit the country following contested presidential election in December 2001, whereas Kenya's former opposition leader and newly elected president, Mwai Kibaki, has worked hard to renew relations with donors.

## Recent Trends in the Domestic Economy

### Economic Growth and Inflation

East Africa has recovered slowly from the severe drought that hit the Horn of Africa in 2002, which was the worst in many years. The slow global recovery meanwhile continued to dampen performance in the region's tourism sector and its Export Processing Zones. Growth in 2003 decelerated, or remained subdued, in all major economies of the region, as a result. Regional GDP increased by an average 2.6 percent in real terms, which is well below population growth and the continental average. Inflation meanwhile accelerated to 8.0 percent, as a result of severe food shortages and higher prices for imported fuel (Figure 2.2).

Political tensions between the three islands of **Comoros** and the Union government have weakened the country's already fragile economy, by paralyzing public administration, postponing economic reforms and blocking disbursements of external assistance.

## Table 2.5: East Africa: Gross Domestic Product and Export Performances

| Country | Real GDP Growth Rate (%) | | GDP Per Capita (US$) | | Real Exports[c/] Growth (%) | | Exports[b/] Per Capita (US$) | |
|---|---|---|---|---|---|---|---|---|
| | Average 1999–2002 | 2003[a/] | Average 1999–2002 | 2003[a/] | Average 1999–2002 | 2003[a/] | Average 1999–2002 | 2003[a/] |
| COMOROS | 1.3 | 2.5 | 312 | 408 | −14.9 | 70.7 | 62 | 50 |
| DJIBOUTI | 1.8 | 3.0 | 838 | 884 | 7.7 | 12.7 | 404 | 462 |
| ERITREA | −0.3 | 5.0 | 180 | 192 | ... | ... | 33 | 42 |
| ETHIOPIA | 5.9 | −4.2 | 94 | 92 | 7.0 | 8.0 | 15 | 16 |
| KENYA | 0.8 | 1.4 | 362 | 444 | 4.6 | 6.0 | 94 | 109 |
| MADAGASCAR | 0.7 | 9.6 | 255 | 317 | 0.3 | 47.5 | 64 | 66 |
| MAURITIUS | 4.9 | 4.4 | 3,794 | 4,593 | 5.2 | 6.4 | 2,314 | 2,406 |
| SEYCHELLES | 0.4 | −5.0 | 7,896 | 8,660 | 29.0 | 2.2 | 5,954 | 6,730 |
| SOMALIA | ... | ... | ... | ... | ... | ... | ... | ... |
| TANZANIA | 5.3 | 5.5 | 262 | 261 | 1.5 | 9.3 | 38 | 45 |
| UGANDA | 6.3 | 5.4 | 244 | 228 | 17.5 | −1.1 | 29 | 32 |
| EAST AFRICA | 4.0 | 2.6 | 242 | 263 | 5.7 | 5.7 | 58 | 62 |

*Notes*: a/ Preliminary estimates
b/ Exports of Goods and Nonfactor Services at Market Prices
c/ Real Exports of Goods Growth
*Source*: ADB Statistics Division, 2004

Economic growth was nonetheless estimated at 2.5 percent in 2003, up from 1.3 percent in 1999–2002. Strong price stability has prevailed in the islands economy, its currency being firmly pegged to the euro. Consumer prices rose by an average 2.5 percent in 2003.

**Djibouti**'s economic prospects have improved since becoming an important base for western forces, including troops from the US, in the war against global terrorism. Growth increased to 3.0 percent in 2003, spurred by strong activity in transit trade, services, and construction. Djibouti's currency board with the US dollar has helped to keep inflationary pressures under control. Inflation was estimated at 2.0 percent in 2003.

The 2002 drought dealt a major blow to **Ethiopia**'s economy. Growth was revised downwards to 2.7 percent in 2002 (reported as 2001/02 in national statistics), before turning negative in 2003, at −4.2 percent. This mostly reflects a 14 percent drop in agricultural and livestock production. Cereal prices surged by an estimated 35 percent by mid-year, despite efforts by the government and donors to tackle the food crisis. As a result, average year inflation accelerated to 14.6 percent in 2003.

**Figure 2.2: East Africa, Selected Economic Indicators, 1999–2003**

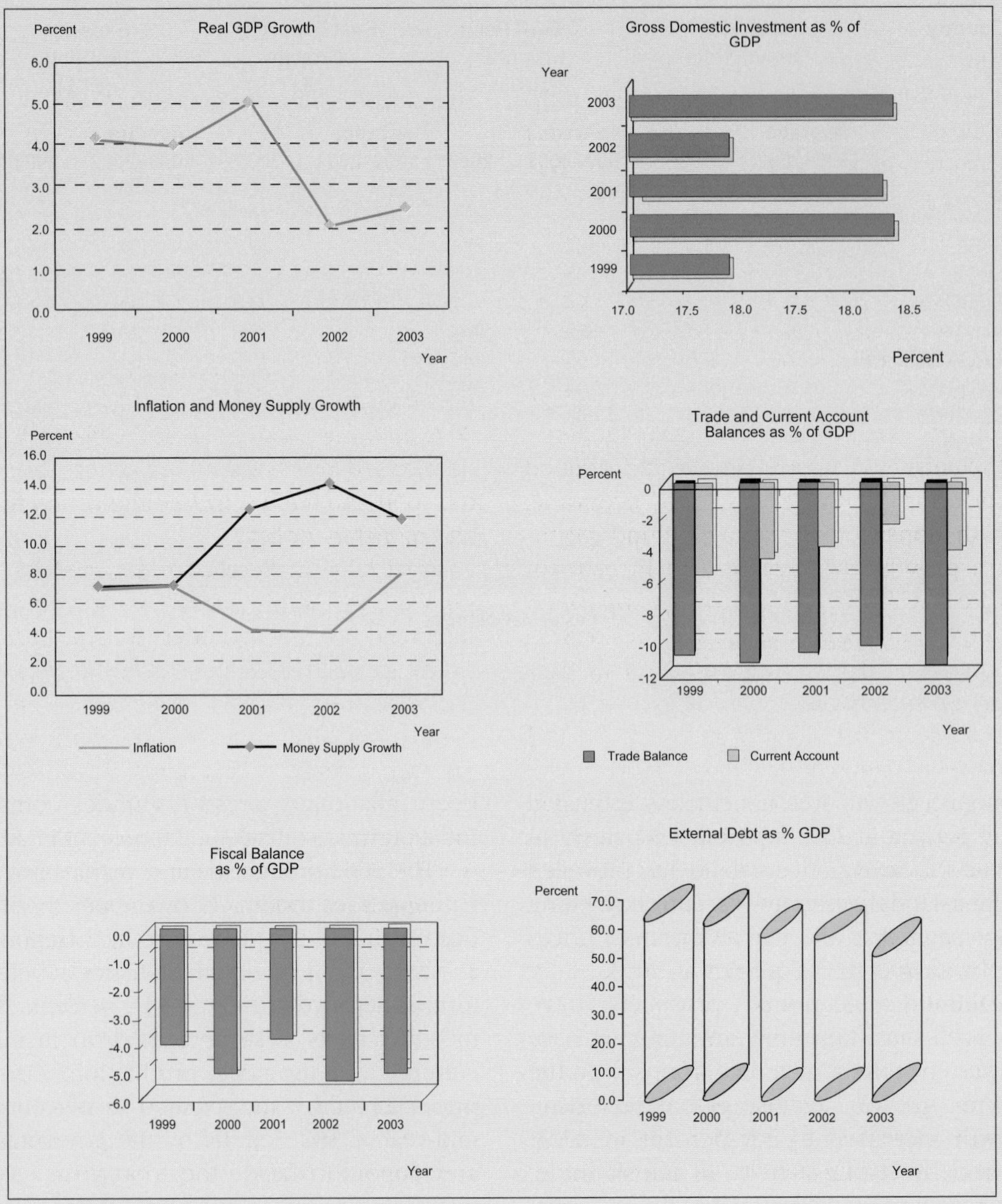
Real GDP Growth
Percent
6.0
5.0
4.0
3.0
2.0
1.0
0.0
1999
2000
2001
2002
2003
Year
Gross Domestic Investment as % of GDP
Year
2003
2002
2001
2000
1999
17.0
17.5
18.0
17.5
18.0
18.5
Percent
Inflation and Money Supply Growth
Percent
16.0
14.0
12.0
10.0
8.0
6.0
4.0
2.0
0.0
1999
2000
2001
2002
2003
Year
Inflation
Money Supply Growth
Trade and Current Account Balances as % of GDP
Percent
0
-2
-4
-6
-8
-10
-12
1999
2000
2001
2002
2003
Year
Trade Balance
Current Account
Fiscal Balance as % of GDP
0.0
-1.0
-2.0
-3.0
-4.0
-5.0
-6.0
1999
2000
2001
2002
2003
Year
External Debt as % GDP
Percent
70.0
60.0
50.0
40.0
30.0
20.0
10.0
0.0
1999
2000
2001
2002
2003
Year

*Source*: ADB Statistics Division, 2004

Growth recovery in **Eritrea** remains fragile. Livestock production improved and the cropping season got off to a good start in the second part of 2003. But the economy continued to suffer from the severe drought that devastated crop production in 2002. Slowness in implementing the post-war reconstruction and demobilization program and inadequacy in the level of external assistance kept economic growth in 2003 below target, at 5 percent. The food situation remained critical in 2003, with tight supply conditions resulting in a sharp acceleration in inflation to 23.9 percent.

**Kenya**'s economy has been affected by years of weak economic management, inefficiency in the public sector, and strained relationships with donors, with economic growth consistently trailing behind population growth as a result. The investment climate has improved since former opposition leader, Mwai Kibaki, was elected President in December 2002, ending 24 years of rule under President Daniel arap Moi. The economy showed first signs of recovery in 2003 (2002/03 in national statistics), with growth edging up to 1.4 percent, as a result of activity in agriculture, manufacturing and services. Inflation meanwhile accelerated to 12.4 percent, mostly reflecting a tightening in the food supply, an increase in the retail price of petroleum products, and a relaxation in monetary policy in the latter part of 2002.

Eroding comparative advantages and the morose external environment continued to dampen growth performance in **Mauritius**. Growth slowed to 4.4 percent in 2003 (2002/03 in national accounts), reflecting the impact of cyclone Dina on sugar output and sluggish growth in the Export Processing Zone and the tourism sector, as a result of the economic slowdown in the EU, the country's main export outlet. Activity in construction and the financial sector continued to be buoyant. Inflation decelerated to 5 percent in 2003, reflecting a tightening in monetary policy.

**Madagascar**'s economic performance in 2003 was impaired by the lingering effects of the 2002 political crisis, which was sparked off by a dispute over the results of the December 2001 presidential elections. Economic recovery was notably slower than expected in tourism, construction and the Export Processing Zone activities. Growth nonetheless resumed from −12.7 percent in 2002 to 9.6 percent in 2003, while inflation decelerated to 3.5 percent, reflecting resumed transport and trade activities and sound fiscal and monetary policy.

Real GDP in **Seychelles** declined by 5.0 percent in 2003. Extensive government intervention and rigidities in the foreign exchange market have created bottlenecks in the economy, while tourism has lost its competitive edge, compared with other, cheaper, destinations in the region. Consumer prices rose by an average 7 percent in 2003, as the government took first steps to liberalize imports and introduce a general sales tax.

**Somalia**'s economy has continued to suffer from civil insecurity, harsh climatic conditions, and an import ban on the country's livestock. Consumer prices in Mogadishu have rocketed, reflecting fuel shortage and fluctuations affecting the Somali currency. Lacking a centralized machinery that exercises monopoly over the use of violence, Somalia continues to exhibit all the symptoms of a divided state, with diminishing economic prospects.

**Tanzania** is the second largest economy of the region after Kenya. The country's performance still largely hinges on agriculture, which accounts for a bit less than half of its GDP. Preliminary estimates for food crop production in 2003/04 indicate a decline compared to last year, owing to dry weather. Economic growth, which decelerated to 5.5 percent in 2003 as a result, was spurred by strong activity in mining, construction and manufacturing. Inflation stood at 5.3 percent in 2003, mostly reflecting higher cereal prices and fiscal and monetary developments.

Growth in **Uganda** decelerated to 5.4 percent in 2003 (2002/03 in national statistics). Agricultural production declined due to adverse weather conditions, while there were delays in the construction of the Bujagali dam construction project. Uganda was the fastest growing economy in the region through most of the 1990s, as a result of successful macro-economic stabilization policy, strong donor support and increased interest from foreign investors. But recent years have seen a slight deceleration in the country's growth, largely because of unfavorable external conditions, notably drought and depressed world coffee prices. Sharp increases in the prices of food and petroleum products, coupled with a weaker Ugandan shilling, raised inflation to 5.9 percent in 2003, against a yearly average of 2 percent in 1999–2002.

## Fiscal Developments

The measures adopted by East African governments to enhance revenue and tighten expenditure control have helped to improve the region's fiscal position over the years, although the overall regional deficit continues to be high by continental standards. East Africa's deficit stood at 5.0 percent of GDP in 2003, against a yearly average 4.5 percent in 1999–2002 (Table 2.6).

The fiscal situation in **Comoros** was particularly troubled in 2003, as local governments and the Union government fought over tax collection. The central government deficit was estimated at 1.2 percent of GDP in 2003.

The government in **Djibouti** has made some progress in introducing greater discipline and transparency in public finances, by notably completing an audit of domestic budgetary arrears and adopting a cash-flow management system. Benchmarks were missed in 2003, however, because of a higher public sector wage bill and lower indirect tax revenues (a harmonized value added tax has yet to be introduced). At the same time, externally-financed public expenditures doubled, reflecting a surge in external assistance from bilateral donors (notably USAID) and the World Bank.

The government in **Eritrea** has resorted to increased domestic credit financing in recent years. It aimed to redirect the bulk of public expenditures towards reconstruction and social spending in 2003. But the fiscal position was still subordinated to the defense budget, as the government only reluctantly begun with the demobilization program of some 200,000 combatants.

The overall government deficit in **Ethiopia** decreased to 8.5 percent of GDP in 2003, in large part reflecting a rise in emergency assistance in the form of grants. The government also made further headways in reforming the tax base, by notably introducing a value-added tax and streamlining the import tariff regime in 2003. The large taxpayer unit was meanwhile

## Table 2.6: East Africa: Macroeconomic Management Indicators

| Country | Inflation (%) | | Fiscal Balance as % of GDP | | Gross Domestic Investment | | Gross National Savings as % of GDP | |
|---|---|---|---|---|---|---|---|---|
| | Average 1999–2002 | 2003[a] | Average 1999–2002 | 2003[a] | Average 1999–2002 | 2003[a] | Average 1999–2002 | 2003[a] |
| COMOROS | 1.9 | 2.5 | −3.3 | −1.2 | 12.1 | 12.9 | 10.7 | 10.0 |
| DJIBOUTI | 1.9 | 2.0 | −2.2 | −1.2 | 9.9 | 11.9 | 5.4 | 6.7 |
| ERITREA | 15.4 | 23.9 | −38.0 | −24.8 | 26.7 | 22.5 | 7.7 | 11.5 |
| ETHIOPIA | −1.6 | 14.6 | −9.0 | −8.5 | 17.5 | 21.2 | 11.6 | 15.1 |
| KENYA | 5.6 | 12.4 | −1.6 | −5.2 | 14.9 | 15.1 | 12.9 | 12.1 |
| MADAGASCAR | 7.8 | 3.5 | −3.8 | −3.3 | 22.7 | 22.8 | 18.1 | 18.2 |
| MAURITIUS | 6.0 | 5.0 | −4.7 | −5.9 | 24.1 | 22.7 | 25.4 | 27.3 |
| SEYCHELLES | 4.7 | 7.0 | −10.9 | 6.4 | 30.6 | 18.4 | 13.5 | 14.1 |
| SOMALIA | ... | ... | ... | ... | ... | ... | ... | ... |
| TANZANIA | 6.3 | 5.3 | −2.3 | −3.2 | 16.9 | 18.9 | 11.0 | 11.4 |
| UGANDA | 2.0 | 5.9 | −4.7 | −4.1 | 20.1 | 21.5 | 13.3 | 15.8 |
| **EAST AFRICA** | **5.5** | **8.0** | **−4.5** | **−5.0** | **18.4** | **19.1** | **14.0** | **14.9** |

Note: a/ Preliminary estimates
*: (Exports & Imports) of Goods and Non Factors Services at Market Prices
Source: ADB Statistics Division, 2004

strengthened. On the spending side, the military budget was curtailed to 5.3 percent of GDP, whereas social spending, which come under special, donor-funded, demobilization and reconstruction programs, was raised to 17.7 percent of GDP.

**Kenya** overshot its budget deficit-GDP target in 2002/03, owing to reduced tax revenue associated with lower-than-expected growth, laxity in expenditure control prior to the elections, additional spending in education, and adjustments in allowances and salaries. As a result, the fiscal deficit rose to 5.2 percent of GDP, the bulk of which being financed through domestic borrowing. The new administration plans to simplify the cumber-

some tax regime, reduce the high public sector wage bill, institutionalize public expenditure reviews and re-activate the medium term expenditure framework. An audit into public domestic debt and unpaid liabilities is soon to be undertaken. The fiscal situation will be enhanced with the resumption of financial support from the IMF in November 2003.

The new administration in **Madagascar** has pursued a relatively sound fiscal policy. In 2003, the government took some bold steps to reform the tax and custom administration and, in so doing, enhance revenue collection. Tax reduction measures on income and customs were meanwhile introduced to promote economic recovery. The revenue-to-GDP ratio, all in all, increased to an estimated 10.6 percent of GDP. Total expenditures in 2003 increased in line with a 12 percent rise in the civil servants base salary and a rebound in externally financed capital expenditures. The fiscal deficit edged down to 3.3 percent of GDP, with net foreign borrowing being the main source of financing.

The central government in **Mauritius** maintained an expansionary policy in 2002/03, with the fiscal deficit at 5.9 percent of GDP. The bulk of the deficit was financed through domestic borrowing. New tax measures included a rise in the VAT rate from 12 percent to 15 percent, a broadening in the VAT tax base, and a reduction in customs tariffs in line with regional trading agreements. The main challenge for the year ahead will be to implement the recent pay review report, which entails a significant rise in civil service wages. Adjustment measures are also needed to avert a possible unsustainable domestic debt situation.

Easy access to foreign financing has traditionally permitted the **Seychelles** government to run wide fiscal deficits. But the sustainability of such a policy has been challenged since the economy fell into recession. The government announced an array of fiscal reforms and belt-tightening measures in July 2003, with notably the adoption of a general sales tax. The fiscal deficit stood at 6.4 percent of GDP in 2003.

**Tanzania**'s fiscal performance in 2003 remained outstanding. The Tanzania Revenue Authority reached its targets in almost all categories, with more taxpayers being brought into the tax base through the implementation of the Taxpayer Identification Number. Earnings were higher than expected as a result. Meanwhile, the cash-flow planning and management system kept expenditures broadly on track, with the share of spending in priority sectors rising to almost 50 percent of total outlays. This, combined with strong donor support, reduced the central government deficit to a low 3.2 percent of GDP.

Fiscal adjustment in **Uganda** concentrates on reinforcing domestic tax efforts, strengthening expenditure management, curbing non-essential public expenditures and raising spending in priority sectors. The government met most of its fiscal targets in 2002/03, with the deficit falling to 4.1 percent of GDP. Additional defense expenditures prompted some donors to scale back budget support, however, as this was made at the expense of social spending. In March 2003, the government agreed on several measures to streamline public administration in the coming years.

### Monetary and Exchange Rate Developments

Monetary policy in East Africa remains expansionary by continental standards. Broad money grew by 11.9 percent in 2003, against a yearly average 10.2 percent in 1999–2002.

Monetary rules in **Comoros** are tight, as the Banque Centrale des Comores conducts its policy within the framework of the Franc Zone. As a member of the Franc Zone, Comoros has its currency pegged to the euro. Strong inflows of foreign currencies boosted money growth in **Djibouti** to 5.1 percent in 2003. This, coupled with a limited increase in domestic credit and the Djibouti franc's unchanged peg to the US dollar, reflected a marked increase in deposits with the commercial banks and an appreciation of the nominal effective exchange rate.

The central bank of **Eritrea** has failed to pursue an independent monetary policy over the years, its lending policy being mostly subordinated to the financing needs of the government. Money supply increased by 26.2 percent in 2003, as a result, while real interest rates were kept negative. Low foreign exchange reserves and the virtual fixing of the official exchange rate have continued to fuel activity on the parallel market. Eritrea introduced its own currency, the nafka, in November 1997 to replace the Ethiopian birr.

The National Bank of **Ethiopia** has sought to reduce some excess liquidity in the banking sector by increasing the sale of government securities. Credit demand remained weak, however, reflecting subdued economic growth and the Commercial Bank of Ethiopia's (CBE's) decision to stop lending to borrowers with non-performing loans (NPLs). The banking sector, which the CBE dominates, needs restructuring. Priority was given to enhancing the supervisory capacity of the central bank in 2003. The CBE meanwhile started to reduce NPLs, through restructuring, cash collection, the issuing of government bonds and write-offs. The exchange rate is market-determined and an interbank foreign exchange market was recently established. The external value of the birr depreciated by 8 percent in nominal effective terms in 2003.

Money growth in **Kenya** picked up to 7.3 percent in 2002/03, as a result of excess government borrowing. The relaxation in monetary policy, coupled with speculative pressures in the run up to the election,

exerted upward pressure on inflation and a substantial weakening of the Kenyan shilling in the latter part of 2002. The Central Bank of Kenya has since tightened its monetary stance, while the new government has shifted emphasis from short-term financing via treasury bills to long-term borrowing through treasury bonds. There was an appreciation in the nominal exchange rate in the first part of 2003, as a result of improved expectations in the aftermath of the election and the weakening of the US dollar. The banking sector has meanwhile continued to carry high level of non-performing loans.

Operations on the foreign exchange market and T-bills auctions in **Madagascar** resumed in October 2002, after an eight months' gap due to the political crisis in that country. The Central Bank of Madagascar relaxed its monetary policy in 2003 to meet additional borrowing requirements from the government and boost credit to the economy. Reserve requirements ratios on demand deposits were reduced to 18 percent in October 2002 and 12 percent in January 2003, while the basis rate fell to 7 percent. Excess bank liquidity was then mopped up through the sale of T-bills. The exchange rate continued to be market determined. The central bank's intervention on the inter-bank foreign exchange market helped to reduce short-term volatility and contain exchange rate appreciation against the US dollar and the euro in 2003. The authorities started to reintroduce currency notes denominated in ariary, the old currency that is still legal tender, towards the end of 2003.

The central bank of **Mauritius** maintained a relatively tight monetary stance in 2002/03, when compared with 2001/02, when lower interest rates, combined with a VAT rise, an increase in utility tariffs, and the depreciation of the Mauritian rupee, led to an acceleration in inflation. The central bank reduced the Lombard rate twice in 2003 on the back of lower economic growth and the widening gap between domestic and foreign interest rates. The bank also intervened on the foreign exchange market to sterilize excess liquidity due to strong foreign currency inflows. The rupee, on average, appreciated against the US dollar, but depreciated against the euro.

Excess liquidity continued to characterize the banking sector in **Tanzania** in 2002/03 notwithstanding a robust growth in private sector credit. This stemmed from strong inflows of donor assistance and an increase in domestic deposits, following the licensing of new banks and the opening of new branches by existing commercial banks. The Bank of Tanzania continued to mop up excess liquidity through open market operations, while the government agreed to securitize central bank deposits into T-bills. The bank intervened on the foreign exchange market to smooth out short-term fluctuations in the exchange rate. There was a 9.7 percent nominal depreciation of the Tanzanian shilling against the US dollar in 2002/03.

The Bank of **Uganda** continued to issue treasury bills and sell foreign exchange to sterilize excess liquidity arising from HIPC-supported government spending and commercial banks' excess reserves from previous years. Growth in credit to the private sector meanwhile picked up as the newly-privatized Uganda Commercial Bank resumed lending activities. Bank supervision and prudential provisions were strengthened with the approval of the new Financial Institutions

Bill in April 2003. The Ugandan shilling depreciated against the US dollar throughout 2003, with the Bank of Uganda occasionally intervening on the foreign exchange market to temper the fall.

## Poverty Reduction Strategies

**Mauritius** and **Seychelles** are both classified as upper middle-income economies. In these two countries, social exclusion, rather than poverty alleviation, is at the top of the domestic policy agendas. All other countries in Eastern Africa, but Tanzania and Kenya, are classified as least developed economies by the United Nations. Four countries — **Ethiopia**, **Madagascar**, **Tanzania**, and **Uganda** — have completed their final PRSPs. Madagascar submitted for appraisal its final PRSP to donors in June 2003, after organizing a final national workshop to discuss the document. Significant resources are being freed in these four countries as part of the Enhanced HIPC debt relief initiative to finance priority sectors, mostly education, health and infrastructure.

**Djibouti** was due to release its PRSP in March 2003, but more time was needed to address data compilation weaknesses and strengthen the participatory framework. The government has since made some progress to update the country's poverty profile and develop broad consultations at a national level. There was also some delay in the preparation of a full PRSP in **Kenya**, where a more comprehensive medium term macro-economic framework is needed. **Eritrea** is in the process of developing a nationwide poverty reduction strategy, which will serve as a basis document for an interim PRSP, as negotiations with the IMF over a PRGF go ahead. **Comoros** is to draw up a poverty reduction strategy under the aegis of the UN Development Program; little progress could be made in 2003 because of the political stalemate.

## Structural Reforms

Structural reforms in East Africa were broadly on track in 2003, as governments introduced new measures to open the banking and utility sectors to private participation and fight corruption.

The difficult process of political reconciliation has switched the focus away from reforms in **Comoros**.

The government in **Djibouti** has worked towards privatizing four main public utilities (water, electricity, telephone and airport); a contract to manage Djibouti's international airport was awarded to a private consortium in 2001. Huge cross-debts, an over-bloated civil service and weak capacity characterize public administration in the country.

**Eritrea**'s program of privatization remained stalled. Rather, the government has increased its control over private sector activity through enacting new trade and business licensing regulations.

Structural reforms in **Ethiopia** have focused on the banking sector. An independent audit of the Commercial Bank of Ethiopia was completed in May 2003, paving the way for the preparation of its restructuring plan. Several small public entities were brought to the point of sale in 2002. The government meanwhile launched a decentralization program, which consists of devolving some fiscal powers to the *woredas* (districts).

The new administration in **Kenya** has placed its anti-corruption program at the top of its policy agenda. Structural reforms to improve infrastructure services and reform the banking sector are also being envisaged. Given the previously poor record in restructuring and privatizing public enterprises, the new government intends to establish a new policy framework for privatization and draw up a new list of state owned enterprises and key parastatals that could be opened to private sector participation. Enterprises previously mooted for sale included Kenya Ports Authority, Kenya Railways, Kenya Telcom, and Kenya Commercial Bank.

The pace of structural reforms in **Madagascar** was satisfactory, despite delays caused by the political and economic crisis in 2002. The sale of the oil distribution company, Solima, which was awarded to a consortium of foreign firms in late 2001, was confirmed in 2002. After a series of major setbacks, the winning bidder for Telma (telecommunications) was appointed in December 2001, although the asset transfer contract was only signed in 2003. Air Madagascar was placed under a two-year management contract with Lufthansa Consulting at end-2002, when a business plan was finalized and a creditors' conference resulted in halving the company's debt.

The most recent privatization in **Mauritius** was that of Mauritius Telecom in 2000, although the government intends to allow greater private sector participation in commercial activities and in the utilities and transport sectors. The financial position of some state owned enterprises, notably the State Trading Corporation (STB), and the Central Electricity Board (CEB), deteriorated through to mid-2003, owing to the non-implementation of an automatic pricing mechanism for petroleum products and electricity tariffs. Efforts are now being made to restructure the CEB, STC and the port and airport. Postal services are also being modernized with the creation of Mauritius Post Ltd.

Although the government in **Seychelles** has privatized some small state-owned enterprises in the fishing and tourism sector, the public sector continues to play a prominent role in the economy.

The government in **Tanzania** has remained committed to pushing through its privatization program and strengthening its national anti-corruption strategy. Private consortiums have now stakes in commercial banking, air transport, port, water, telecommunication and electricity. The government plans to sell the National Micro finance Bank and the national railway company (TRC) in the near future. Agreement was sought between the government and foreign investors over the purchase of the telecommunication utility, TTCL. The government also planned to submit to parliament amendments to the Investment Act and the Labor Act by end-2003, in a bid to improve the investment climate.

In **Uganda**, the main enterprises that have been sold, although with some delay, include Uganda Telecom, in June 2000, Uganda Commercial Bank, in October 2001, and the Uganda Electricity Board's generation division in December 2002. The government remains committed to the sale of the Uganda Development Bank, but liquidation could be envisaged if this fails (Uganda Airlines was liquidated in mid-2001, after an unsuccessful privatization). Other enterprises mooted for privatization include Uganda Railway

Corporation, and Dairy Corporation and Kinyara Sugar Works.

## Recent Trends in the External Sector

### Trade Liberalization

The majority of countries in East Africa have adopted across-the-board liberalization and export-orientated development strategies. External trade in the region as a whole stood at 55.4 percent in 2003, which is low by continental standards. This hides wide discrepancies, however. In Djibouti, Seychelles and Mauritius, exports and imports of goods and non-factor services amounted to more than 100 percent of GDP in 2003.

Five countries in the region (Comoros, Eritrea, Ethiopia, Seychelles and Somalia) are not members of the WTO. **Ethiopia** submitted a request for accession in January 2003. The country has made significant progress in liberalizing its external sector. The average external import tariff was reduced from 19.5 to 17.5 percent in January 2003, with the maximum tariff cut from 40 to 35 percent and the number of bands falling to six.

In June 2003, Kenya, Tanzania, and Uganda agreed to adopt a common external tariff with three bands (0, 10, and 25 percent) under the East African Community (EAC). Arrangements were due to be finalized by November 2003. Intra-regional imports are already charged a preferential 20 percent of the countries' most-favored nation tariff. **Kenya**'s trade regime continues to be relatively restrictive, although the complex structure of *ad valorem* tariff rates and excise duties has been streamlined. The new administration has pledged to grant duty waivers on capital and intermediate goods for 2003/04, but has maintained anti-dumping policy measures on wheat and sugar imports from Common Market for Eastern and Southern Africa (COMESA), to which it belongs. **Tanzania**, which for long used non-tariff barriers to protect its domestic industry, is also committed to streamline its import tariff structure under EAC and Southern African Development Community (SADC). At 9 percent, **Uganda**'s average import tariff rate is the lowest in the sub-region.

All East African countries except Somalia and Tanzania are members of COMESA. The COMESA states plan to establish a custom union by end-2004. COMESA's common external tariff structure entails four tariff bands, with rates ranging from 0 percent on capital goods to 30 percent on final goods. Comoros, Eritrea, Ethiopia and Uganda have made significant progress in reducing intra-regional trade barriers applied to COMESA. But Djibouti, Kenya, Madagascar, and Mauritius are the only four countries in the region to have dropped most intra-regional barriers and in effect joined COMESA's free trade area. In 2002, **Eritrea** streamlined the number of custom tariff rates from a cumbersome 12 to 4, while the maximum rate was slashed from 200 percent to 25 percent. Custom duties in **Madagascar** were reduced from November 2002. Import tariffs on fertilizers and agricultural inputs, construction materials, and inputs used by the textile sector were eliminated in January 2003 to support economic recovery. A duty on mining transactions was introduced to replace royalties. The country, which already belongs to COMESA and the Indian Ocean

Commission (IOC), is reviewing the possibility of joining SADC. **Mauritius**'s trade regime has been shaped by regional trading agreements, preferential market access to the EU and the US, and the development of Export Processing Zones. Mauritius belongs to COMESA, SADC and IOC. EPZ enterprises benefit from sizeable custom duty exemptions and tax reduction. The tariff structure remains relatively complicated elsewhere, although the government is committed gradually to reduce custom duties and non-tariff barriers. All imports are subject to licenses and quotas in **Seychelles**. The number of goods for which the Seychelles Marketing Board has exclusive import rights has nonetheless been reduced.

### Current Account Developments

Tourism is a vital source of foreign currency in East Africa. Soft commodities — mostly tea, coffee and cotton — constitute the second main source of foreign exchange earnings in the region. Some countries like Mauritius and Madagascar have widened their export base through the development of Export Processing Zones to include manufactured goods. Other countries, notably Kenya, Tanzania, and Uganda, hope to take advantage of AGOA, and are committed to progress towards regional integration to boost their exports of manufactured goods. Security concerns, poor international air links and the morose international environment hampered tourism expansion in 2003. The recovery in the world prices of soft commodities helped to compensate for high oil prices, leading to a slight improvement in the region's terms of trade. The current account deficit declined to 4.2 percent of

GDP in 2003, as a result, which is still high by continental standards (Table 2.7).

**Comoros**' external position weakened in 2003, after export receipts from vanilla, the country's main export, reached a peak in 2002. World prices for vanilla were buoyant in 2003, but the volume exported declined. This, coupled with lower export receipts from cloves, contributed to in the current account deficit being flat at 0.0 percent of GDP in 2003, despite rising inflows of workers' remittances and a lower oil import bill resulting from the strengthening of the Comorian franc vis-à-vis the dollar.

**Djibouti**'s current account deficit declined to 4.8 percent of GDP in 2003, reflecting rising official transfers and the impact of the presence of foreign troops in the country. Foreign troops have boosted foreign currency earnings in salaries, re-export activity, and services in public administration, insurance, and air transport.

Despite falling coffee export receipts, large-scale food imports and higher oil prices, the current account deficit in **Ethiopia** remained largely unchanged in 2003 (2002/03 in national statistics), at 6.1 percent of GDP. This was largely explained by the rise in official transfers and robust growth in other exports. Coffee exports declined in 2002/03 because of a combined drop in volume and prices.

### Table 2.7: East Africa: The External Sector, 1999–2003

| Country | Trade Balance as % of GDP | | Current Account as % of GDP | | Terms of Trade (%) | | Total External Debt as % of GDP | | Debt Service as % of Exports | |
|---|---|---|---|---|---|---|---|---|---|---|
| | Average 1999–2002 | 2003[a/] | Average 1999–2002 | 2003[a/] | Average 1999–2002 | 2003[a/] | Average 1999–2002 | 2003[a/] | Average 1999–2002 | 2003[a/] |
| COMOROS | −15.0 | −13.3 | −10.0 | 0.0 | 14.1 | −39.8 | 92.8 | 76.7 | 7.8 | 25.0 |
| DJIBOUTI | −35.4 | −38.7 | −5.3 | −4.8 | 1.2 | 4.9 | 61.5 | 67.7 | 9.8 | 13.3 |
| ERITREA | −61.1 | −75.3 | −5.4 | −11.0 | 0.2 | −7.3 | 25.4 | 78.1 | 4.5 | 11.8 |
| ETHIOPIA | −13.7 | 28.1 | −3.7 | −6.1 | −4.1 | −2.7 | 112.3 | 86.6 | 35.4 | 18.7 |
| KENYA | −8.9 | −3.4 | −2.1 | −3.1 | 1.2 | −1.4 | 63.1 | 33.9 | 23.8 | 14.0 |
| MADAGASCAR | −3.4 | −2.6 | −6.4 | −4.6 | −2.2 | 0.7 | 110.0 | 71.0 | 13.9 | 14.8 |
| MAURITIUS | −7.6 | −4.5 | −0.7 | 4.5 | 1.0 | −2.8 | 28.1 | 21.4 | 8.0 | 7.0 |
| SEYCHELLES | −30.1 | −1.4 | −11.2 | −6.8 | 0.4 | 14.8 | 43.8 | 78.4 | 13.3 | 17.9 |
| SOMALIA | ... | ... | ... | ... | ... | ... | ... | ... | ... | ... |
| TANZANIA | −11.5 | −2.9 | −9.0 | −7.3 | 12.8 | 46.7 | 105.7 | 76.3 | 39.7 | 17.7 |
| UGANDA | −9.1 | −10.1 | −4.7 | −5.7 | −6.3 | 15.6 | 66.3 | 63.2 | 34.5 | 19.8 |
| **EAST AFRICA** | **−11.0** | **−3.7** | **−4.6** | **−4.2** | **0.5** | **15.4** | **82.2** | **56.2** | **22.4** | **13.8** |

*Note*: a/ Preliminary estimates
*Source*: ADB Statistics Division, 2004

Post-reconstruction activities and large-scale food imports in **Eritrea** were the main driving forces behind import growth in 2003. Given the country's narrow export base, consisting of salt, hides and skins and livestock, the trade deficit increased in 2003, which rising external assistance and private transfers, and a small recovery in Assab port transit activities helped to compensate. As a result, the current account deficit fell to 11 percent of GDP in 2003.

**Kenya**'s external current account balance fell from a surplus of 0.5 percent of GDP in 2002 to a deficit of 3.1 percent of GDP in 2003, despite lower inflows of private and official transfers and a wider trade deficit. Tea, horticulture and non-traditional commodities (particularly textile, manufactured goods and raw materials) drove export growth, indicating an improvement in world tea prices and increased market access to the UK, Uganda and Tanzania, while import increased with oil products, machinery and transport equipments. This was more than offset by an improvement in services, indicating rising tourism receipts (despite the Mombasa terrorist attack in November 2002) and lower interest payments.

**Madagascar**'s external position strengthened in 2003. Exports rebounded, as enterprises in the EPZ resumed their activity and routes for traditional exports, such as vanilla, clove and coffee, re-opened. Tourism was slower to resume, however. Imports also grew with the demand for intermediate and consumption goods, leading to a slight widening in the trade deficit. The current account deficit stood at 4.6 percent of GDP in 2003, in large part reflecting larger inflows of

external assistance after the political crisis was solved.

The current account balance in **Mauritius** was in surplus for the third consecutive year in 2002/03. Despite eroding comparative advantages, EPZ exports rose on the back of improved access to the US market under AGOA, the stabilization of the political situation in Madagascar (a major outlet for EPZ output), and the strengthening of the euro. The fall in sugar export earnings and the acceleration in import growth led to a slight trade deficit in 2002/03. With Mauritius seen as a relatively safe tourist destination, the number of tourist arrivals increased by 4 percent in 2002/02, although gross tourism earnings declined. Current transfers meanwhile rose significantly. All in all, the surplus on the current account fell from 5.2 percent of GDP in 2001/02 to 4.5 percent of GDP in 2002/03, reflecting mixed developments in the trade, services and income accounts.

**Seychelles**' current account deficit declined to 6.8 percent of GDP in 2003, reflecting the sluggish demand for imports, good performance in the canned tuna industry, the signing of a new fishing agreement with the EU for 2002–05, but rising external debt payments. Tourism receipts, the country's biggest foreign exchange earner, roughly remained unchanged in 2003.

Minerals (mostly gold) and cash crops (notably coffee, cotton, tea, cashew nuts, and tobacco) constitute the bulk of **Tanzania**'s exports. Soft commodity exports, with the exception of coffee, sisal and cloves, recovered from their poor performance in 2001/02, as a result of a registered increase in export volumes amid good weather conditions in

2002/03 and stronger export prices on the world market. Non-traditional exports, in particular gold and manufactured goods, continued to perform well. There was a significant increase in the imports of oil, capital and intermediate goods, however, as the government started licensing companies to operate in the EPZ. A slight recovery in tourism and a rise in official grants helped to contain the current account deficit at 7.3 percent of GDP in 2002/03. Large food imports are anticipated for 2003/04 given the reduction in strategic grain reserves since the beginning of 2003.

Despite a relatively successful strategy of export-led economic growth, **Uganda**'s export base remains poorly diversified, mostly consisting of weather-dependent agricultural products. Uganda's terms of trade improved for the first time in several years in 2002/03, although poor weather conditions restrained export growth. The current account deficit declined from 6.7 percent of GDP in 2001/02 to 5.7 percent of GDP in 2002/03, reflecting a slightly smaller trade deficit, a slow recovery in tourism receipts and stronger inflows of private and official transfers.

### External Debt

The region's access to external financing is largely limited to official lending. The region's external debt burden has stabilized in recent years, due to prudent borrowing policies and the positive impact of the HIPC initiative. East Africa's debt stock stood at an equivalent 56.2 percent of GDP in 2003, against a yearly average 82.2 percent in 1999–2002.

According to UNCTAD's *World Investment Report 2003*, net foreign direct investment brought in US$765 million to the region in 2002, bringing total FDI inward stock to US$8.5 billion. Tanzania and Uganda were the main recipients of FDI in 2002, reflecting foreign participation in the Bujagali dam construction and mining expansion respectively. Stock exchange markets in Mauritius and Kenya continue to attract small inflows of portfolio foreign investment every year. The perceived level of corruption is a major hindrance for foreign investment in the region, with Uganda, Tanzania, Ethiopia, and Kenya scoring low in Transparency International's *Corruption Perception Index 2003*.

The stock of external debt in **Comoros** totaled US$230 million in end-2003, an equivalent debt-GDP ratio of 76.7 percent. Multilateral debt makes up the bulk of the total debt stock. The country remains current on its obligations with the World Bank, its main lender, but significant payment arrears are owed to bilateral creditors and other multilateral donors, including the African Development Bank.

**Djibouti**'s debt-to-GDP ratio followed an upward trend through most of the last decade, owing to a combination of sluggish economic growth and a continued rise in the nominal debt stock. The country's debt-to-GDP ratio rose to 67.7 percent of GDP in 2003, whereas the debt service ratio edged up to 13.3 percent. The government has yet to settle all arrears vis-à-vis multilateral creditors and negotiations with Paris Club bilateral creditors over rescheduling arrears have remained stalled.

There has been a rapid build-up of external public debt in **Eritrea** since the end of the war. The debt-to-GDP ratio rose from less than 40 percent in 1999 to 78.1 percent in 2003, with the debt service ratio reaching double-digit figures. The authorities are committed to resorting mainly to concessional borrowing.

The government in **Ethiopia** hopes to achieve the HIPC initiative completion point in early 2004. Decision point was reached in November 2001, paving the way for interim debt relief and a Paris Club deal in April 2002. The government has since signed bilateral agreements with all but two Paris Club creditors, and the last two agreements are being finalized. The debt service ratio edged down to 18.7 percent in 2003, reflecting a prudent borrowing policy and improved export performance, while the debt-to-GDP ratio rose slightly to 86.6 percent of GDP in 2003.

The problem of debt sustainability in **Kenya** is compounded by the excessive burden of public domestic debt. External debt fell to 34.0 percent of GDP in 2003, reflecting withheld assistance from multilateral lenders and the government's prudent borrowing policy following the November 2000 rescheduling deal by the Paris Club. Although Kenya is not eligible for debt relief under the Enhanced HIPC initiative, the authorities, in collaboration with the World Bank, have conducted an up-to-date debt sustainability analysis using end-2002 debt statistics, in preparation for a new round of negotiations with the Paris Club.

**Madagascar** reached decision point under the HIPC debt relief initiative in December 2000, paving the way for interim debt relief and a new Paris Club deal in March 2001. The authorities hope to reach completion point in 2004. External debt indicators deteriorated in 2002, as a result of falling GDP, fiscal revenues, and exports. Reflecting improved

economic performance, the debt-to-GDP ratio fell to 71 percent in 2003. After some delays in 2002, the government has remained current on its obligations to multilateral and bilateral creditors.

**Mauritius**' external public debt is low. The debt-to-GDP ratio fell to 21.4 percent in 2003, as capital repayments exceeded loans received. During 2002/03, FDI in Mauritius recorded inflows of Rs1,540 million, while foreign investors divested from the local Stock Exchange to the tune of Rs41 million but purchased Rs163 million of government debt securities.

The growth of **Seychelles**' external public debt has become unsustainable, as the government continued to pile up principal and interest payment arrears. Multilateral and bilateral official lenders have suspended lending to the country, forcing the government to recourse to commercial borrowing. A deal with a consortium of commercial banks was signed in August 2002 to help refinance Seychelles' commercial debt. The debt-GDP ratio rose to 78.4 percent in 2003, whereas the debt service ratio surged to 17.9 percent. Seychelles attracts a small, albeit regular, stream of foreign investment every year, mostly reflecting offshore investment opportunities.

**Tanzania** reached the enhanced HIPC completion point in November 2001, giving rise to US$3.0 billion of debt service relief in nominal terms over a 20-year period. The debt-to-GDP ratio declined to 76.3 percent in 2003, as a result of implementation of the Paris Club bilateral agreements, exchange rate variations, and debt data consolidation. The government has continued to negotiate debt relief with Non-Paris Club official and commercial creditors under terms comparable to the Paris Club. The debt service ratio fell to 17.7 percent in 2003.

**Uganda** was the first country to reach completion point under the enhanced HIPC initiative in May 2000, but debt relief was slower than expected as a result of delays in securing bilateral agreements from Paris Club creditors. The full delivery of assistance under the HIPC initiative, sound external debt management, and fiscal consolidation have since helped to maintain the debt-to-GDP ratio to 63.2 percent in 2003. Timid progress has also been made in securing debt relief agreements from non-Paris Club creditors and commercial lenders. This, combined with stronger export growth, helped to reduce the debt service ratio down in 2003

## Outlook

Economic growth in East Africa is set to accelerate to an average 5.3 percent in 2004, reflecting improved economic management in Kenya, the main economy of the region, satisfactory weather conditions and continued recovery in world commodity prices. Abundant rains since mid-year have improved prospects for the 2003/04 cereal crops and the overall food security situation will improve in the region. Improved security in Eritrea, Ethiopia and north-east Uganda, will also be less disruptive for agricultural activities. In Kenya, growth will accelerate to 2.6 percent, as a result of improved macroeconomic performance under the recently agreed IMF three-year facility and rising external assistance. Growth will accelerate to 2.6 percent as a result. Mauritius will face a more challenging environment, as the EU Sugar Protocol and the Multi-Fiber

Agreement come to an end in 2004, but resumed growth in Madagascar (a major outlet for its EPZ) and access to AGOA, will help to sustain economic growth. The region's external position is also set to improve in 2004, as world prices for soft commodities and tourism receipts recover slowly, in the context of declining oil prices and lower food requirements. Ethiopia and Madagascar are expected to reach completion point under the HIPC enhanced initiative in 2004, which will free up resources for poverty alleviation.

# North Africa

North Africa, which comprises seven countries — Algeria, Egypt, Libya, Mauritania, Morocco, Sudan and Tunisia — is the largest contributor to the continent's wealth, accounting for 38.8 percent of its GDP in 2003. Whereas merchandise exports from Algeria, Libya and Sudan are almost entirely oil and gas related, export composition tends to be wider in other countries. Egypt, Morocco and Tunisia export both traditional products and manufactured goods, notably textile, electronic and equipment goods. Tourism is also a major source of foreign exchange earnings in the region. Egypt is the largest economy of the region, generating an equivalent 31.3 percent of its GDP in 2003.

The region is home to 193.2 million people, representing 21.9 percent of the continent's population. Per capita GDP averaged US$1,352 in 2003, which is roughly twice as high as the continental's average. All countries are classified as middle-income countries, except for Mauritania and Sudan, where per capita GDP is less than US$500. Sparsely populated Libya is the wealthiest country, with an income per head of US$3,853.

The region was affected by escalating violence in the Middle East and by the US-led war in Iraq in 2003. In May 2003, suicide bomb attacks in Casablanca (Morocco) killed 41 people and injured 100. This came a year after a bomb explosion killed 19 tourists in Djerba, a southern city of Tunisia. These terrorist attacks prevented tourism recovery in these two countries in 2003. Another dramatic development in the region was the powerful earthquake that hit north Algeria in May, killing about 2,000 people. There was an attempted coup in Mauritania in June, But President Ould Taya was subsequently re-elected with 67 percent of vote in the first round of elections in November. In September 2003, the UN Security Council voted to lift sanctions against Libya, after the Libyan government agreed to a US$2.7 billion compensation package for the families of the victims of the 1988 Lockerbie bombing. Peace remained fragile in Sudan, after talks between the government and the Sudan People's Liberation Movement resumed in Kenya, Nairobi. The government and the SPLM had signed a first peace agreement in July 2002, after 19 years of civil war.

## Recent Trends in the Domestic Economy

### *Economic Growth and Inflation*

North Africa's growth performance improved in 2003, largely as a result of higher oil output and prices. Real GDP growth accelerated from a yearly average 3.6 percent in 1999–2002 to 4.7 percent in 2003, which is 1.0 percentage point above the continental's average. This reflected improved performance in all countries. Inflation in North Africa has remained roughly stable in recent years, and averaged 3.8 percent in 2003, against an average 2.9 percent in 1999–2002 (Table 2.8 and Figure 2.3).

The economy of **Algeria** is poorly diversified and subject to large fluctuations caused by weather and oil price vulnerability. Despite the May earthquake and the poor state of the banking sector (see monetary developments), growth picked up from 4.1 percent in 2002 to 6.7 percent in 2003. This largely reflected an oil production boost as a

Table 2.8: North Africa: Gross Domestic Product and Export Performances, 1999-2003

| Country | Real GDP Growth Rate (%) | | GDP Per Capita (US$) | | Real Exports[c/] Growth (%) | | Exports[b/] Per Capita (US$) | |
|---|---|---|---|---|---|---|---|---|
| | Average 1999–2002 | 2003[a/] | Average 1999–2002 | 2003[a/] | Average 1999–2002 | 2003[a/] | Average 1999–2002 | 2003[a/] |
| ALGERIA | 3.0 | 6.7 | 1,743 | 2,065 | 3.6 | 4.3 | 617 | 796 |
| EGYPT | 4.3 | 2.8 | 1,359 | 1,093 | 6.7 | ... | 235 | ... |
| LIBYA | 0.8 | 5.6 | 5,340 | 3,853 | ... | ... | ... | ... |
| MAURITANIA | 4.4 | 5.4 | 365 | 389 | –2.6 | 3.7 | 139 | 135 |
| MOROCCO | 2.6 | 4.2 | 1,181 | 1,461 | 5.9 | 5.1 | 359 | 408 |
| SUDAN | 6.3 | 5.8 | 367 | 435 | ... | ... | ... | 71 |
| TUNISIA | 4.3 | 5.5 | 2,127 | 2,535 | 7.9 | 8.3 | 951 | 1161 |
| NORTH AFRICA | 3.6 | 4.7 | 1,365 | 1,352 | 5.7 | 8.1 | 310 | 281 |

Notes: a/ Preliminary estimates
b/ Exports of Goods and Nonfactor Services at Market Prices
c/ Real Exports of Goods Growth
Source: ADB Statistics Division, 2004

result of new investment and higher OPEC quotas, recovery in agriculture following satisfactory weather conditions, and robust activity in construction and services under the government's Economic Recovery Program (ERP). This compares favorably with the yearly average 3.0 percent growth in 1999–2002. Inflation picked up to a still-subdued 2.3 percent in 2003, reflecting a stronger domestic demand.

Economic performance in **Egypt** has remained below the country's potentials, mostly reflecting the slow pace of reforms and, to a lesser extent, the impact of escalating violence in the Middle East and the war in Iraq. The lack of access to credit, red tape and foreign currency shortages have continued to hinder private investment. Growth nonetheless accelerated from 2.2 percent in 2002 to 2.8 percent in 2003, on the back of export growth recovery. Inflation rose from 2.5 percent in 2002 to 3 percent in 2003, as the authorities partly tampered the steep depreciation of the Egyptian pound by an increase in price subsidies for essential goods.

After turning negative in 2002, economic growth in **Libya** accelerated to 5.6 percent in 2003, as a result of rising oil production and receipts. Libya's OPEC production quota rose from 1,232,000 bpd to 1,360,000 bpd in January 2003 before inching down to 1,312,000 bpd in November 2003. Subsidized prices for food, housing and social services have kept inflation relatively low.

# Figure 2.3: North Africa, Selected Economic Indicators, 1999–2003

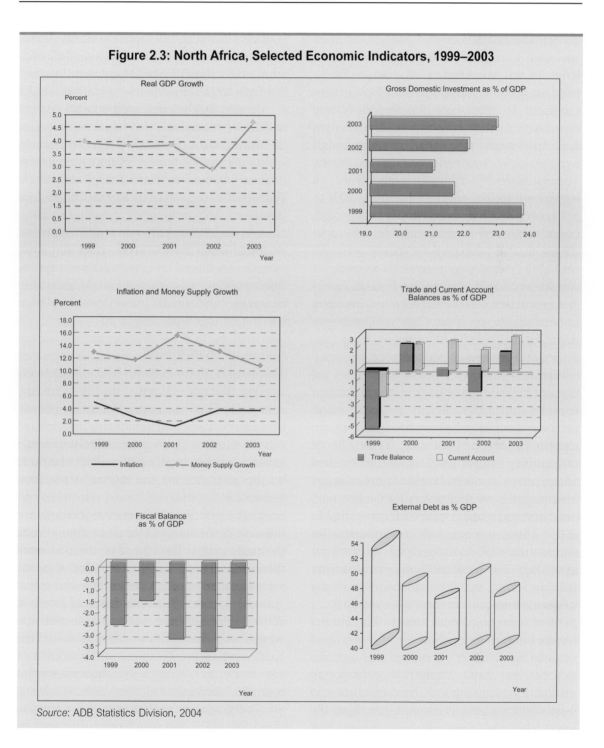

Sound macroeconomic policy, sustained structural reforms, and strong donor support have helped **Mauritania**'s economy successfully to weather external shocks. Growth estimates for 2002 were nonetheless revised down to 3.3 percent, as a result of a drought and the weak demand for Mauritania's exports. Improved weather conditions and the associated rise in agriculture and livestock production fuelled growth recovery in 2003 to 5.4 percent. Activity in oil exploration, construction and services, particularly trade, transport, and telecommunications, was also strong. Oil production is expected to come on stream in 2005. Inflation accelerated to 6.4 percent in 2003, as a result of the lingering impact of the poor harvests and currency depreciation of last year.

In **Morocco**, economic growth accelerated from 3.2 percent in 2002 to 4.2 percent in 2003, on the back of bumper cereal harvests and robust activity in construction and services. Cereal production rose by an estimated 55 percent as a result of outstanding weather conditions. New construction projects at the port, Tanger Méditerranée, as well as in social housing, and road and tourism infrastructure started in 2003. This, coupled with a dynamic telecommunications sector, helped to compensate for subdued activity in tourism, manufacturing and mining. Inflation meanwhile remained under control and averaged 2 percent, reflecting sound fiscal policy and the fixed exchange rate policy.

Real GDP growth in **Sudan** averaged 5.8 percent in 2003, fuelled by rising oil production and good performance in manufacturing and services. Growth in the livestock and agricultural sector was subdued. Annual inflation decelerated to 7 percent, reflecting macroeconomic consolidation under the IMF Staff Monitored Program, but tight food supplies.

Growth in **Tunisia** resumed to 5.5 percent in 2003, after a fall in tourism activity following the April 2002 terrorist attacks on Djerba and a drought-induced drop in agricultural production brought it down to 1.7 percent in 2002. A return to normal weather conditions permitted above-average harvests in 2003. Growth in 2003 was also driven by improved performance in the industrial sector and a rise in both agricultural and manufactured exports. Price stability was maintained by a prudent monetary and fiscal policy, with inflation moving up to 3.3 percent in 2003.

### Fiscal Developments

The fiscal position in North Africa is relatively healthy compared with the rest of the continent. This has permitted to adopt procyclical policies and delay unpopular civil service reforms. The regional fiscal deficit was around 2.9 percent of GDP in 2003, the same as the average for the period 1999–2002 (Table 2.9).

Fiscal policy in **Algeria** has taken on a rather expansionary stance since the ERP was initiated in 2001. The cost of reconstruction of quake-hit areas, combined with rising public sector salaries and higher capital and social spending, inflated public expenditures in 2003. The rise in domestic oil production and world oil prices more than offset the weakening of the US dollar and resulted in a rise in public receipts. The budget surplus rose to 0.7 percent of GDP in 2003, as a result.

The government in **Egypt** has sought to provide a fiscal stimulus to the economy, by

### Table 2.9: North Africa: Macroeconomic Management Indicators, 1999–2003

| Country | Inflation (%) | | Fiscal Balance as % of GDP | | Gross Domestic Investment | | Gross National Savings | |
|---------|---------------|--|----------------------------|--|---------------------------|--|------------------------|--|
| | | | | | as % of GDP | | | |
| | Average 1999–2002 | 2003[a/] | Average 1999–2002 | 2003[a/] | Average 1999–2002 | 2003[a/] | Average 1999–2002 | 2003[a/] |
| ALGERIA | 2.1 | 2.3 | 3.2 | 3.5 | 27.7 | 30.2 | 37.1 | 42.4 |
| EGYPT | 2.9 | 3.0 | −6.2 | −8.3 | 17.8 | 15.4 | 17.1 | 16.4 |
| LIBYA | 2.3 | 2.4 | ... | ... | ... | ... | ... | ... |
| MAURITANIA | 4.0 | 6.4 | 1.3 | −0.7 | 29.6 | 43.0 | 25.8 | 21.6 |
| MOROCCO | 1.5 | 2.0 | −4.6 | −4.2 | 23.1 | 24.6 | 24.6 | 26.2 |
| SUDAN | 9.3 | 7.0 | −0.8 | 0.7 | 17.9 | 20.3 | 2.8 | 10.1 |
| TUNISIA | 2.7 | 3.3 | −2.7 | −2.2 | 26.7 | 25.4 | 23.1 | 22.3 |
| **NORTH AFRICA** | **2.9** | **3.8** | **−2.9** | **−2.9** | **22.0** | **22.9** | **23.2** | **25.8** |

*Note*: a/ Preliminary estimates
*Source*: ADB Statistics Division, 2004

increasing public investment, social spending, subsidies and wages. Measures to strengthen revenue collection and widen the tax base have meanwhile been slow. The budget deficit, which is financed through government bills and external borrowing, rose to 8.3 percent of GDP in 2003 (2002/03 in national statistics). This does not account for the 30 percent rise in subsidies, which the government introduced in its 2003/04 budget to cushion the population against price increases caused by the pound devaluation.

**Libya**'s fiscal performance depends heavily on oil revenues, the bulk of which being used to pay the wages of civil servants. The Libyan government controls almost the entire economy, private activities outside the foreign-owned oil sector being restrained to low-scale activities in retailing and agriculture.

The budget balance in **Mauritania** turned into a manageable deficit equivalent to 0.7 percent of GDP in 2003, after late fishing license payments in 2002 led to an exceptional surplus of 6.2 percent of GDP. Attention focused on reforming the tax system and custom administration, strengthening public expenditure management — by notably tracking HIPC-financed social spending — and enhancing the medium-term expenditure framework. Tax revenues were slightly higher than budgeted in 2003, while government expenditures on social sector continued to increase as expected. No election-related spending overruns were recorded. The government agreed to a 28 percent rise in wages in November 2003, effective from January 2004.

**Morocco**'s fiscal stance has strengthened since 2002, after deteriorating considerably during 1999–2001. Revenue performance improved in 2003, as rising domestic tax receipts, combined with privatization proceeds, more than offset the loss in earnings caused by the phased reduction in external tariffs (the bulk of privatization proceeds was transferred from the central government budget to the special investment fund, Fonds Hassan II). The government meanwhile decided to freeze new hiring in public administration, which partly compensated for agreed wage adjustments in 2003. As a result, the rise in the central government deficit was limited from 4.6 percent of GDP in 2002 to 4.2 percent of GDP in 2003. The government is committed to fiscal consolidation, which implies further revenue consolidation measures and a reduction in the public sector wage bill.

Fiscal revenues in **Sudan** increased with world oil prices in 2003, leading to a small budget deficit of 0.7 percent of GDP. Some of the export-related oil revenues were saved in the government oil savings account (OSA). Non-oil revenues were lower than expected, indicating an array of tax exemptions and room for enhanced revenue collection.

The government in **Tunisia** maintained a tight fiscal stance in 2003, with the budget deficit decreasing to 2.2 percent of GDP. Despite resumed economic growth, fiscal revenues were lower than expected, reflecting slow domestic activity outside the agricultural and export sectors. Measures to widen the tax base and strengthen revenue collection helped to compensate for falling custom revenues. The authorities matched the revenue shortfall by keeping recurrent and capital expenditures below budget. Structural rigidities continued to exist on the expenditure side, with wages and interest payments together absorbing more than 60 percent of total revenues.

### Monetary and Exchange Rate Developments

Monetary policy in North Africa in 2003 strongly focused on maintaining competitive exchange rates and liberalizing foreign exchange markets. Broad money increased by an average 10.5 percent in 2003.

The Central Bank of **Algeria** ordered the closure of the largest private bank, El-Khalifa Bank, in May 2003, over alleged financial irregularities. The Banque commerciale et industrielle d'Algérie (BCIA) was also ordered into liquidation in August. This highlighted the lack of transparency of the banking system and the urgent need for the authorities to reinforce financial supervision. The central bank otherwise maintained a sound monetary policy, by mopping up excess liquidity through the use of a new facility (negative liquidity auctions were introduced in April 2002). Excess liquidity mostly reflected higher deposits at commercial banks by the oil sector. The discount rate was trimmed from 5.5 percent to 4.5 percent in May 2003, reflecting low inflationary pressures and an improved external position. There was a slight depreciation of the Algerian dinar against the euro in 2003.

Two years after the peg to the US dollar was formally abandoned, the Central Bank of **Egypt** (CBE) adopted a free float exchange rate system in January 2003, in a bid to eliminate the differential between the official and parallel rates and liberalize exchange rate transactions. The Egyptian pound subsequently lost 30 percent of its external value, with the CBE temporarily adopting a tight monetary policy. A new law, confirming the independence of the central bank and improving its organizational and management structure, was ratified by parliament in June 2003. Prudential regulations were strengthened, with all banks notably requested to comply with the new minimum capital adequacy ratio of 10 percent, while additional open market tools were developed and introduced to fit the new inflation-targeting monetary policy. In March 2003, the government issued a decree forcing exporters and tourist companies to deliver 75 percent of their foreign currency earnings into the banking channel to help stop capital flight.

There are tight foreign exchange regulations in **Libya**, with often large premium between the black market and the official rates. The Libyan dinar, which is pegged to the SDR, was devalued by 51 percent in December 2001. Slashed import tariffs, administered prices and non-tariff barriers greatly reduced the inflationary impact of the devaluation.

The central bank in **Mauritania** pursued a relatively prudent monetary policy in 2003, by keeping the repo rate and T-bill rate unchanged at 11 percent and 6 percent respectively. Government deposits were meanwhile gradually transferred from commercial banks to the central bank as a means to enhancing liquidity control, while reserve requirement ratios were reduced to compensate for the commercial banks' loss of liquidity. The depreciation of the ouguiya decelerated in 2003, mostly reflecting the weakening of the US dollar. There was still a slight differential between market and parallel rates, indicating flaws in the functioning of the foreign exchange market.

The Bank Al-Maghrib in **Morocco** has successfully tightened the excess liquidity conditions that characterized most of 2002 through money market interventions. Private sector credit growth picked up in 2003, which helped the central bank to sterilize the increase in net foreign assets resulting from the sale of Régie des Tabacs in June 2003. The decline in interest rates meanwhile decelerated. The inter-bank money rate, which dropped from 5.6 percent in end-2001 to 3.2 percent in end-2002, fell to 2.9 percent as of November 2003. There was a slight depreciation in the effective nominal exchange rate in 2003, maintaining Morocco's external competitiveness. The authorities adjusted the fixed exchange rate for the first time in 11 years in April 2001, when the currency basket, to which the dirham is pegged, was modified to reflect the growing importance of the euro area in Morocco's trade.

Monetary developments in **Sudan** in the late 1990s focused on consolidating the independence of the central bank and unifying the exchange rate. The Central Bank tightened its monetary policy in 2003 through open market operations. The exchange rate has *de facto* remained unchanged, since the authorities switched to a managed floating exchange rate system in May 2002.

The Central Bank of **Tunisia** eased monetary policy in 2003, in the context of low inflationary pressures and a sluggish demand for credit. The auction interest rate was cut down twice, from 5.875 percent to 5.5 percent in March and to 5 percent in June. The central bank's main objective is to maintain a constant real exchange rate, through regular intervention on the foreign exchange market and limited convertibility. The Tunisian dinar depreciated by 5 percent against the euro, but appreciated by 6.5 percent against the US dollar in the first nine months of 2003.

## Poverty Reduction Strategies

North Africa as a whole has the least poverty rate among all developing regions in the world, with only 2 percent of its population living under the poverty line of one dollar per day. This hides wide disparities across countries, however.

Mauritania and Sudan are both on the list of the UN's least developed countries. **Mauritania** is in its third year of implementing its PRSP, which was completed in December 2000. A progress report was released in October 2003, highlighting the authorities' commitment to poverty reduction, but mixed progress in the set priority areas, namely rural development, urban development, universal education, health and water supply. **Sudan** is in the process of drawing up an interim PRSP, with the assistance of the World Bank and the UNDP. Once peace is in place, rising oil receipts will support the country's programs for poverty alleviation and rural development, especially in the war-affected areas.

Algeria, Egypt, Morocco and Tunisia are lower middle-income economies. They are expected to reach most MDGs by 2015. While Tunisia has achieved an impressive record of poverty reduction, the social situation has threatened to deteriorate in other countries, indicating a stagnation, if not decline, in GDP per capita and rising unemployment. Unemployment and lack of housing are acute

problems in **Algeria**. Whereas education standards remain satisfactory, access to health services has deteriorated in this country. Education and health indicators in **Egypt** continue to be among the highest on the continent, with social programs concentrating on eliminating gender inequality and pockets of poverty and illiteracy in rural areas. Social housing, access to electricity, safe water and road infrastructure in rural areas, schooling and alphabetization are main priorities in **Morocco**'s Strategy for Integrated Social Development. Poverty reduction strategy in **Tunisia** has largely focused on promoting professional training, creating jobs and fighting social exclusion. Tunisia runs an impressive, but costly, social protection system.

Income disparity is high in **Libya**, the only upper middle-income economy in North Africa. The Libyan authorities are in the process of mapping development indicators throughout the country, with the assistance of the UN Development Program.

## Structural Reforms

The pace of structural reforms in 2003 remained slow in all countries but Morocco. Some changes nonetheless took place in banking and telecommunications.

The government in **Algeria** has been committed since 2001 to a new privatization and economic liberalization program. But progress has been slow, because of the complexity of the reforms (there are more than 1,000 SOEs in Algeria) and strong resistance from trade unions. The first and last major divestiture to take place was that of the steel complex, SIDER, in 2001. A tender to open the capital of state-owned Crédit

Populaire Algérien (CPA) to foreign business banks was issued in April 2003, and a bid for a third mobile phone license was issued in September. But the government has yet to push forward a draft laws to liberalize the hydrocarbon sector (although the oil company, Sonatrach, will not be privatized) and establish concession rights on agricultural land.

The pace of privatization in **Egypt** has been brought to a halt, after being particularly intense in the mid-to-late 1990s, when a total of 192 out of 306 SOEs were sold. In late 2002, the government announced its decision temporarily to suspend the privatization process because of the global, regional and national economic slowdown. The government thus retained control of key public services, such as telecommunication (the 20 percent sale of Egypt Telecom was postponed indefinitely), water and energy. Plans to liberalize the financial sector and privatize state-owned banks were also stalled. The Egyptian Prime Minister has recently announced that a long list of privatizations lined up for 2004 will soon be released.

The government of **Libya** has recently announced plans to privatize 360 public enterprises starting in 2004.

The privatization program in **Mauritania** has almost reached completion, the electricity utility, Somelec, being the only public utility yet to be opened to private capital. The sale of Somelec failed to materialize in 2003. The government has switched the focus of its structural adjustment program towards institutional reforms and capacity building. This notably entails strengthening public administration and pushing through reforms in the judiciary and regulatory framework.

Other reforms include restructuring the National Social Security Fund, as begun in mid-2003, and liberalizing the banking sector. The pace of structural reforms in **Morocco** picked up in 2003. Concerning privatization, 80 percent of the tobacco firm, Régie des Tabacs, was sold to a Franco-Spanish consortium in June, while Renault of France took a 26 percent stake of the automotive plant, Somaca, in September. In the same month, Vivendi of France confirmed its intention to buy an additional 16 percent share in Maroc Telecom. The partial sales of the Banque Centrale Populaire, Sicome and Fertima were meanwhile completed. Other ongoing programs led the government to adopt a new Labor Code in July, while new regulations to speed up the liberalization of the banking and transport sectors were also adopted.

The government of **Sudan** has drawn up a program of privatization, which includes the sale of key public utilities. The audit of the Sudan Petroleum Company was completed and a number of small-to-medium SOEs, including the Friendship Palace Hotel, the Real Estate Bank and Atbara Cement factory, were sold under the IMF staff monitored program in 2002–03.

Structural reforms in **Tunisia** have focused on improving the private investment climate (by notably pushing through the privatization of state enterprises), strengthening banking regulations, and liberalizing the telecommunication sector. The pace of privatization was slow in 2003, indicating near completion of the program. Tunisie Telecom is the only main public utility left that the government plans to open to private participation; a second GSM license was sold in March 2002.

## Recent Trends in The External Sector

### *Trade Liberalization*

The region is moderately open, because Egypt, the main economy of the zone, has traditionally been inward looking, having the largest domestic market in the region. Mauritania, which heavily depends on imports, and Tunisia, which has actively promoted greater integration with the global economy since the mid-1990s, are the most open economies of the region, with a trade openness ratio above 90 percent of GDP.

Four North African countries are members of the WTO, but Algeria, Libya and Sudan are not. **Algeria** has been negotiating its WTO membership since 1998. Algeria's working party met in May 2003, with efforts being made to finish the negotiation for accession in 2004. The authorities have disbanded the former external tariff structure, deemed complex, uncertain and inequitable. Custom tariffs reforms were undertaken in 2001 and 2002, with the elimination of minimum duty values and the adoption of three non-zero tariff bands. Temporary additional duties, which replaced the minimum duty values, are being gradually reduced. **Libya** has been a candidate to join the WTO since December 2001. The country also takes part in the Barcelona Process (see below) as an observer, with the view to soon becoming full partner of the initiative. Import controls remain tight. Custom duties were significantly reduced in 20002, in an attempt to mitigate the price impact of the December 2001 devaluation.

Countries in North Africa have tended to favor bilateral trade agreements and North-South co-operation over regional integration.

Revived in 2001, the Arab Mahgreb Union (AMU), which comprises Algeria, Libya, Mauritania, Morocco and Tunisia, aims to foster regional cooperation and, in particular, seeks the harmonization of custom procedures and the reduction in intra-regional trade barriers. But the continuing deadlock between Algeria and Morocco over the status of Western Sahara has hindered the union's revival. Most countries in North Africa, except Algeria and **Mauritania**, are members of the Community of Sahel-Saharan States (CEN-SAD). Mauritania has eliminated barriers to international trade and liberalized its exchange rate system since the early-1990s. The number of custom duties was reduced from 13 in 1997 to 4 in 2000 and the maximum MFN rate feel from 30 to 20 percent. The average MFN rate stood at a low 10.6 percent in 2002.

Algeria, Egypt, Morocco and Tunisia have pursued trade liberalization under the so-called Barcelona Process (or Euro-Mediterranean Partnership). The Barcelona process seeks to intensify bilateral, multi-lateral and regional cooperation between the European Union and its 12 Mediterranean partners. All four countries have now signed the association agreements (AAEU), under which they agree to establish a free trade zone with the EU by 2010. In **Morocco**, the first round of reduction in custom duties for non-agricultural imports that compete with domestic production kicked off in March 2003. Custom duties on raw materials and non-competitive manufactured goods have already been greatly reduced and were to be abolished in 2003. Measures recently taken under WTO include reducing the number of tariff bands to eight in 2001 and eliminating the use of reference prices on imports in

2002. Implementation of the AAEU was on track in **Tunisia**, with more than half of the tariff reduction already in place. Specific agreements have been signed with the EU on agricultural trade and fisheries. The country's trade regime is relatively restrictive and complex elsewhere, the MFN average tariff averaging 34.5 percent in 2002. Parliament in **Egypt** ratified the Barcelona agreement in April 2003, two years after it was signed. Trade liberalization in the country started in the mid-1990s and included the discontinuation of import licensing requirements, the streamlining of the trade tariff structure, and the reduction in the average tariff from 42 percent to 27 percent. Egypt is the largest economy of the Common Market for Eastern and Southern Africa (see East Africa) and grants preferential access to COMESA partners. **Sudan** is also a member of COMESA and plans to implement tariff reductions in line with the regional grouping's agreed common external tariff structure.

## Current Account Developments

Export diversification makes North Africa as a whole less sensitive to external shocks. Despite preferential access to the EU markets, many North African producers have faced rising external competition for their manufactured exports. Morocco and Egypt recently proceeded with a devaluation of their national currency to boost their competitive edge. Most North African countries, except Mauritania and Morocco, are crude oil exporters. Other commodities that the region exports include cotton, iron ore, phosphate rock, and fish. Tourism is also a major source of foreign exchange earnings in Egypt, Morocco, and Tunisia. The region's external

position remained comfortable in 2003. The current account balance was in surplus, at 2.6 percent of GDP, against a yearly average 1.0 percent of GDP in 1999–2002 (Table 2.10).

Hydrocarbons earnings account for 98 percent of total exports in **Algeria**. The trade surplus rose significantly in 2003, reflecting rising oil prices and higher crude oil exports under OPEC. Although the weakening of the US dollar dampened export earnings in Dinar terms, the current account surplus rose to 12.2 percent of GDP in 2003, compared with an average 9.4 percent of GDP in 1999–2002.

**Egypt**'s external position strengthened in 2003. The sharp devaluation of the Egyptian pound since January 2003 boosted exports, especially textiles, clothing, chemical and leather goods, with an estimated 11.4 percent rise in dollar terms for the 2002/03 fiscal year. The shortage in foreign currencies meanwhile contributed to a fall in imports. There was a marked recovery in tourism receipts, which were hit by the 11 September terrorist attacks the previous year. Despite higher dollar-denominated foreign debt service payments, the current account balance turned into a surplus in 2003, equivalent to 2.8 percent of GDP.

**Libya** heavily relies on oil exports, which accounts for over 95 percent of total export revenues. The current account balance frequently moves from deficit to surplus, given uncompressible outflows in oil-related services and income.

**Mauritania**'s external current account deficit surged to an equivalent 21.6 percent of GDP in 2003, as a result of sluggish export growth (mostly iron ore and fish), large-scale food imports, and rising oil-related machinery and equipment imports and service outflows.

### Table 2.10: North Africa: The External Sector, 1999–2003

| Country | Trade Balance as % of GDP | | Current Account as % of GDP | | Terms of Trade (%) | | Total External Debt as % of GDP | | Debt Service as % of Exports | |
|---|---|---|---|---|---|---|---|---|---|---|
| | Average 1999–2002 | 2003[a] | Average 1999–2002 | 2003[a] | Average 1999–2002 | 2003[a] | Average 1999–2002 | 2003[a] | Average 1999–2002 | 2003[a] |
| ALGERIA | 15.1 | 17.9 | 9.4 | 12.2 | 13.3 | 12.6 | 46.7 | 34.4 | 25.0 | 16.3 |
| EGYPT | −11.1 | ... | −0.7 | ... | 2.9 | ... | 30.3 | ... | 11.7 | ... |
| LIBYA | ... | ... | ... | ... | ... | ... | ... | ... | ... | ... |
| MAURITANIA | −2.1 | −71.2 | −3.8 | −21.6 | 1.3 | −6.3 | 206.1 | 165.8 | 28.1 | 30.8 |
| MOROCCO | −8.4 | −0.3 | 1.5 | 1.6 | −2.7 | −2.5 | 50.5 | 37.1 | 25.3 | 20.4 |
| SUDAN | −4.2 | −1.4 | −15.1 | −10.2 | 3.8 | 0.9 | 169.6 | 138.0 | 5.4 | 7.6 |
| TUNISIA | −11.0 | −9.2 | −3.6 | −3.1 | −0.7 | −2.1 | 60.1 | 59.2 | 18.5 | 16.4 |
| NORTH AFRICA | −1.7 | 3.0 | 1.0 | 2.6 | 4.6 | −0.6 | 49.2 | 46.7 | 19.5 | 16.4 |

*Note*: a/ Preliminary estimates
*Source*: ADB Statistics Division, 2004

The current account deficit had shrunk in 2002, as a result of late receipt of the EU fishing license payment. FDI inflows in the oil sector financed the external gap in 2003.

In surplus for the third year running, **Morocco**'s current account balance stood at 1.6 percent of GDP in 2003. This largely reflected a more pronounced trade deficit, as rising exports in consumption and equipment goods and the moderate import growth failed to compensate for poorer performance in traditional exports, notably fishery, phosphate rock and energy. The services and income balance remained firmly in surplus, despite the stagnation in tourism receipts and private transfers.

**Sudan**'s current-account deficit declined to 10.2 percent of GDP in 2003, reflecting higher exports of oil, cotton, and livestock. While the trade deficit fell significantly in 2003, services

and income outflows were high, because of oil-related payments and expenses.

**Tunisia**'s external position strengthened in 2003. The external current account deficit declined to 3.1 percent of GDP in 2003, indicating continued slack domestic demand and improved export performance, in both agricultural and manufactured goods. Tourism receipts continued to decline in 2003, albeit at a slower rate (receipts dropped by 5.7 percent in the first half of the year compared with 13.8 percent over the same period of 2002, while workers remittances remained roughly unchanged.

### External Debt

The structure of North Africa's capital account indicates greater access to international capital markets. Egypt, Morocco, and Tunisia have secured favorable ratings from several credit rating agencies, enabling their governments and commercial banks to borrow externally from private lenders. The region's external debt burden is low by regional standards. The total debt stock stood at US$110.1 billion in 2003, an equivalent 46.7 percent of regional GDP.

Non debt-creating capital inflows are significant in North Africa. According to UNCTAD *2003 World Investment Report*, FDI inflows in the region totaled US$3.6 billion in 2002, bringing total FDI inward stock at US$53.3 billion. The bulk of foreign participation is oil-related, but also reflects stakes in strategic utilities and in the banking, export and tourism sectors. Morocco, Egypt and Tunisia have opened their stock exchange markets to foreign investors, attracting small amount of foreign portfolio investment every year.

Whereas **Algeria**'s hydrocarbons sector attracts foreign investment, FDI is minimal elsewhere, because of the country's high political risk and the investors' wait-and-see attitude pending changes in the investment code and restructuring of the public sector. The government, which continues mostly to borrow on an official concessional long-term basis, has plans to seek sovereign rating to facilitate its return to the international capital market. The external debt stock has followed a downward trend since the mid-1990s and totaled US$22 billion in 2003, an equivalent 34.4 percent of GDP. While more erratic, the debt-service ratio declined to 16.3 percent in 2003, reflecting rising oil receipts.

**Egypt** is the largest recipient of private capital flows in the region. The country has considerably liberalized and simplified its investment regime since a new code was passed in 1997, but the slow pace of privatization, sluggish economic growth, and the tight foreign exchange regulations have hindered greater foreign participation outside the oil and gas sector. About 90 percent of the country's external debt is publicly guaranteed and concessional. The government has benefited from generous debt relief deals in the past. This, coupled with its prudent borrowing policy, kept the debt-to-GDP ratio at 42.4 percent of GDP in 2003. The debt service ratio stood at 11.7 percent. Greater integration into global capital markets was achieved in June 2001, when Egypt successfully issued Eurobonds, worth US$1.5 billion.

**Libya** is poorly integrated in the world financial markets, having little need for external financing.

The debt-to-GDP ratio in **Mauritania** declined to 165.8 percent in 2003. The country reached completion point under the Enhanced HIPC in June 2002, paving the way for debt service relief equivalent to US$1.1 billion. This is expected to reduce the debt-service/government revenue from 35 percent in 1998 to 11 percent over 2002–11. Private capital inflows have increased dramatically, since oil was discovered in January 2002.

The government in **Morocco** has sought to reduce its external debt burden since the mid-1990s, by notably negotiating debt-for-equity swaps with its major official creditors and buying back some of its commercial debt. The stock of external debt declined to 37.1 percent of GDP in 2003, half of which being owed by the government. The government issued its first eurobonds in July 2003. Foreign investment inflows surged in 2003, as a result of privatization proceeds mostly arising from the sale of Régie des Tabacs. This contributed to an 18.5 percent increase in net foreign assets over the Jan–Aug period.

The oil export boom in **Sudan** has greatly alleviated the country's debt burden. Strong foreign investment inflows in the oil sector have nonetheless failed to bridge the external gap. In addition, official development has remained low, owing to Sudan's external arrears to its main creditors, which prevent the resumption of new disbursements. The debt-to-GDP ratio declined to a still high 138 percent of GDP in 2003.

The stock of external debt in **Tunisia** stood at 59.2 percent of GDP in 2003, 70 percent of which being public. Both the government and private sectors contracted new loans in 2003, mostly from multilateral lenders and the financial market. FDI inflows declined in 2003, after the sale of a second GSM license inflated inflows in 2002. Tunisia's net FDI-GDP ratio is the highest in the region. There were more than 2,000 foreign capital enterprises in the country by end-2000. The bulk of FDI takes place in manufacturing.

## Outlook

Economic growth in North Africa is forecast to decelerate slightly to 3.9 percent in 2004, from 4.7 percent in 2003, reflecting lower OPEC production quotas and a decline in world oil prices. Risks linked to a possible deterioration in the international political environment will remain significant. Security concerns could notably continue to affect both investment and tourism in the sub-region.

The **Algerian** oil sector will continue to produce well below its capacity, as new oil projects come on stream in the context of reduced OPEC production quotas. Growth is likely to decelerate as a result, unless the government successfully pushes through structural reforms, notably with regard to the privatization program and the restructuring of the banking sector. The country's external position will meanwhile weaken with the decline in world oil prices. The government has already based its 2004 budget on an oil price of US$19 a barrel. **Egypt**'s economic outlook will hinge on natural gas development, regional stability, and improved fiscal and monetary policy. The country's business climate is set to improve following the authorities' efforts to enhance foreign exchange liquidity. But excess government borrowing is likely to continue to crowd out domestic borrowing, thereby delaying the private sector recovery. The recovery in tourism activity will meanwhile remain fragile, as tension in the Middle East continues. In **Mauritania**, economic growth will accelerate on the back of rising FDI in the oil sector and satisfactory performance in agriculture. Economic performance in **Morocco** will remain strong, as a result of a good agricultural season, a dynamic construction sector and rising business confidence as reforms proceed at a satisfactory pace. Assuming no external shocks and a modest recovery in demand in Europe. **Tunisia**'s growth is projected to rise to 5.8 percent in 2004, driven by a pick up in exports and tourism. Economic prospects in **Sudan** will be mixed, as domestic oil production increase while world oil prices decline. Much will depend on progress towards restoring peace and security. Netherlands hosted a donor reconstruction conference in April 2003 in a bid to attract grants and long-term concessional loans from bilateral and multilateral lenders to the country.

# Southern Africa

Ten countries make up Southern Africa — Angola, Botswana, Lesotho, Malawi, Mozambique, Namibia, South Africa, Swaziland, Zambia and Zimbabwe. The region is heavily reliant on exports of non-oil minerals (gold, diamonds, copper, platinum) and agricultural products (including tobacco, cotton, horticulture and fruit). All countries but Angola are net crude oil importers. The more developed economies in the region also export labor-intensive manufactured products. In 2003, Southern Africa contributed 32.1 percent of Africa's GDP, making it the second-largest wealth contributor on the continent after North Africa. The region is dominated by South Africa, which accounts for 77.6 percent of total GDP.

The population in Southern Africa totaled 122.6 million in 2003, or 14.1 percent of the continent's total. Per capita income stood at US$1,728 in 2003. But this average hides considerable disparities between middle income countries — Botswana, Namibia, South Africa and Swaziland — where per capita GDP ranges between US$1,729 and US$3,965, and some of the world's poorest — Lesotho, Mozambique, Malawi, and Zambia — where per capita incomes range between US$140 and US$625.

The deepening political and economic crisis in Zimbabwe and the peace process in Angola dominated political news in the region in 2003. The Zimbabwe president, Robert Mugabe, was re-elected in March 2002, paving the way for further opposition crackdown and the forced departure of some 3,000 commercial farmers. National reconciliation meanwhile made good progress in Angola, after the signing of a peace agreement between the government and UNITA ended 27-year of civil war in April 2002. Demobilization neared completion and UNITA was transformed into a political party. Elsewhere, Swaziland held some parliamentary elections in September, while discussions continued over a new constitution that will maintain King Mswati III's position as monarch. In Zambia, former president Frederick Chiluba was arrested and charged with theft and abuse of office.

## Recent Trends in the Domestic Economy

### Economic Growth and Inflation

GDP growth in Southern Africa slowed to 2.2 percent in 2003 (Table 2.11 and Figure 2.4), 1.5 percentage point below the continental average. This largely reflected slower growth in South Africa. The weak international demand and lower export profitability from the stronger rand dampened economic performance in South Africa, but also in Botswana, Lesotho, Namibia and Swaziland. Mozambique was the best performer in 2003, a stark contrast with Zimbabwe, where the slump in domestic production continued. Loose financial policies and the lingering impact of the 2002 drought on regional food prices kept average inflation in Southern Africa well above continental average, at 35.6 percent.

In line with oil production, real GDP in **Angola** grew by 15.3 percent in 2002 (when the Girassol oil field came on stream) and by 4.4 percent in 2003. Despite an end to the 27-year-long civil war, which virtually destroyed all basic infrastructure, the growth

Table 2.11: Southern Africa: Gross Domestic Product and Export Performances, 1999–2003

| Country | Real GDP Growth Rate (%) | | GDP Per Capita (US$) | | Real Exportsc/ Growth (%) | | Exportsb/ Per Capita (US$) | |
|---|---|---|---|---|---|---|---|---|
| | Average 1999–2002 | 2003a/ | Average 1999–2002 | 2003a/ | Average 1999–2002 | 2003a/ | Average 1999–2002 | 2003a/ |
| ANGOLA | 6.2 | 4.4 | 704 | 1,051 | 5.9 | 5.5 | 540 | 695 |
| BOTSWANA | 5.5 | 3.7 | 2,839 | 3,965 | 5.9 | 1.1 | 1784 | 1658 |
| LESOTHO | 2.1 | 4.2 | 455 | 625 | 25.3 | 14.3 | 164 | 306 |
| MALAWI | 0.7 | 5.9 | 155 | 140 | –5.3 | 3.1 | 41 | 46 |
| MOZAMBIQUE | 7.4 | 7.0 | 204 | 229 | 38.3 | 16.2 | 47 | 62 |
| NAMIBIA | 3.0 | 3.7 | 1,696 | 2,324 | 1.6 | 12.0 | 822 | 841 |
| SOUTH AFRICA | 2.9 | 2.2 | 2,717 | 3,572 | 3.3 | 1.4 | 809 | 886 |
| SWAZILAND | 2.7 | 2.3 | 1,248 | 1,729 | –1.3 | 2.6 | 1046 | 1091 |
| ZAMBIA | 3.5 | 4.3 | 327 | 402 | 7.1 | 14.8 | 91 | 118 |
| ZIMBABWE | –8.3 | –11.0 | 622 | 548 | –5.1 | –6.3 | 170 | 119 |
| **SOUTHERN AFRICA** | **2.8** | **2.2** | **1,346** | **1,728** | **3.5** | **2.6** | **451** | **494** |

*Notes*: a/ Preliminary estimates
b/ Exports of Goods and Nonfactor Services at Market Prices
c/ Real Exports of Goods Growth
*Source*: ADB Statistics Division, 2004

of the non-oil sector has continued to lag behind, perpetrating widespread poverty and dependence on imports and food aid. The country continued to face double digit inflation — 95.2 percent in 2003 — underlying a steady rise in food prices, heavy government borrowing and a lax monetary policy.

Growth in **Botswana** accelerated to 3.7 percent in 2003, reflecting higher growth rates in manufacturing, construction and services. There was a decline in agricultural output, however, while growth in the mining sector remained subdued. Inflation decelerated to 4.7 percent in 2003, against a yearly average 6.9 percent in 1999–2002 (Table 2.12).

**Lesotho**'s economic performance remained strong in 2002/03 (reported as 2003 in our tables), with growth picking up to 4.2 percent. This was in large part explained by a growth impetus in the manufacturing sector, particularly the textile sector, and activity in construction. Value-added in agriculture and mining was negative. Despite a slight rise on the previous year's reduced crop, harvests in 2002/03 remained well below average. As a result, inflation decelerated to a still high 9.3 percent, reflecting continued food shortages, the impact of Value Added Tax introduction, and inflation conditions in South Africa.

## Figure 2.4: Southern Africa, Selected Economic Indicators, 1999–2003

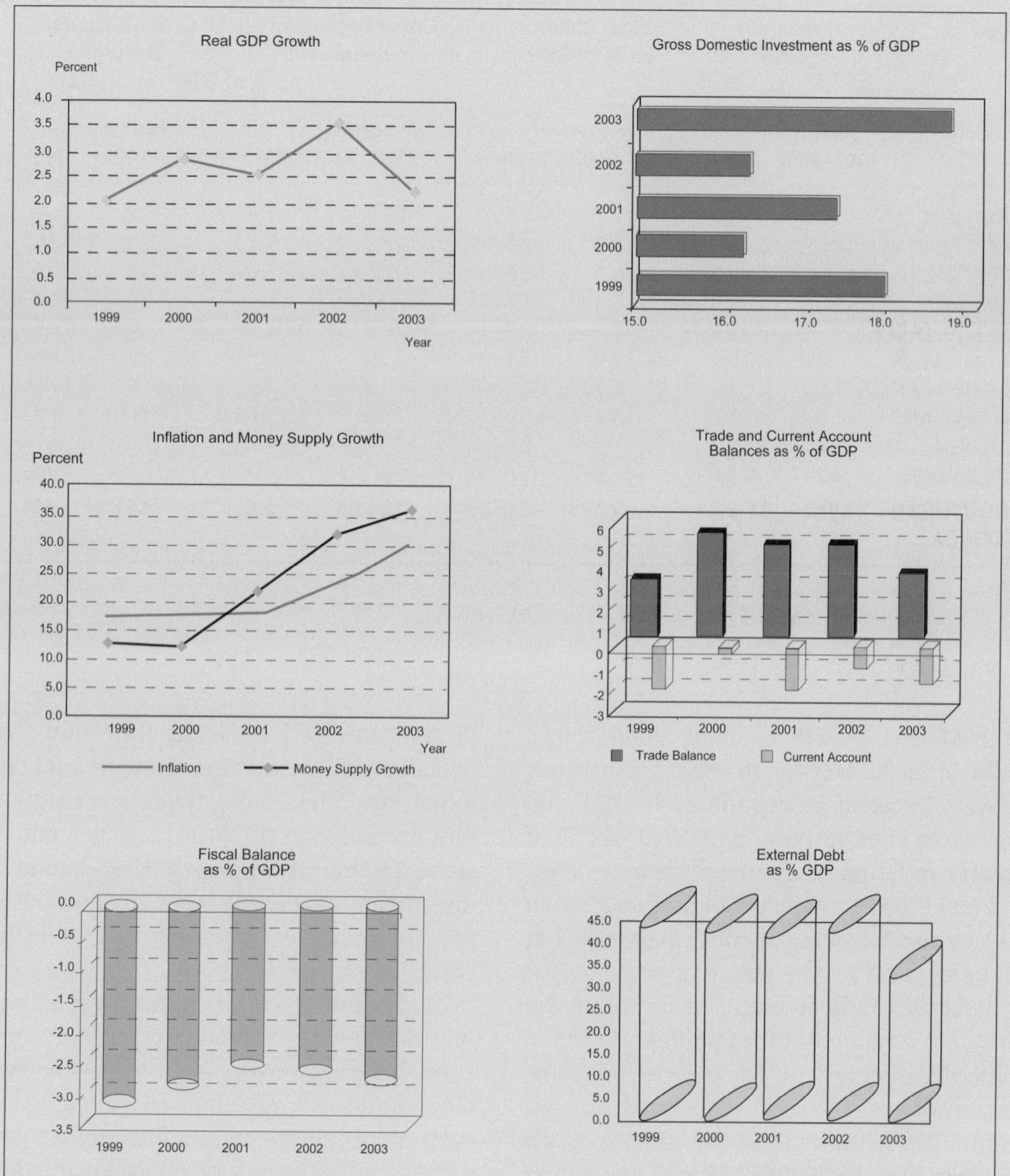
Real GDP Growth
Percent
4.0
3.5
3.0
2.5
2.0
1.5
1.0
0.5
0.0
1999
2000
2001
2002
2003
Year
Gross Domestic Investment as % of GDP
2003
2002
2001
2000
1999
15.0
16.0
17.0
18.0
19.0
Inflation and Money Supply Growth
Percent
40.0
35.0
30.0
25.0
20.0
15.0
10.0
5.0
0.0
1999
2000
2001
2002
2003
Year
Inflation
Money Supply Growth
Trade and Current Account Balances as % of GDP
6
5
4
3
2
1
0
-1
-2
-3
1999
2000
2001
2002
2003
Trade Balance
Current Account
Fiscal Balance as % of GDP
0.0
-0.5
-1.0
-1.5
-2.0
-2.5
-3.0
-3.5
1999
2000
2001
2002
2003
External Debt as % GDP
45.0
40.0
35.0
30.0
25.0
20.0
15.0
10.0
5.0
0.0
1999
2000
2001
2002
2003

*Source*: ADB Statistics Division, 2004

Table 2.12: Southern Africa: Macroeconomic Management Indicators, 1999-2003

| Country | Inflation (%) | | Fiscal Balance as % of GDP | | Gross Domestic Investment | | Gross National Savings | |
| | | | | | as % of GDP | | | |
| | Average 1999–2002 | 2003[a/] | Average 1999–2002 | 2003[a/] | Average 1999–2002 | 2003[a/] | Average 1999–2002 | 2003[a/] |
|---|---|---|---|---|---|---|---|---|
| ANGOLA | 208.7 | 95.2 | −12.1 | −4.6 | 23.0 | 30.3 | 27.2 | 26.0 |
| BOTSWANA | 6.9 | 4.7 | 4.3 | −2.7 | 27.9 | 24.8 | 33.6 | 31.6 |
| LESOTHO | 8.5 | 9.3 | −5.3 | −3.5 | 41.0 | 37.3 | 24.6 | 24.8 |
| MALAWI | 28.9 | 5.0 | −5.5 | −1.3 | 9.6 | 8.5 | 1.3 | 3.2 |
| MOZAMBIQUE | 10.3 | 12.9 | −4.4 | −3.9 | 39.8 | 50.0 | 19.7 | 22.1 |
| NAMIBIA | 9.6 | 9.5 | −2.9 | −3.7 | 23.1 | 25.8 | 27.5 | 27.5 |
| SOUTH AFRICA | 6.4 | 7.7 | −1.7 | −2.1 | 15.6 | 17.2 | 15.4 | 15.3 |
| SWAZILAND | 8.8 | 9.5 | −3.5 | −6.7 | 18.6 | 17.3 | 15.4 | 14.3 |
| ZAMBIA | 24.2 | 18.4 | −5.5 | −5.6 | 18.7 | 22.6 | 1.8 | 5.7 |
| ZIMBABWE | 82.8 | 420.0 | −12.0 | −8.8 | 8.1 | 2.2 | 7.2 | −1.6 |
| **SOUTHERN AFRICA** | **30.1** | **35.6** | **−2.8** | **−2.9** | **16.7** | **18.2** | **15.8** | **15.4** |

*Note*: a/ Preliminary estimates
*Source*: ADB Statistics Division, 2004

In **Malawi**, growth resumed, albeit from a low base, to 5.9 percent, in 2003. There was a recovery in cereal production in the 2003/04-crop year after three consecutive years of drought-induced decline. Inflation decelerated to 5.0 percent in 2003, indicating a fall in food prices following bumper harvests, but still loose fiscal and monetary policy.

Real GDP growth remained strong for the third year running in **Mozambique**, despite a slight deceleration to 7.0 percent in 2003. Mega-projects, notably the Mozal II aluminum smelter and the Temane/Secunda gas pipeline to South Africa, were the catalyst for economic growth. Agricultural production held up well outside some drought-affected areas in the south, with overall cereal production rising to 1.8 million tonnes in 2003. Tight monetary conditions brought inflation down to 12.9 percent. The strengthening of the South African rand and the impact of the drought in the southern provinces drove the rise in consumer prices.

In **Namibia**, real GDP grew by 3.7 percent in 2003, driven by improved activity in the manufacturing sector and a recovery in the agricultural output after last year's reduced crop. Performance in the mining sector was mixed, with a rise in zinc quarrying, but lower production elsewhere, including diamond. Inflation, meanwhile, decelerated to 9.5

percent, supported by a stronger exchange rate and a decline in food price inflation.

Growth in **South Africa** slowed to 2.2 percent in 2003. Falling interest rates supported growth in consumption and investment. But the growth momentum that characterized the export-orientated manufacturing sector in the previous year slowed in 2003, as a result of the stronger currency and weaker international demand. There was a contraction in agricultural production, notably maize, owing to adverse weather conditions, while growth in mining remained modest. Tourism and telecommunication meanwhile continued to fuel activity in services. Inflation decelerated to 7.7 percent in 2003, in response to the rapid strengthening of the currency, prudent fiscal and monetary policy, and improved food market conditions throughout the region.

**Swaziland**'s growth was subdued in 2003 at 2.3 percent, after signs of picking up in 2002 following the completion of the Maguga Dam, a recovery in sugarcane production and rising clothing production. The agricultural production, while rising slightly, remained well below average, as a result of erratic rains. Performance in the construction and manufacturing sector was mixed. Inflationary pressures eased in 2003, although access to food remained tight for about a fifth of the population. The moderate rise in food prices, and the strengthening of the national currency, helped to partly offset the impact of the government's loose fiscal policy.

Real GDP growth in **Zambia** accelerated to 4.3 percent in 2003, on the back of agricultural recovery and buoyant activity in manufacturing, tourism, and construction. The 2003 cereal harvest totaled 1.33m tonnes,

representing an 80 percent increase on the previous year's poor crops. Heavy government borrowing has continued to put pressure on consumer prices. Inflation in 2003 nonetheless decelerated to 18.4 percent, reflecting the relative stability of the exchange rate and lower food price inflation.

**Zimbabwe**'s economic crisis deepened in 2003, with real GDP contracting by −11 percent. Economic mismanagement, international sanctions, adverse weather conditions, and the HIV/AIDS pandemic contributed to the country's economic difficulties. Despite a slight rise on the previous year's output, agricultural production remained well below average in 2003, reflecting drought conditions during the growing season and the impact of the fast-track land reform program. Inflation meanwhile surged to 420 percent, fuelled by acute shortages of basic goods, fuel, and foreign exchange, excessive monetary expansion, and currency devaluation. The government's price control policy — which was relaxed slightly in 2003 — has remained largely ineffective, with prices surging on the informal markets.

### Fiscal Developments

The fiscal situation in Southern African countries weakened in 2003. This in large part reflected the unbudgeted costs of running food relief programs following the 2002 drought. Slack fiscal policy nonetheless continued to characterize countries like Angola, Zambia and Zimbabwe

Weak monitoring of oil revenue inflows and the absence of public expenditure control explain fiscal slippage in **Angola**. The fiscal deficit rose to 4.6 percent of GDP in 2003, the bulk of which being financed through rising payment arrears, central bank borrowing and the depletion of oil bonus payment off-shore accounts. The large increase in spending partly reflected the reclassification of extra-budgetary expenditures into the government accounts.

Mineral export revenues in **Botswana** were lower than expected in fiscal year 2002/03, because of the sluggish world economy and the appreciation of the pula against the US dollar. Corrective actions were taken on the expenditure side, by notably foregoing projects under the ninth National Development Plan, which also freed resources for drought relief and structural salary adjustments. The government contracted a fiscal deficit in 2003 at an equivalent 2.7 percent of GDP. Revenue prospects will improve in 2004 with the full implementation of VAT, adopted in mid-2002.

The government in **Lesotho** missed its fiscal targets in 2002/03, owing to exceptional expenditures towards famine relief and agricultural support to farmers. Revenues were higher than expected, despite declining Southern African Customs Union (SACU) transfers. Efforts to improve tax administration resulted in the establishment of an autonomous revenue authority (LRA) in January 2003 and the introduction of VAT in July.

After two consecutive years of overspending, the government in **Malawi** restored some fiscal discipline in 2003 (2002/03 in national statistics), by notably curtailing non-priority public expenditures. Domestic revenue collection was also better than projected. There was nonetheless significant pressure on public expenditures, because of the cost of running the government's maize

import operation. The deficit, which was 1.3 percent of GDP was mostly financed through domestic borrowing following downward revision of donor support (barring some emergency assistance, the IMF did not resume budget support to the country until October 2003).

Fiscal consolidation has continued in **Mozambique**, with the budget deficit falling to 3.9 percent of GDP in 2003. Revenue collection strengthened through new measures to widen the tax base and improve tax and custom administration — with notably a rise in the tax on fuel products, while capital outlays fell below target. At the same time, the government agreed to a 21 percent rise in the minimum wage in April 2003 and paid for unbudgeted expenditures associated with the cost of organizing local elections. The government consequently reduced domestically-financed capital spending to keep its budget within target.

Public resources management in **Namibia** improved in fiscal year 2002/03. The central government deficit shrunk to 3.7 percent of GDP, reflecting improved expenditure control and enhanced revenue collection. Public salaries were notably frozen in 2002/03, while expenditure allocations were reduced for most ministries.

The government in **South Africa** was in a position to adopt a cautiously expansionary fiscal policy stance for the third consecutive year in 2002/3. The marked increase in government expenditure reflected higher spending on social services, basic infrastructure and HIV/AIDS, which has often involved substantial transfers to provincial governments. Despite continued tax relief, the increase in government revenue was higher than budgeted in 2002/03, reflecting measures to broaden the tax base and enhance tax collection and higher-than-expected growth in taxes on income and profits.

**Swaziland**'s custom revenues have followed a downward trend, as a result of a gradual decline in SACU common external tariffs. The deficit remained substantial in 2002/03 (6.7 percent of GDP), indicating both a decline in tax receipts as a share of GDP and a rise in expenditure on public wages and subsidies to parastatals. The growing deficit was financed through a draw down in the government's foreign exchange reserves and domestic borrowing from the banking sector.

Relations between the **Zambian** government and the IMF remained unstuck in 2003 over budgetary overspending. The government notably agreed to pay higher public sector salaries in April 2003, despite already running a large budget deficit. Faced with pressure from donors, it has attempted to exclude housing allowances from the agreement, which prompted further industrial action from trade unions. The budget deficit will be financed through heavy domestic borrowing and an accumulation in domestic payment arrears.

**Zimbabwe**'s public finances have continued to deteriorate, reflecting quasi-fiscal operations, lax borrowing policy and a freeze in external assistance. Government intervention in the face of soaring inflation has consisted of providing preferential exchange rates to parastatals and introducing direct price controls on essential goods. An emergency supplementary budget was approved in August 2003, to increase spending on pay rises

for state workers and support to farmers. The government aimed to finance the additional budget through removing price controls and increased tax revenues. Preliminary estimates pointed to a fiscal deficit equivalent to 8.8 percent of GDP.

## Monetary and Exchange Rate Developments

Monetary and exchange rate developments in Southern Africa closely follow developments in South Africa, the largest economy of the zone. Three countries, Lesotho, Namibia, and Swaziland, have their currencies pegged to the South African rand at parity under the Common Monetary Area. The rand is also a currency of reference in Botswana. Broad money rose by 35.9 percent in the sub-region against a continental average 15.8 percent in 2003.

The Central Bank in **Angola** has continued to run a sizeable operational deficit and accommodate lax fiscal policies. Interest rates remained negative in real terms in 2003, as a result of galloping inflation. Hyperinflation also contributed to a high level of dollarization of the economy and a steep depreciation of the nominal exchange rate, despite the Central Bank's heavy interventions on the foreign exchange market.

The Bank of **Botswana**'s monetary policy remained tight under a pegged exchange rate system. The central bank raised its lending rate by 100 basis points in 2002 to bear down on inflationary pressures. The rate was left unchanged at 15.25 percent through much of 2003, before being gradually reduced to 14.25 percent in December. This reflected a downward trend in inflation from mid-year. In the meantime, the pula, which is pegged to a currency basket comprised of the South African Rand and the SDR, appreciated against the US dollar, with a negative impact on export competitiveness.

Monetary policy in **Lesotho** focused on maintaining an adequate level of foreign reserves to support the peg per par of the loti to the South African Rand. Rising domestic credit to the government fuelled money expansion in 2003, which the central bank offset through the sale of treasury bills. The Central Bank's 2003 policy also reflected the downward trend in South African interest rate.

Despite pursuing a relatively tight monetary stance (the bank rate was raised from 40 percent to 45 percent in mid-year), the Reserve Bank of **Malawi** (RBM) missed its money growth target in 2003, owing to an increase in government borrowing from the banking system. In addition, the level of foreign exchange reserves dropped, as the central bank helped to finance maize imports (donor support was lower than expected) and continued to intervene on the foreign exchange market to reduce pressures on the exchange rate. The kwacha depreciated significantly against the currencies of the country's major trading partners in 2003, reflecting widening external and internal imbalances.

**Mozambique** has taken some bold monetary measures to curb inflation and stabilize the domestic currency over the years. This notably entailed raising the rediscount rates, strengthening the reserve requirements, and stepping up foreign currencies and T-bills auctions. Monetary conditions have eased since mid-2002 in the context of falling inflation. Interest rates on

central bank instruments have gradually been reduced, while the central bank's interventions on the foreign exchange market have reined in the deceleration of the nominal effective exchange rate.

Monetary policy in **Namibia** is geared towards maintaining the 1:1 parity between the domestic currency, the Namibian dollar, and the South African rand. Interest rates were reduced by a cumulative 200 basis points to 10.75 percent in 2003, in line with monetary developments in South Africa and the improved inflation outlook.

The **South African** Reserve Bank (SARB) changed the direction of its monetary policy in 2003, against the backdrop of lower inflationary pressures, the rapid strengthening of the rand, and lackluster economic growth. The Bank notably slashed its repurchase rate four times, bringing it down from 13.5 percent in September 2002 to 8.5 percent in October 2003. This contrasted with the tight monetary stance that the SARB adopted in the previous year to counter a sharp drop in the value of rand. After depreciating by 34.5 percent in 2001, the nominal effective exchange rate of the rand recovered by 24 percent during 2002 and by a further 12 percent in the first half of 2003.

Akin to the currencies in Lesotho and Namibia, the lilangeni in **Swaziland** is pegged to the South African rand. The monetary authorities reduced their interest rates in 2003, in step with monetary easing by the South African Reserve Bank. The lilangeni has appreciated vis-à-vis the U.S. dollar since mid-2002, reflecting the strengthening of the South African rand.

Growth in broad money in **Zambia** in 2003 was largely attributed to an increase in government borrowing. The Bank of Zambia (BoZ) maintained a tight monetary stance through much of 2003 to put downward pressure on money growth and inflation. Statutory reserve ratios on kwacha and foreign currency deposits were finally reduced from 17.5 percent to 14.0 percent in October 2003, reflecting improved macro-economic indicators and the BoZ's efforts to achieve a sustainable reduction in interest rates. An inter-bank foreign exchange system was successfully introduced in July 2003, on the back of increased exchange rate stability of the kwacha against major currencies.

The Reserve Bank of **Zimbabwe** has continued to accommodate the rapid surge in liquidity resulting from excessive government borrowing, while maintaining artificially low nominal interest rates through concessional lending. This, coupled with rising inflation, kept interest rates increasingly negative in real terms. The parallel exchange rate for the Zimbabwean dollar continued to register steep premium, despite a major devaluation of the official exchange rate in February 2003.

## Poverty Reduction Strategies

By far the main challenge for Southern African countries is the spread of HIV/AIDS. South Africa, Swaziland, Zambia and Botswana have the highest prevalence rates in the world. The spread of the illness constitutes a serious restriction on development efforts. Life expectancy is decreasing fast and the general health of the active population has worsened, with strong negative impacts on health costs and labor productivity, notably in agriculture, education and healthcare. Another immediate challenge for Southern Africa is food security. The

region was hit by a major drought-induced food crisis in 2002/03, leaving 14.4 million people at risk. Prospects were mixed in 2003/04. Whereas improved weather conditions signaled a recovery in cereal production in the region, the food situation remained tight in some countries, notably in Angola, Lesotho, Swaziland, and Zimbabwe.

Most governments in Southern Africa have put in place a poverty alleviation strategy that embraces the MDGs. Malawi, Mozambique, and Zambia are heavily indebted poor countries that qualify for debt relief under the HIPC initiative. Their governments have therefore adopted a broad-based participative framework, as sponsored by multilateral institutions, and so has less-indebted Lesotho.

Poverty is widespread in **Angola**. The government has recently produced a first draft document for its interim PRSP, which is in keeping with post-war reconstruction efforts and ongoing negotiations with the IMF over macro-economic stabilization measures and structural reforms.

**Lesotho** submitted its full PRSP for donors' approval in November 2003. The interim version was released in December 2000, but progress towards completion was delayed, owing to national elections in May 2002 and extra time needed to organize workshops with the civil society and incorporate elements of the government's National Vision.

**Malawi** has assessed progress made in implementing its PRSP in a report released in October 2003. The PRSP was completed and launched in April 2002. Little has been achieved since then, however, the progress report pointing to policy slippages and lower-than-targeted pro-poor expenditures.

The government in **Mozambique** finalized its Action Plan for the Reduction of Absolute Poverty (PARPA) in April 2001. PARPA constitutes the country's final PRSP under HIPC. PARPA's overall objective is to reduce the incidence of absolute poverty from 70 per cent to less than 50 per cent by 2010. A National Household Survey is currently being conducted to help measuring progress. Preliminary assessments point to an improvement in the education and health sectors, but there is a need to strengthen the participatory process and push through certain structural reforms, notably to improve public sector management and tackle labor market rigidities.

**Namibia** adopted its Poverty Reduction Action Program in 2000.

Completed in early 2002, the PRSP in **Zambia** top-prioritizes pro-poor development measures in agriculture and rural areas. The document also sets out goals and policy actions in other sectors, such as industry, mining and tourism. Education and health services have worsened in the country over the years, due to economic decline, lack of resources and institutional inefficiencies.

Despite being classified as an upper middle-income country, **Botswana** still suffers widespread poverty, high unemployment rate, and unfair income distribution. In addition, the spread of HIV/AIDS has greatly upset progress in health and education. Botswana National Poverty Reduction Strategy (BPRS) was tabled before parliament in May 2003. In keeping with the National Strategic Vision, the document aims to eradicate poverty by 2016.

**South Africa** has faced formidable challenges since the end of the apartheid regime in 1994. Results of the 2001 census were published in early 2003, indicating progress in improving access to schools and clinics and bringing electricity and water to rural areas. But there are still strong pressures for fairer income distribution and social and economic rights, as exemplified by an array of policy initiatives to tackle unemployment, promote black economic empowerment and accelerate growth in social transfers. After much delay, the government approved a nationwide anti-HIV/AIDS program in November 2003.

Negative growth rates, food shortages, the HIV/AIDS pandemic, and economic mismanagement have fuelled poverty in **Zimbabwe** since the late 1990s. Social and health indicators, notably in terms of malnourishment, life expectancy, and child mortality, have deteriorated sharply as a result. In addition, the government has moved away from supporting an education and health system, whose quality traditionally stood well above the region's average, to concentrate on humanitarian assistance and food relief.

## Structural Reforms

The second generation of privatization, which includes some of the larger and more attractive SOEs, notably utilities in energy and telecommunications, has barely begun in Southern Africa. Performance varies greatly across countries, however.

The pace of structural reforms in **Angola** has been slow. In 2003, progress was made towards encouraging direct foreign investment and liberalizing trade. Although the investment code was revised and streamlined, corruption practices and the lack of transparency in the management of public resources remained major structural impediments to resumed donor support and development in the non-oil sector. The privatization program remained stalled in 2003. This includes the sale of public owned banks, Banco de Comércio e Indústria (BCI) and Banco de Poupança e Credito (BPC).

Privatization in **Botswana** has yet to start. The Public Enterprise Evaluation and Privatization Agency (PEEPA), which was established in 2001, is to draw up a privatization master plan by 2004. This will probably include the national carrier, Air Botswana (previously mooted for sale) and small-scale divestitures in the agriculture and livestock sector.

Structural reforms in **Lesotho** focus on the divestiture of key utilities, together with the introduction of a multi-sector regulatory framework. Following the sale of Lesotho Telecommunications Corporation (LTC) in 2000, priority was given to the divestiture of Lesotho Electricity Corporation. In May 2003, the government approved a new strategy for restructuring LEC based on a 'Public Service Concession' model. The management contract of LEC with Sadelec of South Africa was meanwhile extended for another 18 months.

The government of **Malawi** has been showing increasingly strong commitment to structural reforms. The ongoing program aims to fight corruption, liberalize the agricultural sector, and restructure and privatize SOEs. In 2002, the monopoly of the Agricultural Development and Marketing Corporation (ADMARC) in the marketing of maize was abolished and the Commercial Bank of Malawi was sold. Little progress was made in 2003. The selected bidders for Air Malawi decided not to take over the company, while the sale of textile manufacturer, David Whitehead and Sons, was put on hold in June following disagreement with the company's management over the price offered by the preferred bidders. Several other measures, including the sale of Malawi Telecom, were delayed.

**Mozambique**'s structural reforms gained momentum in August 2002, when the World Bank agreed to a new program. The latter entails strengthening the financial sector, liberalizing telecommunications and air transport, initiating the privatization of the state telecommunications company, TdM, and making progress with the privatization of the petroleum company, Petromoc. More than 1,200 state-owned enterprises, including all state owned manufacturing companies, have already been restructured or privatized in the country. The authorities have also completed the deregulation and the award of concessions for the running of the railways, ports, and water services.

The government of **Namibia** has reiterated its commitment to privatization, although details of a more comprehensive program have yet to be released. The sale of SOEs has so far been partial and on an *ad hoc* basis. The government is facing trade union pressure not to allow the sale of majority stakes in state assets and public utilities, notably the national airline.

The authorities in **South Africa** launched a public enterprises restructuring program in 2000 in a bid to accelerate the pace of privatization. The main SOEs mooted for private participation are Alexkor (mining), Telkom (telecommunication), Eskom (energy), Transnet (air, maritime, and road transport), and Denel (defense). In January 2003, 51 percent of Denel's helicopter maintenance division, Airmotive, was sold to the French Snecma group. Transnet had previously sold 20 percent of its subsidiary, M-Cell. In March 2003, the domestic and New York listing of Telkom brought the government R3.9 billion. There were delays elsewhere. The sale of 30 percent of Denel Aerospace and Ordnance to British Aerospace was notably due to be completed by April. A concession on the Durban container terminal was also in the pipeline for 2003. The government intends to sell 30 percent of Eskom, with 20 percent earmarked for private investors and the remaining 10 percent being reserved for black economic empowerment companies. Other structural reforms include amendments to the country's labor legislation, trade liberalization, and the land reform program (restitution and redistribution).

Little progress has been made in **Swaziland**, since the government submitted its privatization policy to parliament in early 2003. Non-performing SOEs that need restructuring include Swaziland Railways, the Central Transport Authority (CTA), the Swaziland Development and Savings Bank, and the National Maize Corporation.

**Zambia**'s structural reforms program entails the privatization of mining corporations (KCM), banks (ZNCB), telecommunication (Zamtel), and electricity (Zesco). In mid-2003, the government announced its decision to sell a 51 percent stake in Konkola Copper Mines (KCM) to Sterlite Industries, a UK-based Indian company. Sterlite Industries replaces mining giant Anglo American Corporation, which withdrew from KCM in 2002, after incurring substantial losses. Facing strong trade union pressure, the government also reached an agreement with the Bretton Woods Institutions to commercialize, rather than privatize, Zesco. Under the agreement, the government will not sell any of Zesco's shares to a foreign investor but, instead will cede complete control of the company to an independent chief executive. Bids for a 49 percent stake in ZNCB were received in May 2003.

The government in **Zimbabwe** adopted the National Economic Revival Program (NERP) in February 2003 in a bid to tackle the economic crisis. Priorities under NERP have shifted away from privatization and structural reforms to concentrate on macro-economic stabilization and sectoral measures, notably to improve agricultural production and revive exports. The sales of Air Zimbabwe, Zimbabwe Electricity Supply Authority (Zesa), National Railways of Zimbabwe, the National Oil Company of Zimbabwe and TelOne have been put on hold as a result. The last divestitures took place in 2001, when the government notably sold equities in the Cotton Company of Zimbabwe.

## Recent Trends in The External Sector

### Trade Liberalization

Southern Africa is heavily trade-orientated, with a trade-to-GDP ratio of over 75 percent. Botswana, Lesotho, Namibia, Swaziland, and oil-exporting Angola, are the most open economies in the region. In comparison, South Africa is relatively closed, with a trade openness ratio of 66.5 percent, indicating South Africa's large domestic market and the relatively recent lifting of international sanctions.

All ten countries in the region are members of the WTO and SADC. Malawi, Namibia,

Swaziland, Zambia and Zimbabwe also belong to COMESA. The SADC Free Trade Area Protocol was signed in September 2000, under which over 85 percent of SADC trade is expected to be duty free by 2008. Tariffs on sensitive products will be removed over the period 2008–2012. Rules of origin remain an outstanding issue.

**Angola** signed the free trade agreement with SADC in March 2003 and subsequently withdrew its participation in COMESA. Reforms have been introduced to remove non-tariff barriers and lower customs duties in line with SADC.

**South Africa**, which is by far the largest supplier of intra-SADC imports, enjoys a significant trade surplus with the rest of the region. The country has undertaken extensive trade liberalization since the mid-1990s and concluded a bilateral Free Trade Agreement with the EU in January 2000. **Botswana**, **Lesotho**, **Namibia**, and **Swaziland** implement South Africa's tariff policy, under the SACU. All customs receipts are paid into South Africa's National Revenue Fund before being redistributed to member countries. A new SACU agreement was signed in October 2002, leading to significant revisions to the revenue sharing agreement. A Regional Tariff Board is soon to replace the South African Board of Trade to enhance regional consultations over trade policy changes. Customs receipts have declined in South Africa, Botswana, Lesotho, Namibia, and Swaziland in line with SACU's common external tariffs and the imple-mentation of the South Africa-EU Free Trade Agreement.

The government in **Mozambique** further liberalized its trade regime in 2003, by reducing the top tariff rate from 30 to 25 percent. Malawi has maintained a relatively liberal trade system.

**Zimbabwe** is characterized by a highly restrictive trade regime. There are significant tariff and non-tariff barriers to trade, reflecting government monopolies, price control and tight foreign exchange regulations.

*Current Account Developments*

The external position of the sub-region deteriorated in 2003 compared with 1999–2002, with the current account deficit rising from a yearly average 1.4 percent of GDP to 1.9 percent of GDP in 2003 (Table 2.13). This reflected a loss in the region's external competitiveness as a result of the stronger rand. The share of manufactured exports nonetheless continued to increase in the region, reflecting impetus under the AGOA initiative, while there was a recovery in the world price of the region's minerals, notably gold and platinum in South Africa and copper in Zambia.

**Angola** is the second largest oil producer in SSA after Nigeria. The country's trade surplus rose in 2003, which helped to compensate for the outflows of services and income associated with external debt payment obligations and services paid to international oil companies. The current account deficit declined to 4.3 percent of GDP, as a result, against an average deficit of 10.0 percent of GDP in 1999–2002.

**Botswana**'s current account surplus continued to follow a declining trend in 2003, largely because of depressed diamond market conditions. The country is the world's largest exporter of diamonds. Diamond earnings constitute 80 percent of the country's exports, although garment sales have increased under AGOA.

**Table 2.13: Southern Africa: The External Sector, 1999–2003**

| Country | Trade Balance as % of GDP | | Current Account as % of GDP | | Terms of Trade (%) | | Total External Debt as % of GDP | | Debt Service as % of Exports | |
|---|---|---|---|---|---|---|---|---|---|---|
| | Average 1999–2002 | 2003[a/] | Average 1999–2002 | 2003[a/] | Average 1999–2002 | 2003[a/] | Average 1999–2002 | 2003[a/] | Average 1999–2002 | 2003[a/] |
| ANGOLA | 41.4 | 40.1 | −10.0 | −4.3 | 19.0 | 6.7 | 116.2 | 72.6 | 37.1 | 24.0 |
| BOTSWANA | 14.6 | 10.1 | 9.3 | 3.5 | 0.7 | −3.6 | 22.6 | 22.1 | 2.6 | 2.2 |
| LESOTHO | −56.0 | −10.5 | −16.6 | −12.3 | 3.4 | 3.7 | 68.9 | 48.2 | 16.4 | 6.3 |
| MALAWI | −7.0 | −13.1 | −7.2 | −6.6 | −0.5 | 1.6 | 151.7 | 147.0 | 14.5 | 18.0 |
| MOZAMBIQUE | −17.7 | 171.9 | −20.1 | −27.9 | −1.2 | 4.5 | 88.2 | 98.6 | 19.7 | 15.1 |
| NAMIBIA | −5.2 | −5.7 | 3.7 | 3.8 | 2.3 | −8.9 | 2.5 | 3.2 | 1.6 | 1.8 |
| SOUTH AFRICA | 3.8 | −0.1 | −0.2 | −0.7 | −1.0 | −0.5 | 29.2 | 21.1 | 15.4 | 15.2 |
| SWAZILAND | −7.4 | −41.1 | −3.2 | −3.3 | −1.8 | −1.1 | 27.0 | 28.5 | 0.0 | 0.0 |
| ZAMBIA | −6.7 | −7.5 | −17.1 | −16.6 | −2.7 | −0.1 | 168.5 | 125.2 | 16.7 | 14.5 |
| ZIMBABWE | 1.4 | −3.0 | −0.4 | −3.2 | −2.4 | −8.2 | 58.9 | 43.6 | 7.2 | 25.9 |
| **SOUTHERN AFRICA** | **4.6** | **5.4** | **−1.4** | **−1.9** | **0.8** | **0.3** | **40.1** | **30.6** | **16.7** | **15.6** |

Note: a/ Preliminary estimates
*Source*: ADB Statistics Division, 2004

**Lesotho**'s external situation improved slightly in 2003, despite rising food imports. The current account deficit declined to 12.3 percent of GDP in 2002/03, because of the sharp rise in clothing exports to the US under AGOA and an increase in official transfers.

**Malawi** is heavily dependent on commodity exports, in particular, tobacco, tea, sugar and cotton, although textile exports have grown rapidly in recent years. Transportation costs are high, given the country's landlocked position. The current account deficit declined to 6.6 percent of GDP in 2003, reflecting the discontinuation of maize imports as a result of the improved food situation and a modest increase in domestic exports, owing to higher output and prices.

The pace of execution of the mega-projects has continued to dictate current account developments in **Mozambique**. In 2003, the recovery in prawn exports and rising aluminum exports from Mozal I failed to compensate for the surge in imports resulting from strong investment in the gas pipeline to South Africa and Mozal II. The current account deficit rose to 27.9 percent of GDP as a result. The trade balance is expected to turn into a surplus by 2005, as the mega-projects are gradually completed and exports from these projects increase.

**Namibia**'s current account surplus stood at 3.8 percent of GDP in 2003, reflecting rising net service and income outflows and a more pronounced trade deficit. Export performance was mixed with a fall in diamond export earnings but stronger growth for the exports of livestock and nontraditional manufactured products.

**South Africa**'s current account recorded a small deficit of 0.7 percent of GDP in 2003, after recording a mild surplus in 2002. This reflected a weakening in the trade surplus and continued deficit in services and income. The weakness in the international economy and the relative strength of the rand dampened South Africa's export earnings in 2003, despite the recorded world price recovery in gold and platinum. At the same time, import growth accelerated on the back of increased demand for capital goods. The current account deficit also reflected weaker dividend inflows and a decrease in tourism receipts.

**Swaziland's** current account deficit remained roughly constant in 2003, at 3.3 percent of GDP. The strengthening of the currency and the global economic slowdown deflated the demand for Swaziland's products in 2003, with the exception of clothing under AGOA. Food import requirements meanwhile remained strong.

**Zambia**'s external position improved in 2003, on the back of higher copper prices and continued growth in non-traditional exports. As a result, the current account deficit fell to 16.6 percent of GDP in 2003, compared with an annual average of 17.1 percent of GDP during 1999–2002.

**Zimbabwe**'s current account deficit widened to 3.2 percent of GDP in 2003, indicating poor export performance and international isolation. The adoption by the government of an export incentive scheme in February 2003 resulted in a sharp devaluation of the exchange rate. The boost on exports was temporary, however, while the persistent shortages of foreign exchange in the official market, coupled with rising food import requirements, dented resources for non-food imports.

### External Debt

Southern Africa is the least indebted region in the continent. There are wide disparities across countries, however. Malawi, Mozambique, and Zambia, are all classified as heavily indebted poor countries. By contrast, the stock of external debt in Botswana, Namibia, South Africa and Swaziland stood below 30 percent of their respective GDP in 1999–2002. The region's external debt-to-GDP ratio averaged 30.6 percent in 2003.

Most countries in Southern Africa have been successful in attracting FDI over the years, because they are richly endowed in mineral resources, and/or because they have actively pursued broad-based economic reforms. According to UNCTAD *World Investment Report 2003*, the region hosted US$72 billion worth of FDI inward stock in 2002, 70 percent of which went to South Africa The Johannesburg Stock Exchange (JSE) is by far the largest and most developed stock market in the continent. There are plans to link all SADC stock exchange markets to that in Johannesburg. The governments of South Africa and Botswana have access to international capital markets at a relatively low premium, being highly rated by leading credit rating agencies.

External debt in **Angola** declined to 72.6 percent of GDP in 2003, because of rapid economic growth and limited access to international financing. In 2003, the debt service ratio declined to 24.0 percent. FDI inflows in the oil sector are insufficient to meet the country's external financing requirements. As a result, net international reserves declined and the government accumulated new external debt payment arrears in 2003, despite pledges to normalize its relationship with external creditors and seek an IMF staff monitored program.

At 22.1 percent of GDP in 2003, **Botswana**'s stock of external debt is low by regional and continental standards. This, coupled with low corruption, a stable political outlook and significant foreign exchange reserves (despite the deteriorating environment and economic slowdown of the past few years), explain the country's status as the highest-rated African sovereign. The bulk of FDI in Botswana takes place in the mining sector, but foreign participation in the export-oriented manufacturing sector has also increased in recent years.

**Lesotho**'s external debt-to-GDP ratio declined to 48.2 percent of GDP in 2003, indicating the government's prudent borrowing policy. With a debt service ratio at 6.3 percent in 2003, the country's external debt burden is deemed sustainable and the country does not qualify for debt relief under HIPC. FDI has remained robust in recent years, fuelled by the Lesotho Highland Water Project and Asian and South African investment in the textiles and clothing industry.

**Malawi** reached decision point under the HIPC initiative in 2000, but the implementation of debt relief packages by the Paris Club and multilateral creditors has been slow. The IMF approved the resumption of its interim assistance under HIPC in October

2003. The authorities hope to reach completion point by end-2004. The debt-to-GDP ratio inched up to 147.0 percent in 2003. There was no accumulation in external debt payment arrears in 2003, indicating the government's prudent borrowing policy.

**Mozambique** reached completion point under HIPC in June 1999. The country was granted additional relief under the enhanced HIPC at completion point in September 2001. Mozambique's total external debt declined to 98.6 percent of GDP in 2003, as a result of the initiative, prudent borrowing policy and strong economic growth. Disbursements of official loans and grants and large private capital inflows — mostly directed towards the exploitation of natural resources and large-scale, capital-intensive projects — kept the capital account in surplus in 2003.

**Namibia** is one of Africa's least indebted countries, with a foreign debt equivalent to 3.2 percent of GDP in 2003. This notably reflects prudent economic management as well as strong FDI inflows coming to this well-endowed country.

**South Africa**'s external debt declined to 21.1 percent of GDP in 2003. Despite the strengthening of the exchange rate, the stock of external debt increased in nominal terms as a result of new government borrowing on the international capital markets, notably through bond issues. Increased foreign participation in mining and privatized assets resulted in a small FDI inflow in 2003. There was a marked slowdown in portfolio investment outflows, reflecting lackluster performance in global equity markets.

**Swaziland**'s external debt declined to 28.5 percent of GDP in 2003, while the ratio of external debt service payments to exports rose slightly to 1.5 percent in 2003. Swaziland has struggled to boost FDI in recent years, despite the creation of a one-stop investment shop in 1998 and qualification under AGOA in 2000, owing to rising competition from South Africa.

In late 2000, **Zambia** reached decision point under the Enhanced HIPC initiative. In 2003, external debt fell to US$4.7 billion, which is equivalent to a still high 125.2 percent of GDP. Falling export earnings brought a rise in the debt service ratio to 14.5 percent in 2003. The IMF has yet to resume assistance to the country.

**Zimbabwe** has continued to accumulate external payment arrears to all creditors, including the IMF and the African Development Bank. Despite the freeze in foreign assistance, the stock of total external debt rose to 43.6 percent of GDP in 2003, as a result of the currency depreciation and negative growth.

## Outlook

Growth in Southern Africa is forecast to accelerate to 3.9 percent in 2004. Economic projections in **South Africa** largely dictate the regional outlook. Growth is set to accelerate to 3.0 percent in this country, as export activities rebound on the back of improved global market conditions. One of the risks attached to the regional outlook in 2004 is the possibility of fiscal slippages in election years for Mozambique, Botswana and Malawi. Inflationary pressures will nonetheless follow a downward trend in 2004, because of improved food supply conditions in the 2003/04 crop year.

Growth in **Angola** could reach double-digit figures in 2004, with crude oil production exceeding 1 million b/d, as new oil fields come on stream. Fiscal performance in this country is likely to deteriorate, as world oil prices decline and the absence of a deal with the IMF switches attention away from poverty alleviation and post-war reconstruction measures. Economic performance will also remain buoyant in **Mozambique**, as strong FDI inflows continue to finance the country's mega-projects in 2004. Growth will accelerate in **Botswana**, **Lesotho**, and **Swaziland**, as economic recovery in South Africa and the weaker rand provide some growth momentum in manufacturing and agricultural production returns to normal levels. But the high incidence of the HIV/AIDS pandemic on these countries' productive capacity makes an economic rebound unlikely in the medium term. In **Zimbabwe**, growth could turn positive in 2004, if the authorities adopt a comprehensive adjustment package based on price and exchange rate liberalization and assuming a recovery in agricultural production on the back of successful land reforms and a return to normal weather conditions. This remains an unlikely scenario, however. The economic situation in Zimbabwe is in fact more likely to deteriorate further in 2004, as supply bottlenecks and falling investment continue.

# West Africa

West Africa is made up of 15 countries, divided into two distinct groups: the CFA zone comprising eight countries — Benin, Burkina Faso, Côte d'Ivoire, Guinea Bissau, Mali, Niger, Senegal and Togo — and the non-CFA zone, consisting of Cape Verde, Ghana, Guinea, The Gambia, Nigeria, Liberia and Sierra Leone. The sub-region is dominated by Nigeria, which accounts for some 48.7 percent of the region's output. Nigeria is also the region's chief exporter, a reflection of its rich endowment in crude oil and gas. All countries, excluding Côte d'Ivoire and Nigeria, are net oil importers. In 2003, regional GDP constituted 15.3 percent of the continent's total, a contribution roughly equivalent to that of Central and East Africa combined.

The region's population totaled 253.8 million, or 28.6 percent of the continent's total, in 2003. Nigeria, which is one of the most densely populated countries in continental Africa, alone accounts for 51 percent of the region's total. With a GDP per capita of US$410, West Africa ranks far behind the North and Southern regions in terms of living standards, but slightly ahead of the Central and East regions.

The civil war in Côte d'Ivoire has dealt a major blow to economic and social development prospects in the West African region. Côte d'Ivoire is the second largest economy in the region, accounting for 14.1 percent of its GDP. French troops have been deployed to keep the rebels and government sides apart and a peace deal was signed in Marcoussis, France, in January 2003. But the country is in effect still divided between rebel-controlled north and government controlled-south. In

Liberia, President Charles Taylor finally resigned and fled the country in August, after coming under increased domestic and international pressure and being indicted of war crime in neighboring Sierra Leone. A peace agreement was finally brokered by ECOWAS in August, ending 14 years of civil war. After years of chronic instability and economic mismanagement, President Kumba Yala was ousted in a military coup in Guinea Bissau in September. The first civilian-run presidential elections were held in Nigeria in April, with Olusegun Obasanjo elected for a second term. In Togo, the presidential re-election of Gnassingbé Eyadéma after amendment of the constitution did not win international recognition.

## Recent Trends in the Domestic Economy

### *Economic Growth and Inflation*

Growth in West Africa accelerated to 4.0 percent in 2003 (Table 2.14 and Figure 2.5). Performance varied greatly on an individual country basis, however. Nigeria recorded strong growth in 2003, as a result of higher oil production. Other countries that performed well in 2003 included Benin, Cape Verde, Ghana, Senegal and Sierra Leone. Performance in CFA zone countries was overall weak, in large part because of Côte d'Ivoire's crisis and its impact on the sub-region. Reflecting generally tight monetary and fiscal rules, inflation in West Africa averaged 6.5 percent in 2003, which is 4.7 percentage points below the continental average. Double-digit inflation figures in Nigeria, Gambia and Ghana pointed to differences across the region, however.

### Table 2.14: West Africa: Gross Domestic Product and Export Performance, 1999–2003

| Country | Real GDP Growth Rate (%) | | GDP Per Capita (US$) | | Real Exports[c/] Growth (%) | | Exports[b/] Per Capita (US$) | |
|---|---|---|---|---|---|---|---|---|
| | Average 1999–2002 | 2003[a/] | Average 1999–2002 | 2003[a/] | Average 1999–2002 | 2003[a/] | Average 1999–2002 | 2003[a/] |
| BENIN | 5.5 | 5.5 | 385 | 524 | 7.9 | –10.0 | 58 | 75 |
| BURKINA FASO | 4.4 | 2.6 | 234 | 315 | 6.8 | 12.4 | 23 | 28 |
| CAPE VERDE | 7.5 | 5.0 | 1,335 | 1,806 | 11.7 | 8.2 | 372 | 516 |
| COTE D'IVOIRE | –0.6 | –3.0 | 715 | 838 | 2.8 | –4.4 | 298 | 370 |
| GAMBIA | 3.7 | 7.3 | 301 | 219 | 1.7 | 5.3 | 155 | 162 |
| GHANA | 4.2 | 4.7 | 306 | 357 | 3.0 | 3.7 | 127 | 141 |
| GUINEA | 3.6 | 3.6 | 392 | 405 | 4.6 | 5.5 | 93 | 101 |
| GUINEA-BISSAU | 2.0 | 2.4 | 152 | 162 | 22.1 | 4.8 | 49 | 48 |
| LIBERIA | ... | ... | ... | ... | ... | ... | ... | ... |
| MALI | 4.4 | 3.2 | 247 | 330 | 17.5 | –11.3 | 71 | 96 |
| NIGER | 2.0 | 4.0 | 181 | 228 | –3.6 | 1.8 | 30 | 35 |
| NIGERIA | 2.1 | 5.0 | 355 | 387 | 1.2 | 11.1 | 169 | 192 |
| SENEGAL | 4.7 | 6.5 | 495 | 660 | 6.7 | –3.6 | 150 | 185 |
| SIERRA LEONE | 1.9 | 6.5 | 157 | 160 | 13.6 | 0.6 | 25 | 31 |
| TOGO | 1.4 | 3.0 | 283 | 358 | 7.5 | 17.8 | 98 | 136 |
| **WEST AFRICA** | **2.7** | **4.0** | **357** | **410** | **2.6** | **4.5** | **142** | **164** |

*Notes*: a/ Preliminary estimates
   b/ Exports of Goods and Nonfactor Services at Market Prices
   c/ Real Exports of Goods Growth
*Source*: ADB Statistics Division, 2004

**Benin** continued to enjoy robust economic growth in 2003, despite a slight deceleration to 5.5 percent from 6.4 percent in 2002. Cotton production in 2003/04 (as reported in 2003 national accounts) was expected to reach 410,000 tonnes, against a low 336,000 tonnes in 2002/03. This coupled with recovering world cotton prices, helped to compensate for lower growth in cotton ginning and manufacturing in 2003. Inflation remained subdued, at 1.7 percent, reflecting sound monetary policy (despite some fiscal slippage owing to the elections), satisfactory food supply conditions, and the strengthening of the exchange rate to the US dollar.

Growth in **Burkina Faso** decelerated sharply to 2.6 percent in 2003. In the primary sector, the growth of cereal and cotton production accelerated in 2003/04, as a result of improved weather conditions, but activity in other sectors remained depressed, because

# Figure 2.5: West Africa, Selected Economic Indicators, 1999–2003

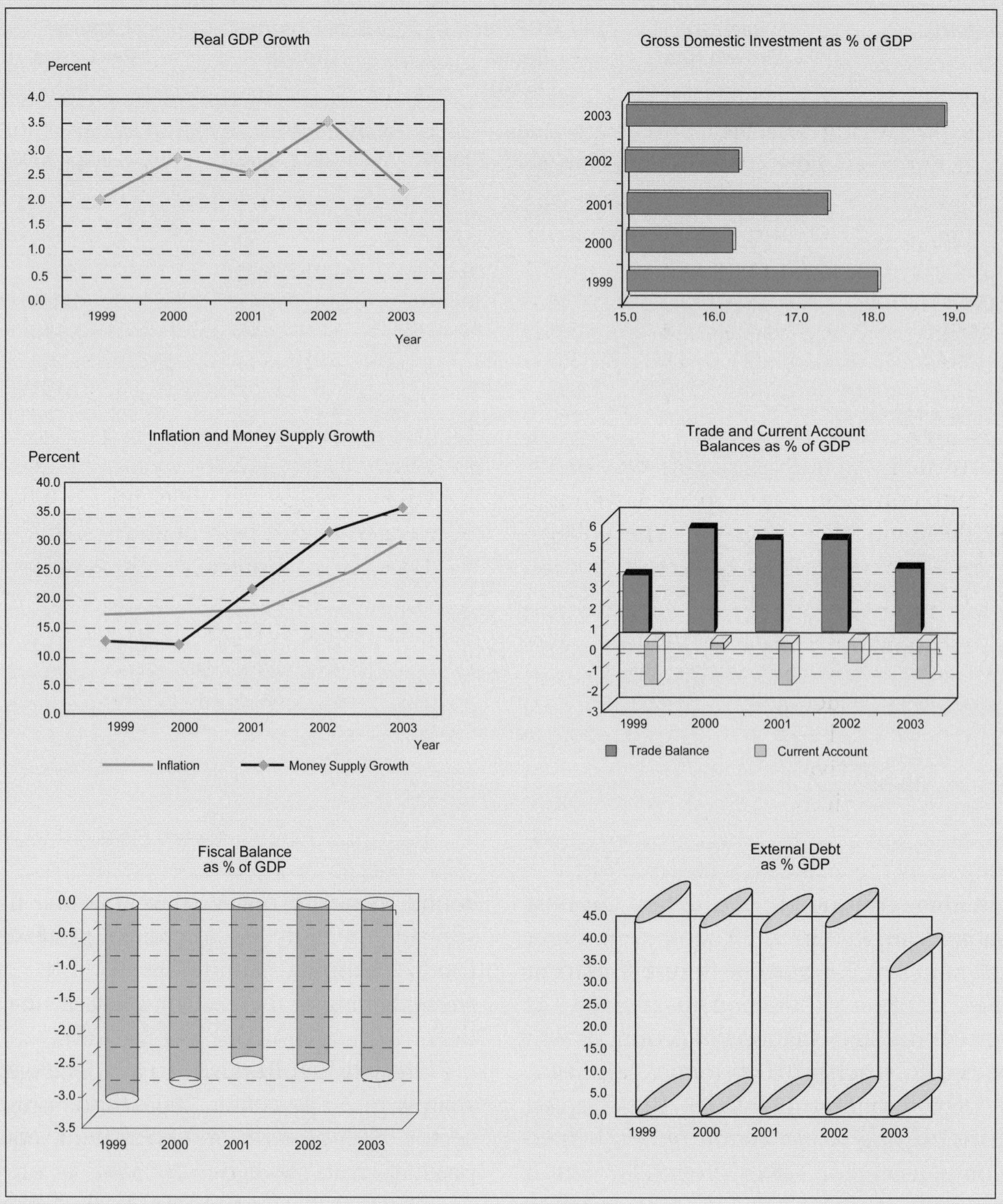

### Real GDP Growth

Percent

### Gross Domestic Investment as % of GDP

### Inflation and Money Supply Growth

Percent

Inflation ——— Money Supply Growth ——◆——

### Trade and Current Account Balances as % of GDP

■ Trade Balance     ☐ Current Account

### Fiscal Balance as % of GDP

### External Debt as % GDP

*Source*: ADB Statistics Division, 2004

of the lingering impact of the crisis in Côte d'Ivoire. The manufacturing sector, in particular, relies heavily on Côte d'Ivoire for its supply of inputs and spare parts. Inflation rose slightly in 2003, as a result of disruptions in trade and transport.

The expanding tourism industry and the associated boom in construction and services pushed economic growth in **Cape Verde** to 5 percent in 2003, on the back of improved macroeconomic stability and strong donor support. Cape Verde's inflation rate averaged 1.1 percent in 2003, disguising a hike in the price of public transport and water and electricity tariffs in January and tight food supply conditions.

Growth in **Côte d'Ivoire** was elusive for the fourth consecutive year in 2003, with real GDP declining by 3.0 percent. The political stalemate took its toll on all sectors, but the impact was the strongest in the manufacturing sector, reflecting the depressed domestic and regional demand and falling investment. Agricultural production meanwhile declined for both food and export crops. There were timid signs of revival in trade, transportation and other services, after borders were reopened and rail services resumed in the latter part of the year. But with the country in effect still divided, growth in services was negative overall. Inflation averaged an above target 3.4 percent in 2003, owing to supply bottlenecks and higher transport costs.

Economic growth in 2002 was revised from a preliminary estimate of 6 percent to –3.0 percent in **The Gambia**, reflecting both statistical weaknesses and the impact of external shocks, notably reduced crops in 2002/03 as a result of poor weather. Growth resumed to an estimated 7.3 percent in 2003,

on the back of a recovery in agricultural production. Exchange rate depreciation, high oil prices and food scarcity fuelled inflation in 2003, with the average rate accelerating to the double-digit figure of 13.0 percent.

Real GDP in **Ghana** grew by 4.7 percent in 2003, against an average 4.2 percent in 1999–2002. Growth was robust in all sectors, the country looking out for a third successive year of favorable food and export crops production. Côte d'Ivoire's crisis has diverted more port and transport activities to Ghana, leading to some congestion. The inflation target for 2003 was revised upward to a double-digit figure, after the authorities raised the price of petroleum products by 95 percent in January. Other inflationary factors included increases in wage and utility prices. Inflation accelerated to 26.4 percent as a result.

Growth in **Guinea** decelerated to 3.6 percent in 2003, reflecting the impact of irregular electricity supply, regional instability, and lower-than-projected activity in agriculture, construction and mining. Inflation picked up to 6.2 percent in 2003, as a result of higher oil prices, expansionary policies and currency depreciation.

Growth in **Guinea-Bissau** resumed in 2003, albeit from a very low base, on the back of a return to satisfactory weather conditions and the associated rise in agricultural production. Real GDP increased by a still subdued 2.4 percent, indicating economic mismanagement and the impact of the September coup. Inflation averaged 3.0 percent, against an average 3.3 percent in 1999–2002, reflecting tight liquidity conditions resulting from the country's membership to the Franc Zone.

**Mali**'s rate of growth slowed down in 2003, from 4.4 percent in 2002 to 3.2 percent, as a result of a combination of external factors, including poor weather conditions in growing season 2002/03 and the prolonged impact of the crisis in Côte d'Ivoire. Value-added in the primary sector was negative, owing to lower crops and the decline in gold production. Supply bottlenecks and the drop in cotton production combined to dampen activity in manufacturing (especially cotton ginning) and construction. Services were meanwhile sustained by the rise in world cotton prices and the rapid creation of alternative trade routes. Inflation in Mali accelerated from 2.4 percent in 2002 to 3.8 percent in 2003, notably reflecting higher transport costs, but effective government intervention on the cereal and energy markets.

Growth in **Niger** accelerated to 4.0 percent in 2003, against a backdrop of an improved socio-political environment and prudent macroeconomic policies. Favorable rainfalls for the third consecutive year led to good performance in agriculture and livestock, the backbone of Niger's economy. Activity in construction was a significant contributor to growth, reflecting the launch of a number of donor-funded projects in road, water, and electricity and rural development infrastructure. Inflation decelerated to an average 0.5 percent, reflecting the abundant supply of food products, import substitution away from Côte d'Ivoire, and the deflationary impact of the currency appreciation on domestic oil prices.

Economic performance in **Nigeria** hinges heavily on oil output and prices. Oil production increased from an average 1.97 million bpd in 2002 to 2.12 million bpd in 2003, following OPEC's decision to raise production quotas. This, combined with good harvests, drove economic growth to 5.0 percent in 2003. Inflation meanwhile decelerated to a still high 12.3 percent, reflecting a satisfactory overall food situation but soaring fuel prices. Fiscal expansion and the fall of the naira also contributed to fuel inflation in 2003.

Economic recovery characterized **Senegal** in 2003, after growth slumped to 2.4 percent in 2002, as a result of a 32 percent fall in agricultural production owing to bad weather. The primary sector rebounded in 2003, reflecting improved weather conditions. While some sub-sectors, notably electricity, construction, and telecommunication, performed well, last year's reduced crops (especially groundnuts) continued to have a dampening impact on manufacturing and services. Inflation decelerated to 2 percent, reflecting sound fiscal and monetary policy.

The improved security situation and increased donor support have supported economic revival in **Sierra Leone**. Growth was estimated at 6.5 percent in 2003, fuelled by a recovery in agricultural production (owing to increased plantings by returning refugees and satisfactory weather conditions) and the implementation of the government's economic rehabilitation program. At the same time, pressure on consumer prices picked up, indicating resumed consumer spending and increased demand for the raw materials and intermediate goods associated with post-war reconstruction. Inflation, which had turned negative in 2002, accelerated to 7.4 percent in 2003, also reflecting higher fuel prices.

**Togo**'s economic performance has remained below its potential since the early 1990s in the absence of external assistance.

The country nonetheless experienced a 3.0 percent economic growth in 2003, fuelled by good performance in mining, bumper crops and rising port and transport activity as a result of trade diversion from Côte d'Ivoire. Togo's inflation was –2.6 in 2003, against a yearly average 2.3 percent in 1999–2002.

## Fiscal Developments

The fiscal position in West Africa improved in 2003 (Table 2.15), despite the impact of Côte d'Ivoire's crisis on the CFA zone's fiscal position. By virtue of their membership to the West African Economic and Monetary Union (WAEMU/UEMOA), CFA zone countries aim to converge towards commonly agreed fiscal targets. These benchmarks, combined with the CFA zone rules on government borrowing, mean that fiscal performance has traditionally been better in CFA countries. At the same time, the fiscal situation in Ghana and Nigeria improved in 2003 despite some overspending, as a result of higher export tax revenues.

### Table 2.15: West Africa: Macroeconomic Management Indicators, 1999–2003

| Country | Inflation (%) | | Fiscal Balance as % of GDP | | Gross Domestic Investment | | Gross National Savings | |
| | | | | | as % of GDP | | | |
| | Average 1999–2002 | 2003[a] | Average 1999–2002 | 2003[a] | Average 1999–2002 | 2003[a] | Average 1999–2002 | 2003[a] |
|---|---|---|---|---|---|---|---|---|
| BENIN | 2.4 | 2.5 | –1.0 | –2.1 | 18.4 | 19.0 | 10.8 | 11.4 |
| BURKINA FASO | 1.4 | 3.0 | –4.0 | –2.5 | 22.3 | 19.6 | 14.1 | 10.2 |
| CAPE VERDE | 1.9 | 2.8 | –9.8 | –1.5 | 20.6 | 22.2 | 9.4 | 10.5 |
| COTE D'IVOIRE | 3.0 | 3.5 | –1.2 | –1.8 | 11.3 | 9.9 | 12.4 | 17.7 |
| GAMBIA | 4.1 | 3.4 | –4.4 | –6.3 | 19.4 | 22.3 | 11.8 | 8.9 |
| GHANA | 21.3 | 26.4 | –7.2 | –2.5 | 22.9 | 23.6 | 16.8 | 22.2 |
| GUINEA | 4.9 | 6.2 | –4.0 | –3.0 | 22.2 | 19.1 | 16.2 | 14.1 |
| GUINEA-BISSAU | 3.3 | 3.0 | –11.1 | –9.0 | 17.1 | 23.6 | 1.3 | 4.3 |
| LIBERIA | ... | ... | ... | ... | ... | ... | ... | ... |
| MALI | 1.4 | 3.8 | –3.6 | –5.4 | 20.1 | 21.3 | 11.0 | 14.0 |
| NIGER | 2.1 | 0.5 | –3.6 | –5.2 | 11.4 | 15.5 | 5.7 | 7.7 |
| NIGERIA | 11.3 | 12.3 | –1.7 | 1.4 | 19.5 | 24.8 | 18.8 | 23.7 |
| SENEGAL | 1.7 | 2.0 | –0.7 | –1.3 | 18.6 | 20.2 | 13.2 | 14.4 |
| SIERRA LEONE | 8.1 | 7.4 | –9.5 | –9.4 | 6.1 | 19.7 | –4.2 | 2.3 |
| TOGO | 2.3 | –2.6 | –2.8 | –0.7 | 18.8 | 20.1 | 6.0 | 10.7 |
| **WEST AFRICA** | **5.4** | **6.0** | **–2.4** | **–0.7** | **18.4** | **21.0** | **15.8** | **19.3** |

*Note*: a/ Preliminary estimates
*Source*: ADB Statistics Division, 2004

**Benin**'s fiscal performance weakened in early 2003, in large part reflecting election-related spending overruns. In addition, the wage bill was still larger than expected as a result of salary adjustments in 2002. Measures to reinforce custom administration and curtail non-priority expenditures were implemented, with the fiscal deficit falling to 2.1 percent of GDP as a result. In August 2003, the government adopted the budget and accounting framework of local governments, as part of the decentralization process, which was launched after local elections in December 2002 and aims to transfer managerial authority to local governments.

The overall fiscal deficit in **Burkina Faso** stood at 2.5 percent of GDP in 2003, in spite of an increase in HIPC Initiative-related social spending (partly reflecting unused resources carried over from 2000–02), and provisions for humanitarian assistance following the crisis in Côte d'Ivoire. Government revenue was projected to rise to 11.4 percent of GDP in 2003, reflecting enhanced tax and customs administration and rising inflows of external assistance. Other steps to strengthen public finance management were taken in 2003, with notably the establishment of the Auditor's General Office and the adoption of the WAEMU budgetary nomenclature.

**Cape Verde**'s fiscal position was sound in 2003, although the implementation of a 15 percent VAT and the adoption of streamlined customs duties were postponed by one year to 1st January 2004. Public outlays as a percentage of GDP decreased in 2003, as a result of falling transfers and subsidies (notably to Electra and former employees of liquidated public enterprises), while revenues continued to increase on the back of higher

customs receipts and the elimination of tax exemptions. This helped to reduce the fiscal deficit to 1.5 percent of GDP and clear most domestic payment arrears.

The government in **Côte d'Ivoire** adopted its 2003 budget in July, after a delay of six months. The budget projected a 17 percent decline in both receipts and expenditures, with a drop of 62.4 percent in external assistance. The budget deficit was estimated at 1.8 percent for the whole year. The underlying growth assumption (+1.8 percent) was unrealistic, however. In addition, transparency in public resources management has deteriorated since the beginning of the war. This has led to a plethora of extra-budgetary procedures (especially regarding military spending) and other financial malpractices. The government resorted to domestic and external payment arrears in 2003 to finance imbalances.

The fiscal situation in **The Gambia** continued to deteriorate in 2003, reflecting a shortfall in custom revenues and delays in grant disbursements. The fiscal deficit rose to 6.3 percent of GDP as a result, the bulk of which being financed through domestic borrowing. The government had plans to reduce non-priority expenditures and reinforce tax administration, with the adoption of a new Income and Sales Tax Act, in 2003/04.

The government in **Ghana** submitted a supplementary budget to parliament in September 2003, to bring nominal expenditure allocations in line with the higher level of prices. Poverty-related expenditures were projected to rise to 6 percent of GDP. Despite higher-than-expected public spending (including the continued rise in the civil service wage bill), the budget deficit declined to 2.5 percent of GDP, owing to improved tax administration and higher-than-expected revenue outturn. There were delays in implementing new tax measures, notably the national health insurance levy. The government did not resort to domestic financing in 2003, which helped to reduce the domestic debt burden on the budget (domestic borrowing overshot in 2002, after the government paid for substantial losses by the state-owned Tema Oil Refinery).

Continued expenditure overruns (due both to security spending and poor expenditure management) and the shortfall in external assistance led to **Guinea**'s fiscal deficit to standing at 3.0 percent of GDP in 2003, thanks to recent progress in revenue mobilization. There was, however, no significant reduction in domestic arrears in 2003.

**Guinea-Bissau** made little progress to strengthen public finances under the ousted regime. Expenditure mismanagement, tax evasion, falling export receipts, and the freeze in external assistance combined to maintain the budget deficit at 9.0 percent of GDP in 2003, all of which being financed through the accumulation of new domestic and external payment arrears. The new administration has committed to pushing through civil service reforms and hopes to settle months of salary payment arrears with the resumption of external assistance in early 2004.

The budget deficit in **Mali** remained above regional average in 2003, rising to an equivalent 5.4 percent of GDP. Revenues were lower than expected, given the economic slowdown and lower-than-anticipated priv-

atization proceeds, while total expenditures rose with subsidies to compensate the electricity utility for the lowering of its tariffs, redundancy packages for former employees at the CMDT (cotton), and HIPC-related social spending. The government meanwhile made progress in bringing its fiscal data in line with the WAEMU framework and improving budget formulation and reporting.

Fiscal consolidation has proceeded satisfactorily in **Niger**. The budget deficit rose to a manageable 5.2 percent of GDP in 2003, when a new budget nomenclature was adopted. There was acceleration in the implementation of the government's poverty reduction program, with a 50 percent rise in HIPC-related capital expenditures. Elsewhere, the government tightened its control on recurrent expenditures, notably the wage bill, and made further progress in settling domestic payment arrears. Niger hoped to meet the WAEMU fiscal criteria on the wage bill (not to exceed 35 percent of fiscal receipts) for the first time in 2003. On the revenue side, corporate income and individual profit tax rates were harmonized to 35 percent, revenue-enhancing tax measures, notably the use of VAT on rice, were introduced, and tax and custom administration was reinforced.

The government in **Nigeria** continued to pursue a pro-cyclical fiscal policy in 2003, with the budget based on a reference crude oil price of US$22 per barrel. Heavy domestic and external debt servicing and election-related spending heavily contributed to the widening of the fiscal deficit in 2002 to 5.3 percent of GDP. But higher-than-expected oil receipts helped the country have a fiscal surplus of 1.4 percent of GDP in 2003 despite some overspending. Efforts to trim down expenditures are made difficult by the lack of transparency and fiscal accountability at all government levels, from local to federal. Recent steps towards the deregulation of the oil market and the end of subsidized prices for domestic fuel will enhance public finances.

In **Senegal**, the government adopted an expansionary fiscal policy in 2003, the year the poverty reduction strategy was launched. The government's fiscal position remained sound, as indicated by the IMF approval of a new three-year PRGF in April. The enhanced HIPC initiative and other concessional assistance in large part financed the increased spending in priority areas. Strong revenue performance helped to contain the widening in the budget deficit to 1.3 percent of GDP in 2003.

Foreign assistance (with notably the World Bank's approval of Economic Rehabilitation and Recovery Credit II in April 2003) continued to finance the bulk of government budget in **Sierra Leone** in 2003. Measures to enhance the tax system and strengthen expenditure controls are planned. The fiscal deficit declined from 9.9 percent of GDP in 2002 (an election year) to 9.4 percent of GDP in 2003.

The fiscal situation in **Togo** was characterized by the continuous freeze in foreign assistance and likely spending overruns associated with the presidential elections in June 2003. The fiscal deficit nonetheless stood at a low 0.7 percent of GDP in 2003, against an average 2.8 percent in 1999–2002.

## Monetary and Exchange Rate Developments

Many countries, except Liberia, Cape Verde and CFA member states, have adopted a flexible exchange rate system, making price stability their main monetary target. Member countries of ECOWAS aim to adopt a common currency by 2005, but delays can be expected. Regional money growth in 2003 decelerated to 15.9 percent, which roughly matches the continental average.

Monetary policy in the West African CFA Zone is conducted at a regional level by the Banque centrale des Etats de l'Afrique de l'ouest (BCEAO) in Dakar, Senegal. The BCEAO has successfully switched to indirect instruments, with the central bank's discount rate, reserve requirements ratio and money market auctions being the main regulators of the zone's liquidity. Direct advances by the central bank to governments, which were frozen and gradually replaced by T-bills since the late 1990s, were no longer permitted in 2003. The regional central bank cut its discount rate twice during the year, from 6.5 percent to 5.5 percent in July, and from 5.5 percent to 5.0 percent in September. The decision to lower interest rates was prompted by success in containing inflationary pressures emanating from the Ivoirian conflict and reduced crops and the economic slowdown in the zone.

The CFA franc, which is pegged to the euro at a rate of CFA656:Euro1, appreciated from an average of CFA697:US$1 in 2002 to CFA584:US$1 in 2003. The strengthening of the regional currency against the US dollar helped to mitigate the inflationary impact of higher world oil prices, but also depreciated the value of export earnings in CFA terms. The convertibility of the regional currency has been limited since the 1994 devaluation.

The Central Bank of **Cape Verde** has pursued a monetary policy consistent with the pegging of the Cap Verdean escudo against the euro. Given the low inflation rate, the Bank gradually reduced domestic interest rates in 2003, its refinance rate being down to 8.5 percent by end-year, but the stock of international reserves fell below target.

The Central Bank in **The Gambia** has bankrolled excess government borrowing and failed to contain the exchange rate depreciation since last year's poor economic performance. The deteriorating balance of payment positions and tighter control on the foreign exchange market have fuelled foreign currency shortage and contributed to a widening gap between the official and parallel exchange rates. Continent Bank collapsed in 2003, indicating the very poor health of the banking sector.

**Guinea**'s central bank pursued an accommodating policy in 2003, by maintaining negative real interest rates and allowing a rapid expansion of domestic credit to the government. The central bank aims to maintain the financing of the budget deficit at an equivalent 10 percent of last year's fiscal receipts and eventually switch to T-bills. Foreign exchange control and rising inflation caused the gap between the official exchange rate and the parallel rate to widen from 2.2 percent in December 2002 to 20.3 percent in September 2003.

Monetary conditions in **Ghana** were tightened in the first quarter in 2003, to counter rising inflationary pressures resulting from the oil price hike. The central bank increased its prime lending rate to 27.5 percent in March 2003 and also used open market operations to keep money growth in line with the revised targets. The bank relaxed its stance in the third quarter of the year, as inflation started to fall. The prime lending rate eventually returned to 24 percent in October 2003. Helped by favorable external conditions, the relative stability of the cedi on the foreign exchange market also contributed to stabilizing prices.

Monetary discipline and price stability have remained elusive in **Liberia**, despite the Liberian dollar being officially at par with the US dollar.

The Central Bank of **Nigeria** (CBN) maintained high interest rates in 2003 to compensate for the large injection of liquidity resulting from heavy government borrowing. Bank credit to the government rose by 69 percent in the first nine months of the year, while bank credit to the private sector rose by 11.4 percent over the same period. Interest rate developments were mixed, as the CBN reduced the minimum rediscount rate to 15 percent, but money market interest rates continued to edge upwards. Despite high interest rates, the money growth target was largely overshot. The naira's depreciation meanwhile accelerated, despite heavy intervention on the foreign exchange auction market, established since August 2002.

Sound monetary policy and greater fiscal discipline have helped to reduce money growth in **Sierra Leone**. The Central Bank conducted weekly foreign exchange auctions in 2003 to mop up excess liquidity and reduce the volatility in the exchange rate.

## Poverty Alleviation Strategies

West Africa hosts the highest number of countries that qualify for debt relief under the enhanced debt relief poor country initiative. **Nigeria**, which does not qualify for the initiative, has no nationwide poverty alleviation strategy and instead favors a sectoral approach to development issues. **Liberia** and **Togo** are the only heavily-indebted countries in the region that have not released an interim PRSP.

Progress towards a fully pledged PRSP document based on a broad-based participatory approach was mixed in Côte d'Ivoire, Guinea-Bissau, Cape Verde, and Sierra Leone. **Côte d'Ivoire**'s PRSP was on the verge of completion, when the civil war broke out in September 2002. The program will no doubt need revising to account for the impact of the fighting on the poor and most vulnerable. The government in **Cape Verde** hoped to complete its PRSP by end-November 2003, as it was given enough time to complete work on the poverty profile and incorporate feedback from the final round of consultations in April 2003 and elements of the 2002–05 National Development Plan, which the government approved in April 2003. As reported in a preparation status report in mid-2003, the government in **Sierra Leone** attributed significant delays in completing its national poverty reduction strategy to delayed completion of the demobilization program, uncertainties from the presidential and legislative elections held in 2002, administrative bottlenecks and the lack of external financial and technical assistance.

Benin, Burkina Faso, The Gambia, Ghana, Guinea, Mali, Niger, and Senegal, have all released their full PRSP. **Benin**, **Ghana**, and **Mali** received donors' approval for their final document in 2003. In 2000, **Burkina Faso** became the first country in West Africa to release its full PRSP. Other countries are still in, or have just completed, their first year of implementation.

## Structural Reforms

The region's commitment to structural reforms was strong in 2003. Bids were launched for shares in export crop marketing boards and strategic utilities, while other market-based reforms made some progress, with notably the adoption of new regulatory frameworks and automatic price adjustment mechanisms. Privatization was brought to completion for only a handful of SOEs, however, Senegal being the the most active in 2003.

Performance was mixed in **Benin** in 2003. Whereas civil service reforms continued to stall (see Fiscal Developments), the liberalization of the cotton sector made some progress. A tender was issued in July for the sale of factories belonging to the public ginning company SONAPRA. Elsewhere, SBEE (electricity and water) was unbundled in October with the creation of SONED (water), while preparation for the private take-over of the Autonomous Port of Cotonou management was well advanced. The government, however, appeared reluctant to bring the sale of public utilities (including telecommunication) to completion. Public enterprises that have been privatized so far are commercial banks and small to medium firms in the agro-manufacturing sector.

**Burkina Faso**'s privatization program was re-activated in 2001, when 13 SOEs, including all strategic utilities, were mooted for sale.

Progress has been slow, partly reflecting strong opposition from trade unions. The privatization process for ONATEL (tele-communication) appeared on track, with the forthcoming sale of a 34 percent stake to a strategic investor. Bids were launched for new shares in cotton ginning parastatal SOFITEX in mid-2003. MEDIFA (pharmaceutical plant) was meanwhile liquidated, after a botched privatization attempt. The management of ONEA (water) has been handed over to a French consortium, pending completion of the ZIGA dam project in 2005. Other state-owned enterprises yet to be privatized include hotels, SONABEL (electricity) and SONABHY (petroleum distribution).

The pace of **Cape Verde**'s structural reforms program has remained satisfactory, despite some delays in 2003. Electricity and water tariffs were raised by 20–25 percent in January 2003 to help resolve deficits in Electra (water and electricity) and the automatic petroleum pricing mechanism was also implemented in January. The government approved a new multisector regulatory framework in April 2003, but progress was mixed in the preparations for the sale of TACV (airline), INTERBASE (cold storage), Emprofac (pharmaceutical distribution) and CABMAR/CABNAVE (shipyards) and the liberalization of the telecommunication sector.

Structural reforms in **Côte d'Ivoire** have been brought to a halt since the country was plunged into civil war in September 2002. Institutional reforms in the cocoa and coffee sector have been finalized, but the new organizations lack transparency and are being audited. SIR (oil refinery) is still awaiting privatization, while CAA (bank) needs auditing and restructuring, before being

opened to private participation. Many agro-industrial plants (rubber, textiles, sugar, palm oil) and commercial banks, and some of the key utilities (electricity, telecommunications, water and port) were already privatized before the war.

**The Gambia**'s Privatization Act adopted in June 2000 has remained stalled. The dispute with the Swiss company, Alimenta, over its ownership of Gambia Groundnut Corporation (GGC) has now been settled, but the processing plants have yet to be returned to the private sector. Other enterprises long mooted for privatization include Nawec (water and electricity) and Gamtel (tele-communications).

**Ghana**'s structural reforms program in 2003 focused on introducing price adjustment mechanisms in the petroleum, water and electricity sectors to help restore the financial viability of loss making utilities. Ghana's largest commercial bank, GCB, was due to be sold in the second half of 2003, after the debt of Tema Oil Refinery (TOR), its main creditor, was restructured. Other SOEs mooted for partial privatization include Ghana Airways. Meanwhile, the Norwegian telecoms company, Telenor Management Partner, concluded a deal with Ghanaian authorities to take over the leadership of Ghana Telecom to prepare it for privatization (Malaysia Telecom has agreed to relinquish its interest in Ghana Telecom, following the expiry of its contract in 2002).

**Guinea**'s difficult political situation and uncertain business environment has hindered the government's privatization program outside mining.

The new administration in **Guinea-Bissau** is committed to civil service reforms and privatization. Progress was slow under the divestiture program launched by the previous government in 2001. This mostly reflected the dismal state of public enterprises, notably EAGB (water and electricity), and the buyers' wait-and-see approach in the face of growing political and social instability. In addition, the outgoing government slashed business confidence in July 2003, when it abruptly rescinded a contract with Portugal-Telecom over its 51 percent share in Guiné-Telecom. About 60 SOEs in the tourism, fisheries, transport and energy sectors could be opened to private participation.

The government in **Liberia** intends to privatize major public utility companies, including telecommunications, water and electricity.

Following the sale of EDM (electricity) in 2001, attention in **Mali** has focused on preparation for the liberalization of the cotton sector. The government laid out its final strategy in 2003, on the basis of a study financed by the World Bank. The CMDT parastatal is to be split into three or four privately-owned regional companies, with each company enjoying exclusive rights to purchase cotton in its region, while also providing support to producers in the form of supply of seeds, fertilizers, pesticides and technical support. The reform is due to take place in 2006. In the meantime, the CMDT will continue to refocus on its core activities, by notably selling its ginning plants in the Kita area and oil producing Huilerie cotonnière du Mali (Huicoma). Bids launched in late 2002 have proven unsuccessful, however.

Structural reforms benchmarks in **Niger** for 2003 entailed the privatization of NIGELEC (electricity) and SONIDEP (petroleum distribution), the establishment of the multi-sector regulatory agency, and the strengthening of the financial sector with notably the restructuring of ONPE (national postal and savings office) and the privatization of commercial bank, CDN. Most of the reforms have suffered implementation delays.

Initially due for completion in 2000, **Nigeria**'s second phase of privatization has been bogged down with problems, in large part because of the parliament's strong opposition to the sale of key public enterprises. After seven months of negotiations with the Nigerian National Petroleum Corporation (NNPC), the Bureau of Public Enterprises announced in May 2003 the impending sale of a 51 percent stake in four refineries (only two refineries are presently in operation). There are 41 SOEs yet to be privatized, among which are Nigeria Telecom (Nitel) and Nigeria Airways. The privatization of Nitel was botched in 2002 after the selected bidder failed to come forward with the pledged US$1.4 billion. Despite the return to civilian rule in 1998, institutionalized corruption, security issues, high energy costs, and decaying infrastructure are major deterrents for private sector development in Nigeria.

The privatization program in **Senegal** made good progress in the cotton, groundnut and transport sectors in 2003. A 51 percent share in Sodefitex (cotton) was sold to Franco-Spanish consortium Dagris-Masa in September 2003. In July, the government issued a tender for the sale of a 51 percent stake in groundnut parastatal Sonacos, with the pre-qualification process completed in October. In May, Canadian CANAC GETMA won (over French group Bolloré) a 25-year concession contract in the national railway. The strategy of privatization in the electricity sector was meanwhile amended, following difficulties encountered in the sector in 2001/02. After two failed privatization attempts, Senelec (electricity) is now due to be sold by end-2004, with a strategic investor taking up a 51 percent share in electricity distribution. Other foreign investors have been invited to bid for stakes in electricity production.

The program of privatization in **Sierra Leone** has gained momentum under the World Bank's Economic Rehabilitation and Recovery Credit, which was approved in April 2003. This is early stage, however. The National Commission for Privatization is in charge of preparing public enterprises for divestiture or private management, while ensuring the efficient delivery of public services.

**Togo**'s privatization program produced mixed results in 2003. The Franco-Spanish consortium, SE2M, increased its stakes at the Port Autonome de Lomé in August 2003, while GTA of Togo was chosen as the winning bidder for the development bank, BTD. The water parastatal was renamed TDE after a ten-year concession contract was signed. The privatization of Togo Telecom (telecoms) and UTB (bank) meanwhile remained stalled.

## Recent Trends in The External Sector

### *Trade Liberalization*

West Africa is relatively open by continental standards. Togo, Ghana, Côte d'Ivoire, and The Gambia and oil exporting Nigeria are the most open economies in the region. This does not necessarily reflect successful export-orientated strategies, but rather the importance of transit activities in these countries, all main transit hubs in the region. All countries but Cape Verde are members of the WTO.

WAEMU/UEMOA, which comprises all eight West African CFA countries, is by far the most integrated economic grouping in Africa. Besides having a common currency, WAEMU has been a customs union since 2000, when all intra-regional tariffs were lifted and a common external tariff structure was adopted. There has also been considerable progress in harmonizing fiscal policies, banking regulations, and business and law procedures. On an individual country basis, all CFA countries have adopted the WAEMU Common External Tariff since January 2000, with four rates running from 0 to 20 percent. A special tax may be imposed to protect goods in sensitive sectors for the first four years of the new regime. Some countries, notably Guinea-Bissau, have yet to achieve full compliance with the region's tariff rate structure and its common classification of goods, which was amended in November 2002. Note that Benin was the only country to benefit from the adoption of the WAEMU Common External Tariff structure, its former trade regime being more liberal. Other WAEMU countries have experienced significant customs revenue shortfalls, which were partly bankrolled by multilateral institutions that supported the trade liberalization scheme and with it, domestic tax reforms.

All 15 West African countries belong to ECOWAS, which is in principle committed to the suppression of customs duties and equivalent taxes within the region and the establishment of a common external tariff. In 2001, all non-CFA ECOWAS countries agreed to adopt WAEMU's common external tariff. Progress under the ECOWAS trade liberalization program has been slow, however. Of all ECOWAS countries, **Nigeria** has one of the most complex external tariff structures, with over 15 tariff bands, and custom duties varying from 0 percent to 150 percent. Trade liberalization is uncertain and inequitable and frequent *ad hoc* changes are made to the tariff and non-tariff nomenclatures. **Ghana**'s trade regime is relatively liberal, since the maximum tariff rate was reduced to 22 percent and the trade tariff structure was simplified to four lines in 2001. The special import tax was abolished in July 2002. **Cape Verde** is to introduce new custom tariffs in January 2004. The new tariff structure will be streamlined into 7 tariff bands, ranging from 0 to 50 percent. This will lower the average tariff rate from 23.5 percent to 12.5 percent.

### Current Account Developments

West Africa's external position improved in 2003, with the current account deficit declining to 1.7 percent of GDP, against a yearly average 2.6 percent in 1999–2002 (Table 2.16). The overall picture was greatly influenced by Nigeria, whose exports

### Table 2.16: West Africa: The External Sector, 1999–2003

| Country | Trade Balance as % of GDP | | Current Account as % of GDP | | Terms of Trade (%) | | Total External Debt as % of GDP | | Debt Service as % of Exports | |
|---|---|---|---|---|---|---|---|---|---|---|
| | Average 1999–2002 | 2003[a] | Average 1999–2002 | 2003[a] | Average 1999–2002 | 2003[a] | Average 1999–2002 | 2003[a] | Average 1999–2002 | 2003[a] |
| BENIN | −10.7 | −9.9 | −7.6 | −7.4 | −4.8 | 24.0 | 72.1 | 55.1 | 13.9 | 15.7 |
| BURKINA FASO | −11.0 | −10.7 | −11.1 | −9.5 | −3.6 | −7.6 | 57.5 | 44.3 | 24.2 | 25.7 |
| CAPE VERDE | −36.4 | −38.9 | −11.2 | −11.1 | −0.8 | 0.0 | 76.4 | 79.2 | 20.5 | 16.7 |
| COTE D'IVOIRE | 16.4 | 21.5 | 1.1 | 7.8 | 2.9 | 6.2 | 98.2 | 78.3 | 22.6 | 16.5 |
| GAMBIA | −18.9 | −287.1 | −7.6 | −12.9 | 3.4 | −10.0 | 132.8 | 183.9 | 12.2 | 13.0 |
| GHANA | −15.3 | 1.2 | −6.2 | −1.4 | −5.1 | −2.6 | 111.0 | 85.4 | 18.1 | 12.0 |
| GUINEA | 2.9 | −1.5 | −5.9 | −5.1 | −3.5 | −2.6 | 101.0 | 87.4 | 14.6 | 11.6 |
| GUINEA-BISSAU | −14.3 | −500.0 | −16.5 | −20.8 | 1.7 | −7.9 | 386.9 | 362.5 | 5.4 | 16.7 |
| LIBERIA | ... | ... | ... | ... | ... | ... | ... | ... | ... | ... |
| MALI | 0.9 | −98.7 | −9.3 | −7.5 | 0.2 | 3.4 | 105.5 | 83.2 | 10.3 | 6.7 |
| NIGER | −2.8 | −0.8 | −5.6 | −7.6 | 5.1 | −1.0 | 88.0 | 73.9 | 10.8 | 16.7 |
| NIGERIA | 15.8 | −1.3 | −0.7 | −1.1 | 20.4 | 10.3 | 72.0 | 63.2 | 9.4 | 8.4 |
| SENEGAL | −8.7 | 56.3 | −5.4 | −4.8 | −1.9 | 7.4 | 68.2 | 58.7 | 13.5 | 12.1 |
| SIERRA LEONE | −9.5 | −6.8 | −10.4 | −17.0 | −1.0 | −2.2 | 171.5 | 123.9 | 64.2 | 50.0 |
| TOGO | −11.8 | −23.0 | −12.9 | −9.2 | −6.9 | −10.8 | 89.7 | 72.4 | 5.9 | ... |
| **WEST AFRICA** | **7.7** | **−1.2** | **−2.6** | **−1.7** | **9.5** | **8.7** | **82.5** | **69.6** | **12.7** | **10.6** |

*Note*: a/ Preliminary estimates
*Source*: ADB Statistics Division, 2004

accounted for 63.9 percent of the region's exports in 2003. The region's export base is poorly diversified and most countries rely on agricultural and/or non-oil mineral exports. Côte d'Ivoire is the only country that exports manufactured goods (including petroleum products), mostly to the sub-region.

The region's terms of trade improved in dollar terms in 2003. The main gainers in 2003 were cotton and gold exporting countries. World cotton prices rose by 31 percent to 60.5 UScents/lb, while world gold prices strengthened for the second consecutive year to 357.8 US$/troy oz. The growth in world oil prices meanwhile decelerated, still benefiting Nigeria. World cocoa prices, which rose by 64 percent to 80.8 US cents/lb in 2002, inched down to a still strong 78.0 US cents/lb in 2003. For CFA countries, the strengthening of the CFA franc against the US dollar deflated export earnings in local currency terms but also reduced the oil import bill.

**Benin**'s current account deficit inched down to an equivalent of 7.4 percent of GDP in 2003. The recovery in world cotton prices helped to compensate for falling export volumes in cotton lint, following reduced harvests in 2002/03. But import growth continued to outpace export growth, with the trade deficit widening in nominal terms as a result. Net service and income outflows remained roughly unchanged, while private and official transfers increased slightly.

**Burkina Faso**'s external position improved in 2003, despite the impact of Côte d'Ivoire's crisis on economic growth, transport costs and workers remittances. This largely reflected rising cotton output and prices and strong inflows of donor support in the form of official transfers. Import growth

remained strong, driven by the demand in capital goods. The current account deficit declined to 9.5 percent of GDP in 2003, against a yearly average 11.1 percent of GDP in 1999–2002.

The current account deficit in **Cape Verde** stood at 11.1 percent of GDP in 2003. The country's export base is slowly shifting away from traditional products (coffee and fish) as a result of tourism expansion, improved access to US and EU markets, and the development of export-oriented industrial parks. Import growth accelerated, however, while private transfer inflows followed a downward trend, reflecting sluggish economic growth in Portugal, where a large migrant community lives.

**Côte d'Ivoire**'s external sector has been somehow sheltered from the political and economic crisis. The current account surplus fell to 7.8 percent of GDP in 2003, reflecting a still large trade surplus and declining public transfer outflows. There was a sharp contraction in imports in 2003, which helped to compensate for the lower export performance, after export receipts reached a peak in 2002, as a result of bumper cocoa harvests, the strong recovery in world cocoa prices, and rising crude oil production.

**The Gambia**'s current account deficit inched up to 12.9 percent of GDP in 2003, with the impact of the weaker dalasi on export earnings and re-export activities, coupled with the suppressed demand for imports, partly compensating for the near-stagnation in tourism receipts and falling public transfers.

**Ghana**'s external payments position improved in 2003, as a result of rising export receipts from cocoa, gold and other exports.

In particular, bumper cocoa harvests (497,000 tonnes in 2002/03), coupled with buoyant export prices, brought a 74 percent rise in cocoa earnings in dollar terms from January to August. This more than offset the rise in oil imports. The rise in official transfers — following the approval of a three-year PRGF arrangement by the IMF in May — also contributed to a decline in the current account deficit to 1.4 percent of GDP, down from a yearly average 6.2 percent of GDP in 1999–2002.

**Guinea**, like Côte d'Ivoire and Nigeria, supports a robust trade surplus. This reflects the country's rich mineral resources, notably bauxite, aluminum, gold and diamonds. The country's current account balance nonetheless remained in deficit in 2003, falling slightly to 5.1 percent of GDP, in large part reflecting bearish export prices and the continued suspension of budgetary assistance.

**Guinea-Bissau**'s current account deficit widened to 20.8 percent of GDP in 2003, as a result of depressed export receipts in cashew nuts, a rising food import bill, and withheld donor support.

**Mali**'s external position deteriorated in 2003. Despite rising world prices in gold and cotton, export earnings declined in 2003, as a result of the stronger currency and falling exports in gold, cotton and livestock in volume terms. This, coupled with depressed workers remittances and higher services outflows, pushed the current account deficit up to 7.5 percent of GDP in 2003.

**Niger**'s current account deficit increased to 7.6 percent of GDP in 2003, reflecting a large increase in imports of capital and intermediate goods under the public investment program and marketing difficulties in live-stock and onion resulting from the closure of borders with Côte d'Ivoire, the main export outlet. Rising grants for budgetary assistance outpaced the fall in private transfers from Côte d'Ivoire.

**Nigeria**'s buoyant oil receipts fell to compensate for rising external debt repayment outflows in 2003, with the current account balance recording a small deficit of 1.1 percent of GDP as a result. The strong demand for imports put further pressure on the exchange rate.

**Senegal**'s current account deficit widened in 2003 to 4.8 percent of GDP, reflecting a more pronounced trade deficit. Export growth was bearish in all products, especially groundnut oil. This followed a remarkable growth in phosphate-derived exports in 2002. Non-food import growth accelerated in 2003 with the rising demand for foreign intermediate and capital goods. This was partly financed by a rise in net public transfers.

Post-war reconstruction efforts and a recovery in domestic consumption continued to fuel imports in **Sierra Leone** in 2003. Rising official transfers and external loans helped to compensate for the widening trade deficit. The current account deficit reached 17.0 percent of GDP in 2003, against 10.4 percent of GDP in 1999–2002.

A boom in transit trade and buoyant growth in export crops and mining products improved **Togo**'s trade position in 2003. The current account deficit shrank to 9.2 percent of GDP in 2003, as a result, against an average 12.9 percent of GDP in 1999–2002.

### External Debt

West Africa's total debt stock, which is mostly made of concessional, long-term official loans, totaled US$64.4 billion in 2003. All countries except Cape Verde, Liberia, Nigeria, and Togo, qualify for debt relief under the enhanced HIPC initiative. Completion point has now been reached in Burkina Faso (2002), Benin (2003) and Mali (2003). West Africa's debt burden eased in 2003, with the debt-GDP ratio declining to 69.6 percent.

West Africa has limited access to international capital markets. In 1996, the Ivorian government transformed some of its commercial debt into Brady Bonds. Ghana received its first credit sovereign rating in 2003. The B+ awarded by Standard and Poor will help the country gain access to cheaper lending and boosted foreign investors confidence. FDI has notably declined in Côte d'Ivoire as a result of political instability but increased in other CFA countries, notably Senegal. According to UNCTAD *World Investment Report 2003*, West Africa hosted US$1.9 billion in FDI inflows in 2002, bringing the total FDI inward stock to US$34.4 billion. Foreign participation on the CFA Bourse régionale des valeurs mobilières (BRVM), and on the Ghanaian and Nigerian stock markets, remains subdued. FDI in West Africa is driven by oil developments in Nigeria, and has proved to be erratic elsewhere.

**Benin** reached completion point under the enhanced HIPC initiative in March 2003, According to the most recent debt sustainability analysis, which assumes full delivery in 2003, the HIPC initiative will free up an estimated US$30 million a year in public resources and make Benin's debt sustainable in the medium to long term, with the debt-to-GDP ratio falling below 150 percent by 2005.

In 2003, the debt-to-GDP ratio fell to 55.1 percent, reflecting both debt relief and prudent borrowing policy.

**Burkina Faso** has benefited from generous debt reduction deals since reaching completion point under HIPC I in July 2000 and under HIPC II in April 2002. But the country's debt burden did not fall as fast as anticipated because of exogenous factors to exports. In response, the IMF and World Bank agreed to top-up the HIPC initiative and bring total nominal debt service relief to US$900 million in 2002. The debt-to-GDP ratio declined to 44.3 percent of GDP in 2003, while the debt service ratio amounted to 25.7 percent.

The government in **Cape Verde** has pursued a prudent borrowing policy since taking office in 2001. Debt payment arrears were cleared with all but two external creditors by mid-2003, while the government remained current on all its external obligations throughout the year. External debt declined to 79.2 percent of GDP in 2003, which is high by regional standards.

**Côte d'Ivoire**'s external debt burden decreased in 2003, with the debt-to-GDP ratio of 78.3 percent. The government had made significant headway in restoring some creditworthiness before the war, by notably signing a major debt rescheduling deal with the Paris Club in April 2002. Loan disbursements had started to resume following the signing of a new PRGF in March 2002 and the country was expected to reach decision point under the HIPC initiative before the end of the year. Most bilateral and multilateral donors withheld their assistance over payment arrears in 2003, while other sources of external financing have virtually dried up.

There was a sharp fall in foreign direct and portfolio investment inflows.

The government in **Ghana** reached decision point under the Enhanced HIPC initiative in January 2002 and hopes to reach completion point in mid-2004. This will trigger full debt relief from all of Ghana's creditors for about US$3.7 billion. A deal was signed with the Paris Club in May 2002 as part of the initiative. The country's total external debt declined slightly to US$6.2 billion in 2003, equivalent to 85.4 percent of GDP, as the government pushed to complete bilateral agreements with Paris Club and to secure similar treatment from non-Paris Club creditors.

**The Gambia**, which reached decision point in December 2000, paving the way for total nominal debt relief worth US$90 million, has yet to negotiate a Paris Club deal. External debt stood at 183.9 percent of GDP in 2003, while the debt service ratio increased to 13.0 percent.

**Guinea**'s external debt-GDP ratio declined to 87.4 percent in 2003. The IMF has suspended its disbursement (including HIPC debt relief assistance) to the country since December 2002 over policy slippages, while the deal signed with the Paris Club in May 2001 expired in April 2003.

**Guinea-Bissau** is the second most heavily indebted country in Africa, with the external debt-to-GDP ratio exceeding 362.5 percent in 2003. Decision point was reached under the HIPC initiative in December 2000, paving the way for a debt relief deal with the Paris Club in January 2001 and a slight improvement in the country's debt indicators. The government continued to fall behind its obligations in 2003, reflecting large fiscal imbalances and depleted foreign exchange reserves.

**Mali** achieved completion point under the enhanced HIPC initiative in March 2003, paving the way for US$675 million in debt relief. The country's debt-to-GDP ratio fell significantly in recent years, as a result of prudent borrowing policy and implementation of debt relief deals with Paris Club and multilateral lenders. The debt-to-GDP ratio fell to 83.2 percent in 2003, while the debt service ratio stood at a manageable 6.7 percent.

The government in **Niger** hoped to reach completion point under HIPC by end-2003, paving the way for a nominal debt relief roughly worth US$850 million. The debt-to-GDP ratio followed a downward trend in 2003, reflecting HIPC interim assistance and prudent borrowing policy. The government was successful in pushing through debt reduction deals with Paris Club and non-Paris Club creditors and with multilateral institutions, such as the EU.

The external debt stock of **Nigeria** stood at US$29.4 billion at end-2003, which is equivalent to 63.2 percent of GDP. The government continued to pursue a Debt Conversion Program (DCP) as part of its debt management strategy and redeemed part of its external debt under the auction system. A number of bilateral agreements were also signed as a follow-up to the debt rescheduling deal signed with the Paris Club of official bilateral creditors in December 2000. Debt servicing resumed in 2003, after a short period of moratorium. The establishment of the country's Debt Management Office has also brought some coherence to the management of debt repayment obligations. FDI inflows to Nigeria totaled US$1.3 billion in

2002, making it the third largest FDI destination in SSA after South Africa and Angola.

**Senegal** is moderately indebted by regional standards. While initially targeted for end-2001, completion point was delayed over policy slippages and was likely to be attained at end-2003. Preliminary estimates indicate a decline in the debt-GDP ratio to 58.7 percent in 2003. There was no accumulation in debt payment arrears, as the authorities continued to pursue a prudent borrowing and debt management policy. Many initiatives have been taken since 2000 to attract foreign investors, with notably the creation of the one-stop investment shop, APIX, the launch of mega-projects in infrastructure and energy, qualification under AGOA and the president's active participation in NEPAD. FDI inflows increased with privatization proceeds in 2003.

**Sierra Leone** reached decision point under the HIPC initiative six months after the signing of a PRGF with the IMF in September 2001. A deal with the Paris Club was subsequently signed as part of the initiative. The country's external debt declined to 123.9 percent as a ratio to GDP in 2003. Foreign investment in richly-endowed Sierra Leone is bound to rise as the post-war reconstruction program kicks off.

The government of **Togo** has pursued a prudent borrowing policy, despite having limited access to concessional lending, because of international sanction over human rights and election issues. Foreign investment in mining and infrastructure has continued, however. The debt-to-GDP ratio has followed a downward trend and stood at 72.4 percent in 2003.

## Outlook

Growth in West Africa will decelerate to 3.6 percent in 2004, down from 4.0 percent in 2003. Good weather throughout the region and progress towards national reconciliation in Côte d'Ivoire will boost growth in the CFA zone. Attention elsewhere will focus on Ghana's presidential elections and Nigeria's commitment to economic reforms. Growth in **Benin** will remain strong in 2004, as a result of higher cotton ginning production and increased public spending in social sectors under HIPC. Agriculture will remain the main source of growth in **Burkina Faso**, as activities in services and industry continue to be affected by the economic crisis in Côte d'Ivoire. The slow re-opening of borders will help to alleviate supply bottlenecks, assuming improved security conditions in Côte d'Ivoire. Growth in **Cape Verde** is set to accelerate in 2004, assuming strong export performance and a resumption in private transfers.

**Côte d'Ivoire**'s economic prospects will improve in 2004, assuming a final resolution to the conflict and enhanced security conditions. Business confidence will be slow to return, however. The government will seek to regularize its relationships with external creditors and foster post war reconstruction efforts in the approach to new elections. The economic situation is likely to deteriorate in **The Gambia**, if the government does not seek to put back on track the IMF PRGF-supported program and restore macro-economic stability.

Growth in **Ghana** will be strong in 2004, assuming satisfactory weather conditions in the next crop year and completion point under the enhanced HIPC initiative. The government hopes to bring inflation down to single digit figures in 2004, but fiscal slippages and delays in the program of structural reforms are more likely, because of presidential elections at the end of the year. **Guinea**'s economic prospects will improve; assuming the government successfully negotiates a staff monitored program with the IMF and security conditions are tightened. Economic prospects in **Guinea-Bissau** could improve in the medium-term, assuming satisfactory weather conditions and stronger commitment to reforms. The interim President, Henrique Rosa, and his interim government have pledged to hold parliamentary and presidential elections by end-2004. In **Liberia**, the UN Security Council has agreed to deploy a 15,000-strong peacekeeping force, which should boost both domestic production and consumption as well as aiding confidence building in the war-torn nation. Economic activity will gain momentum in **Mali** in 2004, reflecting bumper food and cotton harvests in 2003/04

and buoyant activity in the transport, construction and trading sectors as the political situation in Côte d'Ivoire improves. Rising external support under HIPC will boost public investment and growth in **Niger**.

Economic growth will slow in **Nigeria** in 2004, as a result of a lower oil production quota and slippage in oil prices. Performance in the non-oil sector will depend on the government's efforts to push through structural reforms. In **Senegal**, satisfactory harvests in 2003/04 and rising HIPC-funded public investment will prop up growth. Growth prospects in **Sierra Leone** will hinge on continued momentum for post-war reconstruction, including the resettlement of the population, and on strong external assistance. A revival of the mining sector, the main source of foreign exchange earnings, is expected in the medium term. But peace consolidation will be essential for foreign investors to return. **Togo** hopes to regularize its relationship with the EU in 2004.

# PART TWO

# AFRICA IN THE GLOBAL

# TRADING SYSTEM

# CHAPTER 3

# Trade, Development and Africa's Performance

*"The causes which determine the economic progress of nations belong to the study of international trade."* — *Alfred. Marshall, 1890*

## Introduction

The preceding African Development Report (ADR 2003) was devoted to detailed analyses of the phenomenon of economic globalization and on its impact on African development. ADR 2003 argued that trade is the single most powerful vehicle through which the economic gains from globalization are distributed between nations. Historically, trade has acted as an important engine of growth for countries at widely differing stages of development, not only by contributing to a more efficient allocation of resources within countries, but also by transmitting growth from one part of the world to another. The ADR 2003 also showed that not all countries necessarily share equally in the growth of trade or in its benefits and that any such gains depend on: the production and nature and characteristics of the goods that a country produces and trades; the domestic economic policies pursued; and the trading regime it adopts. For these reasons, it was concluded that a disproportionate share of the gains from trade accrues to industrialized countries, to the detriment of developing countries. This is the origin of the claim that the international division of labor, as it now exists, can only lead to the pauperization and further underdevelopment of primary-producing developing countries.

The issue of trade is also at the heart of the debate on Africa's debt, the Highly Indebted Poor Countries (HIPC) initiatives, and the sustainability of debt in the continent's quest for accelerated growth and poverty reduction. One root cause of the heavy indebtedness of African countries, prompting various schemes by the international community to alleviate their debts, lies in their poor trade performance. African countries have consistently imported more than they have exported (i.e. have expended more than they have saved). For many countries, it became a regular necessity to borrow from abroad in order to bridge their financing gaps. The persistence of this pattern led to accumulation of debt and to the kinds of debt repayment problems that are now at the forefront of the development debate in Africa.

This current issue of the African Development Report (ADR 2004) investigates these important concerns in the context of African economies, with this chapter presenting an overview of the role of trade in economic development and discussing Africa's trade performance over the last two decades. The chapter also revisits the debate on the costs and benefits of openness and the implications of liberalization for export performance and growth. The final section discusses some of the key factors and impediments hindering Africa's optimal external trade performance.

## Trade in Economic Development

International trade has been one of the crucial factors behind the growth and prosperity of nations. In the 19th and 20th centuries, trade was, by and large, the engine of growth for the global economy. It has also acted as an engine of growth for particular national economies — such as, in the 19th century, Canada and Australia and, in the 20th century, Japan. International trade has also been a key element in the rise of the newly industrializing countries of Asia, in particular South Korea, Taiwan, Hong Kong, Malaysia and Singapore. It is also the main vehicle of the phenomenal growth rates which China has experienced since the mid-1990s. In the present age of globalization, trade — in concert with the forces of technology and economic liberalization — has served to deepen the internationalization of markets and production, creating unprecedented opportunities as well as challenges for rich and poor nations.

The extraordinary expansion in world output since 1945 has resulted in large part from the massive liberalization of world trade, first under the auspices of the General Agreement on Tariffs and Trade (GATT), established in 1947, and now under the auspices of the World Trade Organization (WTO) which replaced the GATT in 1993. Tariff levels in high-income developed countries have come down dramatically, and now average approximately 4 percent. Tariff levels in developing countries have also been reduced, although they still remain relatively high, averaging 20 percent in the low-and middle-income countries. Non-tariff barriers to trade, such as quotas, licenses and technical specifications, are also being gradually dismantled, but rather more slowly than tariffs. Liberalization of trade has also led to a massive expansion in the growth of world trade relative to world output. While world output (or GDP) has expanded fivefold, the volume of world trade has grown 16 times at an average compound rate of just over 7 percent per annum. In some individual countries, notably in South-East Asia, the growth of exports has exceeded ten percent per annum. Exports have tended to grow fastest in countries with more liberal trading regimes, and these countries have also tended to experience the fastest rates of growth in GDP terms. Clearly, it is difficult, if not impossible, to understand the growth and development process of countries in our epoch without reference to their trading performance.

## Trade Enhances Efficient Allocation of Resources

The complex role of trade in Africa's development has stimulated much new theoretical literature on the links between trade and development and on the merits or otherwise of trade liberalization and openness. Controversy is the stuff of development economics, none more so than on the interrelationship between trade and growth. This should be of little surprise, for trade and development issues are intensely political and have their historical and sociological dimensions too. Much of the theorizing and design of policies relating to trade has been conditioned by the reaction of developing countries to their colonial legacy, and by their belief that international trade is characterized by unequal exchange.

The idea that trade enhances welfare and growth has long and rather distinguished antecedents. Adam Smith (1723–1790), in his famous book, *An Inquiry into the Nature and Causes of the Wealth of Nations* (1776), stressed the importance of trade as a vent for surplus production and as a means of widening the market thereby improving the division of labor and the level of productivity (see Box 3.1). Since the days of Adam Smith the prevailing wisdom in economic science has been that trade leads to specialization and increased division of labor, stimulating in turn greater productivity and increased output. The dynamic gains from trade arise from the effects of trade on the level of investment, and on the state of technical knowledge. The increase in investment and improvements in innovations and technical progress will then lead to increased productivity and com-petitiveness, and trigger a further increase in trade. This positive feedback effect continues and brings about a 'virtuous circle' of increased trade and economic growth.

In the 19th century, Smith's productivity doctrine of the benefits of trade developed into an export-drive argument, particularly in the colonies, which explains why classical trade theory is often associated with colonialism. Smith's Scottish compatriot David Ricardo (1772–1823) extended his analysis through the theory of comparative advantage (which is now known as static nature-given comparative advantage, as opposed to dynamic man-made comparative advantage). He demonstrated rigorously in his *Principles of Political Economy and*

---

**Box 3.1: The Importance of Trade to Economic Development: Quoting Adam Smith (1723–1790)**

Between whatever places foreign trade is carried on, they all of them derive two distinct benefits from it. It carries the surplus part of the produce of their land and labor for which there is no demand among them, and brings back in return something else for which there is a demand. It gives value to their superfluities, by exchanging them for something else, which may satisfy part of their wants and increase their enjoyments. By means of it, the narrowness of the home market does not hinder the division of labor in any particular branch of art or manufacture from being carried to the highest perfection. By opening a more extensive market for whatever part of the produce of their labor may exceed the home consumption, it encourages them to improve its productive powers and to augment its annual produce to the utmost, and thereby to increase the real revenue of wealth and society.

*Source*: Adam Smith, An Inquiry into the Nature and Causes of the Wealth and Poverty of Nations, 1776.

---

*Taxation* (1817) that, on the assumptions of perfect competition and the full employment of resources, countries are enabled to reap welfare gains by specializing in the production of those goods where the country has 'natural' comparative advantage. These are essentially *static gains* that arise from the reallocation of resources from one sector to another as increased specialization based on comparative advantage takes place. These are the *trade-creation* gains that arise within customs unions or free trade areas as the barriers to trade are removed between members. However, once the tariff barriers have been removed and no further reallocation takes place the static gains will be exhausted.

The static gains from trade stem from the basic fact that countries are differently endowed with resources (mostly naturally acquired) and because of this the *opportunity cost* of producing products varies from country to country. The law of comparative advantage states that countries will benefit if they specialize in the production of those goods for which the opportunity cost is low and exchange those goods for other goods, the opportunity cost of which is higher. In other words, the static gains from trade are measured by the resource gains to be obtained by exporting to obtain imports more cheaply in terms of resources given up, compared to producing the goods oneself. Or, to put it another way, the static gains from trade are measured by the excess cost of import substitution, by what is saved by not producing the imported good domestically. The resource gains can then be used in a variety of ways including increased domestic consumption of both goods.

In the classical theory of trade, Ricardo established that differences in comparative advantage (or comparative costs) are the proximate cause of trade. The neoclassical theory of trade, as popularized by Heckscher-Ohlin, also considers inter-country differences in comparative advantage as the proximate cause of trade. Where neoclassical theory diverges from classical theory is in rationalizing the reason for differences in comparative advantage between countries.

While classical theory opts for differences in climate and environment, neoclassical theory is insistent that differences in comparative advantage arise from inter-country differences in relative factor endowments. Both orthodox theories agree that trade leads to specialization and increased division of labor. These help to explain why trade leads to an increase in world output — the 'production gains' from trade.[1]

## Trade Leads to Cumulative Increases in Domestic Resources

As originally proposed in the orthodox theories of trade, the theory of comparative advantage is static; hence it can be questioned whether it has any relevance to the dynamic issues relating to economic development. A consensus has subsequently emerged that the classical and neoclassical theories could be used to address the issue of economic development, utilizing the technique of 'comparative statics'. Harbeler (1988) and others have stressed that the traditional trade theories confer both static gains (direct benefits) and dynamic gains (indirect benefits) on trading countries. In this context, static gains refer to the increase in income that arises from grater efficiency in allocating resources with fixed supplies of factors of production. The 'dynamic benefits' of trade refer to the cumulative increases in income that arise from trade-induced

---

[1] It is also often described as the 'efficiency gains' from trade since it arises mainly from the fact that specialization and increased division of labor lead to more efficient allocation of resources in trading countries.

increases in domestic resources. These dynamic benefits have been dubbed the 'growth effects' of trade in contradistinction to the 'allocative effects' arising from the static gains (Box 3.2)

One of the major dynamic benefits of trade is that export markets widen the total market for a country's producers, making export growth a continual source of productivity growth. There is also a close connection between increasing returns and the accumulation of capital. For a small country with a small market, as is the case of most African countries, there is very little scope for large-scale investment in advanced capital equipment; specialization is limited by the extent of the market. But if a poor small country can trade, there is some prospect of industrialization and of dispensing with traditional methods of production. It is worth remembering that at least 60 countries in the world classified as developing, and 31 in Africa, have populations of less than 15 million. Without export markets, the production of many goods would not be economically viable.

Other important dynamic benefits from trade consist of: the stimulus to competition; the acquisition of new knowledge, new ideas and the dissemination of technical knowledge; the possibility of accompanying capital flows with foreign direct investment; and changes in attitudes and institutions. In the context of 'new' growth theory, these are all forms of externalities that keep the marginal product of physical capital from falling, so that trade improves the long-run growth performance of countries. It is evident that international trade does lead to an increase in income, in the level of investment and in the state of technical knowledge in a given country. Increases in investment in innovations and technological progress then lead to increased productivity and competitiveness, and in turn to more increases in trade and income. This positive feedback continues and brings about a 'virtuous circle' of increased trade, rising income, and economic development. This beneficial effect of international trade on growth and economic development seems to be supported by the empirical evidence.

Moreover, orthodox growth and trade theory predicts the convergence of per capita

---

### Box 3.2: The Growth Effects of Trade

Four vital points may be identified with regard to the growth effects of trade:

- First, trade provides material means (capital goods, machinery and raw and semi-finished materials) indispensable for economic development.
- Secondly, and even more important, trade is the means and vehicle for the dissemination of technological knowledge, the transmission of ideas, for the importation of know-how, skills, managerial talents and entrepreneurship.
- Thirdly, trade is also the vehicle for the international movement of capital especially from the developed to the underdeveloped countries.
- Fourthly, free international trade is the best anti-monopoly policy and the best guarantee for the maintenance of a healthy degree of free competition.

*Source*: Gottfried von Harbeler, The theory of International Trade, 1968, p. 7.

incomes across countries, which is at variance with what we observe in the real world. What appears to happen in practice is that once a country gains an advantage through the capture of export markets it tends to sustain that advantage through the operation of various cumulative forces which generate 'virtuous circles' of success for favored countries (and regions), and 'vicious circles' of slow growth and under-employment for those countries that get left behind. When studies are conducted of the relation between exports and growth, either across countries or over time, it is not always clear whether the relation found is picking up supply-side factors, demand-side influences, cumulative forces interacting with each other, or a combination of all three.

The neoclassical supply-side model of the relation between exports and growth assumes, first, that the export sector, because of its exposure to foreign competition, confers externalities on the non-export sector, and secondly, that the export sector has a higher level of productivity than the non-export sector. Thus, the share of exports in GDP and the growth of exports make an important contribution to overall growth performance. Feder (1983) was the first to provide a formal model of this type to explain the relationship between export growth and output growth. Not surprisingly, the export sector tends to be more 'modern' and capital-intensive than the non-export sector, which to a large extent consists of low-productivity agriculture and petty service activities. The externalities conferred on the non-export sector are part of the dynamic gains from trade discussed at the beginning, associated with the transmission and diffusion of new ideas from abroad relating to both production techniques and efficient management practices.

On the other hand, the 'virtuous circle models' of export-led growth are based on the proposition that exports and growth may be interrelated in a cumulative process. This raises the question of causality, but more importantly such models provide an explanation of why growth and development through trade tend to be concentrated in particular areas of the world, while other regions and countries have been left behind. These models provide a challenge to both orthodox growth theory and trade theory, which try to predict the long-run convergence of living standards across the world. In neoclassical growth theory, capital is assumed to be subject to diminishing returns, so that rich countries should grow slower than poor countries for the same amount of investment undertaken. Neoclassical trade theory predicts convergence through the assumption of factor price equalization. The empirical evidence is at odds with the theory; there is no evidence that living standards across the world are converging (Thirlwall, 1999).

### The Issue for Africa is not Whether to Trade, but in What to Trade

Given the predictions of trade theory, the important point to make is that the issue for developing countries in general, and Africa in particular, is not so much *whether* to trade but in what to trade, and the *terms* on which trade should take place with the developed countries of the world (or between themselves). There can be no doubt that there are both static and dynamic gains from trade, and that trade provides a vent for surplus production (as stressed before). What is in dispute is whether the overall gains to developing countries could be greater if the pattern of trade was different from its present structure, and if the developed countries modified their policies towards the developing world. Specifically, it is still the case that over 60 percent of export earnings of developing countries (and over 80 percent in Africa) are derived from the sale of primary commodities, and the price of primary commodities relative to manufactures has been deteriorating for at least a century at an average rate of approximately 0.5 percent per annum (Thirlwall, 1995). In this regard it has been suggested that for developing countries since the beginning of the post-war era, international trade may in fact be *a lagging sector*, i.e. that it would tend to inhibit rather than promote economic growth. This is the thrust of the Prebisch-Singer hypothesis (1950). According to this thesis, the foreign sector is doomed to lag behind domestic growth partly due to insufficient demand for the primary products of developing countries from industrial countries (as a result of Engel's law, which says that the demand for primary goods increases less than proportionally to increases in global incomes) and partly because of the necessity of developing countries to buy capital goods from the industrialized countries.

The Prebisch-Singer hypothesis finds support in the fact that, in the 20th century, international trade in primary products has not transmitted growth from the developed to the less developing countries the way it did in the 19th century. In particular, income per capita has been growing rapidly in the advanced industrialized countries but it has apparently not led to a proportional increase in the demand for primary products. Thus, an important reason why international trade tends to be a lagging sector in present-day developing countries concerns the existence of adverse demand conditions in the industrial countries. The possible explanations for this phenomenon are many. Ragner Nurkse (1953) advanced six reasons:

- The emphasis of industrial production in the advanced economies is shifting away from 'heavy' industries (such as engineering and chemicals) — that is, from industries where the raw-material content of finished output is high to those where it is low, i.e. towards 'light' industries.
- The share of services in the total output of advanced industrial countries is rising, which tends to cause their raw-material demand to lag behind the rise in their national product.
- The income elasticity of consumer demand for many agricultural commodities tends to be low.
- Agricultural protectionism (in advanced countries) has adversely affected imports of primary products.
- Substantial economies have been achieved in industrial uses of natural materials.
- The leading industrial centers have tended more and more to displace natural raw materials by synthetic and other man-made substitutes.

Thus, in considering the distribution of the gains from trade between developing and developed countries, the problem for many African countries is that the nature of the goods that they are specialized in have characteristics which may cause both the terms of trade to deteriorate and the underutilization of resources to occur. For the same reasons pointed out above, primary commodities have both a low price and income elasticity of demand, which means that when supply increases prices can drop dramatically, and demand grows only slowly with income growth. Also, primary commodities are land-based activities and subject to diminishing returns, and there is a limit to employment in diminishing returns activities set by the point where the marginal product of labor (what an additional laborer can produce given other resources) falls to the minimum subsistence wage.

## Africa's Pattern of Trade and the Balance of Payments Constraint

The above argument leads us to the basic idea of demand-side balance of payments constraint theory in relation to Africa's trading and development experience. The proposition states that the pattern of trade imposes a limit on the pace of economic growth rate of any open economy. This model is rarely articulated in the trade and growth literature, and yet it may be of greater importance for understanding growth rate differences in open African economies, especially when most of them are constrained in their economic performance by a shortage of foreign exchange. The idea of the balance of payments constraint is one important aspect neglected by orthodox trade theory. The balance of payments growth theory postulates that export expansion is vital for a country's growth rate as it is the only component of demand that provides the foreign exchange to allow other components

of demand in an economy to grow faster, such as investment, consumption and government expenditure — all of which have an import content which needs to be paid for in foreign exchange (Thirlwall, 1979; Thirlwall and Hussain, 1982; McCombie and Thirlwall, 1994). Export growth relaxes a balance of payments constraint on demand, as well as impacting on growth through the dynamic effects of trade.

In the case of the balance of payments constraint model, it is clear that in the long run, no developing country can grow faster than a rate consistent with balance of payments equilibrium on current account unless it can finance ever-growing deficits, which in general it cannot. Ratios of deficit to GDP of more than 2–3 percent start to make the international financial markets nervous (witness Mexico, Brazil and the countries of East Asia in recent years), and most borrowing eventually has to be repaid.

For African countries, most of which have been striving for faster growth and poverty reduction, the balance of payments demand-side theory postulates that these goals can only be achieved by changing the pattern of their trade towards the products that are attractive to world income and have higher demand in the international market. It is argued that while there is no disagreement that progress in poverty reduction will come through increased investment that brings about an accelerated and broad-based growth, the theory implies that export expansion plays an important role not only in making such a growth possible, but also sustainable. This is because fast growth generates a large demand for manufactured capital and consumer goods. In the absence of a growing domestic production to satisfy such an increase in demand, the excess demand will spill over into imports, putting pressure on the current account balance. If export expansion is not sufficient to purchase the imported consumer and capital goods associated with faster growth (in addition to servicing foreign debt[2]) the sustainability of fast growth will be threatened, as the heavy burden of foreign indebtedness will eventually close in and capital inflows will eventually dry up (Hussain, 2001)

### The Supply Side Should not be Ignored, but...

The emphasis on the demand side (the characteristics of the goods produced by African countries and the strength of world demand for them) is not to ignore the supply side. There can, of course, be no output without the input of resources. The existence of adverse supply conditions as contributory to the ineffectual role of trade in present-day African economies must be considered. Indeed, it seems clear that internal conditions — poor supply conditions, adverse political and socio-cultural conditions, and imprudent commercial policies — have been critical factors in explaining why primary export expansion has been the mainstay of these countries, both from before and since their political independence. Furthermore, insufficient linkage between the export sector (which appears to be enclaves in many cases) and the rest of the economy has also tended to inhibit the development of processed goods, which use primary products as their

main inputs. Indeed, the role of an appropriate trade regime and trade policy cannot be over-emphasized. According to the World Bank, "... while good trade policy may not by itself lead to development, ill-conceived trade policy can undo the effects of other factors" (World Bank, 1981). Overall, experience has shown that successful export performance requires a broadly supportive policy environment including macroeconomic stability, public investment in infrastructure and human capital, and policies that provide adequate incentives for investment in the export sector. Above all, these policies should be consistent, transparent and steadily maintained over a long period of time, guided by a strategic plan to create new man-made comparative advantages and export niches that attract higher world demand. Such a strategic and visionary plan would need to be formulated by any government in collaboration with all political parties and the private sector so as to ensure consensus and continuity.

Thus, in contrast to the now dominant supply-side development philosophy that emphasizes investment in physical and human capital *per se*, due regard must be given to the question of how these investments will promote export earnings in their totality and in their composition. A growth strategy that concentrates on expanding investment in human and physical capital without due regard to the 'the foreign exchange productivity of investment' will be short-lived because balance of payments constraints will eventually put an end to such an expansion, rendering domestic resources, including human capital, underutilized (Hussain, 2001). This explanation is evident

---

[2] See Elliot and Rhodd (1999).

in the experience of many African countries since their independence.

While investment in the supply-side factors (physical and human) is obviously essential for economic growth, sustainable growth necessitates lifting the balance of payments constraint on growth by producing the goods and services that are attractive to domestic as well as foreign markets. The fundamental objective for countries striving for growth and poverty reduction is to adopt macroeconomic and sector policies that reduce the income elasticity of demand for imports (which measures the proportionate increases in the country's imports as a result of a given increase in its domestic income) and/or increase the income elasticity of demand for exports (which measures the increase in the country's exports as a result of a given increase in world income). Despite the importance of these two income elasticities for Africa's development, they rarely figure in the dominant literature on development economics. The analysis above suggests a long-term visionary model of socioeconomic development, which is firmly anchored on the promotion of income-attractive importable and exportable goods. Regulatory, investment and trade policies, the pursuit of good governance, institutional building, infrastructure development, and human capital formation, all must be designed and implemented with this fundamental objective in mind (Hussain, 2001).

## Trade, Growth, and Debt Sustainability Under HIPC[3]

The issue of trade and trade pattern of African countries is also closely associated with the question of debt and debt sustainability. As noted before, the accumulation of Africa's debt reflects the fact that African countries have consistently imported more than they have exported (invested more than they saved), and hence have borrowed from abroad to bridge their financing gaps. The persistence of this pattern has led to accumulation of debt and to the debt repayments problems. This situation gave rise, in Africa's recent past, to numerous debt-relief schemes, the latest of which is the extended HIPC Initiative.

While the HIPC initiatives have led to marked reduction in Africa's debt indicators in recent years, the pattern of Africa's trade and their specialization in primary product exports pose serious conceptual questions to the sustainability of this scheme. To illustrate, it should be recalled that under the enhanced framework, the sustainability concept, which applies for most[4] HIPC countries, is the ratio

---

[3] See Nureldin Hussain (2003), "A note on HIPC Debt Sustainability and Africa's Development Challenge" presented at the MDBs Vienna meeting on Debt Sustainability.

[4] For those HIPC countries with very open economies where exclusive reliance on external indicators may not adequately reflect the fiscal burden of external debt, an NPV debt-to-export target below 150 percent can be recommended if the country concerned meets two criteria at the decision point: an export-to-GDP ratio of at least 30 percent and a minimum threshold of fiscal revenue in relation to GDP of 15 percent. For these countries, the NPV debt-to-export target will be set at a level that achieves a 250 percent of the NPV debt-to-revenue ratio at the decision point.

of a country's debt to its exports. This measure of sustainability is chosen because of its simplicity and workability, and not because it is tied to any development objectives such as attaining the MDGs. Sustainable debt-to-export levels are defined at a fixed ratio of 150 percent. This measure dictates that once a HIPC country reaches the decision point, it should not allow its debt-to-export ratio to exceed 150 percent. However, this sustainability definition is now under pressure mainly because of the pattern of trade of African countries and their excessive reliance on primary products exports.

There is a threat of external shocks to the sustainability of the HIPC initiatives. Falling prices of primary exports have large negative effects on external indebtedness directly through the transfer of wealth effect and through increasing the domestic currency equivalents of such debts, as well as indirectly through increasing debt service ratios. A fall in debt service ratios tends to further impose a downward pressure on commodity prices when debtor countries attempt to export more of the same commodities for meeting debt service obligations without having to cut back imports. This effect is stronger the lesser the expenditure of creditor countries, which receive debt repayments on the exports of the indebted African countries (AEO, 2003; Thirlwall, 1999; see also Box 3.3). The attempt by debtors to export more affects the terms of trade of all developing countries to the extent that they export similar commodities. There is also the tendency towards currency devaluation, which will also directly lower the terms of trade. African countries that depend on primary commodities seem to be caught in a vicious circle

**Box 3.3: Why Exports are Vital to Growth**

Exports are unique as a growth-inducing force from the demand side because it is the only component of demand that provides foreign exchange to pay for the import requirements for growth. In this sense, it allows all other components of demand to grow faster in a way that consumption-led growth or investment-led growth does not. In other words, the growth of output is determined by the major component of autonomous demand (the demand for exports) to which other components of demand will adapt. In an open economy context, the major component of autonomous demand is export growth, and faster export growth allows all other components of demand to grow faster. Hussain (1995) has applied this model to Africa to contrast the experience of slow-growing African countries with the faster growing countries of Asia over the period 1970–90. The major explanation of the difference in growth rates between Africa and Asia turns out to be the difference in the growth of exports while differences in capital flows and terms of trade movements made only a minor contribution to growth rate differences.

*Source*: Thirlwall, Trade, Trade Liberalization and Economic Growth (2000), p. 18.

where currency depreciation encourages domestic supply of the same primary commodities and reduces the prices of primary commodities still further, so that foreign exchange earnings may not improve, leading to further indebtedness, pressure for currency depreciation and so on.

The other question facing the sustainability of HIPC relates directly to the trade-economic growth nexus. To illustrate, it can be argued, in the extreme case, that any poor country can achieve 'debt sustainability' by curbing its imports, debt repayment, and foreign borrowing to levels that are compatible with its low export earnings. While such a policy can achieve 'sustainability' because it shuts down the sources that can raise the debt-to-export ratio above 150 percent, the price of such practises is to condemn the country to even lower growth rates and an increased incidence of poverty. This, of course, is contrary to the development objectives of African countries, which aspire for higher economic growth and improved living standards. It is also contrary to the objectives of regional and international organizations mandated to help African countries in their development endeavor. Clearly, the sustainability of debt must be defined in such away as to allow African countries to realize their targeted development objectives by expanding their investment beyond the limits permitted by their export earnings — i.e. by borrowing from abroad.

On the other hand, the root cause of the heavy debt of HIPC countries is that these countries consistently had a current account deficit because their imports were persistently more than their exports, and hence borrowed from abroad to bridge the financing gap. The persistence of this pattern indicates that the borrowed funds, to bridge the external financing gap, were either embezzled through corrupt deals, used to finance consumption, or invested in activities that did not alter the pattern of trade to generate sufficient foreign exchange earnings for debt repayment. While it is difficult to ascertain the magnitude of each of these contributory factors, the search for a comprehensive concept of debt sustainability must also relate to the issue of ensuring effective utilization of the borrowed funds, and in particular how the borrowed funds can be used in improving the capacity of foreign exchange earnings of HIPC countries.

Analytically, issues pertaining to the sustainability of HIPC depend on the change in three basic determinants — two related to the numerator of the HIPC-fixed debt-to-export ratio and one related to its denominator. In the numerator, the first determinant is the financing gap, which determines the level of borrowing and the rate of change in the stock of debt given the level of export earnings. The financing gap itself depends on a set of important variables including economic growth and social development targets, investment requirements to achieve those targets and the availability of domestic savings. The second determinant in the numerator is the extent to which any new external borrowing is on concessional terms. In the denominator there is export growth and there are short-term and long-term factors affecting this growth, such as the terms of trade, world demand and the diversification of export baskets. The conceptual challenges facing the issue of debt sustainability as related to nexus of trade, growth and poverty reduction can be summarized as follows:

- **The Challenge of development targeting.** The yardstick for determining sustainability is some arbitrary ratio of debt to exports with no apparent link to any quantifiable developmental outcomes, such as achieving a given growth rate or socio-economic targets such as the MDGs.

- **The Challenge of accommodating concessional borrowing for development.** For debt levels to remain 'sustainable' (i.e. to maintain a given debt-to-export ratio) in the face of shortfalls in exports, a HIPC country might be forced to reduce borrowing, and hence forgo the finance of important development projects.
- **The Challenge of graduating from aid dependency to self-sustainability and private sector flows.** There is no clear policy mechanism in HIPC arrangements to ensure that poor countries escape from the debt trap. The funds released by HIPC programs are essentially used to finance investment in the social sector, which does not generate foreign exchange earnings directly or in the short run.

In nutshell, the accumulation of foreign indebtedness in the case of many African countries is related partly to the structure of their economies and, partly, to the manner in which the borrowed funds are contracted and utilized. These aspects are now the subject of considerable attention and investigations under HIPCs by international development institutions and other MDBs (Box 3.4 provides some thoughts on debt sustainability and the role of MDBs).

## The Debate on Trade Policy and Openness

The dominant orthodoxy of the age is that liberalization and openness are the keys to growth while protectionism is a recipe for economic backwardness. Historically, this was not always the case. Indeed, all developed countries (most recently those of the Asia/Pacific region, India and China) underwent a phase of protectionism to shield their infant industries during their earliest stages of industrialization. If economic history is any guide, Africa's predominantly agrarian economies are being asked to do what most industrial economies never underwent in their course of their industrialization. Under the aegis of the international financial institutions many have liberalized their economies and opened up their domestic markets to an influx of cheap goods. This has triggered de-industrialization and in turn causing massive unemployment.

## Import Substitution Industrialization

The strategy of import-substituting industrialization (IS), in place in most developing countries during the decades of the 1950s and 1960s, was primarily conditioned by the perception that trade would only perpetuate the dependence of developing countries on the developed countries. This is not to say that the inward looking industrialization policies were all an emotional reaction to past history on the part of developing countries; rather, they did have their intellectual underpinnings provided by a number of theoretical models and historical antecedents. Indeed, during the late 1950s and early 1960s several countries, including India, which pioneered the strategy, did experience respectable growth rates and economic stability. But it was the relentless pursuit of the strategy beyond the bounds of what it was capable of delivering which resulted in pervasive inefficiencies and thwarted growth and development. The theoretical design of

## Box 3.4: HIPCs and Debt Sustainability — Challenges Facing MDBs

### Introduction

The issue of debt sustainability and coming up with a forward-looking framework/strategy for low-income countries is obviously critical for the MDBs. There are two dimensions of the problem for MDBs: (a) the need to ensure that low-income countries have access to needed resources for their development while achieving debt sustainability in the long term; and (b) the need for MDBs adjust their lending/non-lending instruments as well as their operations in low-income countries to address the issue of debt sustainability.

Recent discussions on the issue of debt reveal that it is difficult to come up with a single criterion/definition of debt sustainability, as has been done in the case of HIPCs up to now. There seem to be a strong argument to be made for a case-by-case approach, which takes into account the specific conditions of each country. This is particularly the case, as simple ratios like the ones used by HIPCs are subject to wide variations, should a government invest heavily or if a country faces serious external shocks. In this regard, it should be noted that the HIPC criteria of NPV of debt to exports of 150 percent and/or NPV of debt to revenue of 250 percent were chosen for their simplicity and for their workability. With this brief background the following thoughts might be entertained:

- If these criteria are used for future borrowing, it is clear that many low-income countries would not be in a position to borrow on concessional terms to meet their financing needs; in particular if the financing needs of meeting development goals is taken into account, then it is clear that most will not be in a position to access concessional resources.
- There is need to sharpen the tools at our disposal and to make simulations with different approaches to come up with a more realistic framework and one that takes into account a country's specific circumstances.

- There is in particular the need to look in greater detail at the debt dynamics of individual countries to find out the specific factors that influence debt sustainability so that these issues could be addressed by the country with the support of MDBs and other donors.
- To the extent possible, all MDBs should be engaged in this task to ensure that the final agreed framework takes into account their views and perspectives as the final framework will have an impact on their operations An important point, with regard to the operations of the African Development Bank, is that for some of the poorest countries the level of lending could be affected.

### Operational Implications for MDBs

As MDBs now have greater flexibility with the use of grant and loan resources (e.g. IDA13 and ADF-IX), the specific uses of these resources should be looked into closely so that grant resources are used to finance interventions that may not have an immediate pay-off in terms of foreign exchange earnings (e.g. education, health) while loan resources are used for investments that have the potential of contributing directly to economic growth and exports. MDBs will need to invest more resources to understand the process of GDP growth and, as important, the diversification of production and exports (sources of growth) as current economic structures obviously leads to low debt sustainability thresholds (e.g. the case of many low-income HIPC countries where per capita export is one of the lowest in the world and hence its capacity to sustain high levels of debt is obviously limited).

Related to this is the need to increase the efficiency of investments.

In their interventions, MDBs have up to now not sought to clearly link investments they finance with exports (except perhaps in their private sector operations). As the foreign exchange constraint is one of the major factors that contributes to a low

**Box 3.4:** (continued)

debt sustainability threshold, MDBs will need to address the issue of the linkages between export growth, economic growth and debt sustainability much more directly. The policy measures required to promote the growth of exports will also need to be tackled directly.

Similarly, the capacity of governments to raise resources, through more effective taxation to enable them to service their debts, will also need to be looked at more closely.

The debt sustainability issue will also have implications for the country allocation of concessional resources. Currently, allocations are performance-based with a bias on governance issues. The allocation may have to take into account debt sustainability criteria with a view of helping countries relax some of the constraints that may prevent them from having access to concessional resources.

There is a need for close monitoring of the use of resources and country performance both to ensure that resources are effectively used (promote growth); clearly, issues of performance monitoring and measurements of outcomes will need to be given higher priority (in the broader context of development effectiveness).

Debt sustainability issues also require that greater weight be given to improving domestic resources mobilization (to reduce dependence/demand for external resources) — this touches on financial sector reforms in low-income countries

*Source*: H. Kifle, HIPCs sustainability: Some thoughts on its implications for MDBs, October 2003.

the strategy, the mechanics of its implementation and its costs and benefits have been extensively analyzed.

The transition from an IS strategy to outward-looking or open economy policies achieved by several, though, not all developing countries, around the mid-1960s, generated a second bout of controversy and debate, which continues to this day. One of the several reasons for the change in direction of economic policies of countries such as Mexico and Brazil, and in recent years India, is the demonstrated success of the East Asian countries with outward-looking policies. This is not to say that there is consensus in the economics profession on the virtues of the strategy, the mechanics of the strategy or its universal applicability. The issues here are several, including the precise meaning of an outward-looking strategy, the role of the state in shaping and promoting the strategy and the sequencing of the strategy over time. These and other issues have figured in the extensive literature on Africa's growth and development experience in recent years. Several African countries have liberalized their trade and FDI regimes, with some of the countries further ahead than others on the road to economic liberalization. Many of the debated issues relating to trade and development strategies are relevant to these economies in the process of economic liberalization. So too is the experience of the East Asian countries with liberalization, something that is often portrayed as a role model for other countries.

The notion that industrialization is the principal driver of development and that controls over imports were necessary to promote industrialization was the orthodoxy during the decades of the 1950s and 1960s. As noted before, the intellectual underpinnings for the IS strategy were provided by the Singer-Prebisch (Singer, 1950; Prebisch, 1950) thesis that the gains from international trade between the developed and developing countries were unequally distributed in favor of the former. The thesis has several strands to it; export-oriented foreign investments in plantations and minerals generated very little secondary multiplier effects on other sectors of the economy; there was a secular deterioration in the terms of trade for exports of primary products from developing countries *vis-à-vis* manufactures that the developing countries imported; the gains from productivity growth in primary production accrued to the importers of these commodities in the developed countries, but the gains from technological change and productivity growth in manufactures was absorbed in the form of increased wages in developed countries, which in turn increased the price of manufactured goods imported by the developing countries.

The empirical evidence on the terms of trade hypothesis is mixed (Sapsford and Balasubramanyam, 1994). The thesis, though, provided intellectual support for IS policies. According to this argument, specialization in primary commodities does not pay because of the deterioration in the terms of trade and their low multiplier effects. And the market does not function effectively to channel resources away from these activities towards activities in which the economy may possess a comparative advantage. Hence industrialization should be fostered through protection of domestic industries from import competition. Import substitution policies also

drew support from Ragnar Nurkse's well known proposition that exports of primary products including food, could not function as an engine of growth because of the low price and income elasticities these products faced in world markets (Nurkse, 1959). These propositions concerning growth of exports propounded during the post-World War II years, referred to as the first 'export pessimism' (Bhagwati. 1988), were influential in the adoption of IS policies by many developing countries.

Another argument invoked in support of an IS strategy is the time-honored infant industry argument blessed by John Stuart Mill (Box 3.5). The infant industry argument for protection can be formulated in a number of ways (Corden, 1974). The essential argument, however, is that although certain industries may not be able to withstand import competition in the short run, they may be capable of doing so given time to develop. One interpretation of this argument is that time is needed for industries to reap economies of scale; another is that industries capable of generating external economies need protection. The first of these arguments may not hold water as economies of scale need not be time-bound, sufficiently large-scale plants which yield scale economies can be set up without a lapse of time. Another variant of the argument has to do with imperfections relating to information; although private investors may not know the potential for growth of an industry, policy makers are likely to possess the information and they may have to induce firms to invest by offering them protection. Whilst it is arguable, if official policy makers do possess better information than private investors, the

## Box 3.5: John Stuart Mill on Infant Industry Protection

The only case in which, on mere principles of political economy, protecting duties can be defensible is when they are imposed temporarily (especially in a young and rising nation) in hopes of naturalizing a foreign industry, in itself perfectly suitable to the circumstances of the country. The superiority of one country over another in a branch of production often arises only from having begun it sooner. There may be no inherent advantage on one part, or disadvantage on the other, but only a present superiority of acquired skill and experience. A country which has this skill and experience yet to acquire, may in other respects be better adapted to the production than those which were earlier in the field: and besides, it is a just remark of Mr. Rae, that nothing has a greater tendency to promote improvements in any branch of production than its trial under a new set of conditions. But it cannot be expected that individuals should, at their own risk, or rather to their certain loss, introduce a new manufacture, and bear the burden of carrying it on until the producers have been educated up to the level of those with whom the processes are traditional. A protection duty, continued for a reasonable time, might sometimes be the least inconvenient mode in which the nation can tax itself for the support of such an experiment.

*Source*: J. S. Mill, On the Principles of Political Economy, 1867.

first best policy in these cases would be to spread information rather than protection.

The external economies argument rests on the presumption that private rates of return for certain types of investments may be lower than social rates of return, a situation that is unlikely to attract private investors to these industries. Also such economies may be reciprocal in the sense that investments in industry X may benefit industry Y and investments in Y in turn may benefit industry X. These and other arguments for infant industry protection may not be without their merit. The first best policy in all these cases, however, is the institution of production subsidies and not tariff protection (Corden, 1974; Bhagwati and Ramaswami, 1963). The case for subsidies as opposed to tariff protection is that subsidies do not impose the sort of consumer loss of welfare imposed by a tariff.

Whilst there may be a case for protection of one sort or the other on infant industry grounds, the problem arises when infants with little potential for growth are awarded protection, and the essential aspect of the argument that such protection is temporary is ignored. Indeed, the very basis for protection on infant industry grounds may be undermined, when the whole of the manufacturing sector is awarded protection, turning the infant industry argument into an infant economy argument for protection. As Corden remarks, "since protection means favoring one sector of the economy at the expense of the others one cannot protect the whole economy; hence there can be an argument for protection if the external economies are limited to some groups within the economy or if they differ between the groups". Unfortunately many developing countries during the heyday of the IS strategy extended the infant industry argument to the infant economy argument, with the consequence that the economy inherited a highly diversified and unspecialized manufacturing sector, which for the most part survived because of protection from international competition.

Other arguments for protection include the need to correct domestic distortions in labor and product markets. Distortions arise when the market price of goods and factors deviate from their social opportunity costs; for instance the wage rate for labor in manufacturing may be higher than its social opportunity cost, say its marginal product in agriculture, because of minimum wage legislation or the convention that labor should be paid a decent wage. It is now the received wisdom, following the seminal work on the issue by Bhagwati and Ramaswami (1963), that in cases where domestic distortions prevent the economy from realizing its true comparative advantage, the distortion should be dealt at the source of the distortion. Thus, if a distortion is domestic, say of the wage differential variety, then a labor subsidy rather than a tariff on imports is the appropriate policy. A tariff would drive a wedge between international and domestic prices and impose costs on consumers, whilst a subsidy would allow consumers access to imported goods at international prices.

The economic costs of the IS strategy have been analyzed in detail for various economies. The standard analysis of the cost of tariffs, relating to misallocation of resources away from sectors in which the economy has a comparative advantage and the consumer welfare loss that protection imposes, is enshrined in textbooks. The IS policies pursued by countries such as India, with non-tariff barriers such as quotas forming important instruments of protection, inspired novel approaches to the analysis of costs of protection. That non-tariff barriers such as quotas generate rents to quota holders is also well known. The quota licenses, however, can be sold at a premium to those who are unable to obtain them. Quotas, however, are not the only source of rents, for rationing and controls over distribution of commodities too generate rents. Anne Krueger (1974) estimated such rents for the Turkish economy to be around 15 percent of GNP. In the case of India her estimates suggest that the rents obtained from various sorts of controls over economic activity was around 7.3 percent of national income, in the year 1964. Such sizeable rents provide an incentive for economic agents to lobby for protection, seek ways and means, including bribery and corruption, to obtain licenses once quotas are instituted. Bhagwati (1982) christened these sorts of activity that divert entrepreneurial resources from productive activity as 'directly unproductive profit-seeking activities' (Box 3.6). Such activities yield private profits to the rent seekers but do not produce goods and services that would enhance welfare. In addition to this waste of resources, the IS strategy also tilts income distribution in favor of the upper-income groups and reduces employment opportunities as most of the protected industries tend to be relatively capital-intensive. Import substitution policies may also result in substantial amounts of under-utilized capacity, because of the

**Box 3.6: Directly Unproductive, Profit Seeking Activities**

The essential characteristic of the phenomena whose analysis has recently been undertaken, and many of which have been referenced above, is that they represent ways of making a profit (i.e. income) by undertaking activities that are directly unproductive; that is, they yield pecuniary returns but do not produce goods or services that enter a utility function directly or indirectly via increased production or availability to the economy of goods that enter a utility function. In so far as such activities use real resources, they result in a contraction of the availability set open to the economy. Thus, for example, tariff-seeking lobbying, tariff evasion, and premium seeking for gaining import licenses are all privately profitable activities. However, their direct output is simply zero in terms of the flow of goods and services entering a conventional utility function: for example, tariff-seeking yields pecuniary income by changing the tariff and hence factor rewards; evasion of a tariff yields pecuniary income by exploiting the differential price between legal (tariff-bearing) imports and illegal (tariff-evading) imports; and premium-seeking yields pecuniary income from the premia on import licenses. Thus, these are aptly-christened DUP activities. As an acronym, this can be pronounced 'dupe' activities, coming close to the spirit in which economists must view these activities!

J. N. Bhagwati, "Directly Unproductive Profit Seeking Activities". Journal of Political Economy 190 (5), 1982

limited size of domestic markets for the output of several of the protected industries.

These and other costs of the IS strategy have been analyzed and documented extensively (Little, Scott and Scitovsky, 1970; Bhagwati and Srinivasan, 1976; Little, 1982). Even so, it took several decades for many developing countries to modify or abandon the strategy, and many countries in Africa continue to pursue an IS strategy in one form or another. African tariffs during the mid-1990s were more than three times higher than those in the developing countries with the highest growth rates, and more than five times higher than those in OECD countries. In addition, more than a third of African imports encounter some form of non-tariff trade barriers. Admittedly, several African countries, though not all, have initiated economic liberalization policies in recent years. Even so, restrictions on trade in the form of tariff and non-tariff barriers and taxes on exports remain high. And both the growth and trade performance of SSA countries, with rare exceptions, pale into insignificance compared with that of developing countries in general and East Asia in particular. Following the failure of the WTO Cancun trade negotiations in 2003 there is the danger that protectionism may again spread in African countries. Countries may draw support for such policies not only from non-governmental organizations, ever suspicious of liberal economic policies, but also from influential commentators who express doubts about the impact of open economy policies on growth and development.

This zest for protection and the IS strategy, in fact, has its roots in political economy. Protection benefits specific interest groups, and principally the producers who possess the resources to lobby the political party in power — whose prospects of re-election may depend on its willingness to promote the interests of these producers. Thus the interests of the producers and the interests of the elected representatives who are able to supply protection coincide. Consumers who suffer the costs of protection are not able to wield countervailing power because they are too numerous and consumer lobbies are difficult to organize. And if the consumers are largely the poor, and lack the resources to lobby, they are unlikely to be able to reverse such protection. Consumers are either not informed about the costs of protection and, even if well informed, are usually powerless to act. Angus Maddison (1971), commenting on India's IS policies, succinctly noted that the IS strategy:

> *"...won support from the bureaucratic establishment because it added to their power, it was supported by politicians because it encouraged their patronage, it met no opposition from established industry because it did not interfere with vested interests, and it was supported by intellectuals who generally identified capitalism with colonialism. It aroused no opposition because it conflicted with no vested interests."*

Maddison might as well have been referring to the experience of many of African countries. Widespread corruption, poor governance and absence of institutional infrastructure in these countries are all a consequence of the pursuit of power by vested interest groups. It should, however, be emphasized that judicious IS polices do have

a role in promoting growth and development. They may provide the groundwork for developing competitive industries and sectors that can survive and prosper in a liberalized regime. Indeed, none of the analysts of the IS strategy have ruled it out of court nor have they advocated unrestrained free trade. As Bhagwati argues, the sort of IS policies suggested by Nurkse and Prebisch were market-oriented, utilizing import tariffs and export taxes where applicable, rather than widespread controls over trade. In the event, the sort of policies adopted by most developing countries was of the 'slash imports and grow variety' as Bhagwati (1985) puts it. This variety of IS ignores economic costs and benefits and concentrates on providing a ready-made market for entre-preneurs by cutting off imports. Policy makers should recognize the dangers inherent in the indiscriminate use of restraints to trade and interventionist policies of governments that usually complement trade restrictions and provide opportunities for rent seeking.

But what does a transition from IS policies to open economy policies entail? What precisely are open economy policies? Are open economy policies as opposed to the IS strategy effective instruments of growth and development? These and other issues have figured prominently in recent debates.

It is useful to discuss the strategy of import substitution (IS) strategy of industrial-ization that many developing countries pursued with vigor during the decades of the 1950s and 1960s, and until the 1990s in the case of India, for several reasons. First, the origins of the debate on openness and development lie in the IS strategy. Secondly, the IS strategy for all its shortcomings may have laid the foundations for the pursuit of open economy policies. Finally, it may be fallacious to argue that IS strategies and openness strategies are polar opposites. A judicious mix of elements of the two strategies may contribute much more to growth and development than the pursuit of one or the other on its own.

## Economic Liberalisation as Panacea

From the 1980s onwards, international development policy has witnessed a major departure from the protectionist, inward strategies of previous decades. A number of countries, principally the East Asian countries, shifted from an inward-oriented development strategy to an outward-oriented strategy around the mid-1960s. Another group of countries, including Argentina, Chile, Mexico, Turkey, Ghana and Uganda, veered towards an outward development strategy during the decade of the 1980s. These countries were compelled to abandon inward-looking policies, mostly because of the debt crisis in the 1980s which left them not only with heavy debts which they were unable to service and also deprived them of a source of funds required to sustain the inward-looking strategy. Added to this was the demonstrable success of the East Asian countries with outward-looking policies.

Early studies during the 1970s by Balassa (1971, 1978) and Little, Scitovsky and Scott (1970) had established that protection afforded to value added in most developing countries was exceptionally high and had created a bias against exports. Detailed case studies of specific episodes of import

substitution and outward orientation of several developing countries (Bhagwati, 1978; Krueger, 1978; Papageorgiou, Michaley and Choski, 1991) also substantiated the conclusion of the earlier studies that inward-looking policies do not result in sustained growth rates, where as open economy policies do promote growth.

Further corroboration of these conclusions is provided by recent econometric studies that utilize a wide array of data across a number of countries to test the relationship between openness and growth. These studies examine: the differences in price levels for a given basket of goods between specific countries and that in the US (exchange rate distortion index) and the volatility of the exchange rate over the years 1976-85 (Dollar 1992); an index of openness which is constructed on the basis of information on various aspects of trade policy including tariff levels, non-tariff barriers to imports and black market premiums for foreign exchange (Sachs and Warner 1995); and a set of nine indicators which measure the degree of openness including the ones covered in the Sachs-Warner study (Edwards, 1998).[5] Despite this heavy weight of evidence in support of the proposition that openness is likely to be a much more effective strategy for promoting growth than inward-looking policies there are voices of dissent. The controversy appears to center on the precise meaning of openness.

---

[5] These studies, which attempt to quantify openness in various ways and utilize regression techniques to assess the impact of openness on productivity and growth, also endorse the earlier findings that openness promotes growth.

## What does openness mean?

Quite often, trade liberalization is mistakenly equated with openness, resulting in much confusion and subsequently erroneous policy conclusions on the role of trade policy in development. The former is a much broader concept than the latter and includes a variety of factors such as macroeconomic stability as signified by low budget deficits, low rates of inflation, abolition of entry barriers to new investments, elimination of product and factor market distortions which drive a wedge between private and social opportunity costs, improvements in transportation and communications and technological change. Trade policy, however, figures centrally in all this because it is intertwined with domestic economic policies. Restrictions on trade not only result in misallocation of resources but also pervasive inefficiencies that in turn give rise to high inflation rates.

Trade liberalization in turn can be interpreted in several ways. One interpretation is that it is a policy that eliminates tariffs on importable goods and equalizes the domestic price ratio between importables and exportables with the free trade price ratio. A second interpretation is that it is neutral in the provision of incentives between the production of importables and exportables. A third interpretation, referred to as the second best liberalization, is a policy that replaces non-tariff barriers such as import quotas with tariffs (Greenaway, Morgan and Wright, 1998).

In a major study of trade orientation, distortions and growth in developing countries, Edwards (1992) develops a model which assumes that more open economies are more efficient at absorbing exogenously generated technology. Using nine indicators of trade orientation constructed by Leamer (1988) (Box 3.7), he shows for a sample of 30 developing countries over the period 1970–82, that more open economies tend to grow faster. To test the hypothesis, a conventional growth equation is used relating the growth of per capita income of countries to their investment ratio, their initial level of per capita income as a proxy for technological backwardness, and a measure of trade distortion. All but one of the trade distortion measures produce a significant negative coefficient, and the findings are robust with respect to the sample taken, the time period taken and the method of estimation. The findings are also robust to some of the alternative indicators of trade liberalization and distortion mentioned at the beginning. In Edwards' model, however, the only channel through which trade liberalization enhances growth is through the absorption of foreign technology. This is undoubtedly important, but there are other important mechanisms.

Recently Brahmbhatt and Dadush (1996) at the IMF have developed a speed of integration index based on four indicators: (i) the ratio of exports and imports to GDP (the Vamvakidis measure of openness); (ii) the ratio of foreign direct investment to GDP; (iii) the share of manufactures in total exports; and (iv) a country's credit rating. They then divide a sample of 93 countries into four groups — fast, moderate, weak and slow integrators — and find that the fast integrators include most of the rapidly growing East Asian exporting economies, while the weakly and slowly integrating group include most of the low income countries of SSA and some of

### Box 3.7: Measuring Macroeconomic Openness

There are several possible measures of trade liberalization or outward-orientation, and many investigators and organizations (e.g. Leamer, 1988; World Bank, 1987) devise their own measures. Some of the most common measures used are: the average import tariff; an average index of non-tariff barriers; an index of effective protection; an index of relative price distortions or exchange rate misalignment, and the average black market exchange rate premium. In 1987, the World Bank classified a group of 41 developing countries according to their trade orientation in order to compare the performance of countries with different degrees of outward/inward orientation. Four categories of countries were identified:

(i)  Strongly outward-oriented countries, where there are very few trade or foreign exchange controls and trade and industrial policies do not discriminate between production for the home market and exports, and between purchases of domestic goods and foreign goods.

(ii)  Moderately outward-oriented countries, where the overall incentive structure is moderately biased towards the production of goods for the home market rather than for export, and favors the purchase of domestic goods.

(iii)  Moderately inward-oriented countries, where there is a more definite bias against exports and in favor of import substitution.

(iv)  Strongly inward-oriented countries, where trade controls and the incentive structures strongly favor production for the domestic market and discriminate strongly against imports.

Most African countries classified in the list are in the moderately and strongly inward-oriented categories. According to the World Bank, this "suggests that the economic performance of the outward-oriented economies has been broadly superior to that of inward-oriented economies in all respects".

*Source*: Development Research Department, African Development Bank, 2003

---

the middle-income countries of Latin America.

The high performance Asian countries are perhaps the most spectacular examples of economic success linked to exports (notwithstanding the crisis in East Asia of the late 1990s). The economies of Japan, South Korea, Taiwan, Singapore, Hong Kong, Malaysia, Indonesia and Thailand have recorded some of the highest GDP growth rates in the world — averaging 6 percent per annum since 1965 — and also some of the highest rates of export growth, averaging

more than 10 percent per annum. It should be noted, however, that this success has not always been based on free trade and *laissez-faire*.

Japan and South Korea, for example, have been very interventionist, pursuing relentless export promotion but also import substitution at the same time. Indeed, in a meticulous study of *The East Asia Miracle*, the World Bank (1993) concluded that there is no single East Asian model. What is important for growth is not whether the free market rules or the government intervenes, but getting the fundamentals for growth right. Three policies are identified as contributing to the success of these 'tiger' economies: first, industrial policies to promote particular sectors of the economy; secondly, government control of financial markets to lower the cost of capital and to direct credit to strategic sectors, and thirdly, policies to promote exports and protect domestic industry. Crucial to all three policies is good governance. The World Bank concedes that most of the countries deviated from free market economics, but deviated less than other developing countries, and got the fundamentals right (such as high levels of human and physical capital accumulation).

The fact remains that none of these countries could have grown as rapidly as they did without the rapid growth of exports. Apart from the externalities associated with trade and the encouragement of domestic and foreign investment, they simply would not have had the foreign exchange to pay for all the import requirements associated with rapid growth.

The controversy on the impact of liberalization on growth, and the mixed bag of results empirical tests on the issue have produced are mostly due to differing interpretations of liberalization and openness. The debate seems to center on the following issues. Does liberalization, when interpreted to mean lowering of trade barriers alone, result in increased growth? What is the direction of causation? Does trade lead to increased growth rates, or is it the other way round? Is the empirical evidence in favor of the proposition that openness promotes growth seriously flawed? Is it the case that while openness may shift an economy on to a higher level of growth it cannot result in

sustained increases in growth rates over time?

Studies by Rodriguez and Rodrik (1999) elicited propositions that are pertinent to the current debate. According to them, "we are skeptical that there is a strong relationship in the data between trade barriers and economic growth at least for levels of trade restrictions observed in practise" (p. 38) and "we know of no credible evidence — at least for the post 1945 period — that suggests that trade restrictions are systematically associated with higher growth rates. On the other hand we believe that there has been a tendency in academic and policy discussions to greatly overstate the systematic evidence in favor of trade openness" (p. 39). Although they concede that there is no evidence to show that trade restrictions are systematically associated with growth they do suggest that there should be no theoretical presumption in favor of finding an unambiguous, negative relationship between trade barriers and growth rates in the types of cross-national data sets typically analyzed. Indeed, they suggest that "in the presence of certain market failures, such as positive production externalities in import-competing sectors, the long-run levels of GDP can be higher with trade restrictions than without" (p. 5). These arguments do amount to a robust critique of openness and a reluctance to concede that the IS strategy has had its day.

The main thrust of the Rodrigeuz and Rodrik critique of the studies that demonstrate a positive relationship between openness and growth is that the statistical variables and in some cases proxies for trade barriers employed by these studies are flawed. Trade-related variables such as tariff rates and the number of non-tariff barriers to imports in place alone seem to be either statistically insignificant in regression equations relating trade barriers to growth or they lose their significance when other variables are added in the equations. This should be of little surprise, as most trade-related variables such as average tariffs fail to fully capture the extent of protection to imports provided by trade policies.

Admittedly, reduction of trade barriers alone in the absence of other domestic policies designed to eliminate factor and product market distortions may do little to promote growth.[6] By the same token, macroeconomic stability and high rates of investment coupled with excessively high levels of protection may not promote growth either, as exemplified by the Soviet Union and India in the past (Bhagwati and Srinivasan, 1999). This is not to say that there is no positive association between growth and investment, but rather that it is the quality of investment that matters. This quality is influenced by the sectors in which it occurs, which in turn largely determines its efficiency. It is more than likely that the sectoral allocation of investment and its

productive efficiency will be relatively high in an economy that is open to competition both from domestic and external sources than in one which is closed.

Unfortunately, most critics of openness seem to equate openness with the mere reduction in trade barriers. Elaborate case studies of the impact of openness on growth, as opposed to studies based on cross-section regression equations, are at pains to emphasize the significance of domestic policies specifically designed to eliminate factor and product distortions, policies which promote macroeconomic stability, as well as policies which promote savings and investment. These country case studies, such as those by, Bhagwati-Krueger and Papageorgiou, Michealy and Choski, cited earlier, examine the impact of not only trade barriers on growth but also that of monetary and fiscal policies and exchange rates for a number of countries, before and after they liberalized their economic regimes. The significance of these studies is that openness to international trade and competition compels countries to institute growth-inducing macroeconomic policies and eliminate pervasive distortions in product and factor markets found in relatively closed economies.[7]

---

[6] Associated with the problems of quantifying trade variables are the problems of specification and validity of inferences drawn from cross-section regression equations. The results of cross-country regressions crucially depend on the time period to which the equations relate, sample of countries and variables chosen. As Bhagwati and Srinivasan (2001) observe "given these numerous choices, we can confidently expect that there are enough *de facto* degrees of freedom at an analyst's command to reverse any 'findings' that another analyst using similar regressions has arrived at".

---

[7] The so called problem of endogeneity, or the direction of causation between trade liberalization and growth appears to arise because regression exercises by their very nature are unable to identify precisely the impact of openness on these other factors which promote growth. Admittedly growth and trade may be coterminous, but it should be recognized that openness strengthens this relationship between trade and growth.

In fact, some of the variables employed in regression equations do pick up this influence of openness, or the absence of it, on growth. A case in point are the variables relating to black market premiums and state monopoly of major exports included by Sachs and Warner (1995) in their study of the impact of openness on growth. The Sachs-Warner study combines these two variables with variables relating to tariff rates, non-tariff barriers to trade and a variable identifying countries with socialist economic systems to arrive at a single dichotomous variable of openness.[8] The results of the regression estimates, incorporating the dichotomous variable, suggest that open economies do experience higher growth rates than those that are closed. Rodriguez and Rodrik question the conclusion on several grounds, mostly relating to the specification of the variables. One of the points of interest in their wide ranging critique is that none of the trade-related variables, when entered separately in the regression equations, are statistically significant and robust, but that the black market premium variable and the state monopoly over exports variable turn out to be highly significant in their impact on growth. They rightly conclude that it is not trade barriers but the black market premium and export monopolies that have an adverse

impact on growth. But the issue though is whether or not relatively high black market premiums are a consequence of relatively closed economy policies.

Admittedly trade barriers are but one of the several policies which generate black markets with high premiums. But openness is not about trade barriers alone; it encompasses a whole host of other policies including political conflicts, external shocks, and sheer mismanagement of economic policies. Arguably mismanagement of the economy is the chief culprit in the promotion of black markets. This form of administrative mismanagement is much more prevalent in closed as opposed to open economies, simply because of the absence of competition and the bureaucratic control of economic activity which tend to characterize closed economies. As discussed above, pervasive controls over economic activity, and a morass of rules and regulations, are the characteristics of countries which have pursued the IS strategy of industrialization and growth.

Liberalization of trade or openness does not require an all-out export promotion effort. What is required is a policy framework, one which is not biased in favor of either production for export markets or production for domestic markets. We owe this interpretation of openness to Bhagwati, who defines an IS policy as one in which the effective rate of exchange for imports (EERm) exceeds the one for exports and an export promotion (EP) policy is one where the effective rate of exchange for imports is equal to the effective rate of exchange for exports, and a super EP policy is one where the effective rate of exchange for exports (EERx) exceeds the one for imports. The effective rate of exchange is

---

[8] An economy with an average tariff rate higher than 40 percent, with more than 40 percent of its imports subject to non-tariff barriers, with a socialist economic system, with a state monopoly over its principal exports and with a black market premium for its foreign exchange rate exceeding 20 percent during either of the decades of the 1970s and 1980s, assume a value of zero and are classified as closed economies.

defined as the number of units of local currency received or paid for in international transactions.

The analysis postulates that if exports of a particular good were to receive a subsidy of 10 percent, the effective rate of exchange for the good would be the nominal rate plus the subsidy. Similarly if imports of a particular good were subject to a 10 percent tariff, the effective exchange rate for the good would be the nominal exchange rate plus the tariff. The two rates for exports and imports for the economy as a whole are estimated on the basis of average rates of tariffs and subsidies across the spectrum of exports and imports. The estimated averages may conceal large variations in incentives among IS and EP activities. Nonetheless the significant point to note here is that a neutral policy, defined as EP by Bhagwati, does not favor production for either the domestic import substitution activities or the export sectors. And the policy does not preclude tariff protection for import substitution activities; it merely requires that policy incentives offered for production of import substitutes should be matched by incentives for exports. Market orientation of production is guided by market forces, by factor endowments and by managerial as well as entrepreneurial endowments of the country. The promotion of all of these attributes is the hallmark of openness.

### None of the advocates of openness equate it with trade liberalization alone

Anne Krueger, one of the leading proponents of the virtues of openness, much in the same vein as Bhagwati, argues that "an outward-oriented trade strategy is one in which the development strategy itself is based on the growth of domestic economic activity in response to producer incentives that closely mirror international prices. That means that policy makers must focus on delivering adequate transport and communications, permitting imports for exporters at world prices, *and going well beyond simply the easing of restrictions on imports*" (Krueger, 1999, italics added). It is fallacious to equate openness, a much broader concept, with the narrowly defined removal of trade barriers. The weight of the empirical evidence does support the proposition that openness has a positive impact on growth, but removal of trade barriers or trade liberalization alone may or may not do so (Greenaway, Leybourne and Sapsford, 1997).

Trade liberalization orchestrated with other policies, however, is likely to have a sizeable impact on growth. Opinion is divided on whether macroeconomic stabilization policies and trade liberalization should be implemented simultaneously or one should follow the other. The case for simultaneous implementation of the two policies is that if macroeconomic stabilization is in response to a crisis, it may be easier to obtain the consent of interested parties to a package that includes trade liberalization. If stabilization policies result in deflation and unemployment, transitory though they may be, they may be attributed to trade reforms. The case for sequential reforms is that the costs of a combined package may be much higher than when they are implemented singly, and trade reforms may be credible if they are preceded by stabilization. Also, stabilization, which lowers the excess of domestic expenditures over incomes, may serve to reduce the real exchange rate and reduce the bias against exports inherent in the pre-stabilization stage.

These arguments, especially the argument that the move towards openness should minimize the transient welfare costs associated with it, are persuasive. In this context, a schema of sequencing of reforms suggested by Falvey and Kim (1992) is worth noting. The suggested schema runs through four phases:

- macroeconomic stabilization, including conversion of quotas to their tariff equivalents, export incentives and institution of new government revenue measures. In most developing countries tariffs constitute a significant proportion of government revenues and hence the suggestion that quotas should be converted to tariffs and new revenue raising measures should be instituted during the first phase of reforms;
- initial tariff adjustment and announcement of further adjustments;
- a second round of tariff adjustments and the beginning of capital account liberalization; and
- final tariff adjustments and completion of capital account liberalization.[9] This suggested schema of reforms fully recognizes that openness is not to be equated simply with trade liberalization. More to the point, it notes the transient costs of reform packages that

may be contained with a well thought-out schema of sequencing.

A further misconception often associated with trade reforms is the argument that whilst they may increase the value of output at a point in time they may not increase the growth rate.[10] This proposition is based on neoclassical growth models that demonstrate that the rate of growth of an economy converges to the rate of growth of its labor force measured in efficiency units (called the steady state), and increases in savings and investment may increase the level of income temporarily but the economy will eventually converge to a steady state. The models are based on several assumptions including diminishing returns to capital accumulation. As Bhagwati and Srinivasan note, if the tendency of the marginal product of capital to diminish to zero can be arrested per capita income can grow indefinitely and the neoclassical conclusions need not hold. This is precisely the message of the new growth theory or endogenous growth theory, which incorporates technical change and accumulation of human capital into the models to show that the marginal product of capital need not decline to zero. And trade liberalization can result in transmission of new production techniques and know how, all of which can serve to arrest diminishing returns to capital and promote growth.

In sum, the weight of evidence is in favor of the proposition that openness does promote growth. And whilst trade

---

[9] Falvey and Kim's schema is based on theory and accumulated experience with liberalization programs and they do state that these are broad guidelines which can be modified depending on the circumstances of the reforming economy.

[10] Bhagwati and Srinivasan (1999) refer to the former as the 'level effect' and the latter as the 'growth effect'.

liberalization is an integral component of openness it may or may not promote growth on its own, and least of impact favorably on poverty reduction. Trade liberalization does not necessarily imply faster export growth, but in practise the two appear to be highly correlated. The impact of trade liberalization on economic growth outlined above probably works mainly through improving efficiency and stimulating exports which have powerful effects on both supply and demand within an economy. There are several different measures of trade liberalization or trade orientation, and all studies seem to show a positive effect of liberalization on economic performance. Likewise there are several different studies of the relation between exports and growth and the evidence seems overwhelming that the two are highly correlated in a causal sense, but the relative importance of the precise mechanisms by which export growth impacts on economic growth are not always easy to discern or quantify. These and other propositions discussed here are relevant to an analysis of Africa's trade performance and policies.

## Evolution and Trends in Africa's International Trade

Having reviewed the evolving literature on trade and development and revisited the debate on liberalization and openness, the final section of this chapter examines the evolution and performance of Africa in the international trading system.

Available empirical data shows that, apart from the period of the Great Depression of the 1930s, the trend has been towards a rise in world trade for much of the 20th century.

This upward trend accelerated significantly after World War II. In 1900, the value of world exports was US$10 billion; by 1929, it had risen to US$33 billion; in 1950, it was US$61 billion; it jumped to US$278 billion in 1970 and to US$1,998 billion in 1980; by 1987, it had increased to US$2,431 billion. By 2000, world exports had skyrocketed to US$6,356 billion. It is easily verified that between 1900 and 1950, world exports increased at an average annual rate of 3.7 percent; between 1950 and 1970, exports rose at an annual percentage rate of 7.9; between 1970 and 1987, world exports increased at the impressive rate of 13.6 percent per annum and between 1987 and 2000, world exports galloped at the rate of 7.7 percent per annum. The share of manufactured goods in world exports has also changed dramatically since 1950. Between 1900 and 1950, the share of manufactures in world exports averaged 42 percent with primary products accounting for the rest. However, since 1950, the share of manufactured products in world exports has risen steadily, reaching 63 percent in 1968 and exceeding 65 percent in the 1970s. Conversely, the share of primary products (foodstuffs and raw materials) has declined significantly to about 35 percent of world exports.

### Developing Countries are Increasingly Marginalized in Global Trade

Since developing countries depend critically on primary product exports, and developed countries account for the lion's share of manufactured exports, it is clear that world trade has increasingly moved in favor of the developed countries and against developing countries. This is confirmed by evidence from the UN's *World Economic Survey* giving data on the relative export shares of the centrally-planned economies, the market economies of the North (developed economies) and the market economies of the South (the underdeveloped economies). Between 1980 and 1987, the share of world exports of the centrally-planned economies remained stable at 10 percent. However, the share of world exports accounted for by the developed economies rose from 63 percent to 71 percent, while the share of world exports accruing to the underdeveloped economies plummeted from 28 percent to 19 percent. Although developing countries (taken as a group) are being squeezed, it will be seen on further analysis that the sub-group that has born the main brunt of this burden consists of the Sub-Saharan African countries, since available data show that their share of world exports had shrunk to 1.3 per cent by 2001.

The progressive marginalization of the developing countries in international trade has been going on since the end of World War II, pushed along, *inter alia,* by the development of synthetic substitutes for natural raw materials and other technological advances leading to reduction in the raw material content of industrial products. Realizing this, and seeing that there was no salvation in the General Agreements on Tariffs and Trade (GATT), the developing countries agitated within the United Nations General Assembly for the establishment of the United Nations Conference on Trade and Development (UNCTAD) in 1964. UNCTAD has tried valiantly to produce achievements in the areas of generalized preferences and improved market access for the manufactures of developing countries. However, lack of cooperation from developed countries has severely limited its effectiveness in this area.[11]

More than in any other developing region, socioeconomic conditions in African countries deteriorated drastically during the 1980s, a decade that is widely regarded as Africa's 'lost decade'. Available empirical evidence shows that, in SSA, income per capita declined at an annual rate of 2.4 percent; Africa's real GDP per capita fell by 14.3 percent, investment contracted by 15 percent, while exports and imports declined drastically during the same period. By 1990, the total external debt of African countries was in excess of US$270 billion, leading to a crushing debt-service burden and further aggravating Africa's development challenges.

Africa lags behind most other regions on most indicators of growth and development. Judged by conventional indicators such as per capita income levels, life expectancy and literacy rates, absolute levels of poverty, the development record of African countries with rare exceptions is disappointing. Average growth rates of real GDP and real GDP per capita are not only lower than that achieved by other developing regions but they have also declined over the years. Average growth rate of GDP, which was as high as 4.9 percent over the period 1964–69 for SSA, declined to

---

[11] In the late 1970s, the North-South Dialogue underlined inequities in the international trade arena as one of the critical elements in the search for a New International Economic Order (NIEO). In 2004, the same issues persist, with the developed countries continuing to fence off exports of developing countries with tariff and non-tariff barriers to trade, and the income gap between the rich and the poor countries continuing to widen.

around 2 percent per annum during the decade of the 1990s (African Development Report 2003).

The relatively poor economic performance of Africa over the years is the subject of widespread debate with a welter of explanations and policy proposals. Africa's trade performance and policies have figured centrally in these debates. The impressive performance of the East Asian countries, most of which adopted aggressive export promotion policies around the mid-1960s, is often contrasted with the poor trade and growth performance of Africa.

The broad features of Africa's international trade can briefly be sketched. First, with exceptions, Africa's trade measured by its share in world exports, growth of exports and its export composition compares unfavorably to that of other developing regions. The share of Africa as a whole in world exports declined from as high a figure as 7.3 percent in the year 1948 to a low of 1.5 percent in the year 2001 (African Development Report 2003).

Growth rates of exports over the years may be a much more pertinent statistic in judging export performance, rather than export shares, which are influenced by the performance of star performers in world trade. The picture here is less bleak. Although the average annual rate of growth of exports of the region declined from 4.7 percent during the years 1964–69 to around 1.4 percent during the 1980s, it appears to have reached a high of 5.5 percent during the latter half of the decade of the 1990s before declining to around 4 percent in the years 2000–01 (Figure 3.1). The superior performance of the region since the mid-1990s may

reflect the impact of the liberalization policies adopted by several African countries, including Mozambique, Uganda and Ghana. Most of these countries registered above-average growth rates in their exports. Even so, the performance of the region as a whole compares poorly with that of the East Asian countries whose exports grew at an annual average rate per annum of 11 percent, and China that posted the highest rate of growth of exports amongst all regions at 11.4 percent per annum during the decade of the 1990s.

The other features of Africa's exports are the heavy concentration in a few products, principally agricultural products and minerals, and the orientation of much of its trade towards the EU (Figures 3.2 and 3.3). Although the share of manufactures in total merchandise trade has steadily increased in the case of most African countries, agriculture and food continue to be the main export earners. The share of manufactures, which accounted for 14.7 percent of total merchandise exports during the period 1962–69 had increased to around 33 percent by the end of the year 2000. The share of food and agricultural products declined from around 50 percent to around 21 percent over the same period. But these aggregate average figures for SSA conceal the wide variations between countries. South Africa and Mauritius weigh heavily in the category of exports of manufactures. In the case of most others, such as Kenya, Uganda, Côte d'Ivoire, agriculture and food account for relatively large shares of their exports. The composition of African exports is markedly different from that of the East Asian countries whose exports consist mostly of manufactures. The Hirschman concentration index which

## Figure 3.1:  Growth Rates of Exports

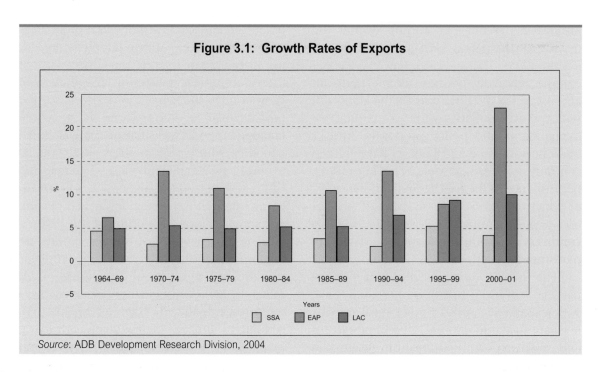

*Source*: ADB Development Research Division, 2004

## Figure 3.2:  Composition of Exports, 2001

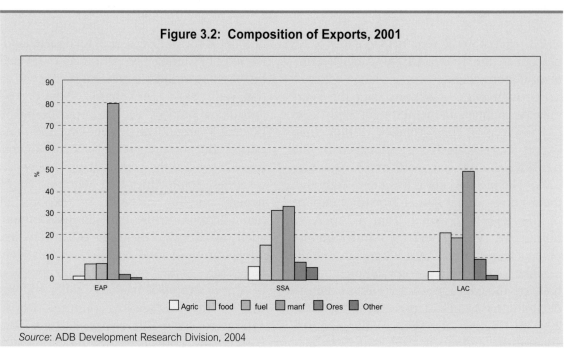

*Source*: ADB Development Research Division, 2004

measures the relative importance of individual products in a country's exports was around 0.49 for SSA countries which compares with 0.15 for middle income Asian countries and 0.11 for the OECD countries during the mid-1990s (Ng and Yeats, 1996).

In the year 2002, 51 percent of Africa's exports were to the EU and 17 percent to North American markets while intra-African trade accounted for only 8 percent of total exports of the region (Figure 3.3). The composition of Africa's exports and its heavy orientation towards a few major markets may be factors in its poor performance. Exports of several countries are concentrated in products that are growing relatively slowly in export markets. Heavy dependence on a few markets also increases the vulnerability of export earnings to fluctuations in demand in the importing countries.

The composition of Africa's exports is heavily in favor of primary products, defined to include processed and unprocessed agricultural products and minerals and appearing to conform to the Heckscher-Ohlin factor endowments explanation of inter-national trade referred to earlier. To recapitulate, the theory simply states that a country exports those products that use its factor endowments intensively. Adrian Wood and Jorg Mayer (1998) put the theory to test in a wide-ranging paper on the composition and prospects for Africa's exports. The basic premise of the paper is that manufactures tend to be intensive in the use of human skills rather than land and primary products tend to be intensive in the use of land rather than labor skills. Thus a country endowed with a relatively high level of skills to land would export manufactures and a country endowed

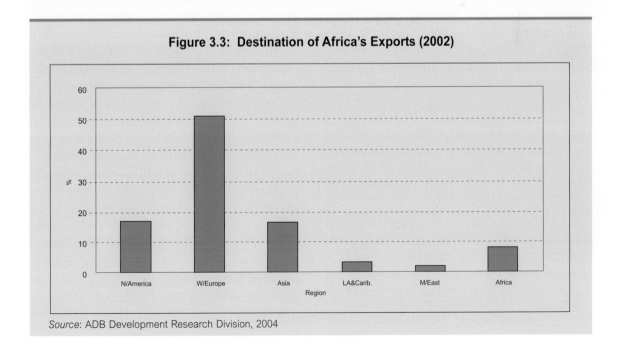

**Figure 3.3: Destination of Africa's Exports (2002)**

*Source*: ADB Development Research Division, 2004

with high proportions of land would export primary products.[12] The results of the exercise provide an explanation both for the small share of manufactures in Africa's exports (because of the region's low ratio of skill to land) and the small share of its primary exports that are processed (because of its low level of skill per worker). In other words, the factor endowments of Africa, that are rich in land but relatively poor in human skills, can help to explain the observed composition of its exports. This conclusion should, however, be qualified to take into account the diversity of the region. As Wood and Mayer note, there are wide variations in the proportion of processed primary products in total exports, share of manufactures in total exports and in factor endowment ratios across the 40 countries in SSA. Exports of manufactures of a dozen mainland countries were below the level that they should have attained given the level of their factor endowments. In the case of Burundi, Côte d'Ivoire, Gambia, Ghana, Malawi, Rwanda, Sierra Leone, Swaziland, Togo and Uganda,

manufactured exports accounted for only 5 percent of total exports — well below the 25 percent predicted by their factor endowments.

The failure of these countries to realize their potential for exporting manufactures resides in a variety of factors mostly related to policy failure, to be discussed later along with the policy proposals for Africa's export promotion, which follow from Wood and Mayer's analysis. It is sufficient to note here that the composition of Africa's exports in general conforms to theoretical explanations and cannot be attributed to policy failure alone.

### African Trade Performance in a Global Context

In global terms, Africa as a region, and especially SSA, has exhibited poor economic performance over at least the past two decades. Most African countries have the lowest export per capita in the world, which explains why they have the lowest GDP per capita, given the fact that in the globalized world of today export performance is one of the most important generators of domestic income. While some countries have been exceptions to the trend and performed very well in recent years (for example Mauritius, Botswana, and Seychelles) the regional performance is cause for concern. The dollar value (in current terms) of exports from Africa actually declined in the 1980s and rose by only 3 percent in the 1990s. The Africa region's share of world merchandise trade, in terms of both exports and imports, declined between 1990 and 2000 (Table 3.1). It is clear that Africa has not shared in the growth of world trade.

---

[12] Wood and Mayer test this proposition for a cross section of 115 countries of which 41 are in SSA, utilizing data for the year 1990. The results of the exercise suggest that the ratio of manufactured exports to primary product exports is positively related to the level of skills per worker and negatively related to the level of land per worker. The ratio of manufactures to processed primary exports is positively related to skill per worker and unrelated to land per worker. Also the ratio of processed to unprocessed primary exports is positively related to skills per worker and unrelated to land per worker. In sum, the proportion of human skills required relative to land increases from unprocessed to processed products and on to manufactures.

Table 3.1:  Regional Shares of World Merchandise Trade, 1990 and 2000

| Region | Exports (%) | | Imports (%) | |
|---|---|---|---|---|
| | 1990 | 2000 | 1990 | 2000 |
| North America | 15.4 | 17.1 | 18.4 | 23.2 |
| Western Europe | 48.3 | 39.5 | 48.7 | 39.6 |
| Asia | 21.8 | 26.7 | 20.3 | 22.8 |
| Latin America | 4.3 | 5.8 | 3.7 | 6.0 |
| Africa | 3.1 | 2.3 | 2.7 | 2.1 |

*Source*: WTO International Trade Statistics 2001

The Africa region accounted for just over 3 percent of world merchandise exports in 1990, but this had declined to a 2.3 percent share in 2000. Over the same period, Africa's share of world merchandise imports also declined. Annual variability in the value of exports was very pronounced in the late 1990s, declining by 17 percent in 1998 but rising by 27 percent in 2000, for example. The value of imports, in contrast, has been quite stable — negligible change throughout the 1980s, and a 4 percent increase in the 1990s.[13]

This variability in exports, as compared with imports, can also be seen in the sector composition of trade. Africa's exports are principally of minerals (mining and petroleum). Sector shares of export earnings are determined more by trends in world prices than changes in export volumes. In the early 2000s, the value of mineral exports declined slightly while the value of agriculture commodities increased slightly,

with manufactures remaining quite stable (Table 3.2). Africa's imports are predominantly of manufactures, and sector shares of imports are quite stable (Table 3.3).

One of the principal factors accounting for the decline in the value of SSA exports is that the world prices of many of the primary commodities they export have declined. Primary commodities dominate African exports. While the export prices of primary commodities overall held their value in the 1990s, this was driven largely by increased world prices for timber and crude petroleum. World prices for many products important to Africa declined between 1990 and 2000: cocoa by 29 percent, sugar by 26 percent, coffee by 9 percent, cotton by 28 percent and copper by 32 percent (while minerals overall declined by 14 percent).[14]

Although primary commodity prices overall recovered in the early 2000s, prices of some commodities important to Africa continued to decline (Table 3.4). For example,

---

[13] Data from World Trade Organization, International Trade Statistics 2001 (Geneva: WTO), p77.

[14] Derived from *ibid*, p212.

### Table 3.2:  Composition of Regional Exports (Sector % Share in Regional Total)

| Region | Agriculture | | Minerals | | Manufactures | |
|---|---|---|---|---|---|---|
| | 2000 | 2002 | 2000 | 2002 | 2000 | 2002 |
| North America | 10 | 10.7 | 7.2 | 7.2 | 78 | 76.9 |
| Western Europe | 9.4 | 9.4 | 7.1 | 6.9 | 80.3 | 80.7 |
| Asia | 6.5 | 6.6 | 7 | 7.1 | 84.2 | 83.6 |
| Latin America | 18.4 | 19.3 | 20.5 | 20.3 | 60.5 | 59.5 |
| Africa | 12.9 | 15.8 | 59.7 | 55 | 24.6 | 25.2 |

Source: WTO (2001 and 2003) International Trade Statistics.

### Table 3.3: Composition of Regional Imports (Sector % Share in Regional Total)

| Region | Agriculture | | Minerals | | Manufactures | |
|---|---|---|---|---|---|---|
| | 1999 | 2002 | 1999 | 2002 | 1999 | 2002 |
| North America | 6.3 | 6.2 | 9 | 11.2 | 80.5 | 78.5 |
| Western Europe | 11 | 10.2 | 8.2 | 10.7 | 77.2 | 75.7 |
| Asia | 10.6 | 9.5 | 14.5 | 16.9 | 72.5 | 71.1 |
| Latin America | 9.6 | 9.8 | 9.1 | 10.9 | 78 | 76.3 |
| Africa | 16.6 | 15.9 | 10.1 | 10.8 | 70.2 | 70.9 |

*Source*: WTO (2001 and 2003) International Trade Statistics.

between 1995 and 2002, prices of cotton, sugar and copper lost almost half of their value while coffee prices collapsed to almost a third of their 1995 value. On the other hand, exporters of cocoa and tea will have seen some recovery, while oil prices showed the largest increase. Even where the trend in prices is upward, Table 3.4 highlights the extreme variations in commodity prices from one year to the next. This variability in prices is the principal cause of instability of African export earnings. Exporters of sugar to the EU under the Sugar Protocol are protected from this instability, as they are allowed to export a quota at a guaranteed European price (well above the world price). This is a significant benefit to countries such as Mauritius, for example, and a benefit to other countries such as Madagascar and Côte d'Ivoire.

Only those countries with high shares of manufactures in their exports are relatively protected from unstable export earnings,

**Table 3.4: Trends in Primary Commodity Export Prices (1995 = 100)**

| Commodity | 1998 | 2000 | 2001 | 2002 |
|---|---|---|---|---|
| All Primary | 79 | 116 | 106 | 106 |
| Food and Beverages | 89 | 77 | 78 | 79 |
|      Cereals | 79 | 67 | 70 | 80 |
|      Sugar | 73 | 66 | 67 | 56 |
|      Coffee | 82 | 50 | 35 | 36 |
|      Cocoa | 117 | 63 | 76 | 124 |
|      Tea | 145 | 151 | 121 | 109 |
| Agriculture Raw Materials | 76 | 81 | 77 | 78 |
|      Cotton | 67 | 60 | 49 | 47 |
| Minerals | 74 | 82 | 74 | 72 |
|      Copper | 56 | 62 | 54 | 53 |
|      Crude Petroleum | 76 | 164 | 141 | 145 |

*Source*: WTO International Trade Statistics 2003.

although they are operating in a competitive world market. Morocco is an example of such a country with relatively stable export earnings (Figure 3.4). South Africa is the only African country with a significant share of

**Figure 3.4: Morocco Trade Trends, 1990–2000**

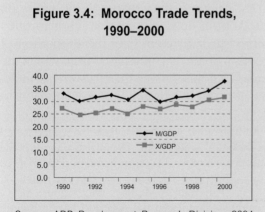

*Source*: ADB Development Research Division, 2004 Statistics.

diverse manufactures in exports. Mauritius and some North African countries have significant exports of textile and clothing manufactures, but these rely to some extent on preferential access to the EU. Other countries, such as Lesotho and Kenya, have increased clothing exports to benefit from preferential access to the US under AGOA. In general, preferential access to developed country markets, especially the EU, has been an important feature of African exports. A downside of multilateral trade liberalization is that it erodes the margin of these preferences.

The African 'export problem' is not simply the general dependence on primary commodity exports, but the heavy dependence of most countries on a narrow range of primary commodities. Even in the late 1990s, 39 African countries still depended for more than half of their export earnings on just two primary commodities.[15] The collapse of world commodity prices in 1998 was estimated to be equivalent to a real income loss of 2.6 percent of SSA's GDP in 1997–98.[16] Commodity prices have not shown any dramatic sign of recovery in recent years. For example, world coffee prices in 2002 were below a third of their level in 1997. The implications of primary commodity dependence and the difficulty of diversifying exports will be addressed below. Zambia illustrates a severe case of dependence on a badly performing commodity — in this case copper — which has impacted unfavorably on the country's exports earnings and development prospects.

Although this chapter is concerned with Africa as a region, it is important to recognize the sharp differences between countries. In particular, a few countries account for most of Africa's exports. In 2000, only six countries had individual shares above 5 percent of total African exports (South Africa, Nigeria, Algeria, Libya, Angola and Morocco), and together accounted for almost 70 percent of African exports (in 1980 they had accounted for 76 percent of African exports).[17] Three of these are very dependent on oil and a fourth (Angola) on minerals more generally. There are other African countries that have had export success, but these are small countries (even relative to Africa) and their success is usually due to specific features. For example, Botswana has managed its diamond resources well and had a steady export performance, while Mauritius has benefited from preferential access to the EU for its sugar and clothing exports. The majority of African countries, however, are economically small and dependent for their exports on relatively low-value primary commodities.

### Regional Integration is Vital to Promoting intra-African Trade

Any discussion of trade and development within the African context would be incomplete without some consideration of the important question of regional cooperation and integration. Since the 1957 Rome Treaty establishing the European Common Market, regional trade Agreements (RTAs) in the form of Free Trade Areas and Customs Unions have become a key feature of international economic relations.[18]

The essence of a Customs Union is that it frees trade between members and imposes a common external tariff on imported goods from the rest of the world (see box 3.8). In a Free Trade Area, by contrast, barriers to trade are brought down within the Area, but there is no common external tariff. Countries are free to impose their own specific tariffs on goods from outside the Area, although often subject to agreement over the proportion of goods that must be purchased from within the Area. Customs Unions therefore *create* trade, but also *divert* it from lower cost suppliers to

---

[15] UNCTAD, Trade and Development Report 1999 (Geneva: UNCTAD) p33.

[16] Ibid. p. 29.

[17] WTO op. cit., p. 77.

[18] The WTO lists 76 that have been established or modified since 1948. The major ones are the European Union (EU); the North American Free Trade Area (NAFTA); Mercosur, covering Argentina, Brazil, Paraguay, Uruguay and Chile; APEC, covering countries in the Asia and Pacific region; ASEAN, covering South-East Asian countries, and SACU, covering countries in southern Africa.

## Box 3.8 Forms of Regional Integration

We may identify five main types or forms of regional integration or RECs, classifying them by a rising degree of intensity. They are: (i) Preferential Trade Agreement (PTA); (ii) Free Trade Area (FTA); (iii) Customs Union (CU); (iv) Common Market; and (v) Economic and Monetary Union (EMU).

*Preferential Trade Agreement*: A PTA is formed with the reduction of custom duties (mainly tariffs) on trade among members relative to those on trade with non-members.

*Free Trade Area*: An FTA involves the elimination of tariffs and quotas on the trade among member countries.

*Customs Union*: A CU goes a step further than the Free Trade Area. In addition to free trade within the union, there is a common external tariff (CET) against non-members.

*Common Market*: This is a CU that allows for the free movement of factors of production among member countries. Thus, it encompasses intra-union free trade, a common external tariff against non-member countries and free movement of factors of production (labor and capital) within the union.

*Economic and Monetary Union*: This is a common market in which there is a single currency and monetary policy, and in which major economic policies (particularly fiscal policy) are coordinated or harmonized. Often, there is a compensation policy, which involves transfer of income to poorer or disadvantaged members of the Union.

**Regional Economic Communities in Africa**

Regional economic integration has a long history in Africa. The South African Customs Union (SACU) was established in 1910 while the East African Community (EAC) was set up in 1919. The East African Community collapsed in 1987 but is now being actively revived. Currently there are 14 regional economic communities in Africa. They are: The Arab Maghreb Union (AMU) established in 1989; the West African Economic Community (CEAO) formed in 1972; the Economic Community of the Great Lakes Countries (CEPGL) established in 1976; the East African Community (EAC) formed in 1919; the Common Monetary Area (CMA); the Economic Community of Central African States (ECCAS); the Common Market for Eastern and Southern Africa (COMESA); the Economic Community of West African States (ECOWAS) established in 1975; the Mano River Union (MRU) formed in 1973; the Central African Customs and Economic Union (UDEAC) established in 1964; the Eastern and Southern African Preferential Trade Area (PTA) formed in 1981; the Southern African Development Community (SADC) formed in 1992 and formerly called SADCC, which was established in 1980; the South African Customs Union (SACU) formed in 1910; and the Indian Ocean Commission (IOC). In addition, there is the proposed continent-wide African Economic Community, whose treaty was signed in 1991 (the Abuja Treaty) and which is expected to be in place by 2025.

*Source*: Development Research Department, African Development Bank, 2003.

higher cost suppliers within the Union. The interesting question is always whether the benefits of trade creation exceed the costs of trade diversion.

Free Trade Areas also create trade, but the extent of trade diversion is likely to be much less, with the presumption that on narrow economic grounds, at least, Free Trade Areas are superior. For the same reason, Customs Unions are likely to be inferior to a policy of unilateral tariff reductions, and therefore need to be justified on other economic or non-economic grounds.[19]

De Melo, Panagariya and Rodrik (1993) suggest three channels through which regional integration could alter economic outcomes for the better (Box 3.9 discusses some of the benefits of regional integration). First, a regional trade agreement entails a larger political community that might lessen the scope for adverse discretionary actions by governments, and in particular restrict the power of growth-retarding political interest groups, unless politically powerful lobbies can form alliances across countries. Secondly, when a regional institution is set up better choices, *ab initio*, may be made than at the nation-state level, where policy-makers have to contend with existing institutions that accommodate factional interests. Thirdly, when participating countries have different economic institutions, policy-making at the regional level will entail a compromise between those institutions and may lead to a superior outcome for at least some member countries. For example, if a Customs Union adopts as its common external tariff, the average tariff of the Union, at least some members must benefit. Notwithstanding the potential political-economic benefits, the World Bank appears to be generally hostile to regional trading blocs because of their relatively inward-looking nature.

Up to now, the general experience of regional trade agreements in developing countries has been disappointing because they have been highly inward-looking and protectionist, with trade diversion exceeding trade creation. Typically, the existing ratio of trade to GDP has been high in the member countries and the ratio of trade with the rest of the world has also been high so that the scope for trade creation has been minimal and the potential for trade diversion has been great. In the Economic Community of West African States (ECOWAS), founded in 1975, the amount of inter-member trade is still less than 10 percent of total exports. According to Robson (1998), most trade-based integration initiatives in Africa have so far made little or no contribution to trade or economic development. Forouton (1993) concludes his study of regional integration in SSA by saying "the structural characteristics of the SSA economies, the pursuit of import-substitution policies, and the very uneven distribution of costs and benefits of integration arising from economic differences among the partner countries, have thus far prevented any meaningful trade integration in SSA". Of the seven or eight groupings in SSA, only SACU has achieved any noticeable degree of integration in the market for goods. Otherwise intra-group trade has remained limited and stagnant. This conclusion is echoed by the authors of many of the applied papers.

## Explaining Africa's Trade Performance

### Dependence on Primary Commodities Exports

It is obvious that, in general, prices of primary commodities, particularly tropical products

---

[19] For a more detailed discussion on the role of regional integration in development, see African Development Report 2000.

and food crops, fluctuate sharply in response to changes in global supply and demand. During the decade of the 1980s, prices of many primary commodities exported by African countries fell to their lowest levels since the end of World War II. Many countries in Africa depend on the exportation of a limited range of primary commodities. Some countries, like Angola, Gabon, Nigeria, Algeria and Libya, obtain the bulk of export revenues from oil. In fact, many African countries obtain over half their export earnings from only one or two primary commodities. In 1988, Uganda derived 100 percent of its export receipts from primary commodities while a further 16 countries were still dependent on primary commodities for over 90 percent of their export revenues.

As a result of this high dependence on exports, the typical African country exhibits a high degree of 'trade openness' which renders it unduly susceptible to external shocks. The adverse effect of this on Africa is increased by the continent's low market share of world trade. Indeed, Africa now accounts for less than 2 percent of world exports. There is thus an unfortunate asymmetry — because of its low market share, Africa has little or no influence on international trade yet because of its openness, it is highly susceptible to internationally transmitted shocks.

The situation is further worsened by the phenomenon of declining terms of trade, which became quite pronounced in the 1980s when the prices for many primary commodities collapsed. By 1989, average commodity prices were still 33 percent lower than in 1980 in spite of a slight recovery in prices in 1988. The World Bank estimates that the fall in commodity prices during the 1980s

cost SSA 15 percent of the real purchasing power of exports. All these factors combined to bring about a drastic fall in Africa's export earnings and a rising trade and current account deficit in the 1980s. In 1988, Africa's export trade totaled US$65.3 billion while its imports amounted to US$65.9 billion. Therefore, in 1988, the import surplus (or trade deficit) amounted to US$0.6 billion while the ratio of the import surplus to total export earnings was an approximately 1 percent. In year 2000, exports of goods and services totaled US$116.3 billion while imports amounted to US$106.6 billion. Thus, the ratio of export surplus to total earnings was 8.3 percent (World Bank, 2002).

It should be pointed out that the increasing marginalization of Africa in world trade has been aggravated by the excessive dependence of African countries on the European export market. In 1988, the European Community alone absorbed over 60 percent of exports of many commodities from Africa. Yet, intra-African trade accounted for less than 6 percent of Africa's total trade. This low degree of intra-regional trade compares unfavorably with Latin America (15 percent) and Asia (43 percent). With the industrialized countries placing more and more tariff and non-tariff barriers on the manufactured exports of developing countries and the attainment of a single European market, it is obvious that continued over-dependence on the European market will become even more unrealistic and counterproductive.

On the basis of the results of the statistical exercise which relates trade volumes to per capita income, population size and geography, Rodrik concludes that "the marginalization of

Africa in world trade is the consequence of two factors: first, Africa's GDP per capita has grown slower than other regions and second, the output elasticity of trade exceeds unity, so that as other countries have grown, their trade volumes have expanded more than proportionately. Taking the region as a whole, there is little evidence that trade policies have repressed trade volumes below cross sectional benchmarks, unless they have done so indirectly through their depressing effect on incomes" (p. 7).

The conclusion that trade volumes are low because per capita incomes are low may seem obvious. The significant questions, however, are: why are per capita incomes low in Africa; and have trade policies contributed to low income levels (as Rodrik suggests they may have done)?

It turns out to be that trade policies do exert a negative influence on income growth and, moreover, they are a significant factor in the considerable variations in trade performance between African countries. Figure 3.5 shows evidence of a basic relationship between the value of exports per capita and per capita incomes. Taxes on trade and black market premia both appear to have a significant negative impact on rate of growth of trade and to a lesser extent on trade shares of African countries. Based on the results of a variety of statistical tests, Rodrik concludes that "trade policies matter in Sub-Saharan Africa, and they matter both in determining the volume of trade and the growth thereof" (p. 15). Particularly significant in this context is the adverse impact of trade taxes including export taxes on trade performance.

The statistical exercises designed to explain inter-country variation in growth rates

**Figure 3.5: Relation Between Exports per Capita and GDP per Capita**

| Countries | GDP per Capita (2000–2002) (US $) | Exports per Capita (2000–2002) (US $) |
|---|---|---|
| Ethiopia | 94.9 | 6.8 |
| Burkina Faso | 220.1 | 19.5 |
| Uganda | 261.5 | 20.6 |
| Tanzania | 269.3 | 22.2 |
| Malawi | 168.5 | 39.1 |
| Kenya | 365.2 | 61.7 |
| Pakistan | 434.4 | 64.1 |
| Zambia | 321.1 | 80.6 |
| Senegal | 472.9 | 101.6 |
| Ghana | 288.5 | 102.3 |
| Cameroon | 558.5 | 130.3 |
| Nigeria | 321.7 | 152.3 |
| Cote d'Ivoire | 629.4 | 222.0 |
| Morocco | 1,193.3 | 254.5 |
| Algeria | 1,762.0 | 640.4 |
| Tunisia | 2,087.1 | 660.5 |
| South Africa | 2,595.5 | 700.2 |
| Thailand | 1,928.3 | 1,022.4 |
| Mauritius | 3,758.3 | 1,335.7 |
| Botswana | 3,303.8 | 1,538.9 |
| Gabon | 3,699.6 | 2,331.3 |
| Seychelles | 7,206.2 | 2,551.7 |
| United States | 35,442.2 | 2,606.0 |
| Korea | 9,406.5 | 3,326.3 |
| Japan | 33,925.3 | 3,415.4 |
| Malaysia | 3,793.0 | 4,060.4 |
| United Kingdom | 25,019.4 | 4,584.5 |

*Source*: ADB Development Research Division, 2004.

of SSA countries suggest that the most important determinants of growth differentials within the SSA countries are human resources (life expectancy), macro fiscal policy (public savings), demography (variations in the dependency ratio), export policy (export taxes) and a catch-up or convergence factor measured by the initial per capita income of countries. Macro fiscal policy and export taxes do determine the openness of an economy broadly defined, as discussed earlier. In addition the Sachs-Warner openness index, which takes the value of one for completely open economies and zero for completely closed economies, appears to exert a significant impact on growth in one of the equations, estimated by Rodrik, which omits public savings as an explanatory variable.

The implication of this finding is that the openness variable, while it may not exert a direct impact on trade performance, does impact on growth. And as growth is an important determinant of trade it has an indirect impact on trade performance, running from growth to trade. Policies such as excessive taxes on trade and overvalued exchange rates, which result in foreign exchange shortages, are the source of black market premia. And most of the econometric exercises on trade and growth report that black market premia have a negative impact on growth.

In sum, there is no escaping the fact that trade policies do matter for trade performance but they impact on trade performance indirectly through their impact on growth. This, in fact, is the message of the advocates of openness; trade policy alone may or may not yield the hoped for benefits, but they are an integral part of open economy policies broadly defined.

### External Barriers to Africa's Trade

Although the fact of external barriers to African trade has sometimes been contested, the historical experience of many countries and the reality on the ground testifies to the existence of various tariff and non-tariff barriers imposed by their major trading partners principally the EU. To assert that such constraints do exist is not, contrary to what critics seem to presume, the same as saying that external barriers are the *sole* explanation for Africa's poor performance in external trade. This view is contested by some World Bank economists (Amjadi, Reinke and Yeats, 1996; Ng and Yeats, 1996) who argue that the tariff barriers facing the African countries in the EU, the principal destination for African exports, are considerably diluted because of the Generalized Scheme of Preferences (GSP) and the EU's Lomé Convention covering the ACP countries.[20] Both of these long standing schemes provide substantial tariff concessions on a range of designated imports into the OECD countries under the GSP and into the EU under Lomé. The least developed countries, a group that includes several African countries, receive substantially higher level of preferences than other developing countries under the GSP. Although the preferences granted African

---

[20] The Lomé Convention expired at the end of the year 2000 and is replaced with a wide-ranging programme of assistance to the ACP countries. The non-reciprocal concessions under Lomé are to be replaced by reciprocal concessions to accord with WTO conventions. However, the Lomé tariff concessions are to continue until the end of 2008.

countries by the EU, for example, have appeared quite generous, *rules of origin* and other factors impede the positive impact that such trade concessions could have had on African economies (Mailafia, 1997).

It is also evident that tariff escalation does deter exports of processed goods from Africa. Tariff escalation occurs when tariffs on final processed goods exceed those on unprocessed raw materials. Such escalation increases the effective rate of protection, the protection afforded to value added on products subject to escalation in the importing countries. Such escalation limits the opportunities for exporters to diversify their exports into processed products and increase the value added content of their exports with beneficial effects on employment generation. This would be so especially in the case of African countries whose exports include a substantial proportion of unprocessed agricultural and mineral products. Following an examination of the structure of EU tariffs on 19 primary commodities exported by Africa, Amjadi et. al conclude that "tariffs do not appear to have been a major general constraint to the further processing and export of African commodities (provided the eligible commodities actually get 'due' preferences), although escalation — which would work against further processing — is evident in several 'MFN covered' chains" (p. 21).

This conclusion, though, is subject to qualifications. First, while all African countries receive full EU duty preferences on all stages of wood, rubber and leather, only the least developed and Lomé Convention countries receive full preferences for wool and cotton products. Countries that receive

GSP preferences therefore would face barriers to processing of cotton and wool yarn. Second, out of the 19 cases examined, only 11 (58 percent) receive full preferences on all stages of processing. Third, in the case of three products (ground nuts, cotton and wool), which are outside of the 11 commodities, preferences are extended only to least developed and Lomé Convention countries, with the result the GSP-eligible countries face a tariff on the processed stage of some goods as high as 10 percent or more (WTO, 2003). This could considerably increase the protection afforded to the value-added chain in the production of final goods in the EU countries, especially so, if unprocessed materials enter duty-free. As the World Bank economists acknowledge, "there are opportunities for OECD countries to improve market access conditions for some processed commodities and one way to do this is to extend existing preferences".

### Non-tariff barriers (NTBs) facing the African exporters may be much more of an impediment than tariff barriers

There is evidence that the extent of NTBs which include quotas, variable levies, voluntary export restraints (VERs) and restrictive licensing arrangements to control imports, facing the developing countries as a whole is much higher than that for intra-OECD trade. Approximately 17 percent of developing country exports (excluding petroleum) encounter NTBs, while the corresponding share for OECD intra-trade is 10 percent. Secondly, approximately 53 percent of developing country exports of textiles face restrictions while the coverage ratio for clothing is 63 percent. In contrast only 5 percent of intra-OECD trade on these items face restrictions. Again, exports of footwear from developing countries face restrictions that are 20 percent higher than that on intra-OECD trade.[21] Thirdly, it is noteworthy that the NTBs facing the African exporters are of a lower magnitude than those encountered by other developing countries. Only about 11 percent of non-fuel exports of African countries face NTBs as opposed to the 17 percent average for all developing countries. This is mainly due to the fact that most of Africa's clothing and textiles are not covered by the Multi-Fibre Agreement. The exception, though, is Mauritius, 88 percent of its textiles and clothing exports face NTBs in the US. Fourthly, food products exports from Africa face higher NTBs than manufactures (23 percent coverage ratio as opposed to 5.7 percent for manufactures). The ad valorem tariff equivalents of these NTBs in the EU and Japan are estimated to be around 50 to 200 percent or more. Finally, agricultural raw materials and minerals encounter relatively low NTBs, only about three-tenths of one percent on agricultural materials and around 6 percent for minerals and metals. In sum, NTBs constitute a much more significant barrier to Africa's exports than tariffs.

In general, however, both tariffs and NTBs for African exporters appear to be lower than that facing other exporters such as the East Asian countries. This, however, does not permit the conclusion that external barriers are of little significance in explaining the relatively poor performance of African exporters. Although because of GSP and Lomé, tariffs on exports of developing countries, especially those on the exports of the least developing countries, are low and in many cases close to zero, specific items of significance to developing countries face tariffs in excess of 100 percent. Such tariff peaks are concentrated in staple food products such as sugar, cereals and fish, tobacco and alcoholic beverages, fruits and vegetables, clothing and footwear. The Uruguay Round trade negotiations, resulted in the conversion of NTBs into their tariff equivalents may have actually increased the dispersion of tariffs around the average. As a result, tariffs that are more than three times higher than the MFN average are not uncommon in the Quad (Canada, USA, EU and Japan). The highest average for tariff for peak products is to be found in the EU with an average of 40.3 percent compared with an average of 7.45 percent for all products. It is estimated that elimination of the peak rates and quotas on imports from the least developed countries into the Quad would increase export earnings of the former by 11 percent or US$2.5 billion (Hoekman, Ng and Olarreaga, 2002).

---

[21] NTB and tariff protection on 54 broad classes of textiles and clothing products in the US is estimated to exceed 100 percent with protection afforded by NTBs accounting for a high proportion of total protection. The magnitude of protection in the EU on these goods could be of a similar magnitude to that in the US.

*It is obvious that peak rates and tariff escalation tend to reduce the real worth of concessions such as the GSP and Lomé*

Indeed, a number of studies have questioned the real worth of the GSP, which is a non-reciprocal concession afforded to developing countries. In the absence of reciprocity, which places these schemes outside the purview of the WTO, these concessions tend to be hemmed in by various qualifications and restrictions. First, once a developing country achieves a specified level of exports it is supposed to have 'graduated', and it is dropped from the scheme.[22] Secondly, exports under the GSP are subject to rules of origin, with limits on the import content of exports. Thirdly, in the absence of reciprocity and WTO rules governing these arrangements, they may be withdrawn at the whim of policy makers in the importing countries. Fourthly, as Amjadi et al note, the growth of regional trade agreements between OECD countries neutralize the tariff preferences provided by GSP and Lomé. This is so because intra-trade between members of the regional groupings is free of duties and NTBs, in the face of which, tariff preferences granted to developing countries do not amount to much. Finally, the most significant drawback of schemes such as the GSP is that they delay trade liberalization if not encourage protectionism in the developing countries. This seemingly perverse outcome may arise because export industries that enjoy tariff preferences in foreign markets are unlikely to oppose protection to import competing sectors. Policy makers can cater to the interests of the import competing industries, as they are not compelled to reciprocate the GSP concessions offered to the export sectors. Also the graduation principle governing GSP may deter exporters from increasing exports beyond the point that qualifies them for graduation.[23]

One other impediment to exports of developing countries, including Africa, is the heavy domestic subsidies — including export subsidies for agriculture — provided by the US and the EU for their own farmers and other producers. The failure of the Cancun negotiations resulted from the intransigence of the EU and the US with regard to the sizeable subsidies they pay their farmers. The WTO agreement on agriculture uses a 'traffic light' approach to categorize different types of domestic support policies. The *amber box* policies are subject to limitations, while *green box* and *blue box* policies, which are aimed at limiting production, are exempt from limitations. The *amber box* policies are deemed to be the most trade-distorting. According to the WTO (2003), total domestic support of the *amber* kind was around US$104 billion, of which the Quad countries accounted for 84

---

[22] The GSP scheme of the EU is due to expire at the end of December 2004. It is to be extended for another year and the graduation clause is to be applied only to the larger beneficiaries whilst the smaller countries will maintain preferences afforded to them.

[23] The case is forcefully demonstrated by Ozden and Reinhart (2002) in a carefully designed econometric study of the impact of GSP, as provided by the US, on trade outcomes of developing countries. The results of the exercise indicate that remaining eligible for GSP makes it less likely for a country to liberalize its own trade policy, and greater the export dependence of a developing country on US GSP, the higher is its resistance to trade liberalization.

percent.[24] The major products affected by the support measures include meat, dairy, cereals and sugar. Between 60 percent and 80 percent of exports of countries such as Benin, Burkina Faso, Burundi, Malawi, Mali, Rwanda, Tanzania, Uganda and Zimbabwe are affected by the domestic subsidies for agriculture in the Quad.

These small, EU-dependent, exporters are also the countries whose exports suffer because of the export subsidies, as distinct from general subsidies to agriculture, for their agricultural products offered by the developed countries. According to the WTO the total value of agricultural subsidies offered by member countries between the years 1995 and 1998 amounted to US$10 billion. Reduction of these subsidies would increase the world prices and benefit net exporters and also raise the incomes of the producers of these commodities. Net importers, however, would have to pay more for the imports of the commodities that now enjoy subsidies.

There is thus reason to believe that the sum of tariff and non-tariff barriers and various sorts of subsidies in the Quad countries do compound the problems faced by the African exporters. Substantial reduction if not elimination of these barriers should facilitate the expansion of exports from these countries. Even so, to take advantage of the opportunities for trade that an elimination of trade barriers could provide them with,

African countries have to set their own houses in order, by eliminating domestic distortions, and by improving the productivity and growth of their export sectors.

*Poor Infrastructure — High Transaction Costs*

Most explanations of trade performance pay little attention to the sort of infrastructure necessary for promotion of exports. In fact, these factors are not accorded a role in traditional theoretical explanations of trade patterns and performance. High transport costs could be as much a barrier to trade as tariffs especially for landlocked countries of which there a re several in Africa.[25] In fact, if transport costs are relatively high, they could translate into relatively high tariffs, as high freight costs increase the CIF value of imports and thus tariffs levied on the total value of imports.

We owe the identification of relatively high transport costs as one of the barriers to expansion of Africa's exports to Ng and Yeats (1996). Their estimates suggest that first, average ad valorem transport costs for all SSA exports (about 8.7 percent) were more than 8 points higher than the average tariffs on these goods in the year 1993. Secondly, there are wide variations in the incidence of transport costs across the region, depending on the type of goods they export. Thirdly, average nominal freight rates for African exports are

---

[24] The UN Human Development Report (2003) puts the total value of agricultural subsidies in the OECD countries at US$311 billion — that compares with the GDP of SSA at US$301 billion in the year 2001.

[25] Ng and Yeats report that in the year 1990 net transport and insurance payments averaged 42 percent of total value of exports for ten landlocked countries (Burkina Faso, Central African Republic, Chad, Ethiopia, Malawi, Mali, Niger, Uganda, Zambia and Zimbabwe).

consistently higher, with the exception of the oil exporters, than those on similar goods shipped by their competitors. For all SSA countries combined, ad valorem freight costs were about 20 percent above those of their competitors. Fourthly, transportation costs appear to increase with the degree of processing, with final products attracting relatively higher transport costs than unprocessed and processed goods. This sort of an escalation increases the effective rate of protection or protection to the value-added content in the industries in the importing countries, and has an adverse impact on processing activities in the exporting countries. This too may provide an explanation for the heavy weight of unprocessed and semi-processed goods in Africa's exports. These heavy transport costs have to be absorbed by the exporters — either by reducing wages or reducing their return on capital.

The proximate reasons for the relatively high transport costs faced by African exporters are mostly inseparable from the anti-competitive cargo reservation policies adopted by most African governments, which are centered around cargo reservation schemes for national carriers. Whilst the policy is intended to promote nationally-owned transport systems, its anti-competitive effect results in increased costs for exporters and importers. This policy is analogous to the infant industry argument for protection with all its attendant costs. It is estimated that freight rates would fall by as much as 50 percent if these reservation schemes were abandoned and transport were subjected to open competition. In addition to the negative impact of these cargo reservation policies, the technologically poor state of African transport

systems also serve to increase transport costs.

Transport costs are but one component of total costs of delivering goods to the external markets from the locale where they are produced. These other costs of transacting business are likely to be relatively high in the absence of developed communication facilities and access to credit markets. Such costs may deter both exports of manufactures and primary products. The thesis that high transaction costs may be a significant factor in the relatively poor performance of Africa's exports is substantiated by statistical tests (Elbadawi, 1998; Oshikoya and Hussain, 2002).

In sum, there are a variety of explanations for the poor export performance of African countries in general. These can be broadly grouped into three categories; those that attribute it to geographical factor, those focused on domestic policies and policy failure; and those that blame failure on the purely external constraints facing Africa's exports.[26] The problem though is that all these explanations tend to be interrelated. For instance, landlocked countries which are further away from ports do face relatively high transport costs and they have to cope with the barriers to trade imposed by neighboring countries. But landlocked countries could trade with each other and enter into agreements to facilitate mutually advantageous trade. Transport costs, although

---

[26] Policy formulation would be that much easier if specific weights could be attached to these differing explanations and to the extent of their impact on the poor performance of African exports. Econometric studies do, however, attempt to quantify the impact of these three categories, with varying degrees of econometric sophistication and coverage of countries and products.

tending to be relatively high for landlocked countries, are often much higher than they should be because of domestic anti-competitive transport policies.

Admittedly, external barriers in the form of escalating tariffs and non-trade barriers are a significant factor in the relatively poor trade performance of African countries. These barriers do not, however, seem to have deterred countries such as Mauritius and Botswana from successfully exploiting their comparative advantage, in clothing and textiles in the case of the former, and diamonds in the case of the latter. Nor did trade barriers deter the East Asian countries from successfully exporting labor-intensive products. In the final analysis, there is no escaping the fact that Africa's domestic economic policies are the primary obstacle to growth in the region's exports. These include a whole array of policies and other shortcomings, ranging from trade policies to the absence of institutions which facilitate trade, foreign direct investment and growth. FDI is closely linked to trade policies both in the ability of countries to attract sizeable volumes of FDI and in its efficient utilization to promote trade and growth.

## Summary and Conclusions

This chapter has reaffirmed the importance and centrality of external trade as a vehicle for overcoming poverty and attaining long-term sustainable growth in Africa. There are static and dynamic gains to be had from trade between countries, but there is nothing in the theory of trade that says that the gains are equitably distributed. The gains from trade to an individual country, based on specialization, may be affected by welfare losses of unemployment and terms of trade deteriora-

tion. In this case, complete specialization is not optimal. Trade liberalization and export growth seem to be positively correlated, and exports act as an engine of growth. How powerful the engine can be, however, depends on the production and demand characteristics of the goods being produced and exported. Countries specializing in the production and export of primary products do not perform as well as countries specializing in the production and export of manufactured goods.

The chapter discussed in some detail the strategy of import substitution and current debates on openness. We have seen that for all its shortcomings the IS strategy laid the foundations for the pursuit of open economy policies that we know of today. It may be fallacious to argue that IS strategies and openness strategies are polar opposites. The historical experience of nations shows that a judicious mix of elements of the two strategies may contribute much more to growth and development than the pursuit of one or the other on its own. It is also worth remembering that, historically, no country has ever developed on the basis of free trade except the United Kingdom, which was the first country to industrialize. The United States, the countries of Europe, Scandinavia, Japan and other successful countries in South East Asia all adopted various means of protection at one time or another. Trade liberalization can be an ultimate goal, but the speed and manner of liberalization needs careful consideration on a country-by-country basis.

Having said this, it is evident, in our globalized world economy, that nations seeking to live in the cocoon of autarky do so only to the long-term detriment of their own individual and collective welfare. Most developing countries are constrained in their growth performance by a shortage of foreign exchange and could therefore grow faster with more exports. However, orthodox trade theory ignores the contribution that export growth makes to the demand for output, and particularly in relaxing a balance of payments constraint on demand by providing the foreign exchange to pay for the import content of higher levels of consumption, investment and government expenditure.

Without doubt, an export-led growth strategy would help African countries overcome their foreign exchange constraints, which have been such a major factor in their stagnating economic predicament for more than two decades.

The imperative of reform and the path of openness are each dictated by economic prudence. For Africa and other developing economies, what is at issue is not whether to trade, but how and on what terms. Deepening and consolidating regional economic communities is also of crucial importance. The vital policy issue for Africa is whether regional trading agreements by themselves, in the form of Customs Unions or Free Trade Areas, can alter the structure of production in favor of commodities with more favorable production and demand characteristics. If not, greater freedom of trade will not necessarily be 'optimal', and protection may be required to acquire comparative advantage in new types of goods based on a judicious mix of tariffs and subsidies, on the lines practised by the successful South East Asian countries.

This chapter has also highlighted some of the factors responsible for Africa's poor export performance. While domestic economic policy inadequacies cannot be ignored, it is also obvious that external economic conditions have also played a significant role. Particularly in the 1980s, escalating external debt and crushing debt-service burden, worsening trade deficits, and the declining inflow of concessional finance and deteriorating terms and conditions of loans were a major obstacle to Africa's external trade. However, the issue of commodity trade seems to be the most fundamental. This is because it is invariably an imbalance in merchandise trade that leads to financing imperatives like borrowing. Specifically, any deficit in the trade or current account balance brings about the need to finance it either by external borrowing (leading to escalation of debt) or other non-debt creating financial flows.

To improve their export performance, African nations must therefore first address those internal factors associated with poor economic and political governance that have impeded macroeconomic stability. Such an export-oriented paradigm has to encourage those cultural and psychological attributes that could release those creative and entrepreneurial energies so central to export performance in Asia and other successful developing economies. But there is also the abiding question of the inequities of the international trading regime itself. African countries find themselves in the impossible position of, once having begun to open up their economies that they are suddenly up against an armada of external tariff and non-tariff barriers to their exports. Clearly, any effective future strategy that aims to put them among key players in international trade would have start from within; but it cannot be expected to end there.

## Box 3.9: Benefits of Regional Economic Integration

*Regional integration and development*

Regional economic communities are formed because of their expected benefits. An important feature of the higher levels of integration is free trade among members. Free trade is expected to lead to rapid expansion of trade among members, which in turn is expected to lead to rapid economic growth. These gains result from the dynamic effects of a Customs Union, which have been shown to overshadow the static effects, viz., trade creation, trade diversion and terms of trade effect. The dynamic effects, which are cumulative in nature, lead to growth. Indeed, the dynamic effects of a Customs Union are often described as the long-run consequences for the economic growth of member countries as a consequence of increased market size and exploitation of economies of scale, increased competition, learning by doing, and increased investment. There is evidence that the larger the Customs Union, the more likely it is to lead to growth, given its potentials to create a larger market for goods and services and the larger scale economies.

*Regional integration and trade*

In general, integration schemes allow for free trade between member countries, but restrict imports from third countries. The free trade element serves to enhance the size of markets whilst the tariff element impedes imports from third countries into the region. It is the expectation that the tariffs will induce the tariff jumping variety of FDI and the increased size of markets following an RTA will induce the market seeking variety of FDI. The received wisdom though is that the market enlargement effect is much more significant than the tariff effect in inducing increased flows of FDI. Furthermore, it is policies designed to eliminate distortions and liberalize trade and investment, which often either precede or accompany integration arrangements, which are likely to induce increased flows of FDI. Integration per se may have little effect on the volume of FDI members of integration schemes are likely to attract.

*Regional integration in Africa*

At the end of the year 2002, some 176 regional trade agreements were in force in the world economy. Developing countries accounted for 30 to 40 percent of all RTAs in force. African countries appear to have embraced RTAs with enthusiasm; there are about eighteen such agreements in Africa. Intra-regional trade of Africa though is relatively low, the highest proportion of regional trade to total trade was between members of the Union Economique et Monetaire (UEMOA) consisting of Benin, Burkina Faso, Côte d'Ivoire, Guinea, Mali, Niger, Senegal and Togo.

*Source*: Development Research Department, African Development Bank, 2003.

# CHAPTER 4

# Economic Reforms and Trade Policy

## Introduction

Having considered the role of trade in the development process and reviewed the evolution and trends in Africa's international trade in the previous chapter, here we look in more detail at questions of trade policy and trade performance. First, we consider the logic of trade policy reforms, and then we examine current trade policy in Africa, including bilateral and multilateral policies and the linkages between policy and performance.

The majority of African countries have liberalized their trade regimes quite significantly in the past two decades. Some countries began the process in the early 1980s, but most have only implemented sustained and significant reduction in barriers to imports since the late 1980s or early 1990s. The major trade liberalization reforms in almost all countries were unilateral — reforms made by the country acting alone. The policies were not implemented as part of an agreement with trading partners. However, various agreements with trading partners have 'locked in' the reform efforts. Most obviously, the multilateral negotiations during the Uruguay Round of the GATT that culminated in the establishment of the WTO in 1995 resulted in African countries making commitments to open trade policies. Numerous regional trading agreements, some of more substance than others, exist whereby African countries have agreed to more open trade

with other African countries. There are also special agreements relating to trade between groups of African countries and the EU and US. Trade and openness are now high on the policy agenda of most African countries. This chapter concentrates on the experience with trade reforms in Africa since the 1980s and African trade performance in the 1990s.

### Measuring Trade Policy Reform

In principle, any policy reform that alters the ease of importing or exporting could be considered as relating to trade. It is obvious that a wide range of policy instruments may be used to affect, directly or indirectly, the price and volume of trade, and there is no ready way of adding together various instruments. Furthermore, to evaluate trade reform one wants to be able to capture the effects on prices, from which one can then evaluate effects on volumes and impacts on the economy. It is quite easy to measure changes in tax instruments, such as tariffs or export taxes, and these have quite direct effects on prices.

While changes in other instruments can sometimes be identified easily, such as reducing quantitative restrictions or relaxing non-tariff barriers, the effects on prices can only be quantified with difficulty. Furthermore, instruments may be applied and altered at varying levels of intensity across different products, making it difficult to provide an aggregate summary of reforms, and even more difficult to evaluate the effect on prices and incentives. This is a major problem for African countries that have reformed complex trade regimes in a piecemeal manner.[1] Consequently, it is extremely difficult to produce comprehensive summary measures of trade policy reform for one country, never mind for comparing countries over time. A common and expedient approach in the face of this difficulty is to use relatively simple measures and acknowledge their weaknesses.

There is a large body of literature on theoretical representation and empirical measurement of trade policy reform,[2] but two relatively simple measures are used most frequently (Box 4.1). The first of these is the ratio of exports plus imports to GDP, often referred to as a measure of openness, but more appropriately considered a trade volume measure. As a country with a less restrictive trade policy is more open to trade, it could be expected to have a larger trade volume relative to countries with restrictive trade policies. Thus, across countries, this is a reasonable measure of openness to trade.

The trade volume measure has particular weaknesses that make it inappropriate as a measure of trade liberalization, i.e. inappropriate to capture changes in trade policy. One of these is that the measure of the

---

**Box 4.1: Measures of Trade Policy**

Many measures of trade policy stance exist in the literature. Some measures look at trade outcomes, implicitly assuming that these reflect policy inputs. For example, the standard openness measure (exports plus imports as a ratio of GDP) interpreted as a measure of trade policy assumes that trade volume increases in line with policy liberalisation. A better volume measure may be the import/GDP ratio, as one would expect imports to increase following liberalisation. Measures of trade policy, especially if they are aiming to capture policy changes, should try to capture the effects on relative prices for importables and exportables. Because of data limitations, such measures are not widely available for many countries. The most commonly used measures of trade policy are measures of protection:

- Nominal protection represents the price raising effects of tariffs. The most common measure is the simple average scheduled tariff, but the implicit tariff (tax collected as a share of price) is a preferable measure.
- Effective protection takes into account the fact that tariffs are paid on intermediate inputs, therefore raise production costs and reduce profitability of protection on the final good.
- True protection allows further for the fact that taxes influence patterns of production and consumption.
- As the data requirements to measure effective and true protection are high, the most widely available measures are simple averages of nominal tariffs.

*Source*: Development Research Department, African Development Bank, 2004

---

[1] See C. Milner and O. Morrissey, 'Measuring Trade Liberalization in Africa', (1999), pp. 60–82.

[2] A reasonably thorough review is provided in D. Greenaway and C. Milner, (1993).

denominator (GDP) can change for reasons unrelated to trade. Another important weakness, especially in the context of African countries, is that exports are largely determined by factors other than a country's trade policy, such as world demand and prices. There are other weaknesses, but these two are sufficient to show that the trade volume measure can change for reasons unrelated to trade policy, so it is unsuitable as a measure of policy reform.

The second simple measure of trade policy is to calculate some average of the scheduled tariffs, a measure of nominal protection. To assess the effects on prices, one would like to know the actual tariff paid (collected tariff as a percentage of the import price). This, however, will depend on other factors such as exemptions, preferences and evasion, and data are often not available. Although the scheduled tariff is not the actual tax paid on imports, one can argue that it captures policy as it represents what policy-makers intended. Furthermore, as one is averaging across all tariffs to get a summary, it is a reasonable summary of the policy intention, and changes should capture at least the direction, if not the degree, of policy reform.

The change in the average scheduled tariff is not a very accurate measure, but is indicative of tariff policy reform (Box 4.2). However, this is only one part of import liberalization, so it may not be good indicator of trade reform. Non-tariff barriers, such as import quotas, are not accounted for. These are important restrictions on trade in many African countries and their removal represents a significant liberalization, the effect of which is not captured by a measure

**Box 4.2:  Measuring Average Tariffs**

There are problems associated with averaging tariffs across all products. Ideally, one would want to weight tariffs on products according to the importance of the product in total imports. For example, a 20 percent tariff on products that account for a large share of imports should be given greater weight in the average than a 5 percent (or 60 percent) tariff on products for which there are negligible imports. Typically, however, the data required to construct weights is not readily available. A related problem is that some scheduled tariffs are redundant as there are no imports of the products to which they apply. To the extent that redundant tariffs are most often those at the highest rates, their presence will mean that the unweighted average tends to overstate the true average. As the unweighted average is simply the average scheduled tariff across the number of products listed, it tends towards the modal rather than the mean value and any bias of redundant tariffs is unlikely to be great. It is generally true that the pattern of unweighted average tariffs across countries will reflect the pattern of tariff protection across those countries.

*Source*: Development Research Department, African Development Bank, 2004.

of tariff changes.[3] As a quota is more restrictive than an equivalent tariff, the process of replacing quotas with tariffs is a liberalization of the import regime. Such a

---

[3] Changes in non-tariff barriers can be captured by measuring trade reform as changes in tariff equivalents. This approach also shows significant liberalization in Africa from the mid-1980s, see V. Ancharaz (2003).

process could give rise to an increase in the measured average tariff as the number of products subject to tariffs is increased. This would be misleading if the products subject to quotas initially had zero scheduled tariffs. As the average tariff measure does not account for this, one should look for information on changes in non-tariff barriers, especially quotas, to obtain a better picture of overall import liberalization.

Finally, it should be noted that the average nominal tariff is not an accurate indicator of the effects of reforms on relative incentives. As it is only an average measure of gross tariff protection on domestic output, i.e. the extent to which domestic producers can raise the price of those outputs, it fails to account for the effect of trade taxes on intermediate inputs. The effective rate of protection accounts for taxes on inputs and outputs, providing a measure of the protection afforded to value added (which more accurately captures the effect on production incentives. Furthermore, nominal protection is generally greater for importables than for exportables (which often have zero protection or are taxed), so that effective protection of exports is frequently negative and invariably less than that for import-competing goods. Unfortunately, the data requirements for estimating effective protection are reasonably demanding and such measures are not readily available for a large number of countries.[4]

*Natural Barriers to Trade*

Policy barriers, and especially trade policy, may be only a part (and often a small part) of the total barriers to trade, the various factors that increase the transactions costs of trade. Some recent literature has measured 'natural' or geographic barriers, such as those associated with distance, being remote or landlocked, usually focusing on transport costs as a major source of trade barriers and of effective 'taxation' of exports.[5] This latter issue can be very important for 'small' countries that have to bear the costs of importing and of exporting, i.e. they are unable to shift trade costs to foreign markets (as competition is intense from more favorably placed producers). It is likely to be the case for many African countries that even if policy barriers to trade are reduced significantly, substantial non-policy barriers remain, and these tend to discriminate against exporters. This is one reason why export supply response is often low for African countries.

Transport costs are one of the more obvious non-policy barriers to trade. It is a particular problem in Africa, not only for the many landlocked countries but also because most countries with seacoasts also have large interiors. One proxy for transport costs is to compare the 'cost, insurance and freight' (CIF) price with the 'free on board' (FOB) price of imports. As the former includes

---

[4] For example, Greenaway and Milner (*op. cit.* p. 92) list 25 studies of effective protection (published in 1990 or earlier), only four of which relate to SSA countries. The number of studies has not increased greatly since then.

---

[5] See, for example, C. Milner, O. Morrissey and N. Rudaheranwa 'Policy and non-Policy Barriers to Trade and Implicit Taxation of Exports in Uganda', (2000).

**Table 4.1: Transport Costs, by World Region, selected years**

| Region | cif/fob ratio | | |
|---|---|---|---|
| | 1980 | 1990 | 1994 |
| Sub-Saharan Africa | 1.112 | 1.115 | 1.157 |
| Asia | 1.093 | 1.086 | 1.086 |
| Central and Eastern Europe | 1.201 | 1.212 | 1.078 |
| Middle East | 1.124 | 1.103 | 1.108 |
| Latin America | 1.094 | 1.091 | 1.083 |
| Western Europe | 1.056 | 1.053 | 1.047 |

*Notes*: Figures are the ratio of cif and fob import prices, averages by region.
*Source*: Derived from IMF (1995).

transport, the ratio captures the significance of transport costs. For example, a cif/fob ratio of 1.2 suggests that transport and related costs are 20 percent of the fob price. Table 4.1 compares such ratios for various regions of the world in 1980, 1990 and 1994.

Two interesting patterns emerge. The first is that for all regions except SSA, transport costs (measured in this way) declined between 1980 and 1994 — SSA is the only region in which transport costs increased. In most regions except for Central and Eastern Europe, this decline was moderate, but by 1994 transport costs were less than 10 percent. The second observation is that, by 1994, SSA had the highest transport costs of any region. Such costs are a barrier to trade: they are equivalent to a tax on exports, making African countries less competitive, and they increase the price of imports (thereby conferring some natural protection on domestic producers).

## Trade Policy Reform in Africa

Since the 1980s, and especially in the 1990s, almost all African countries liberalized their trade regimes to some extent, and many countries reduced trade barriers significantly (especially restrictions on imports). In most cases, these trade policy reforms were undertaken unilaterally under the auspices of a World Bank program. Although the vast majority of African countries signed the Uruguay Round Agreement in Marrakech in December 1994 and therefore were members of the WTO at its establishment, the WTO has not been the driving force for trade liberalization in the continent. Typically, the bound tariffs countries committed to under the WTO are higher than the tariff rates they currently have. Similarly, although there has been a proliferation of regional trading agreements (RTAs) in the continent, few of these have been associated with significant trade policy reform. Consequently, in this section the focus is on unilateral trade reforms.

A broad picture of trade policy reform can be obtained by examining trends in tariffs. Although, as mentioned above, there are limitations of average tariff measures, it is the one measure that is fairly widely available for many countries at different points in time. Even still, the data are patchy. The data presented here are based on average (scheduled, unweighted) tariffs for as many countries as available covering three periods — 1980–85, 1990–95 and 2000–02 (Table 4.2). Where data were available for more than one year in any period, the average for available years is calculated. This indicates the pattern of changes in average tariffs.

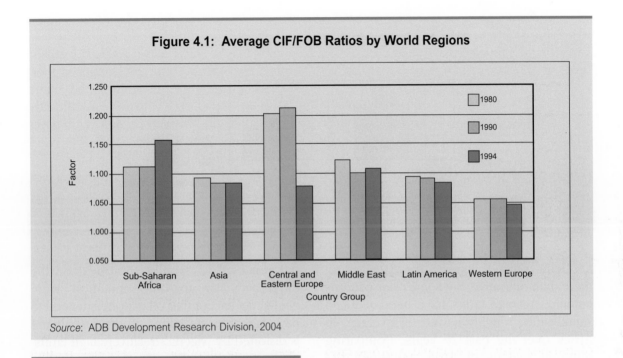

Figure 4.1:  Average CIF/FOB Ratios by World Regions

Source: ADB Development Research Division, 2004

**Table 4.2:  The Pattern of Tariff Changes in Africa**

| | Average Scheduled Tariffs | | |
| --- | --- | --- | --- |
| | 1980–85 | 1990–95 | 2000–02 |
| All Africa | 32.8 | 23.6 | 16.1 |
| Regions | | | |
| North Africa | 31.0 | 27.2 | 22.5 |
| West Africa | 38.5 | 22.8 | 14.2 |
| Central Africa | 30.0 | 21.7 | 16.7 |
| East Africa | 37.3 | 28.3 | 15.9 |
| Southern Africa | 19.5 | 19.7 | 12.7 |
| Export orientation | | | |
| Manufacturing | 28.1 | 20.4 | 16.5 |
| Agriculture | 40.2 | 22.5 | 14.5 |
| Mining/resources | 50.5 | 18.4 | 13.2 |
| Oil | 30.7 | 25.2 | 20.2 |

*Notes*: Averages reported are simple averages across countries in each grouping
*Source*: ADB Development Research Division, 2004

The figures in Table 4.2 are simple averages in three senses. First, for each country they are unweighted averages of scheduled tariffs. Second, within each period they are annual averages for each country (although often there is only one observation for a country in any period). Finally, they are simple averages, not weighted by trade, across countries in each of the groups (and are thus affected by individual countries that may have very low, or very high, values). African countries are grouped by region, and by 'export orientation' — whether it is manufactures, agriculture, mining products or oil that are the major export commodities. The classification by export orientation is useful insofar as manufactures and oil are more stable sources of export earnings than agriculture or mining.

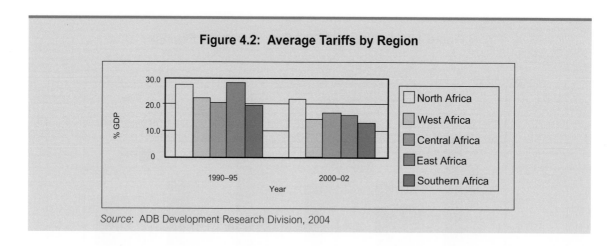

**Figure 4.2: Average Tariffs by Region**

*Source*: ADB Development Research Division, 2004

Being simple averages, the data are no more than indicative, but some clear patterns emerge. Average tariffs have been reduced significantly, roughly halved on average, in Africa over the past 20 years. Comparing different regions of Africa, although the overall variation or spread in tariffs has been reduced, progress varies. North Africa reduced tariffs the least, and by 2000–02 had the highest tariffs of any region (this is influenced by Tunisia having increased tariffs). Southern Africa has consistently had the lowest tariffs (and the trend is influenced by significant reductions in South Africa). Although West Africa appears to show the greatest reduction, the 1980-85 value is distorted by very high tariffs in Guinea, so as a region it is East Africa that reduced the tariffs the most.

Finally, we can observe some differences according to export orientation. In the 1980s, countries whose main exports were agriculture or mining tended to have high tariffs, whereas countries with significant exports of manufactures tended to have relatively low tariffs. By the 2000s, these

differences had largely disappeared: the differences by export orientation were negligible, except that oil exporters tended to have higher tariffs. Although the latter figure is distorted by Nigeria's relatively high tariffs, even excluding Nigeria the average in 2000–02 would be almost 19 percent. Nigeria did very little to liberalize its trade regime in the 1980s and 1990s, and its volatile pattern of trade is determined by world oil prices (Figure 4.3).

**Table 4.3: Changes in Average Unweighted Tariffs in Africa**

|  | Number of Countries | | |
|---|---|---|---|
|  | 1980–85 | 1990–95 | 2000–02 |
| Sample size | 23 | 32 | 26 |
| Average tariff <20% | 3 | 12 | 24 |
| Average tariff >30% | 10 | 7 | 2 |

*Notes*: Gives number of countries in each tariff range
*Source*: Derived from figures in Appendix Tables

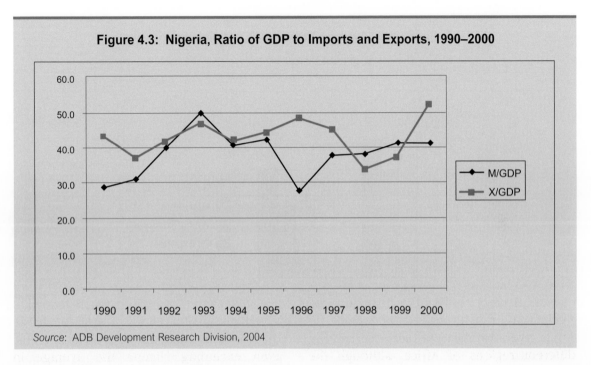

**Figure 4.3: Nigeria, Ratio of GDP to Imports and Exports, 1990–2000**

*Source*: ADB Development Research Division, 2004

The pattern of tariff reductions (trade liberalization) can be observed in almost all African countries, although the timing and extent of reductions varies across countries. Of the 32 countries for which data are available in at least two periods, only two (Tunisia and Zimbabwe) had higher tariffs in 2000–02 than in 1980–85, and one other (Sierra Leone) had higher tariffs in 1990–95 than in 1980–85 (with no data for 2000–02). Table 4.3 shows that whereas only three of 23 countries had average tariffs of less than 20 percent in 1980–85, only two of 26 countries had tariffs higher than 30 percent by 2000–02. In other words, the percentage of countries with tariffs above 30 percent declined from 43 percent in the early 1980s to 8 percent in the early 2000s. The share with tariffs below 20 percent increased from 13 percent to 92 percent over the same period.

**Table 4.4: Distribution of Average Trade-Weighted Tariffs in SSA**

| Average tariff | N=35 1990s | N=26 1980s | N=26 1990s |
|---|---|---|---|
| Under 10% | 6 | 3 | 6 |
| 10-19% | 21 | 2 | 14 |
| 20-29% | 6 | 8 | 4 |
| 30-39% | 2 | 10 | 2 |
| 40% and over | 0 | 3 | 0 |

*Notes*: The column N=35 refers to a sample of observations for the mid to late 1990s, whereas N=26 refers to 26 countries for which values in the 1980s and 1990s can be compared.
*Source*: Derived from data in WTO website.

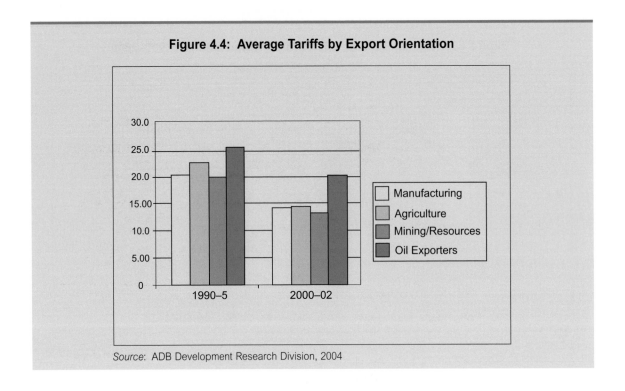

**Figure 4.4: Average Tariffs by Export Orientation**

Legend:
- Manufacturing
- Agriculture
- Mining/Resources
- Oil Exporters

*Source*: ADB Development Research Division, 2004

Table 4.4 reports data on average trade-weighted tariffs for 35 (SSA) countries only. By the 1990s, three-quarters of the SSA countries had an average weighted tariff under 20 percent, and only two countries had an average tariff over 30 percent. We have information to compare average weighted tariffs in the 1980s and 1990s for the 26 countries: 21 countries (80 percent of the sample) had an average over 20 percent in the earlier period, but only six (23 percent of the sample) in the later period. About three-quarters of these countries had average tariffs below 20 percent in the 1990s, suggesting the sample is quite representative of SSA. While this is not directly comparable with Table 4.3, a similar pattern is revealed so we can be confident that the use of unweighted tariffs

gives a fairly reliable picture of the pattern of change.

Table 4.5 provides more detailed data, reporting unweighted average tariffs for all goods, agricultural goods and manufactures (for years generally in the mid-to-late-1990s). Although tariffs are generally higher in agriculture than manufacturing, the gap is rarely large and there are only two countries with average tariffs in agriculture in excess of 30 percent (Burkina Faso and Rwanda). It is interesting to note that SSA averages are relatively close, by this time, to the average for all developing countries, higher than East Asia and Latin America, but lower than South Asia. It is also worth noting that for other regions tariffs are generally lower for manufactures than for other goods (all or agriculture). This

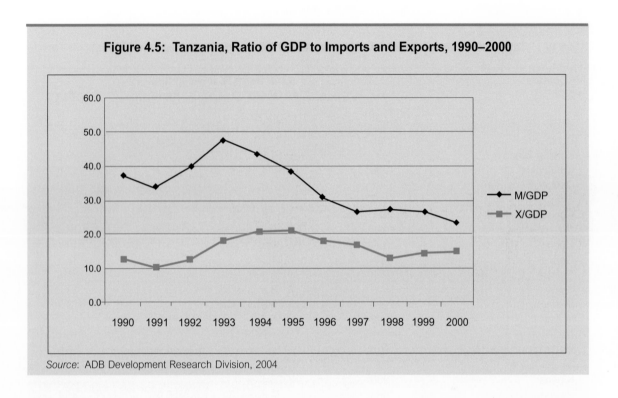

**Figure 4.5: Tanzania, Ratio of GDP to Imports and Exports, 1990–2000**

*Source*: ADB Development Research Division, 2004

suggests that African exporters are globally disadvantaged because they tend to export goods facing relatively high tariffs elsewhere.

Discussion so far has been limited to changes in scheduled tariffs. The broad pattern of trade liberalization is reflected in other aspects of trade reform, but comparative data over time for a large number of countries are not available. Table 4.6 gives some information on coverage of non-tariff barriers (NTBs) in a number of African countries (mostly for the 1980s). This shows quite a mixed pattern, with almost equal numbers of countries reducing and increasing NTB coverage ratios in the 1980s. In the three cases where data are available, coverage ratios were reduced significantly in the 1990s. Furthermore, the coverage ratios only

indicate the percentage of products affected rather than the severity of the restrictions. Other data and evidence suggests that the severity and use of NTBs was reduced significantly during the 1990s.[6] For example, Tanzania is a country that appeared to increase average tariffs during the 1980s because it replaced NTBs with tariffs, but the combined effect was to liberalize imports. Although Tanzania reduced tariffs in the 1990s, imports actually declined, probably because of a reduction in the aid finance available to pay for imports (Figure 4.4).

---

[6] See Judith Dean (1995).

### Table 4.5: Average Tariff Rates by Sector in SSA and Other Regions (1990s)

| Country | Year | Tariff Rate (%, unweighted) | | |
| --- | --- | --- | --- | --- |
| | | All Goods | Agric. | Man. |
| Benin | 1996 | 13.1 | 13.7 | 12.8 |
| Botswana | 1996 | 11.1 | 12.3 | 11.0 |
| Burkina Faso | 1998 | 31.1 | 37.0 | 29.1 |
| Cameroon | 1996 | 18.1 | 24.3 | 17.8 |
| Central Africa Rep | 1997 | 7.0 | 7.6 | 6.8 |
| Chad | 1997 | 15.8 | 17.0 | 15.5 |
| Congo Rep. | 1997 | 17.6 | 18.0 | 17.5 |
| Cote d'Ivoire | 1996 | 19.2 | 21.2 | 18.8 |
| Gabon | 1998 | 20.6 | 25.1 | 19.7 |
| Ghana | 1995 | 15.0 | 20.1 | 14.1 |
| Guinea | 1998 | 16.4 | 16.6 | 16.3 |
| Kenya | 1999 | 18.0 | 16.7 | 18.2 |
| Madagascar | 1998 | 6.8 | 6.4 | 6.9 |
| Malawi | 1998 | 15.7 | 15.6 | 15.7 |
| Mali | 1999 | 11.2 | 16.1 | 10.4 |
| Mauritius | 1998 | 19.0 | 14.9 | 19.5 |
| Mozambique | 1997 | 15.6 | 16.9 | 15.3 |
| Nigeria | 1998 | 23.4 | 23.0 | 24.0 |
| Rwanda | 1993 | 34.8 | 58.0 | 31.1 |
| Senegal | 1996 | 12.3 | 13.5 | 12.1 |
| South Africa | 1999 | 8.5 | 8.0 | 8.6 |
| Tanzania | 1999 | 16.1 | 17.4 | 16.2 |
| Togo | 1997 | 13.3 | 13.6 | 13.3 |
| Uganda | 1996 | 13.2 | 23.7 | 11.6 |
| Zambia | 1997 | 13.6 | 15.9 | 13.0 |
| Zimbabwe | 1998 | 22.2 | 27.0 | 21.7 |
| Averages for Regions (number of countries) | | | | |
| All developing countries (96) | 1993–99 | 13.1 | 17.0 | 12.4 |
| East Asia (15) | 1994–99 | 9.8 | 13.9 | 9.4 |
| South Asia (5) | 1996–99 | 27.7 | 26.3 | 28.0 |
| Sub-Saharan Africa (26) | 1993–99 | 16.5 | 19.2 | 16.0 |
| Middle East & N. Africa (11) | 1995–99 | 14.4 | 20.8 | 13.2 |
| Transition Europe (15) | 1996–99 | 9.6 | 15.7 | 7.8 |
| Latin America (24) | 1995–99 | 10.1 | 13.8 | 9.5 |

*Notes*: Agric refers to agriculture products and Man to manufactures.
*Sources*: WTO, IDB CD ROM 2000 and Trade Policy Review, various issues, 1993–2000; World Bank, World Development Indicators, 2000 and UNCTAD, World Investment Report 2000

**Table 4.6: Non-Tariff Barriers Coverage Ratios in Selected African Countries**

| Country | Coverage Ratios of non-Tariff Barriers (%) | | |
|---|---|---|---|
| | mid-1980s | Late 1980s | Early 1990s |
| Algeria | 67.8 | 93.0 | 9.5 |
| Burundi | 17.1 | 0.3 | |
| Cameroon | 18.1 | 24.3 | |
| Congo DR | 49.6 | 100.0 | |
| Egypt | 32.9 | 45.2 | |
| Kenya | 67.3 | 37.8 | |
| Madagascar | 56.7 | 1.7 | |
| Nigeria | 17.0 | 8.7 | 8.8 |
| Tanzania | 62.2 | 79.7 | |
| Tunisia | 76.2 | 63.7 | 32.7 |
| Zimbabwe | 2.5 | 93.6 | |

*Notes*: The coverage ratio refers to the number of products affected by NTBs as a percentage of the total number of products.
*Sources*: UNCTAD, Directory of Import Regimes 1994 and Handbook of Trade Control Measures of Developing Countries, Supplement 1987.

**Table 4.7  Range of Bound Tariff Rates in SSA Countries**

| Number of Countries with Bound Rates up to:- | | |
|---|---|---|
| in rate range: | Agriculture products | other products |
| 0–40% | 8 | 9 |
| 41–80% | 11 | 24 |
| 81–120% | 6 | 4 |
| 121–160% | 10 | 0 |
| >160% | 1 | 0 |

*Source*: Derived from data in WTO website.

*Multilateral Trade Reforms*

WTO membership will have long-term implications for African countries' trade policies, but has not had significant effects to date for most countries. The most immediate implications of membership have often been regarding legislation and administration, product standards and customs valuation. The majority of African countries did not offer concessions on tariffs or NTBs in the Uruguay Round, and the bound rates, which they did commit to, were generally higher than the rates they currently apply. This is illustrated in Table 4.7, where the majority of countries are seen to have bound rates above 40 percent.

The tariff offers related only to commitments on bound (maximum) rates. Most African countries made general commitments on agriculture, many setting a uniform bound rate above current applied rates. Table 4.7 summarizes the distribution across SSA countries of the ranges that bound rates go up to in agricultural and other products. About half the countries have bound *ad valorem* rates in excess of 80 percent on agricultural products, and twelve countries have a general bound rate on agriculture of 100 percent or more. The bindings are in general lower for non-agricultural products, but this may reflect the absence of a recorded general maximum tariff for other products for many of the countries.

There remains considerable scope for very high rates of effective protection from tariff escalation, and for policy reversals from less to more protectionist positions. However the specification of bound rates and the increased coverage of bindings may provide some constraints on future behavior. Indeed a few countries have identified quite low general bound rates, e.g. Cote d'Ivoire (15 percent), Central African Republic (30 percent), Congo (30 percent). Rates such as these may well signal commitment to open trade policies, and contribute to increasing private sector confidence and to encouraging inward investment. The bindings may also have more significance (be more constraining) in specific sectors.

### Bilateral and Regional Trade Reforms

Unilateral reforms have been the dominant influence on trade regimes in SSA in the last two decades. However, when average tariff barriers are quoted, it is possible that some of the reduction is due to changes in trade preferences and/or changes in the direction of trade (i.e. increasing trade with preferential trading partners). In the present context there are two possible sources of such liberalization of imports, namely imports from preferred intra-regional suppliers and/or from preferred extra-regional suppliers.

The liberalization and expansion of intra-regional trade is a potentially important factor as SSA countries display a high propensity to join regional economic groupings. Most belong to two groupings simultaneously, and a few to three. The overlapping nature of these agreements and the complexities this creates for rules of origin and preferences is an issue for future trade policy. For the moment, the issue is whether the commitments to liberalize intra-regional trade embodied in the protocols of the regional groupings have been a significant source of trade liberalization. The general consensus is that they have not been, which is in line with the evidence on intra-regional trade volumes; by 2000 only 7.6 percent of Africa's exports were to other African countries. A similar conclusion may be drawn about the impact of extra-regional preferential agreements on trade policy openness in SSA.

## Policy and Trade Performance: Why the Linkages are Weak

The presence of import barriers or restrictions creates an anti-export bias by raising the price of importable goods relative to exportable goods. Removal of this anti-export bias through trade liberalization should encourage a shift of resources from the production of import substitutes to the production of exports. Following trade liberalization, one would expect to see an increase in imports and exports, with domestic production of import-competing products declining. Typically, import supply from the rest of the world responds more rapidly than domestic export supply. That is, imports increase faster than exports, imposing adjustment costs, as jobs are lost in import-competing sectors faster than they are created in export sectors, and possibly increasing the trade deficit.

### Trends in Imports

The most obvious trade policy liberalization measures are reducing the average tariff, reducing the dispersion of tariffs and reducing or eliminating non-tariff barriers to imports. All such forms of import liberalization were implemented by African countries in the 1990s. The most immediate effect is to make it easier to import and, specifically,

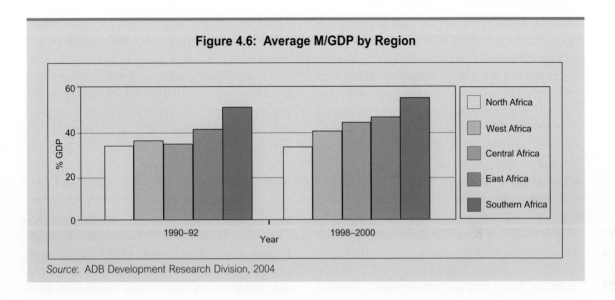

**Figure 4.6: Average M/GDP by Region**

Legend:
- North Africa
- West Africa
- Central Africa
- East Africa
- Southern Africa

X-axis: Year (1990–92, 1998–2000)
Y-axis: % GDP

*Source*: ADB Development Research Division, 2004

to reduce the domestic price of imports. One would therefore expect to observe an increase in imports following liberalization and this was indeed the case. For Africa overall, imports (measured relative to GDP) increased by some 12 percent during the decade of the 1990s.

All regions of Africa recorded an increase in imports over the decade, with the exception of North Africa (Figure 4.6, Table 4.8). Interestingly, North Africa is the region that reduced tariffs the least (proportionally) and that had the highest average tariffs at the end of the decade. Southern Africa, the region that had consistently the lowest average tariffs, also had the highest import/GDP ratio. This high starting point may explain why the percentage increase in imports was relatively low.

For the other three regions, there is no evident correlation of tariffs and tariff reductions to growth in imports. West Africa reduced tariffs the most and to the lowest level (of these three regions), but did not

**Table 4.8: The Pattern of Import Performance in Africa (Country Groups)**

| | Imports (%GDP) | | Change | |
|---|---|---|---|---|
| | 1990–92 | 1998–00 | % points | % |
| All Africa | 39.8 | 44.7 | 4.9 | 12.3 |
| Regions | | | | |
| North Africa | 34.1 | 32.1 | –2.0 | –5.7 |
| West Africa | 35.8 | 40.8 | 5.0 | 14.0 |
| Central Africa | 35.4 | 44.6 | 9.2 | 26.0 |
| East Africa | 41.9 | 45.2 | 3.3 | 7.9 |
| Southern Africa | 51.4 | 54.1 | 2.7 | 5.3 |
| Export orientation | | | | |
| Manufacturing | 33.2 | 37.2 | 4.0 | 12.0 |
| Agriculture | 33.2 | 35.1 | 1.9 | 5.7 |
| Mining/resources | 35.3 | 42.0 | 6.7 | 19.0 |
| Oil | 30.8 | 35.1 | 4.9 | 15.9 |

*Notes*: Change between 1990–92 and 1998–2000 averages is given in percentage points and in percentage terms.
*Sources*: Derived from data in Appendix tables.

have the highest import growth and actually has the lowest import/GDP ratio of the three regions. However, as the data for average tariffs are not weighted, whereas the data on trade performance are relative to GDP, one should not necessarily expect a strong correlation. There is some indication that imports are highest and grow faster in countries with low and declining tariffs, whereas imports are least in countries with relatively high (or slowly declining) tariffs.

Although oil exporting countries had the highest average tariffs in the 1990s, they also showed relatively high growth of imports, probably because buoyant demand for their exports allowed them to finance imports (Figure 4.7). Among the other groups of countries classed by export orientation, import shares and growth tends to be higher in those groups with lower tariffs (in particular, mining exporters tended to have the lowest tariffs but highest imports).

However, the performance of exports is likely to be a more important determinant of import growth.

Trade liberalization increases competition faced by domestic producers. Although some firms may fail, generating production and employment losses, others may respond by increasing efficiency (this is especially relevant for firms using imported inputs). There are potential gains for consumers who can purchase an increasing variety of goods, potentially of better quality, at lower prices. The immediate effect of import liberalization is losses in some sectors offset by gains in other sectors; the net impact is indeterminate. The longer-term impact will depend on how effectively the export sector responds to improved incentives.

### Export Performance

Although trade liberalization does not usually affect actual export prices (as these are typically determined on a world market), it

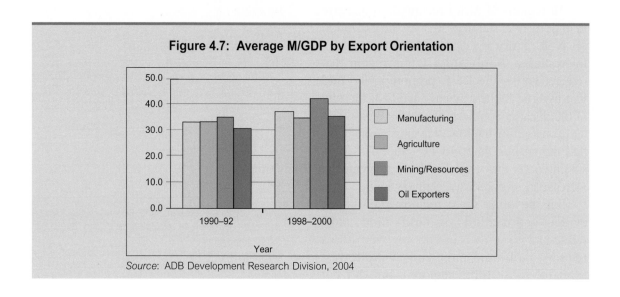

**Figure 4.7: Average M/GDP by Export Orientation**

Legend:
- Manufacturing
- Agriculture
- Mining/Resources
- Oil Exporters

*Source*: ADB Development Research Division, 2004

increases the return to exportables relative to the return to importables. Producers of importables face increased competition from cheaper imports, reducing the profits of those that remain competitive. The competitive position of producers of exportables is not adversely affected, and may be improved if they can access cheaper inputs and/or the trade reform included specific export promotion measures. Thus, the relative incentives to producers of exportables are improved. An adequate export response is usually sufficient to ensure that the net impact of trade liberalization is favorable.

Table 4.9 shows that overall export growth in Africa was quite strong over the decade, with the export/GDP ratio increasing by almost 20 percent. Interestingly, the lowest growth was in North Africa, the least 'liberalized' region, whereas the highest

export/GDP ratio (with moderate growth) is in Southern Africa, the most liberalized region (Figure 4.8). There are many factors affecting export performance. Domestic trade policy is only one, and rarely would it be the most important, at least in the short to medium term. Thus, one would not expect to observe a strong correlation between relative tariff reductions and relative export growth, although it is encouraging that export growth was generally strong throughout Africa. Only a few individual countries recorded sustained export growth in the 1990s, but these are mostly countries that reduced tariffs. Ghana is one example, even if imports may have grown even faster (Figure 4.9).

There was very little difference in export performance across countries classified by export orientation. All groups exhibited similar growth and their relative X/GDP ratios

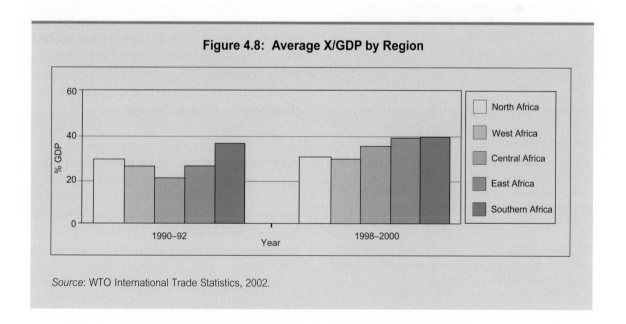

**Figure 4.8: Average X/GDP by Region**

*Source*: WTO International Trade Statistics, 2002.

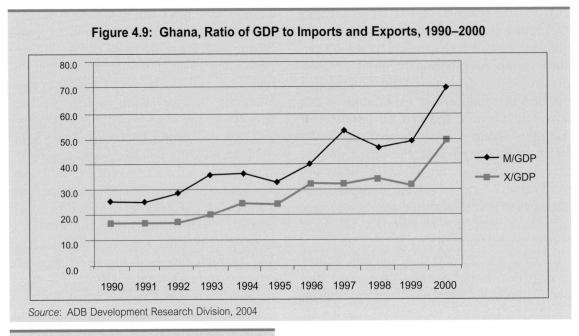

**Figure 4.9: Ghana, Ratio of GDP to Imports and Exports, 1990–2000**

*Source*: ADB Development Research Division, 2004

**Table 4.9: The Pattern of Export Performance in Africa (Country Groups)**

| | Exports (%GDP) | | Change | |
| | 1990–92 | 1998–00 | % points | % |
|---|---|---|---|---|
| All Africa | 27.3 | 32.4 | 5.1 | 18.7 |
| **Regions** | | | | |
| North Africa | 29.5 | 29.9 | 0.4 | 1.4 |
| West Africa | 25.3 | 28.6 | 3.2 | 12.6 |
| Central Africa | 22.2 | 35.2 | 13.0 | 58.6 |
| East Africa | 25.8 | 28.9 | 3.1 | 12.0 |
| Southern Africa | 35.5 | 39.1 | 3.6 | 10.1 |
| **Export orientation** | | | | |
| Manufacturing | 26.6 | 31.2 | 4.6 | 17.3 |
| Agriculture | 21.9 | 25.7 | 3.8 | 17.4 |
| Mining/resources | 29.7 | 33.0 | 3.3 | 11.1 |
| Oil | 34.4 | 38.3 | 3.9 | 11.3 |

*Notes*: Change between 1990–92 and 1998–2000 averages is given in percentage points and in percentage terms.
*Sources*: Derived from data in Appendix tables.

remained similar. As export earnings are the basis of financing imports, one might expect to see a relationship between export and import growth. This is evident comparing Tables 4.9 and 4.10. Regions with the highest export growth also tended to have the highest import growth, although no pattern emerges when countries are grouped by export orientation. The two come together in the effect on the balance of trade.

*Trade Balance*

In percentage terms, export growth exceeded import growth for Africa overall and in most country groups. However, as import/GDP ratios were initially higher than export/GDP ratios, this need not translate into an improvement in the trade balance. The trade deficit for Africa overall was almost unchanged, at just over 12 percetn of GDP at the start and the end of the 1990s. The deficit declined noticeably in North and Central Africa. In the former this can be attributed to a decline in imports (reflecting relatively high trade barriers), whereas in the latter it is due to the dramatic increase in exports (as a number of countries in this region emerged from political and economic instability during the period). The deficit declined slightly in Southern Africa, the region most dependent on imports, and was largely unchanged in East Africa. Only in West Africa was there a noticeable increase in the deficit. This is the region in which average tariffs were reduced the most, highlighting the danger that, following rapid liberalization, imports can increase faster than exports.

When we consider countries classed according to export orientation, only the oil exporters as a group show a trade surplus (and this declined slightly). In terms of the trade balance, the best performance was in agriculture-oriented exporters, for which the deficit declined significantly although it remained high. There is a suggestion of import compression in these exporters, as export/GDP ratios remain very low (exports would have to grow by some 40 percent, given constant imports, to eliminate the deficit). In particular countries, import surges are not unusual, so sustaining a reduction in the trade deficit is difficult if exports are flat (Figure 4.10). Exporters of manufactures reduced the deficit slightly. Exporters of mining resources displayed the worst performance, with the deficit increasing by over a third. As with West Africa, this is a

**Table 4.10: Trade Balance in Africa (as % GDP) (Country Groups)**

| | 1990–92 | | | 1998–2000 | | |
|---|---|---|---|---|---|---|
| | M | X | X-M | M | X | X-M |
| All Africa | 39.8 | 27.3 | –12.5 | 44.7 | 32.4 | –12.3 |
| Regions | | | | | | |
| North Africa | 34.1 | 29.5 | –4.6 | 32.1 | 29.9 | –2.2 |
| West Africa | 35.8 | 25.3 | –10.5 | 40.8 | 28.6 | –12.2 |
| Central Africa | 35.4 | 22.2 | –13.2 | 44.6 | 35.2 | –9.4 |
| East Africa | 41.9 | 25.8 | –16.1 | 45.2 | 28.9 | –16.3 |
| Southern Africa | 51.4 | 35.5 | –15.9 | 54.1 | 39.1 | –15.0 |
| Export orientation | | | | | | |
| Manufacturing | 33.2 | 26.6 | -6.6 | 37.2 | 31.2 | –6.0 |
| Agriculture | 33.2 | 21.9 | –11.3 | 35.1 | 25.7 | –9.4 |
| Mining/resources | 35.3 | 29.7 | -5.6 | 42.0 | 33.0 | –9.0 |
| Oil | 30.8 | 34.4 | 3.6 | 35.1 | 38.3 | 3.2 |

*Notes*: Columns give imports (M), exports (X) and the trade balance (X-M), where a negative sign indicates a deficit, all expressed as percentages of GDP.
*Sources*: Derived from data in Appendix tables.

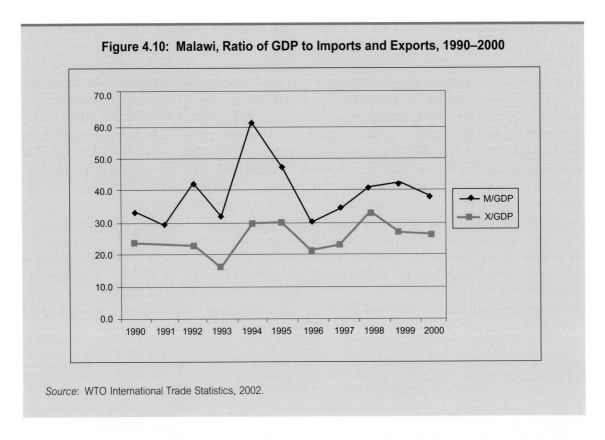

**Figure 4.10: Malawi, Ratio of GDP to Imports and Exports, 1990–2000**

*Source*: WTO International Trade Statistics, 2002.

group that reduced tariffs by the most and suffered the adverse effect of imports growing more rapidly than exports.

These results show that there is a clear danger from relatively rapid liberalization, as import supply is more immediately responsive than export supply. This problem is most pronounced for countries exporting primary commodities subject to weak and volatile world prices. Kenya, for example, has tended to experience an increasing trade deficit (Figure 4.11). Oil exporters have fared reasonably well and maintained a surplus as a group, although this was significantly reduced in the late 1990s (Figure 4.12) agriculture exporters have fared better than

may be expected (reducing the size of the deficit for the group). Countries dependent on mining exports, however, have not fared well in the 1990s. Whilst overall, it would be wrong to conclude that Africa has not gained from trade liberalization in the 1990s, it is true that the export supply response has been a major constraint in many countries. This is one reason why trade reforms may not have delivered the growth dividend anticipated.

*Trade and Growth: The Importance of Exports*

The empirical evidence on the relationship between trade and economic growth can be quite confusing, as often studies are writing

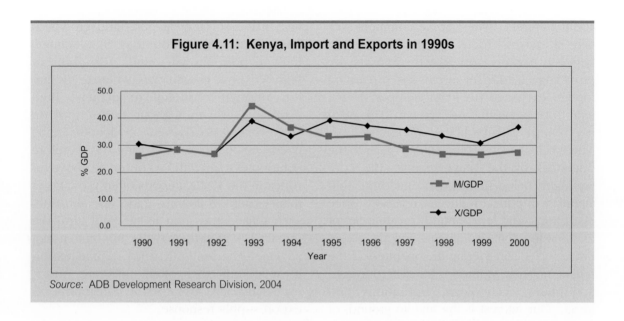

**Figure 4.11:  Kenya, Import and Exports in 1990s**

*Source*:  ADB Development Research Division, 2004

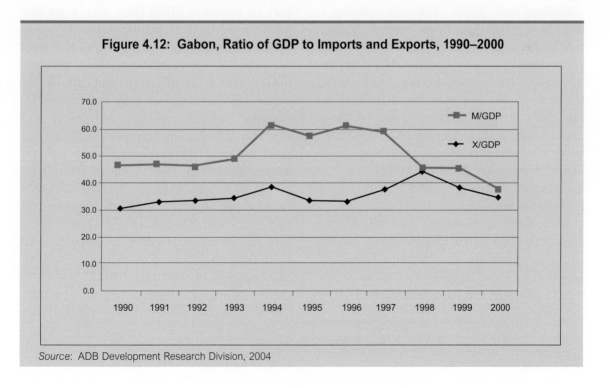

**Figure 4.12:  Gabon, Ratio of GDP to Imports and Exports, 1990–2000**

*Source*:  ADB Development Research Division, 2004

about different issues. Some commentators take a narrow focus on the association between exports and growth. Exports, by providing a market for surplus and by earning foreign exchange (to finance imports), will tend to be associated with growth. This need not require a very liberal import regime. Nevertheless, many commentators refer to the openness of the trade regime, the core argument being that minimizing protection against imports reduces relative price distortions and encourages production of exportables. Some commentators take a very broad focus, considering the openness of the regime not only to imports but also to foreign investment, technology, institutions and ideas.[7] Our interest is the middle ground, of the link between trade policy and growth.

There is very strong evidence that trade is associated with growth, although causality is difficult to prove. Rapidly growing economies will increase their trade, but for very large economies there may not be a big effect on trade/GDP ratios. Initially, it is the demand for imports that increases, but there may be pressure to expand exports to pay for these imports (again, it is usually only very large economies that can finance a sustained trade deficit with capital flows). But this begs the question of where the rapid growth comes from in the first place.

For small economies, and all African economies are small in this sense, export expansion can be the driver of growth. Uganda is an example of a country for which this was the case (Figure 4.13). The

evidence associating exports and growth is also quite strong. Countries that achieve high export growth rates also achieve high economic growth rates, whereas it is rare for a small economy to achieve high economic growth without export growth. However, it is not so clearly evident that trade liberalization increases exports and therefore contributes to growth.[8] As observed above for Africa in the 1990s, imports often grow faster than exports following trade liberalization, such that in the short to medium term the impact on growth may be minimal if not adverse. The long-run gains require export growth, but this often fails in Africa, especially SSA, because of constraints on export supply response.

There are a number of reasons why the beneficial impact of trade policy on growth may be muted in Africa (Box 4.3). A general problem is that there is a weak link between unilateral trade policy reforms and the effect on export trade. Domestic policy reforms have their direct effect on imports, while export performance is largely determined by external factors, notably world prices and demand. In the latter respect, multilateral (and regional) trade liberalization can be important because it increases countries' access to foreign markets. Specific concerns relate to the structure of African exports, and these are most relevant for SSA countries (as few of these are significant exporters of manufactures). First, SSA countries relative endowments of land and natural resources result in export dependency on primary commodities, as shown above. On the one

---

[7] A good example of the broad scope approach is D. Rodrik (1999).

[8] For a review of the evidence see D. Greenaway, C. W. Morgan and P. Wright (1997).

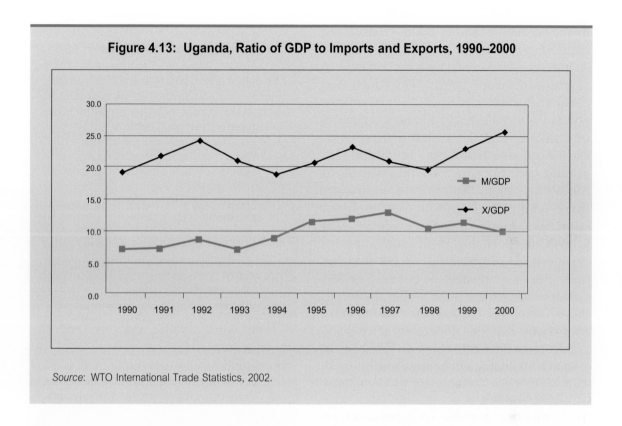

**Figure 4.13: Uganda, Ratio of GDP to Imports and Exports, 1990–2000**

*Source*: WTO International Trade Statistics, 2002.

hand, this subjects exports to the vagaries of a volatile world market. On the other, it means that exports are likely to be relatively bulky with high volume-to-price ratios, hence relatively high unit transport costs.

Second, SSA countries tend to face 'natural barriers' that increase the costs of trade — imports are more expensive and exporting more costly. While these barriers confer protection to producers of importables, they imply effective taxation of exports.[9] Transport

costs are the most obvious such costs. Many SSA countries are landlocked (and suffer the additional costs of slow customs procedures at borders) and many of those that are not have large interiors. The primary commodities they produce have to be transported large distances overland to reach ports; road and rail systems tend to be inefficient throughout SSA, and sea shipping costs are relatively high.[10]

Although the evidence that trade liberalization increases growth is weak,[11]

[9] See, for example, C. Milner (1997), 'On Natural and Policy-Induced Sources of Protection and Trade Regime Bias', *Weltwirtshaftliches Archiv*, 132, 740–752.

[10] For a quantification of these costs see C. Milner, O. Morrissey and N. Rudaheranwa (2000).

[11] For a review, see J. Mbabazi, C. Milner and O. Morrissey, (2003).

there is almost no evidence that trade liberalization retards growth beyond the short-term adverse effect on the balance of payments discussed above. Whilst increased competition from imports could have adverse effects on manufacturing industries, there is no convincing evidence that trade reforms caused de-industrialization in Africa.[12] In general, trade liberalization offers benefits to African countries. The evidence is stronger that exports promote growth, even in African countries. There is some evidence that growth has been higher in more outward oriented SSA economies, suggesting that trade liberalization offers the potential for SSA countries to increase growth rates.[13] Even in those countries dependent on primary commodity exports, a less restrictive trade regime is conducive to increased efficiency of resource allocation and hence growth.

### Trade Structure

Trade structure, in particular dependence on primary commodities, is an important determinant of trade performance, and therefore mediates any link between trade and growth (Box 4.5). Resource endowments will be a major determinant of trade structure. A standard hypothesis is that countries with relatively low endowments of natural resources, thus relatively high labor endowments, will need to industrialize to promote export growth and utilize their comparative advantage. However, countries endowed with natural resources

---

[12] See P. Bennell (1998).
[13] See O. Onafowora and O. Owoye (1998). See also P. Mosley and J. Weeks (1993).

**Box 4.3: Trade and Low Growth in SSA**

A measure of natural resource endowments can capture how comparative advantage relates to exports and growth, as higher endowments are associated with slower growth.

- Countries with relatively low endowments of natural resources, thus relatively high labor endowments, will industrialize to promote export growth.
- Countries endowed with natural resources and low skill levels depend on exports of unprocessed primary commodities.
- Extractive industries and unprocessed commodities have weak linkages with the rest of the economy and tend to face deteriorating terms of trade.
- High transport costs are a greater barrier to trade in primary commodities than manufactures because volume-to-value ratios are generally higher.
- Restrictive trade policies exacerbate the problem by reducing the competitiveness of the exportables sector and the efficiency of resource allocation in the economy.

Given SSA countries' dependence on primary commodity exports, the combination of high transport costs and historically restrictive trade regimes goes a long way towards explaining the poor growth performance of SSA countries.

*Source*: J. Mbabazi, C. Milner and O. Morrissey (2002), 'The Fragility of the Evidence on Inequality, Trade Liberalization, Growth and Poverty', CREDIT Research Paper 02/19.

---

coupled with low skill levels will tend to have export dependence on unprocessed primary commodities. This can retard growth because extractive industries have weak linkages with the rest of the economy, agricultural exports are largely unprocessed and primary commodities tend to face volatile and deteriorating terms of trade.

Box 4.5 identifies the problem faced by countries heavily reliant on a limited number of primary commodities for their export earnings. Under such an environment, trade liberalization will confer limited benefits — the capacity of the export sector to respond is constrained, whereas domestic producers will face increased competition from imports. This may help, in particular, to explain Africa's poor growth performance.

---

### Box 4.4: Trade Structure and Growth

Many African countries are export-dependent upon a few agricultural or mineral commodities. This dependence reflects structural features of the economy. There is evidence that both the underlying structural features and the export dependence retard growth, individually and in combination.

- Having natural resource abundance itself tends to have a positive effect on growth, providing the resources are managed reasonably sensibly.
- Declining world prices for primary commodities reduces export earnings and slows growth in countries dependent on those commodities.

Thus, having an abundance of primary commodities to export is, in itself, beneficial. Problems arise for those countries dependent on a narrow range of primary commodities, especially if these commodities face declining terms of trade.

*Source*: D. Lederman and W. Maloney (2003), 'Trade Structure and Growth', World Bank Policy Research Working Paper 3025.

---

### *Constraints on Export Supply Response*

Trade liberalization is expected to remove the relative disincentive to produce exports and the anticipated beneficial effect is that exports will increase and, in turn, fuel economic growth. However, trade policy is only one factor constraining exports, and relative prices are rarely the major constraint on export supply response. For countries dependent on agricultural exports, non-trade policies (e.g. marketing boards and price controls) have often been biased against agriculture and discouraged export production. In addition, farmers face many constraints in gaining access to factors, inputs and technology that limit their ability to increase production in response to improved (export) price incentives.[14] As mentioned previously, transport costs can be quite high for many SSA countries and this can act as an important constraint on primary commodity exports. The slow pace in implementing institutional reforms is yet another reason for low export supply response.[15] Given the many and varied constraints to increasing production and distribution of primary commodities, one may not observe a quick export response to trade liberalization. This does not mean that trade reforms should not be undertaken; it does mean that one should exercise care in interpreting the evidence.

Transport costs are some 15 percent of unit values on average in Africa, which is

---

[14] For a discussion see A. McKay, O. Morrissey and C, Vaillant (1997). See also F. Noorbakhsh and A. Paloni (1998).

[15] For example, see D. Belshaw, P. Lawrence and M. Hubbard (1999).

considerably higher than the averages for other developing country regions. Table 4.11 illustrates the importance of transport costs, reporting the cif/fob ratio for groups of African countries. Unsurprisingly, landlocked countries (or Central Africa, which is similar) face the highest transport costs, of over 20 percent unit values, while North Africa faces the lowest transport costs (Figure 4.14). In general, transport costs declined slightly between 1980 and 1994. The main exceptions are landlocked, Southern Africa and agriculture groups. The increases in all of these groups are largely due to Malawi, where the ratio in 1994 rose to 1.67 (because the war in Mozambique denied the shortest route to the sea).

Differences in transport costs between groups of countries reflect differences in the direction and composition of trade as well as location characteristics. The latter seems most important, as there are few consistent patterns across countries grouped by export orientation (although manufactures appear to have the lowest costs). Remoteness, poor infrastructure and being landlocked are clearly damaging to trade because they raise trade costs, and such costs are a particular burden on African countries.[16]

A more general point can be made regarding the link between trade liberalization and openness. While the latter may give rise to concerns regarding the competitiveness of domestic producers of importables, access to imported investment goods and the technology embodied in imports may be very beneficial. Furthermore, trade openness and being seen to implement trade reforms may attract foreign investment. Foreign investors tend to be attracted to countries with relatively open trade regimes and increasing trade volumes. Furthermore, the injection of funds, know-how and marketing contacts associated with foreign investment may itself be a boost to exports.

Thus, there are many explanations as to why the export response to trade liberalization in Africa has been limited. These include factors relating to the effectiveness of

**Table 4.11: Transport Costs in Africa, Country Groups**

| Grouping | cif/fob ratio | |
|---|---|---|
| | 1980 | 1994 |
| Landlocked Countries | 1.227 | 1.249 |
| Regions | | |
| North Africa | 1.101 | 1.096 |
| West Africa | 1.196 | 1.191 |
| Central Africa | 1.244 | 1.224 |
| East Africa | 1.161 | 1.146 |
| Southern Africa | 1.137 | 1.222 |
| Export orientation | | |
| Manufacturing | 1.144 | 1.128 |
| Agriculture | 1.168 | 1.196 |
| Mining/resources | 1.197 | 1.139 |
| Oil | 1.148 | 1.152 |

*Source*: Derived from data in IMF (1995).

[16] See also N. Limao and A. Venables (1999). They show that unit transport costs between the US and SSA are more than twice the costs for trade between the US and Germany and the US and Japan. Furthermore, intra-regional transport costs are often higher than extra-regional costs.

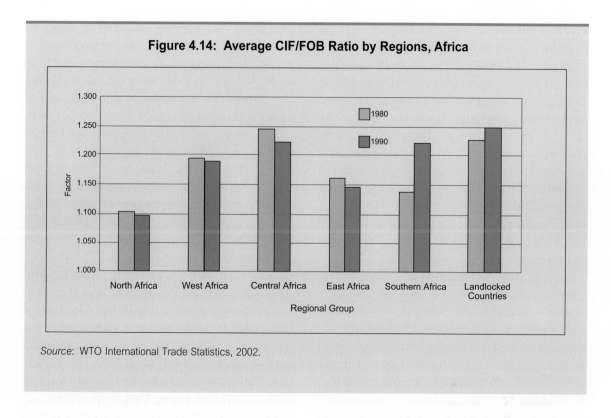

**Figure 4.14: Average CIF/FOB Ratio by Regions, Africa**

Source: WTO International Trade Statistics, 2002.

the liberalization itself (what trade reforms were actually implemented), and to the response of producers to the apparent shift in the incentive structure (do they believe that the reforms are credible and sustainable). However, trade liberalization has now been sustained for some time in most African countries. The issue for the future is how the effectiveness of trade reforms is contingent on the existence of other characteristics of the environment in which production and investment decisions are made. We have identified trade structure and constraints on supply response as predominant among these. Some commentators emphasize the role of institutional (political and legal) and infrastructure factors in affecting private

sector confidence in achieving and securing adequate returns.[17] The simple point is that there are many factors other than trade policy that help explain the poor export performance of African, especially SSA, countries. Consequently, the benefits of trade liberalization may not be immediately apparent. This does not imply that, at the margin, trade policy reform is not beneficial.

## Trade and Poverty

There is almost no empirical evidence directly relating trade performance to poverty in Africa. One major reason is the absence of

---

[17] For example, M. Söderbom and Teal, F. (2003).

cross-country data on poverty in African countries over time. While there is more opportunity to study the effects of trade on poverty in country case studies, the potential linkages are complex and few quantitative studies currently exist. There is evidence for developing countries on the effect of trade and other variables on growth, and economic growth is posited as being the most consistent indicator of potential gains in the incomes of the poor. This helps to identify factors that may indirectly affect poverty via their influence on growth, and trade (in particular export growth) is one such factor.

It is only over the last five or so years that economists have started to address, in a rigorous manner, the ways in which trade may impact on the poor.[18] Data permitting, the unit of analysis would be the household as producer and consumer. As a producer, the household earns income by selling the factors it possesses (e.g. renting land, wage labor) or by utilizing the factors directly for production (e.g. combining household land and labor to grow food, for sale or own-consumption). The distinguishing feature of poor households is that they possess few or low-value factors (e.g. they do not have access to land and their labor is of very low quality). Trade expands market opportunities and increases the demand for, and return to, factors.

International trade provides access to (and competition from) a larger market, but also one that is more competitive, so success in exporting or import-competition requires increased efficiency in producing high quality goods. The major share of the benefits from trade will accrue to those households owning the factors that are most in demand, and in general these will not be poor households. This does not mean that trade will not benefit the poor, but rather suggests that the poor will derive the least direct benefit from trade. Insofar as trade expansion fuels economic growth, aggregate demand in the economy increases and this potentially benefits all.

From the perspective of producers, exports are beneficial (increased demand leads to increased production and incomes) but imports pose a challenge. Increased competition from imports can lead to a reduction of production of import-competing sectors, at least in the short-run. This means that the owners of factors supplied to those sectors will suffer a reduction in income; in poor countries this is mostly wage labor in manufacturing. If the economy is flexible it will adjust over time and, in the long run, the economy should become more efficient. In the short run, and in general, there will be winners and losers from trade. Producers and those earning their incomes from expanding sectors will gain, whereas those earning incomes in contracting sectors will lose. One implication is that in countries where exports are very flat, i.e. there is no evidence of a sustained increase, trade offers no potential to reduce poverty (Figure 4.15).

From the perspective of households as consumers, trade is generally beneficial. Import competition implies that imports and the products of import-competing sectors will be cheaper. Imports also increase the variety

---

[18] The ways in which trade can affect prices, employment and government revenues and how these effects then impact on households are outlined in N. McCulloch, L. A. Winters and X. Cirera (2001).

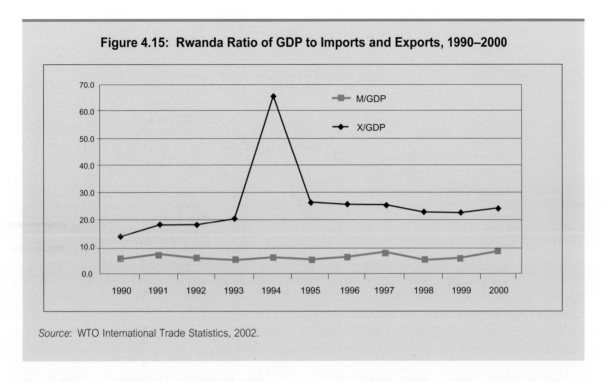

**Figure 4.15: Rwanda Ratio of GDP to Imports and Exports, 1990–2000**

*Source*: WTO International Trade Statistics, 2002.

and quality of goods available. This benefits consumers (including firms using the products as inputs). Expansion of export sectors, if they also sell on the local market, should mean lower prices and/or higher quality. Trade is generally good for households as consumers, whereas it may have good, bad or almost no effect on households as producers or suppliers of factors of production. Trade and in particular export promotion is likely to be one of the more important factors determining poverty, but an economic crisis (typically a cause of increased poverty) will usually be reflected in a downturn in trade, especially exports. For example, the political and economic instability in Zimbabwe since the late 1990s can be seen in the deterioration in its strong trade performance (Figure 4.16).

It is important to distinguish trade policy from trade performance, especially as it is the latter that results in effects on poverty. Trade performance is an outcome, while trade policy is one of the inputs that influences that outcome. Trade policy reforms affect relative incentives, and the performance outcome depends on the ability of agents and sectors to respond to these altered incentives.

The link between policy and performance is not a simple direct one. Trade policy reforms have economic effects on:

(a) Prices of traded products. This is the major direct effect. Import liberalization reduces the price of importables. Although the relative price of exportables rises, unilateral liberalization does not affect export prices.

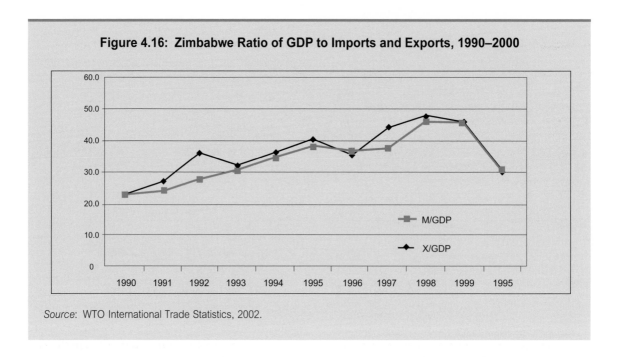

**Figure 4.16: Zimbabwe Ratio of GDP to Imports and Exports, 1990–2000**

*Source*: WTO International Trade Statistics, 2002.

(b) Output, wages and employment opportunities in affected sectors. Producers of import-competing goods face increased competition and these sectors may contract. Producers of exports and those using imported inputs should benefit and may expand.

(c) The government's fiscal position (Box 4.5). Tariffs are an important source of revenue, so tariff reductions can reduce tax revenue. In practice, tax revenues have tended to decline, even if only slightly, in the poorest countries (including those in Africa).[19]

The presence of import barriers or restrictions creates an anti-export bias by raising the price of importable goods relative to exportable goods. Removal of this anti-export bias through trade liberalization would induce a shift of resources from the production of import substitutes to the production of exports. The factors used intensively in the production of exports, land and rural or unskilled labor in poor countries, should benefit most. On the other hand, factors employed in the production of import-competing goods, mostly urban capital and labor, can anticipate losses. Typically, import supply from the rest of the world responds more rapidly than domestic export supply, so liberalization imposes adjustment costs (losses tend to be immediate whereas export gains can take time).

The immediate effect of import liberalization is losses in some sectors, gains in other

---

[19] For a review of evidence see B. Khattry and J. Mohan Rao (2002), 'Fiscal faux pas? An analysis of the revenue implications of trade liberalization' *World Development*, 30:8, 1431–1444.

**Box 4.5: Fiscal Effects**

Import liberalization might be expected to reduce government revenue, as tariffs are typically an important tax. Despite the significant trade liberalization since the early 1990s, tariffs have continued to be a major source of tax revenue. There are a number of reasons why import liberalization may not be associated with lower tariff revenues.

First, the lower tariff rates discourage evasion and avoidance so collection efficiency increases.

Second, quantitative restrictions may be converted into tariffs.

Third, the tariffs may apply to an increasing value of imports. This may arise either because demand is elastic or, more commonly, because there was also devaluation (which increases the domestic price of imports).

In practice, the effect of devaluation on import prices (in domestic currency) may be greater than the effect of tariff reductions. This is a beneficial combination: tariff-induced relative price distortions are reduced, tax revenue does not decline, and there is an incentive for exporters (who receive more domestic currency for the given world price at which they sell). If tariff revenue declines, as it typically does, the revenue can in principle be compensated by increased revenue from other taxes (mostly domestic sales).

*Source*: Development Research Department, African Development Bank, 2004.

sectors, gains to consumers and possible revenue losses to government; the net impact is indeterminate *a priori* (Box 4.6). The longer-term impact will depend on how effectively the export sector responds to improved incentives: although trade liberalization does not usually affect actual

export prices, it increases the return to exportables relative to the return to importables. An adequate export response is usually sufficient to ensure that the net impact of trade liberalization is favorable. Even if one expects an aggregate gain for the economy, it is important to know which types of households or sectors are most likely to gain and which are most likely to lose.

Computable General Equilibrium (CGE) models are useful in this respect, as they allow one to trace through how relative prices alter production and factor incomes, and how this in turn affects real incomes of specific types of households. Such models suggest that trade liberalization does benefit the economy. Although the distribution of gains and losses across households is uneven, the net effect is positive, but often very small. The more flexible and responsive the economy, the greater the net gains (Box 4.6).

The manner in which trade liberalization, growth and poverty are related is an important empirical question. Trade liberalization is an indicator of economic policy reform in which distortions are reduced and market incentives increased. Consequently, it should promote growth. In general, higher growth is associated with lower levels of poverty, although the empirical evidence is fragile for developing countries. There is a lack of robust evidence that differences in growth rates or inequality are determinants of cross-country variations in levels of poverty (Box 4.7).

Countries with less restrictive trade policies and that invested in human capital over a sustained period tend to have higher growth and this reduces levels of poverty. Policies that promote growth and reduce inequality are the most likely to reduce poverty. Openness, including trade liberalization, is one such policy but is only likely to reduce poverty (over time) if associated with investment in human capital so that the economy overall, and more households, can derive gains from trade.

There has been considerable interest in the apparent distinctiveness of the Sub-Saharan African experience relative to other parts of the developing world in terms of countries' abilities to grow out of poverty.[20] This reveals considerable disagreement about what are the critical binding constraints, and about the relative importance of geography, history and current governance in accounting for Africa's generally poor growth and trade performance. What is now less contested is that future improvements in growth performance will require SSA to improve its export performance, which has been at best weak in all but a few countries.[21] The evidence of the experience from other parts of the developing world over the last few decades shows that improved growth performance is associated with exporting, and success in reducing poverty is more likely in growing economies. Indeed the increasing pace of globalization makes the need for the increased international integration of Africa even more pressing.

## Trade Initiatives and Direction of Trade

There is no doubt that African countries have liberalized their trade regimes quite significantly over the past decade or so. The pace and

---

**Box 4.6: Distribution Effects of Trade**

Simulations from a CGE model of Uganda, considering the distribution of impacts for various types of households (differentiated by main source of income) provide three broad conclusions.

- In a relatively inflexible and constrained economy, increases in world prices of exports alone (unless they are very large) or import liberalisation alone will not provide a benefit on the aggregate.
- Trade liberalisation is more likely to provide aggregate benefits if there are also efficiency gains and factors are mobile (this captures the ability of the economy to respond and adjust).
- There are significant distribution effects of trade liberalisation. The largest proportional gains are to the urban self-employed, but there are also significant gains in agriculture. The non-working households are the major losers, and these household types will tend to include the poorest.

In Uganda, trade liberalisation was associated with a period of rapid growth and significant poverty reduction. Exports certainly contributed to growth and poverty reduction, and trade liberalisation contributed to export growth. One cannot say how much of the poverty reduction was attributable to trade liberalisation, but it was a contributory factor.

*Source*: A. Blake, A. McKay and O. Morrissey (2002) 'The Impact on Uganda of Agricultural Trade Liberalisation', Journal of Agricultural Economics, 53:2, 365-381.

---

pattern of trade reforms varies from country to country, but the broad trend is towards lower barriers to imports. The anticipated export supply response has not, however, mater-

---

[20] For wide ranging discussions see D. Belshaw and I. Livingstone (2002).

[21] Söderbom and Teal, F. (2003).

## Box 4.7: Influences on Cross-Country Variations in Poverty

There is limited evidence on the determinants of levels of poverty across countries over time. Partly this is because of the lack of good comparative time series data on levels of poverty in many countries. More generally, it reflects the complex relationship between the determinants of growth and the effect of growth and other factors on poverty. Available evidence suggests:

- Economic growth does not have a consistent influence on variations in poverty across countries over the short to medium term. Growth appears to have a long run effect of reducing poverty, and is associated with poverty reduction in specific countries at specific times.
- More open countries tend to have lower poverty, and openness tends to be associated with growth. A sustained relatively open trade regime appears to be part of a pro-poor growth pattern, perhaps because it supports long run growth.
- It is the sources of growth, such as accumulation and technical change and whether in agriculture or other sectors, that determines the effect on poverty. Trade can reduce poverty if

it provides for a sustainable increase in employment and/or benefits the sectors in which most of the poor are located (typically agriculture).

- Higher levels of human capital are associated with lower poverty. Wider provision of education and health services not only increases the welfare of the poor but also contributes to higher and more widely distributed growth. Countries with higher levels of human capital are in a better position to respond to and benefit from trade.
- Even controlling for the other influences on poverty, poverty is higher in SSA. This can largely be explained by the specific features of SSA countries that explain their poor economic performance.
- There is no robust evidence that inequality is a determinant of poverty although poverty, like inequality, is consistently higher in SSA. Measures of inequality may capture country-specific policy distortions that retard growth and therefore may tend to be associated with higher poverty.

*Source*: Mbabazi, J., C. Milner and O. Morrissey (2003), 'The Fragility of Empirical Links between Inequality, Trade Liberalisation, Growth and Poverty', in R. van der Hoeven and A. Shorrocks (eds), Perspectives of Growth and Poverty (United Nations University Press).

ialized with any consistency in African countries. To a large extent this is because, for most African countries, export performance depends on what happens elsewhere in the world more than on the policy reforms implemented in the countries themselves. Four issues relating to policies in other countries deserve focus: the trade policies of the EU and the US, Africa's major trading partners, the WTO, and regional trade agreements.

### Trade Policies in the EU

Most African countries have benefited from some form of preferential access to the EU market. For North African countries, the preferences have applied mostly to textiles and clothing and certain (seasonal) agricultural products, and a new Euro-Mediterranean Agreement is under negotiation. The EU-South Africa Free Trade Agreement provides for reciprocal preferences covering a wide range of products. The majority of African countries have benefited from preferences granted to African, Caribbean and Pacific (ACP) countries under successive Lomé Conventions, which offer quota and duty-free access for many goods from most SSA countries. Some countries (e.g. Botswana, Côte d'Ivoire, Mauritius and Zimbabwe) have derived significant benefits from the sugar and beef protocols. The Lomé preferences are being eroded on a number of fronts, principally as they come under challenge within the WTO. Preferences granted to specific developing countries can only be maintained in a WTO-consistent manner if there is reciprocity. In order to continue preferences, the EU has proposed introducing reciprocity through the establishment of a series of Economic Partnership Agreements (EPAs), under which the EU and regional groupings of ACP countries offer reciprocal trade preferences to each other. The principle of EPAs is included in the Cotonou Agreement for future EU-ACP relations, and negotiations between the EU and ACP regional groups are being initiated (Box 4.8).

In fact, the least developed among SSA countries are entitled to preferential access without reciprocity. The Everything But Arms (EBA) initiative of March 2001 grants least developed countries both quota and duty free access to the EU market for (almost) all products except arms, although relatively stringent rules of origin apply. Quota restrictions will continue to apply to imports of rice and sugar until 2009, and bananas until 2006. The EBA is an 'offer' rather than an agreement: the EU could suddenly change the terms or terminate access, and could implement safeguard clauses if there was a

---

**Box 4.8: Economic Partnership Agreements**

Two features of EPAs under the Cotonou Agreement, the successor to Lomé, are of particular relevance. First, the EU proposal is that groups of ACP countries form regional integration arrangements among themselves, and these regional groups negotiate with the EU. The EU does not want to negotiate an EPA with the ACP as a whole nor with individual ACP countries. This should stimulate the formation of deeper RTAs amongst African countries, at least those that are ACP. Second, the EPA is reciprocal so the regional ACP groups ultimately have to remove tariffs and barriers to imports from the EU. It is not obvious that EPAs offer any benefit to the majority of SSA countries; offering reciprocity suggests they will be worse off than they have been previously.

*Source*: Development Research Department, African Development Bank, 2004.

---

sudden and significant increase in imports of any commodity. However, EBA only offers a real benefit to those least developed countries that currently face restricted access to the EU market. In practice, it reduces slightly the preference margins of African countries as they already had such preferences under Lomé whereas EBA extends preferential access to a few non-ACP countries.

Irrespective of how beneficial preferential access to the EU has actually been for African countries in the past, the likelihood is that the true margin of preference will be diminished in future years. Partly, this is because the EBA extends tariff-free access to all least developed countries. More significantly, the EU is negotiating reciprocal preferential agreements with other regions, notably Mercosur. Furthermore, whether through EPAs or the WTO, African countries will be lowering barriers to imports from the EU, increasing competition for local producers.

### Trade Policies in the US

African countries have been granted some preferential access to the US market because they are low-income or least developed countries. The US Africa Growth and Opportunity Act (AGOA) of 2000 aimed to alter this by granting tariff-free access to most goods from SSA. AGOA reduced or eliminated tariffs and quotas on more than 1,800 products. Although the range of products is large, ranging from umbrellas and steel to tobacco and fresh yams, clothing exports dominate. This has drawn foreign investors, mostly apparel manufacturers from Asia, to establish factories across Africa and gain quota-free access to the US market. Job creation has been significant in some countries, is often achieved rapidly, and is mostly of young women.

Although it has allowed a number of countries to increase their exports to the US, and US imports of textiles and clothing increased by over 20 percent in the first year. Less than half of the duty free exports to the US of beneficiary countries are under AGOA, and less than half the imports from these countries are duty free. In the major sector, clothing, less than 40 percent of US imports from AGOA beneficiaries are duty-free, and the share is much lower for other products, such as sugar and tobacco. To date, Kenya and Lesotho appear to have been the major beneficiaries of AGOA. Kenya estimates that

almost 50,000 AGOA-related jobs will have been created by 2004. Lesotho created some 10,000 new jobs by 2003, becoming the largest African apparel exporter to the US (exports grew from about US$130 million in 2001 to US$270 million in 2003).

Even where countries are benefiting from AGOA, there are real concerns about how significant and sustainable the benefits are. The greatest concern, in respect to clothing, is that the rules of origin may be tightened in future years, reducing if not eliminating the profitability of African exporters. AGOA has provided opportunities to SSA countries to expand and diversify exports. Whether the benefits can be sustained depends largely on the willingness of the US to continue the preferences with weak rules of origin. Of equal importance is the ability of 'AGOA exporters' to use this stimulus as a base to establish a competitive sector.

### The WTO and African Trade Policy

WTO membership has not to date required African countries to make major new direct commitments on access to their markets, and tariff bindings agreed under the Uruguay Round are not a real constraint. As for developing countries in general, however, the WTO does have many implications for Africa. Although actual progress has been slow, the most important in principle is market access to developed market economies, especially for specific sectors (textiles and clothing, agriculture and natural resources). It is important to note that insofar as African countries have enjoyed preferential access to developed country markets, especially the EU, multilateral negotiation of greater access may actually reduce the margin of preferences extended to Africa. Consequently, African countries, especially the least developed, can find themselves in an ambiguous situation during WTO market access negotiations.

There are also ambiguities regarding the effects of reducing or eliminating agricultural subsidies in developed country markets. African countries that are net food importers, of which there are many, have legitimate concerns about the impact of removing export subsidies on world food prices. Against this must be balanced against the impact on African countries that are actual or potential food exporters. While the removal of export subsidies is in general to be supported as welfare increasing, it is appropriate that special measures are in place to compensate food deficit countries from any increase in world prices. Similar ambiguities arise for some products exported by African countries. West African cotton producers are evidently disadvantaged by the large subsidies given to cotton producers in the US. On the other hand, full liberalization of world sugar trade would be costly to those African (and other ACP) countries that benefit from the EU's Sugar Protocol. As with food, while liberalization of world trade is in general beneficial, one must recognize that some countries may be adversely affected. Often, these will be African countries that currently benefit from preferences.

Many of the new issues covered by the Uruguay Round Agreement have, or may have, important policy implications for Africa (even if they do not relate directly to trade barriers). The Agreement on Trade Related Investment Measures (TRIMs) limits the types

of performance requirements governments can impose on investors. The agreement on Trade Related Aspects of Intellectual Property Rights (TRIPs) is contentious. For SSA, this has achieved greatest prominence in the context of access to cheap (generic) medicines for treatments of major diseases. The General Agreement on Trade in Services (GATS) was limited in scope but took an important first step in bringing disciplines to the area and providing a schedule for progressive liberalization. For financial services, telecommunications and air transport services detailed schedules were provided. Although GATS operates as a 'menu' agreement, with countries choosing what commitments to make and request in each sector, it is important in an environment of privatization of services sectors in African countries. All of these are trade-related issues, but do impose costs on government: officials have to find out what agreements mean and whether there are relevant concerns for the country.

Many of the commitments under the WTO actually relate to technical and administrative issues such as standards and customs valuation. The administrative costs of identifying and implementing commitments can be very high in practice. This is especially true in the many African countries where Trade Ministries, and related agencies such as the Standards Board, Attorney General (for legislation) and Customs, have severely limited resources and few highly trained staff. These administrative costs are very high and constitute a real economic cost, in addition to the costs of negotiating and implementing actual trade policy reforms. Thus, while the WTO may not have been a major source of trade liberalization in Africa, it is central to the detail of trade policy.

### Regional Trade in Africa

There are over ten different RTAs among African countries, many with overlapping membership. However, most of these have not, at least to date, involved significant trade among members nor elimination of tariffs on intra-regional trade. A major exception is the Southern African Customs Union (SACU), which has progressed quite far relative to African RTAs, even compared to the wider Southern African Development Community (SADC) of which its members are part. The largest RTA is the Common Market for Eastern and Southern Africa (COMESA), established in 1994, which has some 20 members stretching from Egypt to Zambia.

COMESA has made some significant achievements in terms of trade liberalization. A free-trade area (FTA) was established in November 2000 as a sub-set of COMESA. Nine members eliminated their tariffs on COMESA originating products, while another five offered very significant preferences to COMESA imports. A Customs Union is proposed from November 2004, with a common external tariff (CET) comprising four rates of 0, 5, 15, and 30 percent. This would be a significant step towards trade liberalization for most of the member countries, although some, such as Uganda, would not necessarily be reducing their tariffs as they are already quite low. However, trade between COMESA countries remains quite low.

As African countries tend to export similar products (and do so mostly to the same developed country markets), and in only a few cases do they export what other African countries import, RTAs offer only limited potential to increase (intra-regional) trade. However, they can offer significant benefits in reducing trade costs, especially for landlocked members. The real benefits of RTAs can be a combination of shared investment, reducing transport costs, improving distribution and marketing systems and reducing customs delays and simplifying procedures. These are vital elements of African trade policy, as one of the most important objectives must be to reduce trade costs, especially for exports.

## Conclusion

This chapter has reviewed the policy efforts that African countries have made within the last decade or more to revamp their external sector. And as we have seen, several have experienced marked improvements in their exports performance. It is evident that preferential access to overseas markets, especially the EU, has been a cornerstone of trade policy for many African countries, especially the poorer SSA countries. Such preferences can be justified as compensating for dependence on primary commodities and the high trade costs faced by many African countries. It is likely that trade policy developments during the next decade will see an erosion of the margins of these preferences. African countries will even more exposed to competition in the markets for their exports than they have previously been. It is also likely that African countries will have to offer increased access to their trading partners. To some extent this will be in line with multilateral negotiations under the WTO, but preferential agreements with the EU will involve some degree of reciprocity in the future, and African countries will offer concessions to each other in regional agreements.

African countries have already taken major steps in liberalizing import regimes. Evidence for this can be found in lower average tariffs, and perhaps more significantly in increases in imports as a share of GDP. Multilateral and regional agreements have committed them to these reforms — the clock cannot be turned back, although the appropriate pace of future liberalization is an important policy issue. To date, there is little aggregate evidence that the trade policy reforms and liberalization since the late 1980s have produced a significant export response. Exports have not increased consistently, and there is no evident correlation between the extent of trade liberalization and the rate at which exports have grown. African countries contemplating further liberalization should aim to do so from a solid export platform.

One of the keys to Africa's future prospects is 'discovering' how to bring about improved export performance. A core element of any strategy is the need to diversify exports. Trade liberalization can do no more than provide opportunities — unilateral reforms increase relative incentives to exporters, and multilateral or regional liberalization increase market access. Domestic policies are necessary to reduce the varied constraints on supply response, increase transport and marketing efficiency, and encouraging investment. To benefit from trade, and channel these benefits into helping reduce poverty, African countries need to increase the flexibility and efficiency of resource use so that they can be competitive in global markets. African countries should concentrate on their own policies and not rely on actions by other countries. Policies in other countries, and especially multilateral and regional agreements, will be important in the long term, but will not ensure that any particular country is able to benefit from the opportunities provided by trade rather than succumbing to the challenges and costs. The major benefit to African countries of acting together is not that it increases trade volumes but that it reduces trade costs.

# CHAPTER 5

# Africa's External Trade Relations

## Introduction

Africa's external trade relations comprise a network of bilateral and multilateral linkages, some of them dating as far back as colonial times. At the dawn of decolonization, Africa's relations with the European Union were enshrined in the 1957 Rome Treaty establishing the European Common Market, when the French dependencies were incorporated into an Association status with the emerging New Europe. Economics alone cannot explain the dynamics of such complex relationships. We necessarily have to take on board time-tested economic and political interests, some of them colored by post-colonial ambition; the need to safeguard sources of strategic natural resources for advanced industrial economies; and the need to protect and stabilize prices for Africa's raw materials exports (Mailafia, 1997).[1] At independence most African countries also acceded into membership of the GATT at the same time as they joined the United Nations and the Bretton Woods Institutions. Some 41 African countries have already become members of the WTO and several more are planning to join.

This chapter extends the analysis of trade policy in the previous chapter into the wider global arena by examining the dynamics of Africa's external trade relations. It examines the evolving bilateral and multilateral trading linkages that Africa has with the rest of the world and evaluates the various policy agendas, negotiations and bargaining and the implications for Africa's long-term prospects in terms of its export performance and overall economic development. First, we consider Africa in the WTO system and in the Doha Round multilateral negotiations. We then discuss recent trade initiatives such as the AGOA, Cotonou and the EBA in the context of the changing global trade regime.

The year 2004 falls within a pivotal period for Africa's position in world trade policy.

---

[1] Another dimension of such relationships is inter-regional cooperation, by which is meant the phenomenon of group-to-group cooperation between different regions of the world. Most interregional relations were largely confined to the European Community's 'association' dialogues with other regional groupings such as the African, Caribbean and Pacific (ACP) states or with the Mediterranean group of countries. Although the EU is still the major actor in the expanding network of relations between regional groupings, the number of interregional arrangements beyond the EU's external relations has been increasing. The Asia Pacific Economic Cooperation (APEC) and Asia- Europe Meeting (ASEM) processes are a good case in point. In recent years, similar arrangements have been established, such as the Europe-Latin America Summit, the Africa-Europe Summit and the East Asia Latin America Forum (EALAF). With regard to Africa, the main regional groupings with which the continent has strong continuing relationships are: (a) the EU-African partnership, (b) the United States, (c) Asia, and (d) the Group of G8 Countries.

Patterns of trade are changing so fast that the effects are likely to be significant in the medium term. This is true for all countries, but especially so for Africa: change is under way in relation to the goods that are exported, imported and consumed locally. In brief, Africa is being squeezed. Its status as a favored recipient of trade preferences in some markets (but not in others) is being eroded rapidly. Increasingly its terms of access to non-regional markets will be on the same basis as its competitors'. Consequently, the attention of trade policy makers has shifted from Brussels to Geneva and yet, as the stalled Doha process attested in 2003, the multilateral system is still perceived as insufficiently attuned to Africa's needs. At the same time the region is being asked by some of its traditional trade partners to offer reverse preferences under the guise of free trade agreements (FTAs). These are being presented as supportive of both regional integration and the multilateral system, but it is not certain that the result will be either of these.

A corollary of this newfound instability in the region's global trade relations has been its exposure of the frailty — at all levels — of Africa's capacity to strategize and negotiate. The well-publicized problems faced by overstretched (or non-existent) diplomatic missions in Geneva to cope with the WTO agenda is merely the tip of an iceberg comprising multiple overlapping trade negotiations. As old relationships come under strain and new ones need to be forged, so the demands for a clear line of communication from economic stakeholders through line ministries to trade negotiators become ever more marked, and the gap between the ideal and reality becomes ever more stark.

Despite these disadvantages, Africa's trade negotiators 'punched above their weight' during 2003 and its immediate predecessors. Between them, the states of Africa are engaged in a very wide range of negotiations both regionally and externally. Trade integration within the Southern African Development Community (SADC), the Common Market for Eastern and Southern Africa (COMESA) and the Union Economique et Monétaire Ouest Africaine (UEMOA/ WAEMU) is already under way. In West Africa, the seven Economic Community of West African States (ECOWAS) — predominantly English speaking — countries have launched a program of monetary integration that can be expected to further deepen intra-regional trade among them. Africa played a prominent role in the WTO. And negotiations for a successor to the current trade regime with the EU are underway. This chapter reviews some of the key areas of negotiation during this period, the issues involved — and the challenges that lie ahead.

## Africa and the WTO Regime

The WTO is the successor to GATT, which was established in 1947, as an interim organization to oversee world trade issues after the failure of the US Congress to ratify the Havana Treaty on the International Trade Organization. GATT was to last for nearly half a century, with its successor coming into force in 1995 following the Uruguay Round of multilateral trade negotiations. The key legal instruments of the WTO include the 12 Multilateral Trade Agreements on Goods (MTAs), the General Agreement on Trade in Services (GATS), the Agreement on Trade-Related Aspects of Intellectual Property Rights

(TRIPs), the Understanding on Rules and Procedures Governing the Settlement of Disputes, and the Agreement on the Trade Policy Review Mechanism. The main functions of the WTO are to (a) facilitate the implementation, administration and operation of the Uruguay Round Agreements; and (b) provide a forum for negotiations among members concerning their multilateral trade relations.

The WTO's key mandate is to manage the liberalization of world trade and to act as a forum for governments to negotiate trade agreements and provide mechanisms for the judicial settlement of trade disputes between any Contracting Parties. The organization is also a fount and repository of international rules for the management and operation of the international trading system, binding governments to a rule-based regime that facilitates free international commerce for exporters and importers, guaranteeing the free flow of goods and services in conformity with internationally accepted ecological and social norms. The key principles of the WTO system focus on promotion of non-discrimination between its trading partners through the Most Favored Nation (MFN) principle and fostering 'national treatment' (NT) for corporate business entitities that operate in foreign jurisdictions; the creation of a more transparent and predictable framework for global trade in terms of reduced tariff and non-tariff barriers and 'market-opening' commitments; fostering a more competitive environment for global trade and discouraging unfair trade practices, such as export subsidies and the dumping of products at below cost price in order to gain unfair market advantage; and the negotiation

of a development-oriented global trade regime that better serves the interests of the poorest nations by giving more elbow room to adjust to changed market conditions and granting them greater flexibility and special privileges to make them better able to compete with advanced industrial economies.

According to WTO protocols, all the Contracting Parties of GATT 1947 wishing to become members of the Organization are required to accept all 12 MTAs incorporated into the Agreement without exceptions or reservations. They are also required to submit their schedules of tariff concessions and of specific sectoral and sub-sectoral concessions with respect to market access and national treatment for trade in service to the WTO for vetting. In essence, this has led to a substantial increase in the scope of obligations for all GATT contracting parties. The developing countries of Africa have been saddled with a quantum increase in the level of their obligations because of the fact that they have high tariffs on agricultural commodities. They have also been adversely affected since they face a higher level of obligations arising from the new General Agreement on Trade in Services (GATS) and even more stringent obligations emanating from the TRIPS agreement on intellectual property rights. In addition, the WTO Agreement has substantially reduced the flexibility hitherto enjoyed by developing countries under the multilateral trading system regarding their trade policies.

## WTO Provisions on Agriculture

The long-term objective of the WTO Agreement on Agriculture is to establish a fair and market-oriented agriculture trading system. It is also aimed at initiating a reform process through the negotiation of commitments on support and protection and through the establishment of strengthened and more operationally effective GATT rules and disciplines. This long-term objective is to provide for substantial progressive reductions in agricultural support and protection sustained over an agreed period of time, resulting in the correction and prevention of restrictions and distortions in world agricultural markets. The WTO embodies provisions, as agreed on by developing countries, aimed at boosting developing countries performance in world trade in agricultural commodities. The WTO members agreed to have specific binding agreements on the key areas of (a) market access; (b) domestic support; and (c) export competition and subsidies.

Many signatories to the Agreement, especially Canada, the EU and many developing countries have seen the WTO not only as a mechanism for implementing the results of the Uruguay Round within a common institutional framework but also as a device for imposing more stringent discipline to preclude unilateral trade measures. According to UNCTAD's *Trade and Development Report, 1994*, the successful completion of the Uruguay Round and the signing of the WTO Agreement would lead to a substantial strengthening of the multilateral trading system by:

(i)   Providing much more detailed rules to govern the application of a variety of trade policy measures;

(iii)  Devising new multilateral trade rules to cover intellectual property and trade in services;

(iv)  Achieving a substantial degree of tariff liberalization so as to maintain the momentum towards ever freer multilateral trade;

(v)   Reducing the discriminatory aspects of regional trade agreements;

(vi)  Effectively raising the multilateral obligations of all countries to broadly comparable levels, with differential and more favorable treatment for developing countries being delineated in a more specific, contractual manner; and

(vii)  Linking together the various agreements concluded within a formal institutional framework (i.e. the WTO), subject to an integrated dispute settlement mechanism.

*Market Access*

An often-mentioned problem of developing countries' agricultural exports has been the lack of access to developed countries' markets, due to the institution of a myriad of import controls and other restrictions. This has largely undermined the growth prospects of developing countries whose development strategy relied on agricultural exports. In the WTO Agreement, developed country members have agreed to take fully into account

"... *the particular needs and conditions of developing country members by providing for a greater improvement of opportunities and terms of access for agricultural products of particular interest to those members, including the fullest liberalization of trade in tropical-agricultural products..., and for products of particular importance to the diversification of product from the growing of illicit narcotic crops."*

Market access concessions relate to bindings and reductions of tariffs and to other market access commitments, as specified in the WTO Agreement. The agreement further provides that members shall not maintain, resort to, or revert to any measures of the kind which have been required to be converted into ordinary customs duties. These measures include quantitative import restrictions, variable import levies, minimum import prices, discretionary import, licensing, non-tariff measures maintained through state-trading enterprises, voluntary export restraints and similar border measures other than ordinary customs duties. This is contained in Article 4 of the Agreement on Agriculture.

### Farm Support in Developed Countries

A basic source of distortion in the world market for agricultural commodities and primary products has been the differential level of domestic support that developed and developing countries can give to the production of these commodities. This has tended to reduce the price competitiveness of developing countries. Thus, the WTO provides for a commitment by each developed country to reduce its domestic support measures in favor of agricultural products. However, for developing countries, government measures of assistance, whether direct or indirect, to encourage agricultural and rural development, are regarded as an integral part of their development programs. Hence, the WTO provides that investment and agricultural input subsidies (e.g.

fertilizers) which are generally provided to low-income or resources-poor producers in developing countries shall be exempted from domestic support reduction commitments that would otherwise be applicable to such measures in developed countries. This is contained in Article 6 of the Agreement on Agriculture.

### Export Competition and Export Subsidies

Domestic support and export subsidy policies have been employed largely by developed economies to protect their agricultural sectors. Under the Export Competition commitments, each member undertakes not to provide export subsidies or any financial contribution other than in conformity with the Agreement and with the commitments as specified in that member's schedule. The financial contribution may involve a direct transfer of funds, potential direct transfers (such as loan guarantees), the forgoing of revenue by the government, or the public provision of goods and services, other than infrastructure, or the government purchase of goods, or any form of income or price support. The Agreement prohibits subsidies contingent upon export performance or upon the use of domestic goods in preference to imported goods. GATT members have also entered into commitment to reduce those classes of subsidies specified in the Agreement as actionable with accompanying target dates and a desired level of action required. The bound reduced of export subsidies are defined in Article 9 (1) of the Agreement. These are to be reduced by 24 percent in terms of value (budget outlays) and 14 percent in volume over a ten-year period by developing countries. For developed countries, the corresponding figures are 36 percent and 21 percent for six years.

## Africa and the Doha Agenda

One arena in which African countries have done rather well — relative to their actual economic power — is with respect to the leverage that they have been able to wield as a result of their collective bargaining strength. This was manifested by the impact they were able to make at the Doha Round. The Africa Group submitted almost two-thirds of all the specific submissions to the Committee on Trade and Development (CTD) and over one-third of the proposals on systemic 'cross-cutting' issues in the period to July 2002. African countries also played a prominent role at the Cancun Ministerial, as well as in the committee-rich WTO negotiating process. But, at the same time, the experience emphasized the asymmetry of influence within the WTO. Groups with greater numerical than economic and technical strength have a greater power to prevent than to mould in cases where other members are not actively sympathetic. As was demonstrated most prominently at Cancun, they can prevent the adoption of proposals to which they object substantially on principle. But, by the same token, they cannot force other countries to accept their own proposals. The only way to move forward positively within the WTO, therefore, is to mould the technical details of proposals as they evolve in order to deal with African concerns — and then only if other members are receptive.

One of the problems for the Africa Group is that, despite the statements made in the Doha Declaration, some key WTO members

have been far from receptive to their perceived needs. The unhappy debates around Special and Differential Treatment (SDT) in the CTD illustrate a wider problem that contributed to the collapse at Cancun. Resolving these difficulties is a challenge not just for Africa but for the entire multilateral system, since the evolution of the WTO as the custodian of trade rules that are relevant to the rapidly evolving realities of international commerce may depend upon it.

The collapse of the 2003 trade talks was a major setback for the international community as a whole and for the poor countries in particular, especially at a time when the world needs to build a consensus on viable partnerships for international cooperation for development. As is well known, the contentious issues centred on the so-called Singapore issues — investment, competition, government procurement, transparency and trade facilitation — which were being handled by a small, exclusive 'Green Room' meeting group. Developing countries feared — and rightly too — that a new international investment regime would benefit multinational corporations at the expense of their own industries and at the expense of what they regard as the more critical issues of agricultural subsidies. This was the main reason for the deadlock situation that developed. But we also cannot overlook the apparent lack of transparency in the WTO system itself. The agenda-setting process, with the unilateral inclusion of such issues as procurement, trade facilitation and investment with little prior consultation with the group of developing nations, led to understandable frustration and created what amounted to a crisis of confidence in the talks.

Failure of the talks means further delay in the creation of an orderly, rules-based international trading regime that would ultimately benefit rich as well as poor nations.

The emergence of the 'Group of 21', the new alliance of developing countries with Brazil, India and China at its heart — which represents more than half the world's population and some two-thirds of its farmers — marked an important shift in the balance of power at Cancun. The fact that developing countries have been able to act together as a bloc could be seen by some as a victory for South-South solidarity. But we have to be careful not to go back to the experiences of the 1970s, when North-South confrontation merely served to erode global inter-dependence whilst weakening the basis for collective action on behalf of a common world interest.

African countries, more than any other group, want full integration into the world economy and the world trading system. As we have seen, Africa's current global trade amounts to less than 3 percent of the world's total. With nearly 300 million people living on less than one dollar a day, Africa is the one region where poverty remains a growing threat. In spite of encouraging trade initiatives such as the US Africa Growth and Opportunity Act (AGOA) and the EU 'Everything But Arms' (EBA) initiative, Africa continues to face considerable tariff as well as non-tariff barriers for its products.

All these obstacles will contribute to slowing economic growth in Africa, which in turn will mean slower progress in poverty reduction and slower progress in meeting the targets of the Millennium Development Goals

for the year 2015. It is can also be expected to impact negatively on the prospects of the New Partnership for African Development (NEPAD), which focuses on renewed partnership with its external stakeholders and hinging African development on re-engagement with the world community on the basis of 'open regionalism'.

## SDT in the Doha Round

The WTO negotiating process is not one that is designed to throw up automatically development friendly results, and nor does it do so in practice. Negotiations in GATT were typically hard-nosed, with negotiators following very narrow, mercantilist agendas. The evidence from Doha so far is that the ethos has not changed and the commitment to strengthened Special and Differential Treatment (SDT) has not yet been translated into practise (Box 5.1). Instead of agreeing broad new provisions, the talks up to Cancun were more about negotiating tactics and the eventual price to be paid than on the substance of what needs to be done. SDT must, if it is to be worthwhile, confer on developing countries some tangible and enforceable benefit that would not otherwise accrue. The industrialized countries have been unwilling so far to agree to this outside the sectoral negotiations in which they would expect some concessions in return.

This has caused concern among many developing countries, not just those in Africa, because the sea change from the GATT to the WTO has made 'formal SDT' much more important. The crucial changes have been the introduction of binding dispute settlement, the related increased litigiousness of

---

**Box 5.1: SDT — the Doha promise and reality**

The Doha Declaration accorded SDT a central place in the current round of rule negotiations. It stated that:

> ...provisions for special and differential treatment are an integral part of the WTO Agreements ... We therefore agree that all special and differential treatment provisions shall be reviewed with a view to strengthening them and making them more precise, effective and operational. (WTO 2001).

Over 85 proposals were submitted at Doha for changes to existing provisions on SDT, but by December 2002 there was agreement on only five of these. All were of limited scope: one concerned the principle of a monitoring mechanism and three were for measures benefiting least developed states only (Gillson and Rios, 2003: 11).

---

members, and the extension of multilateral rule-making into many new areas. Scope for special differentiation applied extensively in the GATT and benefited a very wide range of members (Box 5.2). This 'informal' SDT was achieved by incorporating into the GATT texts vague phrases that could be interpreted in different ways by different members. Such vagueness included such current *causes célèbres* as the Article XXIV requirements that an FTA/Customs Union should cover 'substantially all trade' and be completed 'within a reasonable period of time'. This allowed countries with different views of what should be done to sign up to the same set of words, secure in the knowledge that they could

apply them in their chosen way once the ink was dry.

The innovation of the Uruguay Round to make dispute settlement binding removed this escape route. This fact was not necessarily fully recognized by all (or even most) parties. The subsequent striking down by the WTO of the US offshore tax regime and the EU banana regime, for example, has concentrated minds. In neither case was the defendant willfully flouting WTO rules: both believed that, on their interpretation of the rules, they had a strong defence. A second implication of change is that binding dispute

---

**Box 5.2: SDT for the OECD**

The GATT provided a highly permissive framework — one that mainly benefited the OECD states. The exemptions for temperate agriculture and the quantitative restrictions on developing country textile and clothing exports of the Multifibre Arrangement (MFA) represented only the most visible signs that 'non-discrimination' remained a goal and not an achievement.

Substantial exceptions still exist, and developing countries would argue that many are to their disadvantage. Hence, the proponents of SDT are not pressing for loopholes to be inserted into a well-established system based upon uniform treatment. They are arguing merely for the reality, rather than the rhetoric, of the WTO to apply, and to recognize that binding dispute settlement requires that this be done ex ante rather than ex post. Some go further and argue that 'special' treatment for developing countries now is required to offset bias against them in the present rules that were drafted under heavy industrialized country influence.

*Source*: ADB Development Research Division, 2004.

---

settlement has altered the character of the WTO and its image. All sorts of policies that had been in existence for years have been placed in the WTO's dispute settlement spotlight. And the proportion of cases brought by industrial against developing countries has increased: a review of cases brought between 1995 and 2000 found a threefold increase compared with the GATT period in the proportion of cases that were brought by industrialized countries against developing countries (Delich, 2002). A corollary is the vastly more controversial image of the WTO, compared with the GATT.

### The Status Quo

The presumption of many was that the Uruguay Round represented the beginning of the end for SDT (Box 5.3). Increasingly WTO members would accept the same obligations. But this presumption appears now to have been misplaced, with binding dispute settlement and the spread of WTO rules into new areas making SDT more relevant than in the past. The SDT incorporated into the Uruguay Round texts is unsatisfactory for many members and observers. There are currently three areas of SDT, and they apply to three principal groups of countries. The types of treatment are modulation of commitments, trade preferences and declarations of support, while the main country groups are the industrialized countries, the developing countries and the least developed. Developing countries want Doha to improve some of the types of treatment; some industrialized countries propose a re-visiting of the country groups.

The most substantial SDT provisions are those that allow for a modulation of

---

**Box 5.3: The origins of SDT**

The history of SDT in essence is that:

- SDT had its origins in a view of trade and development that questioned the desirability of developing countries liberalizing border measures at the same pace as industrialised countries;

- the popularity of this approach was (possibly temporarily) in decline in many developing country governments during the negotiation period for the Uruguay Round Agreement;

- consequently, many SDT provisions on border measures and subsidies envisage developing countries (other than the least developed) following a similar path to that of the industrialized countries but at a slower pace;

- other SDT provisions (particularly those covering positive support to developing countries via financial and technical assistance or technology transfer) were not agreed in a form that is enforceable within the WTO system.

*Source*: ADB Development Research Division, 2004.

---

commitments by different type of member. Hence, for example, the Agreement on Agriculture requires the industrialized countries to reduce their tariffs by 36 percent over six years, but developing countries have to do so by only 24 percent over ten years and least developed countries do not need to cut their tariffs at all. This aspect normally meets the minimum requirement for SDT: it is 'legally enforceable' in the sense that a WTO member may use the dispensations granted under SDT in its defense, if its trade policies are challenged by another WTO member on the grounds that they do not conform with the

Uruguay Round commitments. Hence, for example, if India were challenged on the grounds that it had not reduced its agricultural tariffs by 36 percent, it would have a watertight defence in dispute settlement by pointing to the fact that it is required to liberalize by only 24 percent.

### Market Access for Developing Country Exports

The second area is the provision of enhanced market access via trade preferences (mainly by industrialized countries to developing and least developed countries). Under the 1979 Enabling Clause, WTO members are permitted to suspend the granting of MFN treatment in cases where they are offering better-than-MFN tariffs to developing countries. There are many other areas where SDT *could* be provided on market access, but the industrialized countries do not do so; on the contrary, they target their restrictions on developing countries. The misuse of anti-dumping actions is a case in point. Far from using the provisions that exist within the WTO sensitively to reduce the disruption to developing country trade, the Organization for Economic Co-operation and Development (OECD) states are frequently accused of claiming that dumping has occurred when it is simply a case that developing countries are more competitive than domestic suppliers. As in so many cases, the WTO status quo provides the industrialized countries (that largely drafted it) with substantial opportunities for SDT in their own cause, but only limited opportunities in that of the developing states!

The extent to which the provisions on trade preferences meet the requirement of legal enforceability is questionable and is in the process of being clarified by the current dispute of India against the EU (Box 5.4). A strong case can be made that the standard Generalized System of Preferences (GSP) of most industrialized countries can be justified under the SDT provisions of the Enabling Clause where it provides equal treatment to all developing countries. In other words, if the EU were to be challenged in dispute settlement by, say, the US on the grounds that

---

**Box 5.4: India vs. the EU**

The EU's 'generalized' system of preferences actually offers several different regimes. Some beneficiaries are treated more favourably than others.

In 2002 India challenged in the WTO an element of this intra-GSP differentiation: the provision of especially favorable treatment to exports from certain Latin American states. During 2003 the WTO panel set up to examine this dispute concluded in India's favour (WTO 2003b).

If upheld unamended by the Appellate Body, the panel's conclusions could have some wide-ranging effects. Among other things, it considered whether or not the Enabling Clause is a 'positive rule establishing obligations' (as is, for example, Article I.1 of GATT establishing the principle of non-discrimination) or is in the nature of an 'exception' (that can, under certain circumstances, be used as a 'defence' by a member to a finding that its policies are inconsistent with its obligations). It concluded that they were an exception. In other words, it confirmed the 'negative' SDT of the current WTO in relation to trade preferences by emphasizing that they provide members with the opportunity to offer special advantages to developing countries, but not the obligation to do so.

*Source*: ADB Development Research Division, 2004.

the standard GSP tariff available to all developing countries was lower than the MFN tariff being applied to imports from the US, the EU would probably be able to cite the SDT provisions of the Enabling Clause in its defence.

The WTO panel for the India dispute found that the EU could not justify — under the Enabling Clause — the provision of special trade preferences to the Andean and Central American countries that were not also made available to other developing countries. The EU claimed that these countries faced a special problem of fighting drugs, and that its extra preferences were an appropriate support to this struggle. But whilst the panel asserted the right of developed country members to limit GSP preferences in cases where a particular supplying country had an established competitiveness, and to provide special preferences for Least Developed Countries (LDCs), it concluded that the Enabling Clause did not justify any other discrimination between developing countries.

The practical implications of this finding, should it be confirmed by the Appellate Body, would depend on how the EU reacts. In principle, it could adjust policy either by scaling down the benefits that it offers to the Andean and Central American countries or by improving the 'standard' GSP to the same level. Taking the first course of action would enhance the preference margin obtained by some African exporters in cases where they face significant competition from the Andean/ Central American states (notably in the area of horticulture). Taking the second course would, in the first instance, reduce the competitive margin of Africa's current preferences (by widening the number of develop-

ing countries that receive similar access terms). But in the medium term it might also make the current Economic Partnership Agreement (EPA) negotiations less problematic for Sub-Saharan Africa (see below). The EU's current stated position with respect to its trade relations with SSA is that those countries that fail to negotiate EPAs will, after 2007, trade on the basis of the GSP. If the GSP were to be improved during the intervening years (whether as the result of autonomous decision or in response to the WTO ruling), the 'cost' of not joining an EPA would be reduced.

### Ancillary Support

The third area of SDT is wholly unenforceable. It comprises the large number of declarations of support for developing countries that litter the Uruguay Round texts. For example, Article 4 of GATS deals with encouraging the increased participation of developing countries in international services trade through 'negotiated specific commitments' relating to the strengthening of their domestic services capacity, improvement of their access to distribution channels and liberalisation of market access in sectors and modes of supply of export interest to them. Similarly, the 'Decision on Measures Concerning the Possible Negative Effects of the Reform Program on Least-Developed and Net Food-Importing Developing Countries' requires members to review the level of food aid to ensure that it is sufficient to meet the legitimate needs of developing countries, to adopt guidelines to ensure that an increasing proportion is provided to LDCs and net food-importing developing countries and to give full consideration in their aid programs to help improve agricultural productivity and infrastructure. There are many other such references.

There is no action that an aggrieved developing country can take either inside or outside the WTO to force another member (or an international organization) to take actions that it believes are consistent with these undertakings. A considerable element of the discontent expressed by developing countries in the WTO about the failures of SDT derives from resentment that they were 'hoodwinked' into signing the Single Undertaking through promises that were not worth the paper they were written on. The Doha negotiations need to resolve these problems either by making the SDT provisions enforceable in some sense or by amending current rules (or tailoring future rules) to take account of their non-enforceability.

### Problems with the Status Quo

To summarize, there are two principal problems with the status quo. One is that the existing, legally enforceable provisions are eroding assets. The other is that large areas of trade policy are without any legally enforceable SDT. Both are combined in the case of agriculture.

Most legally enforceable SDT is an eroding asset in the sense that it provides modulation of commitments, the vitality of which will decline directly (if time limited) and indirectly (if it relates to removal of barriers that all members are reducing over time). Hence, the implementation delays under the Agreement on TRIPs and the Agreement on Agriculture cease to provide differential treatment once the extended timetable has expired. Similarly, SDT provis-

ions that require developing countries to liberalize/reduce subsidies etc., but to a lesser extent than industrialized countries, will in due course cease to have validity when the developing countries' remaining barriers reach very low levels.

It is true that in cases where least developed countries have been exempted from tariff/subsidy reduction altogether their concessions will not be eroded in this way. But many vulnerable developing countries do not fall within the least developed group.

The other problem, found especially severely in the 'new areas' of trade policy (such as TRIPs, services, government procurement and competition policy) is that no effective SDT exists and it is often far from clear what form more robust provisions would take. Evidently, the removal of formal market access barriers is either irrelevant or a minor aspect of rule formation (Box 5.5).

---

**Box 5.5: Upside-down SDT: agriculture**

An example of the problem of identifying appropriate SDT is found in the Agreement on Agriculture. This aims primarily to solve a problem that developing countries do not have: excessive direct and indirect subsidies to inefficient domestic agriculture. Given this 'wrong' focus (and the very partial coverage of the new rules) the existing SDT provisions have been described as 'upside down': developing countries are allowed flexibility in reducing distortions that they do not have, but face potential gaps in coverage over vital aspects of food security.

*Source*: Michalopoulos, 2003.

Hence, the 'traditional recipe' of slower, more limited barrier-removal is not relevant, as is evident in the case of TRIPs (see below).

### The Doha Impasse

Because existing SDT provisions are not adequate, the Doha Declaration made a commitment to strengthen them and make them more operational. But translating this commitment into operational practise has so far proved to be beyond the grasp of the WTO members, and so there is an impasse (Box 5.6). The major problem in dealing with the deficiencies to the status quo is not

technical but political. It is possible to identify, even at this early stage in the negotiations, flexibilities that would address major concerns. But, they must necessarily be couched in quite broad terms given the absence of specific texts for new rules. And there is an evident unwillingness on the part of industrialized countries to agree broad, enforceable provisions at this time.

If there is a problem with broad provisions now, how about more tightly drawn ones at a later stage when this becomes feasible because there are draft texts that can be amended? The problem here is likely to be the dynamic of the negotiations. If the Doha Round proceeds in the same way as its predecessor, introducing appropriate SDT at a later stage will not be easy (Box 5.7). Whilst some broad positions had been established in the Uruguay Round by 1991, many of the critical details were not agreed until the final months, weeks (and even hours) of the 11-year marathon. Many of these details were hammered out in forums from which the majority of GATT members were excluded. Some of the non-actionable SDT provisions that are causing the greatest developing country bitterness were hatched in this way.

The Doha dynamic will probably be similar because it appears to be inherent to the task of negotiating a wide range of complex provisions simultaneously. There can be no agreement until the major WTO members have obtained compromises with which they can live, and then there is a strong imperative to finalise the deal as quickly as possible before this consensus is disturbed. One close observer of the process attributes a significant part of the final success in the Uruguay Round to Peter Sutherland's

---

**Box 5.6: The SDT impasse**

To be effective, any development provisions must be actionable within the WTO. In the absence of agreed details to any WTO rule changes, such a guarantee can be provided only in broad terms.

In the absence of agreement on sub-groups of developing countries, these broad, actionable provisions would apply either to all developing countries or just to the least developed countries.

The industrialized countries are unwilling, currently, to agree general exemptions, partly because they want to link them to the negotiations of substance and they are unwilling to agree them for all developing countries; but SDT limited to the least developed would be cast too narrowly.

The developing countries are unwilling to discuss differentiation and graduation, at least until substantial offers are on the table, and are reluctant to link provisions which, to their mind, 'restore the balance' to negotiations on further WTO rules.

*Source*: ADB Development Research Division, 2004.

---

### Box 5.7:  The Uruguay Round precedent

The Uruguay Round made erratic progress. A Draft Final Act had been produced by the end of 1991, but the agricultural proposals were rejected by the EU (Croome, 1995: 328). There followed two years in which most of the 'action' took place in bilateral talks between the EU and the USA from which other states were largely excluded. Even when the formal negotiations were re-launched in July 1993, there were at least three tracks: the discussion in the formal GATT groups, the personal 'facilitating' of the new GATT Director General, Peter Sutherland, who 'kept up a punishing series of whirlwind visits to top-level political leaders in the major countries' (ibid.: 349), and bilateral negotiations between the EU and USA, with their respective chief negotiators, Sir Leon Brittan and Mickey Kantor, having from November 'a crucial series of meetings ... that were to continue with only short breaks over a period of more than three weeks' (ibid.: 364).

refusal to countenance any further delay (Croome, 1995). A consequence is that all other members have to scuttle around to establish their willingness to accept the compromises and to secure their own interests.

The TRIPs Agreement is a standing warning of the danger that arises from not introducing binding SDT at an early stage of negotiations. Hailed by many at the time of Marrakech as both modest and desirable, the agreement has long been criticised by trade economists such as Jagdish Bhagwati as 'turning the WTO, thanks to powerful lobbies, into a royalty-collection agency' (letter to the *Financial Times*, 20 February

2001). Its developmental appropriateness was questioned in detail during 2002 by the Commission on Intellectual Property Rights (CIPR), established by the then UK Secretary of State for Development, Clare Short, with a secretariat staffed mainly by officials drawn from the UK Department for International Development. Its final report (CIPR, 2002) stated that:

> "... *we are not persuaded by the arguments that developing countries at very different stages of development should be required to adopt a specific date ... when they will provide the TRIPS standards of protection within their domestic IP regimes, regardless of their progress in creating a viable technological base.*" (p. 161)

Not least of the lessons of TRIPs is that once WTO agreements have been signed, whatever imperfections are subsequently discovered, they are virtually impossible to revise. It is for this reason that the CIPR recognized that:

> "*While we have reservations about the extension of TRIPS standards to all developing countries, we recognize that it is most unlikely that any WTO members would be keen to renegotiate the agreement. Many members fear that in seeking particular amendments they would be obliged to compromise elsewhere in ways that may not bring a net benefit to them.*" (ibid. p. 160)

## The Agreement on Agriculture

Africa's attitude towards multilateral liberalization is necessarily conditioned by the anticipated effects that this will have on its preferential trade regime with the EU, which is its main export market. The relative merits of multilateralism and regionalism have been much debated, and there are clearly both pluses and minuses in shifting fundamentally from the status quo to a significantly more liberal world trade regime. The relative attractions depend critically upon the time period considered and the socioeconomic actors involved. But this academic discussion is not necessarily directly relevant to the issues that have come before the Doha Round. The worst-case scenario for Africa is one in which few if any of the identified benefits from multilateral liberal trade accrue to the region (because WTO change is too limited) but key advantages of the current preferential regime are lost. During 2003 and its immediate predecessors, it became increasingly clear that such a worst-case scenario could be played out. This would be the result of changes in the multilateral arena and the preferential one.

The multilateral arena of most interest is that concerned with agriculture. This is not because Africa does not obtain preferences on non-agricultural products, but because the erosion of the key one — on clothing — is already pre-ordained (Box 5.8). In the case of temperate agriculture, however, robust preferences still exist. But they could be eroded by any combination of change under the following three headings:

- Significant multilateral liberalization to reduce OECD market access barriers to agricultural imports;
- Autonomous actions by OECD states that have the effect of reducing the returns to preferential exporters;
- Changes to the preferential trade agreements.

**Box 5.8: Negotiating modalities**

These are intended to establish the quantitative targets for liberalization in the Doha Round. This follows the precedent of the Uruguay Round when, for example, the industrialized countries agreed to convert all their market access restrictions into tariffs which they then reduced by 36 percent over six years. These figures are not mentioned in the Agreement on Agriculture and, by implication, neither will any that are produced for the Doha Round. Rather, the modalities established the cuts that the WTO members had to make to their tariff schedules when producing their 'comprehensive draft commitments'. It is then up to their negotiating partners to check whether the schedules accord with the benchmarks.

According to the Doha timetable, the draft commitments were to have been adopted at the Cancun Ministerial meeting in September 2003, but this deadline was missed. Even if the meeting had not been brought to a premature close, the 'modalities' being discussed were still skeletal in the sense that they contained no numbers for the tariff/subsidy cuts that would be made. These would still have had to be negotiated post-Cancun.

The first of these is dealt with in the next three sub-sections. The area of autonomous OECD action of most important for Africa — change to the EU's Common Agricultural Policy (CAP) is covered in the following section. This is followed by a review of the preferences for Africa offered by the Quad and, then, the change of most current importance for Africa — the replacement of the Cotonou trade regime with a set of EPAs.

*Market Access*

The most fundamental change in the WTO Agreement on Agriculture that could alter Africa's preferences would be substantial liberalization. Preferences are the other side of the coin to protectionism. If a country has a liberal trade regime it cannot, by definition, offer preferential access to some suppliers. Only if it restricts imports in some significant way does the possibility arise of reducing these barriers to some extent for favored trade partners. OECD market access barriers for agriculture fulfill comfortably the first criterion: no fewer than 19 of the 33 Harmonized System (HS) chapters covered (in whole or in part) by the Agreement on Agriculture face tariff peaks in at least one (and usually two or three) of the Quad states.[2] The evidence so far from Doha is that even a successful conclusion to the Round will leave most of these peaks in place.

Whilst the 1994 Agreement on Agriculture began a process of reinforcing rules and liberalizing trade in temperate agricultural goods, this still has a long way to go. In return for accepting rules that *could* become constraining after further rounds of negotiation, members were allowed to defer major pain by setting import restrictions and subsidies at high initial levels. The OECD countries retain a huge number of agricultural 'tariff peaks', some of which run into thousands of percent.[3] The products that most frequently encounter tariff peaks in the Quad are:

- Beef: Canada and EU;
- Dairy products: EU, Japan, US;
- Vegetables, fresh or dried: EU, Japan, US;
- Fresh fruit: EU, Japan, US;
- Cereals and products: EU and Japan;
- Sugar: Canada, EU, Japan, US;
- Prepared fruit and vegetables: Canada, EU, Japan, US;
- Wine: Canada, EU, Japan, US;
- Spirits: EU, Japan, US;
- Tobacco: Japan, US.

Of these, the product groups with the greatest *absolute* importance for Africa are tobacco and sugar. In *proportional* terms (i.e. Africa's share in world imports), the most important are fruits such as oranges, avocados, dates and grapes, fresh cut flowers and tea (in Japan). Whilst the Cotonou and Euro-Med Agreements cover many of these, Africa still faces tariff peaks in other Quad markets. The existence of peaks is important because it means that apparently substantial tariff cuts may still leave in place barriers so high as to keep imports at very low levels. How likely is it that the Doha Round will bring down tariff peaks to levels at which substantial imports become viable? 'Not very likely' seems to be the answer.

What are known in the jargon as the 'negotiating modalities' were due to have been agreed by 31 March 2003 but were in fact not (Box 5.9). While the modalities are not the final word in the negotiations, they are certainly the most important 'first steps'. Only if the formula adopted commits the industrialized countries to reduce their import protection to non-constraining levels will it be possible for the Doha Round to result in

---

[2] Canada, EU, Japan and the USA.

[3] The operational definition of a tariff peak is over 15 percent *ad valorem*.

## Box 5.9: Preference erosion on clothing

The decision in the Uruguay Round to phase out the MFA by the end of 2004 means that Africa will lose the most substantial element of the current preferential regimes on clothing. This is that they are either free from quotas (as with SSA exports to the EU) or that the quotas are much less restrictive than those applied to major competitors (notably the countries of Asia). Even though tariff preferences may remain from 2005 onwards, these are relatively minor compared with the situation on quotas.

There are bound to be significant shifts in the global pattern of clothing production as a result. African industries that have depended upon Cotonou, the Euro–Med Agreements and the African Growth and Opportunity Act (AGOA) for their growth may face serious adjustment problems.

increased export opportunities for developing countries in Quad markets. Even then, there will be much to negotiate. On past precedent, the formulas will allow members some latitude in liberalizing to a greater extent on some items and to a lesser extent on others. It will be important to follow the negotiations closely to urge that the greater reductions are made on items of importance to Africa.

Since the draft Cancun text left out the numbers it is not possible to establish its effects, but in the run-up to the earlier March 2003 deadline the WTO Secretariat produced a summary of member state positions, known colloquially as the revised Harbinson draft, H1 (Rev.1) (WTO 2003a). This did contain numbers but it failed to win consensus, partly

because some members felt that it was too drastic and others felt it did not go far enough (Box 5.10). The application of the proposal to the Quad's current tariffs would have left many product groups largely immune to imports. The principal product areas that would retain tariff peaks of over 50 percent post-H1 (Rev.1) are:

- In the EU: beef, dairy products, bananas, prepared meat, sugar and grape juice;
- In Japan: meat, dairy products, cereals, sugar, coffee/tea essences and silk;
- In the US: peanuts and tobacco.

## Box 5.10: The Harbinson draft

The Harbinson approach would have reduced higher tariffs proportionately more than lower ones. The square brackets in the text indicate the figures suggested for industrialized countries. These were not agreed.

(i) For all agricultural tariffs greater than [90 percent *ad valorem*] the simple average reduction rate shall be [60] percent subject to a minimum cut of [45] percent per tariff line.

(ii) For all agricultural tariffs lower than or equal to [90 percent *ad valorem*] and greater than [15 percent *ad valorem*] the simple average reduction rate shall be [50] percent subject to a minimum cut of [35] percent per tariff line.

(iii) For all agricultural tariffs lower than or equal to [15 percent *ad valorem*] the simple average reduction rate shall be [40] percent subject to a minimum cut of [25] percent per tariff line (WTO 2003a: para. 8).

In addition to these ultra-constrained products, those facing 25–50 percent tariff peaks (which will reduce, if not suffocate, trade) include:

- EU: meat (other than beef), fruit, vegetables, cereals, fruit juices, food industry residues, and tobacco;
- Japan: cereal preparations, miscellaneous food preparations;
- US: dairy products, sugar, butter substitutes.

As long as world agricultural trade remains relatively illiberal, preferential exporters have a strong interest in avoiding or delaying the erosion of their preferences. The African sugar exporters were especially active — and achieved some success in the Harbinson draft. Under this the EU (and other preference givers) would have been permitted to extend tariff reductions 'affecting long-standing preferences in respect of products which are of vital export importance for developing country beneficiaries of such schemes ...' over a period of eight rather than five years, with a first installment being deferred until the start of the third year of the implementation period (WTO, 2003a). This was seen as important to allow Sugar Protocol beneficiaries to reduce their production costs in advance of increased competition in the EU market.

### Subsidies

Cotton, the African *cause célèbre* at Cancun, does not feature on these lists of tariff peaks. This is because the principal problem with the Agreement on Agriculture for African cotton producers is not the market access barriers in the Quad but the domestic subsidies of the US. Almost all of West Africa's cotton exports to the EU in 2002 were 'cotton, neither carded nor combed' (HS 520100).[4] In the EU, Canada and Japan items in this HS sub-head face zero percent MFN duties, and although they face a tariff of up to 31.4 cents/kg in the USA this is equivalent to only about 10 percent *ad valorem*. One concern is of OECD exports that have benefited from subsidies (either direct or indirect) that disrupt African trade. There have been concerns over the years, for example, with heavily subsidised EU beef exports to Western and Southern Africa. At Cancun there was prominent discussion of the hindrances posed to West African cotton exporters by US subsidies to American cotton producers. Many commentators attributed the perceived inadequacy of the US offer on cotton as a significant factor contributing to the stalling of negotiations.

As substantial net importers of cereals, Africa as a region also had an interest in any rule changes that would tend to increase import costs and, hence, result in deterioration in their terms of trade. The region has become increasingly dependent upon imports (Figure 5.1). Contrary to some popular opinion, this is not primarily a result of food aid, which has formed a relatively small (and declining in the last decade covered) share of the total. A significant part of the foreign exchange used to pay for the imports comes from agricultural exports,

---

[4] 100 percent of Chad's, 99 percent of Mali's, 97 percent of Benin's and 88 percent of Burkina Faso's; their exports to the US are so small as not to figure in the United States International Trade Commission data.

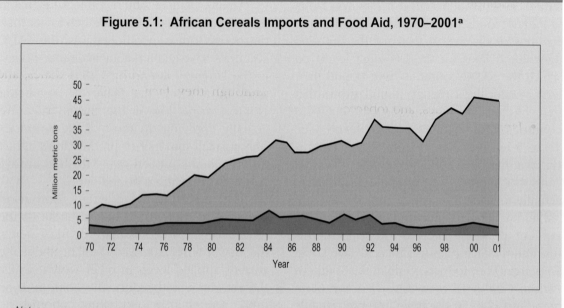

**Figure 5.1: African Cereals Imports and Food Aid, 1970–2001[a]**

*Note*:
(a) It is not clear from the data whether FAO figures for total imports include food aid. It should be clear, since figures for imports should include all imports, but since the figure for food aid comes from WFP and, presumably, is compiled from what donors say they have sent, it is not known if all of what is reported under food aid is also noted under imports.To the extent that food aid is additional, its share of the total is even smaller than the graph suggests.
*Source*: FAO FAOSTAT Agriculture Data (http://apps.fao.org/page/collections?subset=agriculture).

which are also affected by WTO rules (especially those on preferences). Hence, any change in either side of the trade equation could affect indirectly the food security of individuals by altering either the total volume of food available in a country or its distribution between different types of food (over which individuals have different entitlements).

### Africa and Tariff Cuts

Will the next round of multilateral agricultural tariff cuts leave African agriculture dangerously vulnerable to dumped imports? It is certainly a potential outcome, given that

Doha is unlikely to remove the direct and indirect OECD subsidies that artificially depress world prices. But until the modalities for developing and least developed country tariff reduction are known it is not possible to determine how likely this potential is to be realized. An analysis of the effects of applying the Harbinson draft in Southern Africa, though, suggests that the danger is not high — this time around.

The reason why agriculture, at least in Southern Africa, would not be thrown open to the winds of global competition by the Harbinson formula is that this has either happened already (largely as a result of structural adjustment) or, if it has not, Doha would not fundamentally affect the status quo for most items. An analysis of the 600–700 agricultural lines (at the HS6-digit level) on which the SADC countries have bound their tariffs under the Uruguay Round shows that many followed the example of the OECD countries and set them at high levels (see Table 5.1). In the jargon, a 'bound' tariff is one that has been submitted to the WTO and cannot be exceeded; 'applied' tariffs are those actually in force. In all the countries listed in Table 5.1 the maximum bound tariff is 100 percent or more and, in most cases, this maximum rate applies to almost all (well over 90 percent) of products. Only in the Southern African Customs Union (SACU) is the ultra-high tariff cited in the table unrepresentative of the entire range, and tariffs in excess of 90 percent are more typical of the maximum.

An important feature of Table 5.1 is that in most cases applied rates are much lower than the bound ones. In other words, the SADC countries have taken out an 'insurance policy' in the Uruguay Round by setting the bound tariff at a level that leaves a significant comfort zone above the tariffs they are actually applying. In most of the countries only a small minority of product lines attract the maximum applied rate, which is always below the maximum bound rate.

The application of the Harbinson proposal to the current bound tariffs of the SADC countries shows that, for most items, the 'new' bound tariff would still be above the current applied level. In other words, whilst the reform would reduce the comfort zone (and, for this reason alone, should be accompanied by other reforms — see Stevens et al, 2000), it would not, in itself, result in any significant cuts to the tariffs actually applied at present. Except in the cases of SACU and Mauritius, fewer than one percent of agricultural lines would see the bound rate brought below the current applied level and, in the great majority of cases, the products concerned are alcohol and tobacco; the only 'staples' are some categories of fruit, vegetables and maize in Mauritius. For SACU the list is longer, at almost one-eighth of the items, and broader since it includes a range of meats, dairy products and sugar. However, the 'free trade' agreement between the EU and South Africa, accompanied by autonomous SACU liberalization, is likely to be a much more important factor in liberalization than any outcome of Doha.

**Table 5.1: SADC Tariff Ranges for Agriculture (percent)**

| Country | Maximum | | Minimum | |
|---|---|---|---|---|
| | Bound | Applied | Bound | Applied |
| Malawi | 125 | 30 | 125 | 0 |
| Mauritius | 122 | 55 | 37 | 0 |
| Mozambique | 100 | 35 | 100 | 0 |
| SACU | 597 | 115 | 0 | 0 |
| Tanzania | 120 | 30 | 120 | 0 |
| Zambia | 125 | 25 | 45 | 0 |
| Zimbabwe | 150 | 40a | 25 | 0 |

Note:
(a) Excluding tobacco, alcohol and aerated mineral water, which face high rates but are not food items.

## Change to the EU's Common Agricultural Policy

Relief (full or partial) from the CAP's protectionism is currently one of the most commercially valuable African trade preferences, and its relative importance will grow as other preferences are eroded (see below). But autonomous change to the CAP may erode these preferences more rapidly than the Doha Round. Unless the Doha modalities go much further than Harbinson, the EU will retain tariff peaks for many of the items on which preferences are offered. It will retain, therefore, the capacity to continue preferences if it wishes. But the changes to the CAP being introduced and discussed could reduce significantly the commercial advantage that Africa obtains — without any change to the actual text of the trade agreements.

It is important not to confuse 'CAP change' with 'liberalization'. What would a more liberal agricultural regime look like? Liberalization, in the textbook sense, means reducing the government taxes and subsidies (and amending protectionist rules) that stop high-cost domestic producers losing market share to lower-cost imports. It implies that the global location of production will change over time, with lower-cost producers increasing output and higher-cost producers declining. An absolutely essential part of this process is the removal of OECD barriers to imports from developing countries. Whilst tariff slashing would not in principle prevent OECD governments from subsidizing their farmers sufficiently for them to be able to compete with imports, the fiscal cost would be very high, making the cuts improbable. Without the tariff cuts, it will remain feasible for governments to avoid production relocation through the payment of subsidies.

The EU portrays its CAP changes as an exercise in liberalization, but they have little in common with the concept just described. EU 'liberalization' aims to sustain European production but to reshuffle the subsidies and taxes to make them less costly to the European budget and more easily defensible in the WTO. The EU currently provides €43 billion per year of direct support funded at the Union level. In addition, there is the indirect support of tariffs that make imports artificially expensive, as well as national-level assistance to farmers. The Commission proposals of 2002 seek to shift €25 billion of direct, EU-level income support from one type of support to another. This will have very limited effects on the EU's overall agricultural trade since it will neither decrease production nor increase market access. But it will erode African preferences.

### Implications for Preferences

Because of the complex ways in which Cotonou assists SSA agricultural exporters, it is often hard to calculate the extent to which an EU policy change will result in erosion — even though the broad direction of change is clear enough. Take the examples of the EU's Agenda 2000 reforms, its mid-2002 proposals on the preference for beef and rice (EC 2002), and its recent 'discussion paper' on sugar (EC 2003). They aim to alter the mix of policies that support domestic producers, not to reduce significantly the overall subsidy they receive. In broad terms, market prices are set to fall but European farmers will receive income supports to offset this. If European market prices fall, so will those received by

ACP exporters. If ACP exports are unrestricted, it may be possible for some states to offset a part of this by increasing the volume of exports. But where exports are limited by a tariff quota (TQ) (as they are for beef, rice and sugar), they will have no opportunity to offset the decline in their return per tonne exported by increasing the volume of sales.

It is important for ACP exporters to know how far EU prices will fall — but that is not clear. The EU proposals on beef and rice refer only to the 'intervention price' — the price at which the state steps in directly or indirectly to buy up produce that cannot find a buyer. Agenda 2000 cut the intervention price for beef, but also introduced subsidies for storage aimed to encourage the private sector to sustain market prices. It also retains export subsidies, so supporting the domestic market price by offloading some supplies on to the world market. The 2002 proposal recommends for rice the same combination of a sharp (50 percent) cut in the intervention price, private storage subsidies to encourage the maintenance of prices above this level, and a 'safety net' price below this at which the state will intervene. The link between changes to EU policy and to market prices is even more indirect in the case of sugar.

Actual market prices will depend upon how farmers and traders react to these changes — and also on the Euro equivalent of world market prices (which, in turn, depends both on underlying prices and on the exchange rate). Hence, whilst it is easy to see that a 50 percent price cut is proposed, it does not follow that actual market prices will fall by exactly this proportion. But the trend is clear. The EU's aim is to reduce European market prices close to world market levels. This is so that it will not have to pay WTO-vulnerable export subsidies to get rid of surpluses on the world market. It would remove one of the two benefits of ACP preferences.

## Africa and the Quad

The evidence from the Doha process so far, therefore, is that it seems unlikely to herald the imminent arrival of a liberal trade regime, at least in the area of agriculture. Even if the collapse at Cancun does not lead to a renewed bout of regional trade bloc creation, it seems inevitable that preferential and regional trade agreements with particular trade partners will continue to figure prominently in Africa's trade profile. But change is under way which could alter significantly the gains that the region has traditionally obtained under these agreements.

In relation to the Quad, the EU is overwhelmingly Africa's most important market importing almost 50 percent more items than the other three Quad states put together. There are very few items that are imported into one of the other three Quad members and not into the EU. In 2000 the EU imported 1,710 items from Africa to a value of $1 million or more and of these no fewer than 1,692 were covered by a preference for at least one exporter from the region. The US, which was the next largest Quad importer, took only 491 items, of which preferences were available for one-half.

The EU has no fewer than eight trade agreements with Africa. All African states are eligible for the GSP. Those south of the Sahara (except South Africa) also benefit from the

Cotonou trade regime[5] and, in the case of the least developed countries, the 'Everything but Arms' (EBA) regime. In addition, South Africa and most of the North African countries have their own bilateral agreements. In the case of the North African countries, these are of long standing but are in the process of being transformed into reciprocal FTAs, many of the provisions of which are similar (Table 5.2). This follows the Barcelona Declaration objective of creating a Euro–Mediterranean free trade area by 2010. Negotiations for revised trade agreements have already been concluded with Tunisia (1995), Israel (1995), Morocco (1996), Jordan (1997), Egypt (1999), Algeria (2001), and Lebanon (2002). Those with Tunisia, Morocco and Israel have been ratified and are already in force. At the same time, the five Cooperation Agreements which the European Community concluded in the mid-1970s with Algeria, Egypt, Jordan, Lebanon and Syria continue to be implemented.

**Table 5.2: North Africa's Most Recent Trade Agreements with the EU**

| Agreement | Most recent extension signed in |
| --- | --- |
| EU–Algeria | April 2002 |
| EU–Tunisia | March 1998 |
| EU–Morocco | March 2000 |
| EU–Egypt | June 2001 |

For Japan and Canada, the GSP is the basic building block of their preferential trade regimes with Africa. Both provide special arrangements for least developed countries within the GSP framework which offer wider and deeper preferences. In the case of the USA, the GSP is also the building block, but the AGOA provides the most favorable treatment within the GSP framework for 125 of the 491 items (26 percent) for which data are available for US imports from Africa.

At the same time a higher proportion of imported products faces zero MFN tariffs in countries other than the EU. The proportion ranges from almost two-thirds for Canada to just over a half for Japan and 42 percent for the US; in the EU it is just over one-quarter (although in absolute terms the EU offers a zero MFN on more items than all the other three combined).

The two sets of figures are related. One reason why Canada cannot offer preferences on a large proportion of its imports from Africa is that it levies a zero MFN duty on many. As indicated above, preferences are the obverse of protectionism. This is the underlying reason why liberal-trade economists will normally prefer multilateral liberalization to preferences. Additionally, there is the political assessment that the vested interests created by preferences may prove to be a 'stumbling block' rather than a 'building block' to multilateralism, to adapt Bhagwati's celebrated aphorism. But in cases such as the present, where multilateral liberalization is not on offer (because there is no consensus in the WTO), regionalism may be a second-best.

---

[5] South Africa is formally a party to the Cotonou Agreement, but is not eligible for the trade regime.

## The Protection–Preference Nexus

Central to the argument on how Africa may be affected by change to its regional agreements is the concept of 'trade policy rents' (Box 5.11). An important paradox emerges: that Africa's greatest gains from exporting to Europe have been in the products that appear at first glance to be the most heavily protected and to receive the least generous preferences.

Africa's exports fall into three groups in terms of their market characteristics. These are:

1. Traditional products (such as beverages) that are exported to a relatively undifferentiated, liberal world market;
2. Other traditional exports (such as clothing, beef, sugar, citrus and olive oil) that are exported to markets that are heavily influenced by agricultural protectionism;
3. Non-traditional products (such as horticulture) that are exported to markets characterized to a greater or lesser extent by protectionism.

The reason for differentiating between these groups is that they face very different 'value chains' and price characteristics. The secular decline in the terms of trade for the first category (beverages, etc.) was forecast over half a century ago in the pioneering work of Raúl Prebisch and Hans Singer; forecasts that have been borne out in reality. African exporters are price-takers on a declining world market. Some appear to have 'lost' their comparative advantage to new entrants such as Malaysia (as in the case of West African palm oil production). The second category

> **Box 5.11:  How rents are created**
>
> What are termed 'trade policy rents' arise when a market is distorted but certain suppliers of imports receive preferential access. The purpose of the distortion is to enable domestic producers to sell goods that consumers would otherwise prefer to buy from foreign producers (whether because they are cheaper, of a preferred quality or whatever).
>
> One way to do this is to subsidize the domestic producers — but this tends to be politically unpopular because it is visible, and results either in higher taxes or lower government expenditure on other things. Another, less visible and less politically costly way is to rig the domestic market so that consumers have to pay the higher prices at which domestic producers can compete.
>
> One of the fundamental mechanisms to achieve this is to impose protectionist trade barriers that, by squeezing imports, restrict supply and maintain prices at higher levels than would otherwise apply. In some cases, these restrictions (and their price effects) are substantial. The principal intention of these distortions is normally to confer the rents on producers in the distorting state, but there is leakage — often through preferences. All of the OECD countries offer some form of preferential market access to certain developing countries.

would have been expected, on the basis of the Prebisch–Singer analysis, to have suffered a secular decline in their terms of trade, were it not for the fact that OECD governments (and especially the EU) have stepped in with policies to support the prices received by their own farmers and have passed on some of these 'benefits' to some African exporters. Consequently, the relative returns from exporting these products have been much more attractive than for other traditional commodities (Stevens and Kennan, 2001). The third category (non-traditional exports) shares the same characteristic — but the scale of the price boost is less marked than for some category 2 items (such as sugar and beef) and the structure of the value chain through which the final price is distributed is very different. In broad terms, Africa's gains from the non-traditional exports have been less substantial than those from the protected traditionals, but the gains are less vulnerable to policy change in the EU.

### The Scale of Rents

In general terms, the protection–preference nexus makes sourcing imports from some suppliers more attractive than from others, but who gains what depends upon the power distribution within a value chain. The trade policy rent may:

- Accrue to the producers (processors or shippers) in the preferred countries, increasing the profitability of production and allowing them to:
  - increase supply relative to that of non-preferred countries; or
  - compensate for production, processing, storage or transport inefficiency relative to that of non-preferred countries; or
  - invest in the human and physical capital required for upgrading;
- Accrue to the buyers in the importing country (if the price they pay to their suppliers does not increase by the full amount of the import tax cut), increasing the profitability of importing from preferred countries relative to non-preferred ones leading to:

- increased imports from the former;
- a need/willingness to shift value-adding processes to the producing country.

The balance between these outcomes is affected by both the overall scale of the rent and the architecture of the rules that create it. Rents are most substantial in product markets that face protectionism so severe that it restricts sharply the possibility of importing from non-preferred sources (Box 5.12). At the other end of the scale are items for which protection is so modest as to render any preferences of limited commercial value. For example, the tariff paid by non-preferred countries on exports to the EU of shelled almonds is only 3.5 percent, compared with preferential rates of 0–3.1 percent.

In the middle are commodity groups like horticulture. EU tariffs are moderately high (for example, 12.8 percent for aubergines) and so the duty-free access provided to a range of developing countries is significant. The advantage is available to a large number of countries, and does not appear sufficiently large by itself to exclude totally non-preferred suppliers. The preference is insufficient to offset any substantial price uncompetitiveness on the part of producers or transporters or, of course, any other failings in the fiercely rigorous supply chain required to get perishable items from an African field to a European supermarket shelf within hours (Dolan et al, 1999).

### The Effects of Agreement Architecture

For the recipient the existence of a preference is better *ceteris paribus* than its non-existence, and a deep cut in protection is better than a shallow cut, but the matter does not end here. There are features of a preference agreement that can enhance or retard its development impact in addition to the simple matters of breadth (number of items covered) and depth (reduction in protection). And these can change.

Who gains this rent within the value chain depends upon the bargaining power of the various elements — retailers, importers, shippers, exporters or producers — which depends in turn partly upon their inherent characteristics and partly upon the architecture of the preference agreement. There exists a host of ways in which the rules and procedures of a preference agreement can bias the result in favour of one party or another. For example, if (as is normally the case) it is importers who are legally liable for penalties for tax evasion should a good be shown *ex post* not to have been eligible for a

preference, then the preferential tariff may not even be claimed. A review of EU importers indicates that this is a very real concern (Cerrex 2002). In such cases, the potential tax cut will not translate into any actual tax cut at all. The main effects of agreement architecture are summarised in Table 5.3. In broad terms, the closer a specific agreement is to the right-hand column the better.

The first row, central column, of Table 5.3 deals with the number of beneficiaries. A preference is sometimes available to effectively all potential suppliers. In such cases it is as if the preference did not exist and MFN tariffs were set at the preferential level. A similar effect occurs when the margin of preference is very small. In this case, the margin may be either over MFN levels or over the preferential rates enjoyed by a significant number of other suppliers. In all these cases, there will be no discernible effect of the

**Table 5.3: Factors Affecting the Impact of a Preference**

| Feature | Characteristics tending to: reduce country impact | enhance country impact |
|---|---|---|
| 1. Geographical coverage | Most supplying states receive preference | Few supplying states receive preference |
| 2. Depth of preference | Small improvement in market access compared with competitors | Substantial improvement in market access compared with competitors |
| 3. Tariff quotas | Global quotas | Country-specific quotas |
| 4. Duration | Short | Long |
| 5. Legal basis | Autonomous, subject to arbitrary change | Contractual, with effective dispute settlement |
| 6. Origin rules | High domestic processing requirement with limited cumulation | Lower domestic processing requirement with broad cumulation |

preference on the exports of any particular country.

At the other end of the scale are cases where only a small number of potential supplying countries receive the preference (row 1, right-hand column). And the bargaining power of the supplying country is enhanced most substantially when importers cannot obtain the tax cut if they import from other sources (row 3). For example, the TQs under the Cotonou Beef Protocol are country specific, as are those under the Sugar Protocol. Hence, for example, if the EU monopsony importer of cane sugar does not buy raw cane from Mauritius, it cannot 'make it up' from other suppliers.[6] This enhances the bargaining power of the supplier. But, at the same time, when preferences are quota restricted it is vital that the exporting country obtain an increase in its price as a result of the tax cut because it cannot raise the volume of exports.[7]

The worst case, therefore, is one in which preferences are heavily constrained by volume but apply to many suppliers. This is the case, for example, with the TQs under the Agreement on Agriculture for frozen beef.

---

[6] East Asian MFA quotas tend to fall into the same category.

[7] The sugar case also illustrates in an extreme form the potential 'downside' of preferences. By guaranteeing high prices for fixed volumes, the regime may have contributed to the high cost of production in the Caribbean. Mauritius illustrates the balance between the positive and negative features. The rents earned on sugar contributed to economic diversification into clothing, but may also have delayed the quest for efficiency in the sugar sector, which is now attempting to position itself to compete in a post-Sugar Protocol world.

The effect can be inferred by comparing the import prices of chilled beef (CN 02013000, for which there are country-specific TQs) and frozen beef (CN 02023050, for which there is a global TQ) with the 'reference prices' obtained by, say, Namibia (which has a country-specific TQ for both under Cotonou). The average EU unit import value for chilled beef from all sources in 2000 was higher (107 percent) than the unit value of imports from Namibia. By contrast, the average unit value for the selected category of frozen beef was lower (86 percent) than Namibia's (see Stevens et al, 2003).

Other factors that may affect the division of the spoils are those that impact on the certainty and duration of an agreement (Table 5.3, rows 4–6). In cases where preferences may be withdrawn (for example because they are subject to ceilings or anti-surge provisions), importers may not know until after the event whether or not they will receive the tax reduction. In such circumstances they are unlikely to pass on in the form of higher prices a tax cut that they may not receive, and their incentive to increase imports from the preferred source may also be muted.

The capacity of a preference-receiving country to benefit from an increase in the volume of its exports is also likely to be restricted if an agreement is of limited duration or uncertain future. In cases where increased supply requires investment, this is particularly likely to be the case. The AGOA derogation on clothing inputs for LDCs is particularly interesting because a finger is often pointed towards rules of origin as the main example of the 'small print' that can prevent a preference that exists on paper having an impact because it imposes conditions that cannot be met. Unduly onerous requirements in relation to the value added or processes that must be undertaken in a country before it can claim 'ownership' of the goods and, hence, the tax reduction, can negate the purpose of the agreement. Rules may be made less onerous either directly (by altering them to require less added value/ fewer processes to be undertaken domestic- ally) or by enlarging the range of countries from which imports may be sourced without the end-product losing originating status. The second of these is known as cumulation: some agreements allow for inputs to be derived from a very large number of countries, but others are more restrictive.

A change in agreement architecture can affect the distribution of gains. This is well illustrated by comparing the treatment of sugar under the EU–ACP Sugar Protocol and the EU's EBA initiative (Box 5.12).

A single EU processor/distributor is the monopsony buyer of exports to the EU under the Sugar Protocol and is substantially

---

**Box 5.12: The EU's EBA**

Since March 2001 the EU has imported duty free from all least developed countries any product except arms. Implementation of the EBA has been partially deferred for bananas (until 2006), sugar and rice (until 2009). In the interim the tariff faced by least developed countries is being reduced progressively, and they have duty-free access for an increasing quota of sugar and rice that is set at levels comfortably above past flows. See the next section of the main text for further details.

---

dependent for its supplies on preferential sugar imports. As a cane sugar refiner, the company needs access to imports since domestic European sugar production is of beet. And, because of the high EU tariff, the financial viability of its operations depends upon the continuation of supplies from preferred sources. Since each beneficiary of the Sugar Protocol has a fixed quota, the company cannot play one off against another; if it cannot agree a price with Malawi, it cannot buy more from Zimbabwe. At the same time, as the owner of the main cane sugar refineries in Europe, it is the only feasible purchaser of African (and Caribbean/ Pacific) exports to the EU. The alternative of exporting already refined sugar to the EU is not considered to be commercially viable on a substantial scale. The only, very partial, alternative would be to sell outside the European harvesting season to EU beet refiners. But the beet and cane industries are in competition for market share.

Under EBA there are (or will be) no quantitative limits on the sugar that least developed African countries are able to export, in contrast to the position under the Sugar Protocol. But neither is there any built- in protection against the sole feasible large- scale importer playing one supplier off against another and driving down the price received, or of the beet refiners doing the same if they compete for market share. For this reason, the least developed sugar- exporting countries have so far agreed to what is effectively a market-sharing agree- ment with the non-least developed ACP Sugar Protocol beneficiaries. The former will voluntarily limit the quantity of their exports and, in return, will receive a price that is linked to the EU level. Whether or not this arrangement will survive full EBA liberalization of sugar in 2009 remains to be seen.

### Impact on Producers

The comparison between sugar exported under the Sugar Protocol and under EBA illustrates how the effect of the protection–preference nexus on any given group of producers or countries will depend on many features of the regime's architecture. Another influencing factor is the way in which any tariffs are calculated. Many of the tariffs imposed by OECD countries on 'sensitive' agricultural products are in the form of specific duties. In other words, instead of the tariff being set at 100 percent it is fixed at, say, €50/kg. Such specific duties, unlike *ad valorem* ones, increase the post-tax price of a product with a high unit value by a proportionately smaller amount than one with a low unit value. Because of this, importers may be encouraged to purchase top-quality items that attract higher unit values. This is particularly likely if the item is subject to a TQ limiting the volume of imports that can be made. The EU's preferences for Southern African beef include specific duties and also apply TQs.[8] One consequence is that imports from Botswana, Namibia, Swaziland and Zimbabwe are only of higher-quality beef.

This has a range of effects — including on the type of producer able to benefit from the protection–preference nexus and on prices in

the domestic market. It will always tend to be the case that 'export quality' will be higher than 'average domestic quality'. But when a specific duty combined with a TQ encourages exports to be of only the highest-quality items this disparity is widened. It reduces the chances of poorer producers participating in the lucrative trade because they lack the ability to finance quality production (unless the government makes appropriate provision). At the same time, because each animal contains both higher-value and lower-value cuts, an increase in herd take-off to supply the higher-quality cuts to Europe also increases the supply of lower-quality ones to the domestic market. In turn, this will tend to depress domestic market prices to the benefit of consumers (including poor ones) and the detriment of producers (including poor ones).

## The Architecture of Africa's Trade Agreements

### Broad Framework

Among the most important trading arrangements aimed at improving market access for African countries are the Cotonou Agreement, the EBA initiative and AGOA. Most of Africa's trade agreements with Quad countries have been around in one form or another for many years, but there are two recent new additions — the EU's EBA initiative and the US AGOA. The first introduces new differentiation within SSA that may have an impact on the current negotiations for a successor to the Cotonou trade regime, whilst the latter has opened up in a more substantial way than in the past the US market for SSA clothing exports.

The Cotonou Agreement ensures the continuation of Euro-African economic

---

[8] The TQs are: Botswana 18,916 tons, Namibia 13,000 tons, Swaziland 3,363 tons, Zimbabwe 9,100 tons. Swaziland is a relatively modest exporter.

cooperation. A successor to the Lomé treaties between the ACP states and the EU was signed in Cotonou in 2000, it covers 77 countries, of which 48 are in Africa, aims to promote economic, cultural and social development of the ACP states, with a view to enhancing peace and security and to promoting a stable and democratic political environment. The objective of the Agreement is the integration of ACP economies into the world economy, leading to the stimulation of growth and poverty reduction. The Agreement has four main components: reinforcement of the political dimension of relations between ACP States and the EU; poverty reduction within the context of the objectives and strategies agreed at international and an innovative trade and economic cooperation framework. Unlike the Lomé Convention under which trade cooperation was based essentially on preferential tariffs, the new Agreement's main objective is to promote the progressive integration of the ACP countries into the global economy, by enhancing production and the capacity to attract investment, and by ensuring conformity with WTO rules. The new approach emphasizes trade liberalization, including the adoption of transparent competition policy, the protection of intellectual property rights, standardization and certification. Financial cooperation, which is to be based on assessment of need and policy performance, will cover debt (support for debt relief) and structural adjustment support; support in cases of short-term fluctuations in export earnings; support for sectoral policies; and micro projects and decentralized cooperation. Over the 2000–2007 period, the EU has committed financial resources amounting to €25.1 billion to support development in the ACP States.

The EBA, which grants LDCs non-reciprocal, duty-free access to their markets, is an important gesture by the EU. Effectively, 34 African countries would benefit but it would help if it were extended to all middle and low-income developing countries — and most African countries would then be eligible. For Europe, the potential short-run negative impact of such a policy is negligible, compared to the potential medium to longer term gains — with a more prosperous Africa providing larger markets for European goods, requiring less aid from Europe, and less migration pressure on Europe. Furthermore, by granting EBA status to almost all African countries, it would eliminate the potential complications of the rules of origin. Nevertheless, it is argued that if EBA is strictly enforced to benefit only the LDCs, it runs the risk of hindering the integration efforts of the African sub-regions. There is a problem of capacity to exploit the benefits from these preferences. The EBA made the EU the world's first major trading power to commit itself to opening its market fully to the world's poorest countries. While this initiative may improve trading opportunities for LDCs significantly, concerns still remain on its immediate impact. However, it must be noted that reducing policy barriers — in developing countries themselves, as well as in developed countries — is important, but not enough to guarantee expansion of trade. For example, under the Lomé Convention, the EU gave preferential market access to ACP countries, but exports from these countries to the EU fell from £16 billion in 1985 to £14 billion in 1994. Barriers that prevent poor people from engaging in trade, or from increasing production in response to new market opportunities, need to be removed. Transport costs are often a particular obstacle to trade. A halving of transport costs could double the volume of trade.

AGOA offers a new opportunity to strengthen US-Africa trade and economic relations. In recognition of the achievements of many countries in Africa pursuing economic and political reform, and wishing to offer special support to those countries committed to pursuing further accelerated reforms, the US administration has proposed a US Africa Trade and Investment Initiative. In 2000, the US adopted AGOA to promote exports from some African countries. As part of US general policy to support the development of Africa and to end the marginalization of the continent, the Act provides duty free access to the US markets of products originating from African countries. One of the premises of the Act is that it is more beneficial to developing and low-income countries, particularly African countries to have unrestricted export access to markets in developed countries than to be denied access and given aid. The program is based on an approach toward accelerated growth and development of Africa and the integration of the continent into the world economy and involves trade liberalization, enhanced market access, finance and investment. This approach is consistent with some of the basic elements of Africa's economic development strategy, in particular NEPAD, which, like AGOA, places a premium on good governance and transparency. The stated aim of AGOA is to help reforming African nations spur their export sectors through favourable trade benefits centered on duty-free and quota-free entry of products like textiles into the US market.

In January 2003, the US announced that 38 nations have qualified for preferential treatment under AGOA. This designation signifies that more African countries are making continued progress toward a market-based economy, the rule of law, free trade, economic policies that will reduce poverty, and protection of workers' rights in specific economic and social areas. AGOA-based eligibility to duty free access is, however, conditional on these countries demonstrating determination to have established, or to be making progress towards, the establishment of the following: market-based economies; the rule of law and political pluralism; elimination of barrier to US trade and investment; protection of intellectual property; efforts to combat corruption; policies to reduce poverty; increasing availability of healthcare and educational opportunities; protection of human rights and worker rights; and, elimination of certain child labor practises.

In summary, for the EU and US there are special agreements for SSA (Cotonou and AGOA respectively), but in the case of Canada and Japan the region is served by the standard GSP (designated General Preferential Tariff — GPT — in Canada). In addition three of the four states offer Africa accords which are in some respects superior to or broader than the main agreement and, hence, may be of operational importance, at least for some countries in relation to some products. In the case of the EU, for example, EBA provides broader and deeper preferences than does Cotonou for least developed countries (not exclusively those in SSA), although it does not contain some of the other desirable architectural features of

Cotonou. In the case of Canada, the Commonwealth Developing Countries Remission Order (CDCRO) provides preferences on textile products (which are partially excluded from the GPT) for Commonwealth developing countries. In the case of the US, AGOA, which is an enhancement of the standard GSP, operates on items that are not covered by the GSP, especially textile and clothing articles. Table 5.4 sets out in summary form a number of key features of the principal G8 agreements affecting most of SSA that are relevant to the foregoing discussion, while Table 5.5 does the same for North Africa. These tables are similar, but the former is the more extensive (because SSA has better preferences); for this reason the rest of this section follows Table 5.4. The top row in Table 5.4 identifies which of the multiple agreements serving SSA are the most preferential and, effectively therefore, the ones normally in use.

### Coverage

The third row of Table 5.4 shows that the main agreement applies to all the countries of SSA with the following exceptions: South Africa for Cotonou; and Angola, Burkina Faso, Burundi, Comoros, Congo Democratic Republic, Equatorial Guinea, Liberia, Somalia, Sudan, Togo and Zimbabwe for AGOA.[9] In the case of both Japan and Canada, Africa

---

[9] Of the AGOA exclusions, only three have failed to request access; the others have requested but been denied. Although Congo Democratic Republic was added to the eligibility list for AGOA benefits on 31 December 2002, implementation of the Act's duty-free trade benefits was only to be activated when a transitional government was formed.

shares its preferences with many other developing countries. Hence any trade advantage will be limited because many other competitors have identical terms of access.

Cotonou and AGOA cover most products. In the case of Cotonou, the only significant exceptions are some CAP items which are either excluded altogether or are subject to TQs. However, as explained above, the commercial advantage that SSA countries receive *could* be higher on items that are covered but subject to TQs than on others. This is because the commercial value of a preference is directly linked to the relative liberality of treatment of competitors. Hence, while the Cotonou beef and sugar prefer- ences are heavily constrained by TQs, they confer very substantial commercial advan- tages on their beneficiaries because the price at which goods are sold reflects the artificial restriction of the supply on to the European market achieved *inter alia* by the EU's very restrictive MFN and other preferential trade policies.

### Rules of Origin

The next two rows of Table 5.4 cover the rules of origin. It is methodologically impossible to compare across the board the extent to which the rules are light or heavy since the Quad use different methods for establishing originating status. Both the US and Canada require a given percentage of the ex-factory value to have been added domestically. In the case of Canada, for example, 60 percent must be added domestically, i.e. non-originating imports must not make up more than 40 percent of the ex-factory value. At first sight it would seem easy to compare this with the 35 percent value-added requirement of the US,

## Table 5.4:  Preferences for SSA: Main Architecture

| Aspect | EU | Canada | Japan | USA |
|---|---|---|---|---|
| 1. Main agreement | Cotonou | GPT | GSP | AGOA |
| 2. Geographical coverage[a] | All except South Africa | All | All | 38[b] (out of 48) |
| 3. Product coverage[c] | Most | Excludes sensitive manufactures | Excludes sensitive agriculture and manufactures, and has some ceilings | Most |
| 4. Depth of preferences[c] | Duty-and quota-free except for some CAP products | Variable | Variable | Duty- and quota-free |
| 5. Rules of origin — type[c] | Mixture | 60 percent domestic value added | Change of tariff heading | 35 percent domestic value added + extra rules on clothing |
| 6. Rules of origin — cumulation | Full ACP and EU | Full GPT and Canada | Japan only | SADC[d], WAEMU + extra cumulation for clothing |
| 7. Legal basis | Contractual | Autonomous | Autonomous | Autonomous |
| 8. Overt political conditionality | Low | Low | Low | High |
| 9. Expiry | 2008 | 2004 | 2011 | 2008 — but 2004 for some clothing preferences |
| 10. Formalities | Customs declaration on prescribed form | Exporter declaration | Customs declaration | USTR-approved visa system |

*Notes*:
(a)  Of main agreement.
(c)  But one (Congo Democratic Republic) does not yet benefit from duty-free trade.
(d)  Of main agreement for least developed countries.
(e)  Only Botswana, Mauritius, Tanzania.

## Table 5.5: Preferences for North Africa: Main Architecture

| Aspect | EU | Canada | Japan | USA |
|---|---|---|---|---|
| 1. Main agreement | FTAs | GPT | GSP | GSP |
| 2. Product coverage | Most | Excludes sensitive manufactures | Excludes sensitive agriculture and manufactures, and has some ceilings | Excludes most textiles and clothing |
| 3. Depth of preferences | Duty-and quota-free except for some CAP products | Variable | Variable | Duty-free |
| 4. Rules of origin — type | Mixture | 60 percent domestic value added | Change of tariff heading | 35 percent domestic value added |
| 5. Rules of origin — cumulation | Limited | Full GPT and Canada | Japan only | USA only |
| 6. Legal basis | Contractual | Autonomous | Autonomous | Autonomous |
| 7. Overt political conditionality | Low | Low | Low | Trade policy[a] |
| 8. Expiry | 2008 | 2004 | 2011 | 2006 |
| 9. Formalities | Customs declaration on prescribed form | Exporter declaration | Customs declaration | No special initial documentation |

*Note*:
(a) The standard GSP does not include the overt political conditionality of AGOA but specifies *inter alia* that beneficiaries may lose some or all benefits if they fail to protect intellectual property rights, respect labour rights and resolve investment disputes.

which appears to be more liberal. But the Canadian rule applies across the board, whereas the US has additional rules in relation to clothing under AGOA, some of which are very liberal (until November 2004) whilst others are not. Moreover, account must also be taken of the rules on cumulation. Canada's are much more liberal. The 60 percent 'domestic' value added can include any imported inputs from either Canada or from another GPT state. In the case of the US, by

contrast, cumulation only applies under the standard GSP between the three SADC states and WAEMU members; in addition there is full AGOA cumulation on many of the clothing extensions.

Once the comparison is extended to EU and Japan, the technical impossibility of the task becomes quite apparent. Japan uses an entirely different system for establishing originating status. It is the system that the EU used to employ, and goes by the name of 'change of tariff heading'. Essentially, a good may incorporate imported inputs and not lose originating status provided that the 4-digit HS heading under which the imports are classified is different from the heading under which the resulting export is classified. Because the HS classification system was not designed primarily to establish originating status, this simple rule is flanked by additional provisions on some products. In some cases these are liberal: originating status is safeguarded even if the imported input is classified under the same 4-digit heading. But often it is illiberal: additional processes have to be undertaken to retain originating status even if all imported inputs are classified under a separate heading. Hence the origin rules can be established only on a product-by-product basis.

The same is the case in the EU system, which has evolved away from the change of tariff heading to a heterogeneous, product-specific regime. In effect, the EU uses three systems for establishing originating status, sometimes in combination, depending upon the product. The three are change of tariff heading, percent of value added or the undertaking of a specified production process. What really matters is whether a particular rule makes it more or less easy for a country to acquire originating status given its production structure and the commercial realities of the product in question. Hence, a genuine comparison between the Quad countries is only possible with respect to precisely defined products.

In one area, though, it is possible to make a comparison at a general level; this is on the provisions for cumulation. Other things being equal, the broader the range of countries with which cumulation is allowed, the easier it will be for a country to fulfil the rules of origin. In this respect, the EU and Canada have the most liberal rules, the US is in the middle (except in the case of clothing under AGOA, for which some rules are especially liberal), and Japan is the least liberal.

### Security of Access

The four bottom rows of both tables provide various indicators of security of access. The assumption is that investment to increase supply capacity is more likely to occur if the terms of access are guaranteed for a reasonable period of time, are not vulnerable to arbitrary action by importing countries, and do not require onerous bureaucratic formalities. For SSA, only Cotonou is provided on a contractual basis and, hence, has provisions for dispute arbitration. All the other three, because they are based on the GSP, are autonomous and could be withdrawn or varied at any time. In practise, however, this has tended not to happen except in those cases where the granting country specifically establishes ceilings and other objective criteria that allow it to terminate or vary the level of preference. Only the US imposes overt political conditionality on countries that are eligible for AGOA, in that the countries cannot undermine US national security or foreign policy interests. Formal conditionality for the other three providers tends to be limited to more general rules (such as gross human rights violations or use of prison labor).

None of the agreements has a long shelf-life. The future of Cotonou is under negotiation at the present time. Unless the ACP countries agree EPAs or the EU identifies, vaguely defined, 'alternative' arrangements, the preferences will cease at the end of 2007. Canada's GPT expires in 2004, and US GSP expires in 2006, but the assumption is that these will be rolled over; Japan's GSP expires in 2011. AGOA is in force until 2008.

Economic performance of several countries under AGOA gives room for some optimism. In 2001, the first full year of the program, although total US imports of goods from SSA declined, SSA producers sold $8.2 billion more in goods to the US under AGOA, representing a 61.5 percent increase over the previous year. Also in 2001, US exports to SSA increased, rising by 17.5 percent, even as US exports elsewhere in the world fell by 6.3 percent. Currently, the US trades more with Africa than with the nations of the former Soviet Union and Eastern Europe combined. However, most of AGOA exports from Africa were accounted for by the energy sector, suggesting that there has not been much variety in US-Africa trade activity. Of the total $8.2 billion in exports of AGOA-qualifying goods in 2001, the energy-sector share was about 83 percent, accounted for largely by Nigerian crude oil. The non-energy-sector share of exports was only about 17 percent of the total. Non-energy-sector exports consisted of small quantities of textiles and apparel, minerals and metals, transportation equipment, agricultural products, and chemicals and related products. It is still too early to statistically measure the impact of AGOA on Africa's access to and participation in global trade.

### Administration

Two of the countries represented in Table 5.4 require a formal customs declaration for goods to receive preference: these are the EU and Japan. The US requires a US Trade Representative-approved visa system to benefit from the textile and clothing provisions of AGOA; other imports require only the letter 'A' to be inserted on the entry document. If eligibility is queried, though, a declaration is required according to a prescribed format. In Canada all that is required is a declaration by the exporter. Neither the US nor the EU system appears to create problems for regular users, and neither appears more suitable in all circumstances.

## Everything But Arms (EBA)

Because of its policy relevance to SSA's post-2007 trade regime with the EU — and the important differences between its architecture and that of Cotonou — it is vital to understand EBA's scope and intent. Forty African and other ACP states belong to the UN list of least developed states and, hence, are eligible for EBA. It is reported that some are reconsidering their position with respect to the post-Cotonou negotiations. There is a possibility that some may choose not to enter into EPAs negotiated by their regional partners and to rely upon EBA instead, even though it suffers certain limitations (Box 5.14). This could adversely affect regional integration in Africa.

The EU removed, with effect from 5 March 2001, all tariffs and quotas on imports from LDCs (34 of which are in Africa) of all products other than those classified as armaments[10], bananas, rice and sugar. This has been achieved by amending the current GSP. For bananas, rice and sugar, the removal

---

[10] Those falling in Chapter 93 of the HS.

**Table 5.6: EBA Timetable for Bananas, Sugar and Rice**

| | 2001 | 2002 | 2003 | 2004 | 2005 | 2006 | 2007 | 2008 | 2009 |
|---|---|---|---|---|---|---|---|---|---|
| Bananas[a] | | | | | | | | | |
| Tariff reduction | | 20% | 20% | 20% | 20% | Free | | | |
| Sugar[b] | | | | | | | | | |
| Tariff reduction | — | — | — | — | — | 20% | 50% | 80% | Free |
| Tariff-free quota (tonnes) | 74,185 | 85,313 | 98,110 | 112,826 | 129,750 | 149,213 | 171,594 | 197,335 | None |
| Rice[c] | | | | | | | | | |
| Tariff reduction | | | | | | 20% | 50% | 80% | Free |
| Tariff-free quota (tonnes) | 2,517 | 2,895 | 3,329 | 3,828 | 4,402 | 5,063 | 5,822 | 6,696 | None |

*Notes:*
(a) Changes take effect on 1 January each year.
(c) Changes take effect on 1 July each year.
(d) Changes take effect on 1 September each year.

of restrictions will be undertaken over the period to 2006 (for bananas) and 2009 (for rice and sugar). During the intervening period there will be a combination of progressive tariff cuts for all three products plus an increasing tariff-free quota for sugar and rice. The effects are shown in Table 5.6.

From an African perspective EBA has three potential sets of implications:

- for the beneficiaries it may improve their access to the EU market;
- for non-beneficiaries it may erode their existing preferences (in relation to all least developed countries, not just African ones);
- for SSA states (both least developed and non-least developed) it adds a new dimension to the negotiation of EPAs.

In the first two cases, the scale of effect will depend upon two factors:

- the extent to which the initiative represents an improvement on their current terms of access to the EU market;
- their capacity to increase their exports of the newly favored products.

*Changes to Market Access*

The EBA initiative will have a direct effect on LDCs only in cases where there currently exist restrictions on their access to the European market. At present the LDCs already receive highly preferential access to the EU market. They have benefited for some years from a special tranche of the GSP which provides them with additional preferences over those available to most developing countries.[11] Hence many of their exports are already free

---

[11] The 40 that are part of the ACP group also obtain access under the Cotonou Agreement.

of tariff restrictions and so will not be affected by EBA, which applies only to tariffs. The Commission has estimated that in 1998 taxes on imports from LDCs totalled €7 million. Under EBA this will fall to zero: the loss to the European treasuries of this €7 million will be the gain of the suppliers. As explained above, it is not possible to determine across the board who in the supply chain will receive this €7 million. It will depend upon relative negotiating power, which will vary between products and countries. Hence, for example, the removal of customs duties could simply mean that importers or retailers make a larger profit (or reduce retail prices). Or it could mean that the supplying countries (or the producers therein) receive higher prices. Or, most likely, it could be some combination of these two.

### Supply Capacity

If least developed country producers earn more they may be able to afford to increase the volume of their exports. If so, the ultimate impact of EBA could be much greater than suggested by the static figure of €7 million. If, for example, Malawi or Mozambique were able to divert some of their existing exports from lower-priced markets to the EU, or even to increase production so that they could export more *in toto*, the additional export revenue would be a dynamic gain from the EBA change. The impact of EBA could be significant for competitors for one or both of two reasons. First, even an absolutely small increase in exports could be important in *relative terms*. The costs to competing developing countries could be relatively high if exports were concentrated in products of particular sensitivity or in intricately regulated

EU markets; this may be the case with sugar. Secondly, LDCs may increase their exports to the EU above current levels by:

- Diverting sales from other markets;
- Increasing imports for domestic consumption to allow a higher proportion of production to be exported;
- Or, in the longer term, by increasing total production.

All three ways, but especially the first two, are more likely to occur if EU prices are significantly higher than those elsewhere. And this is more likely to be the case for products in which EU protectionism (from which least developed countries will be relieved) is high. The extreme case is provided by sugar, with EU prices 3–4 times higher than world market prices.

### Products Affected

This sub-section identifies the LDC exports on which the EU levied an import tax prior to EBA.[12] **Table 5.7** provides a detailed list of the very small number of items that are least developed country exports to the EU and for which EBA has resulted in a change in import

---

[12] The methodology used to identify this core group of affected commodities involved a review of 1997 EU trade statistics to identify some 2,939 items imported from at least one least developed country. These were often narrowly defined varieties or types of broader products (e.g. there are many sub-categories of rice, of which two are significant least developed country exports). Of these, 502 items were exported to a value from the least developed group as a whole of €500,000 or more. And of these, only 11 did not have duty- and quota-free access. These are the items for which EBA made an immediate difference.

**Table 5.7: LDC Exports to the EU Affected by EBA**

| CN_1997 | Description | Pre-EBA (1999) import restrictions[a] | |
| --- | --- | --- | --- |
| | | non-ACP least developed countries | ACP least developed countries |
| 02023090 | frozen bovine boned meat | 9.8%+€332.6/100kg | 0%+€332.6/100kg; Protocol K0%+€28.8/100kg |
| 04069021 | cheddar (excl. grated or powdered and for processing) | No preference | K€63.9/100kg |
| 07099060 | fresh or chilled sweetcorn | No preference | €10.1/100kg |
| 08030019 | bananas, fresh (excl. plantains) | No preference | €508/1000kg (K0) |
| 10059000 | maize (excl. seed) | No preference | €75.19/T b |
| 10062017 | long grain husked –brown- rice, length/ width ratio >=3, parboiled | Bangladesh K€109.82/1000kg; no preference | P€75.57/1000kg |
| 10063098 | wholly milled long grain rice, length/width ratio >= 3, (excl. parboiled) | Bangladesh K€232.09/1000kg; no preference | P€160.51/1000kg |
| 17011110 | raw cane sugar, for refining (excl. added flavouring or colouring) | No preference | K0; Protocol 0 |
| 17011190 | raw cane sugar (excl. for refining and added flavouring or colouring) | No preference | K0; Protocol 0 |
| 17019910 | white sugar, containing in dry state>= 99.5 % sucrose (excl. flavoured or coloured) | No preference | K0; Protocol 0 (for 1 item out of 2) |
| 17031000 | cane molasses resulting from the extraction or refining of sugar | No preference | K0 |

*Note*:
(a) 'K' denotes rate within quota; 'P' denotes ceiling.
*Sources*: Eurostat 1998; Taric 1999.

regime. The broader product groups into which these fall, half of which face delayed implementation, are: beef, cheese, maize, bananas, rice and sugar. The small number of products affected directly is not surprising. All least developed countries already received duty-free access to the EU for all of their industrial exports and for most of their primary product exports other than those covered by the Common Agricultural or Fisheries Policies. Hence, EBA has resulted in a change in access only for the limited number of temperate agricultural products that were previously restricted.

Which LDCs have seen the greatest improvement in market access? The answer is that the gains from the EBA are greatest for the non-ACP LDCs because the *status quo ante* was less favorable for them than it was for the ACP states. For eight out of the 11 items in Table 5.7, non-ACP LDCs received no preference over the standard tariff payable by industrialised countries (the EU's MFN tariff), and for two items only one non-ACP LDC — Bangladesh — obtained a preference. In all cases, the import regime facing non-African LDCs was highly protectionist. In broad terms, the African (and other ACP) least developed countries (or some of them) already received preferences on all 11 items. But these preferences were in most cases less favorable than those provided under EBA. Hence even the African LDCs have gained in tariff terms. There are several reasons for this. First, not all SSA states previously received a preference on all items. In the case of sugar and beef, only those countries that were parties to the Cotonou Sugar and Beef Protocols benefited.[13] But, as explained above, the price regime for sugar is different.

## Recent Policy Initiatives

### Renegotiation of the EU Trade Regime

The basic arguments over the pros and cons of EPAs are over five years old, dating back to the EU's proposal at the outset of negotiations for a successor to Lomé IV that the trade

---

[13] All the ACP least developed exporters of the sugar items identified (Madagascar, Malawi, Tanzania and Zambia) are Sugar Protocol beneficiaries. Of the beef item exporters, only Madagascar benefits from the Beef Protocol: Burkina Faso, Chad, Liberia and Uganda do not.

---

**Box 5.13: The work of the CRTA**

The CRTA has a large backlog of work and, since it operates by consensus, has reached very few 'decisions' on whether or not agreements conform. Of the 25 regional trade agreements that had been notified to GATT/WTO and were still in force at 5 May 2003:

for six the CRTA's factual examination had not started;

    14 were in the factual examination stage;

    in two cases the factual examination had been concluded;

    in three cases there were on-going consultations on the draft report.

---

regime be revised (Box 5.15). The Commission obtained from the EU member states its draft mandate for the current negotiations in June 2002 (EU Council 2002). The ACP agreed their 'Guidelines for the Negotiations of Economic Partnership Agreements' in July (ACP, 2002). Neither document goes much beyond general principles.

### WTO Rules on FTAs

A key element of the EU case is that EPAs are more supportive of the multilateral trade system than is the non-reciprocal Cotonou Agreement, and that they can be justified under Article XXIV. This is the WTO provision that allows members to discriminate in favor of some trade partners (and, hence, against others) provided that they are creating a customs union or FTA. Because they would involve reciprocal tariff cuts, the EU claims that EPAs would pass the Article XXIV test.

But what, exactly, are the requirements of Article XXIV? The formal requirements for an agreement to be treated as an FTA are fairly straightforward, but practice is not so clear cut. This is because Article XXIV is vague — by design rather than by accident, because members have been unwilling to restrict themselves through a more precise formulation. One salient requirement of Article XXIV is that the FTA must be completed 'within a reasonable length of time' (defined in the WTO as a period that 'should exceed ten years only in exceptional cases'). Another is that 'duties and other restrictive regulations of commerce ... are eliminated on substantially all the trade between the constituent territories' (GATT, 1947: Part 3, Article XXIV, paras 5(c) and 8(b); WTO, 1995: 32). There is a similar difference between the formal requirement for legitimizing any proposed regime (clear cut) and practise (murky). The formal hurdle for approving an agreement as in conformity with Article XXIV is high. The agreement must have the universal support of members because of the WTO practice of requiring a consensus for all decisions. But in the past a failure to achieve a consensus has not proved to be a barrier to those countries wishing to create an FTA.

The first step is for the parties to the agreement to notify the WTO following signature of an FTA. Such notification will be followed by the referral of the FTA to the WTO Committee on Regional Trade Agreements (CRTA) for consideration (Box 5.13). Membership of the CRTA is open to any country that feels it to be in its interests to belong. In theory the CRTA will produce a report on the compliance, or otherwise, of the FTA with Article XXIV for adoption by consensus of the WTO membership. But practise is a lot less clear cut (Box 5.16). There is no reason to expect a change in practise anytime soon. The CRTA's backlog of agreements is growing. On past form, it is unlikely to give a straightforward approval or disapproval of any agreement — not least because of the need for consensus. Parties to an agreement are unlikely to acquiesce in an unfavorable verdict, but those who face discrimination (or would do so in an analogous agreement between other countries) will not wish to see the precedent of a favorable report.

But this does not mean that countries can sign up to anything and just call it an FTA. In the absence of clear guidance from the Committee, it would still be open to any aggrieved WTO member to file a complaint under the dispute settlement mechanism. This could pass to a quasi-judicial body the task of defining such terms as 'substantially all' trade. In other words, approval or disapproval of an EPA is likely to happen by default. Unless a WTO member challenges it on the grounds that it does not comply with Article XXIV, WTO compatibility will never be tested.

It follows that the EU's insistence on the need for WTO conformity as a *raison d'être* for EPAs could come back to haunt it. The WTO conformity, or otherwise, of the EPA approach (and its operation and interpretation of the Article XXIV requirements — see below) could be determined in the coming years through a dispute. It might be a dispute over an existing agreement (such as the Trade, Development and Co-operation Agreement (TDCA) with South Africa), or over an EPA following its introduction, or even over an agreement that does not involve the EU and Africa at all. But whatever the proximate cause of a dispute that defines the meaning of terms in Article XXIV, it would henceforth apply to all.

### The Commission's Mandate

The mandate adopted by the Council in June 2002 does little to open up the potential gains from EPAs. The scope for further improvements in the EU's market access regime is limited by the commodity composition of ACP exports, as well as the political sensitivity of further liberalization on CAP products and of significant improvements to the rules of origin for sensitive, labor-intensive manufactures. Of these, the agricultural products covered by the CAP are probably the most important. The EU has pointed out for a long time, correctly, that a very high proportion of the goods actually exported by ACP states to the EU already enter duty free. Given the supply constraints in many ACP states, the agricultural goods covered by the CAP represent the only substantial product area in which useful additional market access preferences could be given. The only other significant way in which ACP export diversification could be encouraged would be by deliberately reducing the processing requirements needed to fulfill the rules of origin. This would be effective only if more of the processing could be done in a non-ACP state and less in an ACP one.

In other words, to be of use for ACP goods exports, the post-2007 regime must offer substantially improved access on CAP items and/or better rules of origin. The mandate is silent on both. It defers discussion of improvements for ACP access to the European market until later in the negotiations. The only mention made of improved rules of origin is that the EU will "assess any specific request for change... presented by the ACP..." This is particularly worrying since earlier drafts of the mandate included more concrete initiatives. An early Commission proposal was to extend EBA access to all ACP states. This would have addressed adequately the objective of extending product coverage. The agreed version, therefore, represents a step backwards. A non-binding declaration by Sweden supported by UK and Denmark attached to the mandate argues in favor of full EBA access. But the fact that it is endorsed by only three of the 15 EU members shows that this outcome is by no means assured.

In the absence of any indications of 'gains' it is unsurprising that most discussion has tended to focus on potential 'costs'. The mandate has sharpened some of the concerns. For a start, the mandate recognizes no alternative regime to an EPA and emphasizes the centrality of reciprocity. It states that the 'Objective' of EPAs will be 'establishing free trade areas'. Moreover, the mandate contains a number of demands that should ring alarm bells in the ACP. These include the following:

1. It proposes that 'charges having equivalent effect' to tariffs should be abolished immediately on entry into force of EPAs (i.e. in 2008), and not at the end of a transition period. How many SSA states are even aware of the charges they currently impose (such as excise duties, that may apply with differential effect to imported items) that the EU might construe as 'charges having equivalent effect'? And what would be the consequences of their

summary abolition?

2. It seeks 'national treatment' (NT) for the EU in relation to trade in goods rather than MFN treatment. Again, the implications of this have not been identified by many, or indeed any, SSA states.

3. It proposes that all tariff reductions be made from the rates applied on entry into force, rather than those currently bound in the WTO. In other words, the starting point for negotiation of an EPA will be much lower than it will be in the WTO Doha negotiations. This presents a problem. Liberalization based on applied rather than bound rates makes the issue of safeguards much more important (since ACP states will have lost — from the outset — the leeway to protect themselves from subsidized imports or import surges by raising tariffs to the bound level). It may also raise expectations among the ACP's other trade partners and result in more being asked of them in the WTO negotiations.

4. The mandate's provisions on safeguards and anti-dumping appear to ignore the concerns expressed by ACP states in relation to import surges for products subsidized by the EU. The section on safeguards refers only to Cotonou Annex V, Article 8; this deals only with the rights of the EU to impose safeguard restrictions, not to the reciprocal rights of the ACP (obviously enough, given that Cotonou does not provide for reciprocity). It may be the Commission's intention that identical rights will apply to the ACP — but since the EU subsidizes exports whilst the ACP do not, the safeguard needs of the two groups are different. The Article on anti-dumping appears to limit action to the rights that the ACP states already possess under the WTO.

5. The mandate also makes a sweeping demand that 'quantitative restrictions and measure have equivalent effect' be abolished on entry into force of EPAs. Without any qualification, this could be interpreted to cover TQs as well as formal quotas. In other words, it would restrict significantly the scope for modulation of liberalization through the application of TQs to reduced tariff rates during the initial phase. It also implies that the ACP national export quotas under the Sugar and Beef Protocols would disappear. This could result in a very sharp fall in exports in 2008 from the higher cost ACP producers.

### The ACP Guidelines

The ACP's formal guidelines for the negotiations make a number of important points of principal and practise. Of particular importance, the guidelines stress the need of ACP states to build or develop their analytical and negotiating capacity not only at the national but also at the regional, inter-regional and international levels (ACP, 2002: para. 11). This is in recognition of the inter-relatedness of parallel negotiations in different forums. The guidelines propose that the two-phase negotiating process (Box 5.15) should include in Phase I the objectives and principles of EPAs and issues of common interest to all ACP states. These include sanitary and phytosanitary measures, the treatment of commodity protocols, evaluation of the impact of CAP reform on food exports and fisheries (ACP, 2002: para. 12a). Only when a clear, universal framework of rules that will apply to all EPAs had been agreed should region-specific negotiation fill out the 'local details'.

The guidelines also identify a number of specific ACP objectives in the negotiations on trade. These include:

- Export subsidies and domestic support for all agricultural products originating from ACP states;
- Preservation of existing preferential arrangements;
- Negotiation of an increase in quotas under the commodity protocols in order to accommodate new entrants;
- Restoration of lost quotas under the Sugar Protocol; and
- Attention to the special needs of net food importing states, single commodity producers and non-trade concerns such as rural development (ACP, 2002: para. 35a1).

### The EU's Non-Paper

In addition to these two formal documents that have been the foundations for the initial negotiations, several informal papers have circulated in the last 24 months or so. One of these deserves attention because it provides one of the most extensive statements of the Commission's views about the potential membership of EPAs. It is known as the 'non-paper' (EC, 2001). The EU and ACP are agreed that a large part of the negotiations will be done at a regional level. But which regions? The ACP group includes only one regional organization in which significant formal responsibilities for trade negotiations have been transferred from national to regional bodies (i.e. the Caricom Caribbean Community). Instead it has a large number of, partly overlapping, regional agreements that are moving (sometimes slowly, and sometimes crab-wise) towards closer economic and/or political integration.

The practical implications for any given ACP state of conceding reciprocity in an EPA will be heavily influenced by which other countries are members. Also, it may be impractical for some existing trade groups to co-exist with EPAs if their memberships are not identical. This may be a particular problem for Botswana, Lesotho, Namibia and Swaziland which, as members of SACU, are affected *de facto* by the TDCA. Under the Cotonou Agreement it is the prerogative of the ACP to decide upon the membership of the groups that may engage with the EU to negotiate EPAs. However, it is politically unrealistic to expect that the EU will not have views on the matter that it will seek to further. These need to be borne in mind when assessing the relative merits of the alternative potential negotiating con-figurations.

The Commission's underlying rationale is that EPAs should promote genuine economic integration. Accordingly, 'a high degree of economic integration within the ACP is desirable...'. Whilst 'requiring deep integration between the ACP as a pre-requisite for negotiation would ... not be practical ... EPAs should aim, within reasonable timeframes, to build on these principles...' (EC 2001: 6). This establishes a preferred 'order of priority' that ranks existing regional organizations in terms of their inherent suitability as EPA partners. A basic condition is that the negotiations must take place in a single setting and lead to a single agreement. Additionally, the order of preference is as follows.

- Customs unions 'offer the best conditions' (EC, 2001: 9);
- FTAs should also be considered provided either that they have already been implemented or that legally binding interim agreements exist and are being effectively implemented;
- Regional economic integration initiatives lacking legally binding interim agreements or effective implementation should not be considered unless all members agree to negotiate with the EU in a single setting with a harmonized position and the aim of a single agreed plan and schedule.

The non-paper also reflects upon various issues that have cropped up, such as the obligations of least-developed EPA members, overlapping group membership, non-ACP group members, and the conditions for a bilateral EPA with a single ACP state. It is at pains to deny that least developed members of an EPA are exempt from reciprocity. Whilst there is scope for 'differentiation' in their favor, this should take the form of a delayed start or a slower pace of tariff dismantling (EC, 2001: 13).

In cases where some members of a larger FTA belong also to a smaller customs union it is up to the ACP to decide which of the two should negotiate the EPA. If two or more regional groupings have overlapping membership, the members should normally decide which one agreement they wish to use as the EPA negotiating umbrella. However,

negotiations could occur with more than one group if each is willing to harmonize closely its negotiating position with the other(s) so that the negotiations take place in one setting with all ACP states having the same access arrangements (EC, 2001: 11). According to the non-paper 'there is no legal reason which prevents the negotiation of an EPA with a free trade area which has non-ACP countries as members.' (EC, 2001: 11). The EPA will simply not apply to the non-ACP state. But this may lead to trade diversion. This is especially likely in cases where the EU already has a trade agreement with the non-ACP state (as would be the case, for example, with both Egypt in COMESA and South Africa in SADC). Consideration should be given, therefore, to bringing the non-ACP state into the EPA. The Commission's view is that bilateral EPAs should not be allowed to weaken regional economic integration. The non-paper states that ACP countries which are members of a customs union or FTA through which they would be eligible to negotiate with the EU 'should ... not be eligible for such negotiations on an individual basis.' (EC, 2001: 12).

### The Question of Reciprocity

Most of the discussion on the successor to the Cotonou trade regime has focused so far on the perceived costs to the ACP arising from reciprocity in the proposed new EPAs. Under Lomé and Cotonou the ACP were required merely to treat the EU no less favourably than any other industrialized trade partner. In complete contrast, the new EPAs will offer duty-free access for 'substantially all' EU exports to the ACP. There are two reasons why the reciprocity debate has taken center-stage, to the virtual exclusion so far of the other vital issues. They are that:

- ACP liberalization required for reciprocity is bound to have adjustment and fiscal costs for these states in the form of increased competition for domestic producers and lower trade taxes for governments;
- There is not much else to debate since neither the EU nor the ACP have been able so far to put forward in any detail other specific innovations for an EPA.

But it is difficult to advance the analysis of reciprocity without knowing which countries will be in each EPA (and the potential terms of the agreement). The regional configurations within which ACP states will negotiate EPAs are only just emerging. Although the negotiations began officially in October 2002, the period since then has been concerned largely with plenary discussions between the whole ACP on the one hand and the EU on the other. During the second half of 2003, Western and Central Africa formally launched regional negotiations with the EU and discussions are at an advanced stage in Eastern and Southern Africa on the appropriate geographical configurations. But not substantive discussions have yet occurred with any of the groups. It now seems likely that detailed negotiations will not begin until 2005. But we can at least identify the benefits that SSA states currently obtain from Cotonou, and how these may change.

About the only thing that is certain on EPAs is that the EU wants them to be reciprocal, i.e. that in return for preferential access to the EU market the ACP members must offer Europe preferential access to their own markets. Moreover, the EU talks of the

preferences being in the form of duty-free access (not least because of the requirements of WTO Article XXIV). Beyond that are many details which still have to be determined, including:

- Will reciprocity also apply to trade between the ACP members of EPAs?
- Can different members maintain different preferences *vis-à-vis* the EU (and each other)?
- What proportion of ACP imports must be duty free?
- Over what period must reciprocity be introduced?

Answers to these questions are needed from an assessment of the effects of reciprocity on domestic competition and government revenue. The net effect of the EPA will be determined not just by its specific provisions, but also by its incremental costs and benefits over and above those deriving from parallel negotiations. Hence, any assessment must be put in its broader context. As with CAP change it is very important not to fall into the trap of equating automatically a new policy like EPAs with 'trade liberalization' as it is normally understood in economic textbooks (Box 5.17). EPAs will result in textbook change only if the price of imports into ACP members falls and this reduction is passed on to users (who need not be the final consumers). If an imported good that competes with a domestic good becomes cheaper to the consumer, they will switch purchases; if it becomes cheaper to the retailer/wholesaler then they are more likely to stock it. In either case, imports of the good increase and domestic production goes down. There are at least four reasons why

## Box 5.14: EPAs may not be textbook liberalization

In the 'textbook model', liberalization results in a shift in the international division of labour because returns go up for some activities and down for others. There are short-to-medium-term adjustment costs for the economic actors who lose out (and also while alternative government revenue sources are put in place) but aggregate economic welfare increases (at least in the medium-to-long term).

There are many controversies surrounding these liberal views: but they are not the most immediate area of concern with EPAs. The primary question to be asked is: will EPAs actually result in liberalization according to the textbook model? Only if the answer is 'yes' will the effects forecast in the textbooks — good and/or bad — actually follow.

EPAs alone might not produce this effect. These are if:

1. There is no tariff cut;
2. The exporter appropriates the tariff cut by charging a higher price;
3. The importer appropriates the tariff cut and on-sells at the same price;
4. EPAs are overtaken by other trade liberalization.

The first point arises because EPAs will not liberalize all trade, only 'substantially all'. Some goods will not need to be subject to any tariff reduction. Points 2–4 are interlinked. Tariff cuts towards one trade partner will not necessarily result in any price falls. Competitive markets need to be created — they don't necessarily 'just happen'. Take the case of a piece of industrial equipment that can be imported from either the EU or, say, Japan for the same price, and which faces a 25 percent tariff. If the tariff is cut to zero percent under the EPA, the EU exporters *could* try to gain market share from Japan. But they might also prefer to increase their prices by 25 percent, which would have no effect on the price paid by the customer or on the volume of sales, but would result in greater profits. They are more likely to choose the second option if the chance of increasing sales volume is small (perhaps because Japan could cut prices too).

The same arithmetic will be done by importers. If domestic trade is not competitive they need not pass on any price cut.

A tariff cut is more likely to result in a fall in domestic prices if:

- it applies to many potential sources of imports;
- there is a competitive domestic market.

The more general the liberalization the harder it becomes to sustain the restrictive business practices that allow exporters or importers to make enhanced profits (at the expense of government revenue). Multilateral liberalization through the WTO would be the most general — and the most likely to result in both the gains and the adjustment costs associated with market opening. A regional agreement with *only* the EU would be much narrower. A set of regional agreements (with other African and non-African states) would fall in between these two extremes. So the ultimate impact of an EPA is likely to be affected heavily by Africa's negotiations with trade partners other than the EU.

## *The EU–South Africa TDCA*

Whilst it is not yet possible to provide a definitive assessment of 'benefits' or 'costs' of EPAs (let alone an economic analysis of their effect on Africa's economies), there is a clear and urgent need for a set of 'what if' analyses. These would identify the potential product exemptions from EPAs of different memberships. In case a challenge is made, it is important that the requirements of Article XXIV be taken seriously in structuring any EPAs. But, of course, these requirements could change either in the Doha Round or as a result of dispute settlement. The ACP Guidelines state that the ACP should champion such change by preparing and submitting concrete proposals within Doha (ACP, 2002: para. 16).

At present it is difficult to be sure what all this means for the structure of EPAs but some guidance is available from the EU–South Africa TDCA. This not only makes clear what the EU interprets Article XXIV to require, but it is also possible that, between now and 2007, it could be subject to a WTO challenge and so provide a test case for the interpretation of Article XXIV (Box 5.18).

## *Non-Tariff Issues*

The tariff cuts on products included in the EPA are not the only defensive issues facing the ACP. It might be thought that there would be no effects of increased import competition on the goods excluded from reciprocal tariff cuts. But there could be two types of impact. One is through indirect effects: if, for example, imports of a substitute were liberalized, consumption of the excluded good might fall as the price difference

---

**Box 5.15:  The TDCA and Article XXIV**

In the TDCA the EU has stated that it believes the Article XXIV requirement that an FTA must cover 'substantially all' trade can be fulfilled if both parties reduce to zero tariffs on products that account for 90 percent on average of the current trade between them. It has also indicated that it believes this average figure can be achieved asymmetrically, with the EU liberalizing on more than 90 percent and its partner on less. In the specific case of the EU–South Africa TDCA, South Africa has liberalised on products accounting for 86 percent of its imports from the EU while Europe has liberalised on 94 percent. The agreement also indicates that the EU believes the Article XXIV requirement that liberalization occur 'within a reasonable period of time' can be achieved through a transitional period of up to 12 years.

---

between the two items shifted consumption patterns in favor of imports. Another is if excluded products receive additional protection from excise duties, licensing or other measures with a tariff-like effect. The EU wants these abolished at the start of the negotiations (Box 5.19). Even if it fails in this demand, the ACP must expect it to push hard for the elimination of 'charges having equivalent effect' to tariffs, even on goods that will be excluded from formal liberalization.

A related piece of preparatory research that could ease the negotiations substantially would cover mechanisms to collect value-added tax (VAT). It is well understood that a fall in tariffs will necessarily shift the source of government revenue from trade taxes to a

**Box 5.16: Which taxes are quasi tariffs?**

The definition of 'charges having equivalent effect' is open to debate. Clearly, if a country imposes an excise duty on imported spirits at a higher level than on domestically produced ones there is a *prima facie* case that the difference is a 'charge having equivalent effect'. But what about the situation in a country that does not produce spirits domestically (although it does produce other alcoholic beverages) yet imposes a high excise duty on spirits?

There is a lot of preparatory work to be done. Each ACP state needs to know which of its current taxes might be construed as a 'charge having equivalent effect', on which of these it can mount a strong defence, and what the effect would be on government revenue of changing its current policy. Until this information is available, the implications of the EU's demand that such charges be abolished in 2008 cannot be assessed.

but also of the EU's initial position that 'charges having equivalent effect' be abolished and also that the ACP offer the EU national treatment (NT). What is required in these cases is baseline research that will establish for each ACP state the extent to which these are relevant issues.

A similar requirement for baseline research is needed in respect to NT. Much of the discussion on services negotiations concerns NT, whereas goods negotiations have tended to be more concerned with market access. This is because Article III of GATT 1947 already requires members to offer NT in 'like' goods. NT in goods trade is often misunderstood as allowing a foreign firm to take advantage of all the support available to its domestic competitors yet also to benefit from lower-cost production in its home base. For example, it might be thought NT would allow China to sell on the African market garments produced at a fraction of local cost without any offsetting import taxes. The predictable effect would be a sharp fall in prices and a loss of existing domestic clothing production capacity. But this is incorrect. Offering NT in goods does not require a country to liberalize its border measures; it merely requires it to impose no other discriminatory measures on imported goods *other than* any bound tariff or other border measures. The severity of such border measures is determined by negotiations and concessions on 'market access'. But, of course, if as a consequence of reciprocity African states *do* remove their border measures, the NT provision will prevent them from introducing any other discriminatory measure. Moreover, the reciprocity exercise may throw into sharper focus some existing

sales tax or VAT. The latter are economically superior but administratively more difficult to collect. Hence government revenue is expected to fall, since a smaller share of the tax collectable will actually be collected under a VAT system. This administrative problem could be reduced by using a country's customs department to collect VAT on imports (as is common practise). If the VAT system were to operate well, this initial payment would be rebated against the payments made by the users of imports. If the VAT system worked poorly, the government would at least continue to have revenue related to import value taxed 'at source'. The analysis of competitive and fiscal effects needs to take account not only of tariff cuts discrimination that is technically contrary to NT but has been overlooked because its effects are dwarfed by the high tariffs. Market access liberalization could lead to new demands for such measures to be removed.

Two parallel sets of research are required. One is to identify within ACP countries areas where there is a perception that domestic suppliers are treated differently. The other is to seek clarification from the EU of instances in which it believes NT would result in a change to the status quo additional to the removal of tariff barriers.

## Africa's External Interests

Although ACP interests have been heavily focused on the implications of reciprocity, the negotiations need to address several other very important issues. These all center on the fact that the existing trade regime is eroding fast and needs to be revived. Since the EU's mandate contains no specific proposals for improving its import regime, and merely offers to respond to ACP requests in certain areas, it is important that the ACP take the initiative to articulate their demands. This will require research. The ACP Guidelines specifically refer to the need to assess the impact of CAP reform. In addition, the ACP's demands for treatment of its agricultural exports under EPAs need to take account of (and seek to influence) the EU's positions in the WTO. It seems very likely that the current negotiations on the Agreement on Agriculture will not result in a substantially liberal EU import regime for products covered by the CAP. Hence, the possibility will continue to exist for significant ACP preferences. The task for the negotiations will be to ensure that this potential is realized.

Given that the EU has proposed, in its mandate, to remove all quantitative restrictions, a high priority for initial research is on those products currently subject to TQs. These include sugar, beef and rice. An early study should be to identify the implications for ACP exporters of the removal of any quantitative restrictions on their exports to the EU in order to help articulate a negotiating position that serves all ACP interests.

### Improved Access of Goods

The two key changes needed on goods cover market access on agriculture and rules of origin. The proposal in the initial draft Commission mandate to extend EBA coverage to all ACP states needs to be revived (and included in the Euro–Med Agreements with North Africa). Not only would it represent the removal of all existing barriers to African exports, but also it would defuse the incipient tension within African regional agreements between least developed countries and the others. On the rules of origin, the experience with AGOA and its liberal rules on the use of imported inputs to clothing for the LDCs provides convincing evidence that the Cotonou rules are unrealistic. There is a need for more liberal rules on cumulation and the reduction in the level of processing required.

### A Services EPA

Perhaps the most intriguing area for Africa is the proposal that EPAs include a services component. SSA must decide whether to embrace this enthusiastically as an opportunity to obtain better conditions for its services exports, or defensively as a challenge to domestic providers. But in either case all states will need to understand better what might be involved. International trade in services is riven with barriers. Whereas barriers to international trade in goods have fallen substantially over the past 50 years, services trade is still subject to a wide range of laws and other regulations. The barriers that these create are often complex, indirect and opaque — and may be quite invisible until someone tries to export.

The task of identifying barriers to services trade is a tricky one. The problem is partly one of unfamiliarity: because international trade in many services is of recent origin, we are much less familiar with the ways in which policy can affect trade. But it is also because services trade (and regulation) is inherently more complicated than trade in goods. It is easy to understand how tariffs can affect trade in goods. All internationally traded goods have to cross a border (whether they be clothes, computers or copper) and the effect on them of an import tax of 100 percent can easily be seen as more severe than one of 5 percent. While there is increasing concern in trade negotiations with 'behind-the-border' measures (such as investment policies) much attention is still given to the old-fashioned tariff.

In services trade, behind-the-border measures are of the essence. Indeed, it may not be the service that crosses a border at all (Box 5.20). It may be the customer who crosses the border (as with tourism) or the supplier (on-site auditing or computer services). Moreover, the impact of any regulation on the commercial viability of trade will depend on the specifics of the services activity. Immigration and visa problems may be merely tiresome for one firm (that does most business over the web or

> ### Box 5.17: The EU–South Africa Agreement on Services
>
> 'The Parties will *endeavour to extend* the scope of the Agreement with a view to further liberalising trade in services between the Parties ... [which] shall provide for the absence or elimination of substantially all discrimination between the parties *in the services sectors covered* and should cover all modes of supply ...' (Article 30: 1, emphasis added).

phone) but ruinous for another (for which frequent close contact with the client is essential).

Yet again, whether or not a regulation is constraining may depend on the way a service is delivered. For example, if an airline wishes to sell paper tickets it may be advantageous to set up a travel shop in its market. This will require it to conform to all the host government's requirements for setting up, staffing and marketing a business, and will probably require the movement of people across borders and, hence, immigration controls. If, by contrast, electronic tickets are sold over the web, none of this need necessarily be required; instead there may be other regulations.

A further illustration is provided by the case of insurance which, like airline tickets, can also be sold either through a shop or over the web. Governments may have prudential regulations applying to the validity in their domestic market of policies purchased from a non-resident supplier over the web. *Selling* over the web may not be a problem, but no one will *buy* the policies because they are not

**Box 5.18:  The different forms of services trade**

Services trade is not as transparent a concept as trade in goods. The GATS has identified four 'modes of supply' for services which represent different forms of international trade.
- Cross-border (Mode 1): trade takes place from the territory of one country into that of another, e.g. information and advice being transmitted electronically, or cargo transportation.
- Consumption abroad (Mode 2): consumers or firms make use of services in another country, e.g. tourism, education.
- Commercial presence (Mode 3): a firm from one country sets up in another in order to supply services. Establishment can take several forms: incorporation, branches, representative offices, and joint ventures. It is a particularly common mode of supply in financial services and telecommunications.
- Presence of natural persons (Mode 4): natural persons from one country stay in another for a limited period in order to supply services. Includes the self-employed and employees of service providers, e.g. construction and professional services.

valid in the export market due to government rules. And given the heterogeneity of services trade (and trade restrictions) it is vital to specify precisely what is to be traded and how. Only then can the most constraining trade restrictions be identified.

There are a few precedents on what might be in a services accord, but they point in different directions. For example, the EU–South Africa TDCA shows that the provisions are largely of a formal kind. They introduce

the possibility of negotiations taking place on services but include no specific provisions. Similarly, while they allude to the need to make any provisions compatible with WTO requirements, they only talk about the need to offer substantial liberalization.

The EC–Bulgaria Agreement[14] provides universal sectoral coverage for services but establishes that this will be 'gradual' in the case of some activities. But the accord may not be a true precedent as it is a European Association Agreement. Bulgaria has adopted a transitional period arrangement of ten years maximum, divided into two five-year stages. The EU–Mexico Agreement follows the South African precedent of an initial accord that provides only a broad framework establishing that the two parties would endeavor to negotiate a services agreement, but it has gone further in subsequently filling in the details.[15] This task was passed to the EU-Mexico Joint Council established under the agreement. The Council decided on 27 February 2001 an initial set of provisions in the area of services.[16]

There are two important features to note about this 2001 decision. The first is that it is very restricted in terms of specific coverage. But the second is that it sets a timetable for adding further detail. Since the timetable expires well before the conclusion of the EPA negotiations, Africa needs to monitor subsequent agreements to determine more

---

[14] WT/REG1/S/C/N55 currently under factual examination.
[15] Official Journal of the European Communities, L276, 28 October 2000 (pp 45–61).
[16] Official Journal of the European Communities, L70, 12 March 2001 (pp 7–50).

clearly the extent to which the EU is willing to liberalize. Chapter 1 of the 2001 Mexico agreement establishes a range of general provisions in relation to market access, MFN, NT, mutual recognition and 'regulatory carve-out'. The provisions on regulatory carve-out (Article 16) are replicated in more detail in some of the subsequent sectoral chapters. The key point is that both parties are permitted to continue to regulate (for prudential or other reasons) the service sector in question provided only that such regulations do not discriminate against the service providers of the other party.

There are subsequent sectoral chapters on maritime transport and financial services as well as general exceptions. The maritime transport chapter appears only to offer each Party MFN treatment. The financial services chapter goes further, not only offering NT but also making a range of specific provisions such as that 'no Party may require a financial service supplier of the other party to engage individuals of any particular nationality as senior managerial or other key personnel' (Article 16: 1) and that neither party 'may require more than a simple majority of the board of directors … be composed of nationals' (Article 16: 2). Whilst the commitments entered into might restrict the freedom of manoeuvre of Parties to some degree as compared to the *status quo ante*, there are a range of 'let-outs' in the main text. But, above all, the parties are permitted to continue with restrictions listed in the annexes — which appear to reproduce either in whole or in substantial part the restrictions bound into the GATS by each Party.

The broad conclusion to be drawn from the EU-Mexico Agreement, therefore, is that it provides a framework for establishing NT in an initial tranche of sectors, for the extension of such provisions in due course by negotiation to other sectors, and for dispute settlement and other discussion. But it is far from 'opening up' the market of the one to the other. Most importantly, there is absolutely no provision for a relaxation of rules governing the movement and employment of natural person *except* for senior management, yet these may be crucial for removing obstacles to services trade.

The EU–Chile Association Agreement of 26 April 2002 goes much further than either the initial or the revised Mexico accord. It provides extensive schedules, similar in format to GATS ones, detailing the treatment that each side will accord to the other. The schedules, which run to many pages of very tightly worded text, give the impression that they bear very close similarity to the EU's position in the GATS.

*Potential Gains from Services*

Countries trade because it allows them to consume a larger volume and/or more desirable range of goods and services than they would be able to do without trade. Imports can supply items that cannot be produced (or not competitively) at home; exports supply the foreign exchange for the imports. But there are differences between goods and some services over how these gains accrue. An increase in exports of goods will affect directly how many imports can be obtained: the wages paid to those who produce the goods will increase domestic purchasing power and the foreign exchange received by the local exporting firm will finance imports. Services exports under

Modes 1 and 2 (cross-border and consumption abroad) have similar effects. Work is undertaken in the exporting state and the foreign exchange accrues to local firms (even though, as with goods, a part may also be held abroad by them or accrue to foreign associates).

But the situation with Modes 3 and 4 (establishment abroad and presence of natural persons) is different. The extreme case is provided by the individual migrant worker: s/he works, consumes and saves abroad; unless and until a part of their savings is repatriated (and/or the person returns with new skills), there is no direct economic gain to the 'exporting country'; rather, there is a loss of human resources. The contrast is less stark with Modes 3 and 4 undertaken by employees of home-based companies, but the direct economic gains for the home state will still be smaller than for goods.

The primary gains to the exporting country under Modes 3 and 4 are indirect. If an African firm sets up an office in UK employing mainly British individuals it will contribute little directly to employment in its home country or, except to the extent it repatriates its profits, to foreign exchange receipts. But it may contribute indirectly — for example by increasing 'follow-on' orders for goods and services produced in its home country, by enhancing the skills of citizens who are employed abroad, or by making the firm (including its domestic operations) more globally competitive. The important negotiating point is that Modes 3 and 4 are often a means to an end (increased exports of goods and of services under Modes 1 and 2) rather than a national economic objective in their own right. This may affect a government's

negotiating strategy and lead to a paradox. Restrictions on Modes 3 and 4 exports may be more obvious and severe than those on Modes 1 and 2. Hence there is 'more to negotiate about'. Yet the national gains from reducing Mode 3 and 4 restrictions may be less obvious.

The objective of importing is to provide consumers with either lower prices or an enhanced quality and range of services. The term 'consumers' includes domestic producers for whom the service is an input. The competitiveness of a country's exports and non-competing services may be influenced by the (non) availability of imported service inputs. Since 'services' actually account for a high proportion of the value of Africa's 'goods' exports, an uncompetitive services sector can stymie good trade.

A difference between goods and services is that the competitiveness of imports of the latter is less easy to judge objectively. It is easy to determine whether or not a Japanese machine is cheaper/higher quality than an Italian or African one. Provided that standards are monitored and markets are reasonably competitive, a government can be confident of the effect that a reduction of restrictions on imports of Japanese machines will have. Not so with services, for which price and quality will vary — partly according to the individuals involved and partly because of the regulatory framework. Without knowing more about a government's regulatory objectives with respect to a services sector, it is not possible to predict whether any given change in import regime is likely to enhance the welfare of citizens either directly (by allowing them to consume more or better services) or indirectly (by enhancing the competitiveness of service-consuming producers).

An increasing range of internationally traded services do not fall within the reach of a government that has abandoned a restrictive exchange control or passport policy. Any Mode 1 services that can be marketed, supplied and paid for remotely (e.g. computer software downloaded from the internet, airline tickets purchased on the web/phone, or life assurance) are outside the control of governments save in those (limited) cases where part of the business process occurs in an area where they can act. Hence, government can make it more difficult for its citizens to use telephone call-back services by controlling local access numbers, and it can control imports of car insurance by making it a legal requirement for drivers to have cover with a locally incorporated company. But these are increasingly the exceptions, not the rule. The same applies *a fortiori* to Mode 2. In a real sense, therefore, the import restrictions that exist apply primarily to Modes 3 and 4, and it is these that Africa most needs to assess. But the impact on the economy of any change to these modes is likely to be indirect. Among other things, this makes it difficult to generalize. It also makes it likely that preconceptions drawn from experience with goods trade will be misplaced.

## Differences between Goods and Services

It is easier to generalize about the effects of removing restrictions to trade in goods than in services, partly because the most usually assessed restriction (the tariff) is common to many goods flows and because the ways in which changes to it feed through into markets are reasonably well understood. Where the 'normally expected' feed-through does not occur (e.g. if foreign exchange is rationed) the forecast effects of tariff cuts are likely to be wrong. This problem of 'special circumstances' applies widely to services. If all tariffs are cut by half, for example, several immediate effects are likely (provided markets are reasonably competitive and efficient). The task is to strike a balance between the interests of consumers, producers, taxpayers and recipients of government expenditure.

- All sectors will be affected and any differences between them in proportional effect can be easily calculated by reference to their initial tariff level.
- There will be a transfer from the government revenue of the importing state to elements in the supply chain. The distribution of this transfer between the stages in the supply chain will vary according to circumstance, but one way or another the net effect is likely to be an increase of international trade.
- Import prices are likely to fall to the benefit of consumers (including industrial users) but to the cost of domestic producers of competing products.

With services trade everything is different. For a start, there are far fewer universal effects than there are in the case of goods. Zero tariffs for goods are likely to benefit international trade in all sectors; in services, by contrast, a change to the rules of establishment may be of central importance to one sector but of only tangential relevance to another, depending upon the extent to which the business process favours locally established companies. For car insurance it may be the difference between a sale and no sale at all; for niche life assurance it may be less important than the ability to undertake comparative marketing. Whereas a single change for goods (cutting tariffs by 50 percent) will tend to have similar effects across the board, a single change for services is likely to have a much more localized effect.

## Different Negotiating Agendas

Much of the discussion on services negotiations concerns national treament, whereas goods negotiations have tended to be more concerned with market access. This is because, as explained above, Article III of GATT 1947 already requires members to offer NT in 'like' goods. In the case of those services that are controllable by government (mainly Modes 3 and 4), NT is still offered only on a limited basis. This is one reason why negotiations give it a high profile. Another is that the constraints on market access in Modes 3 and 4 are either shadowy (is a restriction on the number of banks a market access restriction or an exercise of prudential regulation?), or very controversial (e.g. work permits and visas), or both. But just as NT for goods does not necessarily result in competition (e.g. for an item facing a very high *ad valorem* equivalent tariff), so in the case of services NT by itself may make only a limited difference to consumer choice in the importing state. National treatment means exactly what it says: foreign firms are treated no worse — but no better — than their domestic competitors. Given the nature of services trade, this could remove, in whole or in part, their competitive advantage even if there were no protectionist intent on the part of the regulating government.

This could happen by virtue of the features of a foreign service-provider that might allow it to offer services more competitively than the domestic supplier. One possible factor in its competitiveness would be its ability to draw upon resources (technical, financial or personnel) from its home base. But NT by itself does not necessarily give the firm the right to draw freely upon its resources abroad. Prudential requirements concerning reserves may require a firm to hold deposits in the host country rather than using those in its home base. Immigration and work permit restrictions as well as non-recognition of qualifications may frustrate its attempt to utilise its foreign holdings of technical and human resources. There are GATS rules against the deliberate misuse of qualification recognition as a protectionist (or discriminatory) device, but as the EU's experience in creating a single services market demonstrates, rules in this area can be evaded. A restrictive set of policies could stifle the competitive advantages of a foreign supplier by much more than, say, a 40 percent tariff.

In other words, whereas it is reasonable to assume that NT for goods that do not face very high tariffs will generally lead to lower domestic prices, in services no such generalizations are warranted; the effect may be context specific. This is the more likely because some services (finance, telecoms etc.) are legitimately regulated by government to control the level or quality supply. In these cases it is the decision of government (or an independent authority) as *regulator* that is more likely to affect the level of competition than its *trade policy* stance.

This is not to say that offering NT to foreign firms will have no impact. It may affect the quality of services offered and reduce the proportion of current and future business conducted by wholly domestic firms (which may in turn have indirect economic effects if, say, they are more likely to re-invest profits domestically). But the economic and political effects may be less clear-cut than would be the case with goods. The political costs of redundancies and closures in competing domestic firms may be lower, but so will the gains of lower consumer prices and the economic benefits arising from a redistribution of investment and employment into more competitive sectors.

And partly because trade in many services is of such recent origin (and still far from fully developed), public attitudes are very different in some cases from those for goods. The issues are not fundamentally different, but whereas the populace has grown used to the trade-offs and priority setting that are intrinsic to trade in goods, these still jar when it comes to services. It is axiomatic, for example, that goods exports reduce the welfare of a country's citizens if no account is taken of the imports made available by the foreign exchange earned. Exporting involves using scarce factors of production to produce commodities that are then not available to be consumed by those who produced them. Often this attracts no controversy at all. Few complain that clothing made in Mauritius, Madagascar or Tunisia is exported and not available for locals to buy and wear. From

time to time, cases emerge which cause some public discussion (for example on the merits of smallholder farmers producing export crops rather than food for their own consumption). But these are the exception rather than the rule — and arise because the trade-off accepted implicitly elsewhere is called into question in relation to the goods involved.

Such controversy is more fundamental in some potential areas of services trade and for the same reason as the export/food crop debate is controversial; the trade-offs are not necessarily accepted. In the case of health, the use of local hospital beds and doctors to treat foreign patients, or the export under Mode 1 of teams of medical staff, are likely to provoke indignation that vital national resources are not being made available to citizens. From an economist's standpoint there is no fundamental difference between a country exporting health services and using the foreign exchange to import other necessities and doing the same thing with cherry tomatoes. But public perceptions are not the same as those of economists. A government that fails to take account of this difference does so at its own peril.

## Conclusions

As this chapter has shown, Africa has not been in short of the political capital of good-will in its external trade diplomacy. Several trade agreements have been put in place to improve market access for African exports. As we have seen, some of these have not produced the desired results due to a multi-plicity of factors. With regard to the evolving WTO regime, despite the many welcome improvements contained in the new trade framework, it is somewhat inevitable that developing countries will continue to have a relatively weak bargaining position, as trade liberalization in the WTO remains dependent upon developed countries' willingness to reduce tariffs and domestic support in areas of vital interest to developing countries' exports trade. Trade in commodities has over the years been governed by Commodity Trade Agreements. There is, however, no reference in the WTO of what will become of these Agreements. Their sustained use in the determination of commodity bargains side by side with the WTO Agreements could continue to impoverish commodity producers.

Aside from the observed internal weakness of the WTO, it is also evident that other factors relating to Africa's poor competitiveness might hinder her ability to truly exploit opportunities presented by the WTO. One of the most critical is the problem of the unfavorable supply conditions for cash crops due to insufficient domestic production, relatively poor quality of outputs as a result of poor handling of crops, underdeveloped agronomic research and lack of proper link between research organisations and producers; and lack of improved seeds and seedlings. Other critical factors relate to poor and unreliable infrastructures (energy, water supply, transportation); poor access to credit and foreign exchange; lower labor productivity in relation to most Asian countries; rural-urban migration away from agriculture to industrial and white-collar employment; pervasive poverty and poor health; and the existence of cumbersome export procedures.

Africa can be regarded as one of the biggest losers at Cancun. African countries,

more than any other group, want full integration into the world economy and world trading system. As we have seen, Africa's current global trade amounts to less than 3 percent of the world's total. With nearly 300 million people living on less than one dollar a day, Africa is the one region where poverty remains a growing threat. In spite of encouraging trade initiatives such as AGOA and the EBA, Africa continues to face considerable tariff as well as non-tariff barriers for its products. All these obstacles will contribute to slowing economic growth in Africa, which in turn will mean slower progress in poverty reduction and slower progress in meeting the targets of the Millennium Development Goals for the year 2015. It is can also be expected to impact negatively on the prospects of NEPAD, which focuses on renewed partnership with its external stakeholders and hinges African development on re-engagement with the world community on the basis of 'open regionalism'.

Clearly, Africa stands to benefit from the emergence of a more equitable global trading system. Cancun was meant to be the 'development round' of trade talks to make good on pledges made at Doha two years earlier. Its chief goal was to lower trade barriers in areas where freer trade would help poor countries most, especially agriculture. A global trade and development pact would be expected to lift within a decade some estimated 150 million people — most of them in Sub-Saharan Africa — out of poverty. At the very least, Cancun's failure has delayed progress towards concluding a trade round that would have given poor countries the biggest economic gains. With the Doha

Round in seeming jeopardy, the prospects for the removal of rich countries' farm subsidies and market access barriers or concluding the trade talks by the original deadline of 31 December 2004 have retreated farther into the unknown future.

# CHAPTER 6

# Trade and Structural Transformation: Towards a New Agenda for Policy

## Introduction

In a changed international environment, trade is likely to remain at the forefront of the global policy agenda for much of the foreseeable future. As this study has shown, trade has been a crucial element in the growth of nations; and it is even more so for low-income developing economies. This chapter brings together the main findings and divergent strands of analysis in the previous chapters into a coherent summary and conclusion. It is premised on the need for Africa to pursue an export-oriented policy agenda anchored on structural transformation.

Here we highlight the domestic and external policy measures needed to optimize Africa's export performance and the experiences of Mauritius and East Asia are discussed as examples of the sorts of policy choices that African countries need to undertake. The question of global governance and coordination of policies on trade between international development institutions, including the African Development Bank Group is also discussed.

## Structural Transformation and Export Diversification

African countries have never been short of policy advice since their attainment of independence in the 1960s. For the last two decades much of the policy advice has been centered on structural reforms, which a good number of countries have implemented under the aegis of the Bretton Woods Institutions (BWIs). Whilst some embraced reforms with conviction, others did so merely out of the need to maintain credible relations with external creditors. It could be said that given the dire straits in which the overwhelming majority of countries found themselves after the 'second oil shock' in 1979, if structural reforms had not existed, they would have had to be invented. The combination of mounting indebtedness, dwindling foreign reserves and growing food deficits, among other symptoms of economic crisis, required structural measures to stem a downward economic spiral.

Over the years much has been learned about what works or does not work with regard to orthodox structural reform programs, and there has been a mutually beneficial learning process between Africa and the multilateral finance institutions. Gradually, we are returning to the realization that nations and peoples must be the ultimate owners of their own development. Externally inspired models may work for a while, but they could never be sustainable in the long run.

### A New Vision of Development

The development experiences of the recent past reinforce the need for a new development paradigm in Africa, in particular one that exploits the linkages between agriculture, manufacturing and export markets. Without industrialization and without structural transformation, no developing economy can survive in the 21st century. The countries of Africa need to adopt and prosecute a policy of structural transformation in order to achieve rapid and sustainable economic growth, raise living standards and reduce the incidence of widespread poverty in which the majority of their peoples are currently entrapped.[1] The strategy of structural transformation refers to the restructuring of the productive and institutional foundations of a predominantly agrarian economy to increase productivity and enhance diversification of exports through creating rural-urban and inter-sectoral linkages in an increasingly open economy (Box 6.1).

In this regard, it is encouraging that some countries have gradually shifted the composition of their exports from unprocessed to processed traditional products (such as Côte d'Ivoire and its semi-processed cocoa products, Senegal and its phosphate derivative products, and Cameroon and its processed timber).

The only countries in Africa that have convincingly diversified their production and exports away from traditional products include Tunisia, Mauritius, Morocco, Egypt and South Africa. Diversification efforts towards manufactured exports in these countries have initially relied on labor-intensive products, ranging from chemicals, basic metals, and leather through to motor vehicles manufacturing, textile and footwear, and electronic goods. These countries, however, would need to make their export sectors more dynamic, in order to maintain a competitive edge for their manufactured products on the world market. According to UNCTAD, the sharp increase in the number of low-skilled workers participating in trade-related activities is an important reason why developing countries may face increasingly saturated markets for their manufactured exports. It is recognized, for instance, that increasing labor costs in Mauritius have eroded the competitiveness of its textile industry over the years.

*Successful Diversification is a Dynamic Process*

Early African diversifiers must, however, learn from economic history which tells us that successful diversification is not an event, but is rather, a dynamic process where old leading industries would have to hand on the lead to new industries in response to challenges emanating from the domestic and international competitive environments. It is indeed encouraging to note that Africa's early diversifiers are responding positively to this challenge. For instance, in the face of high domestic labor costs and international competition in textiles, Mauritius is gradually shifting its labor-intensive, low technology production to a relatively more capital-intensive, high technology production base. The development of new industries (including printing, publishing, jewelry, watches and clocks, sporting goods, etc.,) is expected to complement existing industries, thereby creating 'advantages of conglomeration', particularly in the country's Export Processing Zone.

---

[1] For a more detailed discussion of the policy of structural transformation, see the African Development Report, 2003.

## Box: 6.1: Towards a New Policy Agenda in Africa

Africa is endowed with abundant but largely untapped potentials of natural resources — fertile soils, water, oil, gas, minerals and metals — and a population that is full of energy, vigor and ingenuity. Significant socio-political changes have swept the continent in the last decade. Some 35 countries have been implementing structural adjustment programs while civil wars have ended in several others, with the prospects that the path towards peace and progress will be restored. A new wave of democratization has also swept through the continent, and the progress towards change, though slow and fragile, seems headed for the better. For the first time in two decades, aggregate growth in income per capita has been significantly positive since 1996, perhaps signaling an escape from an enduring trap. Africa accounts for more than 10 per cent of the world's population. Its long-term development vision could be driven by the goal to account for at least 10 percent of world output and exports within the next 30 years. This is daunting but not impossible. But such a goal in the context of globalization requires a coherent strategy, or in other words a business plan. This should seek to minimize the risks of globalization while maximizing its benefits. To be effective, such a plan must be comprehensive and involve consistent and coherent actions/programs at three major levels:

- *Domestic strategy*, anchored on building the institutions and enabling environment for a private sector-led, competitive market economy. More fundamentally such a domestic strategy must be guided by the ideology of aggressive outward or export-orientation, using regionalism as a building block.
- *Regional strategy*, driven by the need to enlarge markets and to exploit complement-

arities, economies of scale and synergies in provision of regional public goods — infrastructure, security/defense and collective regional institutions as agencies of restraint — so that domestic reforms and policies can be locked in for credibility. Such a regional strategy must also involve defining and mainstreaming regional best practices in political and economic governance, and exert collective peer pressures on erring countries to conform to the regional 'convergence criteria'.

- *Global strategy*, aimed at addressing many of the asymmetrical power relations and inequities in globalization, creating a level playing field, redesigning the global financial architecture, provision of global public goods, and strengthening the programs and institutions for preferential and differential treatments to Africa.

The new strategies would require fundamental changes in the existing ways of doing business. It is axiomatic that growth in living standards results from the accumulation of physical capital (investment) and human capital (labor), and through advances in technology. Experiences of countries that have increased output most rapidly demonstrate that it is necessary to create the conditions that are conducive to long-run per capita income growth. Economic stability, institution-building, and structural reforms are as important for long-term development as financial transfers. What matters is the whole package of policies, financial and technical assistance as well as debt relief. Sub-Saharan African countries need to grow at 7 percent a year on average to reduce poverty by half by 2015. They have to be fuelled by much higher domestic savings, and by a flow of grants, loans and investments.

*Source*: African Development Report, 2003

Early diversifiers in Africa, including South Africa, Tunisia, Egypt and Morocco, will need to continue building dynamic export sectors and acquiring new comparative advantages in products and services where world demand is high, in a changing global competitive environment.

### Strengthening the Links between FDI and Trade

A strategy of structural transformation requires, among other things, the creation of dynamic linkages between export expansion and inward investments. Available estimates suggest that nearly two-thirds of world trade, including both intra-firm trade and third party transactions, during the latter half of the decade of the nineties, involved the participation of multinational corporations (UNCTAD, 2002). Foreign investment is considered a potent instrument of development because of its ability to transfer technology and skills to developing countries. The technology and know-how, especially marketing know-how, which accompany FDI, also makes a significant contribution to growth of exports of host countries. This they do through transferring specific production and labor skills required for enhancing export competitiveness in the sectors in which they invest. Equally important is the spill over of technology and know-how from foreign firms to locally owned firms. The channels for such a spillover include sub-contracting arrangements for the production of components between foreign-owned and locally owned firms, movement of trained labor from foreign-owned to locally owned firms, and imitation.

Like many other developing countries, most African countries have actively sought FDI. Several countries have liberalized FDI regulatory regimes through privatizing publicly-owned enterprises, relaxing mandatory joint-venture requirements (Nigeria), reducing the number of industries which were previously closed to foreign investors (Ghana) and expediting investment approval procedures (Kenya). The growth in the share of FDI in total external resource flows to Africa since the mid-1990s reflects these policy initiatives. Even so, Africa lags behind in the total volume of FDI it has attracted, especially so considering its resource endowments and potential for attracting FDI. Its share in annual global inflows of FDI is a mere 2 percent compared with Asia's share of 14 percent, and its share in FDI flows to developing countries as a whole is around 4 percent compared with around 45 to 50 percent in the case of Asia and around 35 to 40 percent in the case of Latin America and the Caribbean. Again its share in the stock of FDI in developing countries is around 6.8 percent compared with 55 percent for Asia and 30 percent in Latin America.

There are countries that are not endowed with an abundance of oil and mineral resources but have succeeded in attracting relatively large volumes of FDI. Apart from the well-known examples in East Asia such as Singapore and Hong Kong this set includes the African countries of Mozambique, Uganda, Mali and Ghana. Here there are a variety of explanations, all of which suggest that African countries too are capable of attracting large volumes of foreign investments. For Africa, two of the nine factors listed in Box 6.2, namely macroeconomic stability and distortion-free factors, are

**Box 6.2:  Determinants of Foreign Direct Investment in Africa**

Much of the FDI in Africa is concentrated in a handful of countries. In recent years three countries- South Africa, Nigeria, and Angola have accounted for around 50 to 75 percent of the total inflows into the SSA region. Other countries that have received significant volumes of FDI in recent years include Botswana, Mauritius, Lesotho, Uganda, Swaziland, Namibia and Mozambique. He primary sector including oil and minerals accounted for around 40 per cent of the accumulated stock of FDI at the end of the year 1999, manufacturing for another 30 percent and services for around 27 per cent. It is easy to conclude that whatever FDI African countries have attracted in recent years is largely due to their endowments of resources including minerals and oil as in the case of Nigeria and Angola and large potential markets as in the case of South Africa. Non-oil exporting countries such as Mozambique, Uganda and Mauritius have figured significantly in the FDI league tables in Africa. The success of these countries in attracting sizeable flows of FDI which have contributed to the growth of their exports and income is to be attributed to a number of factors identified in the literature. The extant theoretical and empirical literature on determinants of FDI yields the following broad propositions.

1   Host countries with sizeable domestic markets, measured by GDP per capita and sustained growth of these markets, measured by growth rates of GDP attract relatively large volumes of FDI

2   Resource endowments including natural resources and human resources are a factor of importance in the investment decision process of foreign firms.

3   Infrastructure facilities including transportation and communication net works are an important determinant of FDI.

4   Macro economic stability, signified by stable exchange rates and low rates of inflation is a significant factor in attracting foreign investors.

5   Political stability is conducive to inflows of FDI

6   A stable and transparent policy framework towards FDI is attractive to potential investors.

7   Foreign firms place a premium on a distortion free economic and business environment.

8   Fiscal and monetary incentives in the form of tax concessions do play a role in attracting FDI, but these are of little significance in the absence of a stable economic environment.

9   Regional groupings and preferential trading arrangements between prospective recipients of FDI may induce increased inflows.

Natural resource endowments attract what Dunning (1993) refers to as resource seeking FDI. The relatively large volumes of FDI in Nigeria, Angola, Namibia and Botswana, for example, are of the resource seeking variety. FDI appears to have been attracted to Nigeria and Namibia despite political instability in these countries. Perhaps the stability that matters for foreign investors is not the stability of regimes be they dictatorships or democracies but the stability of policies, especially assurances against expropriation, which the successive government in these countries appear to have provided, principally because they are reluctant to kill the goose that lays the golden egg. The joint venture arrangement between the Nigerian government (through the Nigerian National Petroleum Corporation — NNPC) and oil companies, such Shell, ExxonMobil, and BP, provides adequate guarantees against expropria- tion. Indeed, most MNEs seek stability of policies irrespective of the governments in power.

*Source*: African Development Bank, Research Department, 2004.

especially crucial in promoting inward investment.

Low inflation rates and stable exchange rates are also important factors in attracting FDI for more reasons than one. First, they attest to the stability and underlying strength of the economy. Secondly, they provide a degree of certainty relating to the future course of the economy and impart confidence in the ability of firms to repatriate profits and dividends. Weak economies with high levels of domestic borrowing and debt (measured by the ratio of budget deficits to GDP and total volume of borrowing to GDP) are often compelled to institute exchange controls on the capital account of the balance of payments. Thirdly, more often than not a stable macroeconomic environment also implies a stable political environment. Political and economic stability are usually intertwined.

It is a well known fact that countries with a distortion-free market environment — free of policy induced incentives and restrictions — tend to attract relatively larger volumes of FDI than distortion-ridden economies. We owe a precise enunciation of this proposition to Jagdish Bhagwati who argued that, with adjustments "for differences among countries for their economic size, political attitudes towards FDI and political stability, both the magnitude of FDI inflows and their efficacy in promoting economic growth will be greater over the long haul in countries pursuing the export promotion (EP) strategy than in countries pursuing the import substitution (IS) strategy" (Bhagwati, 1978).

Several features of Bhagwati's hypothesis are noteworthy. First, is the reference to the trade policy framework of countries host to foreign investment. The inward looking IS strategy, pursued with vigor in the past by countries such as India, is exemplified by tariffs and quotas on imports, and in many cases, restrictions on spheres of activity and on volumes of investment by both domestic and foreign investors. Quite often, IS regimes are also characterized by subsidies on exports, a sort of second-best policy to promote exports, but the protection from import competition afforded to import-substituting industries exceeds the incentives for exports provided by subsidies. The policy orientation of EP regimes, as defined by Bhagwati, is its neutrality. In other words, the policy regime favors the production of neither import-substitutes nor exportables. The importance of trade and macroeconomic reforms in attracting FDI is well illustrated by Uganda's experience (Box 6.3).

Macroeconomic stability and a distortion-free economic environment presuppose transparency of policies and an efficient administration, with a minimum of red tape and bureaucratic hurdles, in the functioning of the FDI regime. Corruption in Africa and its adverse impact on both inflows and the efficacy of FDI is often noted. Amongst other reasons, the high levels of corruption in several African economies are a consequence of highly regulated and opaque trade and FDI regimes. As discussed earlier, import substitution regimes foster rent-seeking and other activities which could deter FDI in the long-term.

Judged by the principal determinants of FDI, African countries do have the potential to attract much higher volumes of FDI than they receive at present. This need not be confined to resource-seeking FDI, such as investments

---

**Box 6.3:  Uganda**

Since the mid-nineties Uganda's real GDP has grown at around 6 percent per annum on an average. Growth has attracted FDI mainly into the manufacturing sector. Inflows of FDI which averaged around $65 million during the years 1991-96 increased more than four fold and stood at $ 275 million in 2002. Foreign investment accounts for around 24 per cent of the gross fixed capital formation in the economy. Uganda's success in attracting FDI and promoting growth is to be attributed to fiscal discipline, trade policy reforms and the institution of a favourable climate for FDI. Since 1995 Uganda has eliminated all quantitative restrictions on trade except for restrictions in place for moral, health, security and environmental reasons. Tariffs are now the main trade policy instrument. The simple average rate of Uganda's applied MFN tariff rate is 9 per cent. However, withholding tax and commission on import licence move it up to 15 per cent. The tariff structure has been simplified through the reduction of number of bands from 5 to 3 (zero, 7 per cent and 15 per cent). The only export tax that is levied is on 15 exports revenues on coffee collected by the Uganda Coffee development Authority.

*Source*: Based on information in Uganda Trade Policy Review, WTO, 2002.

services. The FDI potential index, a rough measure of the ability of a country to attract FDI, based on various determinants of FDI, also suggests that these countries do possess the sort of ingredients necessary to attract increased volumes of foreign investments.[2] Botswana, in fact, provides an excellent example of a country that has graduated from the ranks of LDCs to that of a low middle-income country with prudent economic policies and efficient utilization of foreign investment capital (Box 6.4).

In sum, although most African countries rank relatively low in the FDI league tables, they cannot be dismissed as countries with little potential for attracting and efficiently utilizing FDI in the development process. The success stories narrated above suggest that, given the sort of domestic policies and business climate favorable to their operations, foreign firms do seek investment outlets in these countries and they do play a role in the promotion of trade and growth.

---

[2] The FDI performance index is estimated as the ratio of the share of a country's FDI in global flows of FDI to its share in global GDP. Countries with an index of greater than unity receive volumes of FDI than that suggested by their GDP. For the years 1998–2000 the index was 1 for Malawi, 1.8 for Mozambique, 1 for Uganda and 1.7 for Zambia. The FDI potential index is a rough measure of the attractiveness of a country for foreign firms. It is estimated as an unweighted average of a set of variables which are the principal determinants of FDI. These include GDP growth rates, share of exports in GDP, telephone lines per 1,000 inhabitants and a set of human skills. The FDI potential index for Malawi was estimated at 0.150, for Mali 0.216, Mozambique 0.178, Uganda 0.228 and Zambia 0.160. The highest rating was for Singapore at 0.64.

in minerals and oil. Africa has the potential to attract efficiency-seeking FDI, defined as investments designed to take advantage of low labor costs and establishment of specific segments of the value added chain in host countries. Countries such as Uganda and Mozambique have been successful in attracting investments into manufacturing and

## Box 6.4: Botswana — Success Based on Sound Policies

Botswana was one of the poorest countries in the world, with a per capita income of US$80, when it attained political independence in 1966. At the turn of the century its per capita income measured in PPP dollars was US$6,032 (US$3,240 at market exchange rate) For the year 2001 per capita income in PPP dollars was as high as US$7,820 (US$2,970 at market exchange rate).

This impressive performance of Botswana is to be attributed to prudent management of its public finances, an efficient civil service and effective utilization of FDI. Botswana maintained budget surpluses until the year 2001 when it registered a deficit of 3.1 percent of GDP for the first time in years. The deficit was on account of increased development expenditures, but the accumulated reserves of Botswana can meet the deficits without recourse to public borrowing. Foreign exchange reserves are estimated to be around 32 months of import coverage. The Bank of Botswana's principal monetary policy objective is controlling inflation and it tries to maintain inflation rate at no higher than the weighted average level of its major trading partners. The Bank maintains the nominal effective exchange rate constant and seeks to achieve an inflation rate that, at a minimum also maintains a relatively stable real exchange rate, so as to promote export competitiveness and economic diversification. The credit rating for Botswana given by Moody's, and by Standard and Poor's, at 'A' for long-term debt, puts the country well ahead of many others in the world.

Botswana has been open to FDI since 1966. The government acknowledges the critical role of private, especially foreign, capital in stimulating growth, sustainable employment and poverty alleviation. Foreign investment is allowed in all sectors except those reserved for small and micro enterprises. Foreign investors are encouraged, but not compelled, to establish joint –ventures. No foreign equity limits apply. All foreign and locally owned companies with ten or more employees must be licensed. License applications are processed by the Ministry of Trade, Wildlife and Tourism within four to five weeks. A foreign investment code was released in 2001 to guide investors and to consolidate Botswana's investment policies and legislation.

Foreign firms have played a significant role in Botswana's development. They developed the mining sector, principally diamonds, in joint ventures with the government. They also have a significant presence in Botswana's services sector, commercial banks are foreign controlled. In tourism of a total of 331 enterprises operated between March 1997 and February 2001, more than two-thirds of them foreign, half of them being joint ventures with local partners. FDI has provided the impetus for diversification of the economy from agriculture towards mining and services and has contributed to the country's impressive growth. Even so, there are challenges ahead for the country. If it is to develop strong backward linkages from foreign firms to the local economy and reduce its relatively high levels of unemployment, the country has to develop local capabilities. Unfortunately, Botswana has the highest incidence rate of HIV/AIDS in the world, however the government has in place a comprehensive program for combating the disease.

## Promoting Trade and Export Expansion

As part of the policy mix of a strategy of structural transformation, African governments need to devise more effective methods for promoting trade and export expansion. Devising such strategies must begin with the capacity of policy operatives to analyze and implement sound trade and export policies. Linked to such capacity is the need to strengthen trade missions and the quality of their economic diplomacy, including trade negotiations skills.

Clearly, growth in the export of manufactured goods depends on a combination of domestic industrialization and vigorous export promotion. In addition to the production of high-quality manufactured goods, successful export requires creative marketing, attractive packaging, information on demand conditions in foreign markets, flexibility, adaptability and zeal in penetrating foreign markets. Africa has the potential in terms of human resources, raw materials and access to the requisite technology. What are needed are adequate will, organizational acumen and persistence to succeed.

The policy of export promotion is being canvassed as a means of encouraging the diversification of production and exports. It is also a vehicle for improving the balance of trade and balance of payments and for galvanizing capital inflows and improving the competitiveness of domestic industries. Export promotion is a wide-ranging policy initiative that has many components and dimensions. Policies and strategies for export promotion are designed to:

(i)     Enhance the marketability of exportables through product diversification and quality improvement;

(ii)    Strengthen and improve the institutional framework for providing better support services to exporters and export-oriented industries;

(iii)   Establish backward linkages between export-oriented industries and primary sectors for the utilization of local raw materials;

(iv)    Attract an increased number of entrepreneurs for setting up export-oriented industries and encourage them through the provision of suitable incentive packages, as well as appropriate human resources development programs for the promotion of entrepreneurial and managerial skills in the context of a competitive international environment;

(v)     Expand and consolidate existing export markets as well as create new markets for African exportables;

(vi)    Ensure the removal of procedural and regulatory bottlenecks incompatible with the attainment of the objectives of an export-led growth policy;

(vii)   Promote programs for developing export-oriented knowledge-based resources, including computer software, Internet facilities and electronic commerce, engineering and consultancy services;

(viii)  Diversify and increase export of high value-added manufactured products, that depend on the natural resources where Africa has comparative advantage;

(ix) Encourage the acquisition and adaptation of environment-friendly technologies to ensure that African products meet the required international standards.

In addition to the traditional export commodities, Africa has significant potential for export of horticulture, soya beans, shrimps, fish, cashew nuts, and gum Arabic. To have a reasonable chance of success, governments must vigorously promote improvements in rural infrastructure, enhance extension delivery services, undertake aggressive marketing, provide comprehensive agricultural trade information and offer other requisite incentive packages and trade support infrastructure. It is well known that the gains from export of processed and manufactured goods are greater than those from exporting primary commodities largely because of the higher value-added and countries therefore need to gradually diversify into manufacturing exports. This also requires confronting constraints such as inadequate infrastructure facilities, policy instability and lack of predictability, price and exchange rate instability, lack of requisite financing for industrial development, insufficient emphasis on R&D activities, inappropriate technologies, and ineffective regulatory institutions, which manifest bureaucratic bottlenecks and rent-seeking activities.

### EPZs as Part of a Package

One of the new approaches that can be used to foster trade development in Africa is establishment of export processing zones (EPZs). As in the case of Mauritius, the advantages that EPZs offer include the rapid expansion of the industrial base, stimulation of the domestic sector through linkages with the rest of the economy, and alleviation of the problem of unemployment in the host country. The Asian and Pacific countries have used free trade zones as instruments of development more than any other developing nations. EPZs have had a marked success in Hong Kong, Singapore, China, Taiwan and South Korea.

The incentives provided by the EPZs include an absence of tariffs and other barriers on imports into the zones, an absence of duties on exports from the zones, the provision of infrastructure facilities, including electricity, often at subsidized rates to firms located in the zones. The objective of setting up these zones is that they can attract FDI which in turn will generate employment, promote backward linkages with domestic firms, promote exports and thus foreign exchange earnings and result in the importation of technology and skills. EPZs, in most cases, are oases of free trade in an economy that may be rife with policy-induced distortions including tariffs and other barriers to imports. They are designed to lure foreign firms away from the protected domestic markets towards export markets. They are an example of the 'second-best' policy in the sense that they are an attempt to offset distortions elsewhere in the economy by another distortion. Introduction of new distortions in the form of export incentives, EPZs are in the nature of export incentive schemes, in order to correct existing distortions results in a proliferation of distortions, which may cause more harm than good for the promotion of exports.

There are, however, several issues relating to the social costs and benefits of export processing zones. The first of these relates to the social opportunity costs of establishing these zones. These costs include the costs of infrastructure in the zones, subsidies of various sorts provided to the firms on the zones and the social opportunity costs of labor employed in the zones. To the extent the opportunity cost of labor is negligible and the economy is endowed with a fairly elastic supply of relatively cheap labor the employment created on the zones and the exports they generate should be counted as benefits. This could be so even in the presence of a protected domestic sector alongside the zones, provided the social opportunity cost of labor is negligible. The zones then serve as a focal point for the organization of labor and production of labor-intensive manufactures. This seems to explain the success of China. When the supply of cheap labor tapers off and isolating the zones from the rest of the economy becomes problematic, the usefulness of the zones comes into question. This would be so especially in the case of economies where EPZs are established as an antidote to protection elsewhere in the economy rather than as a part of a well designed export promotion policy. It could however be argued that EPZs are unnecessary if the economy pursues an outward-looking strategy of development with few policy-induced distortions.

*Good Governance is Imperative*

To reverse the spread of poverty and improve human welfare, the present rate of growth in Africa would have to double. Yet this is impossible without the political and the economic underpinnings for sustained economic development, namely, good governance. Good governance requires that citizens have the means to hold their rulers accountable. It requires responsive, responsible political leadership that respects the rule of law. Good governance requires social reciprocities: different groups within a country and their political leaders must transcend religious, kinship, ethnic, and racial differences. These principles are essential for good political governance. They also establish the basis for good economic governance, i.e. a state's capacity to initiate, design, and implement policies that realize a shared development vision of accelerated growth and poverty reduction.

During the 1990s, Africa gradually began to move towards more acceptable norms of political and economic governance. A new ethos is emerging that increasingly favors democracy and the rule of law against the old discredited habits of personal rule, 'neo-patrimonialism' and corrupt rulership. During the last decade, some 42 African countries have held multi-party presidential or parliamentary elections, with mixed results but also some notable successes. In low-income African countries, for example, approximately 68 percent of the population now live in partially free conditions compared to approximately 22 percent in the 1980s. Most countries have also begun to improve economic governance, a fact underlined by the new development path that has been adopted. The path is guided by a set of strategic choices. It acknowledges the pivotal role of the private sector in economic growth, and places poverty reduction at the heart of the development process.

Notwithstanding these positive developments, democracy remains an expression of ethnic allegiances in some cases, especially where popular judgment makes no impact on government programs. The number of African countries struggling with instability and conflict points to the tenuous hold of democracy and social cohesion on the continent. Corrupt practices in the public and private sectors, including fiscal fraud and tax evasion, continue to distort free markets, hamper economic development and hamstring the institutional capacity to deliver on public services. State regulatory, fiscal, administrative and technical capacities remain inadequate in many African countries. Lack of expertise and institutional capacity to meet the challenges of globalization, and participate effectively in the global economy, are the most critical of these lacunae.

The recent momentum for appropriate change needs to enhance political and economic governance so that African countries achieve a level of socioeconomic development that reflects their potential and the aspiration of their populations. African countries still need to move away from authoritarianism towards effective forms of governance through greater popular participation and decentralization. These improvements have to be reflected in effective, transparent systems of financial supervision and legal accountability, of public administration, in an operational legal framework and with predictable regulatory structures, alongside socially-responsible corporate governance.

Experience does show that good political governance is a prerequisite for good economic governance (African Development Report, 2001). In the area of economic management, the privatization process must seek to avoid fraud and any concentration of economic power. Central bank independence, which prevents using monetary instruments for political or material gain, is essential for effective monetary policy. Debt management units that monitor the borrowing and repayment processes, and conduct periodic analyses of the foreign exchange productivity of borrowed funds, have to be created to avoid future debt crises. Fiscal management must be efficient and fair. African countries must build capacities in areas that support the functioning of political and economic governance and the activities of the private sector and civil society. Linked to this is the need for an efficient civil service, which is essential to meet the challenges of development management in the 21st century. This means not only containing costs and rationalizing civil service systems but also providing incentives to attract and retain high quality administrative officials. Clear policies must be adopted that focus on fighting corruption. A legal and social environment hostile to corrupt practices has to be an integral part of this process. Improving governance and fighting corruption should go hand in hand with efforts to enliven Africa's image in the world.

### Mauritius as a success story

Mauritius provides a case study of a successful strategy of structural transformation in Africa (Box 6.5).

## Box 6.5: Mauritius — Economic Success Based on Structural Transformation

Despite its small land area and population, Mauritius is one of the fastest-growing economies of Africa and is generally considered as an African success story. Since gaining independence in 1968, the country has succeeded in making the transition from a low-income, agricultural economy to a more diversified, middle-income country. Political stability and democracy have provided an attractive business climate for foreign investment. Tourism has boomed and services have also grown side-by-side with manufacturing and industry. Its modern port, airport and telecommunications links have given it an advantage as a strategic area for investment and have helped to accelerate economic growth.

Mauritius, a small economy with a population of 1.19 million in 2000, is a success story in Africa. The average annual growth rate of the economy was around 5.7% per annum during the years 1995-2000. Per capita income of Mauritius at UU$3,750 in the year 2001 was one of the highest among African countries. A mono crop economy until 1970, with sugar being the mainstay, Mauritius has successfully diversified. Textiles and clothing, tourism, financial services and sugar are now the main pillars of the economy. The services sector, dominated by tourism and financial services, is the most important segment, accounting for 74 percent of real GDP. Service exports account for more than one-third of the total foreign exchange earnings of the economy. Manufacturing accounts for 75 percent of merchandise exports, with textiles and clothing accounting for more than 40 percent of manufacturing output and 60 percent of merchandise exports followed by sugar at 20 percent.

During the last two decades, the economy has expanded at an annual average rate of 5.75 percent. Mauritius was a poor country with per capita income of US$260 in the early 1960 and,

today, it has been transformed to a middle-income country. Successive governments have pursued policies to foster economic transformation by diversifying into manufacturing for export. The options included: purchase of new machinery and equipment and hiring consultants; encouragement of a massive inflow of foreign direct investment (FDI); purchase of licenses for new technology for domestic production of new products. The adopted strategy was a mixture of all these options. The object was to participate in the international best practice for the production of textiles and clothing, and so an EPZ was created.

The strategy consisted of unrestricted tariff-free imports of machinery and raw materials, no restrictions on ownership or repatriation of profits, a ten-year income-tax holiday and a policy of centralized wage setting to ensure industrial peace and promote moderate wage increases. Thus, the tax-free zone was designed not as a geographical area but as an economic activity, specifically, the manufacturing of textiles and clothing. There was a strong and positive response to this EPZ package as demonstrated by large inflows of FDI from Hong Kong and a few other countries. An international technology transfer took place and local investors also joined in the process. The local investment component was financed from the surpluses of the sugar sector, which was facilitated by a series of sugar booms beginning in the 1970s. The import of equipment and technical skills was supported by the availability of relatively cheap labor and by an enabling macroeconomic policy environment.

The EPZ scheme, coupled with preferential market access provided by some of the developed countries, has contributed to the success of Mauritius in diversifying the economy away from sugar towards low wage and low skill intensive exports, principally textiles and clothing.

*Source*: Trade Policy Review of Mauritius, 2002, and WTO World Trade Report 2003.

In the early years of independence, Mauritius relied on sugar exports for its foreign earnings. As the authorities sought to sustain and accelerate economic growth, they realized that this could never be achieved by sole reliance on sugar exports. Thus a deliberate effort was made to diversify the economy and encourage domestic production activities through backward linkages. This led to the legislation of an Act establishing an EPZ in 1970. An attractive set of incentives was offered to both foreign and domestic investors, including duty-free entry of capital goods and raw materials, tax holidays on corporate profit, tax holidays on dividends, wide availability of infrastructure and cheap credits.

As a result of the success of the EPZ, the manufacturing sector benefited from substantial foreign investment and grew rapidly. In just over 20 years, Mauritius transformed itself from a mono-cultural sugar exporting economy to one in which manufacturing comprised one third of GDP.

There was also a second important factor — preferential trade agreements. Mauritius was a country of origin not subject to quota limits set by the EU and the United States. Mauritius has thus benefited greatly from trade agreements, such as the Lomé/Cotonou conventions (preferential access to Mauritian exports to the European market), and the Multi-Fiber Agreement (MFA), which allowed Mauritius to build up its export-oriented garment industry.

The expansion of value-added through upgrading of technology or diversification of the product range has also been vital. FDI technology has had significant spill over effects in terms of buoyant R&D expenditures and widely available on-the-job training.[3] The success of the Mauritian experiment shows that a country can move forward by implementing imported ideas and allowing the economy to generate high rates of growth based on them.

### Africa Can Also Learn from East Asia

The relative success of East Asia in achieving structural transformation within less than a generation poses significant lessons for Africa. The group of East Asian countries include the so-called tigers, namely Singapore, Republic of Korea, Hong Kong, Taiwan, and Malaysia and Thailand. The growth rates which these countries achieved from around the mid-1960s to the mid-1990s is remarkable, more so because of the vigor with which most of these countries have recovered from the financial crisis which afflicted them during the mid-1990s.

It could be argued that the structure of these economies, their historical antecedents, their geophysical characteristics, the ethnic composition of their population, and the types of external constraints they were faced with during their miraculous growth phase are all so significantly different from those facing other developing countries, especially the African countries, it would be futile to seek lessons from their experience.

---

[3] The case of Mauritius illustrates the limitations of the strategy of export growth based on EPZ situated in the midst of a protected domestic market. In the absence of competition in the domestic market productivity growth has been low and the country seems to have run out of cheap labour. Foreign firms, in labour –intensive sectors are likely to be foot loose and migrate to other locales of relatively cheap labour.

Admittedly no two developing countries are alike; they differ from each other in their resource endowments, size of their economies, political institutions, ethnic composition and historical antecedents. Thus Singapore and Hong Kong are small in terms of population and geographical size relative to Malaysia and South Korea. They are also much more homogenous in terms of the ethnic composition of their population than Malaysia. These countries, however, do share one common feature, i.e. their broad economic policy framework that can best be described as an outward-looking strategy of development or openness, discussed earlier. Here again, these countries differ from each other in the precise mechanics of the policy and policy instruments they have employed.

Even so, there are several elements of the East Asian experience that are relevant to African countries that have recently embarked on economic liberalization (Yanagihara and Sambommatsu, 1997). These can be grouped into the following broad categories: trade and FDI policies; role of the state; education policies; and policies designed to promote both equity and growth.

The Asian tigers switched from an import-substitution strategy of development to an export-oriented outward looking strategy around the mid-1960s. Whilst free trade has been the norm in the case of Hong Kong, the other tigers adopted a vigorous export promotion policy through the provision of a variety of incentives to exporters of labor-intensive manufactured goods. These included provision of infrastructure facilities, such as port facilities and improved transportation systems, adequate supply of electricity and telecommunication systems. In addition, export-oriented firms were provided with access to credit markets and foreign exchange.

Although the tigers adopted an export-oriented growth strategy, they did continue to foster import-competing industries until recent years. This was done through a judicious use of protection and policies designed to build technology and human capabilities. Protection in most cases was temporary, true to the spirit of the infant industry argument, and the performance of the domestic industries was closely monitored.

Foreign know-how and technology have played a significant role in industrialization and growth of the East Asian countries. The contractual modes of foreign enterprise participation, though, differ between the countries of the region. Korea differs markedly from Singapore, Hong Kong and Taiwan in its policies towards foreign enterprise participation in its economy. Singapore and Taiwan pursued an open-door policy towards FDI, although it was targeted to enter specific sectors. Taiwan moved from a policy which did not guide the sectoral allocation of FDI during the decade of the 1950s to one of encouraging FDI in labor-intensive exports such as textiles, garments and assembly of electronics during the 1960s, to one of targeting FDI towards high-tech industries such as informatics and precision instruments during the 1970s and 1980s. Singapore provided open and liberal entry to foreign investors, actively sought to move FDI from labor-intensive activities towards skills and technology-intensive activities. This it did through by investments in infrastructure and building up of the sort of human skills attractive to foreign firms.

The role of the government in the development process in the East Asian countries has attracted widespread attention. Government intervention in Korea, Taiwan and Singapore was extensive, and governments did intervene selectively, and such interventions contributed to the sophisticated industrial structure in place in these countries. In all three of these countries, the basic thrust of interventions was to overcome market failures that deterred technological deepening; upgrading into more complex products and processes within existing activities and extending into new activities, raising local content, and developing the base of technological abilities (Lall, 1995). Most of the interventions were well-coordinated, and thus credit market interventions were integrated with technology policies and skills formation. In sum, the state played a significant role in the growth process of the East Asian countries, not just in getting the fundamentals right but also in directing and monitoring industrial development, and in propelling economies from the production of low-tech goods into the production of high-tech goods.

An integral part of the economic policy design of the East Asian countries was promotion of education. Primary education is almost universal in the East Asian countries and secondary education (judged by the percentage of the relevant age group enrolled in secondary schools) is also high in all of the tiger economies, with Korea and Taiwan at developed country levels and Singapore and Hong Kong not far behind. Again Korea and Taiwan have tertiary education enrolment ratios close to that of developed countries, followed by Singapore and Hong Kong. The data on enrolment ratios in tertiary education

does not reveal the fact that Taiwan and Korea are ahead of the technological leaders in the OECD countries in terms of providing the sort of skills needed for industrialization (natural sciences, mathematics, engineering) and Singapore and Hong Kong also rank high on the league tables of science and technology oriented education (Lall, 2000). Singapore has large enrolments in polytechnics devoted to the development of vocational skills. In addition, these countries have encouraged on the job learning and development of knowledge, through investments in R&D both by the private sector and public enterprises.

The other significant aspect of development policy in the East Asian countries is the promotion of 'growth with equity'. In most of these countries, levels of poverty and income inequalities are relatively low, strikingly low in comparison with those in the African countries. Promotion of equity is not just a function of fiscal policy designed to tax the rich and subsidize the poor. Much more important is the structure of incentives and design of policies which promote employment and productivity of labor. In this context, the land reforms carried out in Taiwan and Korea and the development of agriculture, more so in Taiwan than in Korea, during the early growth phase significantly contributed to both growth and equity. Taiwan provides a classic example of a country that cashed in on its agricultural sector to promote industrialization.

As Ranis (1995) notes in the case of Taiwan, "agriculture played a critical historical role, not only as a provider of savings, foreign exchange and labor but also as a contributor to the dynamic non-agricultural sector in the rural areas". During the 1950s agricultural output increased at 4 percent a year, the output of traditional crops increased by 50 percent and that of non-traditional crops such as cotton, fruits and vegetables approximately doubled. Alongside the growth in production, mostly due to changes in total factor productivity brought about through govern-ment sponsored research and technology diffusion activities, employment in agriculture increased by a substantial 12 percent during the 1950s. The demand for non-agricultural products generated by the growth in agricultural incomes was largely met by small and medium scale enterprises. These enter-prises were largely in the rural areas and strengthened the backward and forward linkages between agricultural and non-agricultural activities. Although Korea's rural development was not as marked as that of Taiwan, the contribution of agriculture to growth and equity was not insignificant.

Provision of free education and subsidized housing for workers in most of these countries have also contributed to the promotion of equity. Malaysia provides an example of a country that has managed the problems posed by an ethnically diverse population through positive discrimination policies for the economically disadvantaged groups. The foregoing review of the factors that contributed to the growth miracle of East Asia is by no means exhaustive. It has merely skimmed the surface to identify possible lessons from the East Asian experience for the African countries. It should be reiterated that not all of the policies adopted by these countries a re applicable to African countries, especially so when there is no one model which can be identified as the Asian model.

Nonetheless, the Asian experience provides some broad lessons. First, is the need to get the fundamentals right, meaning macroeconomic discipline, competitiveness and openness to trade and FDI. This wisdom, though, does not arise from the Asian experience alone; indeed, most studies on economic policy emphasize the need for these fundamentals, and several of the African countries have attempted to get them right.

Secondly, is the role of education and human capital development. Especially significant for the African countries is the promotion of primary and secondary education. There is a welter of evidence to show that the social and private rates of return to primary education are substantial. It not only contributes to productivity growth, especially in agriculture, but it also lowers the fertility rate and promotes the participation of women in the labor force. The data on gross enrolment rates suggests that the African countries are on par with other developing countries in terms of primary education. In fact, the ratio of education expenditures to GDP in some of the African countries is higher than that in Korea, and yet the contribution of education to growth and development is not obvious (Easterly, 2002). None of this suggests that education has little impact on growth; it is just that the quality of education matters. The opportunity cost of education tends to be high, despite the relatively high private rates of return to primary education, because parents apply a high discount rate in assessing the present value of the future flows of incomes of their children. High teacher-to-pupil ratios, lack of adequate training and low salaries for teachers, inadequate spending on classroom materials and corruption all contribute to the low quality of education.

The one lesson that can be drawn from East Asia's experience is the attention to quality of education and the emphasis they have placed on vocational skills, which are essential for technological change and growth. This sort of an education policy is eminently transferable to the African countries. Much the same can be said of tertiary education policies that have emphasized science and engineering.

Another lesson of relevance from Taiwan's experience relates to agricultural development. Apart from state-sponsored research and development, the development of rural industries which utilize both rural labor and agricultural raw materials is to be recommended for most African countries which rely on exports of processed agricultural products. The significance of the policy here is the establishment of small-scale enterprises in rural areas that forge backward and forward linkages with agriculture. Policies of land reform which not only establish property rights for those who cultivate the land but also provide inputs and essential technical know-how would also contribute to both equity and growth. It should be emphasized that mere redistribution of land with little regard to the capabilities of farmers is likely to do little for growth.

The other much-discussed issue relates to trade and FDI policy. Although openness to trade and FDI is the received wisdom, several caveats are in order. First, openness, as discussed earlier, does not exclude promotion of import competing industries. A well-designed system of protection that closely monitors the productive efficiency of the protected industries and one that does not impart an anti-export bias could contribute to the build up of technological capabilities and industrialization. This, however, requires state support for the development of human skills and R&D innovations. Both Korea and Taiwan provide examples of the sort of government interventions that are likely to yield fruit. The experience of Korea and Taiwan with regard to protection-induced industrialization may not be transferable to each and every African country. It pre-supposes the presence of an efficient system of monitoring and appraisal of the protected industries, one which does not encourage rent–seeking or fall prey to protectionist lobbies.

The lessons for Africa from the East Asian experience mostly relate to education policies designed to build local technical capabilities which in turn pave the way for efficient utilization investment. Another lesson of importance is the need to promote the sort of policies that can promote equity along with growth. Finally, there are also lessons to be learned from Korea and Taiwan with the sequencing of liberalization policies, directed at not only mitigating the transitory costs of liberalization but also the promotion of domestic capabilities.

## Africa Will Continue to Need External Support

In order to enhance their performance in external trade, African authorities must reform their domestic productive base so as to enhance competitiveness and ensure long-term diversification. But the international development community would also have to provide assistance especially in those key sectors where such assistance would enable them diversify their exports base, improve capacity in managing trade policy, ensure market access, and participate more effectively in multilateral trade negotiations and in global governance of international trade.

### The need for differentiated treatment

External assistance for trade and development in Africa needs to appreciate the differentiation between countries and regions. For the middle-income countries of North Africa, such as Morocco and Tunisia, which are rapidly diversifying their exports and productive base, the most important development challenge in the coming decade is to create enough jobs for their rapidly growing workforces. During the 2000–2010 period, the number of new entrants to the labor force will average 4 million a year — double that of the last two decades. Unemployment rates in the region, which average 15 per cent today, have doubled in the past two decades and are now among the highest in the world. Unemployment rates for the young, educated, female and first-time job seekers are even greater. With countries facing a steady decline in per capita oil revenues, aid inflows and workers' remittances, the need for a viable alternative to public sector employment has become critical. Such countries can meet these challenges by deepening and accelerating economic reforms that many have already started. They will need to implement trade policy reforms as well as embark upon massive export development. They will need to make three fundamental shifts in their sources of growth: from oil to non-oil sectors; from state-dominated to market-driven activities; and from protected import-substitution to competitive export-oriented activities.

### Pointers for Development Assistance

African countries require international assistance in making large investments in trade-creating and trade-facilitating infrastructure, such as telecommunications and transportation, and in trade-related government institutions, such as customs and tax administrations and export promotion and servicing units (Hussain, 1996). In this regard, recent initiatives such as AGOA and EBA will need to be sustained and deepened if African countries are to expand their exports, accelerate economic growth and reduce poverty. Concessional assistance in this regard would need to be complemented by intensified efforts to reduce the debt burden of low-income countries.

It has been argued that the sweeping price-oriented reforms implemented by the majority of African countries were focused mainly on improving price competition, through currency devaluation and demand management policies. But Africa's price competition explains only a small proportion of the changes in its market shares. Non-price factors appear to be of much greater importance in determining the success, or otherwise, of a country in the international market. Increased attention would, thus, need to be devoted to improving aspects pertaining to non-price competition, particularly in the area of marketing and product sophistication. These include: improvement of packaging; communication and foreign contacts; export processing services and quality controls; transport and the speed of delivery of products; and the provision of export credit through financial reforms. Improving these non-price aspects will tend to increase the income elasticity of demand for Africa's exports.

Much as most countries realize the benefit of export diversification, the actual process of diversifying exports is a slow and rather difficult task. The Doha Declaration of November 2001 by WTO ministers underlined the importance of trade capacity building as a crucial element of the development dimension of the evolving global trading system. It also highlighted the need to mainstream trade into development and poverty reduction, in full awareness of the fact that trade is not an end in itself, but a means or vehicle for attaining long-term sustainable development. International development assistance needs to focus on helping African countries upgrade their export capacity and devise viable strategies for export diversification in several areas.

### Institutional Capacity

One of the most important challenges to transformation of Africa's export baskets is the upgrading of the technological capabilities of medium, small and micro enterprises which form the bulk of private sector industry and provide employment for a large number of people. This is the backbone of modern industrial entrepreneurship in Africa, and could lead to the growth of new manufactured exports. The support of donor community would be needed to establish and promote the institutions that can provide extensive extension services by delivering

comprehensive packages of assistance comprising technical know-how, finance, management skills, training and sales information. Box 6.6 provides a checklist of the sorts of questions that would need to be addressed by policymakers as well as donors in terms seeking to improve the institutional environment for trade policy and implementation.

### Technology

The promotion of technology development in Africa is a vital but neglected aspect of development policy. Technology development refers to the ability of enterprises to use modern technologies efficiently, to master imported knowledge and equipment, to adapt them to local needs, to use local inputs and to offer an efficient supply base for foreign investors. It covers both large-scale enterprises and smaller ones; in Africa, both show striking weaknesses in their technological capabilities. There is also the question of technology infrastructure, which includes metrology, standards, testing and quality institutions, public research institutions and university research concerned with industry. Donor support would be needed to improve the provision of the technology infrastructure. This might be pursued through, among others, technical and financial support to public research institutes and universities; technical and financial support to establish and promote quality, standards and metrological institutions which provide the basic framework for firms to communicate on technology, and keep the basic measurement standards to which industry can refer in accessing foreign markets; and technical and financial support to encourage and foster links

## Box 6.6: Checklist for Trade and Development Policy Action

The Checklist for Trade and Development Policy Acton, designed by DFID, provides a comprehensive diagnostic tool for evaluating trade policy in any developing economy.

**Role of trade in the macroeconomy**
- How important is trade and foreign investment to the country?
- What are the key products and markets?
- How have trading patterns evolved?
- How much government revenue comes from trade taxes?

**Evolution and structure of trade policy**
- Is there a clear trade policy and trade development strategy?
- How has the policy evolved?
- What are the key trade policy issues at present?
- What are the main trade policy instruments?
- What protection measures, tariffs and subsidies are in place?
- What is the regulatory framework affecting trade and foreign investment?
- Is trade policy considered in parallel with other development policies?

**Government and trade administration**
- Who is in charge of trade policy?
- How are roles divided within government?
- What are the mechanisms for coordination between ministries?
- What is the role of external trade missions?
- What are the decision making processes?
- How are consultations undertaken on trade policy? Where are the bottlenecks?
- Are resources sufficient? Have extra requirements been identified?
- What capacity is there outside government?

- What role have trade officials had in preparing national development strategies?

**Trade agreements and regional integration**
- How much awareness is there about WTO and the multilateral trading system?
- Are their difficulties implementing WTO agreements?
- Have adequate preparations been made for new WTO negotiations?
- How active is the country in setting international product standards?
- Are regional and bilateral trade agreements delivering benefits?
- What are the opportunities and challenges for integration?
- Do regional organizations play an important part?
- What are the country's key objectives for future trade negotiations?

**Trade development promotion and assistance**
- Is trade development a high national priority?
- What are the main external barriers for export development?
- Are technical product standards a problem in export markets?
- What are the main domestic constraints facing traders?
- Have donors agreed an assistance strategy for trade development?
- Are donors currently providing trade and development or related assistance?

*Source*: International Trade Department, DFID, 2001.

between industry and research institutions, technical colleges and universities.

### Human Capital

The design of current liberalization programs hardly takes into account the need to build human resources to cope with the ensuing international competition. The speed of liberalization is usually much faster than the ability of any African country to provide the new skills and capabilities that industry needs. Many existing industries can become competitive if their human resources are improved. There are several kinds of skills development relevant to industrial competitiveness that can be provided by the donor community. Countries would benefit from technical and financial support for the provision of training in specific industrial skills for the most important industry clusters that would form the dynamic edge of industrial growth. It might be possible to set up wood-working, food processing, metal-working and so on, to bring them within striking distance of modern levels of quality and productivity. Often training has to go together with the provision of new equipment, better layout, improved process know-how and more modern product technology. All these may need specific policies addressing their informational, financial and other needs.

### Financing Industrial Restructuring

The financing of industrial restructuring in the context of policy reform and liberalization is an important issue in much of Africa. Most adjustment programs were accompanied by stringent stabilization measures that curtailed

sharply the supply of investible resources to industry. The donor community can play an active role by supporting establishment of specialized institutions that meet the financing needs of industries; provide technical assistance to establish and promote capital markets which facilitate the mobilization of foreign and domestic resources for investment; and financial support to provide new financing instruments and modalities, particularly for small-scale medium enterprises.

### Debt Reduction Can Help

The issue of donor assistance to Africa is closely related to the question of debt reduction and debt sustainability. The accumulation of Africa's debt reflects the fact that African countries have consistently imported more than they exported (invested more than they saved), and hence have borrowed from abroad to bridge their financing gaps. While the HIPC initiatives have led to marked reduction in Africa's debt indicators in recent years, the pattern of Africa's trade and their specialization in primary product exports pose serious questions about the sustainability of this scheme. Falling prices of primary exports have large negative effects on external indebtedness directly through the transfer of wealth effect and through increasing the domestic currency equivalents of such debts, as well as indirectly through increasing debt service ratios.

The other question facing the sustainability of HIPC relates directly to the trade-economic growth nexus. To illustrate, it can be argued, in the extreme case, that any poor country can achieve 'debt sustainability' by curbing its imports, debt repayment, and foreign borrowing to levels that are compatible with its low export earnings. While such a policy can achieve 'sustainability' because it shuts down the sources that can raise the debt-to-export ratio above 150 percent, the price of such practices is to condemn the country to even lower growth rates and an increased incidence of poverty. Clearly, the assistance of the international community would be needed to in revisiting sustainability of HIPCs in such away as to allow African countries to realize their targeted development objectives by expanding their investment beyond the limits permitted by their export earnings — i.e. by borrowing from abroad.

On the other hand, it is now apparent that the funds that Africa has borrowed historically to bridge the external financing gap, were either embezzled through corrupt deals, used to finance consumption, or invested in activities that did not alter the pattern of trade to generate sufficient foreign exchange earnings for debt repayment. While it is difficult to ascertain the magnitude of each of these contributory factors, the donor community must work with international and regional organizations in ensuring effective utilization of the borrowed funds, and in particular how the borrowed funds can be used in improving the capacity of foreign exchange earnings of HIPC countries.

### Improved Market Access is Vital

In spite of recent market access initiatives, Northern subsidies and other protectionist measures have severely hampered African exports. The case of cotton in West Africa is instructive (Box 6.7). There is also the inevitable erosion of preferences that would come with the full implementation WTO rules in the coming decade. Clearly, there remains a high level of protectionism in the developed economies, which has reduced the potential benefits of the Uruguay Round to most developing countries, including Africa. Ironically, the highest barriers remain for those products in which African countries have (or could develop) a comparative advantage. These barriers, typically in the form of tariff peaks, tariff escalation and non-tariff barriers, persist for products like textiles and clothing, leather products, fish and fish products, fruits and vegetables, and semi-processed primary products like coffee, cocoa, and fruit juices.[4]

While the decision to integrate international trade in agriculture into the WTO disciplines is commendable, implementation problems have dogged the process. Agriculture has remained distorted by protection and domestic subsidies in the EU, which spends about US$360 billion per annum supporting European farmers — an amount that exceeds the entire GNP of SSA. The Farm Bill passed by the US legislature will also increase government spending on agriculture by 80 percent — that is, conservatively an additional US$ 82 billion over the next ten years. Subsidies in Europe and the US continue to hamper African agricultural exports. It has been estimated that the

---

[4] A recent World Bank study concludes that unrestricted market access into the Quad countries for sub-Saharan Africa would boost non-oil exports by 14 percent and incomes by 1 percent without creating any major trade diversion effects (Ianchovichina, Mattoo and Olarreaga, 2001).

## Box: 6.7:  African Cotton Producers Challenge Northern Subsidies

**Some Key Facts:**
- In the year 2002, world prices stood at US$ 0.42/lb, in contrast to the average of US$ 0.72/lb for the preceding 25 years;
- In 2002 subsidies to US and EU cotton producers led to an estimated loss of US 300 million to African farmers, which was higher than the US$230 million that the HIPC Trust Fund approved as debt relief to the nine West and Central African cotton exporting countries of Benin, Burkina Faso, Cameroon, Chad, Guinea, Guinea-Bissau, Mali, Niger and Senegal;
- In 2001, Mali suffered a loss in cotton earnings amounting to US$43 million, which was exactly the amount that the country was offered as debt relief under the enhanced HIPC Initiative.

**Cotton Producers Demand Fairness**
Four African nations challenged the WTO ministerial meeting in Cancun, Mexico, in September, to agree to rapidly phase out all production and export subsidies for cotton. The countries — Benin, Burkina Faso, Chad and Mali — are all heavily dependent on cotton and their economies have been hit hard by a depressed world market flooded with a highly subsidized crop from rich nations. In a proposal submitted to the WTO in June, the countries stress that their 'only specific interest' in the current round of negotiations, launched in Doha, Qatar, in 2001, was the elimination of cotton subsidies. The proposal, supported by 13 other West and Central African countries, called on the Cancun meeting to set up a mechanism to progressively reduce subsidies and eventually eliminate them by a fixed date. As an immediate and interim measure, it suggested that farmers in least developed countries be compensated for losses incurred because of the subsidies.

In West and Central Africa, where more than 90 per cent of Africa's cotton is grown for export, cotton revenues fell by 31 per cent between 1999 and 2002, mainly as a result of the massive subsidies paid to cotton farmers in the US, Europe and China. While African cotton has many advantages — high quality and the world's lowest costs of production — it cannot compete with subsidized cotton. President Compaoré noted that African producers are ready to face world competition, "on the condition that it is not distorted by subsidies."

*Source*: UNCTAD, 2003; *Africa Recovery*, UN, July 2003.

average American gets up to US$21,000 in subsidies whilst EU farmers each receive an estimated US$14,000 in support. In a decade that donors discouraged any form of subsidies for African farmers in the context of structural reforms, this contradictory attitude amounts to a Machiavellian illusion.

Tariff barriers also remain a problem. Manufactured products, including processed food exports of developing countries fall into categories that attract tariffs on average about four times higher than those applied to categories of manufactured goods exported by industrialized countries to the same markets. Tariff escalation (higher tariffs on processed primary commodity exports) is a disincentive for African countries wishing to diversify into higher-value added products as a means of promoting industrialization and increasing their foreign exchange earnings and employment. Tariff escalation has generally been reduced, but a number of product chains of export interest to Africa continue to face tariff escalation (e.g. cocoa pastes, coffee extracts, crude vegetable oil, leather, fish and fish products).

Also, ambiguities and loopholes in the WTO agreements on contingency protection measures, such as anti-dumping, enable the rich countries to place excessive restrictions on imports from developing countries on the grounds of injury to domestic industry. There has been in recent times a significant increase in the number of anti-dumping investigations and in the use of technical barriers, and, in particular, sanitary and phyto-sanitary measures by developed countries.

## Restoring Confidence at the WTO

The breakdown of the multilateral trade talks at Cancun may have dealt a severe blow to the multilateral trading system itself — a system that, for more than half a century, has underpinned the international liberal trading system and has been the basis for global economic prosperity. Concerted action needs to be taken in order to restore confidence and to get the talks back on track. In particular, it is time to reconsider whether the 'Singapore Issues' that the developed countries have insisted upon belong to the WTO. Indeed, they are strictly non-trade issues, which is why the attempt to bring them into the system has caused so much acrimony and division for the past many years.

### Trade, Development and Global Governance

Governance of the international trade system is in a state of flux. The erstwhile GATT was accused of many of the same ills that afflicted the other key institutions of global governance, namely, non-accountability, non-transparency and a democratic deficit in their decision-making processes (Keohane and Nye, 2001). Whilst the WTO Doha Round has highlighted the importance of development and poverty reduction as central pillars of global trade liberalization, the reality on the ground shows that the richest nations treat this as a matter of only symbolic importance (Rodrik, 2001). After the Cancun debacle, it is clear that a successful outcome cannot be guaranteed. As well as having similar interests to other developing countries on many areas of contention, Africa has special concerns as a result of its current pattern of trade. Africa has already played an active role in the evolution of international trade policy, and is likely to continue to do so given the range of trade negotiations in which it is necessarily involved.

The negotiating teams of the larger OECD countries are huge compared with those of African states, but it is worth remembering that the disparity in size also reflects a difference in composition. The OECD delegations include representatives of producer and consumer interests. It is their task to identify the commercial implications of proposed rules and, in turn, to make drafting suggestions for the rules which would have commercial implications that they favor. The whole delegation operates within an environment in which civil society organizations assess and lobby in order to produce country positions that reflect the interests of socioeconomic groups other than producers. To this extent the oft-cited problem that many African delegations in Geneva (let alone Brussels, Washington and Tokyo) are understaffed slightly misses the point. Of even greater importance is the absence of an integrated mechanism that links trade negotiators with producer and consumer groups within a country that can identify society's offensive and defensive interests in any set of negotiations. Without this, the Geneva delegations, however well staffed, are operating in something of a vacuum.

### Policy harmonization

The Doha Declaration by WTO ministers in November 2001 committed Contracting Parties to working together to improve trade and development capacity as a vehicle for exports expansion in developing economies. In particular, it underlined the crucial role of the Development Assistance Committee in the "coordinated delivery of technical assistance with bilateral donors.... and relevant inter-national and regional intergovernmental institutions, within a coherent policy framework and timetable" (OECD, 2003). In Africa, the question of developing trade capacity for effective participation in the global trading system is critical. In particular, African countries need to improve their capacity to negotiate as well as implement WTO regulations. Globally, donor countries have provided more than US$2.5 billion in funding for trade capacity building in 2003, an 18 percent increase from the preceding year. In the case of the WTO, its technical assistance scheme provides for trade-related support in such areas as customs administration, negotiation skills and electronic governance. Considering all the needs and the gaps to be filled, this level of assistance remains far short of what is required to meet the trade capacity needs of the poorest countries.

The African Development Bank (ADB) has come together with the World Bank and other development agencies to form the 'Integrated Framework for Technical Assistance for Trade Development of Least Developed Countries'. It is an initiative that aims to provide technical assistance to LDCs in the areas of trade and development and assist those countries that are seeking to integrate trade into their own national economic planning processes, particularly in the context of their PRSPs. The initiative also aims to enhance policy coordination in trade capacity-building programs sponsored by donors (United Nations, 2001).

Policy coherence can be viewed at two levels: at one level, it refers to harmonization of policies and procedures regarding the delivery of development aid by donors; at another, it refers to the joint coordination of national poverty reduction activities. Support for policy harmonization began to gain momentum following the global consensus on the value of the comprehensive develop-ment framework, the launching of the Enhanced HIPC Initiative, and the adoption of the PRSP strategy for coordination of national poverty reduction efforts. Resources and strategies need to be harmonized and coordinated in order to achieve effective results on the ground.

A consensus is emerging on the desirability of focusing aid and multilateral development bank (MDB) operations in areas where they could contribute most effectively to supporting systemic change, through, for example, policy-based lending and successful investment projects with significant demonstration effects that are aligned with country priorities. In order to enable the regional member countries (RMCs) move forward on PRSPs through reducing high transaction costs and the burden on partner country capacities, the various development agencies have also been moving to harmonize policies. In particular, the five MDBs (including the ADB) and OECD-DAC have worked together along with other institutions to harmonize policies in several areas, including financial management, procurement procedures, environmental procedures and evaluation methodologies. During the 'High-Level Forum on Harmonization' that took place in Rome in February 2003, an endorsement was received for the work accomplished in each of the four areas. It was acknowledged that there was a need to shift from institutional-level harmonization to country-level harmonization.

## Role of the African Development Bank

Although traditional ADB financing did not focus on trade as such, this is not to say that the whole issue has been ignored. In reality, a great deal of the Bank's interventions — from project lending to debt relief and capacity building — have direct or indirect bearing on external trade performance of recipient countries. Moreover, the Bank has been a strong player in the promotion of regional economic communities in Africa, which are essential vehicles for the development of intra-African trade. The Bank is aware that it cannot duplicate the efforts of such institutions as the WTO and UNCTAD, but it needs to redefine the scope and nature of its interventions so as to strengthen the effectiveness of its programs in

trade and development, especially in those sectors that can impact favorably on poverty reduction.

Indeed, the new Strategic Plan underscores that international trade increases competition and productivity growth and can lead to significantly reduce poverty in RMCs. Openness to trade allows exporters to sell their outputs in a larger market and workers in exporting countries benefit as the resulting higher prices for the they make translate into higher wages in income. Despite some successes in certain of its emerging markets such as Mauritius, South Africa, Morocco, and Egypt, RMCs' trade performance continues to be weak both because of domestic factors (trade policy, trade facilitation, 'behind the border' issues) that have both constrained traditional exports and limited diversification, and because of trade barriers and heavily distorting subsidies in major markets. Weak export performance has been a major factor in raising concerns over debt sustainability, particularly for the RMCs of the African Development Fund.

Given its development mandate and because of its current staff skills mix constraints, the Bank is not adequately positioned strategically to play a leadership role in promoting trade reforms but, in the context of the growing global attention to trade issues in developing countries, the Bank, in particular through its private sector window, will continue to undertake actions to assist RMCs in implementing the 'Integrated Framework' exercise — an international initiative undertaken by a consortium of international organizations and bilateral donors to assist developing countries in their integration into the international market.

Africa is the principal focus of this initiative because Africa accounts for three-quarters of the eligible countries.

At the corporate level, the Bank will continue to take action, in close coordination with the major seven regional economic communities (RECs), in lobbying for a genuinely pro-development Doha Round and for the elimination of agricultural subsidies, which at US$350 billion per year, are 25 times the ODA flows to Africa. To support this advocacy role, including capacity building for trade negotiations and support to private sector initiatives, the Bank will continue to collaborate more closely with the WTO in helping to build capacity within its RMCs, through well-targeted training for trade analysis and negotiation.

The timely, effective and efficient response to the 'new wave of development initiatives' such as NEPAD, the Water Initiative, and the fight against HIV/AIDS, malaria and other communicable diseases, are also being given particular attention by the Bank Group. However, for the Bank to play an active or leading role in these key areas of intervention, and thus assist its RMCs in meeting the MDGs by 2015, the Bank Group requires a significantly greater proportion of the anticipated increases in ODA funding, and the ADF-X replenishment, that are expected over the Plan period and beyond.

The Bank recognizes that meeting these goals will require strong commitment on the part of all stakeholders, and hence, attaches great importance to the need for effective collaboration among all relevant development partners. While ensuring that the Bank's efforts complement the work of the BWIs and its other key developmental partners, Bank interventions will increasingly focus on strengthening its capacity in policy-based lending and related sectors, including trade and development. For the 12 ADB-only and two Blend-RMCs, which constitute the Bank Group's middle-income clientele, it is understood that the majority have established well-articulated goals in their National Development Programs and closely linked macroeconomic policies. Bank Group support to these RMCs will continue to vary in line with the guiding principles of the Plan. Nevertheless, the Bank will continue to play an active role in advising on specific sectoral strategies, including privatization reforms and the promotion of economic and financial governance. It can also be expected that most of these interventions will eventually impact positively on the trade and exports sector.

To bring the poor closer to the monetized economy, the provision of social services would be complemented by the provision of basic infrastructures.

By virtue of its founding mandate, the ADB places high priority on national, sub-regional/regional development operations which strengthen intra-African economic cooperation and regional integration. The Bank is mandated to further the economic development and social progress of African countries, individually and collectively. In pursuit of its mandate, the Bank has since its establishment collaborated with other regional institutions, financed integration-enhancing studies, supported multinational projects, provided resources to regional development finance institutions for on-lending, co-operated with regional integrating institutions, and promoted and facilitated the creation of regional capacity-building institutions.

The overall thrust of the Bank's operational activities is guided by the need to assist its regional member countries achieve the MDGs agreed upon by the international community. Bank interventions therefore focus on contributing to the goal of halving poverty by 2015, through the promotion of high and sustainable rates of growth. Such a strategy, which is fully consistent with the Bank's Vision, aims at improving the social conditions of African women and men, while promoting employment and wealth creation.

The Bank has followed this approach for the past few years by establishing various mechanisms to enhance the operational quality and development impact of its projects and programs. This has involved channeling the bulk of the Bank's concessional resources to perform-ing countries, which possess the requisite institutions to use them effectively. The Bank has also enhanced the quality-at-entry of projects through rigorous screening of all proposals to filter out those that are unlikely to succeed. The process ensures that project and program proposals are consistent with its policy framework and with the agreed country strategy. It also seeks to ensure that Bank interventions have clear development objectives, and that the means adopted are consistent with the goals set.

Another way in which the Bank endeavors to keep the operations on course is by expanding and increasing its field supervision missions, and by introducing mandatory mid-term reviews to facilitate implementation of timely corrective measures. Further, the Annual Portfolio Performance Review has contributed to the identification of implementation constraints, thereby helping to take the required corrective measures to improve project implementation and effectiveness. In this connection, it is gratifying to note that in the course of 2003 the Bank received a special commendation from the US Congress for improvements in the quality of its portfolio.

In addition to these measures, the Bank has stepped up and undertaken a number of major initiatives that are aimed at reinforcing the focus on development effectiveness. First, the Bank has launched a program of administrative reforms, starting with the new structure that became effective as of 1 January 2002.This is intended to provide the Bank with the means and institutional capacity to carry out its Vision. A substantial strengthening of the Bank's human resources capacity, and filling the skills gap, particularly in the crosscutting areas of governance, gender, environment, and regional integration, has accompanied the reorganization. Secondly, the Bank has designed a program of establishing up to 25 field offices in its RMCs. This is intended to provide effective field presence to strengthen policy dialogue and participatory appro-aches, as well as ensuring closer coordin-ation with other key development partners who operate largely at the country level. Thirdly, the Bank has drawn up its first comprehensive Strategic Plan covering the period 2003–07. The Plan sets out to operationalize the Vision Statement that was adopted in 1999 with poverty reduction being the overarching objective for Bank Group operations over the next five years.

## Summary and Conclusions

Compared to other developing regions, Africa has never fared so poorly in international trade performance as it has in the last two decades. This study has revisited many of the contending explanations for Africa's increasingly marginal status in international economic relations. None of them taken singly can provide a definitive account for Africa's poor exports performance. In general, the distortions introduced by pro-tectionist policies appear to be a major explanatory factor, followed by external barriers to trade facing most African exporters in the form of high effective rates of protection and tariff peaks.

As shown in this study, several African countries have taken bold measures to reform their economies and liberalize their import regimes. Evidence for this can be found in lower average tariffs, and perhaps more significantly in increases in imports as a share of GDP. Multilateral and regional agreements have committed them to these reforms and the clock cannot be turned back, although the appropriate pace of future liberalization remains an important policy issue. To date, there is little aggregate evidence that the trade policy reforms and liberalization since the late 1980s have produced a significant export response. Exports have not increased consistently, and there is no evident correla-tion between the extent of trade liberalization and the rate at which exports have grown. African countries contemplating further

liberalization need to do so by building a solid export platform. It is also evident that Africa's economic prospects will considerably be influenced by progress in international debt relief efforts. The question of debt sustainability is crucial; so also the need to target ODA and funding by multilateral finance institutions into those sectors that promise greater value added in terms of exports development while minimizing the risks of further deterioration in the debt burden of nations (Kifle, 2003). Clearly, expanding the enhanced HIPC framework and increasing the magnitude of resources available to the HIPC Trust Fund is imperative.

To reverse this situation, this report has argued, African countries need to pursue a strategy of export-oriented industrialization with much more conviction than ever before. The process, however, has to begin with the rationalization of the agrarian sector, and creating those linkages with the urban-industrial sector that would generate new synergies in terms of exports diversification. In this regard, trade liberalization can do no more than provide opportunities — unilateral reforms increase relative incentives to exporters, and multilateral or regional liberalization increase market access. Domestic policies are necessary to reduce the varied constraints on supply response, increase transport and marketing efficiency, and encourage investment. To benefit from trade, and to channel these benefits into helping reduce poverty, African countries need to increase the flexibility and efficiency of resource use so that they can be competitive in global markets.

Exports diversification requires the building up of local capabilities in conjunc-tion with technology and know-how provided by foreign firms. The proposition that Africa's comparative advantage in the immediate future lies in primary products, including processed and unprocessed agricultural products and minerals, is not without its merit. This thesis does not necessarily rule out diversification, but it would be within the group of primary products. Processing of agricultural products would constitute diversification and it would also enhance local value-added. Here too there would be a need for managerial and marketing know-how imparted by foreign-owned enterprises. One constraint to such diversification is the high effective rates of protection in the importing countries and the agricultural subsidies in the Quad. Allied to the issue of export diversification is the potential for the export of services from Africa. Much of the FDI in services in African countries is in financial services. Apart from financial services, the other sector in which Africa has a substantial comparative advantage is tourism. It is here that both FDI and non-equity forms of foreign enterprise participation could contribute to the sector. Their contribution would range from the establishment of hotels to promotion of Africa's tourist attractions in other developed countries.

Perhaps more than any other developing region, Africa also has a huge stake in the emergence of a world order that is based on lawful conduct between states and on sound and predictable international economic regimes. It is therefore crucial that the developed countries respect the emergence of the developing world. The decision-making system within WTO must therefore be reformed so that there is more transparency and democracy, so that developing country members can participate more effectively. Measures must be taken to make the WTO an organization that truly serves the interests of rich and poor equally, without which there can only be more crises and loss of confidence in the system.

It was Nobel laureate Sir Arthur Lewis who once remarked that developing countries have within themselves all the requisites for their own development; and that they could still successfully develop were even the rest of the world to be sunk under the sea. He was underlining the fact that Africa and the developing world *ultimately* do not need to look to others for their own development. The new generation of African leaderships will need to marshal a bolder vision of their continent's future, based on democracy, good governance and the rule of law.

Linked to this is the need to evolve effective institutions for sound public management and development of a vibrant private sector. NEPAD provides a rallying focus for this collective new vision towards a better future. The recent launching of the African Peer Review Mechanism also shows that there is indeed commitment to ensuring that Africa will evolve a set of 'minimum standards' for economic and political governance. In today's economy, good governance is an open process whereby all countries endeavor to adhere to the emerging universality of laws. Resolving such critical governance problems as a corruption, environmental degradation, excessive military expenditure and civil war would require supportive actions on the part of Africa's development partners. African countries also need assistance in preparing for the new rules-based WTO trading system, and to ensure that the problems of globalization do not outweigh the benefits.

For its part, the ADB Group, as the continent's leading development finance institution has the enormous responsibility of helping Africa realize its new vision of reformation and rebirth. Recognizing the magnitude of the challenge of poverty reduction and the finite capacity of its human and financial resources, the Bank will seek to maximize the development impact of its activities through a clearer definition of its areas of strategic focus, and through greater selectivity of operations and through better targeting of resources at country, regional, and sectoral levels. To effectively meet its global and regional responsibilities, the Bank will actively participate in, and play a lead role when appropriate as well as continue to liaise with other international development agencies, in building a more harmonized framework for trade, development and global governance. In our troubled and divided world, the fight against poverty and the resentment and alienation that it breeds is a vocation of lasting value.

# BIBLIOGRAPHICAL NOTE

## Introduction

The background papers prepared specifically for the Report are listed below, along with the selected bibliography used in the Report. These papers synthesize relevant literature. The Report has drawn on a wide range of African Development Bank reports, including ongoing research as well as countries' economic, sector and project work. It has also drawn on outside sources, including published and unpublished works of institutions such as the IMF, the World Bank, IFC, the United Nations and its agencies such as the ECA, FAO, ILO, IFAD, UNAIDS, UNCTAD, UNIDO, UNDP, WHO, WTO and OECD.Other sources include publications from various national economic and statistics agencies, African Economic Digest, Africa Financing Review, Africa Research Bulletin; Business Africa, The Economist, Economist Intelligence Unit, Financial Times; International Capital Markets; Middle East Economic Digest; and Southern Africa Monitor.

## Background papers

(i)   Oliver Morrissey (2003), "Trade Policy and Performance in Africa"

(ii)  Milton Iyoha (2003), "Africa in the Global Trading System"

(iii) Christopher Stevens (2003), "Africa in the Global Trading System"

(iv)  V.N. Balasubramanyam (2003) "Africa: Trade Performance, Policies and Prospects"

## Selected Bibliography

**African Development Bank.** (1997). *African Development* Report 1997. Oxford: Oxford University Press.

—— (1999). *African Development Report 1999*. Oxford: Oxford University Press.

**Ajayi, S.I. (2001).** What Africa needs to do to benefit from globalisation. *Finance and Development*, vol.38, no.4, December.

**Akinlo, A.E & Akinbobola, T. O. (2003).** "Good house keeping and return to economic growth", in *Development thought, policy advice and economic development in Africa in the 20th century: lessons for the 21st century.* Edited by A. G. Garba. Ibadan: Ibadan University Press.

**Amjadi, A. Rienke, & Yeats, A. (1996).** *Did external barriers cause the marginalisation of Sub-Saharan Africa in world* trade? Washington D.C.: World Bank. (Policy Research Working Paper no 1586).

**Ancharaz, V. (2003).** "Determinants of trade policy reform in Sub-Saharan Africa". *Journal of African Economies,* vol. 12, no. 3, pp. 417–443.

**Bajulaiye-Shasi, T. (1992).** "Concepts and processes of economic integration", in *The challenges of African economic integration.* Ibadan: Nigerian Economic Society. (selected papers for the 1992 Annual Conference of the Nigerian Economic Society).

**Balassa, B. (1961).** *The theory of economic integration.* London: George Allen & Unwin.

—— "Exports and economic growth: further evidence". *Journal of Development Economics,* vol. 5, pp. 181–189, June.

—— et.al. (1971). "The structure of protection in developing countries" Baltimore: Johns Hopkins.

**Balasubramanyam, V N & Salisu, M A. (1991).** "Export promotion, import substitution and direct foreign investment in less developed countries", in *International trade and global development,* edited by A. Koekkoek and L.B. M. Mennes. London: Routledge.

—— —— & Sapsford, D. (1996). "Foreign direct investment and growth in EP and IS countries". *The Economic Journal,* vol. 106, no. 434, pp. 92–105.

**Baldwin, R.E. (1997).** "Review of theoretical developments on regional integration", in *Regional integration and trade liberalization in Sub-Saharan Africa,* vol. 1, edited by T.A. Oyejide, I.A. Elbadawi & P. London: Macmillan.

**Belshaw, D. & Livingstone, I., eds. (2002).** *Renewing development in sub-Saharan Africa: policy, performance and prospects,* London: Routledge.

**Belshaw, D. & Lawrence, P. & Hubbard, M. (1999).** Agricultural tradables and economic recovery in Uganda: the limitations of structural adjustment in practice, *World Development,* vol.27, no. 4, pp. 673–690.

**Bennell, P. (1998).** Fighting for survival: manufacturing industry and adjustment in sub-Saharan Africa. *Journal of International Development,* vol. 10, no. (5), pp. 621–637.

**Bhagwati, J N, & Srinivasan, T. N. (1976).** *Foreign trade regimes and economic development: India.* London: Macmillan.

—— (1978). *Anatomy and consequences of exchange control regimes,* vol. 1. New York: National Bureau of Economic Research. (Studies in International Economic Relations, 10)

—— —— & Ramaswami, V.K. (1963). Domestic distortions, tariffs, and the theory of optimum subsidy. *Journal of Political Economy,* vol. 71, no. 1, February, pp. 44–50.

—— Srinivasan, T.N. (1999). *Outward orientation and development: are revisionists right?* New Haven: Yale University. (Economic Growth Centre discussion paper no. 806).

—— (1982). Directly unproductive, profit seeking DUP activities. *Journal of Political Economy,* vol. 90, no. 5, pp. 988–1002.

—— (1988). Export-promoting trade strategy: issues and evidence, *World Bank Research Observer,* vol. 3.

**Blake, A., McKay, A. & Morrissey, O. (2002).** "The impact on Uganda of agricultural trade liberalization". *Journal of Agricultural Economics*, vol.v 53, no. 2, pp. 365–381.

Blomstrom, M., & Kokko, A. (1998). "Multinational corporations and spillovers", *Journal of Economic Surveys*, vol.12, no.3, pp. 247–277.

Bowden, Rick (2001), IMF-WB-WTO Synthesis Report: an overview of the increased coordination of the International Monetary Fund (IMF), the World Bank, and the World Trade Organization (WTO) Trade Liberalization Policies, October 2001.

Bowen, H.P., Hollander, A. & Viaene, J.M. (1998). *Applied international trade analysis*. London: Macmillan.

Brander, J.A. & Spencer, B.J. (1983). "International R & D rivalry and industrial strategy". *Review of Economic Studies,* vol. 50.

Calomiris, Charles W. (2000) "When will economics guide IMF and World Bank reforms?" *Cato Journal,* vol 20, no. 1, Spring/Summer, pp. 85–103.

Chen, T. (1992). "Determinants of Taiwan's direct foreign investment". *Journal of Development Economics*, vol.39, pp. 397–407.

CIPR (Commission on Intellectual Property Rights). (2002). *Integrating intellectual property rights and development policy.* London: CIPR.

Collier P. & Gunning J. (1999). "Why has Africa grown slowly?" *Journal of Economic Perspectives*, vol. 13, no. 3, pp. 3–22.

—— Gunning, J. (1999). "Explaining African economic performance". *Journal of Economic Literature,* vol.37, no. 1, pp. 64–111.

—— (1997). "The welfare effects of customs unions: an anatomy". *Economic Journal,* vol. 89, pp. 84–95.

Cooper, C.A. & Massell, B. F. (1965). "Towards a general theory of customs union for developing countries". *Journal of Political Economy*, vol. 73, no.5, pp. 461–476.

Corden, W.M. (1974). *Trade policy and economic welfare.* Oxford: Oxford University Press.

Croome, J. (1995). *Reshaping the world trading system: a history of the Uruguay Round.* Geneva: World Trade Organization.

Dabee, R. & Milner, C. (1999). "Evaluating trade liberalization in Mauritius", in *Regional integration and trade liberalization in Sub-Saharan Africa.* vol. 2, edited by A. Oyejide, et. al. London: Macmillan.

Daouas, M. (2001). "Africa faces challenges of globalisation". *Finance and Development,* vol. 38, no. 4, December.

Dean, J. (1995). "The trade policy revolution in developing countries" *The world economy global trade policy review,* pp. 173–90.

—— Desai, S. & Riedel, J. (1994). *Trade policy reform in developing countries since 1985: a review of the evidence.* Washington D.C: World Bank. (World Bank Discussion Papers no. 267)

**Delich, V. (2002).** "Developing countries and the WTO dispute settlement system", in *Development, trade, and the WTO,* edited by B. Hoekman, A. Mattoo & P. English. Washington DC: World Bank.

**Din, M. (1994).** "Export processing zones and backward linkages". *Journal of Development Economics,* vol. 43, pp. 369–385.

**Dolan, C., Humphrey, J. & Harris-Pascal, C. (1999).** *Horticulture commodity chains: the impact of the UK market on the African fresh vegetable industry.* Brighton: Institute of

**Development Studies, University of Sussex. September.** (Working Paper no. 96).

**Dollar, D. (1992).** "Outward oriented developing economies: really do grow more rapidly: evidence from 95 LDCs, 1976–85". *Economic Development and Cultural Change.*

**Dunning, J. H. (1993).** *Multinational enterprises and the global economy.* Workingham: Addison-Wesley.

**Easterly, W & Levine, R. (1997).** "Africa's growth tragedy; policies and ethnic divisions". *The Quarterly Journal Of Economics,* vol.112, no.4, pp. 1203–1250.

**Edwards, S. (1993).** "Openness, trade liberalization, and growth in developing countries". *Journal of Economic Literature,* vol. 31, no. 3, pp. 1358–1393.

**Ekpo, A.H. & Egwaikhide, F. O. (1994).** "Export and economic growth in Nigeria: a reconsideration of the evidence". *Journal of Economic Management,* vol. 1, no. 1.

**Elbadawi, I.A. (1998).** *Can Africa export manufactures? The role of endowment, exchange rates and transaction costs.* Washington D.C.: World Bank.

**Emery, R.F. (1967).** "The relation of exports and economic growth". *Kyklos,* vol. 470–486.

**Eurostat. (1998).** *Intra- and extra-EU trade annual data: combined nomenclature.* Luxembourg: Statistical Office of the EC. (CD-Rom, supplement 2/1998).

**Fajana, O. (1979).** "Trade and growth: the Nigerian experience." *World Development,* vol. 7, pp. 73–78.

**Falvey, R & Kim, C.D. (1992).** "Timing and sequencing issues in trade liberalization". *Economic Journal,* vol.102, no. 413, pp. 908–924.

**FAO (Food and Agricultural Organization). (2003).** *State of Food Security Report, 2003.* Rome: FAO.

**Finch, D. & Michaelopoulos, C. (1988).** "Development, trade, and international organizations", in. *Development with trade.* Edited by A.O. Krueger. San Francisco: International.

**Foroutan, F. & Pritchett, L. (1993).** "Intra-sub-Saharan African trade: is it too little?" *Journal of African Economics,* vol.2, no. 1.

**Fosu, A. K. (1990).** "Exports and economic growth: the African case." *World Development,* vol. 18, no. 6, pp. 831–835.

Fowdar, N. (1992). *Textile outlook international*. London: Economist Intelligence Unit.

Frankel, J. & Romer, D. (1999). "Does trade cause growth?" *American Economic Review,* vol.89, no.3, pp. 379–399.

Gillson, I. & Rios, N. (2003). *Report on special and differential treatment in the WTO Seminar*. London: Department for International Development.

Gondwe, G.E. (2001). "Making globalisation work in Africa". *Finance and Development,* vol. 38, no. 4, December.

Gorg, H., & Greenaway, D. (2001). *Foreign direct investment and intra-industry spillovers: a review of the literature*. Nottingham: Nottingham University. (Research Paper Series, Centre for Research on Globalization and Labour Markets Programme, School of Economics, Nottingham University).

Greenaway, D. & Milner, C.R. (1993). *Trade and industrial policy in developing countries,* London: MacMillan.

—— Morrissey, O. (1994). "Trade liberalisation and economic growth in developing countries", in *Trade transfers and development,* pp. 210–230, edited by S. M. Murshed & K. Raffer. London: Edward Elgar.

—— Sapsford, D. (1994). "What does liberalization do for exports and growth?" *Weltwirtschaftliches Archive*, vol.130.

—— (1993). "Liberalising foreign trade through rose-tinted glasses." *Economic Journal*, vol. 103, no. 416, pp. 208–222.

—— (1998). "Does trade liberalisation promote economic development?" *Scottish Journal of Political Economy*, vol.45, pp. 491–511.

—— Morgan, C. W. & Wright, P. (1997). "Trade liberalisation and growth in developing countries". *World Development*, vol. 25, no. 11, pp. 1885–1892.

—— —— —— (1998). "Trade Reform, Adjustment and Growth: what does the evidence tell us?" *Economic Journal*, vol. 108, pp. 1547–1561.

Guisinger S.E. (1986). "Do performance requirements and investment incentives work?" *The World Economy*, vol.l.9, no.1.

Harbeler, G. (1988). *International trade and economic development*. San Francisco: International Center for Economic Growth.

Hine, H.C. (1994). "International economic integration", in *survey in international trade,* edited by D. Greenaway L. A. Winters. Oxford: Basil Blackwell.

Hoekman B.; Ng F. and Olarreaga M. (2002). "Eliminating excessive tariffs on exports of least developed countries". *World Bank Economic Review*, vol.16, no.1, pp. 1–21.

Hussain, N.M. (October 2003), A Note on HIPC Debt Sustainability and Africa's Development Challenge. Being Text of a Paper Presented at the MDBS Meeting on Debt Sustainability, Vienna.

Ianchovichina, Elena, Mattoo Aaditya and Olarreaga, Marcelo. (2001). *Unrestricted market access for Sub-Saharan Africa: how much is it worth and who pays?* Development Research Group, The World Bank, Washington (mimeo).

IMF. (International Monetary Fund) (1997a). *World economic outlook: globalisation, opportunities and challenges.* Washington, D.C: IMF.

—— (1997b). *IMF Survey,* July 7.

—— (2001). *Mauritius 2001.*Article IV Consultations. Washington, D.C: IMF. (Staff Reports).

—— 2003). *IMF Report 2003*

—— (2003). *World economic outlook, September,*

Iyoha, M.A. (1977). « Economic growth in the customs union: a theoretical analysis." *Nigerian Journal of Economic and Social Studies,* July.

—— (1995). "Traditional and contemporary theories of external trade", in *External trade and economic development in Nigeria.* Ibadan: Nigerian Economic Society. (Selected papers for the 1995 Annual Conference of the Nigerian Economic Society).

—— (1996). "Debt, commodities and resource flows", in *The political economy of development: an African perspective,* edited by S. Rasheed, & S. Tomori. Accra, Ghana: ICIPE Science Press.

—— (1998). "An econometric analysis of the impact of trade on economic growth in ECOWAS countries". *Nigerian Economic and Financial Review,* vol 3, December.

—— (1999). *External debt and economic growth in sub-Saharan African countries: an econometric study.* Nairobi: African Economic Research Consortium. (AERC Research Paper Series, no. 90, March).

—— (2002). "Globalisation, trade and economic growth: the African experience". *Nigerian Economic and Financial Review,* vol. 7, no. 2, December.

—— (2003). The impact of globalization on agricultural exports and economic development in Africa. *African Notes,* November/December . (Cornell University).

—— (2003). The global patterns of development in the 20th century and their lessons", in *Development thought, policy advice and economic development in Africa in the 20th century: lessons for the 21st century,* edited by A. G. Garba. Ibadan: Ibadan University Press.

Jebuni, C.D., Ogunkola, E.O. & Soludo, C.C. (2001). "A case study of the Economic Community of West African States ECOWAS", in *Regional integration and trade liberalization in Sub-Saharan Africa,* vol.3, edited by T.A Oyejide, I.A Elbadawi & S. Yeo. London: Macmillan.

Jones, B. (2002). "Economic integration and convergence of per capita income in West Africa". *African Development Review,* vol. 14, no.1, pp. 18–47.

Khattry, B. & Mohan, J. Rao. (2002). "Fiscal faux pas? An analysis of the revenue implications of trade liberalization" *World Development,* vol. 30:8, pp. 1431–1444.

**Kifle, H (2003).** HIPCS Sustainability: Some Thoughts on its Implications for MDBS, Text of a paper Presented at the Vienna Technical Meeting on Debt Sustainability, vienna, Austria, October 2003 (mimeo).

**Kindleberger, R. M. (1965).** *Economic development* . New York: McGraw-Hill.

**Kreinin, M.E. (1964).** "On the dynamic effects of a customs union". *Journal of Political Economy,* vol. 72, no. 2, April, pp. 193–195.

**Krueger, A. (1999).** "Why trade liberalization is good for growth?" *Economic Journal,* vol. 108, pp. 513–1522.

**Krueger, A.O. (1978).** *Foreign trade regimes and economic development: liberalization attempt and consequences.* Cambridge: National Bureau of Economic Research and M.A. Ballinger Publication Co.

—— **(1983).** *The new multinationals: the speed of third world enterprises.* New York: Wiley.

—— **(1994).** "The East Asian miracle: does the bell toll for industrial strategy". *World Development,* vol. 22, no. 4, pp. 644–654.

—— **(1995).** "Structural adjustment and African industry." *World Development,* vol. 23, no. 12, pp. 2019–2031.

—— **(2000).** *Selective industrial and trade policies in developing countries: theoretical and empirical issues.* Queen Elizabeth House, Oxford University. (Working Paper no 48).

**Lancaster, Kelvin (1980).** Intra-industry trade under perfect monopolistic competition. *Journal of International Economics,* vol. 10, no. 2, pp. 151–175.

**Lawrence, P. & Thirtle, C, eds. (2001).** *Africa and Asia in comparative economic perspective.* London: Palgrave.

**Lecraw, D. (1977).** "Direct investment from firms in less developed countries". *Oxford Economic Papers,* vol.29, pp. 442–457.

**Limao, N. & Venables, A.J. (1999).** Infrastructure, geographical disadvantage and transport costs. Washington D.C.: World Bank. (World Bank Research Paper, no. 2257).

**Little, I.M.D. (1982).** *Economic development: theory, policy and international relations.* New York: Basic Books Inc. Publishers.

—— **Scitovsky, T. & Scott, M. (1970).** *Industry and trade in some developing countries.* London: Oxford University Press.

**Lyakurwa, W., A. McKay, Ng'eno, N, & Kennes, W. (1997).** "Regional integration in Sub-Saharan Africa: a review of experiences and issues" in *Regional Integration and trade liberalization in Sub-Saharan Africa. vol. 1: framework, issues and methodological perspectives.* Edited by T.A Oyejide, et. Al. London: Macmillan.

**Maddison, A. (1971).** *Class structure and economic growth: India and Pakistan since the Moguls.* London: George Allen & Unwin .

**Mailafia, Obadiah. (1997).** *Europe and economic reform in Africa: structural* *adjustment and economic diplomacy*. New York and London: Routledge.

**Massell, B.F., Pearson, S.R. & Fitch, J.B. (1972).** "Foreign exchange and economic development: An empirical study of selected Latin American countries". *Review of Economics and Statistics*, May.

**Mauritius Central Office of Statistics. (2002).** *Annual Digest of Statistics*.

**Mbabazi, J., Milner, C. & Morrissey, O. (2003).** "The fragility of empirical links between inequality, trade liberalisation, growth and poverty*"*, in *Perspectives of growth and poverty*, edited by R. van der Hoeven, and A. Shorrocks. Tokyo: United Nations University Press.

**McCarthy, C. (2000).** "Regional integration in sub-Saharan Africa: Past, present and future", in *Regional integration and trade liberalization in Sub-Saharan Africa, vol. 4: Synthesis, edited by T. A.* Oyejide, B. Ndulu, & D. Greenaway. London: Macmillan.

**McCulloch, N., Winters, L. A, & Cirera, X. (2001).** *Trade Liberalisation and Poverty; a handbook*, London, Centre for Economic Policy Research.

**McGillivray, M. & Morrissey, O. eds. (1999).** *Evaluating Economic Liberalisation*, London: Macmillan.

**McKay, A., O. Morrissey & C, Vaillant (1997).** "Trade Liberalisation and Agricultural Supply Response: Issues and Lessons", *European Journal of Development Research*, vol. 9, no. 2, pp. 129–147.

**Michaely, M. (1977).** Exports and growth: An empirical investigation. *Journal of Development Economics*, March. Ram, R. 1985. Exports and economic growth: Some additional evidence. *Economic Development and Cultural Change*, vol.v. 33, no. 2, pp. 415–425, January.

**Michalopoulos, C. (2003).** "Special and Differential Treatment in Agriculture: Proposals for a Development Round", in C. Stevens, ed., *Special and Differential Treatment in Terms of Trade*, IDS Bulletin vol. 34, no. 2, April.

**Milner, C. & Morrissey, O. (1999).** "Measuring Trade Liberalisation in Africa", in M. McGillivray & O. Morrissey, eds., *Evaluating Economic Liberalisation*, pp. 60–82. London: Macmillan.

—— —— **N. Rudaheranwa (2000).** Policy and non-Policy Barriers to Trade and Implicit Taxation of Exports in Uganda, *Journal of Development Studies*, vol. 37, no. 2, pp. 67–90.

**Milner, C.R. (1996).** Discovering the Truth about Protection Rackets, *The World Economy*, vol. 19, pp. 517–532.

—— **(1997).** On Natural and Policy-Induced Sources of Protection and Trade Regime Bias, *Weltwirtshaftliches Archiv*, vol. 132, pp. 740–752.

—— **(1998).** Trade Regime Bias and The Response To Trade Liberalisation in Sub-Saharan Africa, *Kyklos,* vol. 51, pp. 219–236.

Minford, P., Riley, J. & Nowell, E. (1995). *The elixir of growth: Trade, non-traded goods and development.* Centre for Economic Policy Research Discussion Paper no. 1165.

Morisset J. (2000). *Foreign Direct Investment in Africa.* International Trade and Capital Flows, Washington, D.C: World Bank. (Working paper no. 2481).

Morrissey, O. (1995). Politics and Economic Policy Reform: Trade Liberalisation in sub-Saharan Africa, *Journal of International Development*, vol. 7, no. 4, pp. 599–618.

—— (2002). *Trade Policy Reforms in sub-Saharan Africa: Implementation and Outcomes in the 1990s* in Belshaw and Livingstone eds, pp. 339–353.

Mosley, P. & Weeks, J. (1993). Has recovery begun? Africa's adjustment in the 1980s revisited. *World Development*, vol. 21, no. 10, pp. 1583–1606.

Mundell, R. (1957). International Trade and Factor Mobility, A*merican Economic Review*, vol. 47, no. 3, pp. 321–335.

Ng, F. & Yeats, A. (1996). *Open economies work better!. Did Africa's protectionist policies cause its marginalisation in world trade?* Washington, D.C.: World Bank. (Policy Research Working Paper, no 1636).

Noorbakhsh, F. & Paloni, A. (1998). Structural adjustment programmes and export supply response, *Journal of International Development*, vol. 10, no. 4, pp. 555–573.

Nurkse, R. (1959). *Patterns of Trade and Development.* Stockholm: Almqist & Wicksell.

O'Connell, S.A. & Ndulu, B. (2000). *Africa's growth experience: a focus on the source of growth.* AERC Explaining African Economic Growth Project.

OECD Observer (2003), "Trade Capacity Building: Critical for Development", Paris, August 2003.

Ogun, O. & Adenikinju, A. (1992). *Integrating the African region: Lessons from historical experiences.* In *The Challenges of African Economic Integration.* Selected papers for the 1992 Annual Conference of the Nigerian Economic Society. Ibadan: Nigerian Economic Society.

Onafowora, O. & Owoye, O. (1998). "Can trade liberalization stimulate economic growth in Africa?" *World Development*, vol. 26, no. 3, pp. 497–506.

Osagie, E. (1992). "African economic integration: lessons from outside Africa", in *The challenges of African economic integration.* Ibadan: Nigerian Economic Society. (Selected papers for the 1992 Annual Conference of the Nigerian Economic Society).

Oyejide, T.A. & Njinkeu, D. (2002). *African preconditions and positive agenda for a new round of multilateral trade negotiations.* Nairobi: AERC. (AERC special paper no. 40).

—— (1997). *Regional integration and trade liberalization in sub-Saharan Africa..* Nairobi: AERC. (AERC special paper no. 28).

Ozden, C & Reinhardt, E. (2002). *The perversity of preferences; GSP and developing country trade policies, 1976–2000*. Washington, D.C.: World Bank. (World Bank Working Paper Series on International Economics, Trade and Capital Flows).

Panagariya, A. (2000). *Evaluating the case for export subsidies*. Washington D.C.World Bank. (World Bank Policy Research working paper, 2276).

Papageorgiou, D., Michaely, M. & Choksi, A. (1991). Liberalising Foreign Trade, Oxford: Blackwell.

Prebisch, R. (1950). *The economic development of Latin America and its principal problems*. New York: U.N. Department of Economic Affairs

Ranis, G. (1995). "Another look at the Asian miracle". *The World Bank Research Observer*, vol. 9, no.3, pp. 509–534.

Robertson, D. H. (1938). "The future of international trade". *Economic Journal*, vol. 48.

Rodriguez, F & Rodrik, R. (1999). *Trade policy and economic growth: a skeptic's guide to the cross national evidence*. Cambridge: National Bureau of Economic Research. (Working paper no. 7081).

Rodrik, D. (1999). *The new global economy and developing countries: making openness work*. Washington, DC: Johns Hopkins University Press. (ODC policy essay no. 24.)

—— (2001). *The global governance of trade as if development really mattered*: report submitted to the UNDP, Kennedy School of Government, Harvard University (mimeo).

Rodrik, R. (1998). *Trade policy and economic performance in Sub-Saharan Africa*. Cambridge: National Bureau of Economic Research. (Working paper no. 6562).

Rondinelli, D. A. (1987). « Export processing zones and economic development in Asia: A review and reassessment of a means of promoting growth and jobs". *American Journal of Economics and Sociology*, vol. 46, no. 1.

Sachs J & Warner A. (1995). "Economic reforms and the process of global integration". *Brookings Papers on Economic Activity*, no.1

—— & —— (1995). "Sources of slow growth in African economies". *Journal of African Economies*, vol. 6, pp. 335–376.

Salisu, M. A. (2003). *Foreign direct investment in Africa*. Lancaster: Department of Economics, Lancaster University. (International Business Group Discussion papers).

Salvatore, D. (1983). "A simultaneous equations model of trade and development with dynamic policy simulations". *Kyklos*, vol. 36, no. 5, pp. 66–90.

Sapir, A. (1993). "Regionalism and the new theory of international trade: do the bells toll for the GATT? A European outlook". *The World Economy*, vol. 16 4, July.

**Sapsford, D. & Balasubramanyam, V.N. (1994).** "The long-run behavior of the relative price of primary commodities: statistical evidence and policy implications". *World Development,* vol. 22, no. 11, pp. 1737–1745.

**Servern, A.K. (1968).** "Exports and economic growth: comment". *Kyklos,* vol. 21.

**Sharer, R. (1999).** Trade: an engine of growth for Africa. *Finance and Development,* vol.36, no. 4, December.

—— **(2001).** "An agenda for trade, investment and regional integration." *Finance and Development, vol.* 38, no. 4, December.

**Singer, H.W. (1950).** "The Distribution of gains between investing and borrowing countries". *American Economic Review,* Papers and Proceedings.

—— **(1988).** "The world development report 1987 on the blessing of outward orientation: a necessary correction". *Journal of Development Studies,* vol. 24.

**Söderbom, M. & Teal, F. (2003).** "Are Manufacturing Exports the Key to Economic Success in Africa?" *Journal of African Economies,* vol.12, no. 1, pp. 1–29.

**Södersten, B. (1980)** *International Economics.* New York: Macmillan.

**Stern, Joseph J. and Gugerty, Mary K. (1996).** *Structural barriers to trade in Africa.* Harvard Institute of International Development and the Kennedy School of Government, Harvard University (mimeo).

**Stevens, C. & Kennan, J. (2001).** "Food Aid and Trade" in *Food security in Sub-Saharan Africa.* Edited by S. Devereux and S. Maxwell. London: ITDG Publishing.

—— **Greenhill, R., Kennan, J. & Devereux, S. (2000).** *The WTO agreement on agriculture and food security.* London: Commonwealth Secretariat. (Economic Paper 42).

—— **et. al. (2003).** *The impact and poverty reduction implications of foot and mouth disease control in southern Africa, with special reference to Zimbabwe.* Nairobi: International Livestock Research Institute.

**Stiglitz, J.E. (1996).** "Some lessons from the East Asian miracle". *The World Bank Research Observer,* vol. 11, no. 2.

**Subramanian, A & Roy, D. (2001).** *Who can explain the Mauritius miracle: Meade, Romer, Sachs, or Rodrik?* Washington D.C: IMF. (IMF Working Paper no 01/116).

**TARIC (The Integrated Tariff of the Community). (1999).** *Integrated tariff of the European Communities,* C212–C212A, 23.7.1999 CD-Rom. Luxembourg: Office for Official Publications of the European Communities.

**Teshome, M. (1996).** "Multilateralism and Africas regional economic communities". *Journal of World Trade,* vol.32, no. 4.

**Thirlwall, A. P. (2000).** Trade, Trade Liberalization and Economic Growth: Theory and Evidence. Background Paper Prepared for the African Development Report 2000 (mimeo).

—— (2003) *Trade, the balance of payments and exchange rate policy in developing countries.* Cheltenham: Edward Elgar.

Tyler, G. W. (1981). "Growth and export expansion in developing countries: Some empirical evidence". *Journal of Development Economics*, vol. 9, no. 1, August, pp. 121–130.

UNCTAD. (1994). *Trade and Development Report.* Geneva, UNCTAD.

—— (1998). *World Investment Report.* Geneva. UNCTAD.

—— (1999). *Trade and Development Report 1999*, Geneva: UNCTAD.

—— (2000). *The post-Uruguay Round tariff environment for developing country exports: Tariff peaks and escalation.* UNCTAD. (UNCTAD/WTO Joint Study).

—— (2002). *World Investment Report*, Geneva: UNCTAD.

UNDP (United Nations Development Program). (2003). *Human Development Report 2003: millennium development goals: a compact among nations to end human poverty.* New York: Oxford University Press.

UNECA (United Nations Economic Commission for Africa) (2003) Economic *Report on Africa, 2003: Accelerating the Pace of Development,* Addis Ababa: ECA.

—— (2000). *Africa and the WTO: the challenges of negotiations on trade in agricultural products.* Addis Ababa: ECA.

—— (2003). *Economic report on Africa 2003: accelerating the pace of development.* Addis Ababa: ECA.

UNECLA (United Nations Economic Commission for Latin America). (1950). *The development of Latin America and its principal problems.* New York: UNECLA.

Vernon, R. (1966). "International investment and international trade in the product cycle". *Quarterly Journal of Economics*, May.

Viner, J. (1950). *The customs union issue.* New York: Carnegie Endowment for international Peace.

Voivodas, C. (1973). "Exports, foreign capital inflow and economic growth". *Journal of International Economics,* vol. 3, no. 4, pp. 337–349.

Warr, P. (1984). "The Jakarta Export Processing Zone: benefits and costs". *Bulletin of Indonesian Economic Studies*, 19.

Watson, P. L. (2001). "Export processing zones in sub-Saharan Africa". *Africa Region Findings, World Bank*, no. 193.

Wells, L. (1983). Third world multinationals. Cambridge: MIT Press.

WHO. (World Health Organization). (2003) Summary of the Report of the Commission on Macroeconomics and Health, 2003

Winters, L. A., McCulloch, N & McKay, A. (2002). Trade liberalisation and poverty: the empirical evidence. Nottingham: University of Nottingham. (CREDIT Research Paper 02/22) <www.nottingham.ac.uk/economics/credit/>

**Wood, A & Mayer, J. (1998).** "Africa's export structure in comparative perspective", in Economic development and regional dynamics in Africa: Lessons from the East Asian experience. (UNCTAD Series on economic development and regional dynamics in Africa).

**World Bank (1993).** The East Asian miracle: economic growth and public policy. Washington DC: World Bank (Policy Research Report).

—— **(2003)** Global Development Finance, 2003.

—— **(1981).** World Development Report. Washington, D.C: World Bank.

—— **(1991).** Intra-regional trade in sub-Saharan Africa. Washington, D.C.: World Bank. (Report no. 7685-AFR).

—— **(1997).** World Development Indicators. Washington, D.C.: World Bank.

—— **(2000).** Can Africa claim the 21st century? Washington, D.C.: World Bank.

—— **(2001).** World Bank Policy and Research Bulletin, 12 2. Apr–Jun.

—— **(2003).** Global Economic Prospects 2004.

—— **(2003).** World Bank Africa Database 2003. Washington, D.C.: World Bank.

—— **(2003).** World Development Indicators CD-Rom 2002. Washington, D.C.: The World Bank.

**WTO. (World Trade Organisation). (2003).** World Trade Report, Geneva: WTO.

—— **(1995).** The Results of the Uruguay Round of Multilateral Trade Negotiations: The Legal Texts. Geneva: GATT Secretariat/World Trade Organization.

—— **(2000).** Market access. Committee on Agriculture, Special Session G/AG/NG/W/37. Geneva.

—— **(2001).** Trading Into the Future. Geneva.

—— **(2001).** International Trade Statistics, Geneva: WTO.

—— **(2001).** Ministerial Declaration, WT/MIN 01 /DEC/1, 20 November. Geneva: World Trade Organization http: //docsonline.wto. org.

—— **(2002).** Committee on Trade and Development. Special Session. Draft Report to the General Council. Revision, TN/CTD/W/ 12/Rev.1, 22 July 2002. Geneva: World Trade Organization http: //docsonline.wto.org .

—— **(2003).** Negotiations on agriculture: first draft of modalities for the further commitments revision, TN/AG/W/1/Rev.1, 18 March. Geneva:

—— **(2003).** European communities: conditions for the granting of tariff preferences to developing countries, WT/DS246/R, 1 December 2003. Geneva: World Trade Organization, http: //docsonline.wto.org

**Yangihara T. (1994).** "Anything New in the Miracle Report? Yes and No". World Development. vol.22, no. 4, pp. 663–670.

# PART THREE

# ECONOMIC AND SOCIAL STATISTICS ON AFRICA

# Contents

# Preface

The main purpose of this part of the Report is to present basic data that enable the monitoring of economic and social progress in regional member countries of the African Development Bank (ADB), and provide benchmark data for analysts of African development. The data cover the Bank's 53 regional member countries, with statistics on Basic Indicators, National Accounts, External Sector, Money Supply and Exchange Rates, Government Finance, External Debt and Financial Flows, Labor Force, and Social Indicators.

Throughout this part of the Report, statistical tables are arranged in sections and according to indicators. The tables contain historical data from 1980 to 2003. Period averages are provided for 1980–1990, and 1991–2003.

The data are obtained from various international sources and supplemented, to the extent possible, with data directly obtained from ADB regional member countries, and estimates by the ADB Statistics Division. Statistical practices vary from one regional member country to another with regard to data coverage, concepts, definitions, and classifications used. Although considerable efforts have been made to standardize the data, full comparability cannot be assured. Care should be exercised in their interpretation. They provide only indications on trend or structure that allow for the identification of significant differences between countries.

Technical information on these data is provided in the explanatory notes to facilitate appropriate interpretation. However, users are advised to refer to technical notes of the specialized publications of the main sources for more details.

The designations employed and the presentation of data therein do not imply any opinions whatsoever on the part of the African Development Bank concerning the legal status of any country or of its authorities. They were adopted solely for convenience of statistical presentation.

## Symbols used

...    not available

0    zero or insignificant value

|    break in the comparability of Data

TABLE 1.1
BASIC INDICATORS

| COUNTRY | AREA ('000 SQ. KM) | POPULATION ('000) 2003 | GNI PER CAPITA (US $) 2002 | CONSUMER PRICE INFLATION (%) 2003 | LIFE EXPECTANCY AT BIRTH (Years) 2003 | INFANT MORTALITY RATE (per 1000) 2003 | ADULT ILLITERACY RATE (%) 2003 |
|---|---|---|---|---|---|---|---|
| ALGERIA | 2,382 | 31,800 | 1,720 | 2.3 | 70 | 43 | 30 |
| ANGOLA | 1,247 | 13,625 | 670 | 95.2 | 40 | 138 | ... |
| BENIN | 113 | 6,736 | 380 | 1.7 | 51 | 91 | 59 |
| BOTSWANA | 600 | 1,785 | 3,010 | 4.7 | 38 | 55 | 20 |
| BURKINA FASO | 274 | 13,002 | 250 | 3.0 | 46 | 91 | 73 |
| BURUNDI | 28 | 6,825 | 100 | 7.1 | 41 | 106 | 48 |
| CAMEROON | 475 | 16,018 | 550 | 2.3 | 46 | 87 | 25 |
| CAPE VERDE | 4 | 463 | 1,250 | 1.1 | 70 | 29 | 24 |
| CENT. AFR. REP. | 623 | 3,865 | 250 | 7.0 | 40 | 100 | 49 |
| CHAD | 1,284 | 8,598 | 220 | 4.0 | 45 | 113 | 53 |
| COMOROS | 2 | 768 | 390 | 2.5 | 61 | 65 | 44 |
| CONGO | 342 | 3,724 | 720 | 2.0 | 49 | 82 | 16 |
| | | | 90 | | | | |
| CONGO (DRC) | 2,345 | 52,771 | 720 | 9.1 | 42 | 119 | 35 |
| COTE D'IVOIRE | 322 | 16,631 | 610 | 3.4 | 41 | 100 | 48 |
| DJIBOUTI | 23 | 703 | 900 | 2.0 | 46 | 101 | 32 |
| EGYPT | 1,001 | 71,931 | 1,470 | 3.0 | 69 | 39 | 42 |
| EQUAT. GUINEA | 28 | 494 | .. | 6.6 | 49 | 99 | 14 |
| ERITREA | 118 | 4,141 | 180 | 23.9 | 53 | 72 | 41 |
| ETHIOPIA | 1,104 | 70,678 | 100 | 14.6 | 46 | 99 | 57 |
| GABON | 268 | 1,329 | 3,120 | 0.3 | 57 | 55 | ... |
| GAMBIA | 11 | 1,426 | 270 | 13.0 | 54 | 79 | 60 |
| GHANA | 239 | 20,922 | 270 | 26.4 | 58 | 56 | 25 |
| GUINEA | 246 | 8,480 | 150 | 6.2 | 50 | 100 | ... |
| GUINEA BISSAU | 36 | 1,493 | 410 | 3.0 | 46 | 118 | 58 |
| KENYA | 580 | 31,987 | 360 | 12.4 | 44 | 68 | 15 |
| LESOTHO | 30 | 1,802 | 470 | 9.3 | 34 | 90 | 15 |
| LIBERIA | 111 | 3,367 | 140 | 14.2 | 41 | 145 | 43 |
| LIBYA | 1,760 | 5,551 | .. | 2.4 | 73 | 20 | 18 |
| MADAGASCAR | 587 | 17,404 | 230 | 3.5 | 54 | 90 | 31 |
| MALAWI | 118 | 12,105 | 160 | 5.0 | 38 | 113 | 37 |
| MALI | 1,240 | 13,007 | 240 | 3.8 | 49 | 117 | 72 |
| MAURITANIA | 1,026 | 2,893 | 280 | 6.4 | 53 | 95 | 58 |
| MAURITIUS | 2 | 1,221 | 3,900 | 5.0 | 72 | 16 | 14 |
| MOROCCO | 447 | 30,566 | 1,170 | 2.0 | 69 | 41 | 48 |
| MOZAMBIQUE | 802 | 18,863 | 210 | 12.9 | 38 | 120 | 52 |
| NAMIBIA | 824 | 1,987 | 1,960 | 9.5 | 43 | 58 | 16 |
| NIGER | 1,267 | 11,972 | 170 | 0.5 | 47 | 124 | 82 |
| NIGERIA | 924 | 124,009 | 300 | 12.3 | 51 | 77 | 32 |
| RWANDA | 26 | 8,387 | 210 | 4.7 | 40 | 109 | 30 |
| SAO T. & PRINC. | 1 | 161 | 290 | 9.0 | 70 | 31 | ... |
| SENEGAL | 197 | 10,095 | 460 | 2.0 | 53 | 60 | 60 |
| SEYCHELLES | 0.5 | 84 | 7,050.0 | 7.0 | ... | ... | ... |
| SIERRA LEONE | 72 | 4,971 | 140 | 7.4 | 34 | 175 | ... |
| SOMALIA | 638 | 9,890 | .. | ... | 49 | 115 | ... |
| SOUTH AFRICA | 1,221 | 45,026 | 2,600 | 5.8 | 46 | 47 | 14 |
| SUDAN | 2,506 | 33,610 | 380 | 7.0 | 56 | 75 | 39 |
| SWAZILAND | 17 | 1,077 | 1,240 | 9.5 | 34 | 77 | 18 |
| TANZANIA | 945 | 36,977 | 290 | 5.3 | 43 | 100 | 22 |
| TOGO | 57 | 4,909 | 270 | −2.6 | 50 | 80 | 39 |
| TUNISIA | 164 | 9,832 | 1,990 | 2.7 | 73 | 23 | 26 |
| UGANDA | 241 | 25,827 | 240 | 5.9 | 47 | 84 | 30 |
| ZAMBIA | 753 | 10,812 | 330 | 18.4 | 33 | 103 | 19 |
| ZIMBABWE | 391 | 12,891 | .. | 420.0 | 33 | 57 | 9 |
| AFRICA | 30,061 | 849,491 | 650 | 11.2 | 51 | 81 | 37 |

TABLE 2.1
GROSS DOMESTIC PRODUCT, REAL
(MILLIONS US DOLLARS, CONSTANT 1995 PRICES)

| COUNTRY | 1980 | 1990 | 2000 | 2002 | 2003 | Av. Ann. Real Growth Rate (%) 1980–1990 | Av. Ann. Real Growth Rate (%) 1991–2003 |
|---|---|---|---|---|---|---|---|
| ALGERIA | 31,386 | 41,236 | 48,586 | 51,893 | 55,370 | 2.6 | 2.3 |
| ANGOLA | 5,076 | 6,368 | 6,877 | 8,181 | 8,541 | 1.3 | 2.8 |
| BENIN | 1,256 | 1,635 | 2,610 | 2,917 | 3,076 | 3.1 | 5.0 |
| BOTSWANA | 1,272 | 3,574 | 6,001 | 6,607 | 6,851 | 11.2 | 5.2 |
| BURKINA FASO | 1,475 | 2,044 | 3,039 | 3,325 | 3,411 | 3.1 | 4.0 |
| BURUNDI | 728 | 1,126 | 946 | 1,010 | 996 | 4.2 | −0.8 |
| CAMEROON | 6,310 | 8,752 | 10,040 | 11,017 | 11,457 | 3.1 | 2.2 |
| CAPE VERDE | 171 | 381 | 704 | 772 | 810 | 11.3 | 6.0 |
| CENT. AFR. REP. | 964 | 1,069 | 1,239 | 1,241 | 1,233 | 0.6 | 1.2 |
| CHAD | 787 | 1,309 | 1,673 | 1,991 | 2,172 | 4.5 | 4.2 |
| COMOROS | 167 | 223 | 243 | 254 | 260 | 3.6 | 1.2 |
| CONGO | 1,281 | 2,050 | 2,388 | 2,560 | 2,591 | 6.4 | 1.9 |
| CONGO (DRC) | 7,599 | 8,296 | 4,703 | 4,743 | 4,980 | 1.1 | −3.7 |
| COTE D'IVOIRE | 8,557 | 9,189 | 11,865 | 11,687 | 11,336 | −0.4 | 1.7 |
| DJIBOUTI | 507 | 544 | 495 | 517 | 533 | 1.2 | −0.1 |
| EGYPT | 29,899 | 50,921 | 77,907 | 82,466 | 84,808 | 5.9 | 4.0 |
| EQUAT. GUINEA | 94 | 117 | 640 | 1,035 | 1,188 | 1.2 | 20.7 |
| ERITREA | ... | ... | 571 | 641 | 673 | ... | 5.5 |
| ETHIOPIA | 4,507 | 5,447 | 7,448 | 8,329 | 7,982 | 2.5 | 3.2 |
| GABON | 3,633 | 4,345 | 5,022 | 5,100 | 5,139 | 2.1 | 1.4 |
| GAMBIA | 241 | 344 | 477 | 489 | 525 | 2.4 | 3.3 |
| GHANA | 4,236 | 5,243 | 7,983 | 8,697 | 9,106 | 2.1 | 4.3 |
| GUINEA | 2,265 | 3,075 | 4,530 | 4,899 | 5,076 | 3.3 | 3.9 |
| GUINEA BISSAU | 172 | 218 | 233 | 217 | 222 | 0.5 | 0.6 |
| KENYA | 5,612 | 8,360 | 9,884 | 10,098 | 10,240 | 4.2 | 1.6 |
| LESOTHO | 500 | 768 | 1,076 | 1,151 | 1,199 | 3.8 | 3.5 |
| LIBERIA | ... | ... | ... | ... | ... | ... | ... |
| LIBYA | 40,167 | 27,273 | 33,339 | 33,439 | 35,311 | −3.1 | 2.1 |
| MADAGASCAR | 3,048 | 3,212 | 3,814 | 3,531 | 3,872 | 0.6 | 1.6 |
| MALAWI | 992 | 1,234 | 1,729 | 1,687 | 1,787 | 2.0 | 3.1 |
| MALI | 2,200 | 2,334 | 3,159 | 3,739 | 3,858 | 0.3 | 4.1 |
| MAURITANIA | 752 | 886 | 1,333 | 1,433 | 1,510 | 1.9 | 4.2 |
| MAURITIUS | 1,810 | 3,193 | 5,374 | 5,778 | 6,030 | 4.5 | 5.0 |
| MOROCCO | 21,590 | 31,506 | 39,309 | 43,118 | 44,929 | 4.4 | 2.9 |
| MOZAMBIQUE | 1,938 | 1,967 | 3,379 | 4,112 | 4,400 | −1.8 | 6.5 |
| NAMIBIA | 2,434 | 2,751 | 4,156 | 4,372 | 4,533 | 0.8 | 3.9 |
| NIGER | 1,833 | 1,813 | 2,163 | 2,387 | 2,482 | 0.6 | 2.5 |
| NIGERIA | 22,357 | 24,864 | 32,922 | 34,054 | 35,762 | 1.6 | 2.9 |
| RWANDA | 1,645 | 2,011 | 2,083 | 2,429 | 2,507 | 2.7 | 3.9 |
| SAO T. & PRINC. | 48 | 42 | 50 | 55 | 57 | 0.2 | 2.4 |
| SENEGAL | 3,063 | 4,158 | 5,790 | 6,261 | 6,668 | 2.7 | 3.7 |
| SEYCHELLES | 315 | 442 | 655 | 642 | 610 | 2.9 | 2.6 |
| SIERRA LEONE | 1,123 | 1,227 | 769 | 862 | 918 | 1.4 | −1.8 |
| SOMALIA | ... | ... | ... | ... | ... | ... | ... |
| SOUTH AFRICA | 124,613 | 144,763 | 172,173 | 183,088 | 187,116 | 2.1 | 2.0 |
| SUDAN | 4,485 | 5,751 | 10,187 | 11,402 | 12,064 | 2.6 | 5.9 |
| SWAZILAND | 640 | 1,187 | 1,605 | 1,693 | 1,731 | 6.5 | 2.9 |
| TANZANIA | 3,474 | 4,808 | 6,418 | 7,241 | 7,639 | 3.4 | 3.6 |
| TOGO | 1,175 | 1,304 | 1,485 | 1,537 | 1,583 | 2.4 | 1.7 |
| TUNISIA | 10,509 | 14,915 | 23,699 | 25,268 | 26,658 | 4.0 | 4.6 |
| UGANDA | 3,113 | 4,102 | 7,866 | 8,851 | 9,330 | 2.4 | 6.5 |
| ZAMBIA | 3,366 | 3,733 | 3,992 | 4,326 | 4,512 | 1.3 | 1.6 |
| ZIMBABWE | 4,376 | 6,734 | 7,101 | 5,647 | 5,026 | 5.4 | −2.0 |
| AFRICA | 382,211 | 464,837 | 594,291 | 631,568 | 653,570 | 2.5 | 2.8 |

TABLE 2.2
GROSS DOMESTIC PRODUCT, NOMINAL
(MILLIONS US DOLLARS AT CURRENT MARKET PRICES)

| COUNTRY | 1980 | 1990 | 2000 | 2002 | 2003 | Av. Ann. Nonimal Change (%) 1980–1990 | 1991–2003 |
|---|---|---|---|---|---|---|---|
| ALGERIA | 42,318 | 62,031 | 54,462 | 55,914 | 65,667 | 4.2 | 1.1 |
| ANGOLA | 5,400 | 10,260 | 8,859 | 11,248 | 14,323 | 7.0 | 6.7 |
| BENIN | 1,405 | 1,845 | 2,255 | 2,719 | 3,528 | 3.6 | 6.6 |
| BOTSWANA | 1,057 | 3,516 | 4,973 | 5,053 | 7,077 | 13.8 | 6.1 |
| BURKINA FASO | 1,929 | 3,120 | 2,601 | 3,127 | 4,101 | 5.7 | 3.3 |
| BURUNDI | 920 | 1,132 | 709 | 628 | 592 | 2.3 | −4.6 |
| CAMEROON | 6,741 | 11,152 | 8,879 | 9,642 | 12,066 | 5.7 | 1.6 |
| CAPE VERDE | 107 | 339 | 549 | 643 | 836 | 15.0 | 7.6 |
| CENT. AFR. REP. | 797 | 1,488 | 953 | 1,054 | 1,297 | 7.5 | 0.2 |
| CHAD | 1,033 | 1,739 | 1,406 | 1,968 | 2,745 | 6.0 | 5.0 |
| COMOROS | 124 | 263 | 204 | 247 | 313 | 9.0 | 2.5 |
| CONGO | 1,706 | 2,799 | 3,220 | 3,014 | 4,232 | 5.7 | 5.4 |
| CONGO (DRC) | 14,869 | 9,348 | 4,300 | 5,500 | 6,090 | −3.5 | −1.1 |
| COTE D'IVOIRE | 10,175 | 10,796 | 10,599 | 11,692 | 13,936 | 1.4 | 2.9 |
| DJIBOUTI | 296 | 418 | 553 | 592 | 621 | 3.5 | 3.1 |
| EGYPT | 22,913 | 43,094 | 99,788 | 85,995 | 78,654 | 6.8 | 5.2 |
| EQUAT. GUINEA | 61 | 132 | 1,264 | 2,117 | 2,889 | 9.7 | 31.0 |
| ERITREA | ... | ... | 641 | 632 | 795 | ... | 5.7 |
| ETHIOPIA | 5,024 | 6,854 | 6,364 | 6,041 | 6,481 | 3.5 | 0.2 |
| GABON | 4,279 | 5,952 | 5,065 | 4,813 | 5,762 | 4.3 | 0.5 |
| GAMBIA | 241 | 317 | 421 | 357 | 312 | 3.9 | 0.1 |
| GHANA | 4,446 | 5,887 | 4,978 | 6,160 | 7,462 | 3.3 | 3.0 |
| GUINEA | 6,684 | 2,818 | 3,113 | 3,214 | 3,435 | 4.8 | 1.7 |
| GUINEA BISSAU | 139 | 262 | 215 | 204 | 241 | 8.8 | 0.0 |
| KENYA | 7,265 | 8,531 | 10,453 | 12,309 | 14,189 | 1.9 | 5.1 |
| LESOTHO | 431 | 615 | 859 | 714 | 1,126 | 4.7 | 6.0 |
| LIBERIA | ... | ... | ... | ... | ... | ... | ... |
| LIBYA | 36,273 | 28,905 | 34,441 | 19,204 | 21,386 | −1.8 | −1.3 |
| MADAGASCAR | 4,042 | 3,081 | 3,878 | 4,397 | 5,520 | −1.9 | 5.4 |
| MALAWI | 1,238 | 1,881 | 1,707 | 1,901 | 1,700 | 4.6 | 2.6 |
| MALI | 1,787 | 2,741 | 2,668 | 3,364 | 4,286 | 5.5 | 4.8 |
| MAURITANIA | 709 | 1,019 | 960 | 990 | 1,126 | 4.0 | 1.2 |
| MAURITIUS | 1,153 | 2,667 | 4,554 | 4,743 | 5,608 | 9.6 | 6.1 |
| MOROCCO | 18,805 | 25,821 | 33,335 | 36,094 | 44,668 | 4.2 | 4.7 |
| MOZAMBIQUE | 3,526 | 2,463 | 3,685 | 3,599 | 4,316 | −0.3 | 5.2 |
| NAMIBIA | 2,166 | 2,350 | 3,458 | 2,926 | 4,618 | 1.6 | 6.4 |
| NIGER | 2,509 | 2,481 | 1,798 | 2,171 | 2,733 | 0.9 | 1.8 |
| NIGERIA | 64,202 | 28,472 | 42,077 | 43,802 | 48,039 | −6.4 | 5.4 |
| RWANDA | 1,163 | 2,584 | 1,749 | 1,669 | 1,755 | 8.4 | 1.8 |
| SAO T. & PRINC. | 47 | 58 | 46 | 54 | 60 | 2.9 | 0.8 |
| SENEGAL | 2,987 | 5,715 | 4,374 | 5,096 | 6,662 | 8.1 | 2.4 |
| SEYCHELLES | 147 | 368 | 619 | 699 | 724 | 9.9 | 5.5 |
| SIERRA LEONE | 1,100 | 650 | 636 | 783 | 796 | −0.9 | 2.5 |
| SOMALIA | ... | ... | ... | ... | ... | ... | ... |
| SOUTH AFRICA | 80,423 | 112,014 | 128,022 | 106,339 | 160,825 | 4.5 | 3.8 |
| SUDAN | 6,760 | 9,026 | 11,014 | 13,279 | 14,612 | 7.2 | 5.8 |
| SWAZILAND | 544 | 882 | 1,389 | 1,193 | 1,862 | 6.4 | 6.9 |
| TANZANIA | 4,771 | 4,259 | 9,079 | 9,699 | 9,638 | 2.0 | 6.9 |
| TOGO | 1,136 | 1,628 | 1,206 | 1,360 | 1,757 | 4.9 | 2.0 |
| TUNISIA | 8,743 | 12,314 | 19,444 | 21,155 | 24,923 | 3.7 | 5.9 |
| UGANDA | 1,245 | 4,304 | 5,889 | 5,726 | 5,896 | 16.9 | 3.6 |
| ZAMBIA | 3,878 | 3,288 | 3,238 | 3,697 | 4,349 | 1.4 | 2.6 |
| ZIMBABWE | 6,679 | 8,773 | 7,399 | 9,027 | 7,063 | 3.5 | −0.2 |
| AFRICA | 398,111 | 463,754 | 566,869 | 541,224 | 646,435 | 1.7 | 2.8 |

TABLE 2.3
GROSS NATIONAL SAVINGS
(PERCENTAGE OF GDP)

| COUNTRY | 1980 | 1990 | 2000 | 2002 | 2003 | Annual Average 1980–1990 | Annual Average 1991–2003 |
|---|---|---|---|---|---|---|---|
| ALGERIA | 30.4 | 31.6 | 41.4 | 38.3 | 42.4 | 26.9 | 32.1 |
| ANGOLA | 20.8 | 1.7 | 44.4 | 26.5 | 26.0 | 12.1 | 20.9 |
| BENIN | 29.3 | 12.0 | 10.9 | 9.8 | 11.4 | 9.9 | 11.4 |
| BOTSWANA | 30.7 | 37.8 | 33.8 | 33.4 | 31.6 | 31.5 | 30.3 |
| BURKINA FASO | 12.2 | 15.0 | 16.4 | 7.9 | 10.2 | 15.2 | 14.6 |
| BURUNDI | 4.8 | ... | −4.0 | 3.0 | 4.6 | 6.7 | 1.5 |
| CAMEROON | 20.4 | 16.2 | 14.7 | 12.4 | 11.9 | 20.0 | 13.6 |
| CAPE VERDE | −108.0 | 19.0 | 10.0 | 10.4 | 10.5 | 13.0 | 18.4 |
| CENT. AFR. REP. | −2.9 | 8.5 | 7.4 | 5.2 | 4.0 | 3.2 | 5.6 |
| CHAD | 11.3 | 0.4 | 3.3 | 6.1 | 7.0 | 2.6 | 4.1 |
| COMOROS | 14.7 | 18.3 | 10.5 | 12.1 | 10.0 | 17.1 | 10.8 |
| CONGO | 30.5 | 6.9 | 29.0 | 25.5 | 21.0 | 25.4 | 12.4 |
| CONGO (DRC) | 6.4 | 5.2 | −1.2 | 6.3 | 11.4 | 6.2 | 7.9 |
| COTE D'IVOIRE | 22.1 | −2.1 | 7.8 | 19.8 | 17.7 | 10.3 | 9.2 |
| DJIBOUTI | 25.3 | 11.8 | 5.1 | 4.0 | 6.7 | 8.1 | 6.9 |
| EGYPT | 16.5 | 19.1 | 17.2 | 16.3 | ... | 16.0 | 18.7 |
| EQUAT. GUINEA | −29.4 | −9.0 | 14.3 | 21.3 | 25.1 | −12.3 | 16.9 |
| ERITREA | ... | | 2.1 | 13.3 | 11.5 | ... | 16.7 |
| ETHIOPIA | 7.3 | 10.5 | 10.0 | 14.5 | 15.1 | 9.8 | 13.1 |
| GABON | 54.5 | 24.2 | 28.0 | 24.9 | 25.2 | 37.5 | 25.5 |
| GAMBIA | ... | 17.8 | 12.7 | 10.3 | 8.9 | 18.4 | 13.3 |
| GHANA | 5.8 | 23.4 | 15.6 | 20.3 | 22.2 | 8.4 | 17.5 |
| GUINEA | 9.0 | 2.7 | 14.7 | 16.2 | 14.1 | 7.1 | 14.0 |
| GUINEA BISSAU | 9.5 | 14.2 | 2.8 | 2.2 | 4.3 | 9.3 | 5.3 |
| KENYA | 7.5 | 19.9 | 12.7 | 14.1 | 12.1 | 18.1 | 15.4 |
| LESOTHO | 43.1 | 46.4 | 23.4 | 24.7 | 24.8 | 31.9 | 24.1 |
| LIBERIA | ... | ... | ... | ... | ... | ... | ... |
| LIBYA | ... | ... | ... | ... | ... | ... | ... |
| MADAGASCAR | 1.2 | 4.1 | 25.0 | 10.1 | 18.2 | 3.2 | 9.6 |
| MALAWI | 8.1 | 12.1 | 4.1 | −0.1 | 3.2 | 11.2 | 4.7 |
| MALI | 7.0 | 14.9 | 10.0 | 14.1 | 14.0 | 9.7 | 13.8 |
| MAURITANIA | 14.2 | 6.4 | 29.4 | 27.9 | 21.6 | 11.4 | 17.7 |
| MAURITIUS | 14.9 | 25.9 | 24.2 | 27.0 | 27.3 | 20.5 | 26.6 |
| MOROCCO | 16.5 | 22.9 | 22.3 | 25.7 | 26.2 | 19.3 | 21.9 |
| MOZAMBIQUE | 1.3 | −8.7 | 18.0 | 26.7 | 22.1 | 0.5 | 9.0 |
| NAMIBIA | 21.2 | 29.4 | 26.3 | 29.8 | 27.5 | 19.7 | 25.4 |
| NIGER | 17.1 | 7.4 | 5.0 | 7.4 | 7.7 | 10.0 | 5.2 |
| NIGERIA | 23.3 | 29.5 | 25.9 | 15.4 | 23.7 | 15.4 | 18.6 |
| RWANDA | 8.8 | 3.6 | 12.6 | 11.5 | 8.6 | 8.8 | 7.0 |
| SAO T. & PRINC. | −10.4 | −9.3 | 23.0 | 6.1 | 18.2 | −6.2 | 11.7 |
| SENEGAL | −1.8 | 10.4 | 12.3 | 13.7 | 14.4 | 4.4 | 11.7 |
| SEYCHELLES | 11.5 | 20.0 | 22.8 | 6.8 | 14.1 | 16.6 | 17.4 |
| SIERRA LEONE | 3.6 | −1.5 | −1.8 | −5.8 | 2.3 | 3.2 | −3.6 |
| SOMALIA | ... | ... | ... | ... | ... | ... | ... |
| SOUTH AFRICA | 33.9 | 19.1 | 15.2 | 16.1 | 15.3 | 23.9 | 16.0 |
| SUDAN | −68.7 | 9.1 | ... | ... | 10.1 | 14.2 | 0.8 |
| SWAZILAND | 16.7 | 24.9 | 16.2 | 14.4 | 14.3 | 21.2 | 17.8 |
| TANZANIA | 20.7 | 20.9 | 12.3 | 14.5 | 11.4 | 16.7 | 11.1 |
| TOGO | 18.3 | 20.4 | 4.6 | 9.1 | 10.7 | 14.7 | 7.3 |
| TUNISIA | 24.6 | 21.6 | 23.1 | 21.8 | 22.3 | 22.6 | 22.2 |
| UGANDA | 42.4 | 5.9 | 12.8 | 14.9 | 15.8 | 16.6 | 12.6 |
| ZAMBIA | 11.8 | 14.8 | 0.7 | 3.9 | 5.7 | 8.9 | 6.6 |
| ZIMBABWE | 14.5 | 16.4 | 15.0 | −0.9 | −1.6 | 13.8 | 11.5 |
| AFRICA | 19.5 | 18.5 | 18.7 | 18.3 | 19.1 | 18.0 | 17.3 |

TABLE 2.4
GROSS DOMESTIC INVESTMENT
(PERCENTAGE OF GDP)

| COUNTRY | 1980 | 1990 | 2000 | 2002 | 2003 | Annual Average 1980–1990 | Annual Average 1991–2003 |
|---|---|---|---|---|---|---|---|
| ALGERIA | 39.1 | 28.9 | 24.6 | 30.6 | 30.2 | 33.7 | 28.1 |
| ANGOLA | 20.4 | 2.2 | 5.3 | 32.2 | 30.3 | 16.7 | 26.1 |
| BENIN | 35.6 | 14.2 | 18.9 | 17.8 | 19.0 | 19.8 | 17.2 |
| BOTSWANA | 40.4 | 37.8 | 29.1 | 24.5 | 24.8 | 32.4 | 28.0 |
| BURKINA FASO | 13.3 | 18.2 | 22.7 | 18.3 | 19.6 | 17.3 | 21.7 |
| BURUNDI | 13.9 | 13.5 | 8.4 | 8.6 | 11.5 | 16.3 | 10.6 |
| CAMEROON | 21.0 | 17.8 | 16.4 | 19.6 | 17.4 | 23.3 | 16.6 |
| CAPE VERDE | 38.7 | 24.4 | 20.6 | 21.6 | 22.2 | 43.7 | 26.9 |
| CENT. AFR. REP. | 15.7 | 6.1 | 9.6 | 8.6 | 7.1 | 11.5 | 9.4 |
| CHAD | 11.2 | 11.5 | 17.0 | 62.6 | 41.6 | 10.9 | 22.2 |
| COMOROS | 20.5 | 19.7 | 10.3 | 12.9 | 12.9 | 17.7 | 15.1 |
| CONGO | 12.4 | 15.9 | 21.0 | 23.3 | 22.4 | 17.4 | 28.1 |
| CONGO (DRC) | 24.7 | 34.4 | 3.5 | 9.2 | 15.0 | 31.0 | 15.9 |
| COTE D'IVOIRE | 22.8 | 6.7 | 10.6 | 10.5 | 9.9 | 15.0 | 11.3 |
| DJIBOUTI | 13.1 | 17.4 | 12.2 | 10.2 | 11.9 | 16.1 | 12.0 |
| EGYPT | 35.7 | 29.4 | 18.4 | 15.7 | ... | 30.5 | 17.6 |
| EQUAT. GUINEA | 35.7 | 17.4 | 43.9 | 29.5 | 26.9 | 23.9 | 60.1 |
| ERITREA | ... | ... | 18.4 | 26.5 | 22.5 | ... | 22.1 |
| ETHIOPIA | 12.6 | 12.0 | 15.3 | 20.5 | 21.2 | 13.9 | 15.9 |
| GABON | 32.9 | 21.7 | 21.8 | 24.3 | 25.5 | 36.8 | 25.3 |
| GAMBIA | 41.5 | 20.4 | 17.3 | 21.9 | 22.3 | 24.5 | 19.1 |
| GHANA | 5.6 | 26.7 | 24.0 | 19.7 | 23.6 | 9.9 | 23.2 |
| GUINEA | 13.4 | 12.7 | 22.0 | 22.7 | 19.1 | 14.3 | 20.5 |
| GUINEA BISSAU | 53.4 | 27.9 | 16.0 | 16.9 | 23.6 | 36.3 | 23.3 |
| KENYA | 22.8 | 24.2 | 15.4 | 13.6 | 15.1 | 22.8 | 17.5 |
| LESOTHO | 35.2 | 50.9 | 41.7 | 35.9 | 37.3 | 37.5 | 48.7 |
| LIBERIA | ... | ... | ... | ... | ... | ... | ... |
| LIBYA | ... | ... | ... | ... | ... | ... | ... |
| MADAGASCAR | 15.0 | 14.8 | 30.7 | 16.0 | 22.8 | 11.0 | 16.1 |
| MALAWI | 24.7 | 20.6 | 9.3 | 12.3 | 8.5 | 18.8 | 14.3 |
| MALI | 14.8 | 20.7 | 20.5 | 19.0 | 21.3 | 17.1 | 21.0 |
| MAURITANIA | 36.1 | 18.8 | 32.1 | 33.0 | 43.0 | 28.6 | 24.1 |
| MAURITIUS | 24.8 | 31.2 | 25.8 | 21.8 | 22.7 | 24.4 | 26.9 |
| MOROCCO | 24.2 | 25.3 | 23.7 | 22.7 | 24.6 | 24.4 | 22.3 |
| MOZAMBIQUE | 12.2 | 22.5 | 36.6 | 44.5 | 50.0 | 15.0 | 29.9 |
| NAMIBIA | 20.8 | 28.4 | 19.3 | 26.0 | 25.8 | 18.0 | 22.0 |
| NIGER | 28.1 | 11.0 | 10.8 | 12.9 | 15.5 | 14.9 | 10.1 |
| NIGERIA | 18.5 | 21.3 | 15.9 | 22.3 | 24.8 | 18.8 | 19.8 |
| RWANDA | 12.4 | 11.7 | 17.5 | 18.8 | 19.9 | 15.1 | 15.5 |
| SAO T. & PRINC. | 16.8 | 29.5 | 43.5 | 26.6 | 30.2 | 18.5 | 40.9 |
| SENEGAL | 10.9 | 13.8 | 18.5 | 18.4 | 20.2 | 11.7 | 17.2 |
| SEYCHELLES | 38.3 | 24.6 | 29.3 | 28.4 | 18.4 | 26.2 | 28.8 |
| SIERRA LEONE | 17.7 | 9.4 | 8.0 | 10.0 | 19.7 | 11.7 | 6.4 |
| SOMALIA | ... | ... | ... | ... | ... | ... | ... |
| SOUTH AFRICA | 29.9 | 17.2 | 15.6 | 15.2 | 17.2 | 23.1 | 16.3 |
| SUDAN | −3.6 | 7.3 | ... | ... | 20.3 | 3.5 | 1.6 |
| SWAZILAND | 40.7 | 19.1 | 19.9 | 17.8 | 17.3 | 27.1 | 20.4 |
| TANZANIA | 37.8 | 26.1 | 17.6 | 17.4 | 18.9 | 28.8 | 19.8 |
| TOGO | 28.7 | 26.6 | 18.8 | 20.7 | 20.1 | 21.8 | 16.6 |
| TUNISIA | 29.4 | 27.1 | 27.3 | 25.3 | 25.4 | 28.6 | 26.5 |
| UGANDA | 4.8 | 11.9 | 19.8 | 21.2 | 21.5 | 6.9 | 17.8 |
| ZAMBIA | 27.0 | 17.3 | 18.6 | 18.4 | 22.6 | 19.6 | 15.8 |
| ZIMBABWE | 18.8 | 17.4 | 13.5 | 1.4 | 2.2 | 18.2 | 15.8 |
| **AFRICA** | **25.8** | **21.8** | **18.5** | **19.7** | **20.5** | **23.5** | **19.8** |

TABLE 2.5
TERMS OF TRADE
(1995 = 100)

| COUNTRY | 1982 | 1992 | 1998 | 2002 | 2003 | Annual Average Growth Rate (%) 1982–1992 | 1993–2003 |
|---|---|---|---|---|---|---|---|
| ALGERIA | 169.9 | 120.3 | 88.1 | 130.6 | 147.1 | −1.5 | 3.9 |
| ANGOLA | 267.9 | 121.2 | 90.4 | 158.1 | 168.8 | −4.4 | 6.1 |
| BENIN | 37.1 | 79.3 | 95.0 | 74.2 | 92.0 | 9.5 | 2.4 |
| BOTSWANA | 25.2 | 95.2 | 108.2 | 111.2 | 107.2 | 20.9 | 1.2 |
| BURKINA FASO | 62.5 | 85.5 | 123.3 | 102.6 | 94.8 | 3.8 | 1.9 |
| BURUNDI | 102.4 | 52.7 | 82.9 | 51.2 | 46.8 | −2.9 | 0.9 |
| CAMEROON | 180.5 | 94.7 | 91.7 | 109.5 | 102.8 | −5.7 | 1.6 |
| CAPE VERDE | 288.1 | 132.2 | 71.6 | 69.4 | 69.5 | −3.5 | −5.0 |
| CENT. AFR. REP. | 105.0 | 88.0 | 95.7 | 76.5 | 86.1 | −1.0 | 0.1 |
| CHAD | 49.6 | 70.9 | 103.2 | 93.9 | 104.9 | 4.8 | 4.3 |
| COMOROS | 304.1 | 192.3 | 55.1 | 383.2 | 230.7 | −3.3 | 10.4 |
| CONGO | 200.6 | 109.4 | 89.4 | 149.9 | 142.3 | −5.7 | 4.7 |
| CONGO (DRC) | 62.2 | 77.6 | 95.3 | 105.5 | 96.4 | 3.1 | 2.4 |
| COTE D'IVOIRE | 87.6 | 61.8 | 97.9 | 100.7 | 106.9 | −2.1 | 6.2 |
| DJIBOUTI | 405.8 | 125.2 | 129.3 | 134.9 | 141.5 | −8.7 | 2.2 |
| EGYPT | 127.7 | 103.4 | 101.8 | 112.7 | ... | −1.7 | ... |
| EQUAT. GUINEA | 116.0 | 70.9 | 45.8 | 60.4 | 60.1 | −1.5 | 3.9 |
| ERITREA | ... | 99.5 | 97.5 | 101.3 | 93.9 | ... | −0.5 |
| ETHIOPIA | 137.7 | 103.7 | 99.1 | 46.9 | 45.6 | 1.2 | −5.1 |
| GABON | 72.7 | 117.3 | 74.9 | 140.9 | 138.3 | 6.0 | 7.4 |
| GAMBIA | 84.6 | 100.0 | 98.4 | 111.6 | 100.4 | 2.0 | 0.2 |
| GHANA | 122.2 | 82.3 | 109.1 | 85.8 | 83.6 | 1.2 | 0.7 |
| GUINEA | 87.7 | 140.2 | 124.8 | 107.3 | 104.5 | 5.5 | −2.2 |
| GUINEA BISSAU | 141.5 | 127.1 | 94.4 | 95.1 | 87.6 | −1.7 | −2.6 |
| KENYA | 120.1 | 80.1 | 94.2 | 85.0 | 83.8 | −0.9 | 0.6 |
| LESOTHO | 113.3 | 96.7 | 111.3 | 126.8 | 131.5 | −1.1 | 2.9 |
| LIBERIA | ... | ... | ... | ... | ... | ... | ... |
| LIBYA | ... | ... | ... | ... | ... | ... | ... |
| MADAGASCAR | 122.9 | 85.8 | 93.1 | 67.6 | 68.0 | 1.6 | −1.1 |
| MALAWI | 96.4 | 97.7 | 95.7 | 93.2 | 94.8 | 0.3 | 0.0 |
| MALI | 90.4 | 82.6 | 120.6 | 118.6 | 122.6 | −0.7 | 4.6 |
| MAURITANIA | 58.7 | 84.0 | 103.7 | 108.4 | 101.5 | 4.4 | 3.0 |
| MAURITIUS | 57.8 | 103.0 | 109.5 | 111.0 | 107.9 | 4.7 | 0.5 |
| MOROCCO | 133.2 | 95.5 | 114.0 | 101.5 | 99.0 | −2.6 | 0.5 |
| MOZAMBIQUE | 68.3 | 95.8 | 95.0 | 89.4 | 93.4 | 2.3 | 0.1 |
| NAMIBIA | 142.6 | 105.9 | 113.1 | 124.0 | 113.0 | −3.2 | 0.8 |
| NIGER | 159.8 | 105.7 | 80.5 | 96.8 | 95.9 | −1.5 | −0.3 |
| NIGERIA | 156.5 | 116.3 | 91.8 | 174.2 | 192.1 | 0.4 | 6.8 |
| RWANDA | 146.7 | 62.2 | 106.3 | 87.6 | 80.3 | −5.5 | 4.0 |
| SAO T. & PRINC. | 166.2 | 101.5 | 102.3 | 100.4 | 98.0 | 1.1 | 0.1 |
| SENEGAL | 97.0 | 101.2 | 109.1 | 101.0 | 108.4 | 0.3 | 0.7 |
| SEYCHELLES | 373.9 | 101.6 | 87.4 | 72.7 | 83.5 | 2.1 | 1.2 |
| SIERRA LEONE | 76.9 | 85.0 | 99.3 | 93.0 | 91.0 | 1.2 | 1.0 |
| SOMALIA | 106.2 | 100.3 | 99.7 | 99.3 | ... | −0.4 | ... |
| SOUTH AFRICA | 65.9 | 84.0 | 116.9 | 133.2 | 134.4 | 2.8 | 4.8 |
| SUDAN | 94.4 | 100.7 | 95.8 | 92.1 | 91.6 | −0.3 | −0.8 |
| SWAZILAND | 93.5 | 97.6 | 98.1 | 91.4 | 90.4 | 0.4 | −0.7 |
| TANZANIA | 147.5 | 77.4 | 140.5 | 168.9 | 247.7 | −7.1 | 18.8 |
| TOGO | 180.1 | 107.8 | 110.2 | 79.3 | 70.7 | −5.1 | −1.7 |
| TUNISIA | 129.5 | 101.6 | 96.9 | 94.1 | 92.2 | −2.4 | −0.9 |
| UGANDA | 76.7 | 112.2 | 90.7 | 41.5 | 48.0 | 6.7 | −5.3 |
| ZAMBIA | 112.4 | 95.6 | 78.1 | 69.9 | 69.8 | −1.2 | −2.5 |
| ZIMBABWE | 66.9 | 95.8 | 110.6 | 100.3 | 92.1 | 3.5 | −0.2 |
| AFRICA | 122.9 | 103.2 | 96.3 | 111.2 | 114.3 | −1.8 | 1.1 |

TABLE 2.6
CURRENT ACCOUNT BALANCE
(AS PERCENTAGE OF GDP)

| COUNTRY | 1982 | 1992 | 1998 | 2002 | 2003 | Annual Average 1982–1992 | 1991–2003 |
|---|---|---|---|---|---|---|---|
| ALGERIA | −1.0 | 2.6 | −1.9 | 7.7 | 12.2 | 0.2 | 4.5 |
| ANGOLA | −9.7 | −7.6 | −28.9 | −5.8 | −4.3 | −4.4 | −10.4 |
| BENIN | −30.4 | −4.5 | −5.7 | −8.0 | −7.4 | −8.1 | −6.2 |
| BOTSWANA | 16.6 | 4.8 | 4.1 | 7.3 | 3.5 | 3.4 | 8.2 |
| BURKINA FASO | −4.3 | −5.5 | −9.6 | −10.3 | −9.5 | −3.4 | −8.7 |
| BURUNDI | −12.6 | −15.4 | −7.6 | −6.0 | −6.8 | −10.7 | −7.4 |
| | | | | | | | |
| CAMEROON | 5.0 | −2.5 | −2.5 | −7.2 | −5.6 | −0.9 | −3.7 |
| CAPE VERDE | −9.4 | −5.7 | −11.1 | −11.2 | −11.1 | −4.5 | −10.0 |
| CENT. AFR. REP. | −11.6 | −7.2 | −6.1 | −3.4 | −3.1 | −6.5 | −3.1 |
| CHAD | −3.3 | −9.7 | −10.9 | −56.6 | −34.6 | −9.4 | −19.7 |
| COMOROS | 0.6 | −15.6 | −11.7 | 1.1 | 0.0 | −15.1 | −8.6 |
| CONGO | 18.7 | −10.7 | −20.6 | 2.2 | −1.6 | 1.7 | −15.9 |
| | | | | | | | |
| CONGO (DRC) | −3.5 | −9.2 | −10.2 | −2.9 | −3.3 | −6.4 | −3.6 |
| COTE D'IVOIRE | −7.2 | −11.4 | −2.6 | 9.3 | 7.8 | −6.6 | −0.9 |
| DJIBOUTI | −17.9 | −16.9 | −0.6 | −6.2 | −4.8 | −11.9 | −4.2 |
| EGYPT | −7.2 | 8.7 | −3.0 | 0.7 | 2.8 | −2.2 | 0.3 |
| EQUAT. GUINEA | −85.0 | −22.9 | −80.3 | −8.2 | −1.4 | −27.2 | −44.4 |
| ERITREA | ... | 13.5 | −23.9 | −13.3 | −11.0 | ... | −7.6 |
| | | | | | | | |
| ETHIOPIA | −5.9 | −1.3 | −1.6 | −6.0 | −6.1 | −3.2 | −4.1 |
| GABON | 14.2 | −4.0 | −18.7 | 0.7 | −0.3 | 0.8 | 0.5 |
| GAMBIA | −2.7 | −0.1 | −3.8 | −11.7 | −12.9 | −1.2 | −6.8 |
| GHANA | −0.3 | −5.6 | −5.0 | 0.6 | −1.4 | −2.2 | −5.9 |
| GUINEA | −5.1 | −8.0 | −8.5 | −6.5 | −5.1 | −5.9 | −6.7 |
| GUINEA BISSAU | −32.8 | −37.3 | −12.9 | −14.9 | −20.8 | −26.5 | −16.0 |
| | | | | | | | |
| KENYA | −4.7 | −1.3 | −4.9 | 0.5 | −3.1 | −3.5 | −2.3 |
| LESOTHO | −16.4 | −30.9 | −25.2 | −11.8 | −12.3 | −18.3 | −22.9 |
| LIBERIA | ... | ... | ... | ... | ... | ... | ... |
| LIBYA | ... | ... | ... | ... | ... | ... | ... |
| MADAGASCAR | −8.5 | −7.4 | −7.4 | −5.9 | −4.6 | −7.1 | −6.2 |
| MALAWI | −7.7 | −12.5 | −1.1 | −8.0 | −6.6 | −5.6 | −9.0 |
| | | | | | | | |
| MALI | −7.2 | −4.7 | −7.6 | −5.0 | −7.5 | −6.7 | −8.2 |
| MAURITANIA | −40.1 | −8.8 | −1.1 | −5.2 | −21.6 | −14.2 | −6.0 |
| MAURITIUS | −5.7 | −1.1 | −2.8 | 5.2 | 4.5 | −1.8 | −0.2 |
| MOROCCO | −6.3 | −2.1 | −0.4 | 3.0 | 1.6 | −5.1 | −0.1 |
| MOZAMBIQUE | −13.5 | −21.2 | −14.4 | −17.7 | −27.9 | −14.7 | −20.1 |
| NAMIBIA | −3.3 | 1.7 | 3.8 | 2.2 | 3.8 | 2.4 | 3.6 |
| | | | | | | | |
| NIGER | −11.5 | −1.9 | −7.3 | −5.5 | −7.6 | −3.5 | −5.9 |
| NIGERIA | −13.9 | −4.6 | −5.7 | −7.0 | −1.1 | −5.2 | −1.6 |
| RWANDA | −8.2 | −10.4 | −9.6 | −7.3 | −4.7 | −7.4 | −7.1 |
| SAO T. & PRINC. | −55.4 | −54.4 | −31.2 | −46.3 | −33.3 | −41.1 | −46.1 |
| SENEGAL | −11.9 | −7.9 | −4.2 | −4.7 | −4.8 | −9.1 | −5.3 |
| SEYCHELLES | −29.4 | 0.6 | −16.4 | −11.3 | −6.8 | −9.7 | −11.9 |
| | | | | | | | |
| SIERRA LEONE | −11.5 | −13.4 | −6.3 | −15.8 | −17.0 | −8.1 | −9.6 |
| SOMALIA | −5.7 | −13.0 | −5.8 | −2.8 | ... | −8.3 | ... |
| SOUTH AFRICA | −21.3 | −43.5 | −14.9 | −11.0 | −10.2 | −15.8 | −16.7 |
| SUDAN | −4.3 | 1.5 | −1.7 | 0.3 | −0.7 | 1.2 | −0.6 |
| SWAZILAND | 22.4 | −4.0 | −6.9 | −3.4 | −3.3 | −2.3 | −3.2 |
| TANZANIA | −5.7 | −4.7 | −11.0 | −2.7 | −7.3 | −4.1 | −9.2 |
| | | | | | | | |
| TOGO | −13.3 | −5.7 | −11.9 | −11.6 | −9.2 | −6.2 | −10.1 |
| TUNISIA | −11.7 | −7.8 | −3.4 | −3.5 | −3.1 | −6.3 | −4.0 |
| UGANDA | −2.6 | −4.7 | −5.9 | −6.4 | −5.7 | −2.7 | −4.8 |
| ZAMBIA | −19.1 | −3.6 | −16.7 | −15.7 | −16.6 | −7.7 | −10.7 |
| ZIMBABWE | −10.3 | −8.9 | −4.6 | −2.3 | −3.2 | −3.1 | −2.3 |
| | | | | | | | |
| AFRICA | −6.2 | −1.4 | −4.1 | −1.0 | −0.4 | −2.7 | −1.8 |

TABLE 2.7
BROAD MONEY SUPPLY (M2)
(PERCENTAGE ANNUAL CHANGE)

| COUNTRY | 1980 | 1990 | 2000 | 2002 | 2003 | Annual Average 1980–1990 | 1991–2003 |
|---|---|---|---|---|---|---|---|
| ALGERIA | 17.4 | 11.4 | 13.2 | 5.2 | 12.3 | 14.4 | 16.5 |
| ANGOLA | ... | ... | ... | ... | ... | ... | ... |
| BENIN | 48.9 | 28.6 | 26.0 | −7.0 | −7.2 | 12.7 | 11.2 |
| BOTSWANA | 19.0 | −14.0 | 1.4 | −1.1 | 10.6 | 22.6 | 17.0 |
| BURKINA FASO | 15.1 | −0.5 | 6.2 | 0.6 | 6.1 | 11.8 | 8.4 |
| BURUNDI | 1.4 | 9.6 | 4.3 | 29.5 | 9.3 | 11.6 | 14.7 |
| CAMEROON | 21.4 | −1.7 | 19.1 | 15.9 | −3.4 | 11.1 | 5.2 |
| CAPE VERDE | 30.6 | 14.6 | 13.7 | 13.6 | 4.6 | 18.7 | 11.7 |
| CENT. AFR. REP. | 35.0 | −3.7 | 2.4 | −4.3 | −3.5 | 8.4 | 5.6 |
| CHAD | −15.3 | −2.4 | 18.5 | 26.6 | 3.4 | 8.4 | 10.2 |
| COMOROS | ... | 3.9 | 14.5 | 9.2 | 0.7 | 12.7 | 7.2 |
| CONGO | 36.6 | 18.5 | 58.5 | 13.1 | −3.6 | 14.0 | 6.2 |
| CONGO (DRC) | ... | ... | ... | ... | ... | ... | ... |
| COTE D'IVOIRE | 2.8 | −2.6 | −1.9 | 30.0 | −4.2 | 4.0 | 8.8 |
| DJIBOUTI | ... | 3.6 | 1.1 | 15.7 | 5.7 | 7.6 | 1.4 |
| EGYPT | 51.4 | 28.7 | 11.6 | 12.6 | 9.3 | 25.7 | 12.1 |
| EQUAT. GUINEA | ... | −52.0 | 36.2 | 53.1 | 14.5 | −9.0 | 35.2 |
| ERITREA | ... | ... | ... | ... | ... | ... | ... |
| ETHIOPIA | 4.2 | 18.5 | 14.2 | 13.3 | 4.7 | 11.9 | 11.2 |
| GABON | 24.6 | 3.3 | 18.3 | 5.7 | −0.8 | 8.6 | 6.6 |
| GAMBIA | 10.4 | 8.4 | 34.8 | 35.3 | 12.7 | 18.8 | 16.6 |
| GHANA | 33.8 | 13.3 | 54.2 | 48.9 | 3.2 | 42.2 | 37.3 |
| GUINEA | ... | ... | ... | 19.7 | 16.7 | ... | 13.1 |
| GUINEA BISSAU | ... | 574.6 | 60.8 | 22.8 | 2.4 | ... | 34.4 |
| KENYA | 0.8 | 20.1 | 4.5 | 11.7 | 2.7 | 12.7 | 16.7 |
| LESOTHO | ... | 8.4 | 1.4 | 8.8 | 1.4 | 18.0 | 10.8 |
| LIBERIA | ... | ... | ... | ... | ... | ... | ... |
| LIBYA | 26.6 | 19.0 | 3.1 | 1.1 | 0.4 | 7.2 | 4.8 |
| MADAGASCAR | 20.6 | 4.5 | 17.2 | 8.0 | −0.1 | 16.9 | 19.8 |
| MALAWI | 12.6 | 11.1 | 41.6 | 20.7 | 4.3 | 17.6 | 29.6 |
| MALI | 4.5 | −4.9 | 12.2 | 27.9 | 9.2 | 8.1 | 13.7 |
| MAURITANIA | 12.5 | 11.5 | 16.1 | 8.9 | 5.4 | 13.0 | 5.3 |
| MAURITIUS | 23.2 | 21.2 | 9.2 | 12.5 | 3.0 | 21.0 | 13.2 |
| MOROCCO | 10.8 | 21.5 | 8.4 | 6.4 | 2.2 | 14.1 | 9.3 |
| MOZAMBIQUE | ... | 37.2 | 38.4 | 21.6 | 3.4 | 39.5 | 35.7 |
| NAMIBIA | ... | ... | 13.0 | 6.9 | 8.2 | ... | 17.5 |
| NIGER | 20.8 | −4.1 | 12.4 | −0.5 | −6.2 | 7.5 | 0.5 |
| NIGERIA | 46.1 | 32.7 | 48.1 | 21.6 | 17.8 | 18.1 | 31.6 |
| RWANDA | 8.1 | 5.6 | 15.6 | 12.6 | 6.9 | 7.8 | 14.0 |
| SAO T. & PRINC. | ... | ... | 24.9 | 25.0 | 14.3 | ... | 39.5 |
| SENEGAL | 10.3 | −4.8 | 10.7 | 8.2 | −0.8 | 7.6 | 8.6 |
| SEYCHELLES | 33.2 | 14.5 | 9.1 | 14.3 | 2.9 | 11.7 | 14.9 |
| SIERRA LEONE | 21.6 | 74.0 | 12.1 | 29.6 | 5.9 | 51.8 | 28.2 |
| SOMALIA | ... | ... | ... | ... | ... | ... | ... |
| SOUTH AFRICA | 22.8 | 11.4 | 7.2 | 14.5 | 2.4 | 17.2 | 12.6 |
| SUDAN | 29.4 | 48.8 | 37.5 | 30.3 | 8.2 | 38.0 | 53.2 |
| SWAZILAND | 13.7 | 0.6 | −6.6 | 13.1 | 3.7 | 17.1 | 11.9 |
| TANZANIA | 26.9 | 41.9 | 14.8 | 25.1 | 6.4 | 25.7 | 22.5 |
| TOGO | 9.1 | 9.5 | 15.2 | −2.2 | 6.8 | 9.0 | 4.6 |
| TUNISIA | 18.5 | 7.6 | 14.1 | 4.4 | 2.5 | 14.9 | 9.3 |
| UGANDA | 34.8 | ... | 18.1 | 25.0 | 7.7 | 83.6 | 22.0 |
| ZAMBIA | 9.0 | 47.9 | 73.8 | 31.1 | 5.4 | 38.6 | 40.8 |
| ZIMBABWE | 29.6 | 15.1 | 68.9 | 191.7 | 85.2 | 16.8 | 57.1 |
| AFRICA | 23.2 | 20.6 | 17.3 | 19.2 | 15.8 | 11.2 | 22.9 |

TABLE 2.8
REAL EXCHANGE RATES INDICES (PERIOD AVERAGE)
(NATIONAL CURRENCY PER US $, 1995 = 100)

| COUNTRY | CURRENCY | 1982 | 1992 | 2001 | 2002 | 2003* | Average Percentage Growth 1982–1992 | 1991–2003 |
|---|---|---|---|---|---|---|---|---|
| ALGERIA | DINAR | 42.1 | 85.1 | 134.1 | 138.9 | 135.4 | 9.1 | 4.6 |
| ANGOLA | NEW KWANZA | 0.0 | 36.6 | 88.5 | 85.1 | 76.8 | ... | 15.3 |
| BENIN | CFA FRANC | 87.9 | 77.8 | 137.0 | 131.0 | 109.5 | 2.1 | 4.4 |
| BOTSWANA | PULA | 90.0 | 100.3 | 153.4 | 160.2 | 124.7 | 3.5 | 2.4 |
| BURKINA FASO | CFA FRANC | 67.1 | 66.0 | 145.5 | 137.7 | 113.6 | 1.7 | 6.7 |
| BURUNDI | FRANC | 66.4 | 115.4 | 148.3 | 171.5 | 181.1 | 5.4 | 4.8 |
| CAMEROON | CFA FRANC | 103.4 | 66.6 | 138.1 | 130.0 | 108.0 | −1.9 | 7.1 |
| CAPE VERDE | ESCUDO | 124.6 | 96.6 | 147.4 | 140.2 | 116.1 | −1.3 | 2.2 |
| CENT. AFR. REP. | CFA FRANC | 69.0 | 70.4 | 157.1 | 148.7 | 122.4 | 2.0 | 7.0 |
| CHAD | CFA FRANC | 74.8 | 64.8 | 131.1 | 120.6 | 98.2 | 0.8 | 5.2 |
| COMOROS | FRANC | 123.6 | 89.1 | 151.3 | 141.7 | 149.5 | −0.5 | 5.2 |
| CONGO | CFA FRANC | 102.3 | 79.6 | 129.6 | 121.4 | 101.1 | −0.3 | 3.2 |
| CONGO (DRC) | FRANC | 28.6 | 90.2 | 69.9 | 93.5 | 103.6 | 13.7 | 11.0 |
| COTE D'IVOIRE | CFA FRANC | 91.8 | 71.7 | 142.4 | 132.0 | 108.5 | 0.4 | 5.5 |
| DJIBOUTI | FRANC | 121.7 | 107.4 | 101.3 | 101.6 | 101.8 | −0.9 | −0.5 |
| EGYPT | POUND | 93.9 | 126.5 | 105.1 | 118.3 | 152.0 | 5.5 | 2.3 |
| EQUAT. GUINEA | CFA FRANC | 166.8 | 76.8 | 124.8 | 107.8 | 83.3 | −5.0 | 2.1 |
| ERITREA | NAKFA | ... | ... | 114.8 | 121.4 | 100.5 | ... | 0.9 |
| ETHIOPIA | BIRR | 53.6 | 52.8 | 163.0 | 180.9 | 164.0 | 0.3 | 12.1 |
| GABON | CFA FRANC | 69.4 | 73.5 | 151.5 | 146.3 | 121.9 | 2.1 | 5.9 |
| GAMBIA | DALASI | 87.7 | 98.2 | 160.6 | 193.9 | 239.4 | 2.5 | 8.8 |
| GHANA | CEDI | 6.3 | 83.4 | 173.7 | 170.8 | 151.1 | 33.0 | 7.5 |
| GUINEA | FRANC | 19.1 | 98.8 | 177.0 | 177.9 | 174.6 | 89.3 | 5.5 |
| GUINEA BISSAU | CFA FRANC | 17.7 | 87.7 | 115.6 | 108.3 | 89.4 | 17.8 | 0.5 |
| KENYA | SHILLING | 90.0 | 110.2 | 112.5 | 112.7 | 102.4 | 2.6 | 0.1 |
| LESOTHO | MALOTI | 97.2 | 97.0 | 176.2 | 195.6 | 135.5 | 2.7 | 4.0 |
| LIBERIA | DOLLAR | 168.0 | 119.3 | 3,148.6 | 3,567.6 | 2,843.8 | −2.9 | 358.6 |
| LIBYA | DINAR | ... | 137.9 | 196.7 | 417.1 | 426.5 | −4.4 | 14.6 |
| MADAGASCAR | FRANC | 43.4 | 91.1 | 105.2 | 106.2 | 95.2 | 8.4 | 1.0 |
| MALAWI | KWACHA | 66.9 | 65.7 | 118.6 | 112.4 | 138.2 | 1.3 | 9.1 |
| MALI | CFA FRANC | 71.0 | 68.1 | 151.1 | 142.8 | 116.9 | 2.3 | 6.9 |
| MAURITANIA | OUGUIYA | 94.4 | 74.9 | 172.7 | 180.2 | 167.5 | −1.1 | 8.0 |
| MAURITIUS | RUPEE | 96.2 | 104.1 | 137.2 | 135.0 | 122.9 | 2.4 | 1.7 |
| MOROCCO | DIRHAM | 97.1 | 108.1 | 140.2 | 134.8 | 118.3 | 2.4 | 1.1 |
| MOZAMBIQUE | METICAL | 44.8 | 92.0 | 134.4 | 133.9 | 121.7 | 12.3 | 3.0 |
| NAMIBIA | DOLLAR | 83.9 | 95.6 | 171.1 | 192.1 | 133.1 | 3.6 | 4.0 |
| NIGER | CFA FRANC | 49.0 | 73.2 | 143.5 | 135.2 | 114.3 | 5.6 | 5.4 |
| NIGERIA | NAIRA | 73.6 | 310.3 | 285.8 | 277.5 | 271.8 | 20.6 | 16.0 |
| RWANDA | FRANC | 83.8 | 117.5 | 139.1 | 149.0 | 165.2 | 3.2 | 4.8 |
| SAO T. & PRINC. | DOBRA | 25.5 | 47.6 | 150.9 | 144.6 | 142.3 | 6.7 | 11.5 |
| SENEGAL | CFA FRANC | 82.4 | 69.3 | 158.6 | 150.3 | 125.2 | −0.1 | 6.9 |
| SEYCHELLES | RUPEE | 116.2 | 101.9 | 118.3 | 112.4 | 107.8 | 0.0 | 0.6 |
| SIERRA LEONE | LEONE | 75.8 | 116.4 | 117.9 | 130.9 | 133.2 | 6.2 | 1.8 |
| SOMALIA | SHILLING | 29.1 | ... | 216.9 | ... | ... | 33.1 | ... |
| SOUTH AFRICA | RAND | 96.0 | 93.9 | 189.7 | 216.2 | 147.5 | 2.2 | 5.2 |
| SUDAN | POUND | 6.4 | 114.9 | 10.0 | 9.5 | 9.0 | 153.4 | −13.2 |
| SWAZILAND | EMALANGENI | 92.0 | 103.5 | 179.4 | 198.3 | 165.4 | 3.6 | 4.8 |
| TANZANIA | SHILLING | 30.5 | 102.1 | 94.9 | 101.8 | 106.2 | 12.6 | 0.7 |
| TOGO | CFA FRANC | 73.5 | 78.3 | 152.0 | 142.7 | 121.3 | 2.8 | 5.4 |
| TUNISIA | DINAR | 92.0 | 98.7 | 148.2 | 144.5 | 129.3 | 1.9 | 2.8 |
| UGANDA | SHILLING | 34.5 | 136.2 | 155.9 | 165.8 | 175.0 | 20.2 | 2.9 |
| ZAMBIA | KWACHA | 76.2 | 109.0 | 113.2 | 112.5 | 106.7 | 6.6 | 0.0 |
| ZIMBABWE | DOLLAR | 54.6 | 103.6 | 89.4 | 37.9 | 98.5 | 7.0 | 9.6 |

* estimates

TABLE 2.9
INTERNATIONAL RESERVES
(MILLIONS US DOLLARS)

| COUNTRY | 1980 | 1990 | 2000 | 2002 | 2003 | Average Annual Growth (%) 1980–1990 | 1991–2003 |
|---|---|---|---|---|---|---|---|
| | 4,028.5 | 979.3 | 12,023.9 | 23,237.5 | 28,295.5 | –4.7 | 45.1 |
| | ... | ... | 1,198.2 | 375.5 | 659.5 | ... | 44.5 |
| | 12.4 | 64.9 | 458.1 | 615.7 | 547.7 | 182.7 | 31.3 |
| | ... | ... | 6,318.2 | 5,473.9 | 5,436.1 | ... | 2.1 |
| | 72.4 | 300.5 | 243.6 | 313.4 | 314.5 | 17.1 | 2.1 |
| | 101.1 | 109.8 | 32.9 | 58.8 | 71.6 | 8.1 | 9.2 |
| | 200.3 | 33.7 | 212.0 | 629.7 | 644.8 | 13.4 | 453.4 |
| | ... | ... | 28.3 | 79.8 | 84.0 | ... | 51.0 |
| | 59.0 | 121.7 | 133.3 | 123.2 | 126.8 | 10.7 | –5.3 |
| | 9.0 | 130.8 | 110.7 | 218.7 | 211.9 | 35.8 | –1.7 |
| | 6.6 | 29.9 | 43.2 | 79.9 | 85.0 | 33.9 | 10.4 |
| | 89.9 | 8.9 | 222.0 | 31.6 | 35.4 | –0.5 | 437.0 |
| | 246.3 | ... | ... | ... | ... | 13.0 | ... |
| | 36.6 | 4.0 | 667.9 | 1,863.3 | 2,108.8 | 9.2 | 27.5 |
| | ... | ... | 67.8 | 73.7 | 80.7 | ... | 1.7 |
| | 1,687.0 | 3,194.6 | 13,117.6 | 13,242.4 | 13,290.6 | 11.2 | 16.4 |
| | ... | ... | 23.0 | 88.5 | 125.1 | ... | 389.3 |
| | ... | ... | 25.5 | 30.3 | 35.1 | ... | 28.6 |
| | 89.6 | 20.5 | 306.3 | 881.7 | 907.8 | 9.4 | 59.8 |
| | 112.1 | 277.3 | 190.1 | 139.7 | 167.7 | 115.9 | 186.8 |
| | ... | ... | 109.4 | 106.9 | 103.9 | ... | –0.1 |
| | 243.7 | 298.1 | 232.1 | 539.7 | 705.2 | 4.5 | 14.9 |
| | ... | ... | 147.9 | 171.4 | ... | ... | ... |
| | ... | ... | 66.7 | 102.7 | 128.1 | ... | 40.0 |
| | 505.2 | 205.5 | 897.7 | 1,068.0 | 1,258.5 | –5.3 | 66.7 |
| | ... | ... | 417.9 | 406.4 | 422.6 | ... | –0.3 |
| | ... | ... | 0.3 | 3.3 | 1.5 | ... | 62.9 |
| | 13,242.5 | 6,033.4 | 12,460.8 | 14,307.4 | 16,549.4 | 17.1 | 15.5 |
| | ... | ... | 285.2 | 363.3 | 400.7 | ... | 24.8 |
| | 68.9 | 137.7 | 246.9 | 165.2 | 126.9 | 33.8 | 5.0 |
| | 21.7 | 190.5 | 381.3 | 594.5 | 730.2 | 43.5 | 16.3 |
| | 144.3 | 57.2 | 279.9 | 396.2 | 399.9 | –2.8 | 15.9 |
| | 95.7 | 749.9 | 897.4 | 1,227.4 | 1,382.5 | 61.8 | 6.7 |
| | 414.2 | 2,250.6 | 4,823.2 | 10,132.7 | 11,562.7 | 26.0 | 18.8 |
| | ... | ... | 725.1 | 819.2 | 820.7 | ... | 22.0 |
| | ... | ... | 260.0 | 323.1 | 297.0 | ... | 23.6 |
| | 130.1 | 222.2 | 80.4 | 133.9 | 91.3 | 13.6 | 3.9 |
| | 10,236.9 | 3,864.5 | 9,910.9 | 7,331.3 | 7,324.2 | 18.7 | 25.0 |
| | ... | ... | 190.6 | 243.7 | 226.8 | ... | 11.7 |
| | ... | ... | 11.6 | 17.4 | 20.5 | ... | 25.7 |
| | 19.1 | 11.0 | 384.0 | 637.4 | 688.6 | 1.6 | 4.5 |
| | ... | ... | 43.8 | 69.8 | 68.3 | ... | 17.3 |
| | ... | ... | 49.2 | 84.7 | 73.1 | ... | 13.2 |
| | ... | ... | ... | ... | ... | ... | ... |
| | 2,140.8 | 2,459.3 | 6,082.8 | 5,904.2 | 6,251.9 | 5.9 | 34.8 |
| | ... | ... | 247.3 | 440.9 | 558.6 | ... | 42.6 |
| | ... | ... | 351.8 | 275.8 | 259.3 | ... | –0.7 |
| | ... | ... | 974.2 | 1,528.8 | 1,692.9 | ... | 27.2 |
| | 82.3 | 353.2 | 152.3 | 205.1 | 195.4 | 19.2 | 0.5 |
| | 595.3 | 798.0 | 1,811.1 | 2,290.3 | 2,563.2 | 8.2 | 5.7 |
| | ... | ... | 808.0 | 934.0 | 910.4 | ... | 9.3 |
| | ... | 193.1 | 244.8 | 535.1 | 471.1 | 13.2 | 54.6 |
| | 283.1 | 194.6 | 193.1 | 83.4 | ... | –2.8 | ... |
| | 42,804.9 | 49,840.2 | 79,190.4 | 99,000.7 | 109,514.3 | 0.2 | 6.2 |

TABLE 2.10
CONSUMER PRICE INDICES (GENERAL)
(1995 = 100)

| COUNTRY | 1980 | 1990 | 2000 | 2001 | 2002 | 2003* | Average Annual change (%) 1990–1999 | 2000–03 |
|---|---|---|---|---|---|---|---|---|
| ALGERIA | 11.6 | 29.3 | 135.5 | 141.2 | 143.2 | 146.5 | 17.8 | 2.1 |
| ANGOLA | ... | 0.0 | 419,108.6 | 1,058,668.3 | 2,211,358.3 | 4,316,571.4 | 1,012.3 | 170.4 |
| BENIN | ... | 59.8 | 120.4 | 125.3 | 126.7 | 128.9 | 7.7 | 3.0 |
| BOTSWANA | 20.2 | 55.2 | 149.8 | 160.6 | 169.4 | 177.3 | 10.9 | 6.3 |
| BURKINA FASO | 51.6 | 73.6 | 112.4 | 117.9 | 120.6 | 124.2 | 4.5 | 2.5 |
| BURUNDI | 29.0 | 60.0 | 239.7 | 261.9 | 258.4 | 276.7 | 13.9 | 9.8 |
| CAMEROON | 30.8 | 67.1 | 118.9 | 124.3 | 127.7 | 130.7 | 5.2 | 3.1 |
| CAPE VERDE | | 74.6 | 122.5 | 127.1 | 129.4 | 130.8 | 7.3 | 1.5 |
| CENT. AFR. REP. | 53.3 | 71.9 | 105.0 | 109.0 | 111.5 | 119.3 | 3.9 | 3.1 |
| CHAD | ... | 69.6 | 116.5 | 130.9 | 137.7 | 143.2 | 4.9 | 6.4 |
| COMOROS | ... | 71.4 | 117.6 | 113.4 | 117.2 | 120.1 | 3.9 | 1.7 |
| CONGO | 26.5 | 48.4 | 130.6 | 131.1 | 136.1 | 138.8 | 8.2 | 1.6 |
| CONGO (DRC) | 0.0 | 0.0 | 107,334.9 | 491,486.4 | 627,628.2 | 684,742.4 | 3,386.4 | 237.1 |
| COTE D'IVOIRE | 38.8 | 64.1 | 115.4 | 120.5 | 125.8 | 130.1 | 5.9 | 3.7 |
| DJIBOUTI | ... | 77.4 | 113.3 | 115.3 | 117.1 | 119.4 | 4.4 | 1.9 |
| EGYPT | 11.0 | 52.4 | 127.2 | 130.2 | 133.5 | 137.5 | 10.8 | 2.7 |
| EQUAT. GUINEA | ... | 64.1 | 124.0 | 134.9 | 143.0 | 152.4 | 7.5 | 8.6 |
| ERITREA | ... | ... | 162.8 | 186.6 | 218.1 | 270.2 | ... | 19.3 |
| ETHIOPIA | 35.3 | 54.4 | 105.9 | 98.4 | 91.3 | 104.7 | 7.4 | 1.1 |
| GABON | 41.6 | 73.2 | 111.1 | 113.4 | 113.6 | 114.0 | 5.5 | 1.2 |
| GAMBIA | 14.7 | 72.6 | 114.3 | 119.5 | 128.0 | 144.6 | 5.8 | 6.4 |
| GHANA | 0.8 | 28.3 | 302.4 | 401.8 | 460.1 | 581.6 | 27.6 | 24.8 |
| GUINEA | ... | 61.0 | 123.2 | 129.9 | 133.3 | 141.5 | 8.7 | 5.3 |
| GUINEA BISSAU | ... | 15.1 | 258.1 | 266.6 | 275.2 | 283.5 | 37.5 | 4.5 |
| KENYA | 11.1 | 34.0 | 151.2 | 158.6 | 161.7 | 181.8 | 16.9 | 7.3 |
| LESOTHO | 15.4 | 54.2 | 147.1 | 157.3 | 176.6 | 193.0 | 11.1 | 8.7 |
| LIBERIA | 33.1 | 65.2 | 160.8 | 180.3 | 205.9 | 235.1 | 9.7 | 13.5 |
| LIBYA | ... | 42.0 | 111.3 | 101.8 | 103.8 | 106.3 | 11.7 | –1.8 |
| MADAGASCAR | 7.0 | 35.3 | 163.4 | 171.6 | 179.3 | 185.6 | 17.3 | 6.2 |
| MALAWI | 5.6 | 24.7 | 366.0 | 465.5 | 531.2 | 557.7 | 30.5 | 19.0 |
| MALI | ... | 75.2 | 107.9 | 113.6 | 116.3 | 120.7 | 4.2 | 2.7 |
| MAURITANIA | ... | 70.8 | 127.1 | 133.1 | 138.2 | 147.1 | 6.2 | 4.6 |
| MAURITIUS | 32.2 | 71.0 | 136.7 | 142.7 | 151.8 | 159.4 | 7.8 | 5.3 |
| MOROCCO | 37.0 | 74.6 | 109.6 | 110.3 | 113.4 | 115.6 | 4.5 | 1.8 |
| MOZAMBIQUE | ... | 14.4 | 179.5 | 195.6 | 228.5 | 257.9 | 33.6 | 12.9 |
| NAMIBIA | 17.0 | 57.4 | 148.2 | 162.0 | 180.3 | 197.4 | 10.3 | 9.8 |
| NIGER | 62.0 | 76.4 | 115.0 | 119.6 | 122.8 | 123.4 | 5.0 | 2.8 |
| NIGERIA | 2.0 | 14.3 | 175.9 | 207.6 | 236.0 | 265.1 | 31.8 | 12.7 |
| RWANDA | 22.3 | 34.1 | 137.2 | 141.9 | 144.7 | 151.5 | 17.3 | 3.5 |
| SAO T. & PRINC. | ... | 25.4 | 440.2 | 482.0 | 526.4 | 573.8 | 35.9 | 9.7 |
| SENEGAL | 40.7 | 71.8 | 105.0 | 108.2 | 110.5 | 112.7 | 4.2 | 2.0 |
| SEYCHELLES | 68.5 | 92.3 | 114.7 | 121.5 | 121.8 | 130.3 | 2.0 | 4.9 |
| SIERRA LEONE | 0.1 | 15.6 | 255.0 | 260.7 | 252.6 | 271.3 | 45.9 | 1.4 |
| SOMALIA | 0.2 | 27.5 | 193.2 | 215.4 | 258.5 | ... | 35.0 | 11.5 |
| SOUTH AFRICA | 14.9 | 58.6 | 138.2 | 146.1 | 159.4 | 168.6 | 9.9 | 7.0 |
| SUDAN | 0.1 | 2.8 | 501.1 | 525.6 | 569.2 | 609.1 | 80.4 | 7.1 |
| SWAZILAND | 15.4 | 54.3 | 143.7 | 154.5 | 172.7 | 189.1 | 9.5 | 9.7 |
| TANZANIA | 2.0 | 29.5 | 178.5 | 187.8 | 196.4 | 206.9 | 22.9 | 5.3 |
| TOGO | 43.7 | 62.8 | 108.6 | 112.9 | 116.4 | 113.3 | 6.8 | 1.1 |
| TUNISIA | 34.6 | 75.5 | 117.3 | 119.7 | 122.9 | 126.2 | 4.9 | 2.8 |
| UGANDA | ... | 40.5 | 129.9 | 135.8 | 133.1 | 140.9 | 16.5 | 2.0 |
| ZAMBIA | 0.1 | 3.0 | 354.4 | 431.3 | 527.0 | 624.0 | 76.4 | 22.1 |
| ZIMBABWE | 8.1 | 29.8 | 469.6 | 829.8 | 1,991.5 | 10,355.7 | 28.6 | 173.1 |
| **AFRICA** | **5.9** | **26.4** | **202.4** | **226.3** | **246.5** | **274.5** | **23.3** | **11.5** |

* estimates

TABLE 2.11
OVERALL GOVERNMENT DEFICIT(–) /SURPLUS (+) AS A PERCENTAGE OF GDP AT CURRENT PRICES
(PERCENTAGE)

| COUNTRY | 1980 | 1990 | 2000 | 2002 | 2003 | Annual Average 1980–1990 | 1991–2003 |
|---|---|---|---|---|---|---|---|
| ALGERIA | 9.9 | 3.6 | 9.7 | 0.2 | 0.7 | 1.3 | 0.1 |
| ANGOLA | –9.9 | –23.7 | –6.3 | –9.0 | –4.6 | –10.2 | –16.1 |
| BENIN | 4.2 | –4.1 | –1.8 | –2.4 | –2.1 | –4.7 | –1.4 |
| BOTSWANA | 31.0 | 10.4 | 6.6 | 1.1 | –2.7 | 11.8 | 5.4 |
| BURKINA FASO | –7.0 | –4.1 | –3.6 | –5.0 | –2.5 | –4.5 | –3.1 |
| BURUNDI | –6.2 | –2.7 | –1.8 | –1.3 | –6.2 | –7.6 | –4.4 |
| | | | | | | | |
| CAMEROON | 0.3 | –7.6 | 1.4 | 1.8 | 1.8 | –2.7 | –2.4 |
| CAPE VERDE | 8.0 | –3.3 | –19.8 | –1.9 | –1.5 | –8.7 | –9.3 |
| CENT. AFR. REP. | –8.5 | –6.8 | –1.8 | –1.3 | –1.6 | –2.8 | –3.4 |
| CHAD | 6.4 | –5.9 | –6.8 | –6.3 | –7.0 | –0.5 | –5.7 |
| COMOROS | –16.0 | –1.7 | –1.9 | –6.5 | –1.2 | –8.4 | –3.5 |
| CONGO | –0.9 | –6.6 | 1.2 | –8.1 | 3.1 | 1.3 | –8.6 |
| | | | | | | | |
| CONGO (DRC) | –0.4 | –10.9 | –6.0 | –2.7 | –4.9 | –6.3 | –9.1 |
| COTE D'IVOIRE | –12.8 | –19.3 | –1.3 | –1.6 | –1.8 | –7.7 | –4.3 |
| DJIBOUTI | 6.3 | –7.3 | –1.8 | –3.5 | –1.2 | –4.4 | –5.0 |
| EGYPT | 9.6 | –12.6 | –6.0 | –7.4 | ... | –16.5 | –4.6 |
| EQUAT. GUINEA | –16.3 | –5.3 | 8.0 | 12.7 | 23.2 | –10.5 | 1.0 |
| ERITREA | ... | ... | –32.4 | –30.3 | –24.8 | ... | –21.2 |
| | | | | | | | |
| ETHIOPIA | –3.6 | –9.7 | –11.5 | –9.3 | –8.5 | –6.0 | –6.9 |
| GABON | 7.4 | –4.1 | 11.6 | 3.8 | 8.9 | –2.7 | 0.5 |
| GAMBIA | –23.0 | –1.7 | –1.4 | –5.0 | –6.3 | –7.4 | –3.1 |
| GHANA | –11.6 | –2.1 | –7.9 | –5.0 | –2.5 | –4.0 | –7.3 |
| GUINEA | –0.5 | –5.5 | –3.2 | –5.9 | –3.0 | –2.8 | –3.4 |
| GUINEA BISSAU | 12.2 | –5.9 | –10.8 | –12.2 | –9.0 | –5.3 | –11.6 |
| | | | | | | | |
| KENYA | –7.8 | –6.8 | –0.7 | –3.8 | –5.2 | –5.8 | –2.9 |
| LESOTHO | –10.1 | –0.9 | –1.5 | –3.8 | –3.5 | –9.7 | –0.8 |
| LIBERIA | ... | ... | ... | ... | ... | ... | ... |
| LIBYA | ... | ... | ... | ... | ... | ... | ... |
| MADAGASCAR | –14.2 | –0.6 | –2.8 | –5.5 | –3.3 | –6.1 | –5.0 |
| MALAWI | –11.6 | –2.8 | –4.9 | –5.2 | –1.3 | –7.1 | –6.2 |
| | | | | | | | |
| MALI | 4.2 | –2.7 | –3.2 | –3.8 | –5.4 | –5.2 | –3.5 |
| MAURITANIA | –13.7 | –5.2 | –3.1 | 7.8 | –0.7 | –7.2 | 0.3 |
| MAURITIUS | –10.6 | –2.1 | –3.8 | –5.9 | –5.9 | –6.3 | –4.3 |
| MOROCCO | –11.2 | –0.6 | –6.4 | –4.6 | –4.2 | –7.8 | –3.8 |
| MOZAMBIQUE | –2.0 | –5.9 | –2.0 | –8.1 | –3.9 | –7.7 | –3.7 |
| NAMIBIA | ... | 0.6 | –1.1 | –4.4 | –3.7 | –0.1 | –3.5 |
| | | | | | | | |
| NIGER | –1.0 | –7.0 | –3.5 | –2.3 | –5.2 | –3.7 | –3.7 |
| NIGERIA | –3.4 | 3.1 | 6.3 | –5.3 | 1.4 | –5.2 | –1.3 |
| RWANDA | –3.3 | –7.2 | 0.7 | –2.4 | 0.9 | –4.2 | –4.5 |
| SAO T. & PRINC. | –27.7 | –42.2 | –16.5 | –13.8 | –10.2 | –26.7 | –28.7 |
| SENEGAL | –8.2 | –0.5 | 0.1 | 0.4 | –1.3 | –4.2 | –0.8 |
| SEYCHELLES | –6.6 | 5.6 | –11.7 | –15.1 | 6.4 | –7.0 | –6.2 |
| | | | | | | | |
| SIERRA LEONE | –12.1 | –8.8 | –9.3 | –9.9 | –9.4 | –9.1 | –7.5 |
| SOMALIA | ... | ... | ... | ... | ... | ... | ... |
| SOUTH AFRICA | –1.4 | –3.3 | –2.0 | –1.2 | –2.1 | –3.8 | –4.0 |
| SUDAN | –8.9 | –14.9 | ... | ... | –0.9 | –11.1 | –0.1 |
| SWAZILAND | ... | 6.5 | –1.4 | –6.3 | –6.7 | –0.6 | –1.9 |
| TANZANIA | –5.7 | –3.2 | –1.7 | –2.7 | –3.2 | –5.8 | –2.1 |
| | | | | | | | |
| TOGO | –5.7 | –2.8 | –5.5 | –0.7 | –0.7 | –3.9 | –5.0 |
| TUNISIA | –2.8 | –5.4 | –3.3 | –2.4 | –2.2 | –4.9 | –3.4 |
| UGANDA | –4.7 | –4.1 | –9.7 | –5.6 | –4.1 | –5.7 | –3.5 |
| ZAMBIA | –18.5 | –8.3 | –5.7 | –5.6 | –5.6 | –13.2 | –4.4 |
| ZIMBABWE | –9.6 | –6.2 | –21.9 | –5.4 | –8.8 | –7.8 | –8.4 |
| | | | | | | | |
| AFRICA | –3.6 | –4.8 | –1.9 | –3.4 | –3.0 | –5.8 | –3.9 |

TABLE 2.12
TOTAL EXTERNAL DEBT
(MILLIONS OF US DOLLARS)

| COUNTRY | 1982 | 1992 | 1998 | 2002 | 2003 | Annual Average Growth Rate (%) 1982–1992 | 1993–2003 |
|---|---|---|---|---|---|---|---|
| ALGERIA | 16,683 | 27,078 | 30,450 | 22,997 | 22,190 | 4.3 | −1.5 |
| ANGOLA | 9,574 | 12,041 | 10,588 | 9,300 | 9,710 | 2.4 | −1.5 |
| BENIN | 368 | 1,110 | 1,620 | 1,873 | 1,940 | 24.9 | 5.2 |
| BOTSWANA | 265 | 769 | 1,106 | 1,218 | 1,250 | 15.1 | 4.6 |
| BURKINA FASO | 352 | 875 | 1,422 | 1,676 | 1,780 | 8.1 | 6.7 |
| BURUNDI | 212 | 994 | 1,127 | 1,119 | 1,020 | 17.6 | 0.4 |
| CAMEROON | 1,220 | 7,333 | 8,177 | 5,475 | 5,920 | 19.9 | −1.1 |
| CAPE VERDE | 57 | 167 | 280 | 514 | 570 | 11.7 | 12.4 |
| CENT. AFR. REP. | 247 | 752 | 905 | 1,011 | 1,290 | 12.5 | 5.5 |
| CHAD | 137 | 636 | 1,003 | 1,377 | 1,520 | 19.5 | 8.4 |
| COMOROS | 76 | 190 | 210 | 230 | 230 | 14.8 | 1.9 |
| CONGO | ... | 3,798 | 5,155 | 6,474 | 6,760 | −1.1 | 5.7 |
| CONGO (DRC) | 4,505 | 11,368 | 13,506 | 10,434 | 8,730 | 9.2 | −1.8 |
| COTE D'IVOIRE | 6,226 | 16,661 | 10,851 | 11,029 | 10,880 | 13.0 | −3.5 |
| DJIBOUTI | 24 | 227 | 337 | 395 | 420 | 26.6 | 5.9 |
| EGYPT | 31,700 | 35,200 | 28,076 | 28,661 | 28,748 | 1.9 | −1.6 |
| EQUAT. GUINEA | 90 | 221 | 263 | 283 | 280 | 13.9 | 2.4 |
| ERITREA | ... | ... | 141 | 509 | 570 | ... | 158.5 |
| ETHIOPIA | 1,191 | 9,026 | 5,151 | 5,233 | 5,670 | 24.3 | −2.5 |
| GABON | 1,136 | 2,938 | 3,808 | 2,952 | 2,510 | 11.4 | −0.9 |
| GAMBIA | 268 | 301 | 465 | 575 | 570 | 0.9 | 6.1 |
| GHANA | 1,693 | 3,531 | 6,053 | 6,374 | 6,210 | 7.7 | 6.5 |
| GUINEA | 1,242 | 2,448 | 3,442 | 3,085 | 2,910 | 8.2 | 1.8 |
| GUINEA BISSAU | 494 | 840 | 917 | 848 | 870 | 5.4 | 0.5 |
| KENYA | 4,824 | 6,291 | 5,678 | 4,651 | 4,870 | 3.1 | −2.2 |
| LESOTHO | 124 | 437 | 639 | 531 | 550 | 15.5 | 2.3 |
| LIBERIA | ... | ... | ... | ... | ... | ... | ... |
| LIBYA | ... | ... | ... | ... | ... | ... | ... |
| MADAGASCAR | 1,775 | 3,742 | 3,836 | 3,659 | 3,570 | 9.3 | −0.3 |
| MALAWI | 882 | 1,691 | 2,479 | 2,773 | 2,910 | 7.2 | 5.1 |
| MALI | 867 | 2,264 | 3,017 | 3,198 | 3,110 | 10.0 | 3.1 |
| MAURITANIA | 1,167 | 2,134 | 2,400 | 1,921 | 1,840 | 8.7 | −1.2 |
| MAURITIUS | 533 | 1,000 | 1,223 | 989 | 1,090 | 7.8 | 1.2 |
| MOROCCO | 11,641 | 21,509 | 20,585 | 16,233 | 16,480 | 7.3 | −2.2 |
| MOZAMBIQUE | 1,695 | 4,892 | 4,114 | 3,644 | 4,210 | 13.0 | −0.3 |
| NAMIBIA | ... | 103 | 70 | 89 | 100 | −8.0 | 0.3 |
| NIGER | 603 | 1,193 | 1,617 | 1,886 | 1,950 | 7.2 | 4.9 |
| NIGERIA | 13,681 | 29,006 | 28,221 | 29,807 | 29,390 | 10.9 | 0.2 |
| RWANDA | 220 | 806 | 1,159 | 1,410 | 1,470 | 14.9 | 5.7 |
| SAO T. & PRINC. | 36 | 216 | 295 | 266 | 270 | 25.5 | 2.3 |
| SENEGAL | 1,670 | 3,412 | 3,639 | 3,239 | 3,900 | 9.7 | 1.7 |
| SEYCHELLES | 55 | 127 | 235 | 560 | 580 | 19.1 | 15.7 |
| SIERRA LEONE | 386 | 1,157 | 1,179 | 1,152 | 1,090 | 12.8 | −0.4 |
| SOMALIA | 1,044 | 2,196 | 3,033 | 3,588 | ... | 8.6 | ... |
| SOUTH AFRICA | 7,220 | 10,500 | 18,020 | 21,300 | 21,700 | 5.9 | 6.9 |
| SUDAN | 22,609 | 26,765 | 37,462 | 32,728 | 33,400 | 3.7 | 2.5 |
| SWAZILAND | ... | 209 | 288 | 438 | 430 | 4.4 | 8.2 |
| TANZANIA | 3,468 | 6,777 | 7,652 | 7,061 | 7,260 | 7.6 | 0.7 |
| TOGO | 776 | 1,213 | 1,327 | 1,136 | 1,260 | 5.3 | 0.9 |
| TUNISIA | 3,772 | 8,298 | 11,585 | 13,665 | 15,270 | 8.0 | 5.9 |
| UGANDA | 841 | 2,647 | 3,631 | 3,647 | 3,880 | 13.4 | 3.7 |
| ZAMBIA | 3,463 | 6,772 | 6,232 | 5,119 | 4,670 | 7.9 | −3.1 |
| ZIMBABWE | 1,830 | 3,773 | 4,511 | 5,480 | 5,720 | 11.7 | 4.0 |
| AFRICA | 162,942 | 287,639 | 309,040 | 293,318 | 296,844 | 6.4 | 0.3 |

TABLE 2.13
DEBT SERVICE
(Millions of US Dollars)

| COUNTRY | 1982 | 1992 | 1998 | 2002 | 2003 | Annual Average Growth Rate (%) 1982–1992 | 1993–2003 |
|---|---|---|---|---|---|---|---|
| ALGERIA | 4,560 | 9,490 | 4,590 | 4,090 | 4,140 | 7.7 | −5.9 |
| ANGOLA | 220 | 1,610 | 2,070 | 2,270 | 2,400 | 28.5 | 8.4 |
| BENIN | ... | 30 | 50 | 70 | 80 | 8.3 | 13.9 |
| BOTSWANA | 10 | 90 | 70 | 60 | 60 | 29.7 | −2.3 |
| BURKINA FASO | 20 | 60 | 60 | 70 | 90 | 45.1 | 13.4 |
| BURUNDI | 10 | 40 | 40 | 30 | 20 | 17.1 | −1.8 |
| CAMEROON | ... | 200 | 770 | 270 | 380 | 2.9 | 31.5 |
| CAPE VERDE | ... | ... | 10 | 40 | 40 | −50.0 | 14.6 |
| CENT. AFR. REP. | ... | ... | 20 | ... | 180 | −20.0 | −6.3 |
| CHAD | ... | ... | ... | 30 | 40 | ... | −2.2 |
| COMOROS | ... | 20 | ... | 10 | 10 | ... | −50.0 |
| CONGO | ... | ... | 80 | 230 | 340 | ... | 13.7 |
| CONGO (DRC) | 720 | 2,520 | 810 | 10,410 | 180 | 27.0 | 92.6 |
| COTE D'IVOIRE | 900 | 1,020 | 1,110 | 1,110 | 1,040 | 6.3 | 1.7 |
| DJIBOUTI | ... | 10 | 20 | 20 | 20 | 5.6 | −12.5 |
| EGYPT | ... | ... | ... | ... | ... | ... | ... |
| EQUAT. GUINEA | 10 | ... | 60 | 70 | 60 | −11.1 | 11.7 |
| ERITREA | ... | ... | ... | 30 | 20 | ... | ... |
| ETHIOPIA | 60 | 180 | 200 | 200 | 200 | 17.9 | 56.5 |
| GABON | 790 | 660 | 270 | 520 | 1,640 | 2.6 | 26.9 |
| GAMBIA | 40 | 20 | 20 | 30 | 30 | 28.0 | 6.1 |
| GHANA | ... | 280 | 570 | 450 | 350 | 6.8 | 7.7 |
| GUINEA | 100 | 80 | 160 | 90 | 100 | 3.2 | 35.1 |
| GUINEA BISSAU | ... | ... | 10 | ... | 10 | ... | −60.0 |
| KENYA | 200 | 400 | 780 | 440 | 500 | 12.5 | 9.0 |
| LESOTHO | ... | 30 | 40 | 50 | 40 | 12.5 | 5.5 |
| LIBERIA | ... | ... | ... | ... | ... | ... | ... |
| LIBYA | | | | | | | |
| MADAGASCAR | 300 | 50 | 160 | 170 | 170 | 7.0 | 15.8 |
| MALAWI | 60 | 40 | ... | 90 | 90 | 14.3 | 0.0 |
| MALI | 20 | 60 | 80 | 70 | 80 | 13.3 | 5.6 |
| MAURITANIA | 0 | 90 | 90 | 110 | 120 | −10.0 | 4.5 |
| MAURITIUS | 80 | 140 | 180 | 230 | 200 | 7.0 | 4.8 |
| MOROCCO | 1,550 | 3,110 | 3,020 | 2,710 | 2,620 | 11.8 | −1.4 |
| MOZAMBIQUE | 390 | 80 | 90 | 150 | 180 | 31.9 | 10.9 |
| NAMIBIA | 30 | 30 | 20 | 30 | 30 | 9.7 | 3.0 |
| NIGER | ... | ... | 30 | 60 | 70 | ... | −4.5 |
| NIGERIA | 2,380 | 3,080 | 1,350 | 1,490 | 2,000 | 17.4 | 0.7 |
| RWANDA | ... | ... | 20 | 40 | 40 | ... | 10.0 |
| SAO T. & PRINC. | ... | ... | 10 | 0 | 20 | ... | ? |
| SENEGAL | 190 | 240 | 240 | 210 | 230 | 4.4 | 9.3 |
| SEYCHELLES | 0 | 40 | 60 | 50 | 100 | 9.3 | 19.0 |
| SIERRA LEONE | 70 | 90 | 50 | 70 | 80 | 85.3 | 7.5 |
| SOMALIA | 62 | 1,947 | 2,474 | ... | ... | ... | ... |
| SOUTH AFRICA | 300 | 100 | 10 | 50 | 180 | 1.4 | 63.4 |
| SUDAN | 2,530 | 3,510 | 6,190 | 5,140 | 5,990 | 4.8 | 5.8 |
| SWAZILAND | ... | ... | ... | ... | ... | ... | ... |
| TANZANIA | 150 | 240 | 700 | 230 | 220 | 3.6 | 8.4 |
| TOGO | 60 | 40 | 50 | 10 | 0 | 0.6 | −13.0 |
| TUNISIA | 520 | 1,360 | 1,620 | 1,630 | 1,860 | 4.7 | 3.6 |
| UGANDA | ... | 250 | 140 | 130 | 160 | 31.6 | −1.7 |
| ZAMBIA | 0 | 540 | 150 | 120 | 190 | 45.3 | 18.3 |
| ZIMBABWE | 250 | 520 | 630 | 30 | 410 | 7.9 | 119.2 |
| AFRICA | 20,043 | 33,012 | 28,391 | 35,698 | 29,519 | 5.1 | −0.5 |

TABLE 3.1
LABOUR FORCE BY SECTOR
(PERCENT IN)

| COUNTRY | AGRICULTURE | | | | INDUSTRY | | | | SERVICES | | | |
|---|---|---|---|---|---|---|---|---|---|---|---|---|
| | 1980 | 1985 | 1990 | 1996 | 1980 | 1985 | 1990 | 1996 | 1980 | 1985 | 1990 | 1996 |
| ALGERIA | 31 | 25 | 19 | 14 | 27 | 29 | 32 | 35 | 42 | 46 | 49 | 51 |
| ANGOLA | 74 | 72 | 70 | 68 | 10 | 10 | 11 | 11 | 17 | 18 | 19 | 21 |
| BENIN | 70 | 65 | 59 | 54 | 7 | 7 | 8 | 10 | 23 | 28 | 32 | 36 |
| BOTSWANA | 70 | 61 | 52 | 42 | 13 | 19 | 28 | 41 | 17 | 20 | 20 | 17 |
| BURKINA FASO | 87 | 86 | 85 | 84 | 4 | 5 | 5 | 5 | 9 | 10 | 10 | 11 |
| BURUNDI | 93 | 92 | 92 | 91 | 2 | 3 | 3 | 3 | 5 | 5 | 5 | 6 |
| CAMEROON | 70 | 63 | 56 | 49 | 8 | 10 | 13 | 15 | 22 | 27 | 32 | 36 |
| CAPE VERDE | 52 | 46 | 40 | 35 | 23 | 27 | 31 | 36 | 26 | 27 | 29 | 29 |
| CENT. AFR. REP. | 72 | 67 | 61 | 56 | 6 | 8 | 10 | 12 | 21 | 25 | 29 | 32 |
| CHAD | 83 | 80 | 76 | 72 | 5 | 5 | 6 | 7 | 12 | 15 | 18 | 21 |
| COMOROS | 83 | 81 | 79 | 77 | 6 | 6 | 7 | 8 | 11 | 12 | 14 | 15 |
| CONGO | 62 | 61 | 60 | 58 | 12 | 12 | 12 | 13 | 26 | 27 | 28 | 29 |
| CONGO (DRC) | 71 | 68 | 64 | 60 | 13 | 14 | 16 | 17 | 16 | 18 | 20 | 23 |
| COTE D'IVOIRE | 65 | 60 | 54 | 49 | 8 | 10 | 12 | 14 | 27 | 30 | 34 | 37 |
| DJIBOUTI | ... | ... | ... | ... | ... | ... | ... | ... | ... | ... | ... | ... |
| EGYPT | 46 | 42 | 39 | 36 | 20 | 22 | 24 | 27 | 34 | 35 | 36 | 37 |
| EQUAT. GUINEA | 66 | 61 | 57 | 52 | 11 | 13 | 15 | 18 | 23 | 26 | 28 | 30 |
| ERITREA | ... | ... | ... | ... | ... | ... | ... | ... | ... | ... | ... | |
| ETHIOPIA | 80 | 77 | 74 | 72 | 8 | 9 | 10 | 12 | 12 | 14 | 15 | 16 |
| GABON | 75 | 73 | 71 | 69 | 11 | 12 | 12 | 13 | 14 | 15 | 16 | 18 |
| GAMBIA | 84 | 83 | 82 | 80 | 7 | 7 | 8 | 9 | 9 | 10 | 11 | 11 |
| GHANA | 56 | 54 | 53 | 52 | 18 | 18 | 19 | 19 | 26 | 27 | 28 | 29 |
| GUINEA | 81 | 78 | 76 | 74 | 9 | 10 | 11 | 13 | 10 | 11 | 12 | 13 |
| GUINEA BISSAU | 82 | 81 | 80 | 79 | 4 | 4 | 4 | 5 | 14 | 15 | 15 | 16 |
| KENYA | 81 | 79 | 77 | 75 | 7 | 7 | 8 | 9 | 12 | 13 | 14 | 16 |
| LESOTHO | 86 | 84 | 82 | 81 | 4 | 5 | 5 | 6 | 10 | 11 | 12 | 13 |
| LIBERIA | 74 | 73 | 71 | 70 | 9 | 9 | 9 | 9 | 16 | 18 | 20 | 21 |
| LIBYA | 18 | 14 | 11 | 8 | 29 | 30 | 32 | 34 | 53 | 55 | 57 | 58 |
| MADAGASCAR | 81 | 79 | 78 | 76 | 6 | 7 | 7 | 8 | 13 | 14 | 15 | 16 |
| MALAWI | 83 | 78 | 75 | 70 | 7 | 10 | 13 | 17 | 9 | 11 | 12 | 13 |
| MALI | 86 | 84 | 82 | 80 | 2 | 2 | 3 | 3 | 12 | 14 | 16 | 17 |
| MAURITANIA | 69 | 61 | 53 | 45 | 9 | 12 | 16 | 21 | 22 | 27 | 31 | 34 |
| MAURITIUS | 28 | 25 | 23 | 20 | 24 | 24 | 23 | 23 | 48 | 51 | 54 | 57 |
| MOROCCO | 46 | 40 | 35 | 30 | 25 | 29 | 35 | 40 | 29 | 31 | 31 | 30 |
| MOZAMBIQUE | 84 | 83 | 82 | 81 | 7 | 8 | 9 | 10 | 8 | 8 | 9 | 9 |
| NAMIBIA | 43 | 44 | 43 | 40 | 22 | 20 | 27 | 37 | 36 | 6 | 31 | 23 |
| NIGER | 91 | 89 | 88 | 86 | 2 | 2 | 2 | 2 | 7 | 9 | 10 | 12 |
| NIGERIA | 68 | 67 | 65 | 64 | 12 | 12 | 13 | 13 | 20 | 21 | 22 | 23 |
| RWANDA | 93 | 92 | 92 | 92 | 3 | 3 | 3 | 3 | 4 | 5 | 5 | 5 |
| SAO T. & PRINC. | ... | ... | ... | ... | ... | ... | ... | ... | ... | ... | ... | ... |
| SENEGAL | 81 | 79 | 78 | 77 | 6 | 7 | 7 | 7 | 13 | 14 | 15 | 16 |
| SEYCHELLES | ... | ... | ... | ... | ... | ... | ... | ... | ... | ... | ... | ... |
| SIERRA LEONE | 70 | 67 | 64 | 61 | 14 | 15 | 16 | 17 | 16 | 18 | 20 | 22 |
| SOMALIA | 76 | 74 | 72 | 70 | 8 | 9 | 10 | 11 | 16 | 17 | 18 | 19 |
| SOUTH AFRICA | 17 | ... | 14 | ... | 35 | ... | 32 | ... | 48 | ... | 54 | ... |
| SUDAN | 71 | 68 | 65 | 62 | 7 | 8 | 9 | 11 | 21 | 23 | 25 | 27 |
| SWAZILAND | 74 | 71 | 67 | 64 | 9 | 10 | 12 | 13 | 17 | 19 | 21 | 23 |
| TANZANIA | 86 | 84 | 81 | 79 | 5 | 5 | 6 | 7 | 10 | 11 | 12 | 14 |
| TOGO | 73 | 71 | 69 | 67 | 10 | 10 | 11 | 12 | 17 | 18 | 20 | 21 |
| TUNISIA | 35 | 31 | 28 | 25 | 36 | 43 | 49 | 56 | 29 | 26 | 23 | 19 |
| UGANDA | 86 | 84 | 82 | 81 | 4 | 5 | 6 | 6 | 10 | 11 | 12 | 13 |
| ZAMBIA | 73 | 71 | 70 | 68 | 10 | 11 | 11 | 12 | 17 | 18 | 19 | 20 |
| ZIMBABWE | 73 | 70 | 68 | 66 | 10 | 12 | 13 | 14 | 17 | 18 | 19 | 20 |
| AFRICA | 70 | 67 | 65 | 62 | 11 | 12 | 13 | 15 | 19 | 21 | 22 | 23 |

TABLE 3.2
LABOUR FORCE PARTICIPATION RATE
(Percentage of population of all ages in labour force)

| COUNTRY | TOTAL | | | | FEMALE | | | | MALE | | | |
|---|---|---|---|---|---|---|---|---|---|---|---|---|
| | 1980 | 1990 | 1995 | 2002 | 1980 | 1990 | 1995 | 2002 | 1980 | 1990 | 1995 | 2002 |
| ALGERIA | 26.0 | 27.9 | 30.8 | 35.7 | 21.4 | 21.2 | 24.3 | 29.1 | 78.6 | 78.8 | 75.7 | 70.9 |
| ANGOLA | 49.5 | 47.4 | 46.6 | 45.7 | 47.0 | 46.6 | 46.5 | 46.4 | 53.0 | 53.4 | 53.5 | 53.6 |
| BENIN | 47.9 | 45.1 | 45.2 | 45.5 | 47.0 | 48.3 | 48.3 | 48.3 | 53.0 | 51.7 | 51.7 | 51.7 |
| BOTSWANA | 43.3 | 42.8 | 44.1 | 45.2 | 48.9 | 46.6 | 46.1 | 45.4 | 51.1 | 53.4 | 54.0 | 54.6 |
| BURKINA FASO | 53.1 | 50.4 | 48.9 | 47.0 | 50.2 | 49.3 | 49.0 | 48.4 | 49.8 | 50.7 | 51.0 | 51.6 |
| BURUNDI | 54.9 | 53.8 | 53.0 | 52.5 | 50.2 | 49.2 | 49.2 | 49.0 | 49.8 | 50.8 | 50.8 | 51.0 |
| CAMEROON | 41.9 | 40.1 | 40.6 | 41.4 | 36.8 | 37.0 | 37.5 | 38.4 | 63.2 | 63.1 | 62.4 | 61.6 |
| CAPE VERDE | 32.5 | 35.2 | 37.3 | 40.5 | 34.0 | 37.4 | 37.7 | 38.0 | 66.0 | 62.6 | 62.3 | 61.4 |
| CENT. AFR. REP. | 52.2 | 48.8 | 47.9 | 46.9 | 48.4 | 47.1 | 46.9 | 46.6 | 51.6 | 52.9 | 53.1 | 53.4 |
| CHAD | 48.0 | 47.0 | 46.4 | 45.6 | 43.6 | 44.2 | 44.6 | 45.0 | 56.4 | 55.8 | 55.4 | 55.0 |
| COMOROS | 45.2 | 45.0 | 46.0 | 47.3 | 43.4 | 43.0 | 43.2 | 42.8 | 56.6 | 56.5 | 56.8 | 57.2 |
| CONGO | 42.0 | 41.6 | 41.2 | 40.6 | 41.9 | 42.5 | 42.8 | 43.1 | 58.1 | 57.5 | 57.2 | 57.0 |
| CONGO (DRC) | 44.3 | 42.7 | 42.4 | 41.8 | 44.6 | 44.0 | 43.7 | 43.3 | 55.4 | 56.0 | 56.3 | 56.7 |
| COTE D'IVOIRE | 40.9 | 39.0 | 39.6 | 40.6 | 31.6 | 31.4 | 32.2 | 33.3 | 68.4 | 68.6 | 67.8 | 66.7 |
| DJIBOUTI | 50.5 | 50.6 | 50.2 | 49.6 | 46.1 | 45.7 | 45.6 | 45.6 | 53.9 | 53.9 | 54.0 | 54.4 |
| EGYPT | 33.7 | 33.5 | 35.0 | 37.4 | 27.0 | 27.9 | 29.8 | 32.3 | 73.0 | 72.1 | 70.2 | 67.7 |
| EQUAT. GUINEA | 44.7 | 42.7 | 41.9 | 41.4 | 35.7 | 35.1 | 35.7 | 35.7 | 65.3 | 64.9 | 64.9 | 64.3 |
| ERITREA | ... | ... | 48.8 | 48.7 | ... | ... | 47.7 | 47.6 | ... | ... | 52.3 | 52.4 |
| ETHIOPIA | 45.8 | 44.6 | 43.9 | 43.7 | 42.5 | 42.4 | 42.1 | 42.0 | 57.5 | 57.6 | 57.9 | 58.0 |
| GABON | 48.6 | 44.5 | 44.4 | 44.7 | 45.0 | 44.3 | 44.5 | 44.7 | 55.0 | 55.7 | 55.7 | 55.3 |
| GAMBIA | 51.4 | 49.9 | 50.1 | 50.6 | 45.4 | 45.0 | 45.1 | 45.2 | 54.9 | 55.0 | 54.9 | 54.8 |
| GHANA | 46.4 | 46.4 | 47.7 | 49.7 | 50.9 | 50.9 | 50.7 | 50.3 | 49.1 | 49.1 | 49.3 | 49.7 |
| GUINEA | 51.8 | 50.0 | 49.7 | 49.4 | 47.2 | 47.5 | 47.3 | 47.1 | 52.8 | 52.6 | 52.7 | 52.9 |
| GUINEA BISSAU | 46.5 | 45.1 | 44.2 | 43.1 | 40.1 | 40.4 | 40.7 | 40.8 | 59.9 | 59.6 | 59.5 | 59.2 |
| KENYA | 47.2 | 47.5 | 49.5 | 52.1 | 46.3 | 46.4 | 46.7 | 47.1 | 53.7 | 53.6 | 53.3 | 52.9 |
| LESOTHO | 39.4 | 37.9 | 38.9 | 39.9 | 41.4 | 40.7 | 40.9 | 42.0 | 58.8 | 59.3 | 59.1 | 58.0 |
| LIBERIA | 40.7 | 39.4 | 38.9 | 38.1 | 39.5 | 40.1 | 40.3 | 40.3 | 60.5 | 59.9 | 59.7 | 59.8 |
| LIBYA | 31.0 | 29.5 | 31.8 | 35.0 | 18.6 | 18.4 | 20.8 | 24.2 | 81.4 | 81.6 | 79.2 | 75.8 |
| MADAGASCAR | 49.6 | 48.6 | 48.2 | 47.9 | 44.8 | 44.7 | 44.7 | 44.6 | 55.2 | 55.3 | 55.3 | 55.4 |
| MALAWI | 50.3 | 50.1 | 49.3 | 48.1 | 50.6 | 49.3 | 49.1 | 48.7 | 49.4 | 50.7 | 50.9 | 51.3 |
| MALI | 51.7 | 49.7 | 48.5 | 47.0 | 45.8 | 46.4 | 46.4 | 46.2 | 54.2 | 53.6 | 53.6 | 53.8 |
| MAURITANIA | 48.0 | 45.6 | 45.2 | 44.7 | 45.1 | 44.6 | 44.5 | 44.0 | 54.9 | 55.4 | 55.5 | 56.0 |
| MAURITIUS | 35.5 | 40.9 | 42.2 | 44.0 | 25.7 | 30.3 | 31.6 | 33.3 | 74.3 | 69.7 | 68.6 | 66.7 |
| MOROCCO | 35.9 | 37.1 | 38.8 | 41.1 | 33.5 | 34.5 | 34.6 | 34.9 | 66.5 | 65.5 | 65.4 | 65.0 |
| MOZAMBIQUE | 54.9 | 51.1 | 51.7 | 52.3 | 49.5 | 51.0 | 51.1 | 50.8 | 50.5 | 49.0 | 48.9 | 49.2 |
| NAMIBIA | 41.0 | 40.8 | 40.5 | 39.9 | 41.5 | 41.9 | 42.0 | 42.4 | 58.5 | 58.1 | 57.8 | 57.6 |
| NIGER | 48.1 | 47.2 | 46.7 | 45.9 | 43.8 | 43.2 | 43.2 | 43.2 | 56.2 | 56.8 | 56.8 | 56.8 |
| NIGERIA | 41.2 | 39.5 | 39.6 | 39.9 | 35.5 | 34.6 | 35.1 | 35.8 | 64.5 | 65.4 | 64.9 | 64.2 |
| RWANDA | 51.1 | 52.1 | 52.7 | 53.2 | 49.2 | 49.0 | 49.6 | 51.9 | 50.8 | 51.0 | 50.4 | 48.1 |
| SAO T. & PRINC. | 43.6 | 42.2 | 44.3 | 45.9 | 43.9 | 42.9 | 43.1 | 43.1 | 56.1 | 57.1 | 56.9 | 56.9 |
| SENEGAL | 45.9 | 44.0 | 44.3 | 44.8 | 42.2 | 42.8 | 43.1 | 43.3 | 57.8 | 57.2 | 57.0 | 56.7 |
| SEYCHELLES | 48.4 | 47.9 | 48.0 | 47.5 | 45.2 | 47.1 | 47.2 | 47.4 | 54.8 | 52.9 | 52.8 | 55.3 |
| SIERRA LEONE | 38.6 | 37.5 | 37.4 | 37.2 | 35.6 | 35.5 | 36.1 | 37.1 | 64.5 | 64.5 | 63.8 | 62.9 |
| SOMALIA | 45.2 | 43.7 | 43.3 | 42.6 | 43.4 | 43.3 | 43.3 | 43.4 | 56.6 | 56.6 | 56.7 | 56.6 |
| SOUTH AFRICA | 36.8 | 38.8 | 40.1 | 41.6 | 35.3 | 37.5 | 38.0 | 38.9 | 64.7 | 62.5 | 62.0 | 61.1 |
| SUDAN | 37.0 | 37.7 | 38.5 | 39.7 | 27.0 | 27.1 | 28.3 | 30.0 | 73.0 | 72.9 | 71.7 | 70.0 |
| SWAZILAND | 33.7 | 33.2 | 33.7 | 34.4 | 36.3 | 37.0 | 38.0 | 39.1 | 63.7 | 63.0 | 62.0 | 60.9 |
| TANZANIA | 51.2 | 51.1 | 51.0 | 51.1 | 49.8 | 49.7 | 49.6 | 49.3 | 50.2 | 50.3 | 50.4 | 50.7 |
| TOGO | 42.8 | 41.9 | 42.1 | 42.5 | 39.3 | 39.8 | 40.0 | 40.1 | 60.7 | 60.1 | 60.0 | 59.9 |
| TUNISIA | 34.0 | 34.5 | 37.2 | 41.2 | 29.0 | 29.2 | 30.6 | 32.5 | 71.0 | 70.8 | 69.4 | 67.5 |
| UGANDA | 51.7 | 50.7 | 49.5 | 48.0 | 47.6 | 47.8 | 47.9 | 47.7 | 52.4 | 52.2 | 52.1 | 52.3 |
| ZAMBIA | 42.8 | 43.3 | 42.8 | 42.2 | 44.2 | 44.0 | 44.0 | 43.7 | 55.8 | 56.0 | 56.0 | 56.3 |
| ZIMBABWE | 43.9 | 44.9 | 45.2 | 45.5 | 44.3 | 44.2 | 44.5 | 44.5 | 55.7 | 55.8 | 55.5 | 55.5 |
| **AFRICA** | **42.5** | **42.0** | **42.5** | **43.3** | **40.1** | **40.2** | **40.5** | **41.0** | **59.9** | **59.8** | **59.5** | **59.0** |

TABLE 3.3

COMPONENTS OF POPULATION CHANGE

| COUNTRY | TOTAL FERTILITY RATE (PER WOMAN) | | | CRUDE BIRTH RATE (PER 1,000 POPULATION) | | | CRUDE DEATH RATE (PER 1,000 POPULATION) | | | RATE OF NATURAL INCREASE (PERCENT) | | |
|---|---|---|---|---|---|---|---|---|---|---|---|---|
| | 1980 | 1990 | 2003 | 1980 | 1990 | 2003 | 1980 | 1990 | 2003 | 1980 | 1990 | 2003 |
| ALGERIA | 6.7 | 4.6 | 2.7 | 42.4 | 31.6 | 22.5 | 11.6 | 7.1 | 5.5 | 3.1 | 2.5 | 1.7 |
| ANGOLA | 6.9 | 7.2 | 7.1 | 50.8 | 52.1 | 51.9 | 24.7 | 24.9 | 23.4 | 2.6 | 2.7 | 2.8 |
| BENIN | 7.1 | 6.6 | 5.6 | 51.5 | 47.1 | 41.1 | 19.2 | 15.7 | 14.2 | 3.2 | 3.1 | 2.7 |
| BOTSWANA | 6.1 | 4.7 | 3.6 | 43.8 | 35.6 | 30.0 | 8.3 | 6.2 | 23.3 | 3.6 | 2.9 | 0.7 |
| BURKINA FASO | 7.8 | 7.3 | 6.6 | 50.7 | 49.4 | 47.5 | 20.4 | 17.8 | 17.0 | 3.0 | 3.2 | 3.0 |
| BURUNDI | 6.8 | 6.8 | 6.7 | 46.2 | 46.6 | 44.6 | 18.7 | 21.6 | 20.4 | 2.8 | 2.5 | 2.4 |
| CAMEROON | 6.4 | 5.9 | 4.5 | 45.1 | 41.7 | 34.9 | 16.6 | 13.3 | 17.2 | 2.8 | 2.8 | 1.8 |
| CAPE VERDE | 6.3 | 5.1 | 3.2 | 37.9 | 36.7 | 27.3 | 10.4 | 8.2 | 5.3 | 2.7 | 2.8 | 2.2 |
| CENT. AFR. REP. | 5.8 | 5.6 | 4.8 | 43.1 | 42.1 | 37.4 | 19.6 | 18.1 | 22.0 | 2.4 | 2.4 | 1.5 |
| CHAD | 6.7 | 6.7 | 6.6 | 48.1 | 48.5 | 48.1 | 23.0 | 20.5 | 19.2 | 2.5 | 2.8 | 2.9 |
| COMOROS | 7.1 | 6.1 | 4.8 | 48.7 | 40.6 | 36.1 | 14.3 | 10.8 | 8.2 | 3.4 | 3.0 | 2.8 |
| CONGO | 6.3 | 6.3 | 6.2 | 43.4 | 44.0 | 44.0 | 12.0 | 12.1 | 15.1 | 3.1 | 3.2 | 2.9 |
| CONGO (DRC) | 6.7 | 6.7 | 6.6 | 48.6 | 48.6 | 49.9 | 18.1 | 19.7 | 21.0 | 3.1 | 2.9 | 2.9 |
| COTE D'IVOIRE | 7.4 | 6.4 | 4.6 | 50.1 | 42.6 | 35.1 | 16.5 | 15.3 | 19.7 | 3.4 | 2.7 | 1.5 |
| DJIBOUTI | 6.7 | 6.3 | 5.6 | 44.7 | 43.3 | 38.9 | 19.6 | 17.5 | 17.7 | 2.5 | 2.6 | 2.1 |
| EGYPT | 5.4 | 4.3 | 3.3 | 39.1 | 32.0 | 26.5 | 13.0 | 8.6 | 6.1 | 2.6 | 2.3 | 2.0 |
| EQUAT. GUINEA | 5.7 | 5.9 | 5.8 | 42.9 | 43.6 | 42.6 | 21.8 | 18.9 | 16.5 | 2.1 | 2.5 | 2.6 |
| ERITREA | 6.4 | 6.2 | 5.3 | 45.0 | 43.6 | 39.2 | 19.5 | 15.0 | 11.8 | 2.5 | 2.9 | 2.7 |
| ETHIOPIA | 6.8 | 6.9 | 6.1 | 48.2 | 47.8 | 42.1 | 21.4 | 19.0 | 17.5 | 2.7 | 2.9 | 2.5 |
| GABON | 5.5 | 5.3 | 3.9 | 39.7 | 39.1 | 31.1 | 15.2 | 12.2 | 11.3 | 2.5 | 2.7 | 2.0 |
| GAMBIA | 6.5 | 5.8 | 4.6 | 47.6 | 42.6 | 35.1 | 21.5 | 15.9 | 12.5 | 2.6 | 2.7 | 2.3 |
| GHANA | 6.8 | 5.6 | 4.0 | 46.4 | 39.0 | 31.4 | 14.0 | 11.2 | 9.9 | 3.2 | 2.8 | 2.2 |
| GUINEA | 7.0 | 6.5 | 5.7 | 51.5 | 45.1 | 42.3 | 24.6 | 19.9 | 15.7 | 2.7 | 2.5 | 2.7 |
| GUINEA BISSAU | 7.1 | 7.1 | 7.0 | 49.1 | 49.8 | 49.4 | 26.3 | 22.7 | 19.3 | 2.3 | 2.7 | 3.0 |
| KENYA | 7.7 | 5.9 | 3.9 | 50.8 | 41.4 | 32.0 | 13.4 | 10.4 | 16.9 | 3.7 | 3.1 | 1.5 |
| LESOTHO | 5.6 | 4.9 | 3.8 | 41.9 | 36.3 | 30.8 | 15.7 | 13.7 | 26.6 | 2.6 | 2.3 | 0.4 |
| LIBERIA | 6.9 | 6.9 | 6.8 | 49.8 | 50.0 | 49.6 | 20.2 | 22.1 | 21.4 | 3.0 | 2.8 | 2.8 |
| LIBYA | 7.3 | 4.7 | 3.0 | 46.3 | 27.5 | 23.1 | 11.6 | 4.6 | 4.2 | 3.5 | 2.3 | 1.9 |
| MADAGASCAR | 6.4 | 6.2 | 5.6 | 45.6 | 44.7 | 41.1 | 17.6 | 16.4 | 12.9 | 2.8 | 2.8 | 2.8 |
| MALAWI | 7.6 | 7.0 | 6.0 | 54.6 | 50.3 | 44.1 | 22.0 | 20.0 | 23.9 | 3.3 | 3.0 | 2.0 |
| MALI | 7.0 | 7.0 | 7.0 | 50.3 | 49.7 | 49.7 | 21.0 | 17.7 | 15.9 | 2.9 | 3.2 | 3.4 |
| MAURITANIA | 6.4 | 6.1 | 5.7 | 43.8 | 42.5 | 41.4 | 18.1 | 16.4 | 13.9 | 2.6 | 2.6 | 2.7 |
| MAURITIUS | 2.7 | 2.2 | 1.9 | 23.9 | 20.2 | 15.9 | 6.4 | 6.5 | 6.7 | 1.7 | 1.4 | 0.9 |
| MOROCCO | 5.6 | 3.9 | 2.7 | 38.0 | 28.9 | 22.9 | 12.0 | 8.0 | 6.0 | 2.6 | 2.1 | 1.7 |
| MOZAMBIQUE | 6.4 | 6.2 | 5.5 | 45.8 | 44.2 | 40.7 | 21.3 | 20.8 | 23.5 | 2.4 | 2.3 | 1.7 |
| NAMIBIA | 6.4 | 5.8 | 4.4 | 42.1 | 41.0 | 32.6 | 13.3 | 10.7 | 18.6 | 2.9 | 3.0 | 1.4 |
| NIGER | 8.2 | 8.0 | 7.9 | 56.5 | 55.4 | 54.7 | 24.7 | 22.7 | 18.7 | 3.2 | 3.3 | 3.6 |
| NIGERIA | 6.9 | 6.5 | 5.3 | 47.6 | 44.8 | 38.6 | 18.1 | 14.9 | 13.7 | 3.0 | 3.0 | 2.5 |
| RWANDA | 8.3 | 6.8 | 5.6 | 52.1 | 44.3 | 43.5 | 19.3 | 32.5 | 21.4 | 3.3 | 1.2 | 2.2 |
| SAO T. & PRINC. | 5.4 | 5.1 | 3.9 | 39.7 | 36.0 | 32.6 | 9.6 | 8.8 | 5.7 | ... | ... | ... |
| SENEGAL | 6.9 | 6.3 | 4.9 | 47.3 | 42.5 | 36.6 | 19.6 | 15.0 | 12.0 | 2.8 | 2.8 | 2.5 |
| SEYCHELLES | ... | ... | ... | ... | ... | ... | ... | ... | ... | ... | ... | ... |
| SIERRA LEONE | 6.5 | 6.5 | 6.4 | 48.9 | 49.4 | 49.1 | 28.9 | 28.9 | 29.2 | 2.0 | 2.1 | 2.0 |
| SOMALIA | 7.3 | 7.3 | 7.2 | 51.8 | 51.9 | 51.6 | 22.4 | 23.0 | 17.2 | 2.9 | 2.9 | 3.4 |
| SOUTH AFRICA | 4.7 | 3.6 | 2.6 | 34.5 | 29.1 | 22.3 | 10.8 | 8.3 | 18.1 | 2.4 | 2.1 | 0.4 |
| SUDAN | 6.1 | 5.4 | 4.3 | 42.5 | 38.3 | 32.3 | 16.7 | 13.8 | 11.7 | 2.6 | 2.5 | 2.1 |
| SWAZILAND | 6.7 | 5.9 | 4.4 | 47.3 | 42.1 | 33.9 | 15.1 | 12.0 | 26.5 | 3.2 | 3.0 | 0.7 |
| TANZANIA | 6.7 | 6.3 | 5.0 | 46.6 | 45.0 | 38.8 | 15.2 | 14.5 | 18.0 | 3.1 | 3.0 | 2.1 |
| TOGO | 6.9 | 6.3 | 5.2 | 46.2 | 43.1 | 38.0 | 16.5 | 13.6 | 14.6 | 3.0 | 3.0 | 2.3 |
| TUNISIA | 5.2 | 3.5 | 2.0 | 34.8 | 26.6 | 16.9 | 8.4 | 6.3 | 5.5 | 2.6 | 2.0 | 1.1 |
| UGANDA | 7.1 | 7.1 | 7.0 | 50.5 | 50.5 | 50.4 | 18.3 | 19.8 | 16.1 | 3.2 | 3.1 | 3.4 |
| ZAMBIA | 7.0 | 6.3 | 5.5 | 46.0 | 45.3 | 41.9 | 14.4 | 17.3 | 27.6 | 3.2 | 2.8 | 1.4 |
| ZIMBABWE | 6.9 | 5.5 | 3.8 | 45.5 | 39.7 | 31.8 | 10.4 | 11.1 | 27.5 | 3.5 | 2.9 | 0.4 |
| AFRICA | 6.5 | 5.8 | 4.8 | 45.4 | 41.6 | 37.0 | 16.7 | 14.6 | 15.2 | 2.8 | 2.7 | 2.2 |

TABLE 3.4
MORTALITY INDICATORS

| COUNTRY | INFANT MORTALITY RATE (PER 1,000) | | | LIFE EXPECTANCY AT BIRTH (YEARS) | | | | | |
|---|---|---|---|---|---|---|---|---|---|
| | 1980 | 1990 | 2003 | 1980 | | 1990 | | 2003 | |
| | | | | M | F | M | F | M | F |
| ALGERIA | 98 | 62 | 43 | 59 | 61 | 61 | 67 | 69 | 72 |
| ANGOLA | 161 | 159 | 138 | 40 | 43 | 43 | 46 | 45 | 47 |
| BENIN | 115 | 102 | 91 | 46 | 48 | 50 | 50 | 53 | 56 |
| BOTSWANA | 63 | 48 | 55 | 56 | 60 | 59 | 63 | 37 | 36 |
| BURKINA FASO | 131 | 113 | 91 | 45 | 51 | 46 | 54 | 48 | 50 |
| BURUNDI | 123 | 126 | 106 | 45 | 49 | 42 | 45 | 40 | 42 |
| CAMEROON | 108 | 86 | 87 | 48 | 51 | 51 | 54 | 50 | 51 |
| CAPE VERDE | 66 | 48 | 29 | 59 | 63 | 62 | 68 | 67 | 73 |
| CENT. AFR. REP. | 128 | 111 | 100 | 43 | 48 | 45 | 49 | 43 | 46 |
| CHAD | 149 | 131 | 113 | 40 | 44 | 43 | 46 | 45 | 48 |
| COMOROS | 110 | 88 | 65 | 50 | 54 | 54 | 58 | 60 | 63 |
| CONGO | 88 | 82 | 82 | 47 | 53 | 49 | 54 | 50 | 54 |
| CONGO (DRC) | 118 | 119 | 119 | 47 | 51 | 50 | 53 | 51 | 54 |
| COTE D'IVOIRE | 110 | 99 | 100 | 48 | 51 | 49 | 52 | 48 | 49 |
| DJIBOUTI | 137 | 119 | 101 | 43 | 46 | 46 | 49 | 39 | 41 |
| EGYPT | 114 | 72 | 39 | 54 | 57 | 61 | 64 | 67 | 70 |
| EQUAT. GUINEA | 142 | 122 | 99 | 42 | 45 | 46 | 49 | 51 | 54 |
| ERITREA | 119 | 93 | 72 | 43 | 46 | 47 | 51 | 51 | 54 |
| ETHIOPIA | 144 | 123 | 99 | 42 | 45 | 44 | 47 | 43 | 44 |
| GABON | 85 | 69 | 55 | 47 | 50 | 50 | 53 | 52 | 54 |
| GAMBIA | 143 | 106 | 79 | 39 | 42 | 42 | 45 | 46 | 49 |
| GHANA | 93 | 76 | 56 | 52 | 55 | 54 | 57 | 56 | 59 |
| GUINEA | 161 | 136 | 100 | 39 | 40 | 43 | 44 | 48 | 49 |
| GUINEA BISSAU | 169 | 145 | 118 | 37 | 40 | 41 | 44 | 44 | 47 |
| KENYA | 86 | 68 | 68 | 53 | 57 | 55 | 59 | 49 | 50 |
| LESOTHO | 114 | 101 | 90 | 51 | 55 | 56 | 58 | 40 | 39 |
| LIBERIA | 153 | 170 | 145 | 49 | 52 | 43 | 45 | 55 | 57 |
| LIBYA | 53 | 31 | 20 | 59 | 62 | 67 | 70 | 70 | 74 |
| MADAGASCAR | 119 | 111 | 90 | 47 | 49 | 48 | 50 | 53 | 55 |
| MALAWI | 165 | 143 | 113 | 44 | 45 | 44 | 45 | 40 | 39 |
| MALI | 164 | 135 | 117 | 45 | 47 | 48 | 50 | 51 | 53 |
| MAURITANIA | 124 | 112 | 95 | 45 | 48 | 48 | 51 | 51 | 55 |
| MAURITIUS | 32 | 22 | 16 | 63 | 69 | 66 | 73 | 69 | 76 |
| MOROCCO | 102 | 68 | 41 | 56 | 59 | 62 | 65 | 67 | 71 |
| MOZAMBIQUE | 143 | 139 | 120 | 42 | 45 | 42 | 45 | 37 | 39 |
| NAMIBIA | 88 | 68 | 58 | 52 | 55 | 54 | 56 | 45 | 45 |
| NIGER | 158 | 148 | 124 | 40 | 41 | 42 | 42 | 46 | 47 |
| NIGERIA | 119 | 99 | 77 | 47 | 48 | 50 | 51 | 52 | 53 |
| RWANDA | 128 | 128 | 109 | 44 | 47 | 31 | 32 | 41 | 42 |
| SAO T. & PRINC. | 60 | 53 | 31 | ... | ... | ... | ... | ... | ... |
| SENEGAL | 93 | 72 | 60 | 43 | 48 | 48 | 52 | 53 | 57 |
| SEYCHELLES | ... | ... | ... | ... | ... | ... | ... | ... | ... |
| SIERRA LEONE | 190 | 188 | 175 | 34 | 37 | 34 | 37 | 40 | 42 |
| SOMALIA | 146 | 151 | 115 | 41 | 44 | 40 | 43 | 48 | 51 |
| SOUTH AFRICA | 66 | 50 | 47 | 53 | 60 | 56 | 64 | 46 | 47 |
| SUDAN | 116 | 97 | 75 | 47 | 50 | 51 | 54 | 56 | 59 |
| SWAZILAND | 101 | 81 | 77 | 49 | 54 | 54 | 58 | 38 | 37 |
| TANZANIA | 105 | 98 | 100 | 49 | 52 | 51 | 54 | 51 | 52 |
| TOGO | 110 | 90 | 80 | 48 | 49 | 50 | 52 | 52 | 54 |
| TUNISIA | 68 | 40 | 23 | 61 | 62 | 66 | 68 | 70 | 73 |
| UGANDA | 121 | 110 | 84 | 45 | 49 | 42 | 44 | 46 | 48 |
| ZAMBIA | 98 | 104 | 103 | 49 | 52 | 47 | 48 | 44 | 43 |
| ZIMBABWE | 68 | 59 | 57 | 57 | 61 | 52 | 53 | 44 | 43 |
| AFRICA | 115 | 96 | 81 | 48 | 51 | 51 | 54 | 52 | 54 |

Note : M and F refer to Male and Female respectively

TABLE 3.5
POPULATION WITH ACCESS TO SOCIAL INFRASTRUCTURES
(PERCENT OF POPULATION)

| COUNTRY | SANITATION | | | SAFE WATER | | | HEALTH SERVICES | | |
|---|---|---|---|---|---|---|---|---|---|
| | 1985 | 1990–93 | 2000 | 1985 | 1990–93 | 2000 | 1985 | 1991 | 1992–96 |
| ALGERIA | 59 | 90 | 73 | 69 | 90 | 94 | ... | ... | 98 |
| ANGOLA | 18 | 31 | 44 | 28 | 31 | 38 | 70 | 24 | ... |
| BENIN | 10 | 70 | 23 | 14 | 70 | 63 | ... | 42 | 18 |
| BOTSWANA | 36 | 70 | ... | 77 | 70 | ... | ... | 86 | ... |
| BURKINA FASO | 9 | 42 | 29 | 35 | 42 | ... | 70 | ... | 90 |
| BURUNDI | 52 | 58 | ... | 23 | 58 | ... | 45 | 80 | 80 |
| CAMEROON | 36 | 41 | 92 | 36 | 41 | 62 | 20 | 15 | 80 |
| CAPE VERDE | 10 | 67 | 71 | 31 | 67 | 74 | ... | ... | ... |
| CENT. AFR. REP. | 19 | 18 | 31 | 24 | 18 | 60 | .. | 13 | 52 |
| CHAD | 14 | 33 | 29 | 31 | 33 | 27 | 30 | 26 | 30 |
| COMOROS | ... | 48 | 98 | 63 | 48 | 96 | 82 | ... | ... |
| CONGO | 40 | 27 | ... | 20 | 27 | 51 | ... | ... | 83 |
| CONGO (DRC) | 23 | 60 | 20 | 33 | 60 | 45 | 33 | 59 | 26 |
| COTE D'IVOIRE | 50 | 82 | ... | 17 | 82 | 77 | ... | 60 | ... |
| DJIBOUTI | 37 | 24 | 91 | 43 | 24 | 100 | ... | ... | ... |
| EGYPT | 80 | 64 | 94 | 75 | 64 | 95 | 99 | 99 | 99 |
| EQUAT. GUINEA | ... | 95 | 53 | ... | 95 | 43 | ... | ... | ... |
| ERITREA | ... | 68 | 13 | ... | 68 | 46 | ... | ... | ... |
| ETHIOPIA | 19 | 27 | 15 | 16 | 27 | 24 | 44 | 55 | 46 |
| GABON | 50 | 67 | 21 | 50 | 67 | 70 | 80 | 87 | ... |
| GAMBIA | ... | 76 | 37 | 45 | 76 | 62 | 90 | ... | 93 |
| GHANA | 26 | 57 | 63 | 56 | 57 | 64 | 64 | 76 | ... |
| GUINEA | 21 | 55 | 58 | 20 | 55 | 48 | 13 | 45 | 80 |
| GUINEA BISSAU | 25 | 27 | 47 | 31 | 27 | 49 | 64 | ... | 40 |
| KENYA | 44 | 49 | 86 | 27 | 49 | 49 | ... | ... | 77 |
| LESOTHO | 22 | 62 | 92 | 36 | 62 | 91 | 50 | 80 | 80 |
| LIBERIA | 21 | ... | 37 | ... | ... | 35 | .. | 39 | |
| LIBYA | 91 | 97 | 97 | 90 | 97 | 72 | 100 | 100 | 95 |
| MADAGASCAR | 3 | 16 | 42 | 31 | 16 | 47 | 65 | 65 | 38 |
| MALAWI | 60 | 77 | 77 | 32 | 77 | 57 | 54 | 80 | 35 |
| MALI | 21 | 49 | 69 | 17 | 49 | 65 | 35 | ... | 40 |
| MAURITANIA | ... | 72 | 33 | 37 | 72 | 37 | 30 | ... | 63 |
| MAURITIUS | 97 | 100 | 99 | 99 | 100 | 100 | 100 | 99 | 100 |
| MOROCCO | 46 | 58 | 75 | 57 | 58 | 82 | 70 | 62 | 70 |
| MOZAMBIQUE | 20 | 24 | 43 | 15 | 24 | 60 | 40 | 30 | 39 |
| NAMIBIA | 14 | 60 | 41 | 52 | 60 | 77 | 72 | ... | 59 |
| NIGER | 9 | 52 | 20 | 37 | 52 | 59 | 48 | 30 | 99 |
| NIGERIA | 35 | 40 | 63 | 36 | 40 | 57 | 66 | 67 | 51 |
| RWANDA | 58 | 79 | 8 | 49 | 79 | 41 | 80 | ... | 80 |
| SAO T. & PRINC. | 15 | 70 | ... | 42 | 70 | ... | ... | ... | ... |
| SENEGAL | 55 | 50 | 70 | 44 | 50 | 78 | 40 | 40 | 90 |
| SEYCHELLES | 99 | 97 | ... | 95 | 97 | ... | 99 | 99 | ... |
| SIERRA LEONE | 21 | 34 | 28 | 24 | 34 | 28 | 36 | ... | 38 |
| SOMALIA | 15 | 37 | ... | 31 | 37 | ... | 20 | ... | ... |
| SOUTH AFRICA | ... | 87 | 86 | ... | 87 | ... | ... | ... | ... |
| SUDAN | 5 | 77 | 62 | 40 | 77 | 75 | 70 | 70 | 70 |
| SWAZILAND | ... | 60 | ... | 54 | 60 | ... | ... | 55 | ... |
| TANZANIA | 64 | 49 | 90 | 52 | 49 | 54 | 73 | 93 | 42 |
| TOGO | 14 | 63 | 34 | 35 | 63 | 54 | 61 | ... | ... |
| TUNISIA | 52 | 99 | ... | 89 | 99 | ... | 91 | 100 | ... |
| UGANDA | 13 | 42 | 75 | 16 | 42 | 50 | 42 | 71 | 49 |
| ZAMBIA | 47 | 59 | 78 | 48 | 59 | 64 | 70 | 75 | ... |
| ZIMBABWE | 26 | 74 | 68 | 52 | 74 | 85 | 71 | ... | 85 |
| AFRICA | **35** | **55** | **60** | **42** | **55** | **60** | **61** | **66** | **62** |

\* refers to 1993-95
\*\* refers to 1990-95

TABLE 3.6
SCHOOL ENROLMENT RATIO

| | PRIMARY | | | | | | SECONDARY | | | | | |
|---|---|---|---|---|---|---|---|---|---|---|---|---|
| | 1975 | | 1990 | | 2000/2001 | | 1975 | | 1990 | | 2000/01 | |
| COUNTRY | Total | Ratio F/M | Total | Ratio F/M | Total | Ratio F/M | Total | Ratio F/M | Total | Ratio F/M | Total | Ratio F/M |
| ALGERIA | 93 | 0.69 | 100 | 0.84 | 114 | 0.90 | 20 | 0.53 | 61 | 0.80 | 63 | 0.95 |
| ANGOLA | 130 | 0.60 | 92 | 0.92 | 64 | 0.92 | 9 | 0.40 | 12 | 0.66 | 12 | 0.66 |
| BENIN | 50 | 0.45 | 58 | 0.50 | 86 | 0.58 | 9 | 0.34 | 12 | 0.41 | 18 | 0.44 |
| BOTSWANA | 71 | 1.23 | 113 | 1.07 | 108 | 1.01 | 15 | 1.06 | 43 | 1.12 | 65 | 1.10 |
| BURKINA FASO | 14 | 0.56 | 33 | 0.63 | 43 | 0.65 | 2 | 0.46 | 7 | 0.53 | 9 | 0.55 |
| BURUNDI | 21 | 0.63 | 73 | 0.83 | 62 | 0.83 | 2 | 0.43 | 6 | 0.57 | 8 | 0.61 |
| CAMEROON | 95 | 0.80 | 101 | 0.86 | 91 | 0.90 | 13 | 0.50 | 28 | 0.70 | 25 | 0.68 |
| CAPE VERDE | 127 | 0.90 | 121 | 0.96 | 144 | 1.00 | 7 | 0.86 | 21 | 0.95 | ... | 0.94 |
| CENT. AFR. REP. | 73 | 0.53 | 65 | 0.64 | 56 | 0.65 | 8 | 0.23 | 12 | 0.41 | 10 | 0.42 |
| CHAD | 35 | 0.35 | 54 | 0.45 | 70 | 0.52 | 3 | 0.20 | 8 | 0.23 | 10 | 0.25 |
| COMOROS | 64 | 0.43 | 75 | 0.73 | 84 | 0.86 | 13 | 0.39 | 18 | 0.68 | 24 | 0.81 |
| CONGO | 136 | 0.75 | 133 | 0.88 | 84 | 0.91 | 48 | 0.54 | 53 | 0.69 | 52 | 0.72 |
| CONGO (DRC) | 93 | 0.67 | 70 | 0.62 | 47 | 0.69 | 17 | 0.36 | 22 | 0.48 | 30 | 0.62 |
| COTE D'IVOIRE | 61 | 0.57 | 67 | 0.71 | 77 | 0.87 | 12 | 0.39 | 22 | 0.47 | 24 | 0.48 |
| DJIBOUTI | 30 | 0.54 | 38 | 0.71 | 37 | 0.73 | 7 | 0.36 | 12 | 0.65 | 14 | 0.70 |
| EGYPT | 70 | 0.67 | 94 | 0.85 | 100 | 0.88 | 40 | 0.56 | 76 | 0.81 | 75 | 0.88 |
| EQUAT. GUINEA | 140 | ... | ... | ... | 125 | ... | 14 | 0.25 | ... | ... | ... | ... |
| ERITREA | ... | ... | 23 | 0.96 | 61 | 0.82 | ... | ... | 15 | 0.93 | 20 | 0.71 |
| ETHIOPIA | 21 | 0.49 | 33 | 0.67 | 71 | 0.55 | 6 | 0.38 | 14 | 0.77 | 12 | 0.79 |
| GABON | 178 | 1.65 | 163 | ... | 151 | ... | 30 | 0.55 | ... | ... | ... | ... |
| GAMBIA | 33 | 0.49 | 64 | 0.68 | 75 | 0.77 | 9 | 0.36 | 19 | 0.43 | 26 | 0.56 |
| GHANA | 72 | 0.77 | 75 | 0.83 | 78 | 0.85 | 36 | 0.61 | 36 | 0.64 | 31 | 0.63 |
| GUINEA | 31 | 0.52 | 37 | 0.47 | 63 | 0.58 | 14 | 0.35 | 10 | 0.34 | 13 | 0.35 |
| GUINEA BISSAU | 65 | 0.45 | 56 | 0.58 | 83 | 0.58 | 4 | 0.40 | 9 | 0.45 | 11 | 0.48 |
| KENYA | 104 | 0.86 | 95 | 0.96 | 91 | 1.00 | 13 | 0.55 | 24 | 0.73 | 24 | 0.85 |
| LESOTHO | 106 | 1.42 | 112 | 1.23 | 104 | 1.12 | 13 | 1.17 | 25 | 1.48 | 31 | 1.46 |
| LIBERIA | 40 | 0.52 | 30 | 0.69 | 118 | 0.69 | 17 | 0.32 | 14 | 0.40 | 14 | 0.40 |
| LIBYA | 137 | 0.82 | 105 | 0.94 | 117 | 1.00 | 55 | 0.54 | 86 | 1.03 | 100 | 0.94 |
| MADAGASCAR | 92 | 0.72 | 103 | 1.00 | 102 | 0.97 | 13 | 0.71 | 18 | 0.97 | 16 | 0.99 |
| MALAWI | 56 | 0.62 | 68 | 0.84 | 158 | 0.91 | 4 | 0.34 | 8 | 0.29 | ... | 0.55 |
| MALI | 25 | 0.56 | 27 | 0.57 | 55 | 0.65 | 7 | 0.35 | 7 | 0.48 | 12 | 0.51 |
| MAURITANIA | 20 | 0.56 | 49 | 0.74 | 84 | 0.89 | 4 | 0.12 | 14 | 0.48 | 16 | 0.51 |
| MAURITIUS | 105 | 0.98 | 109 | 1.00 | 108 | 0.99 | 38 | 0.83 | 53 | 1.00 | 65 | 1.04 |
| MOROCCO | 62 | 0.58 | 67 | 0.69 | 90 | 0.76 | 17 | 0.57 | 35 | 0.74 | 39 | 0.76 |
| MOZAMBIQUE | 83 | 0.55 | 67 | 0.75 | 85 | 0.72 | 3 | 0.50 | 8 | 0.62 | 7 | 0.63 |
| NAMIBIA | ... | ... | 129 | 1.10 | 113 | 1.01 | ... | ... | 44 | 1.27 | 61 | 1.18 |
| NIGER | 19 | 0.54 | 29 | 0.56 | 32 | 0.62 | 2 | 0.37 | 7 | 0.43 | 7 | 0.54 |
| NIGERIA | 50 | 0.64 | 91 | 0.76 | 82 | 0.79 | 8 | 0.53 | 25 | 0.73 | 34 | 0.84 |
| RWANDA | 55 | 0.84 | 70 | 0.98 | 122 | 0.97 | 4 | 1.23 | 8 | 0.78 | 13 | 0.77 |
| SAO T. & PRINC. | ... | ... | ... | ... | ... | ... | ... | ... | ... | ... | ... | ... |
| SENEGAL | 40 | 0.73 | 59 | 0.74 | 73 | 0.81 | 11 | 0.40 | 16 | 0.52 | 16 | 0.60 |
| SEYCHELLES | ... | ... | 96 | ... | ... | ... | ... | ... | ... | ... | ... | ... |
| SIERRA LEONE | 39 | 0.64 | 50 | 0.69 | 65 | 0.69 | 12 | 0.46 | 17 | 0.57 | 17 | 0.58 |
| SOMALIA | 42 | 0.71 | 10 | 0.52 | 8 | 0.52 | 4 | 0.30 | 6 | 0.53 | 5 | 0.53 |
| SOUTH AFRICA | 104 | 1.02 | 122 | 0.98 | 119 | 0.98 | 27 | 1.00 | 74 | 1.16 | 84 | 1.19 |
| SUDAN | 47 | 0.57 | 53 | 0.75 | 55 | 0.84 | 14 | 0.44 | 24 | 0.80 | 21 | 0.90 |
| SWAZILAND | 97 | 0.94 | 111 | 0.96 | 125 | 0.87 | 32 | 0.83 | 44 | 0.99 | 54 | 0.99 |
| TANZANIA | 53 | 0.71 | 70 | 0.98 | 63 | 0.98 | 3 | 0.55 | 5 | 0.71 | 5 | 0.88 |
| TOGO | 98 | 0.53 | 109 | 0.65 | 124 | 0.71 | 19 | 0.31 | 24 | 0.34 | 27 | 0.36 |
| TUNISIA | 97 | 0.67 | 113 | 0.89 | 118 | 0.94 | 21 | 0.55 | 45 | 0.80 | 65 | 0.97 |
| UGANDA | 44 | 0.66 | 71 | 0.80 | 141 | 0.84 | 4 | 0.33 | 13 | 0.54 | 14 | 0.59 |
| ZAMBIA | 97 | 0.84 | 99 | 0.93 | 79 | 0.94 | 15 | 0.52 | 24 | 0.61 | 29 | 0.63 |
| ZIMBABWE | 70 | 0.84 | 116 | 0.98 | 97 | 0.97 | 8 | 0.70 | 50 | 0.87 | 49 | 0.85 |
| AFRICA | 71 | 0.68 | 78 | 0.85 | 89 | 0.81 | 14 | 0.54 | 25 | 0.77 | 29 | 0.81 |

# Explanatory Notes

The main objective of the notes below is to facilitate interpretation of the statistical data presented in Part III of the Report. Data shown for all African countries are annual totals or five year averages. Period average growth rates are calculated as the arithmetic average of annual growth rates over the period. These statistics are not shown in the tables when they are not significant or not comparable over years.

## Section 1: Basic Indicators

This section contains one table (Table 1.1) which presents some basic indicators as background to the tables in this part of the Report. The table provides cross-country comparisons for area, population, GNI per capita, Consumer Price Inflation, life expectancy, infant mortality and adult literacy rates. The main sources of data in this table are the United Nations Organizations, the World Bank, Country reports and ADB Statistics Division's estimates.

Area refers to the total surface area of a country, comprising land area and inland waters. The data is obtained from the Food and Agriculture Organization (FAO). The population figures are mid-year estimates obtained from the United Nations Population Division.

GNI per capita figures are obtained by dividing GNI in current US dollars by the corresponding mid-year population. GNI measures the total domestic and foreign value added claimed by residents. It comprises GDP plus net factor income from abroad, which is the income residents receive from abroad for factor services less

similar payments made to nonresidents who contribute to the domestic economy. The data are obtained from the World Bank Atlas.

Life expectancy at birth is the number of years a new born infant would live, if patterns of mortality prevailing at the time of birth in the countries were to remain unchanged throughout his/her life. The infant mortality rate is the annual number of deaths of infants under one year of age per thousand live births. Adult literacy rate is the percentage of people aged 15 and above who can, with understanding, both read and write a short simple statement on their everyday life. The data are obtained from UNESCO.

## Section 2: Macroeconomic Indicators

### Table 2.1. Gross Domestic Product, real

National accounts estimates are obtained from regional member countries data, the World Bank, the IMF and the United Nations Statistical Division. In several instances, data are adjusted or supplemented with estimates made by the ADB Statistics Division. The concepts and definitions used for national accounts data are those of the United Nations 1993 System of National Accounts (SNA). Many countries continue to compile their national accounts in accordance with the 1968 SNA, but more and more are adopting the 1993 SNA.

Gross Domestic Product (GDP) measures the total final output of goods and services produced by a national economy, excluding provisions for depreciation. GDP figures are shown at constant 1995 market prices, and have been converted to US dollars using constant 1995 exchange rates provided by the IMF and the World Bank. For a few countries where the official exchange rate does not reflect effectively the rate applied to actual foreign exchange transactions, an alternative currency conversion factor has been used.

Aggregate growth rates for Africa are calculated as weighted averages of individual country growth rates using the share of the country's GDP in aggregate GDP based on the purchasing power parties (PPP) valuation of country GDPs.

## Table 2.2. Gross Domestic Product, nominal

Data shown in this table are given at current market prices and are obtained by converting national currency series in current prices to US dollars at official exchange rates. Annual changes in GDP are presented in nominal terms.

## Table 2.3. Gross National Savings

Gross National Savings (GNS) is calculated by deducting total consumption from GNI at current prices and adding net private transfers from abroad.

## Table 2.4. Gross Capital Formation

Gross Capital Formation consists of gross domestic fixed capital formation plus net changes in the level of inventories.

## Table 2.5. Terms of Trade

Terms of trade estimates are obtained from the IMF and supplemented by ADB Statistics Division estimates. These are obtained by dividing unit value indices of exports by unit value indices of imports. The terms of trade indices for the entire set of regional member countries are also ratios of the unit value of exports and the unit value of imports.

## Table 2.6. Current Account Balance

Data in this table are obtained from the IMF, and based on the methodology of the fifth edition of the Balance of Payments Manual. The current account includes the trade balance valued f.o.b., net services and net factor income, and current transfer payments. The data is given as percentage of GDP.

## Table 2.7 Broad Money Supply

Broad Money supply (M2) comprises currency outside banks, private sector demand deposits, (and, where applicable, post office and treasury checking deposits) and quasi-money.

## Tables 2.8 Real Exchange Rate Index

The real exchange rate index is defined broadly as the nominal exchange rate index adjusted for relative movements in national price or cost indicators of the home country and the United States of America.

*Table 2.9. International Reserves*

International Reserves consist of country's holdings of monetary gold, Special Drawing Rights (SDRs) and foreign exchange, as well as its reserve position in the International Monetary Fund (IMF).

*Table 2.10. Consumer Price Index*

Consumer price index shows changes in the cost of acquisition of a basket of goods and services purchased by the average consumer. Weights for the computation of the index numbers are obtained from household budget surveys.

*Table 2.11. Overall Fiscal Deficit or surplus*

The overall surplus/deficit is defined as current and capital revenue and official grants received, less total expenditure and lending minus repayments. The data is given as a percentage of GDP.

*Tables 2.12–2.13 Total External Debt; Debt Service.*

The main source of external debt data is the IMF. Total external debt covers outstanding and disbursed long-term debt, use of IMF credit, and short-term debt. Debt service is the sum of actual repayments of principal and actual payments of interest made in foreign exchange, goods, or services, on external public and publicly guaranteed debt.

*Section 3: Labor Force and Social Indicators*

This section presents data on labor force by sector (agriculture, industry and services) and also labor force participation rates, total and by sex.

Other tables in the section give data on components of population change (i.e. fertility, births, deaths and rate of natural increase), infant mortality rates, and life expectancy at birth, access to social infrastructure (sanitation, safe water and health services) and school enrolment ratios for primary and secondary levels.

*Table 3.1. Labor Force by Sector*

The labor force includes economically active persons aged 10 years and over. It includes the unemployed and the armed forces, but excludes housewives, students and other economically inactive groups. The agricultural sector consists of agriculture, forestry, hunting and fishing. Industry comprises mining and quarrying, manufacturing, construction, electricity, gas and water. Services include all other branches of economic activity and any statistical discrepancy in the origin of resources.

*Table 3.2. Labor Force Participation Rates*

The table shows the percentage of the population within each sex and age group that participates in economic activities (either employed or unemployed) from ILO data. Figures shown are ratios of the total economically-active population to the total population of all ages. Activity rates for females may be difficult to compare among countries because of the difference in the criteria adopted for determining the extent to which female workers are to be counted among the "economically active".

## Table 3.3. Components of Population Change

Total fertility rate indicates the number of children that would be born per woman, if she were to live to the end of the child-bearing years; and bears children during those years in accordance with prevailing age-specific fertility rates. The crude birth rate represents the annual live births per thousand population. The crude death rate is the annual number of deaths per thousand population. Rate of Natural increase of the population is the difference between Crude Birth and Crude Death rates expressed as a percentage. The data in the table are obtained mainly from the United Nations Population Division, UNICEF and the World Bank.

## Table 3.4. Mortality Indicators

The variables presented in this table – namely infant mortality rate and life expectancy at births — are as defined in Table 1.1. The sources of data are also the same.

## Table 3.5. Population with Access to Social Infrastructures

The percentage of people with access to sanitation is defined separately for urban and rural areas. For urban areas, access to sanitation facilities is defined as urban population served by connections to public sewers or household systems, such as pit privies, pour-flush latrines, septic tanks, communal toilets, and other such facilities. In the case of the rural population, the definition refers to those with adequate disposal, such as pit privies and pour-flush latrines. Applications of these definitions may vary from one country to another, and comparisons can therefore be inappropriate.

The population with access to safe water refers to the percentage of the population with reasonable access to safe water supply (which includes treated surface water, or untreated but uncontaminated water such as that from springs, sanitary wells, and protected boreholes). The threshold for the distance to safe water in urban areas is about 200 meters, while in rural areas it is reasonable walking distance to and from sources where water can be fetched.

The population with access to health services refers to the percentage of the population that can reach appropriate local health services by local means of transport in no more than one hour. Data in this table are obtained from the World Bank.

## Table 3.6. School Enrolment

The primary school enrolment ratio is the total number of pupils enrolled at primary level of education, regardless of age, expressed as a percentage of the population corresponding to the official school age of primary education. School enrolment ratios may be more than 100 per cent in countries where some pupils' ages are different from the legal enrolment age. Data in this table are obtained from UNESCO.

The secondary school enrolment ratio is the total number of pupils enrolled at secondary level of education, regardless of age, expressed as a percentage of the population corresponding to the official school age of secondary education.

# Data Sources

| | | |
|---|---|---|
| 1. | **Basic Indicators** | Food and Agriculture Organization: FAOSTAT Database, 2003. United Nations Population Division: The 2002 revision. World Bank: African Development Indicators, 2002/2003. Regional Member Countries, ADB Statistics Division. |

**2.**     **Macroeconomic Indicators**

| | | |
|---|---|---|
| 2.1–2.4 | National Accounts | United Nations: National Accounts Yearbook, various years. World Bank: Africa Live Database, February 2004. IMF: World Economic Outlook data files, September 2003. ADB Statistics Division. |
| 2.5–2.6 | External Sector | Regional Member Countries. IMF: World Economic Outlook, Data files, September 2003. |
| 2.7–2.10 | Money Supply Exchange Rates and Prices | IMF: International Financial Statistics, February 2004, and International Financial Statistics, Yearbook, 2002. ILO: Yearbook of Labor Statistics, various years. ADB Statistics Division, Regional Member Countries. |
| 2.11 | Government Finance | IMF: World Economic Outlook Data files, September 2003. |
| 2.12–2.13 | External Debt | IMF: World Economic Outlook, September 2003. ADB Statistics Division. |

**3.**     **Labor Force and Social Indicators**

| | | |
|---|---|---|
| 3.1–3.2 | Labor Force | Food and Agriculture Organization: FAOSTAT Database, 2003 World Bank: African Development Indicators 2001/2002 ADB Statistics Division. |
| 3.3–3.6 | Social Indicators | UNICEF: The State of the World's Children, various years. World Bank: African Development Indicators, 2002/2003. UN: Human Development Report, 2003. UN: Population Division, The 2002 Revision. Regional Member Countries. ADB Statistics Division. |

**This publication was prepared by the Bank's Development Research Department (PDRE). Other publications of the Department are:**

AFRICAN DEVELOPMENT REVIEW
A semi-annual professional journal devoted to the study and analysis of development issues in Africa

ECONOMIC RESEARCH PAPERS
A working paper series presenting the research findings, mainly by the research staff, on topics related to African development policy issues.

COMPENDIUM OF STATISTICS
An annual publication providing statistical information on the operational activities of the Bank Group.

GENDER, POVERTY AND ENVIRONMENTAL INDICATORS ON AFRICAN COUNTRIES
A Biennial publication providing information on the broad development trends relating to gender, poverty and environmental issues in the 53 African countries.

SELECTED STATISTICS ON AFRICAN COUNTRIES
An annual publication, providing selected social and economic indicators for the 53 regional member countries of the Bank.

AFRICAN ECONOMIC OUTLOOK
An annual publication jointly produced by the African Development Bank and the OECD Development Centre, which analyses the comparative economic prospects for African countries.

*Copies of these publications may be obtained from:*

**Development Research Department (PDRE)**
**African Development Bank**

| **Headquarters** | **Temporary Relocation Agency (TRA)** |
|---|---|
| 01 BP 1387 Abidjan 01, | Angle des trois rues, Avenue du Ghana, |
| COTE D'IVORIE | RUES PIERRE DE COUBERTIN |
| TELEFAX (225) 20 20 49 48 | ET HEDI NOUIRA |
| TELEPHONE (225) 20 20 44 44 | BP 323 — 1002 TUNIS BELVEDERE |
| TELEX 23717/23498/23263 | TUNISIA |
| Web Site: www.afdb.org | TELEFAX (216) 71351933 |
| EMAIL: afdb@afdb.org | TELEPHONE (216) 71333511 |
| | Web Site: www.afdb.org |
| | EMAIL: afdb@afdb.org |